Developments in Natural Intelligence Research and Knowledge Engineering:

Advancing Applications

Yingxu Wang
University of Calgary, Canada

Managing Director:	Lindsay Johnston
Senior Editorial Director:	Heather A. Probst
Book Production Manager:	Sean Woznicki
Development Manager:	Joel Gamon
Acquisitions Editor:	Erika Gallagher
Typesetter:	Russell A. Spangler
Cover Design:	Nick Newcomer, Lisandro Gonzalez

Published in the United States of America by
Information Science Reference (an imprint of IGI Global)
701 E. Chocolate Avenue
Hershey PA 17033
Tel: 717-533-8845
Fax: 717-533-8661
E-mail: cust@igi-global.com
Web site: http://www.igi-global.com

Library of Congress Cataloging-in-Publication Data

Developments in natural intelligence research and knowledge engineering / Yingxu Wang, editor.
   p. cm.
  Includes bibliographical references and index.
  Summary: "This book covers the intricate worlds of thought, comprehension, intelligence, and knowledge through the scientific field of Cognitive Science, covering topics that have been pivotal at major conferences covering Cognitive Science"--Provided by publisher.
  ISBN 978-1-4666-1743-8 (hardcover) -- ISBN 978-1-4666-1744-5 (ebook) -- ISBN 978-1-4666-1745-2 (print & perpetual access) 1. Information technology. 2. Knowledge management. 3. Information storage and retrieval systems. 4. Cognitive science. I. Wang, Yingxu.
  T58.5.D496 2012
  153--dc23
                      2012002467

British Cataloguing in Publication Data
A Cataloguing in Publication record for this book is available from the British Library.

The views expressed in this book are those of the authors, but not necessarily of the publisher.

Table of Contents

Section 1
Cognitive Informatics

Yingxu Wang, University of Calgary, Canada
George Baciu, The Hong Kong Polytechnic University, Hong Kong
Yiyu Yao, University of Regina, Canada
Witold Kinsner, University of Manitoba, Canada
Keith Chan, The Hong Kong Polytechnic University, Hong Kong
Bo Zhang, Tsinghua University, China
Stuart Hameroff, The University of Arizona, USA
Ning Zhong, Maebashi Institute of Technology, Japan
Chu-Ren Hunag, The Hong Kong Polytechnic University, Hong Kong
Ben Goertzel, Novamente LLC, USA
Duoqian Miao, Tongji University, China
Kenji Sugawara, Chiba Institute of Technology, Japan
Guoyin Wang, Chongqing Posts and Telecommunications University, China
Jane You, The Hong Kong Polytechnic University, Hong Kong
Du Zhang, California State University - Sacramento, USA
Haibin Zhu, Nipissing University, Canada

Yingxu Wang, University of Calgary, Canada
Davrondzhon Gafurov, Gjovik University College, Norway

Section 2
Cognitive Computing

Section 5
Applications of Cognitive Informatics and Cognitive Computing

Chapter 22
An Evaluation Method of Relative Reducts Based on Roughness of Partitions
Yasuo Kudo, Muroran Institute of Technology, Japan
Tetsuya Murai, Hokkaido University, Japan

Detailed Table of Contents

Section 1
Cognitive Informatics

Chapter 1

    Yingxu Wang, University of Calgary, Canada

    George Baciu, The Hong Kong Polytechnic University, Hong Kong

    Yiyu Yao, University of Regina, Canada

    Witold Kinsner, University of Manitoba, Canada

    Keith Chan, The Hong Kong Polytechnic University, Hong Kong

    Bo Zhang, Tsinghua University, China

    Stuart Hameroff, The University of Arizona, USA

    Ning Zhong, Maebashi Institute of Technology, Japan

    Chu-Ren Hunag, The Hong Kong Polytechnic University, Hong Kong

    Ben Goertzel, Novamente LLC, USA

    Duoqian Miao, Tongji University, China

    Kenji Sugawara, Chiba Institute of Technology, Japan

    Guoyin Wang, Chongqing Posts and Telecommunications University, China

    Jane You, The Hong Kong Polytechnic University, Hong Kong

    Du Zhang, California State University - Sacramento, USA

    Haibin Zhu, Nipissing University, Canada

Cognitive informatics is a transdisciplinary enquiry of computer science, information sciences, cognitive science, and intelligence science that investigates the internal information processing mechanisms and processes of the brain and natural intelligence, as well as their engineering applications in cognitive computing. *Cognitive computing* is an emerging paradigm of intelligent computing methodologies and systems based on cognitive informatics that implements computational intelligence by autonomous inferences and perceptions mimicking the mechanisms of the brain. This article presents a set of collective perspectives on cognitive informatics and cognitive computing, as well as their applications in abstract intelligence, computational intelligence, computational linguistics, knowledge representation, symbiotic computing, granular computing, semantic computing, machine learning, and social computing.

Chapter 2

Yingxu Wang, University of Calgary, Canada
Davrondzhon Gafurov, Gjovik University College, Norway

Comprehension is an ability to understand the meaning of a concept or an action. Comprehension is an important intelligent power of abstract thought and reasoning of humans or intelligent systems. It is highly curious to explore the internal process of comprehension in the brain and to explain its basic mechanisms in cognitive informatics and computational intelligence. This paper presents a formal model of the cognitive process of comprehension. The mechanism and process of comprehension are systematically explained with its conceptual, mathematical, and process models based on the Layered Reference Model of the Brain (LRMB) and the Object-Attribute-Relation (OAR) model for internal knowledge representation. Contemporary denotational mathematics such as concept algebra and Real-Time Process Algebra (RTPA) are adopted in order to formally describe the comprehension process and its interaction with other cognitive processes of the brain.

Chapter 3

J. Anitha, Karunya University, India
C. Kezi Selva Vijila, Karunya University, India
D. Jude Hemanth, Karunya University, India

Fuzzy approaches are one of the widely used artificial intelligence techniques in the field of ophthalmology. These techniques are used for classifying the abnormal retinal images into different categories that assist in treatment planning. The main characteristic feature that makes the fuzzy techniques highly popular is their accuracy. But, the accuracy of these fuzzy logic techniques depends on the expertise knowledge, which indirectly relies on the input samples. Insignificant input samples may reduce the accuracy that further reduces the efficiency of the fuzzy technique. In this work, the application of Genetic Algorithm (GA) for optimizing the input samples is explored in the context of abnormal retinal image classification. Abnormal retinal images from four different classes are used in this work and a comprehensive feature set is extracted from these images as classification is performed with the fuzzy classifier and also with the GA optimized fuzzy classifier. Experimental results suggest highly accurate results for the GA based classifier than the conventional fuzzy classifier.

Chapter 4

Cungen Cao, Chinese Academy of Sciences, China
Yuefei Sui, Chinese Academy of Sciences, China
Yu Sun, Chinese Academy of Sciences, China

In the classical formal logics, the negation can only be applied to formulas, not to terms and predicates. In (frame-based) knowledge representation, an ontology contains descriptions of individuals, concepts and slots, that is statements about individuals, concepts and slots. The negation can be applied to slots, concepts and statements, so that the logical implication should be considered for all possible combinations of individuals, concepts, slots and statements. In this regard, the logical implication at the ontological level is different from that at the logical level. This paper attempts to give such logical implications between individuals, concepts, slots, statements and their negations.

Section 2
Cognitive Computing

Chapter 5

Takeshi Okadome, Kwansei Gakuin University, Japan
Yasue Kishino, NTT Communication Science Laboratories, Japan
Takuya Maekawa, NTT Communication Science Laboratories, Japan
Koji Kamei, Advanced Telecommunications Research Institute International, Japan
Yutaka Yanagisawa, NTT West, Japan
Yasushi Sakurai, NTT Communication Science Laboratories, Japan

In a remote or local environment in which a sensor network always collects data produced by sensors attached to physical objects, the engine presented here saves the data sent through the Internet and searches for data segments that correspond to real-world events by using natural language (NL) words in a query that are input in an web browser. The engine translates each query into a physical quantity representation searches for a sensor data segment that satisfies the representation, and sends back the event occurrence time, place, or related objects as a reply to the query to the remote or local environment in which the web browser displays them. The engine, which we expect to be one of the upcoming Internet services, exemplifies the concept of symbiosis that bridges the gaps between the real space and the digital space.

Chapter 6

Koji Kamei, ATR Intelligent Robotics and Communication Laboratories, Japan
Yutaka Yanagisawa, NTT Communication Science Laboratories, Japan
Takuya Maekawa, NTT Communication Science Laboratories, Japan
Yasue Kishino, NTT Communication Science Laboratories, Japan
Yasushi Sakurai, NTT Communication Science Laboratories, Japan
Takeshi Okadome, Kwansei Gakuin University, Japan

The construction of real-world knowledge is required if we are to understand real-world events that occur in a networked sensor environment. Since it is difficult to select suitable 'events' for recognition in a sensor environment a priori, we propose an incremental model for constructing real-world knowledge. Labeling is the central plank of the proposed model because the model simultaneously improves both the ontology of real-world events and the implementation of a sensor system based on a manually labeled event corpus. A labeling tool is developed in accordance with the model and is evaluated in a practical labeling experiment.

Chapter 7

Tadeusz Wibig, University of Lodz and the A. Soltan Institute for Nuclear Studies, Poland

Standard experimental data analysis is based mainly on conventional, deterministic inference. The complexity of modern physics problems has become so large that new ideas in the field are received with the highest of appreciation. In this paper, the author has analyzed the problem of contemporary high-energy physics concerning the estimation of some parameters of the observed complex phenomenon. This article confronts the Natural and Artificial Networks performance with the standard statistical method of the data analysis and minimization. The general concept of the relations between CI and standard (external) classical and modern informatics was realized and studied by utilizing of Natural Neural Networks

(NNN), Artificial Neural Networks (ANN) and MINUIT minimization package from CERN. The idea of Autonomic Computing was followed by using brains of high school students involved in the Roland Maze Project. Some preliminary results of the comparison are given and discussed.

Chapter 8

Jane You, The Hong Kong Polytechnic University, China
Qin Li, The Hong Kong Polytechnic University, China
Jinghua Wang, The Hong Kong Polytechnic University, China

This paper presents a new approach to content-based image retrieval by using dynamic indexing and guided search in a hierarchical structure, and extending data mining and data warehousing techniques. The proposed algorithms include a wavelet-based scheme for multiple image feature extraction, the extension of a conventional data warehouse and an image database to an image data warehouse for dynamic image indexing. It also provides an image data schema for hierarchical image representation and dynamic image indexing, a statistically based feature selection scheme to achieve flexible similarity measures, and a feature component code to facilitate query processing and guide the search for the best matching. A series of case studies are reported, which include a wavelet-based image color hierarchy, classification of satellite images, tropical cyclone pattern recognition, and personal identification using multi-level palmprint and face features. Experimental results confirm that the new approach is feasible for content-based image retrieval.

Chapter 9

Poonam Bansal, Guru Gobind Singh Indraprastha University, India
Amita Dev, Ambedkar Institute of Technology, India
Shail Bala Jain, GGSIP University, India

In this paper, a feature extraction method that is robust to additive background noise is proposed for automatic speech recognition. Since the background noise corrupts the autocorrelation coefficients of the speech signal mostly at the lower orders, while the higher-order autocorrelation coefficients are least affected, this method discards the lower order autocorrelation coefficients and uses only the higher-order autocorrelation coefficients for spectral estimation. The magnitude spectrum of the windowed higher-order autocorrelation sequence is used here as an estimate of the power spectrum of the speech signal. This power spectral estimate is processed further by the Mel filter bank; a log operation and the discrete cosine transform to get the cepstral coefficients. These cepstral coefficients are referred to as the Differentiated Relative Higher Order Autocorrelation Coefficient Sequence Spectrum (DRHOASS). The authors evaluate the speech recognition performance of the DRHOASS features and show that they perform as well as the MFCC features for clean speech and their recognition performance is better than the MFCC features for noisy speech.

Section 3
Denotational Mathematics

Chapter 10

Kai Hu, University of Calgary, Canada
Yingxu Wang, University of Calgary, Canada
Yousheng Tian, University of Calgary, Canada

Autonomous on-line knowledge discovery and acquisition play an important role in cognitive informatics, cognitive computing, knowledge engineering, and computational intelligence. On the basis of the latest advances in cognitive informatics and denotational mathematics, this paper develops a web knowledge discovery engine for web document restructuring and comprehension, which decodes on-line knowledge represented in informal documents into cognitive knowledge represented by concept algebra and concept networks. A visualized concept network explorer and a semantic analyzer are implemented to capture and refine queries based on concept algebra. A graphical interface is built using concept and semantic models to refine users' queries. To enable autonomous information restructuring by machines, a two-level knowledge base that mimics human lexical/syntactical and semantic cognition is introduced. The information restructuring model provides a foundation for automatic concept indexing and knowledge extraction from web documents. The web knowledge discovery engine extends machine learning capability from imperative and adaptive information processing to autonomous and cognitive knowledge processing with unstructured documents in natural languages.

Chapter 11

Guilong Liu, Beijing Language and Culture University, China
William Zhu, University of Electronic Science and Technology of China, China

Rough set theory is an important technique in knowledge discovery in databases. Classical rough set theory proposed by Pawlak is based on equivalence relations, but many interesting and meaningful extensions have been made based on binary relations and coverings, respectively. This paper makes a comparison between covering rough sets and rough sets based on binary relations. This paper also focuses on the authors' study of the condition under which the covering rough set can be generated by a binary relation and the binary relation based rough set can be generated by a covering.

Chapter 12

Masahiro Inuiguchi, Osaka University, Japan

Rough sets can be interpreted in two ways: classification of objects and approximation of a set. From this point of view, classification-oriented and approximation-oriented rough sets have been proposed. In this paper, the author reconsiders those two kinds of rough sets with reviewing their definitions, properties and relations. The author describes that rough sets based on positive and negative extensive relations are mathematically equivalent but it is important to consider both because they obtained positive and negative extensive relations are not always in inverse relation in the real world. The difference in size of granules between union-based and intersection-based approximations is emphasized. Moreover, the types of decision rules associated with those rough sets are shown.

Chapter 13

Jianhua Dai, College of Computer Science, Zhejiang University, China

The collection of the rough set pairs <lower approximation, upper approximation> of an approximation (U, R) can be made into a Stone algebra by defining two binary operators and one unary operator on the pairs. By introducing a more unary operator, one can get a regular double Stone algebra to describe the rough set pairs of an approximation space. Sequent calculi corresponding to the rough algebras, including rough Stone algebras, Stone algebras, rough double Stone algebras, and regular double Stone algebras are proposed in this paper. The sequent calculi are called rough Stone logic (*RSL*), Stone logic (*SL*), rough double Stone logic (*RDSL*), and double Stone Logic (*DSL*). The languages, axioms and rules are presented. The soundness and completeness of the logics are proved.

Section 4
Computational Intelligence

Chapter 14

Yong Liu, Institute of Cyber-Systems and Control of Zhejiang University, China
Yunliang Jiang, Huzhou Teachers College, China
Jianhua Yang, SCI-Tech Academy of Zhejiang University, China

Feature selection is a classical problem in machine learning, and how to design a method to select the features that can contain all the internal semantic correlation of the original feature set is a challenge. The authors present a general approach to select features via rough set based reduction, which can keep the selected features with the same semantic correlation as the original feature set. A new concept named inconsistency is proposed, which can be used to calculate the positive region easily and quickly with only linear temporal complexity. Some properties of inconsistency are also given, such as the *monotonicity of inconsistency* and so forth. The authors also propose three inconsistency based attribute reduction generation algorithms with different search policies. Finally, a "mini-saturation" bias is presented to choose the proper reduction for further predictive designing.

Chapter 15

Jiayu Zhou, Arizona State University, USA
Shi Wang, Chinese Academy of Sciences, China
Cungen Cao, Chinese Academy of Sciences, China

Chinese information processing is a critical step toward cognitive linguistic applications like machine translation. Lexical hyponymy relation, which exists in some Eastern languages like Chinese, is a kind of hyponymy that can be directly inferred from the lexical compositions of concepts, and of great importance in ontology learning. However, a key problem is that the lexical hyponymy is so commonsense that it cannot be discovered by any existing acquisition methods. In this paper, we systematically define lexical hyponymy relationship, its linguistic features and propose a computational approach to semi-automatically learn hierarchical lexical hyponymy relations from a large-scale concept set, instead of analyzing lexical structures of concepts. Our novel approach discovered lexical hyponymy relation by examining statistic features in a Common Suffix Tree. The experimental results show that our approach can correctly discover most lexical hyponymy relations in a given large-scale concept set.

Chapter 16

Abdesslem Layeb, University Mentouri of Constantine, Algeria
Djamel-Eddine Saidouni, University Mentouri of Constantine, Algeria

In this work, the authors focus on the quantum evolutionary quantum hybridization and its contribution in solving the binary decision diagram ordering problem. Therefore, a problem formulation in terms of quantum representation and evolutionary dynamic borrowing quantum operators are defined. The sifting search strategy is used in order to increase the efficiency of the exploration process, while experiments on a wide range of data sets show the effectiveness of the proposed framework and its ability to achieve good quality solutions. The proposed approach is distinguished by a reduced population size and a reasonable number of iterations to find the best order, thanks to the principles of quantum computing and to the sifting strategy.

Cognitive informatics (CI) is a research area including some interdisciplinary topics. Visual tracking is not only an important topic in CI, but also a hot topic in computer vision and facial expression recognition. In this paper, a novel and robust facial feature tracking method is proposed, in which Kanade-Lucas-Tomasi (KLT) optical flow is taken as basis. The prior method of measurement consisting of pupils detecting features restriction and errors and is used to improve the predictions. Simulation experiment results show that the proposed method is superior to the traditional optical flow tracking. Furthermore, the proposed method is used in a real time emotion recognition system and good recognition result is achieved.

Section 5
Applications of Cognitive Informatics and Cognitive Computing

A sensor network consists of a large number of sensor nodes, which are spread over a geographical area. Sensor networks have found their way into many applications, from military domains to traffic or environmental monitoring, and as sensor networks reach toward wide spread deployment, security becomes a major concern. In this regard, one needs to be sure about the confidentiality, authenticity and tamper-proof of data. The research thus far has focused on how to deploy sensor networks so that they can work efficiently; however, the focus of this paper is on sensor networks' security issues. In this paper, the authors propose a formal model to design and analyze the secure sensor network system. The model is based on an augmented Petri net formalism called Extended Elementary Object System. This proposed secure sensor network model has a multi-layered structure consisting of sink node layer, sensor node layer and security mechanism layer. At the security mechanism layer, a synchronous firing mechanism is utilized as a security measure to detect malicious node attacks to sensor data and information flow. In addition, the model applies SNEP protocol for authentication and confidentiality of sensor data.

Chapter 19

This paper describes how the selection of parameters for the variance fractal dimension (VFD) multiscale time-domain algorithm can create an amplification of the fractal dimension trajectory that is obtained for a natural-speech waveform in the presence of ambient noise. The technique is based on the variance fractal dimension trajectory (VFDT) algorithm that is used not only to detect the external boundaries of an utterance, but also its internal pauses representing the unvoiced speech. The VFDT algorithm can also amplify internal features of phonemes. This fractal feature amplification is accomplished when the time increments are selected in a dyadic manner rather than selecting the increments in a unit distance sequence. These amplified trajectories for different phonemes are more distinct, thus providing a better characterization of the individual segments in the speech signal. This approach is superior to other energy-based boundary-detection techniques. Observations are based on extensive experimental results on speech utterances digitized at 44.1 kilosamples per second, with 16 bits in each sample.

Chapter 20

Tsau Young Lin, San Jose State University, USA
Rushin Barot, San Jose State University, USA
Shusaku Tsumoto, Shimane Medical University, Japan

The concepts of approximations in granular computing (GrC) vs. rough set theory (RS) are examined. Examples are constructed to contrast their differences in the Global GrC Model (2nd GrC Model), which, in pre-GrC term, is called partial coverings. Mathematically speaking, RS-approximations are "sub-base" based, while GrC-approximations are "base" based, where "sub-base" and "base" are two concepts in topological spaces. From the view of knowledge engineering, its meaning in RS-approximations is rather obscure, while in GrC, it is the concept of knowledge approximations.

Chapter 21

Ke-Jia Chen, Nanjing University of posts and telecommunications, China, and Université de
Technologie de Compiègne, France
Jean-Paul A. Barthès, Université de Technologie de Compiègne, France

We consider Personal Assistant (PA) agents as cognitive agents capable of helping users handle tasks at their workplace. A PA must communicate with the user using casual language, sub-contract the requested tasks, and present the results in a timely fashion. This leads to fairly complex cognitive agents. However, in addition, such an agent should learn from previous tasks or exchanges, which will increase its complexity. Learning requires a memory, which leads to the two following questions: Is it possible to design and build a generic model of memory? If it is, is it worth the trouble? The article tries to answer the questions by presenting the design and implementation of a memory for PA agents, using a case approach, which results in an improved agent model called MemoPA.

Chapter 22

Yasuo Kudo, Muroran Institute of Technology, Japan
Tetsuya Murai, Hokkaido University, Japan

This paper focuses on rough set theory which provides mathematical foundations of set-theoretical approximation for concepts, as well as reasoning about data. Also presented in this paper is the concept of relative reducts which is one of the most important notions for rule generation based on rough set theory.

In this paper, from the viewpoint of approximation, the authors introduce an evaluation criterion for relative reducts using roughness of partitions that are constructed from relative reducts. The proposed criterion evaluates each relative reduct by the average of coverage of decision rules based on the relative reduct, which also corresponds to evaluate the roughness of partition constructed from the relative reduct.

Preface

Cognitive informatics (CI) is a new discipline that studies the natural intelligence and internal information processing mechanisms of the brain, as well as the processes involved in perception and cognition. CI was initiated by Yingxu Wang and his colleagues in 2002. The development and the cross fertilization among computer science, information science, cognitive science, and intelligence science have led to a whole range of extremely interesting new research fields known as CI, which investigates the internal information processing mechanisms and processes of the natural intelligence – human brains and minds – and their engineering applications in computational intelligence.

The theories of informatics and their perceptions on the object of information have evolved from the classic information theory, modern informatics, to cognitive informatics in the last six decades. The *classic information theories*, particularly Shannon's information theory, are the first-generation informatics that study signals and channel behaviors based on statistics and probability theory. The *modern informatics* studies information as properties or attributes of the natural world that can be distinctly elicited, generally abstracted, quantitatively represented, and mentally processed. The first- and second-generation informatics put emphases on external information processing, which are yet to be extended to observe the fundamental fact that human brains are the original sources and final destinations of information. Any information must be cognized by human beings before it is understood, comprehended, and consumed. The aforementioned observations have led to the establishment of the third-generation informatics, *cognitive informatics*, a term coined by Yingxu Wang in a keynote to the First IEEE International Conference on Cognitive Informatics in 2002. It is recognized in CI that *information* is the third essence of the natural world supplementing to matter and energy, which is any property or attribute of the natural world that can be distinctly elicited, generally abstracted, quantitatively represented, and mentally processed. On the basis of the evolvement of intension and extension of the term information, *informatics* is the science of information that studies the nature of information, its processing, and ways of transformation between information, matter, and energy.

In many disciplines of human knowledge, almost all of the hard problems yet to be solved share a common root in the understanding of the mechanisms of natural intelligence and the cognitive processes of the brain. Therefore, CI is a discipline that forges links between a number of natural science and life science disciplines with informatics and computing science. CI provides a coherent set of fundamental theories, and contemporary mathematics, which form the foundation for most information and knowledge based science and engineering disciplines.

This book entitled **Developments in Natural Intelligence Research and Knowledge Engineering** is the fourth volume in the IGI Series of Advances in Cognitive Informatics and Natural Intelligence. The book encompasses 22 chapters of expert contributions selected from the *International Journal of Cognitive Informatics and Cognitive Computing* during 2010. The book is organized in five sections on: (i) Cognitive informatics; (ii) Cognitive computing; (iii) Denotational mathematics; (iv) Computational intelligence; and (v) Applications in cognitive informatics and cognitive computing.

SECTION 1. COGNITIVE INFORMATICS

Cognitive Informatics (CI) is a transdisciplinary enquiry of computer science, information science, cognitive science, and intelligence science that investigates into the internal information processing mechanisms and processes of the brain and natural intelligence, as well as their engineering applications in cognitive computing. Fundamental theories developed in CI covers the Information-Matter-Energy-Intelligence (IME-I) model, the Layered Reference Model of the Brain (LRMB), the Object-Attribute-Relation (OAR) model of internal information representation in the brain, the cognitive informatics model of the brain, natural intelligence (NI), abstract intelligence (αI), neuroinformatics (NeI), denotational mathematics (DM), and cognitive systems. Recent studies on LRMB in cognitive informatics reveal an entire set of cognitive functions of the brain and their cognitive process models, which explain the functional mechanisms and cognitive processes of the natural intelligence with 43 cognitive processes at seven layers known as the sensation, memory, perception, action, meta-cognitive, meta-inference, and higher cognitive layers.

According to CI, natural intelligence, in the narrow sense, is a human or a system ability that transforms information into behaviors; while in the broad sense, it is any human or system ability that autonomously transfers the forms of abstract information between data, information, knowledge, and behaviors in the brain. The history of human quest to understand the brain and natural intelligence is certainly as long as human history itself. It is recognized that artificial intelligence is a subset of natural intelligence. Therefore, the understanding of natural intelligence is a foundation for investigating into artificial, machinable, and computational intelligence.

The section on cognitive informatics encompasses the following four chapters:

- Chapter 1. *Perspectives on Cognitive Informatics and Cognitive Computing*
- Chapter 2. *The Cognitive Process of Comprehension: A Formal Description*
- Chapter 3. *A Hybrid Genetic Algorithm Based Fuzzy Approach for Abnormal Retinal Image Classification*
- Chapter 4. *Logical Connections of Statements at the Ontological Level*

Chapter 1, **Perspectives on Cognitive Informatics and Cognitive Computing**, by Yingxu Wang, George Baciu, Yiyu Yao, Witold Kinsner, Keith Chan, Bo Zhang, Stuart Hameroff, Ning Zhong, Chu-Ren Hunag, Ben Goertzel, Duoqian Miao, Kenji Sugawara, Guoyin Wang, Jane You, Du Zhang, and Haibin Zhu, presents *cognitive informatics* as a transdisciplinary enquiry of computer science, information sciences, cognitive science, and intelligence science that investigates into the internal information processing mechanisms and processes of the brain and natural intelligence, as well as their engineering applications in cognitive computing. *Cognitive computing* is an emerging paradigm of intelligent computing methodologies and systems based on cognitive informatics that implements computational intelligence by autonomous inferences and perceptions mimicking the mechanisms of the brain. This chapter reports a set of collective perspectives on cognitive informatics and cognitive computing, as well as their applications in abstract intelligence, computational intelligence, computational linguistics, knowledge representation, symbiotic computing, granular computing, semantic computing, machine learning, and social computing.

Chapter 2, **The Cognitive Process of Comprehension: A Formal Description**, by Yingxu Wang and Davrondzhon Gafurov, presents comprehension as an ability to understand the meaning of a concept or the behavior of an action. Comprehension is an important intelligent power of abstract thought and reasoning of humans or intelligent systems. It is highly curious to explore the internal process of comprehension in the brain and to explain its basic mechanisms in cognitive informatics and computational intelligence. This chapter presents a formal model of the cognitive process of comprehension. The mechanism and process of comprehension are systematically explained with its conceptual, mathematical, and process models based on *the Layered Reference Model of the Brain* (LRMB) and the Object-Attribute-Relation (OAR) model for internal knowledge representation. Contemporary denotational mathematics such as concept algebra and Real-Time Process Algebra (RTPA) are adopted in order to formally describe the comprehension process and its interaction with other cognitive processes of the brain.

Chapter 3, **A Hybrid Genetic Algorithm based Fuzzy Approach for Abnormal Retinal Image Classification**, by J. Anitha, C. Kezi Selva Vijila, and D. Jude Hemanth, presents fuzzy approaches as one of the widely used artificial intelligence techniques in the field of ophthalmology. These techniques are used for classifying the abnormal retinal images into different categories which assist in treatment planning. The main characteristic feature which makes the fuzzy techniques highly popular is their accuracy. But, the accuracy of these fuzzy logic techniques depends on the expertise knowledge, which indirectly relies on the input samples. Insignificant input samples may reduce the accuracy that further reduces the efficiency of the fuzzy technique. In this work, the application of Genetic Algorithm (GA) for optimizing the input samples is explored in the context of abnormal retinal image classification. Abnormal retinal images from four different classes are used in this work. A comprehensive feature set is extracted from these images. Classification is performed with the fuzzy classifier and also with the GA optimized fuzzy classifier. Experimental results suggest highly accurate results for the GA based classifier than the conventional fuzzy classifier.

Chapter 4, **Logical Connections of Statements at the Ontological Level**, by Cungen Cao, Yuefei Sui, and Yu Sun, presents that in classical formal logics, negation can only be applied to formulas, not to terms and predicates. In (frame-based) knowledge representation, an ontology contains descriptions of individuals, concepts, and slots; and statements about individuals, concepts, and slots. The negation can be applied to slots, concepts, and statements, so that the logical implication should be considered for all possible combinations of individuals, concepts, slots, and statements. Hence, the logical implication at the ontological level is different from that at the logical level. This chapter attempts to give such logical implications between individuals, concepts, slots, statements, and their negations.

SECTION 2. COGNITIVE COMPUTING

Computing systems and technologies can be classified into the categories of *imperative, autonomic,* and *cognitive* computing from the bottom up. The imperative computers are a passive system based on stored-program controlled behaviors for data processing. The autonomic computers are goal-driven and self-decision-driven machines that do not rely on instructive and procedural information. Cognitive computers are more intelligent computers beyond the imperative and autonomic computers, which embody major natural intelligence behaviors of the brain such as thinking, inference, and learning.

Cognitive Computing (CC) is a novel paradigm of intelligent computing methodologies and systems based on CI that implements computational intelligence by autonomous inferences and perceptions mimicking the mechanisms of the brain. CC is emerged and developed based on the multidisciplinary research in CI. The latest advances in CI and CC, as well as denotational mathematics, enable a systematic solution for the future generation of intelligent computers known as *cognitive computers* (CogCs) that think, perceive, learn, and reason. A CogC is an intelligent computer for knowledge processing as that of a conventional von Neumann computer for data processing. CogCs are designed to embody *machinable intelligence* such as computational inferences, causal analyses, knowledge manipulation, machine learning, and autonomous problem solving.

The section on cognitive computing encompasses the following five chapters:

- Chapter 5. *The Event Search Engine*
- Chapter 6. *Incremental Knowledge Construction for Real-World Event Understanding*
- Chapter 7. *Autonomic Computing for a Complex Problem of Experimental Physics*
- Chapter 8. *On Hierarchical Content-Based Image Retrieval by Dynamic Indexing and Guided Search* 4-2
- Chapter 9. *Robust Feature Vector Set Using Higher Order Autocorrelation Coefficients* 4-3

Chapter 5, **The Event Search Engine**, by Takeshi Okadome, Yasue Kishino, Takuya Maekawa, Koji Kamei, Yutaka Yanagisawa, and Yasushi Sakurai, presents that in a remote or local environment where a sensor network always collects data produced by sensors attached to physical objects, the engine presented here saves the data sent through the Internet and searches for data segments that correspond to real-world events by using natural language (NL) words in a query that are input in an web browser. The engine translates each query into a physical quantity representation searches for a sensor data segment that satisfies the representation, and sends back the event occurrence time, place, or related objects as a reply to the query to the remote or local environment in which the web browser displays them. The engine, which is expected to be one of the upcoming Internet services, exemplifies the concept of symbiosis that bridges the gaps between the real space and the digital space.

Chapter 6, **Incremental Knowledge Construction for Real-World Event Understanding**, by Koji Kamei, Yutaka Yanagisawa, Takuya Maekawa, Yasue Kishino, Yasushi Sakurai, and Takeshi Okadome, presents that the construction of real-world knowledge is required if people are to understand real-world events that occur in a networked sensor environment. Since it is difficult to select suitable *events* for recognition in a sensor environment a priori, the authors propose an incremental model for constructing real-world knowledge. Labeling is the central plank of the proposed model because the model simultaneously improves both the ontology of real-world events and the implementation of a sensor system based on a manually labeled event corpus. A labeling tool is developed in accordance with the model and is evaluated in a practical labeling experiment.

Chapter 7, **Autonomic Computing for a Complex Problem of Experimental Physics**, by Tadeusz Wibig presents the standard experimental data analysis as based mainly on conventional, deterministic inference. The complexity of modern physics problems becomes nowadays so large that new ideas are highly appreciated. The chapter analyzes the problem of contemporary high-energy physics concerning the estimation of some parameters of the observed complex phenomenon. It confronts the natural and artificial networks performance with the standard statistical method of the data analysis and minimization. The general concept of the relations between CI and standard (external): classical and modern informatics was realized and studied by utilizing of Natural Neural Networks (NNN), Artificial Neural Networks (ANN), and MINUIT minimization package from CERN. The idea of autonomic computing was followed by using brains of high school students involved in our Roland Maze Project. Some preliminary results of the comparison are given and discussed.

Chapter 8, **On Hierarchical Content-Based Image Retrieval by Dynamic Indexing and Guided Search**, by Jane You, Qin Li, and Jinghua Wang, presents a new approach to content-based image retrieval by using dynamic indexing and guided search in a hierarchical structure, and extending data mining and data warehousing techniques. The proposed algorithms include: a wavelet-based scheme for multiple image feature extraction, the extension of a conventional data warehouse and an image database to an image data warehouse for dynamic image indexing, an image data schema for hierarchical image representation and dynamic image indexing, a statistically based feature selection scheme to achieve flexible similarity measures, and a feature component code to facilitate query processing and guide the search for the best matching. A series of case studies are reported, which include a wavelet-based image color hierarchy, classification of satellite images, tropical cyclone pattern recognition, and personal identification using multi-level palmprint and face features. The experimental results confirm that the new approach is feasible for content-based image retrieval.

Chapter 9, **Robust Feature Vector Set Using Higher Order Autocorrelation Coefficients**, by Poonam Bansal, Amita Dev, and Shail Jain, presents a feature extraction method that is robust to additive background noise for automatic speech recognition. Since the background noise corrupts the autocorrelation coefficients of the speech signal mostly at the lower orders, while the higher-order autocorrelation coefficients are least affected, this method discards the lower order autocorrelation coefficients and uses only the higher-order autocorrelation coefficients for spectral estimation. The magnitude spectrum of the windowed higher-order autocorrelation sequence is used here as an estimate of the power spectrum of the speech signal. This power spectral estimate is processed further by the Mel filter bank, log operation, and the discrete cosine transform to get the cepstral coefficients. These cepstral coefficients are referred to as the Differentiated Relative Higher Order Autocorrelation Coefficient Sequence Spectrum (DRHOASS). The authors evaluate the speech recognition performance of the DRHOASS features and show that they perform as well as the MFCC features for clean speech and their recognition performance is better than the MFCC features for noisy speech.

SECTION 3. DENOTATIONAL MATHEMATICS

The needs for complex and long-series of causal inferences in cognitive computing, αI, computational intelligence, software engineering, and knowledge engineering have led to new forms of mathematics collectively known as denotational mathematics. *Denotational Mathematics* (DM) is a category of expressive mathematical structures that deals with high-level mathematical entities beyond numbers and sets, such as abstract objects, complex relations, perceptual information, abstract concepts, knowledge, intelligent behaviors, behavioral processes, and systems.

It is recognized that the maturity of any scientific discipline is characterized by the maturity of its mathematical means, because the nature of mathematics is a generic meta-methodological science. In recognizing mathematics as the *metamethodology* for all sciences and engineering disciplines, a set of DMs has been created and applied in CI, αI, AI, CC, CogC, soft computing, computational intelligence, and computational linguistics. Typical paradigms of DM are such as *concept algebra* (Wang, 2008), *system algebra* (Wang, 2008), *real-time process algebra* (Wang, 2002), *granular algebra* (Wang, 2009), *visual semantic algebra* (Wang, 2009), and *inference algebra* (Wang, 2011). DM provides a coherent set of contemporary mathematical means and explicit expressive power for cognitive informatics, cognitive computing, artificial intelligence, and computational intelligence.

The section on denotational mathematics encompasses the following four chapters:

- Chapter 10. *A Web Knowledge Discovery Engine Based on Concept Algebra*
- Chapter 11. *Approximations in Rough Sets vs. Granular Computing for Coverings*
- Chapter 12. *Further Considerations of Classification-Oriented and Approximation-Oriented Rough Sets in Generalized Settings*
- Chapter 13. *Generalized Rough Logics with Rough Algebraic Semantics*

Chapter 10, **A Web Knowledge Discovery Engine Based on Concept Algebra**, by Kai Hu, Yingxu Wang, and Yousheng Tian, presents a system of autonomous on-line knowledge discovery and acquisition in cognitive informatics, cognitive computing, knowledge engineering, and computational intelligence. On the basis of the latest advances in cognitive informatics and denotational mathematics, this chapter develops a web knowledge discovery engine for web document restructuring and comprehension, which decodes on-line knowledge represented in informal documents into cognitive knowledge represented by concept algebra and concept networks. A visualized concept network explorer and a semantic analyzer are implemented to capture and refine queries based on concept algebra. A graphical interface is built using concept and semantic models to refine users' queries. To enable autonomous information restructuring by machines, a two-level knowledge base that mimics human lexical/syntactical and semantic cognition is introduced. The information restructuring model provides a foundation for automatic concept indexing and knowledge extraction from web documents. The web knowledge discovery engine extends machine learning capability from imperative and adaptive information processing to autonomous and cognitive knowledge processing with unstructured documents in natural languages.

Chapter 11, **Approximations in Rough Sets vs. Granular Computing for Coverings**, by Guilong Liu and William Zhu, presents rough set theory as an important technique in knowledge discovery in databases. Classical rough set theory proposed by Pawlak is based on equivalence relations, but many interesting and meaningful extensions have been made based on binary relations and coverings, respectively. This chapter makes a comparison between covering rough sets and rough sets based on binary relations. The authors also study the condition under which the covering rough set can be generated by a binary relation and the binary relation based rough set can be generated by a covering.

Chapter 12, **Further Considerations of Classification-Oriented and Approximation-Oriented Rough Sets in Generalized Settings**, by Masahiro Inuiguchi presents a view that rough sets can be interpreted in two ways: classification of objects and approximation of a set. From this point of view, classification-oriented and approximation-oriented rough sets have been proposed. In this chapter, the authors reconsider those two kinds of rough sets with reviewing their definitions, properties, and relations. They describe that rough sets based on positively and negatively extensive relations are mathematically equivalent, but it is important to consider both because the positively obtained and negatively extensive relations are not always in inverse relation in the real world. The difference in size of granules between union-based and intersection-based approximations is emphasized. Moreover, the types of decision rules associated with those rough sets are shown. The chapter shows the differences using a numerical example.

Chapter 13, **Generalized Rough Logics with Rough Algebraic Semantics**, by Jianhua Dai presents the collection of the rough set pairs <lower approximation, upper approximation> of an approximation (U, R) by a Stone algebra by defining two binary operators and one unary operator on the pairs. By introducing a more unary operator, one can get a regular double Stone algebra to describe the rough set pairs of an approximation space. Sequent calculi corresponding to the rough algebras, including rough Stone algebras, Stone algebras, rough double Stone algebras, and regular double Stone algebras, are proposed in this chapter. The sequent calculi are called rough Stone logic (RSL), Stone logic (SL), rough double Stone logic (RDSL), and double Stone Logic (DSL). The languages, axioms, and rules are presented. The soundness and completeness of the logics are proved.

SECTION 4. COMPUTATIONAL INTELLIGENCE

Intelligence science studies theories and models of the brain at all levels, and the relationship between the concrete physiological brain and the abstract soft mind. Intelligence science is a new frontier with the fertilization of biology, psychology, neuroscience, cognitive science, cognitive informatics, philosophy, information science, computer science, anthropology, and linguistics. A fundamental view developed in software and intelligence sciences is known as *abstract intelligence* (αI), which provides a unified foundation for the studies of all forms and paradigms of intelligence such as natural, artificial, machinable, and computational intelligence. αI is an enquiry of both natural and artificial intelligence at the neural, cognitive, functional, and logical levels from the bottom up. In the narrow sense, αI is a human or a system ability that transforms information into behaviors. However, in the broad sense, αI is any human or system ability that autonomously transfers the forms of abstract information between *data, information, knowledge,* and *behaviors* in the brain or intelligent systems.

Computational intelligence (CoI) is an embodying form of abstract intelligence (αI) that implements intelligent mechanisms and behaviors by computational methodologies and software systems, such as expert systems, fuzzy systems, cognitive computers, cognitive robots, software agent systems, genetic/ evolutionary systems, and autonomous learning systems. The theoretical foundations of computational intelligence root in cognitive informatics, software science, and denotational mathematics.

The section on computational intelligence encompasses the following four chapters:

- Chapter 14. *Feature Reduction with Inconsistency*
- Chapter 15. *Learning Hierarchical Lexical Hyponymy*
- Chapter 16. *A New Quantum Evolutionary Algorithm with Sifting Strategy for Binary Decision Diagram Ordering Problem*
- Chapter 17. *A Robust Facial Feature Tracking Method Based on Optical Flow and Prior Measurement*

Chapter 14, **Feature Reduction with Inconsistency**, by Yong Liu, Yunliang Jiang, and Jianhua Yang, presents the feature selection as a classical problem in machine learning, and how to design a method to select the features that can contain all the internal semantic correlation of the original feature set is a challenge. The authors present a general approach to select features via rough set based reduction, which can keep the selected features with the same semantic correlation as the original feature set. A new concept named inconsistency is proposed, which can be used to calculate the positive region easily and quickly, with only linear temporal complexity. Some properties of inconsistency are also given, such as the *monotonicity of inconsistency,* et cetera. Then the authors propose three inconsistency based attribute reduction generation algorithms with different search policies. Finally, a *mini-saturation* bias is presented to choose the proper reduction for further predictive designing.

Chapter 15, **Learning Hierarchical Lexical Hyponymy**, by Jiayu Zhou, Shi Wang, and Cungen Cao, presents Chinese information processing as a critical step towards cognitive linguistic applications like machine translation. Lexical hyponymy relation, which exists in some Eastern languages like Chinese, is a kind of hyponymy that can be directly inferred from the lexical compositions of concepts, and of great importance in ontology learning. However, there is a key problem; the lexical hyponymy is so commonsense that it cannot be discovered by any existing acquisition methods. In this chapter, the authors systematically define lexical hyponymy relationship, its linguistic features, and propose a computational approach to semi-automatically learn hierarchical lexical hyponymy relations from a large-scale concept set, instead of analyzing lexical structures of concepts. This novel approach discovered lexical hyponymy relation by examining statistic features in Common Suffix Tree. Experimental results shows that the approach can correctly discover most lexical hyponymy relations in a given large-scale concept set.

Chapter 16, **A New Quantum Evolutionary Algorithm with Sifting Strategy for Binary Decision Diagram Ordering Problem**, by Abdesslem Layeb and Djamel-Eddine Saidouni, presents the quantum evolutionary quantum hybridization and its contribution in solving the binary decision diagram ordering problem. A problem formulation in terms of quantum representation and evolutionary dynamic borrowing quantum operators were defined. The sifting search strategy is used in order to increase the efficiency of the exploration process. Experiments on a wide range of data sets have shown the effectiveness of the proposed framework and its ability to achieve good quality solutions. The new proposed approach is distinguished by a reduced population size and a reasonable number of iterations to find the best order, thanks to the principles of quantum computing and to the sifting strategy.

Chapter 17, **A Robust Facial Feature Tracking Method Based on Optical Flow and Prior Measurement**, by Guoyin Wang, Yong Yang, and Kun He, presents cognitive informatics as a research area including some interdisciplinary topics. Visual tracking is not only an important topic in CI, but also a hot topic in computer vision and facial expression recognition. In this chapter, a novel and robust facial feature tracking method is proposed, in which Kanade-Lucas-Tomasi (KLT) optical flow is taken as basis, and the method of prior measurement consisting of pupils detecting, feature restricting, and errors accumulating is used to improve the predictions. Simulation experiment results show that the proposed method is superior to the traditional optical flow tracking. Furthermore, the proposed method is used in a real time emotion recognition system and good recognition result is achieved.

SECTION 5. APPLICATIONS OF COGNITIVE INFORMATICS AND COGNITIVE COMPUTING

A series of fundamental breakthroughs have been recognized, and a wide range of applications has been developed in cognitive informatics and cognitive computing in the last decade. This section reviews applications of theories, models, methodologies, mathematical means, and techniques of CI and CC toward the exploration of the natural intelligence and the brain, as well novel cognitive computers. The key application areas of CI can be divided into two categories. The first category of applications uses informatics and computing techniques to investigate cognitive science problems, such as memory, learning, and reasoning. The second category adopts cognitive theories to investigate problems in informatics, computing, and software/knowledge engineering. CI focuses on the nature of information processing in the brain, such as information acquisition, representation, memory, retrieve, generation, and communication. Through the interdisciplinary approach and with the support of modern information and neuroscience technologies, mechanisms of the brain and the mind may be systematically explored.

The section on applications of cognitive informatics and cognitive computing encompasses the following five chapters:

- Chapter 18. *Modeling a Secure Sensor Network Using an Extended Elementary Object System*
- Chapter 19. *Amplification of Signal Features Using Variance Fractal Dimension Trajectory*
- Chapter 20. *Some Remarks on the Concept of Approximations from the View of Knowledge Engineering*
- Chapter 21. *Giving Personal Assistant Agents a Case-Based Memory*
- Chapter 22. *An Evaluation Method of Relative Reducts Based on Roughness of Partitions*

Chapter 18, **Modeling a Secure Sensor Network Using an Extended Elementary Object System**, by Vineela Devarashetty, Jeffrey J.P. Tsai, Lu Ma, and Du Zhang, presents a sensor network consisting of a large number of sensor nodes, which are spread over a geographical area. Sensor networks have found their way into many applications, from military domains to traffic or environmental monitoring, to name a few. As sensor networks reach towards wide spread deployment, security becomes a major concern. Practitioners need to be sure about the confidentiality, authenticity, and tamper-proof features of data. The research thus far has focused on how to deploy sensor networks so that they can work efficiently. The focus of this chapter is on sensor networks' security issues. The authors propose a formal model to design and analyze the secure sensor network system. The model is based on an augmented Petri net formalism, called Extended Elementary Object System. This proposed secure sensor network model has a multi-layered structure consisting of sink node layer, sensor node layer and security mechanism layer. At the security mechanism layer, a synchronous firing mechanism is utilized as a security measure to detect malicious node attacks to sensor data and information flow. In addition, the model applies SNEP protocol for authentication and confidentiality of sensor data.

Chapter 19, **Amplification of Signal Features Using Variance Fractal Dimension Trajectory**, by Witold Kinsner and Warren Grieder, presents how the selection of parameters for the variance fractal dimension (VFD) multiscale time-domain algorithm can create an amplification of the fractal dimension trajectory that is obtained for a natural-speech waveform in the presence of ambient noise. The technique is based on the variance fractal dimension trajectory (VFDT) algorithm that is used not only to detect the external boundaries of an utterance, but also its internal pauses representing the unvoiced speech. The VFDT algorithm can also amplify internal features of phonemes. This fractal feature amplification is accomplished when the time increments are selected in a dyadic manner rather than selecting the increments in a unit distance sequence. These amplified trajectories for different phonemes are more distinct, thus providing a better characterization of the individual segments in the speech signal. This approach is superior to other energy-based boundary-detection techniques. These observations are based on extensive experimental results on speech utterances digitized at 44.1 kilosamples per second, with 16 bits in each sample.

Chapter 20, **Some Remarks on the Concept of Approximations from the View of Knowledge Engineering**, by Tsau Young Lin, Rushin Barot, and Shusaku Tsumoto, presents approximations in granular computing (GrC) vs. rough set theory (RS). Examples are constructed to contrast their differences in the Global GrC Model (2nd GrC Model), which, in pre-GrC term, is called partial coverings.

Mathematically speaking, RS-approximations are "subbase" based, while GrC-approximations are "base" based, where "subbase" and "base" are two concepts in topological spaces. From the view of knowledge engineering, its meaning in RS-approximations is rather obscure, while in GrC, it is the concept of knowledge approximations.

Chapter 21, **Giving Personal Assistant Agents a Case-Based Memory**, by Ke-Jia Chen and Jean-Paul A. Barthès, presents Personal Assistant (PA) agents as cognitive agents capable of helping users handle tasks at their workplace. A PA must communicate with the user using casual language, sub-contract the requested tasks, and present the results in a timely fashion. This leads to fairly complex cognitive agents. However, in addition, such an agent should learn from previous tasks or exchanges, which will increase its complexity. Learning requires a memory, which leads to the two following questions: Is it possible to design and build a generic model of memory? If it is, is it worth the trouble? The chapter tries to answer the questions by presenting the design and implementation of a memory for PA agents, using a case approach, which results in an improved agent model called MemoPA.

Chapter 22, **An Evaluation Method of Relative Reducts Based on Roughness of Partitions**, by Yasuo Kudo and Tetsuya Murai, presents the rough set foundations of set-theoretical approximation of concepts and reasoning about data. The concept of relative reducts is one of the most important for rule generation based on rough set theory. In this chapter, from the viewpoint of approximation, the authors introduce an evaluation criterion for relative reducts using roughness of partitions constructed from them.

This book is intended to the readership of researchers, engineers, graduate students, senior-level undergraduate students, and instructors as an informative reference book in the cutting-edge fields of cognitive informatics, natural intelligence, abstract intelligence, and cognitive computing. The editor expects that readers of **Developments in Natural Intelligence Research and Knowledge Engineering** will benefit from the 22 selected chapters of this book, which represent the latest advances in research in cognitive informatics and natural intelligence and their engineering applications.

Yingxu Wang
University of Calgary, Canada

Acknowledgment

Many persons have contributed their dedicated work to this book and related research. The editor would like to thank all authors, the associate editors of *IJCINI*, the editorial board members, and invited reviewers for their great contributions to this book. I would also like to thank the IEEE Steering Committee and organizers of the series of IEEE International Conference on Cognitive Informatics and Cognitive Computing (ICCI*CC) in the last ten years, particularly *Lotfi A. Zadeh, Witold Kinsner, Witold Pedrycz, Bo Zhang, Du Zhang, George Baciu, Phillip Sheu, Jean-Claude Latombe, James Anderson, Robert C. Berwick,* and *Dilip Patel*. I would like to acknowledge the publisher of this book, IGI Publishing, USA. I would like to thank *Dr. Mehdi Khosrow-Pour, Jan Travers, Kristin M. Klinger, Erika L. Carter*, and *Myla Harty*, for their professional editorship.

Section 1
Cognitive Informatics

Chapter 1
Perspectives on Cognitive Informatics and Cognitive Computing

Yingxu Wang
University of Calgary, Canada

George Baciu
The Hong Kong Polytechnic University, Hong Kong

Yiyu Yao
University of Regina, Canada

Witold Kinsner
University of Manitoba, Canada

Keith Chan
The Hong Kong Polytechnic University, Hong Kong

Bo Zhang
Tsinghua University, China

Stuart Hameroff
The University of Arizona, USA

Ning Zhong
Maebashi Institute of Technology, Japan

Chu-Ren Hunag
The Hong Kong Polytechnic University, Hong Kong

Ben Goertzel
Novamente LLC, USA

Duoqian Miao
Tongji University, China

Kenji Sugawara
Chiba Institute of Technology, Japan

Guoyin Wang
Chongqing Posts and Telecommunications University, China

Jane You
The Hong Kong Polytechnic University, Hong Kong

Du Zhang
California State University - Sacramento, USA

Haibin Zhu
Nipissing University, Canada

DOI: 10.4018/978-1-4666-1743-8.ch001

ABSTRACT

Cognitive informatics is a transdisciplinary enquiry of computer science, information sciences, cognitive science, and intelligence science that investigates the internal information processing mechanisms and processes of the brain and natural intelligence, as well as their engineering applications in cognitive computing. Cognitive computing is an emerging paradigm of intelligent computing methodologies and systems based on cognitive informatics that implements computational intelligence by autonomous inferences and perceptions mimicking the mechanisms of the brain. This article presents a set of collective perspectives on cognitive informatics and cognitive computing, as well as their applications in abstract intelligence, computational intelligence, computational linguistics, knowledge representation, symbiotic computing, granular computing, semantic computing, machine learning, and social computing.

INTRODUCTION

Definition 1: *Cognitive Informatics (CI) is a transdisciplinary enquiry of computer science, information science, cognitive science, and intelligence science that investigates into the internal information processing mechanisms and processes of the brain and natural intelligence, as well as their engineering applications in cognitive computing (Wang, 2002a, 2003a, 2003b, 2004, 2005, 2007b, 2008b, 2009a; Wang & Kinsner, 2007; Wang & Wang, 2006; Wang, Kinsner, & Zhang, 2009a, 2009b; Wang et al., 2006, 2009).*

The latest advances and engineering applications of CI have led to the emergence of cognitive computing and the development of cognitive computer that think and learn, as well as autonomous agent systems.

Definition 2: *Cognitive Computing (CC) is an emerging paradigm of intelligent computing methodologies and systems based on cognitive informatics that implements computational intelligence by autonomous inferences and perceptions mimicking the mechanisms of the brain (Wang, 2002a, 2009b, 2009g).*

CC is emerged and developed based on the transdisciplinary research in cognitive informatics, abstract intelligence, and denotational mathemat-

ics since the inauguration of the 1st IEEE International Conference on Cognitive Informatics (ICCI 2002, see Figure 1) (Wang et al., 2002, 2008).

Definition 3: *Abstract Intelligence (αI) is the general mathematical form of intelligence as a natural mechanism that transfers information into behaviors and knowledge (Wang, 2009a).*

Typical paradigms of αI are natural intelligence, artificial intelligence, machinable intelligence, and computational intelligence, as well as their hybrid forms.

Definition 4: *Denotational Mathematics (DM) is a category of expressive mathematical structures that deals with high-level mathematical entities beyond numbers and sets, such as abstract objects, complex relations, perceptual information, abstract concepts, knowledge, intelligent behaviors, behavioral processes, and systems (Wang, 2002b, 2007a, 2008a, 2008c, 2008d, 2008e, 2009d, 2009f; Wang, Zadeh & Yao, 2009).*

In recognizing mathematics as the *meta-methodology* of all sciences and engineering disciplines, a set of DMs have been created and applied in CI, αI, CC, AI, soft computing, computational intelligence, and fuzzy inferences.

The IEEE ICCI series has been established since 2002 (Wang, 2002a, 2003b; Wang et al.,

Figure 1. IEEE ICCI'08 keynote speakers and co-chairs at Stanford University (from right to left: Jean-Claude Latombe, Lotfi A. Zadeh, Yingxu Wang, Witold Kinsner, and Du Zhang)

2002). Since its inception, ICCI has been growing steadily in its size, scope, and depth. It attracts worldwide researchers from academia, government agencies, and industry practitioners. The conference series provides a main forum for the exchange and cross-fertilization of ideas in the new research field of CI toward revealing the cognitive mechanisms and processes of human information processing and the approaches to mimic them in cognitive computing.

The theoretical framework of CI (Wang, 2007b) encompasses a) fundamental theories of natural intelligence; b) abstract intelligence; c) denotational mathematics; and d) cognitive computing as follows.

CI Theories: Fundamental theories developed in CI covers the Information-Matter-Energy-Intelligence (IME-I) model (Wang, 2007a), the Layered Reference Model of the Brain (LRMB) (Wang et al., 2006), the Object-Attribute-Relation (OAR) model of information representation in the brain (Wang, 2007c), the cognitive informatics model of the brain (Wang & Wang, 2006), Natural Intelligence (NI) (Wang, 2007b), and neuroinformatics (Wang, 2007b). Recent studies on LRMB in cognitive informatics reveal an entire set of cognitive functions of the brain and their cognitive process models, which explain the functional mechanisms and cognitive processes of the natural intelligence with 43 cognitive processes at seven layers known as the sensation, memory, perception, action, meta-cognitive, meta-inference, and higher cognitive layers (Wang et al., 2006).

Abstract Intelligence (αI): The studies on αI form a human enquiry of both natural and artificial intelligence at the reductive levels of neural, cognitive, functional, and logical from the bottom up (Wang, 2009a). The paradigms of αI are such as natural, artificial, machinable, and computational intelligence. The studies in CI and αI lay a theoretical foundation toward revealing the basic mechanisms of different forms of intelligence. As a result, cognitive computers may be developed, which are characterized as knowledge processors beyond those of data processors in conventional computing.

Denotational Mathematics (DM): DM is a category of expressive mathematical structures that deals with high-level mathematical entities beyond numbers and sets, such as abstract objects, complex relations, perceptual information, abstract concepts, knowledge, intelligent behaviors, behavioral processes, and systems (Wang, 2008a). It is recognized that the maturity of a scientific discipline is characterized by the maturity of its mathematical (meta-methodological) means. Typical paradigms of DM are such as concept algebra (Wang, 2008c), system algebra (Wang, 2008d; Wang, Zadeh & Yao, 2009), real-time process algebra (Wang, 2002b, 20097a, 2008e), granular algebra (Wang, 2009h), visual semantic algebra (Wang, 2009f), fuzzy quantification/qualification, fuzzy inferences, and fuzzy causality analyses. DM provides a coherent set of contemporary mathematical means and explicit expressive power for CI, αI, CC, AI, and computational intelligence.

Cognitive Computing (CC): As presented in Definition 2, the latest advances in CI, αI, and DM have led to a systematic solution for future generation intelligent computers known as *cognitive computers* that think and learn (Wang, 2006, 2009b), which will enable the simulation of *machinable thought* such as computational inferences, reasoning, and causality analyses. A wide range of applications of CI, αI, CC, and DM is expected toward the implementation of highly intelligent machinable thought such

as formal inference, symbolic reasoning, problem solving, decision making, cognitive knowledge representation, semantic searching, and autonomous learning.

Applications of CI, αI, CC, and DM: The key applications of the above cutting-edge fields in CI can be divided into two categories. The first category of applications uses informatics and computing techniques to investigate problems of intelligence science, cognitive science, and knowledge science, such as abstract intelligence, memory, learning, and reasoning. The second category of applications includes the areas that use cognitive informatics theories to investigate problems in informatics, computing, software engineering, knowledge engineering, and computational intelligence. CI focuses on the nature of information processing in the brain, such as information acquisition, representation, memory, retrieval, creation, and communication. Through the interdisciplinary approach and with the support of modern information and neuroscience technologies, mechanisms of the brain and the mind may be systematically explored within the framework of CI.

COGNITIVE INFORMATICS AND GLOBAL CONSCIOUSNESS

In this section, we emphasize the need for the scalability of the state of cognitive informatics and modeling of human intent, emotions, and perceived reality. Much of the fascination with cognition is due to the learnt experience that surrounds the attempts to automate emotional perceptions in the context of current events. We emphasize the need to scale up the cognitive models to a global consciousness that is now aided by multi-sensory networks interacting with a perceived global awareness facilitated by integrated computer and sensory networks.

Questions of existence have transcended the borders of sciences and non-empirical models of the perceived world surrounding our senses. Are these questions different now than they were five hundred or a thousand years ago? Are our minds evolving? Or, do we perceive a relativistic time dilation effect in the information age? Beginning to understand self-awareness in the context of time and space, that is bringing consciousness to one-self as the subject of consciousness in the current process of cognition is accelerating. The enabling technology is the diversification of computer networks and the Internet.

Many have captured the essence of information exchange in the context of recent past, but few have understood the direction of the evolutionary process ahead of the process itself. On May 26, 1995, Bill Gates sent one of his well known memos, preceding the information technology revolution. Internet would "set the course of our industry for a long time to come." In his "Internet Tidal Wave" memo Gates declares: "In this memo I want to make clear that our focus on the Internet is critical to every part of our business." This was only a year after Netscape launched its browser in 1994. Was this a vision or an accident? What made his "vision" so clear? Was it a random inspiration or was it a time dilation effect in the information exchange domain? In order to answer this question, we must probe deeper into the differences between our synaptic neural networks and the von Neumann machine. It remains to be seen if the answer to this question can be found in the patterns of the Law of Powers of 10 (Pirolli, 2009).

Timely Information: In relativistic terms, time dilates as the speed of a particle approaches c, the speed of light. As we are all becoming aware of global events, such as the financial tidal wave, our receptors are continuously updated with a stream of text, images, video, and sound. The information meta-structures are taking new forms. Their delivery and often their representation have evolved as the speed of transmission and much enlarged memory capacity seem to make our perceptual reference clock slow down.

How is our world different from 1995? One answer is Google. Large quantities of information can now be mined in milliseconds. For example, a simple pattern "*a*" on Google currently gives: "Results 1 - 10 of about 18,860,000,000 for *a*. (0.04 seconds)," that is, 18 billion pages in 40 milliseconds.

Global Consciousness: Most interestingly, information transfer through our receptors has taken almost paradoxical forms such as, for example, in the Global Consciousness Project at Princeton (Nelson, 2000). Started in 1970's by Robert Jahn (2000) with a simple random number generating device, the REG – Random Event Generator, the Global Consciousness Project is currently serving as a seismograph for tremors in the global consciousness medium. Designed as a large scale sensor network, it is intended to capture alterations in the randomness of background noise, potentially showing polarization of group mind activity when events of considerable significance take place.

Since 1998, the Global Consciousness Project (GCP), also known as the Princeton EGG (ElectroGaiaGram = electroencephalogram + Gaia), archives random data in parallel sequences of synchronized 200-bit trials every second continuously from a global network of physical random number generators located in more than 65 host sites around the world. The objective is to capture large scale interactions between physical systems and human emotions expressed through brain activity in the context of perceived reality events. It claims to have accurately indicated the global mourning during Princess Diana's funeral in Sep. 1997, and it spiked off the charts before and during 9/11.

This experiment is certainly one of the most representative scientific awakenings of cognition in search for global consciousness. It is one of the best representations of large scale network sensors that could provide a scientific link between mind-machine interfaces. It is a platform that shows in real-time the dependency between information transfer and time, the basic ingredients of cognitive informatics (Wang, 2002a, 2007b; Wang et al., 2009).

Are we beginning to acknowledge the synaptic formation of a global consciousness? The answer may be realized as the integral relationship between time and awareness in the neural fabric of a network of minds. ICCI 2009 (Baciu, Wang, et al., 2009) is our modest attempt to address the many facets of cognition in the context of perception of reality and the extrapolation of brain power to "machine intelligence." We certainly hope that we are starting to pave the road to the next level of mind-brain interactions and the machines that could support it.

COGNITIVE INFORMATICS AND COGNITIVE DYNAMICAL SYSTEMS

Many developments of the last century centered around adaptation and adaptive systems. The focus in this century appears to be shifting towards cognition and cognitive dynamical systems with emergence (Kinsner, 2007). Although cognitive dynamical systems are always adaptive to various conditions in the environment, adaptive systems of the past have not been cognitive.

The evolving formulation of cognitive informatics (CI) (Wang, 2002a; Wang et al., 2009) has been an important step in bringing the diverse areas of science, engineering, and technology required to develop such cognitive systems. Current examples of various cognitive systems include autonomic computing, cognitive radio, cognitive radar, cognitive robots, cognitive networks, cognitive computers, cognitive cars, cognitive factories,

as well as brain-machine interfaces for physically-impaired persons, and cognitive binaural hearing instruments. The phenomenal interest in this area may be due to the recognition that perfect solutions to large-scale scientific and engineering problems may not be feasible, and we should seek the best solution for the task at hand. The "best" means suboptimal and the most reliable (robust) solution, given not only limited resources (financial and environmental) but also incomplete knowledge of the problem and partial observability of the environment. Many new theoretical, computational and technological developments have been described at this conference and related journals.

The challenges can be grouped into several categories: (a) theoretical, (b) technological, and (c) sociological. The first group of theoretical issues include modelling, reformulation of information and entropy, multiscale measures and metrics, and management of uncertainty. Modelling of cognitive systems requires radically new approaches. Reductionism has dominated our scientific worldview for the last 350 years, since the times of Descartes, Galileo, Newton, and Laplace. In that approach, all reality can be understood in terms of particles (or strings) in motion. A Nobel laureate physicist, Stephen Weinberg said "All explanatory arrows point downward, from societies to people, to organs, to cells, to biochemistry, to chemistry, and ultimately to physics." "The more we know of the universe, the more meaningless it appears." However, in this unfolding emergent universe with agency, meaning, values and purpose, we cannot prestate or predict all that will happen. Since cognitive systems rely on perceiving the world by agents, learning from it, remembering and developing the experience of self-awareness, feelings, intentions, and deciding how to control not only tasks but also communication with other agents, and to create new ideas, CI may not only rely on the reductionist approach of describing nature. In fact, CI tries to expand the modelling in order to deal with the emergent universe where no laws of physics are violated, and yet ceaseless unforeseeable creativity arises and surrounds us all the time. This new approach requires many new ideas to be developed, including reformulation of the concept of cognitive information, entropy, and associated measures, as well as management of uncertainty, and new forms of cognitive computing.

As we have seen over the last decade, cognitive informatics is multidisciplinary, and requires cooperation between many subjects, including sciences (e.g., cognitive science, evolutionary computing, granular computing, computer science, game theory, crisp and fuzzy sets, mathematics, physics, chemistry, biology, psychology, humanities, and social sciences), engineering and technology (computer, electrical, mechanical, information theory, control theory, intelligent signal processing, neural networks, learning machines, sensor networks, wireless communications, computer networks). Special issues of the IEEE Proceedings and IJCINI are dedicated to cognitive systems with their practical perspectives (April 2009), fundamental issues (May 2009), and cognitive computing (October 2009).

COGNITIVE COMPUTING AND COMPUTER VISION

To endow computers with human visual capability is one of the main goals of artificial intelligence (AI) although there still is a long way to go. Taking object recognition as an example in 1980s, a main approach addressing the problem is the 3D reconstruction one, i.e., the reconstruction of 3D object from 2D images. In 1990s since the 3D reconstruction method was confronted with extreme difficulty, most researchers abandoned the attempts and turned to the 2D based approach, i.e., object recognition from 2D images directly. However, the new road is still uneven.

When a huge amount of 2D-image data are obtained by digital cameras in object recognition (or classification), they should be transformed into an object invariant representation. In order to solve the problem, we need two key techniques, i.e., a robust detector and an object invariant describer (Zhang & Zhang, 2002). A number of great efforts have been made on these techniques, but so far few efficient solutions have been found. A new direction emerged to solve the problems of computer vision is that computer science may learn some things from cognitive informatics, neuron science, and brain science, which studies what computer vision can learn from human visual principles and how it will be affected by the new interdisciplinary research on computer vision.

COGNITIVE COMPUTING AND MACHINE CONSCIOUSNESS

The brain is viewed as a computer in which sensory processing, control of behavior and other cognitive functions emerge from 'neurocomputation' in parallel networks of perceptron-like neurons. In each neuron, dendrites receive and integrate synaptic inputs to a threshold for axonal firing as output—'integrate-and-fire'. Neurocomputation in axonal-dendritic synaptic networks successfully accounts for non-conscious (auto-pilot) cognitive brain functions. When cognitive functions are accompanied by consciousness, neurocomputation is accompanied by 30 to 90 Hz gamma synchrony EEG. Gamma synchrony derives primarily from neuronal groups linked by dendritic-dendritic gap junctions, forming transient syncytia ('dendritic webs') in input/integration layers oriented sideways to axonal-dendritic neurocomputational flow. As gap junctions open and close, a gamma-synchronized dendritic web can rapidly change topology, evolve and move through the brain (like a benevolent computer worm might move through computer circuits) as a spatiotemporal envelope performing collective integration and volitional choices correlating with consciousness. The 'conscious pilot' is a metaphorical description for a mobile, gamma-synchronized dendritic web as vehicle for a conscious agent/pilot which experiences and assumes control of otherwise non-conscious auto-pilot neurocomputation. Applications of the conscious pilot in computing have been identified such as a self-organizing mobile agent moving through input/integration layers of computational networks.

COGNITIVE INFORMATICS AND WEB INTELLIGENCE

Artificial Intelligence (AI) has been mainly studied within the realm of computer based technologies. Various computational models and knowledge based systems have been developed for automated reasoning, learning, and problem-solving. However, there still exist several grand challenges. The AI research has not produced major breakthrough recently due to a lack of understanding of human brains and natural intelligence. Ignoring what goes on in human brain and focusing instead on behavior has been a large impediment to understanding complex human adaptive, distributed reasoning and problem solving. In addition, most of the AI models and systems will not work well when dealing with large-scale, dynamically changing, open and distributed information sources at a web scale.

In order to develop a new cognitively inspired web reasoning and problem-solving systems, we need to better understand how humans perform complex adaptive, distributed problem solving and reasoning. Understanding the principles and mechanisms of information organization, retrieval and selection in human memory aims to find more cognition-inspired methods of information memory system, problem solving and reasoning at the web scale. Based on many investigations on information retrieval and selection in human memory system, we can view the human brain as a huge distributed knowledge base with multiple information granule networks. In the light of the brain inspired methodology, we need to investigate specifically the following issues:

- Why humans can give a good answer within a reasonable time by exploring variable precision when receiving a question (i.e., a reasoning problem)?
- How humans select a suitable level of information granules and retrieve in single or multiple information sources, which is based on a trade-off between user needs and certain constraints?

As a result, the relationships between biologically plausible granular reasoning and web reasoning need to be defined and/or elaborated. Granular reasoning describes a way of thinking from the human ability to perceive the real world under various levels of granularity. Granular reasoning provides a solution for web scale reasoning and would have a significant impact on problem solving and reasoning at a web scale. From the viewpoint of granular reasoning, data, information, and knowledge are arranged in multiple levels according to their granularity. A higher level contains more abstract or general knowledge, while a lower level contains more detailed or specific knowledge. Reasoning can be performed on various levels. Results from a higher may be imprecise but can be obtained faster. In contrast, one can move to a lower level to obtain more precise conclusion if more time is allowed. Therefore, granular reasoning offers a multiple-resolution reasoning scheme. One may choose a proper level of granularity to draw a desirable conclusion under certain constraints. In fact, such a reasoning scheme is commonly used by human for practical and real-time decision-making.

Therefore, the study on granular reasoning of human and web can be carried out in a unified way from the viewpoint of cognitive informatics and brain informatics. The web granular reasoning is considered as an application of human-inspired granular reasoning. As for human granular reasoning, based on the previous studies about basic-level advantage and its reversal effect, fMRI/ERP can be adopted to investigate how the neural system cooperates and coordinates with each other when the starting point locates in the basic level and how the brain modulates and adapts to the change when the starting point switches to a more general level. The key question is "can we find a new cognitive model for developing human-level web based granular reasoning and problem-solving?" In order to answer this question, we investigate the cognitive mechanism and neural basis of human problem solving and reasoning, for developing new cognitively inspired web intelligence models. Based on this result, we will implement a Problem Solver Markup Language (PSML) for representing, organizing, retrieving, and selecting web information sources with multiple levels of granularity, and develop PSML based web inference engines for personalized wisdom web problem solving and services.

COGNITIVE COMPUTING AND GRAPH INFORMATION PROCESSING

Many real-world problems can be represented in graphs and better solved with such a representation. For example, finding the best topological configuration for architectural layout design, finding the best molecular structure for drug discovery or finding the best network topology for overlay network optimization, etc. These problems can be formulated as a combinatorial optimization problem and be solved like many other such problems with an evolutionary algorithm (EA). Even though there are EAs that are developed to evolve trees or artificial neural network architecture, many of them are not developed to deal with graphs in general. To deal with the many problems that are represented by graphs, we propose to use a novel EA. The EA represents graphs in adjacency matrices and makes use of reproduction operators that resemble uniform crossover and mutations in linear-string GA to generate better and better graphs until an

optimal or near-optimal solution graphs can be identified. Like human problem solving, this approach can be used to tackle very complex problems. Such a problem can be first broken down into easily manageable sub-problems so that solutions can be found relatively easily. Based on these solutions to the sub-problems, much more complex problems can be solved with the EA based on the use of the sub-problem solutions as building blocks.

Very complex real-world problems are usually characterized by the size of the graph generated. When a very large graph is generated, there is a need for them to be understood. Many problems of practical importance such as biological network, social network, web, marketing, and land-use analysis and planning, etc., involve the handling of large graphs. These graph data captures not only the attributes of different objects but also the multiple relationships among them.

To understand complex problem solutions, there is often a need to discover patterns in the graph that represent them. To do so, graph mining techniques can be used. Existing graph mining techniques can discover frequent sub-graphs in large graphs but frequent sub-graphs may not always represent interesting patterns. An approach is needed to discover interesting patterns that can uniquely characterize a graph and to allow it to be distinguished from the others so that the uniqueness of a solution representable in a graph can be more easily noticeable.

COGNITIVE INFORMATICS AND COMPUTATIONAL LINGUISTICS

Language is one of the most complex of all human cognitive activities. Linguistic output, both in spoken and written form, also offers the most tangible example of cognitive activity, in terms of both its quantity and accessibility: "The quality of language that makes it unique does not seem to be so much its role in communicating directives for action as its role in symbolizing, in evoking cognitive images. We mold our 'reality' with our words and our sentences in the same way as we mold it with our vision and our hearing" (Jacob, 1982); "The 'real world' is to a large extent unconsciously built up on the language habits of the group" (Sapir, 1929).

Reinterpreting Jacob (1982) and Sapir (1929), we could state that cognition is the reality molded and modeled by the convention of language. In contrast, the field of Informatics aims to offer an alternative to the imprecise and redundant nature of language, but still needs to deal with natural language's representational conventions as both the source of information and the as user's preferred representational interface.

The above facts suggest a potential synergy between computational linguistics and cognitive informatics. Should we model 'Reality' or the 'reality molded by language'? Does the modeling of 'reality molded by language' facilitate modeling of 'Reality'? How can cognitive informatics model and express competing preferences, ambiguity and other nuances, in a similar way to natural language? Can the cognitive structures conventionalized by languages be effectively extracted based on linguistic facts? Can cognitive informatics and computational linguistics join forces to build an explanatory model of knowledge, as described by Aristotle's four causes? I believe studies on these provocative issues can lead to productive synergy between cognitive informatics and computational linguistics.

COGNITIVE INFORMATICS AND PATTERN THEORY

Cognitive informatics, at its foundation, posits information as a fundamental aspect of the universe, parallel in importance to matter and energy (Wang, 2003a). Information is conceptualized in this context as "any property or attribute of the natural world that can be distinctly elicited,

generally abstracted, quantitatively represented, and mentally processed by the brain. Informatics is then conceived as the study of the structure and dynamics of information and its interrelation with mass-energy, and is understood to incorporate applied aspects and also fundamental theoretical aspects such as concept algebra, information geometry, etc.

An alternate, but conceptually related foundation for the study of cognition is "pattern theory," as articulated in *The Hidden Pattern* (Goertzel, 2006b) and utilized as the foundation for AI theories and designs of (Goertzel, 2006a, 2009a). In the "patternist perspective," the notions of production and simplicity are taken as foundational, and a pattern in X is defined as some f which is simpler than X but produces X. Pattern theory connects to information theory in several ways, one being that it contains algorithmic information theory (Chaitin, 1987) as a special case. The various aspects of intelligence, including memory, learning, perception, action and creativity, are then articulated in pattern-theoretic terms. In pattern theory, the relation between mass-energy and pattern is seen as one of non-foundational inter-containment, meaning that validity is assigned to both of the following perspectives: a) patterns in the universe arise via combinations and interactions of material and energetic entities, b) matter and energy themselves are examples of patterns arising in "universal mind" (cf. Peirce's aphorism that "matter is mind hide-bound with habit").

In spite of their philosophical differences, cognitive informatics and pattern theory have spawned somewhat related approaches to intelligent systems design; for instance, both focus on the creation of autonomic intelligent systems (Wang, 2004, 2009a). However, pattern theory leads to a greater focus on the emergent patterns that may arise when different cognitive processes interact in the pursuit of common goals and related phenomena such as cognitive synergy (Goertzel, 2009b).

COGNITIVE INFORMATICS AND KNOWLEDGE REPRESENTATION

Cognitive informatics (Wang, 2002a), initiated by Yingxu Wang and his colleagues in 2002, is born from the marriage of cognitive and information sciences. It investigates into the internal information processing mechanisms and processes of the natural intelligence (i.e., human brains and minds) and artificial intelligence (i.e., machines).

Hawkins and Blakeslee (2004) pointed out that there were fundamentally different mechanisms between human brains and machines. Human can focus on different levels during the process of problem solving. This leads to the theory of granular computing (GrC). GrC is a way of thinking that relies on the human ability to perceive the real world under various levels of granularity, in order to abstract and consider only those things that serve a specific interest, and to switch among different granularities. By focusing on different levels of granularity, one can obtain different levels of knowledge, as well as a deeper understanding of the inherent knowledge structure.

Rough set theory, proposed by Pawlak in 1982, is one of the most important models of GrC (Pawlak, 1987). Most existing rough set models are still processing data with a flat data table while the hierarchical attribute values have not been considered. We extended the traditional rough set theory and proposed a hierarchical rough set model. The hierarchical rough sets can be referred to as a model of cognitive informatics. In hierarchical rough set model, hierarchical attribute values are considered. For each attribute, concept hierarchy is constructed. That is, we extend a single attribute to a concept hierarchy tree by introducing the prior knowledge, and thus each attribute can be processed at multiple levels. We can choose any level for each attribute in terms of the requirement of problem solving so as to discover the

knowledge in different levels. From the view of relation, hierarchical rough set model also extends traditional equivalence relation to a nested series of equivalence relations.

It is recognized that human thought and knowledge were normally organized as hierarchical structures, where concepts were ordered by their different levels of specificity or granularity (Yao, 2005; Wang, 2008c, 2009e). With granular structures, the triangle summarizes three mutually supporting perspectives: philosophy (structured thinking), methodology (structured problem solving), computation (structured information processing).

The theory of knowledge spaces, proposed by Doignon and Falmagne in 1985, can be regarded as another model of cognitive informatics and GrC. It represents a new paradigm in mathematical psychology for knowledge assessment. It starts out with rather simple psychological assumptions on assessing students' knowledge based on their ability to answer questions. Knowledge spaces may be viewed as a theory of information presentation and information use. The main objective of knowledge spaces is to effectively and economically solve the problem of knowledge assessment. In knowledge spaces, a person's knowledge states are represented and assessed systematically by using a finite set of questions. A collection of subsets of questions is called a knowledge structure, i.e., a granular structure, in which each subset is called a knowledge state or a cognitive state, i.e., a granule. The family of knowledge states may be determined by the dependency of questions or the mastery of different sets of questions by a group of students. Rough sets and knowledge spaces are two related theories. We introduced two of the central topics in rough sets, approximations and reduction, into knowledge spaces and revealed the strong connection between the two theories based on a common framework of GrC.

COGNITIVE INFORMATICS AND SYMBIOTIC COMPUTING

Motivation for Symbiotic Computing

The growth of the ICT industry enables people to get various kinds of information from the Internet by using high performance computers and advanced network technologies. The recent rapid growth of the ubiquitous technologies provide more convenient services for users, which is expected to lead the traditional ICT society to the ubiquitous society where people can access any information in anyplace and at anytime.

On the other hand, problems in the internet society, such as the digital divide, security, network-based crimes, are going to remain as more serious problems to built safe and secure information society. These problems have been caused due to social and human difficulty rather than due to the computer and network technology. For example, people don't feel comfort if they know that they cannot access important and useful information resources due to lack of IT skills, which can be used easily by skillful users. They also may feel hesitation when they want to access web sites to do something useful in an ICT society if they don't have enough knowledge and skills. A skill-less user probably wants supports by computer systems that know him/her well and has social knowledge for him/her to act in the future ICT society safely and securely. Therefore, new disciplinary is expected to tackle these difficult problems by bringing in the sociality and humanity into computing models.

Concept of Symbiotic Computing

A Licklider's view of Man-Computer symbiosis was extended to a view of Neo-Symbiosis in term of the Human Information Interaction (Griffith and Greiter, 2007). In the context of the symbiosis, the quality of life of people in the Real Space (RS) becomes higher if every person couples tightly with the Digital Space (DS) and has a partnership with DS. However, problems of the Internet age such as digital divide, prevent many people from coupling tightly with the Internet.

According to the above symbiosis, we define Community-Agents Symbiosis as a relation that: 1) People in a community in Real Space are tightly coupled with a special agent in digital space, and 2) A person and a personal agent keep partnership for him/her to act safely and conveniently in RS and DS.

Therefore, the concept of the symbiotic computing is a computing model to built Community-Agents Symbiosis by bringing in the sociality and humanity into computing models. Symbiotic computing consists of four function models of Perceptual Functions, Social Functions, Cognitive Functions and Decision Functions as shown in Figure 2.

Relationship between Symbiotic Computing and Cognitive Informatics

One of goals of Symbiotic Computing is to build a Community-Agent Symbiosis between a person and a Partner Agent which recognize one another to help the partner's activities in RS and DS. Trust between partners will be born when they perceive their existences and intentions mutually. The model of the partner agent is similar as the Layered Reference Model of the Brain LRMB (Wang, 2007b, 2009c; Wang et al., 2006). The Partner Agent is a multi-agent system which will have the characteristics of the Cognitive Machines (Kinsner, 2007; Wang, 2009c).

COGNITIVE INFORMATICS AND GRANULAR MODELING

Cognitive informatics and cognitive science have so far involved the main contents of perception, attention, memory, language, thought,

Figure 2. The conceptual framework of symbiotic computing

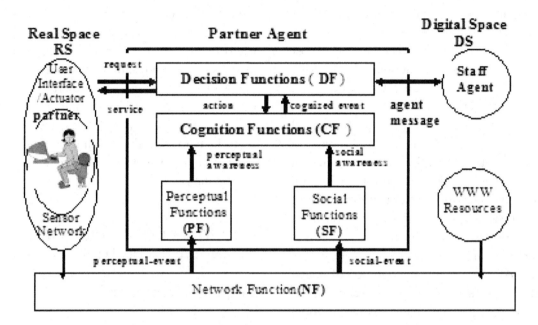

appearance, and consciousness. Researchers with different professional backgrounds use different research methods. Granular Computing (GrC) is a new methodology for solving complex problems in the field of artificial intelligence. Its essence is to analyze the problem from different aspects and granularities, and then to obtain a comprehensive or integrated solution (or approximate solution). Taking problem solving as an interactive communication in different levels, it makes problem solving highly efficient (Zedeh, 1997; Yao, 2008).

The actual cognition environment is a complicated information world. Different cognition theories and methods are studied from different viewpoints respectively, and they are linked to different subjects or areas. There are several typical cognition models, such as psychology cognition model (Robert & Jeffery, 2005), cognitive informatics models of the brain proposed by Wang (2002a, 2003a), concept cognition model proposed by Zhang and Xu (2007) and ontology cognition model by William and Austin (1999). They have a common characteristic, to indicate that humans cognize things from different aspects and levels. Building a hierarchical structure for complex information (granulation) at first, and then mining the characteristics of things on different granularity levels in the hierarchical structure, people can essentially cognize things, and gradually build an information tree which is a cognition model from outside to inside, from shallow to deep, and from simple to complex. GrC provides a new way to simulate human thinking in solving complicated problems.

When people face a chaotic and unlabeled information world, they used to abstract a lot of complex information into some simple concepts in order to analyze and understand them clearly. Yao, Wang, and Zadeh present unifying GrC frameworks on a high-level examination of GrC (Yao, 2008; Wang, 2009h; Wang, Zadeh & Yao, 2009). From the view point of philosophy, GrC tries to abstract and formalize human cognition, and then get a structural thinking pattern. There are three basic elements in cognition mode based on GrC, namely granule, granulation and multi-granularity at multiple layers.

Over 90% of the information captured by human beings is visual information. Computer image information processing is one of the key technologies in computer science. However, most traditional image processing methods describe the characteristics of images by image pixel, color and resolution, while not simulate the human brain. Thus, it is difficult for traditional image processing methods to search image in huge data sets efficiently. Human brain can identify images quickly, because human brain gets the characteristics of things from different granularity levels or different aspects, rather than remembers every characteristic. This process is similar to that of complex problem solving based on GrC. At present, human cognition of image based on GrC attracts many researchers attention. For example, the image cognition model is proposed by Zhang (2002), the computational cognitive model is proposed by Shi et al. (2008), and an automatic face modeling algorithm based on the facial structure of knowledge-based three-dimensional image plane leaflets is proposed by Wang and Gong (2008, 2009). In the process of image cognition, human brain can acquire information in different granularity levels automatically as follows. The first step is the multi-granularity (multi-layer) description of image information which simulates the process of human brain's recognition of image in multi-granularity (as well as the zoom-in and zoom-out process). The second step is image information processing. In order to cognize and identify image information, a concept-tree about image information needs to be built, and it is a stable image information structure (such as pyramid-structure). The top-layer image information is about some basic information, and the bottom-layer information is detailed information (such as pixels, texture, resolution, etc.). Human brain usually does not deal with complex information directly, and it deals with the image information in the hierarchical "pyramid" structure in a top down manner.

In order to let a computer obtain the cognition abilities like human brain for dealing with image information efficiently, two key problems need to be solved, that is, multi-granularity image description and multi-granularity image processing. Multi-granularity image description should be consistent with the human multi-granularity hierarchical cognition model, and multi-granularity image processing (such as searching and identification) depends on image information representation.

COGNITIVE COMPUTING AND GRANULAR COMPUTING

Cognitive Computing

There has been a surge of renewed interest in understanding human cognition and intelligence, in an attempt to unlock the workings of the brain. Cognitive computing is triggered by the fundamental studies in cognitive informatics since 2002 (Wang, 2002a, 2003a, 2007b, 2008b, 2009a; Wang et al., 2009) and followed by IBM and other organizations' initiatives in 2007 (CC, 2007; Wangb, 2009). Research efforts have been made in several directions under various names, including cognitive informatics (Wang, 2002a, 2003b), cognitive computing (or cognitive computation) (CC, 2007; Wang, 2009b; Taylor, 2009), cognitive systems and machines (Kinsner, 2007; Morris et al., 2006), brain informatics (Zhong et al., 2007), and others. Those interdisciplinary studies on the reverse-engineering of the brain aim at understanding the nature of human cognition, as well as designing and implementing cognitive systems and machines.

Cognitive informatics, as an emerging field of study, was initiated by Yingxu Wang in 2002 and further developed by him and his associates since then (Wang, 2002a, 2007b). In cognitive informatics, *cognitive computing* is defined as "intelligent computing methodologies and systems based on cognitive informatics theories that implement computational intelligence by autonomous inferences and perceptions mimicking the mechanisms of the brain (Wang, 2008a, 2009b; Wang & Wang, 2006)." Cognitive Computing 2007 adopts a similar vision developed in cognitive informatics since 2002 where cognitive computing is perceived as "a study of top-down, global, unifying theories that explain observed cognitive phenomena (the 'mind'), that are consistent with known bottom-up neurobiological facts (the 'brain'), that are computationally feasible ..., and that are mathematically principled (CC, 2007). Cognitive computing is a search for computer science-type software/hardware elements that are consistent with known neurobiological facts about the brain and give rise to observed mental processes of perception, memory, language, intelligence, and, eventually, consciousness. Very simply speaking, Cognitive Computing is when computer science meets neuroscience to explain and implement psychology. ... Cognitive Computing is about engineering the mind by reverse engineering the brain."

Granular Computing

As a paradigm of human-inspired computing (Yao, in press), granular computing (GrC) focuses on a special class of approaches to problem solving; these classes are characterized by multiple levels of granularity (Bargiela & Pedrycz, 2009; Lin et al., 2002; Pedrycz et al., 2008; Wang, Zadeh & Yao, 2009). GrC is inspired by humans and aims at serving both humans and machines. A grand challenge for GrC is to reverse-engineer human problem solving. Once we understand the underlying principles, we can empower everyone to be a better problem solver on one hand, and implement machine problem solving on the other (Yao, in press).

The triarchic model of GrC consists of three perspectives: the philosophy of structured thinking, the methodology of structured problem solving, and the computation of structured information processing (Yao, 2006, 2008). The main ideas of the theory are summarized as follows: a) *Granular Structures: Multilevel and Multiview:* A central notion is granular structures characterized by multilevel and multiview. Granular structures consists of inter-connected and inter-acting granules, families of granules interpreted as levels of differing granularity, and partially ordered multiple levels known as hierarchical structures. While a multilevel hierarchy represents a particular view, a collection of many hierarchies represents a multiview description. b) *GrC Triangle:* The vertices of the triangle represent the philosophy of structured thinking, the methodology of structured problem solving, and the computation of structured information processing.

Cognitive Computing and GrC

We consider an important task of cognitive computing, which is to build a conceptual and computational model for explaining human cognition and intelligence. The perspectives of GrC are connected and mutually support the objectives of cognitive computing.

Minsky (2006) portrays a typical brain as containing a great many different parts called resources. The concept of resources is used as an abstract notion without a direct linkage to biological implementation in a brain. A state of mind is explained from the activities of a certain collection of mental resources. In terms of GrC, mental resources may be interpreted as granules. Hawkins (2004) uses the notion of a cortical hierarchy for deriving a memory-prediction framework for explaining intelligence, which may be related to granular structures. These two conceptual models are based on a granule-based description of the brain.

There is evidence from cognitive science that GrC captures some of the essential features of human computing and problem solving. The limited human information processing capacity demands a granulation of a real-world problem so that a complex problem is divided into a small number of granules. The practical daily needs for quick, but suboptimal, decisions require humans to solve a problem at multiple levels of granularity. The selection of the right level of granularity greatly increases the odds of arriving at a satisfactory solution. The notion of granularity may play a key role in explain human intelligence and cognitive computing. GrC can learn from cognitive computing and contribute to cognitive computing.

COGNITIVE INFORMATICS AND MACHINE LEARNING

Cognitive Informatics (CI) is regarded as a convergence of natural and artificial intelligence, which has emerged as a cutting-edge and multidisciplinary research area that tackles the fundamental issues and problems shared by modern informatics, cognitive computing, cybernetics, optimization, fuzzy systems, neural networks, data mining, knowledge discovery, medical science, systems engineering, software engineering, finance computing, management, healthcare and other topics. In other words, CI combines elements of learning, adaptation, evolution and fuzzy logic (fuzzy and rough sets) to create programs and make systems that are, to some extent, *intelligent*. More specifically, CI embraces all of the computational techniques for various topics such as simulated annealing, machine learning, artificial immune systems, expert systems hybrid intelligent systems, hybrid logic, simulated reality, soft computing, Bayesian networks, chaos theory, ant colony optimization, particle swarm optimization, cognitive robotics, developmental robotics, evolutionary robotics, intelligent agents, knowledge-based engineering, theory-based semantics, bioinformatics and bioengineering, autonomous mental development, computational finance and computational economics, intelligent systems, emergence/emergent technologies, data mining, concept mining, etc.

- Cognitive machine learning: Multistrategy learning systems are concerned with the integration of two or more inference types and/or representational mechanisms. These systems make use of the strengths of individual learning strategies, and therefore can be applied to a wider range of problems. It is observed that human learning is clearly not limited to any single strategy, but can involve any type of strategy, or a combination of them, depending on the task at hand. As a result, research on multistrategy learning is the key to understanding learning processes in general, to making progress in machine learning, as well as to extending the applicability of current machine learning methods to new practical domains.

- Knowledge discovery and data mining: Discovery-based science is viewed as a scientific methodology that emphasizes analyses of large volumes of experimental data or text data with the goal of finding new patterns or correlations, leading to hypothesis formation and other scientific methodologies, which includes: a) *Data mining*: looking for associations or relationships in operational or transactional data; b) *Text mining and information extraction*: looking for concepts and their associations or relationships in natural language text such as structured, semi-structured and unstructured text mining; c) *Text summarization*: extracting terms and phrases from large text document collections that summarize their content; and d) *Web mining*: Web structure, content and usage mining; as well as ontology learning from text and databases.

- Knowledge-based systems: The next generation of knowledge-based systems aims to provide support for decision making, and information sharing at any place anytime. Such systems need to tap into large knowledge bases of domain-specific knowledge, which combine machine learning and structured background knowledge representation, such as ontology, and causal representations and reasoning. Information sharing is concerned with creating collaborative knowledge environments for sharing and disseminating information.

COGNITIVE INFORMATICS AND COGNITIVE PENETRABILITY

In the pursuit of engineering cognitive computers, there is an important yardstick against which the performance of such a machine will be measured: an ability to handle contradictory or inconsistent information. Inconsistency is commonplace in the real world and is an accepted part of life. How to manage inconsistency is a multi-dimensional issue. In this article, we focus our attention on the desirability dimension for inconsistency. It turns out that not all inconsistencies are bad, some are even desirable. In the article, we examine a desirable inconsistency that manifests itself as the consequence of cognitive penetrability which is the hallmark of the plasticity of human cognition. Our hope is that the work can help pave the way for developing better inconsistency management and handling methods for cognitive machines (Wang, 2002a, 2007b; Wang, Kinsber & Zhang, 2009).

Cognitive computing strives to engineer holistic intelligent machines that can seamlessly tie together a collection of components that mimic the mental processes dealing with sensation, cognition, perception, emotion, action, and interaction (Zhang, 2007, 2008). The SyNAPSE project, abbreviated for Systems of Neuromorphic Adaptive Plastic Scalable Electronics, and funded by DARPA recently, presents a significant step toward this ambitious goal (DARPA, 2009). One of the desirable features in the SyNAPSE project is to exhibit the adaptation of such a cognitive machine in dynamic, uncertain, probabilistic environments that include partial, erroneous and sometimes contradictory information (DARPA, 2008). Thus, it is an important task in cognitive computing to address the issue of managing and handling inconsistency in knowledge and information.

Desirable Inconsistency

Inconsistency is a multi-dimensional issue in nature (Zhang, 2009). It can arise due to different causes: deficiency in ontological models, epistemic conflicts, defaults that are conflicting, reliability of information sources, incomplete information, defeasible inheritance induced, assertion lifting, deliberate act, or errors. Inconsistency can occur during belief merging, group decision making process, problem solving, or query answering. There are different ways to classify types of inconsistency based the logical forms involved, levels of granularity in knowledge, or categories of knowledge.

Inconsistency has different interpretations depending on the objectives of the circumstances involved. There have been different approaches for detecting inconsistency. How to handle inconsistency once detected is another dimension that includes: tolerating, learning from it, resolving, deferring, or conducting risk analysis. For different manifestations of inconsistency there are significance and degree of information measurements that can be used to differentiate the importance of inconsistent cases.

Temporal property for inconsistency is yet another important dimension. There are several useful temporal properties here: complete temporal inconsistency, partial temporal inconsistency, or fully temporal consistency. Sometimes, an inconsistency is said to be latent because it does not constitute an already established or antagonism or conflict yet, but has the potential of becoming one.

An interesting dimension is the desirability of inconsistency, which addresses the conditions and circumstances under which an inconsistency is considered desirable or useful. Figure 3 summarizes some of the most important aspects of

Figure 3. Dimensions of inconsistency

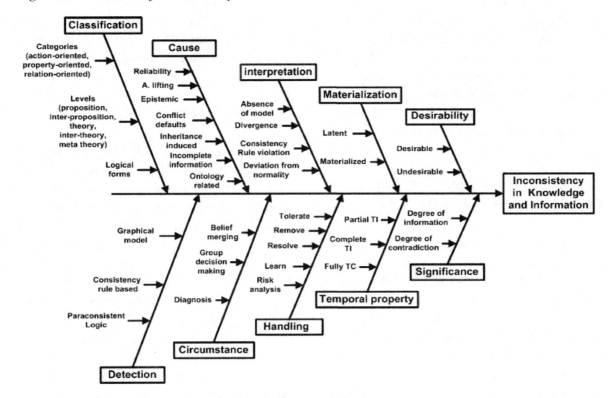

inconsistency management. The focus of this section is on a desirable inconsistency that manifests itself as the consequence of cognitive penetrability (Pylyshyn, 1999).

Cognitive Penetrability

The concept of cognitive penetrability was introduced by Zenon Pylyshsyn to capture the essence of the plasticity of human cognition: the pattern of behavior can be altered in a rational way by changing subjects' beliefs about the task (Pylyshyn, 1989).

The plasticity of human intelligence lies in the fact that many mental processes dealing with sensation, cognition, perception, emotion, action, and interaction are cognitively penetrable: the knowledge, beliefs, goals and expectations a person possesses could influence the experience, behaviors and consequent judgments the person has in those mental processes.

If a system is cognitively penetrable then the function it computes is sensitive, in a semantically coherent way, to the organism's goals, beliefs and expectations, in other words, the function can be altered in a way that bears some logical relation to what the system knows (Pylyshyn, 1999). As exhibited in the natural cognitive systems, human beings can revise their goals, beliefs, expectations, and plans in the face of fresh evidence or as a result of inferences which update previously held beliefs. These human cognitive systems are central processes and depend crucially on the cognitive functions like attention, working memory, executive functions (the ability to hold and manipulate representations in working memory) and inference (the ability to produce consistent sets of beliefs applying rules of procedural rationality) (Gerrans & Kennett, 2006). Cognitive processes not sensitive in the aforementioned way are cognitively impenetrable (cognitive processes whose computational mechanisms are independent of beliefs, goals, and expectations). There are many cognitive processes that are cognitively impenetrable, for instance, visual illusions persist despite our beliefs that they are not veridical representations. Other human cognitive processes that are cognitively impenetrable include: basic emotional responses to stereotypical stimuli, and some classes of automatic and immediate judgment (Gerrans & Kennett, 2006).

Desirable Inconsistency

When cognitively penetrable processes result in revised or updated beliefs, the situation arises where a revised belief may become inconsistent with the previously held belief. The fire alarm example in (Brachman & Levesque, 2004) demonstrates such situation. When responding to a fire alarm, the default action is to evacuate the building. However, if we know that the fire alarm is being tested, then the response is not to evacuate the building. Using AlarmGoingOff(x), AlarmTesting(x), Evacuate(x) to denote alarm going off in building x, alarm testing in building x, and evacuating building x, respectively, we have the following two sentences:

AlarmGoingOff(x) $\wedge$ *¬AlarmTesting(x)* $\supset$ *Evacuate(x)*

AlarmGoingOff(x) $\wedge$ *AlarmTesting(x)* $\supset$ *¬Evacuate(x)*

which are conflicting with each other.

This inconsistency stems from the consequence of cognitive penetrability: what we know determines how we react. It is a reflection of the plasticity of human cognition. As such, it's a desirable inconsistency. Given a conflicting or contradictory circumstance, if it captures the consequence of cognitive penetrability, then we say that it is cognitive penetrability induced inconsistency and refer to it as *CP-inconsistency*. In the real world environment, not all the inconsistent information or knowledge is undesirable and useless. Many are even desirable. The desirability of inconsistency is

predicated on what it can be used to accomplish. There are many plausible circumstances where inconsistency is regarded as having different levels of usefulness.

COGNITIVE INFORMATICS AND ROLE-BASED SOCIAL COMPUTING

Mental (or cognitive) workload is a way to measure the mental demands of complex systems (Tsang, 2001; Young & Stanton, 2001; Yousoof et al., 2006). Mental overload (or information overload, see Grise & Gallupe, 1999) is a situation that a person is not able to deal successfully with all the information presented to him or her. It is a usual phenomenon in our cognitive activities. For example, a researcher may have too many materials to read from different publication resources, such as, books, journals, conferences, reports, and web-based publications and a pilot may see too many signals from the panel of the fighter when an emergency happens.

In a complex system composed of people and computer systems, mental overload is a key issue to make a success for both people (the human users) and the computer system. This is a problem of interaction between natural intelligences and artificial intelligences, i.e., NAII (Natural and Artificial Intelligences Interaction) in the point of view of Cognitive Informatics. Mental overload occurs often in NAII if the interaction is not properly processed.

To restrain the mental overload is the first step for people to efficiently work and interact with machines. Different persons have different ways to deal with workload. A capable person may command a large quantity of soldiers to win a battle by restraining his or her mental overload but an incapable person may make a mess in an easy-going situation because he or she lacks efficient methods to deal with mental workload. Good methods are required to assist people to easily curb mental overload.

Abstraction, classification, extraction, analysis, synthesis and organization are ordinary methods for people to organize and deal with mental workload, because they provide a way to discard useless information and concentrate on real and important information that is critical for people's decision making.

Cognitive models (Wang, 2002a, 2007b; Wang et al., 2006) apply these methods to explain how the brain works. Processes, objects, and classes are conventional mechanisms to model cognitive activities and they are good tools for people to decrease mental overload. However, some of these mechanisms are a little too abstract and too difficult for people to master, e.g., a good abstraction ability requires a person's life long struggle to build and some people may not organize well for a whole life. Therefore, computer-based tools are required. Roles and Role-Based Collaboration (RBC) are one of the promising mechanisms and ways to build such tools.

Roles (Zhu & Zhou, 2008) are a good mechanism to provide abstraction, classification, extraction, analysis, synthesis and organization. They are easy-to-understand components for cognitive thinking beside processes, classes, and objects. The RBC model E-CARGO (Zhu & Zhou, 2006) (Environments, Classes, Agents, Roles, Groups and Objects) provides a way to model the complex world, which can be applied into NI analysis, AI modeling, and NAII assistance.

CONCLUSION

Cognitive Informatics (CI) has been presented as a transdisciplinary enquiry of computer science, information sciences, cognitive science, and intelligence science that investigates into the internal information processing mechanisms and processes of the brain and natural intelligence, as well as their engineering applications in cognitive computing. This article has summarized the presentations of a set of 16 position papers in the ICCI'09 *Panel on Cognitive Informatics and Cognitive Computing* contributed from invited panelists who are part of the world's preeminent researchers and scholars in the field of cognitive informatics and cognitive computing.

Following the successful organization of ICCI 2009 in Hong Kong (Baciu et al., 2009), IEEE ICCI 2010 will be held at Tsinghua University, Beijing, China in July 2010. The theme of ICCI'10 will be "Cognitive Computing and Knowledge Processors". The 10th anniversary event of IEEE ICCI series, ICCI 2011, will be celebrated in Banff, Calgary, Canada where the first event in the series was inaugurated in 2002.

REFERENCES

Baciu, G., Wang, Y., Yao, Y., Chan, K., Kinsner, W., & Zadeh, L. A. (Eds.). (2009). *Proceedings of the 8th IEEE International Conference on Cognitive Informatics (ICCI'09)*. Los Alamitos, CA: IEEE Computer Society Press.

Bargiela, A., & Pedrycz, W. (Eds.). (2009). *Human-Centric Information Processing Through Granular Modelling*. Berlin, Germany: Springer.

Brachman, R. J., & Levesque, H. J. (2004). *Knowledge representation and reasoning*. San Francisco: Morgan Kaufmann Publishers.

CC. (2007). *Cognitive Computing, A Multidisciplinary Synthesis of Neuroscience, Computer Science, Mathematics, Cognitive Neuroscience, and Information Theory*. Retrieved from http://wwwbisc.eecs.berkeley.edu/CognitiveComputing07/

Chaitin, G. (1987). *Algorithmic Information Theory*. Reading, MA: Addison-Wesley.

DARPA. (2008). *Systems of Neuromorphic Adaptive Plastic Scalable Electronics* (Defense Sciences Office, DARPA-BAA08-28). Alrington, VA: Author.

DARPA. (2009). *SyNAPSE Project*. Retrieved from http://www.fbo.gov/index?s= opportunity&mode=form&id= b7b66ad9c 0d5a7df21d9488b107256ae&tab=core&_ cview=1&cck=1&au=&ck=

Gerrans, P., & Kennett, J. (2006). Is cognitive penetrability the mark of the moral? *Philosophical Explorations*, *9*(1), 3–12. doi:10.1080/13869790500492284

Goertzel, B. (2006a). *Patterns, Hypergraphs and General Intelligence*. Paper presented at WCCI-06, Vancouver, BC, Canada.

Goertzel, B. (2006b). *The Hidden Pattern*. Boca Raton, FL: Brown Walker.

Goertzel, B. (2009a). *Cognitive Synergy: A Universal Principle of Feasible General Intelligence?* Paper presented at ICCI'09, Hong Kong.

Goertzel, B. (2009b). *OpenCogPrime: A Cognitive Synergy Based Architecture for Embodied General Intelligence*. Paper presented at ICCI-09, Hong Kong.

Gong, X., & Wang, G. Y. (2008). A novel deformation framework for face modeling from a few control points. In G. Wang, et al. (Eds.), *RSKT 2008* (LNAI 5009, 434-441).

Gong, X., & Wang, G. Y. (2009). Based on the feature points of three-dimensional face variable model. *Journal of Software*, *20*(3), 724–733.

Griffith, D., & Greiter, F. L. (2007). Neo-Symbiosis: The next stage in the evolution of human information interaction. *International Journal of Cognitive Informatics and Natural Intelligence*, *1*(1), 39–52.

Grisé, M. L., & Gallupe, R. B. (1999). Information overload: Addressing the productivity paradox in face-to-face electronic meetings. *Journal of Management Information Systems*, *16*(3), 157–185.

Hawkins, J., & Blakeslee, S. (2004). *On Intelligence*. New York: Henry Holt and Company.

Jahn, R., Dunne, B. J., Bradish, G., Dobyns, Y., Lettieri, A., & Nelson, R. (2000). Mind/Machine Interaction Consortium: PortREG Replication Experiments. *Journal of Scientific Exploration*, *14*(4), 499–555.

Kinsner, W. (2007). Towards cognitive machines: Multiscale measures and analysis. *International Journal of Cognitive Informatics and Natural Intelligence*, *1*, 28–38.

Lin, T. Y., Yao, Y. Y., & Zadeh, L. A. (Eds.). (2002). *Data Mining, Rough Sets and Granular Computing*. Heidelberg, Germany: Physica-Verlag.

Minsky, M. (2006). *The Emotion Machine: Commonsense Thinking, Artificial Intelligence, and the Future of the Human Mind*. New York: Simon & Schuster.

Morris, R., Tarassenko, L., & Kenward, M. (Eds.). (2006). *Cognitive Systems: Information Processing Meets Brain Science*. New York: Elsevier.

Nelson, R. (2000, July 2-7). *Subtle Energies and Uncharted Realms of the Mind*. Paper presented at the Esalen Conference.

Pawlak, Z. (1987). Rough Logic. *Bulletin of the Polish Academy of Science . Technical Science*, *5-6*, 253–258.

Pedrycz, W., Skowron, A., & Kreinovich, V. (Eds.). (2008). *Handbook of Granular Computing*. Chichester, UK: Wiley.

Pirolli, P. (2009). Powers of 10: Modeling Complex Information-Seeking Systems at Multiple Scales. *IEEE Computer*, *42*(3), 33–40.

Pylyshyn, Z. (1989). Computing in cognitive science. In M. I. Posner (Ed.), *Foundations of cognitive science* (pp. 49-92). Cambridge, MA: MIT Press.

Pylyshyn, Z. (1999). Is vision continuous with cognition? The case for cognitive impenetrability of visual perception. *The Behavioral and Brain Sciences*, *22*, 341–423.

Robert, J. S., & Jeffery, S. M. (2005). *Cognition psychology*. Belmont, CA: Wadsworth.

Shi, Z. W., Hu, H., & Shi, Z. Z. (2008). A computational cognitive model for the brain. *International Journal of Cognitive Informatics and Natural Intelligence, 2*(4), 85–99.

Taylor, J. G. (2009). Cognitive computation. *Cognitive Computation, 1*, 4–16. doi:10.1007/s12559-008-9001-8

Tsang, P. S. (2001). Mental workload. In *International encyclopedia of ergonomics and human factors* (pp. 809-813).

Wang, Y. (2002a, August). Keynote: On Cognitive Informatics. In *Proceedings of the 1st IEEE International Conference on Cognitive Informatics (ICCI'02)*, Calgary, Alberta, Canada (pp. 34-42). IEEE CS Press.

Wang, Y. (2002b). The Real-Time Process Algebra (RTPA). *Annals of Software Engineering, 14*, 235–274. doi:10.1023/A:1020561826073

Wang, Y. (2003a). On Cognitive Informatics. *Brain and Mind: A Transdisciplinary Journal of Neuroscience and Neurophilosophy, 4*(2), 151-167.

Wang, Y. (2003b). Cognitive Informatics: A New Transdisciplinary Research Field. *Brain and Mind: A Transdisciplinary Journal of Neuroscience and Neurophilosophy, 4*(2), 115-127.

Wang, Y. (2004, August). On Autonomic Computing and Cognitive Processes (Keynote Speech). In *Proceedings of the 3rd IEEE International Conference on Cognitive Informatics (ICCI'04)*, Victoria, BC, Canada (pp. 3-4). IEEE CS Press.

Wang, Y. (2006, July). Keynote: Cognitive Informatics - Towards the Future Generation Computers that Think and Feel. In *Proceedings of the 5th IEEE International Conference on Cognitive Informatics (ICCI'06)*, Beijing, China (pp. 3-7). IEEE CS Press.

Wang, Y. (2007a). *Software Engineering Foundations: A Software Science Perspective, CRC Series in Software Engineering, Vol. II*. New York: Auerbach Publications.

Wang, Y. (2007b). The Theoretical Framework of Cognitive Informatics. *International Journal of Cognitive Informatics and Natural Intelligence, 1*(1), 1–27.

Wang, Y. (2007c). The OAR Model of Neural Informatics for Internal Knowledge Representation in the Brain. *International Journal of Cognitive Informatics and Natural Intelligence, 1*(3), 64–75.

Wang, Y. (2008a). On Contemporary Denotational Mathematics for Computational Intelligence. In *Transactions of Computational Science* (Vol. 2, pp. 6-29). New York: Springer.

Wang, Y. (2008b). Novel Approaches in Cognitive Informatics and Natural Intelligence. In *ISR Series in Advances of Cognitive Informatics and Natural Intelligence* (Vol. 1). Hershey, PA: Information Science References.

Wang, Y. (2008c). On Concept Algebra: A Denotational Mathematical Structure for Knowledge and Software Modeling. *International Journal of Cognitive Informatics and Natural Intelligence, 2*(2), 1–19.

Wang, Y. (2008d). On System Algebra: A Denotational Mathematical Structure for Abstract System Modeling. *International Journal of Cognitive Informatics and Natural Intelligence, 2*(2), 20–42.

Wang, Y. (2008e). RTPA: A Denotational Mathematics for Manipulating Intelligent and Computational Behaviors. *International Journal of Cognitive Informatics and Natural Intelligence, 2*(2), 44–62.

Wang, Y. (2009a). On Abstract Intelligence: Toward a Unified Theory of Natural, Artificial, Machinable, and Computational Intelligence. *International Journal of Software Science and Computational Intelligence, 1*(1), 1–18.

Wang, Y. (2009b). On Cognitive Computing. *International Journal of Software Science and Computational Intelligence, 1*(3), 1–15.

Wang, Y. (2009c). A Cognitive Informatics Reference Model of Autonomous Agent Systems (AAS). *International Journal of Cognitive Informatics and Natural Intelligence, 3*(1), 1–16.

Wang, Y. (2009d). Paradigms of Denotational Mathematics for Cognitive Informatics and Cognitive Computing. *Fundamenta Informaticae, 90*(3), 282–303.

Wang, Y. (2009e). Toward a Formal Knowledge System Theory and Its Cognitive Informatics Foundations. *Transactions of Computational Science, 5,* 1–19. doi:10.1007/978-3-642-02097-1_1

Wang, Y. (2009f). On Visual Semantic Algebra (VSA): A Denotational Mathematical Structure for Modeling and Manipulating Visual Objects and Patterns. *International Journal of Software Science and Computational Intelligence, 1*(4), 1–15.

Wang, Y. (Ed.). (2009g). Special Issue on Cognitive Computing, On Abstract Intelligence. *International Journal of Software Science and Computational Intelligence, 1*(3), 1–116.

Wang, Y. *(2009h, June).Granular Algebra for Modeling Granular Systems and Granular Computing. In* Proceedings of the 8th IEEE International Conference on Cognitive Informatics (ICCI'09), *Hong Kong, China (pp. 145-154). IEEE CS Press.*

Wang, Y., Johnston, R. H., & Smith, M. R. (Eds.). (2002). *Proceedings of the 1st IEEE.* Los Alamitos, CA: IEEE Computer Society Press.

Wang, Y., & Kinsner, W. (2006). Recent Advances in Cognitive Informatics. *IEEE Transactions on Systems, Man and Cybernetics. Part C, Applications and Reviews, 36*(2), 121–123. doi:10.1109/TSMCC.2006.871120

Wang, Y., Kinsner, W., Anderson, J. A., Zhang, D., Yao, Y., & Sheu, P. (2009). A Doctrine of Cognitive Informatics. *Fundamenta Informaticae, 90*(3), 203–228.

Wang, Y., Kinsner, W., & Zhang, D. (2009a). Contemporary cybernetics and its facets of cognitive informatics and computational intelligence. *IEEE Transactions on Systems, Man and Cybernetics . Part B, 39*(4), 1–11.

Wang, Y., Kinsner, W., & Zhang, D. (2009b). Contemporary Cybernetics and its Faces of Cognitive Informatics and Computational Intelligence. *IEEE Trans. on System, Man, and Cybernetics . Part B, 39*(4), 823–833.

Wang, Y., & Wang, Y. (2006). Cognitive Informatics Models of the Brain. *IEEE Transactions on Systems, Man and Cybernetics. Part C, Applications and Reviews, 36*(2), 203–207. doi:10.1109/TSMCC.2006.871151

Wang, Y., Wang, Y., Patel, S., & Patel, D. (2006). A Layered Reference Model of the Brain (LRMB). *IEEE Transactions on Systems, Man, and Cybernetics . Part C, 36*(2), 124–133.

Wang, Y., Zadeh, L. A., & Yao, Y. (2009). On the System Algebra Foundations for Granular Computing. *International Journal of Software Science and Computational Intelligence, 1*(1), 64–86.

Wang, Y., Zhang, D., Latombe, J.-C., & Kinsner, W. (Eds.). (2008). *Proceedings of the 7th IEEE International Conference on Cognitive Informatics (ICCI'08).* Los Alamitos, CA: IEEE Computer Society Press.

William, S., & Austin, T. (1999). Ontologies. *IEEE Intelligent Systems,* 18-19.

Yao, Y. Y. (2005). Perspectives of Granular Computing. In *Proceedings of the 2005 IEEE International Conference on Granular Computing* (Vol. 1, pp. 85-90).

Yao, Y. Y. (2006). Three perspectives of granular computing. *Journal of Nanchang Institute of Technology, 25*, 16–21.

Yao, Y. Y. (2008). A unified framework of granular computing. In W. Pedrycz, A. Skowron, & V. Kreinovich (Eds.), *Handbook of Granular Computing* (pp. 401-410). New York: Wiley.

Yao, Y. Y. (in press). Human-Inspired Granular Computing. In J.T. Yao (Ed.), *Novel Developments in Granular Computing: Applications for Advanced Human Reasoning and Soft Computation.*

Young, M. S., & Stanton, N. A. (2001). Mental workload: Theory, measurement, and application. In *International encyclopedia of ergonomics and human factors* (pp. 818-821).

Yousoof, M., Sapiyan, M., & Kamaluddin, K. (2006). Reducing Cognitive Load in Learning Computer Programming. In *Proceedings of the World Academy of Science, Engineering and Technology* (Vol. 12, pp. 259-262).

Zadeh, L. A. (1997). Towards a theory of fuzzy information granulation and its centrality in human reasoning and fuzzy logic. *Fuzzy Sets and Systems, 19*, 111–127. doi:10.1016/S0165-0114(97)00077-8

Zhang, B., & Zhang, L. (2002). Granular computing and human cognition. In *Proceedings of the KAIST-Tsinghua Joint Workshop on Brain Science and Human-like Technology* (pp. 37-49).

Zhang, D. (2007). Fixpoint Semantics for Rule Base Anomalies. *International Journal of Cognitive Informatics and Natural Intelligence, 1*(4), 14–25.

Zhang, D. (2008). On temporal properties of knowledge base inconsistency. *Springer Transactions on Computational Science, 2*, 20–37.

Zhang, D. (2009). Quantifying knowledge base inconsistency via fixpoint semantics. *Springer Transactions on Computational Science, 2*, 145–160.

Zhang, W. X., & Xu, W. H. (2007). Granular computing based on the cognition model. *Journal of Engineering Mathematics, 6*(24), 957–971.

Zhong, N., Liu, J., Yao, Y. Y., Wu, J., Lu, S., & Li, K. (Eds.). (2007). *Web Intelligence Meets Brain Informatics (LNAI 4845)*. Berlin, Germany: Springer.

Zhu, H., & Zhou, M. C. (2006). Role-based Collaboration and its Kernel Mechanisms. *IEEE Transactions on Systems, Man, and Cybernetics . Part C, 36*(4), 578–589.

Zhu, H., & Zhou, M. C. (2008). Roles in Information Systems: A Survey. *IEEE Transactions on Systems, Man, and Cybernetics . Part C, 38*(3), 57–589.

This work was previously published in volume 4, issue 1 of the International Journal of Cognitive Informatics and Natural Intelligence, edited by Yingxu Wang, pp. 1-29, copyright 2010 by IGI Publishing(an imprint of IGI Global).

Chapter 2
The Cognitive Process of Comprehension:
A Formal Description

Yingxu Wang
University of Calgary, Canada

Davrondzhon Gafurov
Gjovik University College, Norway

ABSTRACT

Comprehension is an ability to understand the meaning of a concept or an action. Comprehension is an important intelligent power of abstract thought and reasoning of humans or intelligent systems. It is highly curious to explore the internal process of comprehension in the brain and to explain its basic mechanisms in cognitive informatics and computational intelligence. This paper presents a formal model of the cognitive process of comprehension. The mechanism and process of comprehension are systematically explained with its conceptual, mathematical, and process models based on the Layered Reference Model of the Brain (LRMB) and the Object-Attribute-Relation (OAR) model for internal knowledge representation. Contemporary denotational mathematics such as concept algebra and Real-Time Process Algebra (RTPA) are adopted in order to formally describe the comprehension process and its interaction with other cognitive processes of the brain.

INTRODUCTION

Despite of several-decade advances in computer science and artificial intelligence (AI), computers are still passive machines (Wilson & Keil, 2001; Wang, 2002a, 2009b). However, human beings are much active and intelligent in problem solving and decision-making, although they are not good at memory and retrieving of information. In general, computers can store a huge amount of data efficiently; while human beings make sense of or comprehend them in order to make them useful for the society and everyday lives.

DOI: 10.4018/978-1-4666-1743-8.ch002

Cognitive Informatics (CI) is a new and interdisciplinary research area that studies how information is processed and represented by human brain and how this knowledge can be applied in computing and information sciences (Wang, 2002a, 2003, 2007b; Wang, Kinsner, & Zhang, 2009; Wang et al., 2009). Cognitive informatics treats the natural world as a triple *<I, E, M>* where *I* is information, *E* energy, and *M* matter. *Information* is used to model the abstract world, whereas *energy* and *matter* are used to model the physical world. A Layered Reference Model of the Brain (LRMB) is developed in (Wang et al., 2006) that identified 43 cognitive processes at seven layers known as the sensation, memory, perception, action, meta-cognitive, meta-inference, and higher cognitive layers from the bottom up.

In cognitive informatics, cognitive science, AI, and computational intelligence, comprehension is identified as an ability to understand something, which indicates an intelligent power of abstract thought and reasoning of humans or intelligent systems. It is curious to explore the internal process of comprehension in the brain and to explain its basic mechanisms, because comprehension is one of the fundamental processes of brain at the higher cognitive layer according to LRMB. Two denotational mathematical means known as concept algebra (Wang, 2008c) and Real-Time Process Algebra (RTPA) (Wang, 2002b, 2007a) will be introduced in order to formally deal with the modeling of the highly abstract cognitive entity and process of comprehension and other cognitive processes.

This paper attempts to build a formal model for the fundamental cognitive process of comprehension. The mechanism and process of comprehension are systematically explained with its conceptual, mathematical, and process models. The paper discusses the conceptual model of comprehension in cognitive informatics and cognitive psychology based on the computational, functional, and cognitive models of the brain developed in (Wang & Wang, 2007).

The Object-Attribute-Relation (OAR) model for internal knowledge representation (Wang, 2007c) and concept algebra are introduced, which forms a foundation for explaining the cognitive mechanisms of comprehension. The mathematical model of comprehension is developed based on OAR and concept algebra. Then, comprehension as a cognitive process is conceptually elaborated and formally modeled in RTPA, which provides a rigorous description of the comprehension process and its interaction with other cognitive processes of the brain.

THE CONCEPTUAL MODEL OF COMPREHENSION

The linguistic meaning of *comprehension* is an ability to understand the meaning of a concept or an action based on the intelligent power of abstract thought and reasoning. The basic unit of comprehension is a concept (Wallas, 1926; Hurley, 1997; Ganter & Wille, 1999; Wang, 2008c). Therefore, large scope comprehension at sentence and article levels may be analyzed and synthesized by concept-level comprehensions from the top down or the bottom up.

Concepts, Semantics, and Comprehension

The conceptual mode of comprehension to a given concept can be described by the analysis of the intension and extension of the concept and its relations to the entire knowledge of a person in term of an OAR model.

Definition 1. A *concept* is a basic cognitive unit to identify and/or model a real-world concrete entity and a perceived-world abstract subject.

A *concept* in linguistics is a noun or noun-phrase that serves as the subject of a *to-be* statement (Hurley, 1997; Ganter & Wille, 1999; Wang,

2008c). Concepts in cognitive informatics (Wang, 2002a, 2003, 2007b; Wang et al., 2009) are an abstract structure that carries certain meaning in almost all cognitive processes such as comprehension, thinking, learning, and reasoning.

A concept can be identified by its intension and extension (Smith & Medin, 1981; Hurley, 1997; Ganter & Wille, 1999; Wang, 2008c). The *intension* of a concept is the attributes or properties that a concept connotes. The *extension* of a concept is the members or instances that the concept denotes. For example, the intension of the concept *pen* connotes the attributes of being a writing tool, with a nib, and with ink. The extension of the pen denotes all kinds of pens that share the common attributes as specified in the intension of the concept, such as a ballpoint pen, a fountain pen, and a quill pen.

Definition 2. *Semantics* is the meaning of symbols, notates, concepts, functions, and behaviors, as well as their relations that can be deduced onto a set of predefined entities and/or known concepts.

Semantic analysis and comprehension are a deductive cognitive process. According to the OAR model for internal knowledge representation (Wang, 2007c), the semantics of a sentence in a natural language may be considered having been understood when: a) The logical relations of parts of the sentence are clarified; and b) All parts of sentence are reduced to the terminal entities, which are either a real-world image or a primitive abstract concept.

Definition 3. *Comprehension* is a higher cognitive process of the brain that searches relations between a given concept and a set of attribute (A), object (O), and/or relations (R) in long-term memory (LTM) in order to establish a representative OAR model for the concept by connecting it to appropriate clusters of the LTM.

In cognitive psychology, comprehension involves constructing an internal representation based on existing knowledge previously gained in the brain (Quillian, 1968; Matlin, 1998). Polya (1957) considered that when solving a problem one goes through the following four phases: a) Understanding (comprehending) the problem; b) Generating one or more hypotheses; c) Testing hypotheses; and d) Checking the result. In Polya's generic problem solving model, problem comprehension is the first and important step toward problem solving. In cognitive psychology, comprehension involves constructing an internal representation according to Matlin (1998). Both Polya and Matlin agree that comprehension has a relation with the comprehender's background knowledge. This indicates that whatever one is trying to comprehend one relies on one's existing knowledge previously gained in the brain.

The OAR Model for Internal Knowledge Representation

It is recognized that the natural intelligence is memory-based. There are sensory-buffer memory (SBM), short-term memory (STM), long-term memory (LTM), and action-buffer memory (ABM) in the brain. The cognitive model of LTM is developed in (Wang, 2007c) as an OAR model where the object is an abstract model of a physical entity or an abstract artifact, and the attribute is a sub-object that describes detailed properties of an object.

To rigorously explain the hierarchical and dynamic neural cluster model of memory at neurological and physiological levels, a logical model of memory is needed as given below known as the OAR model.

Definition 4. The *Object-Attribute-Relation (OAR) model* of LTM can be described as a triple, i.e.:

$$OAR \triangleq (O, A, R) \tag{1}$$

Figure 1. The OAR model of logical memory architectures

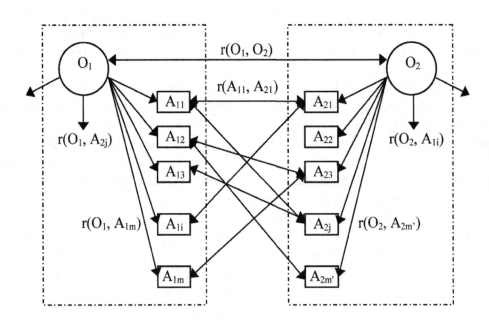

where O is a finite set of objects identified by unique symbolic names, i.e.:

$$O = \{o_1, o_2, ..., o_i, ..., o_n\} \qquad (2)$$

For each given $o_i \in O$, $1 \leq i \leq n$, A_i is a finite set of attributes for characterizing the object, i.e.:

$$A_i = \{A_{i1}, A_{i2}, ..., A_{ij}, ..., A_{im}\} \qquad (3)$$

where each $o_i \in O$ or $A_{ij} \in A_i$, $1 \leq i \leq n$, $1 \leq j \leq m$, is physiologically represented by a neuron in the brain.

For each given $o_i \in O$, $1 \leq i \leq n$, R_i is a set of relations between o_i and other objects or attributes of other objects, i.e.:

$$R_i = \{R_{i1}, R_{i2}, ..., R_{ik}, ..., R_{iq}\} \qquad (4)$$

where R_{ik} is a relation between two objects, o_i and $o_{i'}$, and their attributes A_{ij} and $A_{i'j'}$ $1 \leq i \leq n$, $1 \leq j \leq m$, i.e.:

$$R_{ik} = r(o_i, o_{i'})$$

$$| r(o_i, A_{ij})$$

$$| r(A_{ij}, o_{i'})$$

$$| r(A_{ij}, A_{i'j'}), 1 \leq k \leq q \qquad (5)$$

To a certain extent, the entire knowledge in the brain can be modeled as a global OAR model as illustrated in Figure 1.

According to the OAR model, the result of knowledge acquisition or learning can be embodied by the updating of the existing OAR in the brain. In other words, learning is a dynamic composition of the existing OAR in LTM and the currently created sub-OAR as expressed below.

Theorem 1. The *entire knowledge model* maintained in the brain, or the representation of learning results, states that the internal memory in the form of the OAR structure can be updated by the composition operation â between the existing OAR and the newly created sub-OAR (*sOAR*), i.e.:

$$OAR'\mathbf{ST} \triangleq OAR\mathbf{ST} \uplus sOAR'\mathbf{ST} = OAR\mathbf{ST} \uplus (O_s, A_s, R_s) \tag{6}$$

The above theory of knowledge acquisition lays an important foundation for learning theories and pedagogy. The OAR model can be used to describe information representation and its relation to the external world. The external world is described in terms of real entities whereas the internal world represented by virtual entities and objects. The internal world consists of two layers: the image and abstract layers. Virtual entity is an image of the real entity in internal world and located at the image layer. Objects in the abstract layer are grouped into two classes: the meta and derived objects. Meta objects have direct relations to virtual entities, while derived objects are represented internally without direct relations to virtual entities.

Investigation into the cognitive models of information and knowledge representation in the brain is perceived to be one of the fundamental research areas that help to reveal the mechanisms of the brain. The OAR model developed by Wang (2007c) describes human memory, particularly LTM, by using the *relational* metaphor, rather than the traditional *container* metaphor that used to be adopted in psychology, computing, and information science. The OAR model shows that human memory and knowledge are represented by relations, i.e., connections of synapses between neurons, rather than by the neurons themselves as the traditional container metaphor suggested. The OAR model can be used to explain a wide range of human information processing mechanisms and cognitive processes.

Knowledge as the content of memory is conventionally represented by the *container* metaphor (Hampton, 1997; Wilson & Keil, 2001), which was not able to explain how a huge amount of knowledge may be retained without increasing the number of neurons in the brain. However, the *relational* metaphor based on the OAR model may better explain the dynamic mechanisms of knowledge and memory (Wang, 2008c).

Definition 5. The *relational metaphor of knowledge* perceives that the brain does not create new neurons to represent new information, instead it generates new synapses between the existing neurons in order to represent new information.

The relational model of knowledge is supported by the physiological foundation of neural informatics known as the dynamic neural cluster model.

Corollary 1. The *Dynamic Neural Cluster* (DNC) model states that the LTM is dynamic, where new neurons (to represent objects or attributes) are assigning, and new connections (to represent relations) are creating and reconfiguring over time in the brain.

THE MATHEMATICAL MODEL OF COMPREHENSION

The mathematical model of comprehension is a mapping from a certain concept to a concept network expressed by the OAR model, which involves concept establishment, OAR interpretation, OAR updating, and memorization.

Abstract Concept and Concept Comprehension

A *concept* is a basic cognitive unit of knowledge and inferences by which the meanings and semantics of a real-world entity or an abstract entity may be represented and embodied based on the OAR model. Before an abstract concept is defined, the semantic environment or context (Medin & Shoben, 1988; Murphy, 1993; Codin, Missaoui, & Alaoui, 1995; Hampton, 1997; Hurley, 1997; Ganter & Wille, 1999; Wang, 2008c) in a given language, is introduced.

Definition 6. Let O denote a finite nonempty set of *objects*, and A be a finite nonempty set of *attributes*, then a *semantic environment* or *context* Θ is denoted as a triple, i.e.:

$$\Theta \triangleq (\mathcal{O}, \mathcal{A}, \mathcal{R})$$
$$= \mathcal{R}: \mathcal{O} \to \mathcal{O} | \mathcal{O} \to \mathcal{A} | \mathcal{A} \to \mathcal{O} | \mathcal{A} \to \mathcal{A} \qquad (7)$$

where R is a set of relations between O and A, and | demotes an alternative relation.

Concepts in denotational mathematics (Wang, 2008a, 2009d, 2010b; Wang, Zadeh, & Yaom, 2009) are an abstract structure that carries certain meaning in almost all cognitive processes such as thinking, learning, and reasoning.

Definition 7. An *abstract concept c* is a 5-tuple, i.e.:

$$c \triangleq (O, A, R^c, R^i, R^o) \qquad (8)$$

where

- O is a finite nonempty set of objects of the concept, $O = \{o_1, o_2, ..., o_m\} \subseteq \text{Þ}O$, where $\text{Þ}O$ denotes a power set of O.
- A is a finite nonempty set of attributes, $A = \{a_1, a_2, ..., a_n\} \subseteq \text{Þ}A$.
- $R^c = O \times A$ is a set of internal relations.
- $R^i \subseteq A' \times A$, $A' \sqsubseteq C' \wedge A \sqsubseteq c$, is a set of input relations, where C' is a set of external concepts, $C' \subseteq \Theta_C$. For convenience, $R^i = A' \times A$ may be simply denoted as $R^i = C' \times c$.
- $R^o \subseteq c \times C'$ is a set of output relations.

Definition 8. The *intension* of a concept $c = (O, A, R^c, R^i, R^o)$, c^*, is represented by its set of attributes A, i.e.:

$$c^*(O, A, R^c, R^i, R^o) \triangleq A = \bigcap_{i=1}^{\#O} A_{o_j} \subseteq \text{Þ}A \qquad (9)$$

where $\text{Þ}A$ denotes a power set of A, and # is the cardinal operator that counts the number of elements in a given set.

Definition 8 indicates that the *narrow* sense or the exact semantics of a concept is determined by the set of common attributes shared by all of its objects. In contrary, the *broad* sense or the rough semantics of a concept is referred to the set of all attributes identified by any of its objects as defined below.

Definition 9. The *extension* of a concept $c = (O, A, R^c, R^i, R^o)$, c^+, is represented by its set of objects O, i.e.:

$$c^+(O, A, R^c, R^i, R^o) \triangleq O = \{o_1, o_2, ..., o_m\} \subseteq \text{Þ}O \qquad (10)$$

where an *object* of a concept o is a derived instantiation of the concept that implements an end product of the concept, $o \subset O$, i.e.:

$$\forall c(O, A, R^c, R^i, R^o), o = c.o_i, o_i \subset O, R^o_o \equiv \varnothing$$
$$\Rightarrow o(A_o, R^c_o, R^i_o | A_o \supseteq A, R^c_o = o \times A_o, R^i_o = \{(c, o)\}) \qquad (11)$$

The formation of a concept by indentifying its intention (attributes) and extension (objects) is the fundamental cognitive approach to concept comprehension. Higher level comprehension at sentence and article levels can be manipulated by concept relational and compositional operations as defined in concept algebra.

Concept Algebra for Modeling the Mechanisms of Comprehension

Based on the abstract concept model, any real-world and concrete concept can be rigorously modeled. Further, a set of algebraic operations can be defined on abstract concepts, which form a mathematical structure known as concept algebra (Wang, 2008c).

Definition 10. A *concept algebra CA* on a given semantic environment Θ_C is a triple, i.e.:

$$CA \triangleq (C, OP, \Theta_C) = (\{O, A, R^c, R^i, R^o\}, \{\bullet_r, \bullet_c\}, \Theta_C) \qquad (12)$$

where $OP = \{\bullet_r, \bullet_c\}$ are the sets of *relational* and *compositional* operations on abstract concepts.

Definition 11. The *relational operations* $\bullet_r$ in concept algebra encompass 8 comparative operators for manipulating the algebraic relations between concepts, i.e.:

$$\bullet_r \triangleq \mathcal{R} = \{\leftrightarrow, \leftrightarrow, \prec, \succ, =, \cong, \sim, \triangleq\} \qquad (13)$$

where the relational operators stand for *related, independent, sub-concept, super-concept, equivalent, consistent, comparison,* and *definition,* respectively.

Definition 12. The *compositional operations* $\bullet_c$ in concept algebra encompass 9 associative operators for manipulating the algebraic compositions among concepts, i.e.:

$$\bullet_c \triangleq \Gamma = \{\stackrel{-}{\Rightarrow}, \stackrel{+}{\Rightarrow}, \stackrel{\sim}{\Rightarrow}, \stackrel{}{\Rightarrow}, \uplus, \mathbb{m}, \Leftarrow, \vdash, \mapsto\} \qquad (14)$$

where the compositional operators stand for *inheritance, tailoring, extension, substitute, composition, decomposition, aggregation, specification,* and *instantiation,* respectively.

Concept algebra deals with the algebraic relations and associational rules of abstract concepts. The associations of concepts form a foundation to denote complicated relations between concepts in knowledge representation. Detailed definitions of the algebraic operations in concept algebra have been provided in (Wang, 2008c).

On the basis of concept algebra, a generic model of human knowledge may be rigorously described as follows.

Definition 13. A *generic knowledge K* is an *n*-nary relation R_k among a set of *n* concepts in *C*, i.e.:

$$K = R_k : (\underset{i=1}{\overset{n}{X}} C_i) \to C \qquad (15)$$

where $\underset{i=1}{\overset{n}{\cup}} C_i = C$, and $R_k \in \Gamma$.

In Definition 13 the relation R_k is one of the concept operations defined in concept algebra (Eq. 14) that serves as a set of knowledge composing rules.

A complex knowledge is a composition of multiple concepts in the form of a concept network.

Definition 14. A *concept network CN* is a hierarchical network of concepts interlinked by the set of nine associations R defined in concept algebra, i.e.:

$$CN = R_\circ : \underset{i=1}{\overset{n}{X}} C_i \to \underset{i=j}{\overset{n}{X}} C_j \qquad (16)$$

where $R_k \in \Gamma$.

Because the relations between concepts are transitive, the generic topology of knowledge is a hierarchical concept network. The advantages of the hierarchical knowledge architecture in the form of concept networks are as follows:

a) *Dynamic*: The knowledge networks may be updated dynamically along with information acquisition and learning without destructing the existing concept nodes and relational links.

b) *Evolvable*: The knowledge networks may grow adaptively without changing the overall and existing structure of the hierarchical network.

THE COGNITIVE MODEL OF THE COMPREHENSION PROCESS

The cognitive informatics model of comprehension is a cognitive process at the high-level cognitive layer according to LRMB (Wang et al., 2006). The cognitive model of the comprehension process can be conceptually modeled by the following steps:

a. To search relations from *real entities* to *virtual entities* and/or existing *objects* and *attributes*.

b. To build a partial or adequate OAR model of the entity.

c. To wrap up the sub-OAR model by classifying and connecting it to appropriate clusters of the entire OAR in LTM.

d. To memorize the new OAR model and its connections in LTM.

The cognitive process of comprehension is informally modeled as shown in Figure 2. We assume that three other low-level cognitive processes, *search, memorization,* and *knowledge representation,* as shown in Figure 3, have already been defined (Wang et al., 2006) according to the LRMB. As shown in Figure 2, in the first step to comprehend a given real entity or concept, the knowledge manipulation engine of the brain searches the corresponding virtual entity and its relations to objects in the abstract layer of the memory. Depending on the results of the search for relations, the outcomes of the next step may be different. The ideal search result is that adequate relations have been found. In his case, comprehension is almost reached. The other possible result is that a partial comprehension, a very low level of comprehension, or a virtually no comprehension is obtained when a partial OAR model is built. In the first two cases, the partial OAR model is built as a sub-OAR model, where no sufficient relations have been found. In the last case, for a totally new concept, the search result is incomprehension where only an ID corresponding to the concept is created without any known relations to existing knowledge. All the cases indicate that, in cognitive informatics, everything is comprehensible except the extent of comprehension may vary in a range of 0% to 100%.

The comprehension process starts with identifying an input object (Box 2), which is a *virtual entity* or concept. For instance, when one is reading a text, a word or term may be identified whose meaning is not obvious. This triggers a cognitive process to comprehend the meaning of the concept. Another example can be that when one watches a picture one may not understand what it denotes or the meaning of some part of it may not be clear. In the above examples, the input objects can be a word, concept, formula, shape, picture, and the like.

When the object has been identified, the brain searches for possible relations between existing objects in the OAR model of LTM and the input object from external world. The brain looks for relations at the image layer and then the abstract layer of memory, respectively (Boxes 3 and 4). Once a connection with existing objects is found, the next step is to find out related attributes and relations in order to build an sOAR model for the object under comprehension (Box 5). If the problem domain is familiar to be understood, it is more likely that more related objects exist in LTM. After these steps, the brain checks if the result of searching is adequate for building a sOAR model for the object (Box 6).

If the findings are sufficient, the brain builds an sOAR model for the given object (Box 7). When the model is built, it needs to be connected with a cluster of existing knowledge. The brain classifies the sOAR model and connects it to the most appropriate cluster in the entire OAR model of LTM (Box 8). Only after this step, comprehension is achieved.

However, if the findings are inadequate after the search, the comprehension process builds a partial sOAR with limited information and then, requires further actions to obtain additional information from external resources (Box 10). For example, if one could not recall or does not understand the meaning of a given word by existing knowledge, one may check a dictionary or encyclopedia. The search from external resources may be a repetitive process. For instance, if one cannot find the meaning of the word in the dictionary, then someone may be asked for its meaning as an alternative.

After searching several times in external resources, the brain checks again whether findings are adequate (Box 11). If so, Steps 7 and 8 will be repeated. Otherwise, it is regarded as an incomprehension has been achieved (Box 12) at this given moment. But still the results are remembered in LTM. In the latter case, a partial sOAR model is stored and it may be simply an ID for an unknown concept for future comprehension. For example,

Figure 2. The cognitive model of the comprehension process

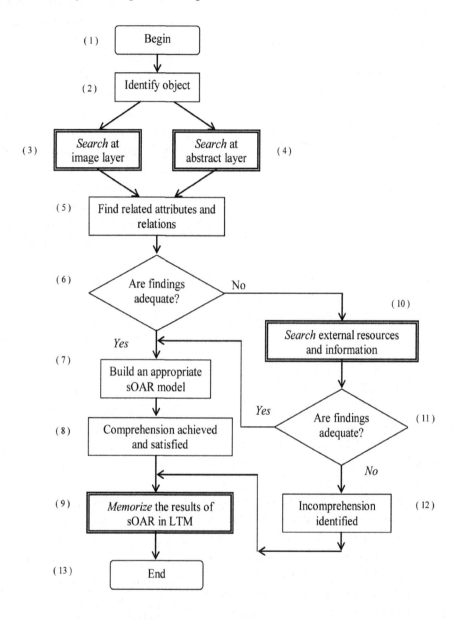

when reading one may come across completely a new word that may neither be found from a dictionary nor from all friends. Therefore, the word may simply be remembered by rote, without understanding its meaning. In this incomprehension case, one may remember the result as "the word has seven letters", "it starts with letter *k*", and "it resembles the word ..." etc. without any significant attribute. For another example, when one watches a picture of something but cannot figure out what it may denote, one can see that some parts of the picture resemble a hand, and other parts may resemble something else, but what the whole picture expresses cannot be understood. In both examples, the brain builds a partial sOAR model with few insignificant attributes and relations for the limited clues in existing knowledge. The final step in the comprehension process is to

Figure 3. Interaction between the comprehension process and other meta-cognitive processes

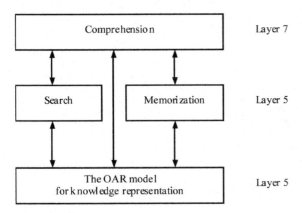

memorize the sub-OAR model and the updated entire OAR in LTM (Box 9), by which a comprehension process is completed.

FORMAL DESCRIPTION OF THE COMPREHENSION PROCESS

On the basis of the explanation of the comprehension process based on the abstract concept and the OAR models as developed in proceeding sections, a rigorous description of the cognitive process of comprehension can be formally modeled using Real-Time Process Algebra (RTPA). An RTPA description of the comprehension process is provided in Figure 4 based on the OAR representation of internal information and knowledge. The process numbers, PNN, used in Figure 4 are corresponding to the labels identified in the boxes of Figure 2, by which each part of the formal description can be mapped onto the flowgraph of the comprehension process.

The relationship between the comprehension process and other meta-processes, such as search, memorization, and knowledge representation, are illustrated in Figure 3 and specified in Figure 4. According to the LRMB model, the comprehension process belongs to Layer 7 – the higher

cognitive functions of the brain. When it is functioning, the Layer 5 meta-processes such as search and memorization have to be called as supporting cognitive processes.

The formal description of the comprehension process serves for two important purposes. First, it demonstrates that how the cognitive functions of the brain may be explicitly described and simulated by a real-time computational process. Second, it shows that, in general, the human behavior in terms of a set of cognitive processes can be formally and accurately described by denotational mathematics, particularly concept algebra and real-time process algebra.

CONCLUSION

Comprehension has been identified as one of the fundamental processes of the brain at the higher cognitive layer according to LRMB. Although knowledge and information are powerful, before any information can be possessed and processed in the brain, it has to be comprehended properly. This paper has explored the cognitive mechanisms and process of comprehension as one of the fundamental cognitive functions of the brain. The conceptual mode of comprehension has been described by the analysis of the intension and extension of a given concept and its relations to the entire knowledge of a learner in term of the OAR model. The mathematical model of comprehension is a mapping from a certain concept to a concept network in the form of OAR. The cognitive informatics model of comprehension is a cognitive process that implements the mapping between the given concept and the OAR model with the support of lower-level cognitive processes such as concept establishment, OAR interpretation, OAR updating, and memorization.

The cognitive mechanisms and process of comprehension can be applied in a wide range of applications in cognitive informatics and com-

Figure 4. Formal description of the comprehension process in RTPA

```
ComprehensionProcess (I:: TheConceptS;
                        O:: OAR(TheConceptS)ST, LcomprehensionN) ≜
{// I. Identify concept/object
 oS := TheConceptS                                                    // PNN = 2
 // II. Search for related attributes and objects
 → ( // PNN =3
     ( ScopeS := ImageLayerOfLTMS
       ↣ Search (I:: (oS, ScopeS);  O:: (ArST, RrST))
     )
    || // PNN = 4
     ( ScopeS := AbstartcLayerOfLTMS
       ↣ Search (I:: (oS, ScopeS);  O:: (ArST, RrST))
     )
   )
 // III. Built sub-OAR
 → ArST = {a₁, a₂, ..., aₙ}                                            // PNN = 5
 → RrST = {o₁, o₂, ..., oₘ}
 → ( ◆ (Ar ST ⊆ AmetaST) ∧ (RrST ⊆ OmetaST)
       ∧ (ArST = φ ∨ RrST = φ)                                        // PNN = 6
       → PL1S: sOAR(oS)ST = {oS, ArST, RrST}                          // PNN = 7
     | ◆ ~
       → ScopeS := ExternalResourcesS                                 // PNN = 10
       ↣ Search (I:: oS, ScopeS; O:: A'rST, R'rST)
       → ( ◆ (ArST ⊆ Ameta ) ∧ (RrST ⊆ Ometa ) ∧
             (ArST = φ ∨ RrST = φ)                                    // PNN = 11
             →PL1S
           | ◆ ~
             → sOAR(oS)ST = {oS, ArST, RrST}                          // PNN = 12
         )
     )
 // IV. Memorization
   → OAR'ST := OARST ⊎ sOARST
   ↣ Memorization (OAR'ST )                                           // PNN = 9
}                                                                     // PNN = 13
```

putational intelligence such as machine learning, problem solving, and on-line document retrieving. In software engineering, program comprehension plays an important role in evolution and maintenance of legacy systems. Comprehension and elicitation of reusable part of code plays an important role in object-oriented programming as well. The cognitive informatics theory for the comprehension process provides inside to the study on program comprehension, and to the development of easy-to-comprehend software systems in software engineering.

ACKNOWLEDGMENT

The authors would like to acknowledge the Natural Science and Engineering Council of Canada (NSERC) for its partial support to this work. We would like to thank the anonymous reviewers for their valuable comments and suggestions.

REFERENCES

Codin, R., Missaoui, R., & Alaoui, H. (1995). Incremental Concept Formation Algorithms Based on Galois (Concept) Lattices. *Computational Intelligence*, *11*(2), 246–267. doi:10.1111/j.1467-8640.1995.tb00031.x

Ganter, B., & Wille, R. (1999). *Formal Concept Analysis*. Berlin: Springer.

Hampton, J. A. (1997). *Psychological Representation of Concepts of Memory* (pp. 81–110). Hove, UK: Psychology Press.

Hurley, P. J. (1997). *A Concise Introduction to Logic* (6th ed.). Belmony, CA: Wadsworth.

Matlin, M. W. (1998). *Cognition* (4th ed.). New York: Harcourt Brace College Pub.

Medin, D. L., & Shoben, E. J. (1988). Context and Structure in Conceptual Combination. *Cognitive Psychology*, *20*, 158–190. doi:10.1016/0010-0285(88)90018-7

Murphy, G. L. (1993). Theories and Concept Formation . In Mechelen, I. V., (Eds.), *Categories and Concepts, Theoretical Views and Inductive Data Analysis* (pp. 173–200). New York: Academic Press.

Polya, G. (1957). *How to Solve It*. Garden City, NY: Doubleday Anchor.

Quillian, M. R. (1968). Semantic Memory . In Minsky, M. (Ed.), *Semantic Information Processing*. Cambridge, MA: MIT Press.

Smith, E. E., & Medin, D. L. (1981). *Categories and Concepts*. Cambridge, MA: Harvard University Press.

Wallas, G. (1926). *The Art of Thought*. New York: Harcourt-Brace.

Wang, Y. (2002a, August). Keynote: On Cognitive Informatics. In *Proceedings of the 1st IEEE International Conference on Cognitive Informatics* (ICCI'02), Calgary, Canada (pp. 34-42). Washington, DC: IEEE.

Wang, Y. (2002b). The Real-Time Process Algebra (RTPA). *Annals of Software Engineering*, *14*, 235–274. doi:10.1023/A:1020561826073

Wang, Y. (2003). On Cognitive Informatics. *Brain and Mind: A Transdisciplinary Journal of Neuroscience and Neurophilosophy, 4*(2), 151-167.

Wang, Y. (2007a, July). *Software Engineering Foundations: A Software Science Perspective* (CRC Series in Software Engineering, Vol. 2). New York: Auerbach Publications.

Wang, Y. (2007b). The Theoretical Framework of Cognitive Informatics. *International Journal of Cognitive Informatics and Natural Intelligence, 1*(1), 1–27.

Wang, Y. (2007c). The OAR Model of Neural Informatics for Internal Knowledge Representation in the Brain. *International Journal of Cognitive Informatics and Natural Intelligence, 1*(3), 64–75.

Wang, Y. (2008a). On Contemporary Denotational Mathematics for Computational Intelligence. *Transactions of Computational Science, 2*.

Wang, Y. (2008c). On Concept Algebra: A Denotational Mathematical Structure for Knowledge and Software Modeling. *International Journal of Cognitive Informatics and Natural Intelligence, 2*(2), 1–19.

Wang, Y. (2009b). On Cognitive Computing. *International Journal of Software Science and Computational Intelligence, 1*(3), 1–15.

Wang, Y. (2009d). Paradigms of Denotational Mathematics for Cognitive Informatics and Cognitive Computing. *Fundamenta Informaticae*, *90*(3), 282–303.

Wang, Y. (2010b). Keynote: Cognitive Informatics and Denotational Mathematics Means for Brain Informatics. In *Proceedings of the 1st Int'l Conference on Brain Informatics* (ICBI'10), Toronto, Canada.

Wang, Y., Kinsner, W., Anderson, J. A., Zhang, D., Yao, Y., & Sheu, P. (2009c). A Doctrine of Cognitive Informatics. *Fundam. Informatic.*, *90*(3), 203–228.

Wang, Y., Kinsner, W., & Zhang, D. (2009b). Contemporary Cybernetics and its Faces of Cognitive Informatics and Computational Intelligence. *IEEE Trans. on System, Man, and Cybernetics . Part B, 39*(4), 823–833.

Wang, Y., & Wang, Y. (2006). Cognitive Informatics Models of the Brain. *IEEE Transactions on Systems, Man and Cybernetics. Part C, Applications and Reviews, 36*(2), 203–207. doi:10.1109/TSMCC.2006.871151

Wang, Y., Wang, Y., Patel, S., & Patel, D. (2006). A Layered Reference Model of the Brain (LRMB). *IEEE Trans. on Systems, Man, and Cybernetics . Part C, 36*(2), 124–133.

Wang, Y., Zadeh, L. A., & Yao, Y. (2009a). On the System Algebra Foundations for Granular Computing. *International Journal of Software Science and Computational Intelligence, 1*(1), 64–86.

Wilson, R. A., & Keil, F. C. (2001). *The MIT Encyclopedia of the Cognitive Sciences*. Cambridge, MA: MIT Press.

This work was previously published in volume 4, issue 3 of the International Journal of Cognitive Informatics and Natural Intelligence, edited by Yingxu Wang, pp. 42-54, copyright 2010 by IGI Publishing (an imprint of IGI Global).

Chapter 3
A Hybrid Genetic Algorithm based Fuzzy Approach for Abnormal Retinal Image Classification

J. Anitha
Karunya University, India

C. Kezi Selva Vijila
Karunya University, India

D. Jude Hemanth
Karunya University, India

ABSTRACT

Fuzzy approaches are one of the widely used artificial intelligence techniques in the field of ophthalmology. These techniques are used for classifying the abnormal retinal images into different categories that assist in treatment planning. The main characteristic feature that makes the fuzzy techniques highly popular is their accuracy. But, the accuracy of these fuzzy logic techniques depends on the expertise knowledge, which indirectly relies on the input samples. Insignificant input samples may reduce the accuracy that further reduces the efficiency of the fuzzy technique. In this work, the application of Genetic Algorithm (GA) for optimizing the input samples is explored in the context of abnormal retinal image classification. Abnormal retinal images from four different classes are used in this work and a comprehensive feature set is extracted from these images as classification is performed with the fuzzy classifier and also with the GA optimized fuzzy classifier. Experimental results suggest highly accurate results for the GA based classifier than the conventional fuzzy classifier.

DOI: 10.4018/978-1-4666-1743-8.ch003

INTRODUCTION

Abnormal retinal image classification system is highly essential in the field of ophthalmology. Classification is a type of pattern recognition system which categorizes the different types of diseases. The effects of the eye abnormalities are mostly gradual in nature which shows the necessity for an accurate abnormality identification system. Most of the ophthalmologists depend on the visual interpretation for the identification of the types of diseases. But, inaccurate diagnosis will change the course of treatment planning which leads to fatal results. Hence, there is a requirement for a bias free automated system which yields highly accurate results. Besides being accurate, the system should be effective in terms of convergence rate which is highly essential for real time applications.

Automating the classification process is a challenging task. Besides being automated, the technique should be accurate and robust. Several computer assisted methods have been proposed for the classification and quantification of brain tumors. Vector fields based pathology identification in retinal images is available in the literature (Benson, 2008). But this technique yields superior results only if the abnormality is highly visible. Contrast enhancement based abnormality detection in retinal images has been implemented (Alan et al., 2006). The drawback of this system is the over estimation of the contrast in the image. Literature survey also reveals the application of wavelet transform for abnormality detection in retinal images (Quellec et al., 2008). The availability of other superior transforms shows the scope for improvement of this technique. Image processing based techniques are also used for retinal exudates detection (Osareh et al., 2003). Diabetic retinopathy detection is also successfully implemented using machine learning techniques (Niemeijer et al., 2007). Though these techniques are highly impressive, they fail to incorporate the intelligence techniques which

have proved to be much better than the image processing techniques.

The intelligence techniques form the subset of cognitive informatics which is the emerging trend in the area of engineering. The theoretical framework of cognitive informatics is proposed by (Wang, 2007). The concept of intelligence techniques is analyzed in detail in this report. The difference between the natural intelligence techniques and the artificial intelligence techniques is explained with the mathematical theorems. The foundation of autonomic computing is also explained by (Wang, 2007). Autonomic computing is the branch of artificial intelligence techniques which mainly deals with automation. The work proposed in this paper is also an automated system and hence it is closely related to cognitive informatics. The recent advances in the area of cognitive informatics is demonstrated by (Wang, 2007; Kisner, 2007). These artificial intelligence techniques which comprise the concepts of cognitive informatics can be used for various applications including the medical field. In this work, the application of intelligence techniques for eye disease identification is explored.

Artificial intelligence techniques generally yield highly accurate results and it includes neural networks, fuzzy theory, etc. Neural network based diabetic retinopathy identification system is reported in the literature (Yun, 2007). Exudate classification based on Support Vector Machine has been successfully implemented (Osareh, 2002). The application of perceptron neural network for retinal disease identification is explored (Treigys, 2007). Radial Basis Function neural networks based abnormality identification system is reported in the literature (Acharya, 2007). Multi layer neural networks are successfully used for keratoconus detection in retinal images (Accardo, 2003). Fuzzy logic techniques based disease identification techniques are also proposed in the literature (Sopharak, 2007). These artificial intelligence based techniques are highly efficient in terms of accuracy. But, the major drawback of these techniques is the convergence rate. Since most of the techniques are iterative in nature, they are computationally slow. Another reason for the inferior convergence rate is the large number of feature set used for the training process.

Several feature selection techniques are available in the literature to reduce the dimension of the dataset. These optimization techniques yield highly accurate results besides reducing the computational time period. Sequential forward selection method based optimization is reported in the literature (Staal, 2004). A modification of the sequential algorithm namely sequential floating selection algorithm is used for feature optimization (Niemeijer, 2006). But evolutionary optimization algorithms have claimed to yield much better results than these techniques. One of the widely used nature based optimization algorithm is Genetic Algorithm (GA). The application of GA based feature selection techniques are explored for improving the performance of the statistical classifiers (Peterson, 2005) and the neural classifiers (Palaniappan, 2009). Literature survey reveals the limited usage of GA for disease identification in the field of ophthalmology.

In this work, an attempt has been made to show the effectiveness of GA technique for abnormality identification in the field of ophthalmology. Real time images from four different categories are used in the work. Real time images collected from scan centers are used in this work. An extensive feature set is extracted from these images. These features are based on the statistical data and the histogram of the input image. GA based optimization is performed on these feature set to select the optimal feature set. Experiments are conducted using the fuzzy classifier with the whole feature set and the optimal feature set. An extensive analysis shows the superior performance of the GA based fuzzy classifier in terms of accuracy and convergence time period. Thus this work highlights the application of GA for abnormality detection in retinal images.

MATERIALS AND METHODS

The basic components of the proposed image classification system are shown in Figure 1. The various stages of the proposed technique are retinal image database (collected from ophthalmologist), pre-processing, feature extraction, feature selection and classification. A detailed explanation is provided in the subsequent sections.

In this study, 460 abnormal retinal images are used for classification. All the images are acquired by Aravind Eye Hospital, Coimbatore, India. The images are stored as colour TIFF images and are 1504×1000 pixels in size for all the objects. The real time images are collected from four abnormal categories namely non-proliferative diabetic retinopathy (NPDR), Central retinal vein occlusion (CRVO), Choroidal neo-vascularisation membrane (CNVM) and Central serous retinopathy (CSR).

As a pre-processing step, the green channel of the raw RGB image is extracted. Since most of the information is available in the green channel, this pre-processing step improves the accuracy of the subsequent steps.

Feature extraction is the technique of data reduction to find a subset of informative variables based on the image. In this work, twelve features

Figure 1. Proposed methodology

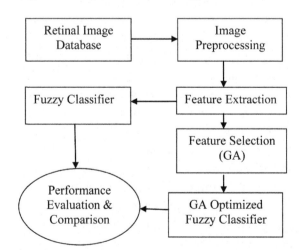

based on texture, shape, size, etc. are extracted from each image.

All the extracted features does not account for high accuracy. Feature selection technique removes the insignificant features besides reducing the dimensionality of the input feature set. In this work, Genetic Algorithm (GA) is used as an optimization algorithm. GA involves several procedures such as cross over, mutation to select the optimal features. The performance measures used in this work are classification accuracy and convergence time period.

In this work, fuzzy nearest neighbor classifier is used for image classification. The experiments are conducted individually with the optimized feature set and the un-optimized feature set. The results are analyzed in terms of the performance measures. The final results are validated with the human experts from the Aravind Eye Hospital, Coimbatore.

IMAGE PRE-PROCESSING

Pre-processing algorithms are implemented to enhance the original image so that it can increase the chances for success of subsequent processes. In this work, the objective of the pre-processing technique is twofold: (a) improving the contrast and (b) converting the original 3D image to 2D pixel values. Literature survey shows that the vessels/background contrast effect is high in the green channel than in the blue and red channels. Again, the subsequent feature extraction process will be made simpler if the 2D pixel values are used. To satisfy these two conditions, the green pixel values are extracted from the input image and stored in the 2D matrix.

FEATURE EXTRACTION

The purpose of feature extraction is to reduce the original data set by measuring certain properties, or features, that distinguish one input pattern from another pattern (Haarlick, 1979). The extracted feature should provide the characteristics of the input type to the classifier by considering the description of the relevant properties of the image into a feature space. Five features based on shape, size of the blood vessels and six features based on texture are used in this work.

Features based on Shape and Size of Blood Vessels

Initially, the blood vessels are segmented using thresholding technique. The resultant image is a binary image and from this image, the following features are calculated.

Area:

The area of an image is obtained by summing the areas of each pixel in the image. The area of an individual pixel is determined by looking at its 2-by-2 neighborhood. There are six different patterns, each representing a different area: Patterns with zero on pixels (area = 0) Patterns with one on pixel (area = 1/4) Patterns with two adjacent on pixels (area = 1/2) Patterns with two diagonal on pixels (area = 3/4) Patterns with three on pixels (area = 7/8) Patterns with all four on pixels (area = 1).

Perimeter:

The perimeter of an image is estimated by counting the number of perimeter pixels. A pixel is part of the perimeter if it is nonzero and it is connected to at least one zero-valued pixel. The pixel connectivity used is a 4-connected neighbourhood.

Circularity:

Circularity is a shape based feature which involves the characteristics of area and perimeter.

$$C = \frac{\left(perimeter\right)^2}{area} \quad (1)$$

Compactness:

Compactness is defined as the weighted circularity measure.

$$CO = 4\pi \left(area \Big/ \left(perimeter\right)^2 \right) \quad (2)$$

Tortuosity:

Tortuosity is a property of curve being tortuous (twisted; having many turns). There have been several attempts to quantify this property. The simplest mathematic method to estimate tortuosity is arc-chord ratio: ratio of the length of the curve to the distance between the ends of it.

Features Based on Texture

The textural features such as mean, standard deviation, skewness, kurtosis, energy and entropy based on the first order histogram are computed using the formulae given next.

The first order histogram estimate of p (b) is simply

$$p(b) = \frac{N(b)}{M} \quad (3)$$

where b = a gray level in the image

M = total number of pixels in a neighbourhood window centered about an expected pixel.

N(b) = the number of pixels of gray value b in the same window that $0 \leq b \leq L-1$.

Mean:

The average value of the pixel intensity values is called as mean. This feature is purely dependent on the gray values.

$$S_M = \bar{b} = \sum_{b=0}^{L-1} bp(b) \quad (4)$$

Standard deviation:

The deviation of each and every pixel intensity values from the mean intensity value is given by standard deviation.

$$S_D = \sigma_b = \left[\sum_{b=0}^{L-1} \left(b - \bar{b}\right)^2 p(b) \right]^{1/2} \quad (5)$$

Skewness:

The measure of symmetry of the input image is given by skewness.

$$S_S = \frac{1}{\sigma_b^3} \sum_{b=0}^{L-1} \left(b - \bar{b}\right)^3 p(b) \quad (6)$$

Kurtosis:

Kurtosis is a measure of whether the data are packed or flat relative to a normal distribution

$$S_K = \frac{1}{\sigma_b^4} \sum_{b=0}^{L-1} \left(b - \bar{b}\right)^4 p(b) - 3 \quad (7)$$

Energy:

The summation of the squares of gray levels of the image is known as angular second moment.

$$S_N = \sum_{b=0}^{L-1} \left[p(b)\right]^2 \qquad (8)$$

Entropy:

It measures the randomness of a gray level distribution. The entropy is expected to be high if the gray levels are distributed randomly throughout the image.

$$S_E = -\sum_{b=0}^{L-1} p(b) \log_2 \left\{p(b)\right\} \qquad (9)$$

The source of the statistical features for medical image analysis is illustrated in (Hemanth, 2010). These features are selected based on the previous work (Chung, 2005; Jelink, 2005). These features work especially well for retinal images.

FEATURE SELECTION

The features extracted from the retinal image database form the initial, high-dimensional feature space. All the features do not contribute to high figure of merit and hence feature space reduction technique is very much essential. Feature selection refers to the problem of dimensionality reduction of data, which initially consists of large number of features. The objective is to choose optimal subsets of the original features which still contain the information essential for the classification task. In this work, Genetic algorithm is proposed for feature selection.

Genetic Algorithm

Genetic Algorithm (Goldberg, 1989) can be viewed as a general purpose search method or an optimization method based on biological evolution. GA is a widely preferred optimization algorithm for many engineering applications. It

falls under the category of evolutionary algorithms since the operations are based on natural theory of evolution. GA maintains a set of candidate solutions called population and repeatedly modifies them. There are several mathematical operations used to modify the candidate solutions. At each step, the GA selects individuals from the current population to be parents and uses them to produce the children for next generation. Candidate solutions are represented as strings of fixed length called chromosomes. Each bit in the string is called as gene. A random population size is initialized and then a fitness function is used to reflect the goodness of each member of population. The fitness function may be a maximization function or minimizing objective function. The computational flowchart of GA is shown in Figure 2.

In this work, each of the twelve features are represented by a chromosome (string of bits) with

Figure 2. Flow diagram of genetic algorithm

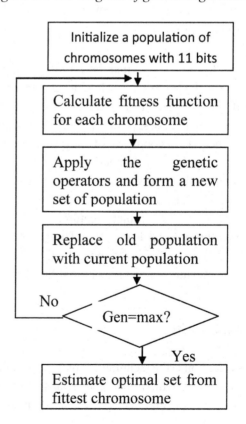

11 genes (bits) corresponding to the number of features. An initial random population of 20 chromosomes is formed to initiate the genetic optimization. A suitable fitness function is estimated for each individual. The fittest individuals are selected and the crossover and the mutation operations are performed to generate the new population. This process continues for a particular number of generations and finally the fittest chromosome is calculated based on the fitness function. The features with a bit value "1" are accepted and the features with the bit value of "0" are rejected. The fitness function used in this work is given by

$$Fitness = (\alpha * \gamma) + \beta * \left(\frac{|c| - |r|}{|c|} \right) \qquad (10)$$

where γ = classification accuracy

$|c|$ = total number of features
$|r|$ = length of the chromosome (number of '1's)
$\alpha \in [0, 1]$ and $\beta = 1 - \alpha$

This formula shows that the classification accuracy and the feature subset length have different significance for feature selection. A high value of α assures that the best position is at least a rough set reduct. The goodness of each position is evaluated by this fitness function. The criteria are to maximize the fitness values. After feature selection, two set of input features are stored among which one is the complete feature set and the other is the optimal feature set. The process of classification is carried out individually with the complete feature set and the optimal feature set.

CLASSIFIER

Classification is the technique of pattern recognition in which the unknown input data is allocated to one of the different categories based on some criteria. In this work, four groups are used corresponding to the four abnormal categories. The classifier used in this work is the fuzzy based classifier namely fuzzy nearest center classifier.

Fuzzy Nearest Neighbor Classifier

This classifier operates in two phases. In the first phase, each of the training data set is clustered into three clusters (background, blood vessels and the defective region) using the fuzzy C-means (FCM) algorithm. The centroid value of any one of the clusters is stored. This process is repeated for all the images from the four categories and the centroid values of all the four categories are stored. Now, for an unknown testing data, the corresponding cluster center is observed using FCM algorithm and the Euclidean distance is calculated with the trained four categories. The testing data is allotted to the category for which the Euclidean distance is minimum.

Algorithm

Fuzzy c-means algorithm is based on minimization of the following objective function:

$$J(U, c_1, c_2, ..., c_c) = \sum_{i=1}^{c} J_i = \sum_{i=1}^{c} \sum_{j=1}^{n} u_{ij}^{m} d_{ij}^{2} \qquad (11)$$

u_{ij} is between 0 and 1;
c_i is the centroid of cluster i;
d_{ij} is the Euclidian distance between i_{th} centroid (c_i) and j^{th} data point.
$m \in [1, \infty]$ is a weighting exponent.

Step 1:
Fuzzy partitioning of the known data sample is carried out through an iterative optimization of the objective function shown in eqn (11), with the update of membership u_{ij} and the cluster centers c_i by:

$$u_{ij} = \frac{1}{\sum_{k=1}^{c} \left(\frac{d_{ij}}{d_{kj}} \right)^{2/(m-1)}} \; ; \; c_i = \frac{\sum_{j=1}^{n} u_{ij}{}^{m} x_j}{\sum_{j=1}^{n} u_{ij}{}^{m}} \qquad (12)$$

At the $(k+1)^{\text{th}}$ iteration, if $\|u(k+1) - u(k)\| < \varepsilon$, then the classifier is assumed to have reached the stabilized condition. A detailed explanation is given in Ross (2004).

Step 2:

Observe the cluster center of the defective region for all the training samples. Store the cluster centers A_1, A_2, A_3 and A_4 which corresponds to the four abnormal categories namely CNVM, CRVO, CSR and NPDR.

Step 3:

For a new data, calculate the Euclidean distance between the data and all the cluster centers of the training samples.

Step 4:

Assign the data to the class with the cluster center whose Euclidean distance is minimum.

$$d(X, A_i) = \min_{1 \le k \le 4} \left\{ d(X, A_k) \right\} \qquad (13)$$

The threshold value (ε) used in this work is 0.01. This algorithm associates the image into any one of the four different abnormal categories based on the defective region. This classifier is tested individually with the whole feature set and with the optimal feature set. The experiments are carried out on an IBM PC Pentium with processor speed 700 MHz and 256 MB RAM. The software used for the implementation is MATLAB (version 7.0) developed by Math works Laboratory.

COMPARATIVE ANALYSIS OF GA BASED FUZZY CLASSIFIER AND CONVENTIONAL FUZZY CLASSIFIER

In this work, two classifiers are used to distinguish the different abnormal retinal images.

The first classifier is the conventional fuzzy nearest centre classifier which accepts the entire feature set as input and provides the classified output. In the proposed hybrid approach, the optimal feature set provided by the GA alone is used for classification. This usage of optimal feature set has substantially enhanced the performance of the conventional classifier. Initially, the two classifiers are analyzed in terms of accuracy which is followed by analysis on convergence rate and computational complexity.

All the extracted features do not guarantee high accuracy. Some of these features may be insignificant which tends to degrade the quality of the output. But the usage of an optimization algorithm eliminates the insignificant features which ultimately improves the accuracy of the classifier. The removal of insignificant features by the optimization algorithms depend on the initial parameter settings.

The convergence rate is the time taken by the classifier for training and testing. A quick convergence rate is always preferred. The training and testing time depends on the number of input features. More the size of the data set, higher will be the training time consumed by the classifier. In the hybrid classifier, the convergence time period is significantly reduced since the numbers of input features are minimized. At the same time, the accuracy will not be affected since the insignificant features alone are eliminated by the optimization algorithm.

Finally, the computational complexity of the hybrid classifiers are minimized to a greater extent since the mathematical operations required for the algorithm has to be performed only for a small size data set in the hybrid classifier. An extensive experimental analysis is provided in the next section to estimate the performance of the classifiers quantitatively in terms of the quality measures.

Figure 3. Sample input images

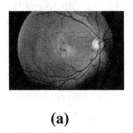 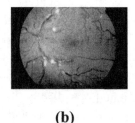 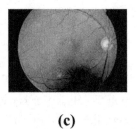

(a)   **(b)**   **(c)**

RESULTS AND DISCUSSIONS

Experiments are conducted on the 460 abnormal retinal images and an extensive analysis is performed based on the results. The performance measures used in this work are classification accuracy and convergence rate. Classification accuracy is the ratio of correctly classified images to the total images. Convergence time period is the time period required for the classification process. Higher classification accuracy and lower time period are preferred by the classification process. Initially, a suitable feature set is extracted from the input images. The features such as area and perimeter are calculated from the segmented blood vessels. These feature values are unique for each category which improves the results of the classification process. Some samples of the input images and the segmented images are shown in Figure 3 and Figure 4.

In Figure 4, the white pixels correspond to the extracted blood vessels. The size and shape of the blood vessels are based on the abnormalities and hence the area and perimeter feature values are unique for each class. Some other features are extracted from the pre-processed images. Even though high segmentation efficiency is not guaranteed, the feature values obtained are sufficient enough to yield high classification accuracy. Then, an extensive GA based feature selection process is performed to obtain the optimal feature set. Table 1 shows the features selected by the genetic algorithm.

From the above table, it is evident that three features are selected from the first category and three features are selected from the second category. Since area and perimeter are primitive shape based features, they are sidelined by the optimization technique. The other three features indirectly depend on area and perimeter and hence the loss of the primitive features does not make any significant change in the accuracy. But, the reduction in the feature size reduces the convergence time period. From the second category, mean and standard deviation are eliminated since they are purely dependent on the intensity values

Figure 4. Sample segmented retinal blood vessels

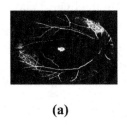 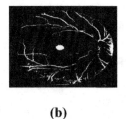 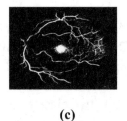

(a)   **(b)**   **(c)**

Table 1. Optimal feature set

Feature type	Whole feature set	Features selected by GA
Features based on size and shape	Area, Perimeter, Circularity, Compactness & Tortuosity	Circularity, Compactness & Tortuosity
Features based on first order histogram	Mean, Standard deviation, Skewness, Kurtosis, Energy, Entropy	Skewness, Energy & Entropy

of the input data. Skewness is preferred over kurtosis since the asymmetry property proves to be significant in classification process. Thus, the feature set dimension is highly reduced from eleven to six which indirectly reduces the convergence time period. Classification is then performed with the un-optimized fuzzy classifier and the GA optimized fuzzy classifier.

In the case of image classification, 460 abnormal images from four different classes are used. 30 images from each class are used for training and the remaining images are used for testing. The classification accuracy for the un-optimized fuzzy classifier is shown in Table 2.

From the above table, it is evident that CNVM images have been classified to a higher extent and the level of misclassification in the CRVO images is comparatively higher than the other types.

Then, the fuzzy classification is performed with the optimal feature set and the classification accuracy is noted. Table 3 lists the classification accuracy results of the GA optimized classifier.

Table 3 clearly shows the superior classification accuracy results of the CNVM images and the comparatively lower accuracy results of the CRVO images. The classification accuracy results of all the types are significantly higher than the un-optimized classifier. Table 4 depicts the overall classification accuracy of the classifiers.

The superior nature of the GA optimized classifier in terms of classification accuracy is clearly proved from the above results. The classification accuracy of the GA optimized classifier is significantly higher because of the absence of the insignificant features. Genetic Algorithm eliminates the unwanted features through the

Table 2. Performance measure of un-optimized classifier for the different abnormal types

Type	No.of training images	No.of testing images	Number of correctly classified images	Classification accuracy (%)
CNVM	30	99	88	88.8
CSR	30	83	72	86.7
CRVO	30	67	54	80.6
NPDR	30	91	79	86.8

Table 3. Performance measure of GA optimized classifier for the different abnormal types

Type	No. of training images	No. of testing images	Number of correctly classified images	Classification accuracy (%)
CNVM	30	99	93	93.9
CSR	30	83	77	92.8
CRVO	30	67	61	91.0
NPDR	30	91	85	93.4

Table 4. Overall performance measure of the classifiers

Classifier	Classification accuracy (%)
Un-optimized classifier	85.7
GA optimized classifier	92.7

Table 5. Convergence rate of the classifiers

Classifier	Average time period (CPU secs)
Un-optimized classifier	13784
GA optimized classifier	7120

optimization methodology. Thus, the effectiveness of GA for enhancing the efficiency of the classifiers has been explored.

The performance of the classifiers is further analyzed on the basis of the convergence rate i.e, the training time and the testing time. Training time refers to the time required by the classifier to derive classification rules that will allow it to classify the images. Testing time refers to the time required by a trained classifier to classify the untrained images. The training time and the testing time for the classifiers are shown in Table 5.

The time taken by the un-optimized classifier is almost two times higher than the GA optimized classifier. The reason is that the number of features used by the un-optimized classifier is eleven and the GA optimized classifier is six. Thus, a twofold increase in the convergence time period is observed in the un-optimized classifier. These results show the superior nature of the GA optimized classifier in terms of convergence rate.

Thus, this work highlights the application of Genetic Algorithm for performance enhancement in abnormal retinal image classification system.

CONCLUSION AND FUTURE WORK

In this paper, the application of Genetic Algorithm for abnormal retinal image classification has been highlighted through an experimental analysis. The classification accuracy of GA based classifier is sufficiently high when compared with the conventional classifier. The convergence time period is approximately halved for the un-optimized classifier over the GA based classifier. This analysis shows the necessity for an optimiza-

tion technique irrespective of the classifier used. This work effectively explores the characteristic feature of the Genetic Algorithm which is suitable for performance improvement of the classifiers.

One of the main challenges of this research work is the feature extraction. Different set of features may yield a higher accuracy. More shape and size based features can be used to improve the accuracy. The fuzzy classifier also can be replaced with the different classifier to achieve a higher accuracy. More experiments can be conducted on different abnormal types to show the effectiveness of Genetic Algorithm.

ACKNOWLEDGMENT

The authors wish to thank M/s. Aravind Eye Hospital, Coimbatore, Tamilnadu for the image database and validation.

REFERENCES

Accardo, P., & Pensiro, S. (2003). Neural network based system for early keratoconous detection from corneal topography. *Journal of Biomedical Informatics, 35*, 151–159. doi:10.1016/S1532-0464(02)00513-0

Acharya, R. (2007). Automatic identification of anterior segment eye abnormality. In . *Proceedings of the ITBM-RBM, 28*, 35–41.

Benson, S., & Yan, H. (2008). A Novel vessel segmentation algorithm for pathological retinal images based on the divergence of vector fields. *IEEE Transactions on Medical Imaging, 27*(2), 237–246. doi:10.1109/TMI.2007.909827

Chung, A. J., Deliganni, F., & Yang, Z. (2005). Extraction of visual features with eye tracking for saliency driven 2D/3D registration. *Image and Vision Computing, 23*, 999–1008. doi:10.1016/j.imavis.2005.07.003

Clark, M. C., Hall, L. O., Goldgof, D. B., & Murtagh, F. R. (2004). Brain tumor segmentation using knowledge-based and fuzzy techniques. *Journal of Fuzzy and Fuzzy-Neuro Systems in Medicine, 8*, 57–68.

Fleming, A. D. (2006). Automated microaneursym detection using local contrast normalization and local vessel detection. *IEEE Transactions on Medical Imaging, 25*(9), 1223–1232. doi:10.1109/TMI.2006.879953

Goldberg, D. E. (1989). *Genetic algorithm in search, optimization and machine learning*. Reading, MA: Addison Wesley.

Haarlick, R. M. (1979). Statistical and structural approaches to texture. *Man and Cybernatics, 67*, 786–804.

Hemanth, J., Selvathi, D., & Anitha, J. (2010). *Artificial Intelligence Techniques for Medical Image Analysis: Basics, Methods, Applications*. Berlin: VDM-Verlag.

Jelink, H. F., et al. (2005). Classification of pathology in diabetic eye diseases. In *Proceedings of the ARPS workshop on digital image computing* (pp. 9-13).

Niemeijer, M. (2006). Image structure clustering for image quality verification of color retinal images in diabetic retinopathy screening. *Medical Image Analysis, 10*, 888–898. doi:10.1016/j.media.2006.09.006

Niemeijer, M. (2007). Automated detection and differentiation of exudates in digital color fundus photographs for DR diagnosis. *Investigative Ophthalmology & Visual Science, 48*(5), 2260–2267. doi:10.1167/iovs.06-0996

Osareh, A. (2002). Comparative exudate classification using support vector machine and neural networks. In . *Proceedings of MICCAI, 2489*, 413–420.

Osareh, A. (2003). Automated identification of diabetic retinal exudates in digital colour images. *The British Journal of Ophthalmology, 87*, 1220–1223. doi:10.1136/bjo.87.10.1220

Palaniappan, R., & Eswaran, C. (2009). Using genetic algorithm to select the presentation order of training patterns that improves ARTMAP classification performance. *Applied Soft Computing, 9*, 100–106. doi:10.1016/j.asoc.2008.03.003

Peterson, R., Doom, T., & Raymer, M. (2005). GA facilitated KNN classifier optimization with varying similarity measures. In *Proceedings of Conference on Genetic and evolutionary computation* (pp. 1549-1550).

Quellec, G. (2008). Optimal wavelet transform for the detection of microaneurysms in retinal photographs. *IEEE Transactions on Medical Imaging, 27*(9), 1230–1241. doi:10.1109/TMI.2008.920619

Solis, M., et al. (2001). Pattern recognition of wavelets decomposition using ART2 networks for echoes analysis. In *Proceedings of the IEEE ultrasonic symposium, 1*, 679-682.

Sopharak, A., & Uyyanonvara, B. (2007). Automatic exudates detection from DR images using FCM and morphological methods. In *Proceedings of the IASTED International conference on advances in computer science and technology* (pp. 359-364).

Stall, J. (2004). Ridge based vessel segmentation in color images of the retina. *IEEE Transactions on Medical Imaging, 23*(4), 501–509. doi:10.1109/TMI.2004.825627

Timothy, J. R. (2004). *Fuzzy logic with engineering applications* (2nd ed.). New York: Wiley and sons.

Treigys, P., & Saltenis, V. (2007). Neural network as an ophthalmologic disease classifier. *Information Technology and Control, 36*(4), 365–371.

Wang, Y. (2007). The theoretical framework of cognitive informatics. *International Journal of Cognitive Informatics and Natural Intelligence, 1*(1), 1–27.

Wang, Y. (2007). Toward theoretical foundation of autonomic computing. *International Journal of Cognitive Informatics and Natural Intelligence, 1*(3), 1–16.

Wang, Y., & Kisner, W. (2006). Recent advances in cognitive informatics. *IEEE Transactions on Systems, Man and Cybernetics. Part C, Applications and Reviews, 36*(2), 121–123. doi:10.1109/TSMCC.2006.871120

Yun, W. (2008). Identification of different stages of Diabetic Retinopathy using retinal optical images. *Information Sciences, 178*, 106–121. doi:10.1016/j.ins.2007.07.020

This work was previously published in volume 4, issue 3 of the International Journal of Cognitive Informatics and Natural Intelligence, edited by Yingxu Wang, pp. 29-41, copyright 2010 by IGI Publishing (an imprint of IGI Global).

Chapter 4
Logical Connections of Statements at the Ontological Level

Cungen Cao
Chinese Academy of Sciences, China

Yuefei Sui
Chinese Academy of Sciences, China

Yu Sun
Chinese Academy of Sciences, China

ABSTRACT

In the classical formal logics, the negation can only be applied to formulas, not to terms and predicates. In (frame-based) knowledge representation, an ontology contains descriptions of individuals, concepts and slots, that is statements about individuals, concepts and slots. The negation can be applied to slots, concepts and statements, so that the logical implication should be considered for all possible combinations of individuals, concepts, slots and statements. In this regard, the logical implication at the ontological level is different from that at the logical level. This paper attempts to give such logical implications between individuals, concepts, slots, statements and their negations.

INTRODUCTION

In the first-order logic, there are three logical connectives $\vee$, $\wedge$ and negation $\neg$, where $\neg$ can only be applied on formulas to form new formulas, and for any formula $\neg\varphi$ and any model M, $\neg\varphi$ is true in M if and only if φ is not true in M.

In natural languages, the connectives and negations have many forms. For example, the exclusive disjunction (exclusive or) and inclusive disjunction (inclusive or). For the negation, the forms are varying. The negation can be applied to a statement (He is not happy), a concept (not a happy man), an individual (Not he is happy) and a value of an attribute (unhappy).

To formalize the different forms of the negation in natural languages, we consider the nega-

DOI: 10.4018/978-1-4666-1743-8.ch004

tion at the ontological level, where the levels are a classification of the various primitives used by knowledge representation systems, firstly defined by Brachman (1979), based on which Guarino (1994) added the ontological level to the levels:

- The logical level;
- The epistemological level;
- The ontological level;
- The conceptual level, and
- The linguistic level.

We believe that every level has its own negation.

The negation at the logical level is the logical negation $\neg$ on formulas. In the first order logic, the negation $\neg$ is applied only to formulas, i.e., if φ is a formula then so is $\neg\phi$; and φ is false if and only if $\neg\varphi$ is true. Hence, φ and $\neg\varphi$ are contradictory.

The negation at the epistemological level is the negation on formulas and on modalities. For example, let B be the epistemological modal *believe*, and φ be a first-order formula. Then, we have the following formulas:

$$B\varphi, (\neg B)\varphi, B(\neg\varphi), \neg(B\varphi);$$

where the negation in $(\neg B)\varphi$ is at the epistemological level; the negations in $B(\neg\varphi)$ and $\neg(B\varphi)$ are at the logical level. For example, the following sentences

Lois believes that Clark Kent is strong.
Lois does not believe that Clark Kent is strong.
Lois believes that Clark Kent is not strong.
It is not true that Lois believes that Clark Kent is strong.

are represented as

$$B\varphi, (\neg B)\varphi, B(\neg\varphi), \neg(B\varphi).$$

It is clear that $(\neg B)\varphi$ is different from $B(\neg\varphi)$ and $\neg(B\varphi)$. In a consistent mind, $B\varphi$ and $B(\neg\varphi)$ are contrary, i.e., $B\varphi$ and $B(\neg\varphi)$ cannot be both true, though they may be both false. For example, either it is not true that *Lois believes that Clark Kent is strong,* or it is not true that *Lois believes that Clark Kent is not strong.* In a consistent mind, $B\varphi$ and $(\neg B)\varphi$ are contradictory; in an inconsistent mind, $B\varphi$ and $(\neg B)\varphi$ are not. $B\varphi$ and $\neg(B\varphi)$ are contradictory.

At the ontological level, the negation can be applied not only to statements, but also to concepts and slots, even to the components in concepts and slots, such as the negation on values.

- The negation can be applied to slots. Let a be an attribute. If the domain of a comprises a Boolean algebra then the negation on values is the complement in the Boolean algebra. For example, let a be an attribute to say whether a person is happy, and then D_a, the domain of a, has three values: *happy, not happy and not unhappy, unhappy,* where the complement of *happy* is *unhappy;* the complement of *unhappy* is *happy,* and the complement of *not happy and not unhappy* is itself. *unhappy* is applied on a concept C (for example, C is concept *man*) and a new concept $unhappy \sqcap C$ (unhappy man), where $happy \sqcap C$ and $unhappy \sqcap C$ are contrary, i.e., there is no individual which is an instance of both $happy \sqcap C$ and $unhappy \sqcap C$, and there may be an individual which is an instance of both the complements of $happy \sqcap C$ and $unhappy \sqcap C$.

- The negation can be used relative to some concept. For example, the logical negation $\neg^C$ relative to C is applied on concept $happy \sqcap C$ (happy man) and a concept $(\neg happy) \sqcap C$ (a not-happy man) is formed, where $happy \sqcap C$ and $(\neg happy) \sqcap C$ are contradictory with respect to C, i.e., for any individual c which is an instance of C, either c is an instance of $happy \sqcap C$, or c is an instance of $(\neg happy) \sqcap C$ but not an instance of both.

- The negation can be applied to statements. For example, *a man is an animal* (represented as $C \sqsubseteq D$ in description logics) is a statement; and *a man is not an animal* (represented as $C ! \sqsubseteq D$) is another statement, and $C \sqsubseteq D$ and $C ! \sqsubseteq D$ are contradictory. Hence, *unhappy* and *not − happy* are taken as the negations of *happy*; $\neg C$ is the negation of C, and $C ! \sqsubseteq D$ is the negation of $C \sqsubseteq D$.

According to the classification of the statements in an ontology language (Gomez-Perez & Corcho, 2002), the negation at the ontological level can have more forms. We take a simple definition of the statements in ontologies: an ontology contains the following three levels of statements:

- The individual level;
- The concept level;
- The slot level.

Each level may have several forms of statements. For example, at the concept level, a statement is either $C \Rightarrow \phi$ or their negations (i.e., $C ! \sqsubseteq D, C \not\Rightarrow \phi, C \not\Rightarrow_d \phi$), where C, D are concepts, φ is a slot statement, $\sqsubseteq$ is the subsumption relation, $\Rightarrow$ is the inheritance relation, and $\Rightarrow_d$ is the default inheritance relation; $C \sqsubseteq D$ mans that C is a sub-concept of D; $C \Rightarrow \varphi$ means that each instance of C has property ϕ; $C \Rightarrow_d \phi$ means that each instance of C by default has property φ. At the individual level, a statement is either $a \Rightarrow \varphi$ or its negation $a \not\Rightarrow \varphi$, where $a \Rightarrow \varphi$ means that a instantiates φ. At the slot level, a statement is either $\varphi \rightarrow \psi$ or its negation, where $\varphi \rightarrow \psi$ means that φ logically implies ψ.

Correspondingly, there are three kinds of negations at the ontological level:

◊   The negation on concepts;
◊   The negation on slots; and
◊   The negation on statements.

And, in an ontology, the negation $\neg$ may be applied to

(a)   Statements, such as $C ! \sqsubseteq D$, or
(b)   Concepts, such as $\neg C$ (the complement of C), or
(c)   Slots, such as $\neg \varphi$,

where C, D are concepts and φ is a slot.

There is another negation on slots, denoted by $\sim$, such that for any slot ϕ, $\sim \phi$ is a slot, and $\phi, \sim \phi$ are contrary, comparing to that $\phi, \neg \phi$ are contradictory. The negation $\sim$ on slots induces a negation $\sim$ on concepts. For example, $\sim happy$ is *unhappy* and if C is concept *person* the $happy \sqcap C$ is concept $happy \sqcap person$ and $\sim happy \sqcap C$ is concept $unhappy \sqcap person$.

In this paper we shall discuss the logical connections of statements of different forms in ontologies.

The paper is organized as follows: the next section gives a formal definition of ontologies and statements in ontologies; the third section discusses the logical implication, contrary and contradiction relations between statements; and the fourth section gives the definition of the negations on concepts and slots, and discusses the logical implication between the statements containing these negations; the last section concludes the paper.

ONTOLOGIES

An ontology is an explicit specification of conceptualization (Gruber, 1995). McGuinness (2002) gave the following ontology spectrum:

catalog, terms/glossary, thesauri, information is-a, formal is-a, formal instance, frames, value restraints, disjointness/inverse/part of, general logical constraints,

Specifications satisfying the following properties are referred to as simple ontologies.

- Finite controlled (extensible) vocabulary
- Unambiguous interpretation of classes and term relationships
- Strict hierarchical subclass relationships between classes

Ontologies can contain other specifications. Gómez-Pérez and Corcho (2002) proposed that the ontology languages for the semantic web should contain the following ingredients

○ Concepts, described by general issues, attributes and facets;
○ Taxonomies, including statements about *subclass of, exhaustive decompositions, disjoint decompositions,* and *not subclass of;*
○ Relations and functions, including n-ary relations/functions, type constraints, integrity constraints and *operational definitions;*
○ Axioms, including the ones in first order logic, second-order logic, independent axioms, and embedded axioms,
○ Instances, including instances of concepts, facts, claims.

For the simplicity, we assume that an ontology language L contains:

◇ A set I of individuals (denoted by $a_1, a_2, ...$);
◇ A set C of atomic concepts (denoted by $C_1, C_2, ...$); there is the top concept $\sqcap$ and the bottom concept $\perp$;

◇ A set S of atomic slots (denoted by $\varphi_1, \varphi_2, ...$) to describe individuals and concepts;
◇ $\sqsubseteq$, The subsumption relation between concepts; $\Rightarrow$, the inheritance relation between concepts and slots; $\Rightarrow_d$, the default inheritance relation between concepts and slots, and $\rightarrow$, the logical implication between slots;
◇ The concept constructors: $\neg, \sqcap, \sqcap, \mapsto$; and
◇ The two negations: $\neg, \sim$.

Definition 1. Each atomic concept is a concept;
If C, D are concepts then so are $\neg C, \sim C, C \sqcap D$ and $C \sqcap D$;
Each atomic slot is a slot;
If φ is a slot then so are $\neg\varphi$ and $\sim \phi$; where $\sim \phi$ and φ are contrary;
If φ is a slot then $\mapsto \varphi$ is a concept.

For any concepts C and D, if $C \sqsubseteq D$ we say that C is a sub-concept of D, or D is a super-concept of C. We define a relation $\equiv$ between concepts, such that for any concepts C and D,

$$C \equiv D \ iff \ C \sqsubseteq D \ \& \ D \sqsubseteq C.$$

From the definition, we know that (1) both concepts C, and slots φ have negation concepts $\neg C$ and negation slots $\neg\varphi$, respectively, where $\neg C$ means that for any x, x is an instance of $\neg C$ iff x is not an instance of C; and $\neg\varphi$ means that for any x, x instantiates $\neg\varphi$ iff x does not instantiate φ; (2) Both concepts C and slots φ have another kind of negation concepts $\sim C$ and negation slots $\sim \phi$, respectively, where when $C = (\mapsto \phi)$, $\sim C$ means that for any x, x is an instance of $\sim C$ iff x instantiates $\sim \phi$.

For example, let φ mean *being happy.* Then, $\sim \phi = \sim$ *being happy* is *being unhappy,* comparing to that $\neg\varphi = \neg$ *being happy* is *not being happy.* $\mapsto \varphi$ is a concept whose instances are being happy. The negation ~ on concepts is induced by the negation ~ on slots.

Let $C = D \sqcap \mapsto \phi$, where D is concept *man*, and $\mapsto \varphi$ is the concept whose instances are happy. Then, $\sim \phi$ (*unhappy*) induces a concept of form $\mapsto (\sim \phi)$ (whose instances are unhappy), and another concept of form $\sim C = D \sqcap (\mapsto \sim \phi)$, a concept *unhappy man*.

Definition 2. A statement Φ in L is defined as follows:

$$\Phi = C \sqsubseteq D \mid C \Rightarrow \phi \mid C \Rightarrow_d \phi$$

$$\mid \phi \rightarrow \psi \mid a \sqsubseteq D \mid a \Rightarrow \phi$$

$$\mid \neg(C \sqsubseteq D) \mid \neg(C \Rightarrow \phi) \mid \neg(C \Rightarrow_d \phi)$$

$$\mid \neg(\phi \rightarrow \psi) \mid \neg(a \sqsubseteq D) \mid \neg(a \Rightarrow \phi),$$

where $C \sqsubseteq D$ means that C is a sub-concept of D; $C \Rightarrow \phi$ means that every instance of C has property φ; $C \Rightarrow_d \varphi$ means that every instance of C by default has property ϕ; $a \sqsubseteq D$ means that a is an instance of D; $a \Rightarrow \varphi$ means that a instantiates property φ.

To simplify the notation, we use

$$C\,!\sqsubseteq D, C \not\Rightarrow \phi, C \not\Rightarrow_d \phi,$$
$$\phi \not\rightarrow \psi, a\,!\sqsubseteq D, a \not\Rightarrow \phi$$

to denote

$$\neg(C \sqsubseteq D), \neg(C \Rightarrow \phi), \neg(C \Rightarrow_d \phi),$$
$$\neg(\phi \rightarrow \psi), \neg(a \sqsubseteq D), \neg(a \Rightarrow \phi),$$

respectively.

For any concept $C, C \sqsubseteq \sqcap$ and $\bot \sqsubseteq C$ are true.

By the definition of $\neg C$ and $\sim C$ given above, we have the following statements: for any concept C and slot φ,

$$C \sqcap \neg C \equiv \bot;$$

$$C \sqcap \neg C \equiv \sqcap;$$

$$C \sqcap \sim C \equiv \bot;$$

$$C \sqcap \sim C \equiv \sqcap;$$

$$(\mapsto \phi) \sqcap (\mapsto \neg \phi) \equiv \bot;$$

$$(\mapsto \phi) \sqcap (\mapsto \neg \phi) \equiv \sqcap;$$

$$(\mapsto \phi) \sqcap (\mapsto \sim \phi) \equiv \bot;$$

$$(\mapsto \phi) \sqcap (\mapsto \sim \phi) \equiv \sqcap.$$

That is, the union of C and $\neg C$ is the top concept; the intersection of C and $\neg C$ is the bottom concept; the union of C and $\sim C$ is a concept, which may not be the top concept; and the intersection of C and $\sim C$ is the bottom concept. Similarly for $\mapsto \varphi$ and $\mapsto \neg \phi, \mapsto \sim \phi$.

Hence, we have that for any concept C,

$$\sim C \sqsubseteq \neg C;$$
$$\sim \phi \rightarrow \neg \phi;$$
$$(\mapsto \sim \phi) \sqsubseteq (\mapsto \neg \phi),$$

where $\sim \phi \rightarrow \neg \phi$ means that $\sim \phi$ logically implies $\neg \varphi$. That is, $\sim C$ is a sub-concept of $\neg C$. For example, *an unhappy man is a not-happy man*. $\sim \phi$ logically implies $\neg \varphi$. For example, *being unhappy* implies *not being happy*. Correspondingly, $(\mapsto \sim \phi)$ is a sub-concept of $(\mapsto \neg \varphi)$. For example *anything unhappy is a not happy thing*.

For any concept C and slot $\varphi, C \Rightarrow \varphi$ and $C \not\Rightarrow \varphi$ are contradictory; and $C \Rightarrow \varphi$ and

$C \Rightarrow \neg\varphi$ are contrary; and $C \Rightarrow \varphi$ and $C \Rightarrow\sim \phi$ are contrary. For example,

every man is happy

not every man is happy

are contradictory;

every man is happy

every man is not happy

are contrary; and

every man is happy

every man is unhappy

are contrary. Correspondingly, $C \Rightarrow \varphi$ and $\neg C \Rightarrow \varphi$ are consistent; and $C \Rightarrow \varphi$ and $\sim C \Rightarrow \phi$ are consistent. For example,

every happy man feels good

every not happy man feels good

are consistent; and

every happy man feels good

every unhappy man feels good

are consistent too.

Given a statement Φ, let $\neg\Phi$ be the negation of Φ. Then, Φ and $\neg\Phi$ are contradictory.

Definition 3. A set S of statements is consistent if S does not contain contradictory statements.

Definition 4. An ontology O is a consistent set of statements, satisfying the following conditions:

◊ There are no concept C and slot φ such that $C \Rightarrow \varphi, C \Rightarrow \neg\varphi \in O$;

◊ There are no concept C and slot φ such that $C \Rightarrow_d \varphi, C \Rightarrow_d \neg\varphi \in O$;

◊ There is no cycle in concepts, that is, there are no concepts $C_1, ..., C_n$ such that

$$C_1 \sqsubseteq C_2, C_2 \sqsubseteq C_3, ..., C_n \sqsubseteq C_1 \in O;$$

and

◊ for any concept $C, C \sqsubseteq \sqcap, \perp \sqsubseteq C \in O$

By translating an ontology into a first order theory, statement $C \,! \sqsubseteq D$ is translated to be a sentence of form

$$\neg\forall x(C(x) \rightarrow D(x)),$$

i.e., $\exists x(C(x) \wedge \neg D(x))$.

To represent the negation of concepts and slots, let $(\neg C)$ be a new unary predicate such that

$$\forall x((\neg C)(x) \leftrightarrow \neg C(x));$$

and let $(\neg\varphi)$ be a new unary predicate such that

$$\forall x(\neg\varphi(x) \leftrightarrow (\neg\varphi)(x)).$$

Remark. Notice that in $(\neg C)(x), (\neg C)$ is the negation of concept C; and $\neg C(x)$ is the logical negation of $C(x)$, i.e., $\neg(C(x))$. For the negation $\sim$, $\sim C \sqsubseteq \neg C$ is translated to be

$$\forall x((\sim C)(x) \rightarrow (\neg C)(x)),$$

which implies that

$$\forall x((\sim C)(x) \rightarrow \neg C(x));$$

and $\sim \phi \rightarrow \neg\phi$ is translated to be

$$\forall x((\sim \phi)(x) \rightarrow (\neg\phi)(x)),$$

which implies that

$$\forall x((\sim \phi)(x) \rightarrow \neg\phi(x)).$$

For example, $\varphi(x)$ means that x is happy, and $\sim \phi(x)$ means that x is unhappy. Then, each unhappy person is not a happy person; and any one who is unhappy is not happy. Hence, $\varphi(x)$ and $\neg\varphi(x)$ are contradictory, and $\varphi(x)$ and $\sim \phi(x)$ are contrary; i.e., $\neg$ is the contradictory negation and $\sim$ is the contrary negation.

$\sim C \Rightarrow \phi$ is translated to be a first-order formula of the following form:

$$\forall x((\sim C)(x) \rightarrow \phi(x)).$$

For example, for each x, if x is a unhappy person then x feels good. Comparing to the translation of $\neg C \Rightarrow \varphi$:

$$\forall x((\neg C)(x) \rightarrow \varphi(x)).$$

For example, for each x, if x is a not-happy person then x feels good.

Therefore, in ontologies, there are two kinds $\neg, \sim$ of the negation applied to concepts or slots and only one kind $\neg$ of the negation applied to statements.

Ontologies have the following inference rules:

- The transitivity of the subsumption relation: for any C, D, E,

$$\frac{C \sqsubseteq D, D \sqsubseteq E}{C \sqsubseteq E};$$

- The inheritance of weaker slots: for any C and slots $\varphi, \psi,$

$$\frac{C \Rightarrow \varphi, \varphi \rightarrow \psi}{C \Rightarrow \psi};$$

- The default inheritance of weaker slots: for any C and slots $\varphi, \psi,$

$$\frac{C \Rightarrow_d \varphi, \varphi \rightarrow \psi}{C \Rightarrow_d \psi};$$

- The implicative inheritance of negative slots: for any C and $\varphi,$

$$\frac{C \Rightarrow \sim \phi}{C \Rightarrow \neg\phi}.$$

LOGICAL CONNECTIONS OF STATEMENTS IN ONTOLOGIES

In this section we consider the logical connections of statements in ontologies, where the statements are of the following forms:

$$C \sqsubseteq D, C \Rightarrow \phi, C \Rightarrow_d \phi,$$
$$C \sqsubseteq \neg D, C \Rightarrow \neg\phi, C \Rightarrow_d \neg\phi,$$
$$C \sqsubseteq \sim D, C \Rightarrow \sim \phi, C \Rightarrow_d \sim \phi,$$

and their negative statements (we omit $\phi \rightarrow \psi, a \sqsubseteq D$ and $a \Rightarrow \varphi$ and their negations). This section consists of two subsections: the following subsection discusses the logical connections of pairs of the above statements; the second subsection gives the logical connections of triples of the above statements.

Two Pairs of Statements

Definition 5. Given two statements Φ and Ψ, we say that Φ and Ψ are *contrary* if both Φ and Ψ cannot be true; *subcontrary* if both Φ and Ψ cannot be false; *contradictory* if both Φ

and Ψ cannot be true or false; and Φ is *subalternate* to Ψ if Φ logically implies Ψ, that is, Φ being true implies Ψ being true.

We first consider the connection between $C \Rightarrow_d \neg\varphi$ and $C \not\Rightarrow_d \varphi$:

- $C \Rightarrow_d \neg\varphi$ means that normally (or by default), every C has $\neg\varphi$;
- $C \not\Rightarrow_d \varphi$ means that "it is not the case that normally (or by default), every C has φ."

For example, let C be a concept of *fish*, φ *being able to fly*. Then, $C \Rightarrow_d \neg\varphi$ means that *by default, each fish is not able to fly*, and $C \not\Rightarrow_d \varphi$ means that *it is not true that by default, each fish is able to fly*.

The logical relation between $C \Rightarrow_d \varphi$ and $C \Rightarrow_d \neg\varphi$ is given by the following square of opposition (Figure 1):where $--$ denotes the contrary relation; $==$ denotes the sub-contrary relation; $\leftrightarrow$ denotes the contradictory relation; and $\downarrow$ denotes the sub-alternate relation.

That is, when C is not the bottom concept, $C \Rightarrow_d \varphi$ logically implies $C \not\Rightarrow_d \neg\varphi$; and $C \Rightarrow_d \neg\varphi$ logically implies $C \not\Rightarrow_d \varphi$. Hence, we have the following inference rules: if $C \neq \perp$ then

$$\frac{C \Rightarrow_d \varphi}{C \not\Rightarrow_d \neg\varphi}; \tag{1}$$

Figure 1. The square of opposition for $C \Rightarrow_d \varphi$.

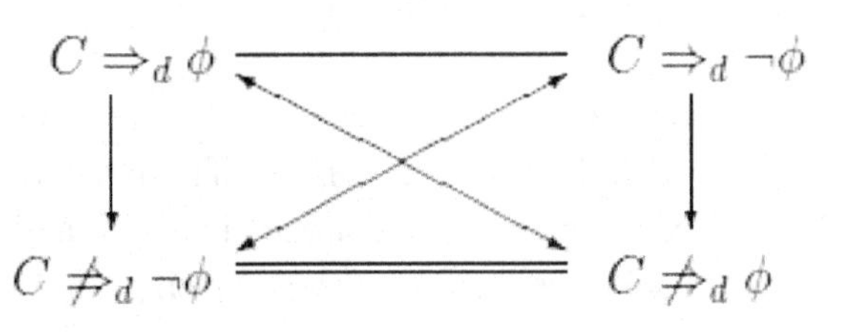

$$\frac{C \Rightarrow_d \neg\varphi}{C \not\Rightarrow_d \varphi}. \tag{2}$$

Remark. As in the traditional square of opposition, both (1) and (2) hold unless $C \neq \perp$. If $C = \perp$ then both $C \Rightarrow_d \varphi$ and $C \Rightarrow_d \neg\varphi$ are true.

Definition 6. An ontology O is *contradictory* (inconsistent) if there is a statement θ such that $\theta, \neg\theta \in O$; O is *contrary* if there are statements θ and δ such that θ and δ are contrary and $\theta, \delta \in O$; O is *sub-contrary* if there are statements θ and δ such that θ and δ are sub-contrary and $\theta, \delta \notin O$.

By the definition, a theory containing both $C \Rightarrow \varphi$ and $C \not\Rightarrow \varphi$ is contradictory, and a theory containing both $C \Rightarrow \varphi$ and $C \Rightarrow \neg\varphi$ is not contradictory, but contrary.

Example 7. Let t denote the water, $h(x)$ denote that x is hot, and $c(x)$ that x is cold. An ontology O containing sentences

The water is hot;

The water is not hot

is represented by $O = \{h(t), \neg h(t)\}$, and O is contradictory.

Let O_1 be an ontology containing the following sentences

The water is hot;

The water is cold

and be represented by $O_1 = \{h(t), c(t)\}$. Then, O_1 is a contrary ontology.

Let O_2 be an ontology such that O_2 is consistent and

$\neg h(t) \notin O_2$

$\neg c(t) \notin O_2.$

Then, O_2 is subcontrary.

The logical relation between $C \Rightarrow \varphi$ and $C \Rightarrow \neg\varphi$ is given in the following square of opposition:

In Figure 2, $C \Rightarrow \varphi$ and $C \Rightarrow \neg\varphi$ are contrary; $C \not\Rightarrow \neg\varphi$ and $C \not\Rightarrow \varphi$ are sub-contrary; and when $C \not\equiv \perp, C \Rightarrow \varphi$ implies $C \not\Rightarrow \neg\varphi$, and $C \Rightarrow \neg\varphi$ implies $C \not\Rightarrow \varphi$. Hence, we have the following inference rules: if $C \neq \perp$ then

$$\frac{C \Rightarrow \varphi}{C \not\Rightarrow \neg\varphi}; \tag{3}$$

$$\frac{C \Rightarrow \neg\varphi}{C \not\Rightarrow \varphi}. \tag{4}$$

The logical relation between $C \sqsubseteq D$ and $C \sqsubseteq \neg D$ is given in the following figure:

In Figure 3, $\neg T \equiv \sim T \equiv \perp$; and $C \sqsubseteq \neg D$ are contrary, $C! \sqsubseteq \neg D$ and $C! \sqsubseteq D$ are sub-contrary, and when $C \not\equiv \perp, C \sqsubseteq D$ implies $C! \sqsubseteq \neg D$, and $C \sqsubseteq \neg D$ implies $C! \sqsubseteq D$. Hence, we have the following inference rules: if $C \neq \perp$ then

$$\frac{C \sqsubseteq D}{C! \sqsubseteq \neg D}; \tag{5}$$

$$\frac{C \sqsubseteq \neg D}{C! \sqsubseteq D}. \tag{6}$$

Similarly for the following pairs:

$$(C \Rightarrow_d \phi, C \Rightarrow_d \sim \phi),$$
$$(C \Rightarrow \phi, C \Rightarrow \sim \phi),$$
$$(C \sqsubseteq D, C \sqsubseteq \sim D);$$

and we have following inference rules: for any C, D with $C \not\equiv \perp,$

$$\frac{C \Rightarrow_d \phi}{C \not\Rightarrow_d \sim \phi}; \tag{7}$$

$$\frac{C \Rightarrow_d \sim \phi}{C \not\Rightarrow_d \phi}; \tag{8}$$

$$\frac{C \Rightarrow \phi}{C \not\Rightarrow \sim \phi}; \tag{9}$$

$$\frac{C \Rightarrow \sim \phi}{C \not\Rightarrow \phi}; \tag{10}$$

$$\frac{C \sqsubseteq D}{C! \sqsubseteq \sim D}; \tag{11}$$

Figure 2. The square of opposition for $C \Rightarrow \varphi$. contradictionary

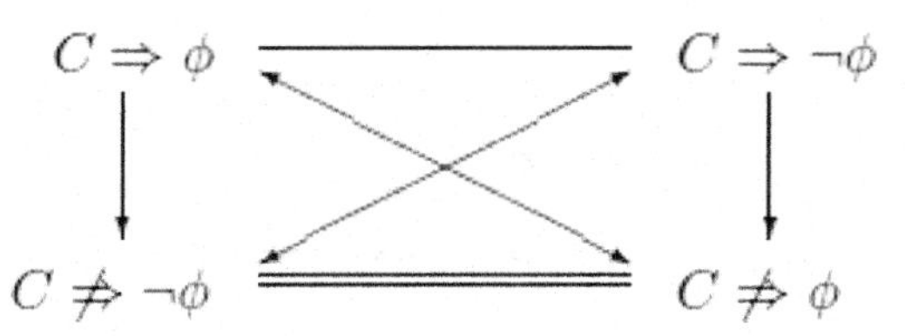

Figure 3. The square of opposition for $C \sqsubseteq D$. contradictionary

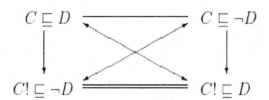

$$\frac{C \sqsubseteq\sim D}{C! \sqsubseteq D}.$$ (12)

Three Pairs of Statements

About the inheritance and default inheritance, we have the following rules: if $C \neq \perp$ then

$$\frac{C \Rightarrow \varphi}{C \Rightarrow_d \varphi};$$ (13)

$$\frac{C \not\Rightarrow_d \varphi}{C \not\Rightarrow \varphi}.$$ (14)

Then, from these rules, we have the following double square of opposition:

In the double square of opposition, the contradictory pairs are

$$(C \Rightarrow \varphi, C \not\Rightarrow \varphi),$$
$$(C \not\Rightarrow \neg\varphi, C \Rightarrow \neg\varphi),$$
$$(C \Rightarrow_d \varphi, C \Rightarrow_d \neg\varphi);$$

where the last pair is because the ontological assumption on O that there is no concept C and slot φ such that $C \Rightarrow_d \varphi$ and $C \Rightarrow_d \neg\varphi \in O$; the contrary pairs are

$$(C \Rightarrow \varphi, C \Rightarrow \neg\varphi),$$
$$(C \Rightarrow \varphi, C \Rightarrow_d \neg\varphi),$$
$$(C \not\Rightarrow \neg\varphi, C \Rightarrow_d \neg\varphi);$$

the sub-contrary pairs are

$$(C \Rightarrow_d \varphi, C \Rightarrow \neg\varphi),$$
$$(C \Rightarrow_d \varphi, C\neg \Rightarrow \varphi),$$
$$(C \not\Rightarrow \neg\varphi, C \not\Rightarrow \varphi);$$

the sub-alternates are

$$(C \Rightarrow \varphi, C \Rightarrow_d \varphi),$$
$$(C \Rightarrow_d \varphi, C \not\Rightarrow \neg\varphi),$$
$$(C \Rightarrow \neg\varphi, C \Rightarrow_d \neg\varphi),$$
$$(C \Rightarrow_d \neg\varphi, C \not\Rightarrow \varphi).$$

The above discussion is similar to the double square of opposition for modalities $\square$ and $\lozenge$. Let φ be a formula. Then, we have the following formulas:

$$\square\phi, \phi, \lozenge\phi, \square\neg\phi, \neg\phi, \lozenge\neg\phi.$$

In Figure 5, the implication pairs are

$$(\square\phi, \lozenge\phi), (\square\neg\phi, \lozenge\neg\phi);$$

the weak implication pairs are

$$(\square\phi, \phi), (\phi, \lozenge\phi), (\square\neg\phi, \neg\phi), (\neg\phi, \lozenge\phi);$$

the contrary pairs are $(\square\phi, \square\neg\phi)$; the sub-contrary pairs are $(\lozenge\varphi, \lozenge\neg\varphi)$; and the contradictory pairs are

$$\sim (C_1$$

Figure 4. The double square of opposition for $C \Rightarrow \varphi, C \Rightarrow_d \varphi$ and $C \not\Rightarrow \neg\varphi$. contradictionary

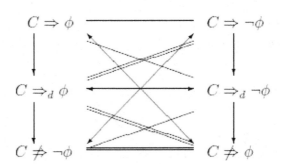

Figure 5. The double square of opposition for
$\neg C_{2}$; *and* $\neg\Box\phi$. *contradictionary*

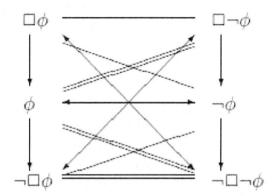

By replacing $\neg$ by $\sim$ in Figure 4, we have the following double square of opposition for (Figure 6) $C \Rightarrow \phi, C \Rightarrow\sim \phi$ and $C \Rightarrow_{d} \phi, C \Rightarrow_{d}\sim \phi$.

THE NEGATIONS ONTOLOGIES

In this section we discuss two kinds of negations, and give a logical connection of the corresponding statements with the negations.

The Two Kinds of Negations: Contrary and Contradictory

In natural languages, there are two kinds of negations of concepts:

- $\neg C$, which means 'not C';
- $\sim C$, which has no intuitive meaning, where C and $\neg C$ are contradictory; and C and $\sim C$ are contraries.

Example 8. To express the following sentences in natural languages:

Nothing is impossible;
Everything is possible,

Figure 6. The double square of opposition for
$C \Rightarrow\sim \phi, C \Rightarrow_{d}\sim \phi$ *and* $C \not\Rightarrow \varphi$. *contradictory*

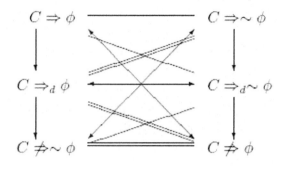

we use $p(x)$ to denote that x is possible, and $\neg p(x)$ impossible. Then, the sentences are expressed in the first-order logic as

$\neg\exists x\neg p(x);$
$\forall x p(x) \equiv \neg\exists\neg p(x).$

That is, both sentences are logically equivalent. In ontologies, two sentences are represented as

$\perp \sqsubseteq \neg C$;$\sqcap \sqsubseteq C$;

where C denotes the possible things; $\neg C$ the impossible things.

Example 9. To express the following sentences in natural languages:

Nothing is bad;
Everything is good,

we use $q(x)$ to denote that x is good, and $\sim q(x)$ bad. Then, the sentences are expressed in the first-order logic as follows:

$\neg\exists x \sim q(x);$
$\forall x q(x) \equiv \neg\exists\neg q(x) \not\equiv \neg\exists \sim q(x).$

In ontologies, two sentences are represented as

$$\sqcap \sqsubseteq D \;;\;\; \perp \sqsubseteq \sim D \;;$$

where D denotes the good things; $\sim D$ the bad things; $\sqcap$ the things, and $\perp$ nothing.

From $\sim \phi \rightarrow \neg \phi$, we usually assume that $\forall x \sim p(x)$ implies $\forall x \neg p(x)$, and dually, $\exists x \sim p(x)$ implies $\exists x \neg p(x)$.

We have that: for any concept C or slot φ,

$$\neg \neg C \equiv C; \;\; \sim \sim C \equiv C;$$
$$\neg \neg \phi \equiv \phi; \;\; \sim \sim \phi \equiv \phi.$$

To consider $\neg \sim C$ or $\sim \neg C$, we take a look at the following examples:

It is not unlikely that ϕ

$$\not\equiv \text{ It is likely that } \phi$$

It is not unnatural that ϕ

$$\not\equiv \text{ It is natural that } \phi$$

It is not inconceivable that ϕ

$$\equiv \text{ It is conceivable that } \phi$$

It is not impossible that ϕ

$$\equiv \text{ It is possible that } \phi,$$

where $\Phi \equiv \Psi$ means two sentences Φ and Ψ express the logically equivalent propositions.

The examples show that for some modality $\square$, for any formula φ,

$$\neg \sim \square \phi \not\equiv \square \phi,$$

that is, $\neg \sim \square \phi$ and $\square \phi$ are not logically equivalent; and for some other modality $\square$, for any formula φ, it may be that

$$\neg \sim \square \phi \equiv \square \phi,$$

where $\square$, denotes the modalities: *likely, natural, conceivable and possible,* respectively.

Therefore, for some concepts C or slots φ, we have the following $\neg \sim C \not\equiv C$, or $\neg \sim \phi \not\equiv \phi$; and for other concepts C or slots φ, we have $\neg \sim C \equiv C$, or $\neg \sim \phi \equiv \phi$. Similarly, for some concepts or slots C, it holds that $\sim \neg C \not\equiv C$; and for other C, it holds that $\sim \neg C \equiv C$. What we have is that for any concept C,

$$\neg \sim C \sqsupseteq C;$$
$$\sim \neg C \sqsubseteq C.$$

Definition 10. A concept C is *contradictory* if

$$\neg \sim C = \sim \neg C = C.$$

Given a concept E, there are two negations with respect to $E: \neg^{E}, \sim^{E}$, such that for any $C \sqsubseteq E$,

$$\neg^{E} C \equiv E \sqcap \neg C \;;$$

$$\sim^{E} C \equiv E \sqcap \sim C \,.$$

A concept $C \sqsubseteq E$ is *contradictory with respect to E* if

$$\neg^{E} \sim^{E} C = \sim^{E} \neg^{E} C = C.$$

Example 11. Let $C = happy\ man =$

$man \sqcap happy$, $D = happy\ thing$. Then

$\sim happy\ thing = unhappy\ thing$;

$\neg happy\ thing = not - happy\ thing$;

$unhappy\ man = man \sqcap \sim happy\ thing$;

$not\ happy\ man = man \sqcap \neg happy\ things$.

Let $E = man$. Then,

$\sim^{E} C = E \sqcap \sim D$;

$\neg^{E} C = E \sqcap \neg D$,

where $\sim^{E} C$ means *unhappy man*, and $\neg^{E} C$ *not-happy man*.

About the happiness and unhappiness, we have the following sentences in the first order logic and the corresponding statements in ontologies: where the sentences are corresponding to the following sentences in natural languages:

everyone is happy;
everyone is not happy;
everyone is unhappy;
everyone is not unhappy;
someone is happy;
someone is not happy;
someone is unhappy;
someone is not unhappy.

The Negations in Description Logics

Description logics are a class of logics, where the concepts are first-order objects in description logics, instead of the statements in the classical logics.

A description logic language contains the following symbols:

- Individual symbols: $c_0, c_1, ...$;
- Atomic concept symbols: $A_0, A_1, ...$;
- Role symbols: $R_0, R_1, ...$;
- Concept constructors: $\neg, \forall, \exists, \sqcap, \sqcup$, and
- Statement constructor: $\sqsubseteq$.

A string C of symbols is a concept if

$$C = A \mid \neg C \mid C_1 \sqcap C_2 \mid C_1 \sqcup C_2$$

$$\mid \forall R.C_1 \mid \exists R.C_1,$$

where A is an atomic concept, and R is a role.

A statement ψ is defined as follows:

$$\psi = C(c) \mid R(c, d) \mid C \sqsubseteq D,$$

where c, d are individuals.

To introduce two kinds of negations in description logics, we add another concept constructor: $\sim$, such that for any atomic concept $A, \sim A$ is a concept.

Given any concept C, define $\sim C$ as follows:

$$\sim C = \sim A \mid \sim C_1 \sqcap \sim C_2 \mid \sim C_1 \sqcup \sim C_2$$

$$\mid \forall R. \sim C_1 \mid \exists R. \sim C_1,$$

comparing to the definition of negation $\neg$:

$$\neg C = \neg A \mid \neg C_1 \sqcap \neg C_2 \mid \neg C_1 \sqcup \neg C_2$$

$$\mid \forall R. \neg C_1 \mid \exists R. \neg C_1.$$

We have the following axioms: for any atomic concept A,

$$\neg\sqcap \equiv \sim\sqcap \equiv \bot;$$

$$\neg\bot \equiv \sim\bot \equiv \sqcap;$$

$$\sim A \sqsubseteq \neg A;$$

$$A \sqcap \neg A \equiv \bot;$$

$$A \sqcap \neg A \equiv \sqcap;$$

$$A \sqcap \sim A \equiv \bot;$$

$$A \sqcap \sim A \equiv \sqcap;$$

and for any concepts C_1, C_2,

$$C_1 \sqcap \bot \equiv \bot;$$

$$C_1 \sqcap \bot \equiv C_1;$$

$$C_1 \sqcap \sqcap \equiv C_1;$$

$$C_1 \sqcap \sqcap \equiv \sqcap;$$

$$C_1 \sqcap C_2 \equiv C_2 \sqcap C_1;$$

$$C_1 \sqcap C_2 \equiv C_2 \sqcap C_1;$$

$$\neg(\neg C_1) \equiv C_1;$$

$$\neg(C_1 \sqcap C_2) \equiv \neg C_1 \sqcap \neg C_2;$$

$$\neg(C_1 \sqcap C_2) \equiv \neg C_1 \sqcap \neg C_2;$$

$$\neg(\forall R.C_1) \equiv \exists R.\neg C_1;$$

$$\neg(\exists R.C_1) \equiv \forall R.\neg C_1;$$

$$\exists R.C_1 \sqcap \forall R.\neg C_1 \equiv \bot;$$

$$\exists R.C_1 \sqcap \forall R.\neg C_1 \equiv \sqcap;$$

$$\sim(\sim C_1) \equiv C_1;$$

$$\sim(C_1 \sqcap C_2) \equiv \sim C_1 \sqcap \sim C_2;$$

$$\sim(C_1 \sqcap C_2) \equiv \sim C_1 \sqcap \sim C_2;$$

$$\sim(\forall R.C_1) \equiv \exists R.\sim C_1;$$

$$\sim(\exists R.C_1) \equiv \forall R.\sim C_1;$$

$$\sim\neg C_1 \sqsubseteq C_1;$$

$$\neg\sim C_1 \sqsupseteq C_1;$$

and for any concepts C_1, C_2, C_3,

$$C_1 \sqcap (C_2 \sqcap C_3) \equiv (C_1 \sqcap C_2) \sqcap C_3;$$

$$C_1 \sqcap (C_2 \sqcap C_3) \equiv (C_1 \sqcap C_2) \sqcap C_3;$$

$$C_1 \sqcap (C_2 \sqcap C_3) \equiv (C_1 \sqcap C_2) \sqcap (C_1 \sqcap C_3);$$

$$C_1 \sqcap (C_2 \sqcap C_3) \equiv (C_1 \sqcap C_2) \sqcap (C_1 \sqcap C_3);$$

We have the following inference rules:

sentences	statements
$\forall x h(x)$	$C \Rightarrow \phi$
$\forall x \neg h(x)$	$C \Rightarrow \neg\phi$
$\forall x (\sim h)(x)$	$C \Rightarrow\sim \phi$
$\forall x \neg(\sim h)(x)$	$C \Rightarrow \neg \sim \phi$
$\exists x h(x)$	$C \sqcap \mapsto \phi \not\equiv \bot$
$\exists x \neg h(x)$	$C \sqcap \mapsto \neg\phi \not\equiv \bot$
$\exists x (\sim h)(x)$	$C \sqcap \mapsto\sim \phi \not\equiv \bot$
$\exists x \neg(\sim h)(x)$	$C \sqcap \mapsto \neg \sim \phi \not\equiv \bot$

$C \sqsubseteq D \Rightarrow E \sqcap C \sqsubseteq E \sqcap D$;

$C \sqsubseteq D \Rightarrow E \sqcap C \sqsubseteq E \sqcap D$;

$C \sqsubseteq D \Rightarrow \forall R.C \sqsubseteq \forall R.D$;

$C \sqsubseteq D \Rightarrow \exists R.C \sqsubseteq \exists R.D$,

where E is a concept.

Proposition 12. For any concept C,

$C \sqcap \neg C \equiv \bot$;

$C \sqcap \neg C \equiv \sqcap$.

Proof. We prove the proposition by the induction on the structure of C.

Case 1. $C = A$. By the axioms, we have the proposition.

Case 2. $C = \neg C_1$, assume that the proposition holds for C_1. Then, $C \sqcap \neg C \equiv (\neg C_1) \sqcap \neg(\neg C_1)$

$\equiv \neg(C_1 \sqcap \neg C_1) \equiv \sqcap \equiv \bot$.

Case 3. $C = C_1 \sqcap C_2$, assume that the proposition holds for C_1 and C_2. Then,

$C \sqcap \neg C$

$\equiv (C_1 \sqcap C_2) \sqcap \neg(C_1 \sqcap C_2)$

$\equiv (C_1 \sqcap C_2) \sqcap (\neg C_1 \sqcap \neg C_2)$

$\equiv (C_1 \sqcap C_2 \sqcap \neg C_1) \sqcap (C_1 \sqcap C_2 \sqcap \neg C_2)$

$\equiv (C_2 \sqcap \bot) \sqcap (C_1 \sqcap \bot)$

$\equiv \bot \sqcap \bot \equiv \bot$;

Case 4. $C = C_1 \sqcap C_2$ assume that the proposition holds for C_1 and C_2. Similar to case 3.

Case 5. $C = \forall R.C_1$, or $C = \exists R.C_1$, assume that the proposition holds for C_1. From the axioms,

$$\forall R.C_1 \sqcap \neg \forall R.C_1 \equiv \forall R.C_1 \sqcap \exists R.\neg C_1 \equiv \bot; \text{ and}$$

$$\exists R.C_1 \sqcap \neg \exists R.C_1 \equiv \exists R.C_1 \sqcap \forall R.\neg C_1 \equiv \bot.$$

Similarly for $C \sqcap \neg C \equiv \sqcap$.

Proposition 13. For any concept C,

$$\sim C \sqsubseteq \neg C.$$

Proof. By induction on the structure of C.

Assume that $C = A$ is atomic. Then, by axioms, $\sim A \sqsubseteq \neg A$;

Assume that $C = \neg C_1$, and the proposition holds for C_1. Then,

$$\sim C =\sim (\neg C_1) \sqsubseteq C_1 \equiv \neg(\neg C_1) \equiv \neg C;$$

Assume that $C = C_1 \sqcap C_2$, and the proposition holds for C_1 and C_2. Then, $\sim C =\sim (C_1 \sqcap C_2) \equiv (\sim C_1) \sqcap (\sim C_2) \sqsubseteq (\neg C_1) \sqcap (\neg C_2) \equiv \neg(C_1 \sqcap C_2) \equiv \neg C$; Similar for case $C = C_1 \sqcap C_2$,

Assume that $C = \forall R.C_1$, and the proposition

$$\sim C =\sim (\forall R.C_1)$$

holds for C_1. Then, $\equiv \exists R. \sim C_1 \sqsubseteq \exists R.\neg C_1$

$$\equiv \neg(\forall R.C_1) = \neg C;$$

Figure 7. The double square of opposition for $C \sqsubseteq \sim D, C \sqsubseteq \neg D$ and $C \sqsubseteq \neg D$.

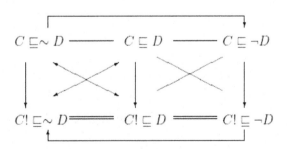

Similar for case $C = \exists R.C_1$.

Corollary 14. For any concept C,

$$C \sqcap \sim C \equiv \bot;$$

$$C \sqcap \sim C \sqsubseteq \sqcap.$$

For the statements in the description logics with two negations $\neg$ and $\sim$, the square of opposition becomes the following double square of opposition (Figure 7).

The principle of conversion by contraposition holds in description logics, that is, for any concepts C and $D, C \sqsubseteq D$ if and only if $\neg D \sqsubseteq \neg C$, even when $\neg D$ is empty. When $\neg D$ is empty, the principle seems strange in natural languages. For example,

Every man is a being;
$C \sqsubseteq D$
(*) *Every non − being is a non − man;*
$\neg D \equiv \bot \sqsubseteq \neg C$
A chimera is not a man;
(*) *A non − man is not a non − chimera.*

CONCLUSION

The paper attempted to show that from the logical level to the linguistic level in the classification of knowledge representation given by Guarino ([10]), the negation has the different forms. The degree of implications, existences and truth is given as follows (Table 1).

The table also gives the connection between statements in ontologies and in the modal logic.

Different from the classical logics, the description logics can contain two kinds of the negation: $\sim$ and $\neg$; and an ontology has the negation on statements and the negations on concepts and

Table 1. Connection between Statements in Ontologies.

$\Rightarrow$	$C \Rightarrow \phi$	$C \Rightarrow_d \phi$	$C \not\Rightarrow \phi$
$\exists$	$\Box \exists x \phi(x)$	$\exists x \phi(x)$	$\Diamond \exists x \phi(x)$
$\Diamond$	$\Box \phi$	ϕ	$\Diamond \phi$
$\Rightarrow$	$C \not\Rightarrow \neg\phi$	$C \Rightarrow_d \neg\phi$	$C \Rightarrow \neg\phi$
$\exists$	$\Diamond \neg \exists x \phi(x)$	$\neg \exists x \phi(x)$	$\Box \neg \exists x \phi(x)$
$\Diamond$	$\Diamond \neg\phi$	$\neg\phi$	$\Box \neg\phi$

slots. The logical connections between these negations are given in this paper.

The strange reading of the principle of conversion by contraposition when $\neg D$ is empty shows that the negation at the linguistic level should have more forms than at the ontological level, and the logical connections between the statements and their negations at the linguistic level should be more complicated than at the ontological level too. For example, in sentence *He is not the one who is unhappy*, the negation is applied to an individual (*not the one*, someone else), and a value (*unhappy*). *He is not the one who is unhappy* implies *Someone else is unhappy*, and *It is not true that he is unhappy* does not.

ACKNOWLEDGMENT

This work is supported by the Natural Science Foundation (grant no. 60273019, 60496326, 60573063, and 60573064), the 863 programme(grant no. 2007AA01Z335) and the National 973 Programme (grants no. 2003CB317008 and G1999032701).

REFERENCES

Baader, F., Calvanese, D., McGuinness, D. L., Nardi, D., & Patel-Schneider, P. F. (Eds.). (2002). *The Description Logic Handbook*. Cambridge, UK: Cambridge University Press.

Baader, F., & Hollunder, B. (1992). Embedding defaults into terminological knowledge representation formalisms. In *Proceedings of the 3rd International Conference on Principles of Knowledge Representation and Reasoning (KR-92)* (pp. 306-317). San Francisco, CA: Morgan Kaufmann.

Borgida, A., & Brachman, R. J. (2002). Conceptual Modeling with description logics . In Baader, F., Calvanese, D., McGuiness, D. L., Nardi, D., & Patel-Schneider, P. F. (Eds.), *The Description Logic Handbook* (pp. 359–381). Cambridge, UK: Cambridge University Press.

Brachman, R. J. (1979). On the epistemological status of semantic networks . In Findler, N. V. (Ed.), *Associative Networks: Representation and Use of Knowledge by Computers*. New York: Academic Press.

Fensel, D., van Harmelen, F., Horrocks, I., Mc-Guinness, D., & Patel-Schneider, P. F. (2001). OIL: An ontology infrastructure for the semantic web. *IEEE Intelligent Systems*, *16*, 38–45. doi:10.1109/5254.920598

Fitting, M. C., & Mendelsohn, R. (1998). *First-order modal logic*. Dordrecht, The Netherlands: Kluwer.

Ginsber, M. (Ed.). (1987). *Readings in Nonmonotonic Reasoning*. San Francisco, CA: Morgan Kaufmann.

Gómez-Pérez, A., & Corcho, O. (2002). Ontology languages for the semantic web. *IEEE Intelligent Systems*, 54–60. doi:10.1109/5254.988453

Gruber, T. R. (1995). Toward principles for the design of ontologies used for knowledge sharing. *International Journal of Human-Computer Studies*, *43*, 907–928. doi:10.1006/ijhc.1995.1081

Guarino, N. (1994). The ontological level. In Casati, R., Smith, B., & White, G. (Eds.), *Philosophy and the Cognitive Science* (pp. 443–456). Vienna, Austria: Höder-Pichler-Tempsky.

Guarino, N. (1995). Formal ontology, conceptual analysis and knowledge representation. *International Journal of Human-Computer Studies*, *43*, 625–640. doi:10.1006/ijhc.1995.1066

McGuinness, D. (2002). Ontologies come of age . In Fensel, D., (Eds.), *The Semantic Web: Why, What, and How*. Cambridge, MA: MIT Press.

Parsons, T. (2006). *The traditional square of opposition*. Stanford Encyclopedia of Philosophy.

Quantz, J., & Royer, V. (1992). A preference semantics for defaults in terminological logics. In *KR-92* (pp. 294-305).

Touretzky, D. S. (1986). *The Mathematics of Inheritance Systems*. San Francisco, CA: Morgan Kaufmann.

This work was previously published in volume 4, issue 3 of the International Journal of Cognitive Informatics and Natural Intelligence, edited by Yingxu Wang, pp. 55-74, copyright 2010 by IGI Publishing (an imprint of IGI Global).

Section 2
Cognitive Computing

Chapter 5
The Event Search Engine

Takeshi Okadome
Kwansei Gakuin University, Japan

Koji Kamei
Advanced Telecommunications Research Institute International, Japan

Yasue Kishino
NTT Communication Science Laboratories, Japan

Yutaka Yanagisawa
NTT West, Japan

Takuya Maekawa
NTT Communication Science Laboratories, Japan

Yasushi Sakurai
NTT Communication Science Laboratories, Japan

ABSTRACT

In a remote or local environment in which a sensor network always collects data produced by sensors attached to physical objects, the engine presented here saves the data sent through the Internet and searches for data segments that correspond to real-world events by using natural language (NL) words in a query that are input in an web browser. The engine translates each query into a physical quantity representation searches for a sensor data segment that satisfies the representation, and sends back the event occurrence time, place, or related objects as a reply to the query to the remote or local environment in which the web browser displays them. The engine, which we expect to be one of the upcoming Internet services, exemplifies the concept of symbiosis that bridges the gaps between the real space and the digital space.

INTRODUCTION

Background

Many surveillance applications based on sensor networks monitor the physical world and detect events that occur in the world on the basis of sensor data. In the applications, events are named according to attributes that have scalar values or ranges of scalar values, such as temperature and light levels. These events, which are described by SQL-like languages (Madden et al., 2003; Bonnet, Gehrke, & Seshadri, 2000; Xue & Luo, 2005; Jiao, Son, & Stankovic, 2005; Li et al., 2002), depend on the value of a particular sensor reading. For example, Li et al. (2002) designed a distributed index that scalably supports multidimensional range queries such as "List all events that have temperatures between 50 and 60° C, and light levels between 10 and

DOI: 10.4018/978-1-4666-1743-8.ch005

Figure 1. The event search engine—overview

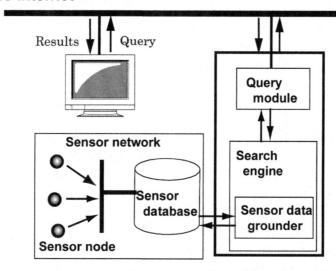

Overview of the Event Search Engine

20 luces." The event descriptions given by the SQL-languages enable surveillance applications to provide services that are activated by the occurrence of certain events. The languages, however, describe only events that can be represented using values obtained from sensors. That is, the weak descriptive power of the languages shows us a typical gap between the real space and the digital space.

As with a Web search using Google, through the Internet, the engine presented here accepts a word set that denotes events that have occurred in the real world and facilitates a search of these events occurred in a remote or local environment. Instead of queries related to sensor reading values, the system embedded in the sensor-networked environment permits us to pose such queries as "drop," "door open," and "who hide book." Because the engine that can accept natural language words in a query provides us a natural interface between a man and a machine, it exemplifies the concept of symbiosis (Griffith & Greitzer, 2007) that can be expected to bridge the gap.

Figure 1 shows an overview of this engine, which consists of two modules: a query module and a search engine that refers to the sensor data grounder. Assuming a remote or local environment in which a sensor network always collects data produced by sensors attached to physical objects, the engine saves the data sent through the Internet and returns information about an event that matches an intuitive interpretation of a set of NL words in a query. A web browser in the remote or local environment displays the returned information. Using a simple Google-like interface, users input queries in a word set that may contain a preposition and/or an adverb such as "drop," "what hide," "book move:horizontally," or "who drop vase on:2006.12.31." The engine returns the event occurrence time, place, or related objects as a reply to the query. Also it answers by, for example, displaying a video image recorded by video cameras.

Before describing the event search engine, the next section summarizes an event representation that is a middle language between sensor values and NL-phrase-like descriptions. Section 3 explains the event search engine using the event representation. We then evaluate our engine and compare it with related work. The final section offers some concluding remarks on our future work.

EVENT REPRESENTATION

This section briefly describes an event representation for an event search that uses a word set as a query. For more details, see Okadome (2006). The event representation, which consists of event descriptors and their concatenation rules, generates observable event descriptions that have their own unique physical quantity expressions. Let us assume that we found a vase that was broken because someone had dropped it and that we want to know when the base dropped. To use the event search engine, we input the word "drop" as a query in an web browser. The verb "drop" has multiple meanings including "fall vertically" and "unload." The event representation reflects the ambiguity of NL words and the verb "drop" is, for example, associated with such event descriptors as fall-vertically and unload whose physical meanings are described by respective physical quantity expressions that the search engine interprets; the search engine tries to find data segments compatible with them. For example, fall-vertically has a physical quantity expression that represents the free and vertical (gravitational) movements:

$$\frac{\frac{d\lambda(t)}{dt}}{\left|\frac{d\lambda(t)}{dt}\right|} \cdot \frac{g}{|g|} = 1 \wedge \frac{d^2\lambda(t)}{dt^2} = g, \; t_1 \leq t \leq t_2,,$$

where $\lambda(t)$ denotes the object location at time t and g does the gravitational constant vector. The

term $\frac{\frac{d\lambda(t)}{dt}}{\left|\frac{d\lambda(t)}{dt}\right|} \cdot \frac{g}{|g|} = 1$ means the direction of the velocity coincides with that of the gravitational vector. The term $\frac{d^2\lambda(t)}{dt^2} = g$ denotes the acceleration is equal to the gravitational vector. The search engine finds corresponding data segments that satisfy the expression.

In general, the following simple form is assigned to each observable event:

$$\forall t \left((t_0 \leq t < t_1 \to P_1) \wedge (t_1 \leq t \leq t_2 \to P_2) \wedge (t_2 < t \leq t_3 \to P_3)\right)$$

where t_0, t_1, t_2, and t_3 are free variables and P_1, P_2, and P_3 are mathematical expressions including variables and physical constants that denote physical quantities such as position and temperature. In this form, the expression $t_0 \leq t < t_1 \to P_1$ represents the *precondition* in which t is a parameter denoting time and P_1 expresses the physical state of objects connected with the event before the event occurs. The expression $t_1 \leq t \leq t_2 \to P_2$ specifies the *ongoing condition* in which the event starts at t_1 and finishes at t_2, and P_2 denotes the state change of the physical object. The last expression $t_2 < t \leq t_3 \to P_3$ describes the *post-condition*. The event result remains until t_3, which is expressed by P_3. Formally, the physical quantity expression of fall-vertically is in the form of

$$\forall t \left((t_0 \leq t < t_1 \to True) \wedge (t_1 \leq t \leq t_2 \to P) \wedge (t_2 < t \leq t_3 \to True)\right)$$

, where P is $\frac{\frac{d\lambda(t)}{dt}}{\left|\frac{d\lambda(t)}{dt}\right|} \cdot \frac{g}{|g|} = 1 \wedge \frac{d^2\lambda(t)}{dt^2} = g$.

Let us here give two more examples. The event descriptor change-location that associates with the verbs "move," "travel," "go," and "locomote" has a physical quantity expression

$\left|\dfrac{d\lambda(t)}{dt}\right| > 0 \;\; (t_1 \le t \le t_2)$. Also, the event descrip-

tor reach-destination(ρ: region) that associates with the verbs "reach," "make," "attain," "hit," "arrive at," and "gain" has a physical quantity expression

$$D(\lambda(t), \rho) > 0 \;\; (t_0 \le t < t_1),$$

$$\left|\dfrac{d\lambda(t)}{dt}\right| > 0 \wedge D(\lambda(t), \rho) > 0 \;\; (t_1 \le t \le t_2),$$

$D(\lambda(t), \rho) = 0 \;\; (t_2 < t \le t_3)$, where ρ denotes a region and $D(p, q)$ is the distance between p and q.

Using a recently constructed electronic lexical database, WordNet (Fellbaum, 1998), we collect words denoting event concepts and construct an event representation and a grounding method that suit the event search on the basis of data produced by such tiny sensors as an accelerometer, a thermometer, and an illuminometer.

Incidentally, the event representation system summarized here is related to the denotational description for knowledge, and other abstract systems which is developed in the field of Cognitive Informatics. (See Wang, 2008a and Wang 2008b for the denotational description.)

EVENT SEARCH SYSTEM

Of the 160 event concepts that we constructed, the present version of the search system can detect 40 kinds of events with which 101 verbs are associated without using a location detector.

Query and Answer

Query

A query that is input in an web browser is assumed to be a word set that corresponds to a simple sentence such as "vase move," "cup:temperature increase" "when vase:move:horizontally," "person move:horizontally vase," and "who move:vase:horizontally." A query may include such interrogatives as "when" and "who." We assume that a verb followed by a colon and an adverb such as "move:horizontally" forms a verb phrase. Also, we assume that a noun followed by a noun such as "cup:temperature" forms a noun phrase that denotes "the temperature of a cup." Likewise, a preposition followed by a colon and a word in a query is assumed to form a prepositional phrase as with "on:2006.12.31," "at:14.35.33," and "on:table." For simplicity, we assume that the time and date given in the form *hh.mm.ss* and *yyyy.mm.dd* are 12.15.30 and 2006.3.31, respectively.

The query module first translates a verb, a noun, prepositions, and adverbs in the query into their respective event descriptors and physical quantity expressions. In the event descriptor set with partial ordering described in Section 2.3, it chooses the most general descriptors associated with the verb. Then, using the binding nouns in a query directed at the person or object related to the verbs, it constructs an event description from the event descriptors and their physical quantity expressions. When a query has prepositions or adverbs as well as a verb, the query module concatenates the event descriptor associated with the verb and the adjuncts for the prepositions or adverbs. It also forms a physical quantity expression for the concatenation. The query module then sends the concatenation and its physical quantity expression to the search engine.

For example, let "vase drop on:2006.12.31 in:room" be a query. Because the verb "drop" is associated with fall-vertically and drop-to-lower-place and the latter is a more general event descriptor than the former, the query module chooses drop-to-lower-place and extracts its physical quantity expression. The choice strategy of most general descriptors assures a fast search because fewer conditional tests are required in the subsequent search phase.

By binding the noun "vase" to the object of the verb "drop," the query module translates the input "vase drop" into the event descriptor drop-to-lower-place$_{(vase)}$, where vase is an adjunct translated from "vase." Also, it translates "on:2006.12.31" and "in:room" to on$_t$(2006.12.31) and inp(room). Finally, the query module constructs a physical expression for the observable event "vase drop on:2006.12.31 in: room" from those of drop-to-lower-place, on$_t$(2006.12.31), and in$_p$(room).

Let us take "cup raise" as another query example, where "raise" is associated with raise-amount-of-something$_{(a,o)}$(Q_s:scalarQuantity) and move-upward$_{(a,o)}$. Because there is no partial order between them, the query module selects both the event descriptors, extracts their respective physical quantity expressions, binds the noun "cup" to the object arguments of the event descriptors, substitutes the variable T (temperature) and L_u (light intensity) for the meta-variable Q_s and sends the three event descriptors raise-amount-of-something$_{(a,cup)}$ (T), raise-amount-of-something$_{(a,cup)}$ (L_u), and move-upward$_{(a,cup)}$ with their physical quantity expressions to the search engine. If the query is "cup:temperature raise" instead of "cup raise" in this example, the query module translates "cup:temperature" into temperature(cup) and sends only raise-amount-of-something$_{(a,cup)}$ (T) with its physical quantity expression.

Answer

The query module also replies to a query. That is, it sends back to the web browser:

1. The event start and finish times in reply to a query that includes "when."
2. The names of physical objects related to the event in reply to a query that includes "what."
3. All of the above information in reply to a query without interrogatives.

In our experimental environment, because we record the video images with four video cameras mounted on the ceiling, the query module can also answer by displaying a video image of the event as a reply to a query including "who," "where," and "how."

Search Engine

The search engine accepts event descriptions produced by the query module and calls the sensor data grounder that searches for sensor data segments that satisfy the physical quantity expressions assigned to the event descriptions.

Sensor Data Analysis

Sensor signals are noisy and fluctuate even in a stable environment. Using a method developed as a speech processing technique based on the signal energy (Rabiner & Sambur, 1975) together with trend analysis using a Kalman predictor (Kitagawa & Gersh, 1984), we eliminate noise in sensor data, smooth them with a lowpass filter, and extract signal activity segments that are not in a stable state.

Also because sensor data vary depending on the individual differences between sensors and the mode of attachment, we calibrate the sensors on each sensor node in advance and normalize the data obtained from the sensors.

Sensor Data Grounding

Beginning with the most recently saved data, the sensor data grounder checks the data over a length that can be adjusted by a parameter until it finds or fails to find a data segment that satisfies the physical quantity expression assigned to the observable events. Because even normalized data has errors, the data check permits those in a range of 10% of the maximum absolute value in a signal activity segment as permissible errors. Let us, for example, assume that we test whether an expression $a > 0$ $a > 0$, holds for acceleration data in a signal activity segment whose maximum value is 10.0 m/sec². Then we judge $a > 0$ holds for data at a time if a is greater than 1.0 m/sec² at the time.

Let

$$\forall t((t_0 \leq t < t_1 \rightarrow P_1) \wedge (t_1 \leq t \leq t_2 \rightarrow P_2) \wedge (t_2 < t \leq t_3 \rightarrow P_3))$$

be the physical quantity expression assigned to an observable event. Starting from the latest collected data, the sensor data grounder seeks a continuous data segment within the segment length ranges that correspond to those of the time intervals, $t_1 - t_0$, $t_2 - t_1$, and $t_3 - t_2$. The sensor grounder judges that the observable event occurs between t and t', if and only if P_1, P_2, and P_3 hold for a data segment within the respective ranges of the intervals and $t' - t$ is within the $t_2 - t_1$ range for the data segment.

For example, the grounder judges that the event fall-vertically$_{(vase)}$ occurs, if and only if the ongoing condition $\dfrac{\dfrac{d\lambda(t)}{dt}}{\left|\dfrac{d\lambda(t)}{dt}\right|} \cdot \dfrac{g}{|g|} = 1 \wedge \dfrac{d^2\lambda(t)}{dt^2} = g$ or its equivalent expression holds for a continuous segment of sensor data produced by such sensors as an accelerometer or a location detector attached to a vase. That is, the grounder calculates the velocity of the vase from an acceleration data segment. When the direction of the vase velocity coincides with that of the gravitational vector and its acceleration is equal to the gravitational vector, the grounder concludes that fall-vertically$_{(vase)}$ occurs at the data segment. Because the ceiling height in environments such as an office are at most 300 cm, the segment search length is less than 785 msec., which corresponds to the time interval required for falling from a height of 300 cm. Note that the grounder does not check the pre- or post-conditions for fall-vertically because they are irrelevant.

Also the grounder detects that the event raise-amount-of-something$_{(a,cup)}$ (T) happens, if and only if the ongoing condition $\left|\dfrac{dT(t)}{dt}\right| > 0$ holds for a continuous segment of sensor data produced by a thermometer attached to a cup.

Note that a physical quantity expression assigned to an observable event does not depend on the type of sensor. In the example fall-vertically$_{(vase)}$, the test for the condition requires data about the vase's velocity and acceleration. Thus, if a sensor node has only an accelerometer, we must calculate its time integral to obtain the velocity. When a sensor node has a location detector that uses a micro-wave- or ultrasonic sensing technique, we need the second-order differential of the position to obtain the acceleration.

The present version of the sensor data grounder can only deal with calculus expressions. The sensor data grounder includes primitive methods, each of which performs the arithmetic operations, time differentials, the inner product, the norm, and the Euclidean distance. By interpreting a calculus expression described as a TeX source and calling on the primitive methods required, it builds a procedure that judges whether the expression holds for a continuous segment of sensor data. When an event description contains temperature or light and its physical quantity expression has a meta-variable, the sensor data grounder binds the meta-variable to T(temperature) and L_u(light).

The sensor data grounder returns the start and finish times of the data segments that it finds and the names of objects whose sensor data vary during the segment intervals to the search engine, which then passes them to the query module.

Expanding Vocabulary

There are many non-associated verbs that denote events related to physical objects. For example, the word "sit," which is strongly related to chairs, is not associated with any event descriptor. To expand the vocabulary that we can deal with, we focus on a word subcategorization approach that defines a lexical usage for a word that tells us how other words or phrases are related to it. Using a method similar to that of the automatic extraction of subcategorization (Briscoe & Carroll, 1997), we first collect verbs related to twenty four object classes in offices such as staplers, chairs, trash cans, and pens, from textual corpora (1.4 Gbytes of data from the New York Times), then select verbs that are not associated with any event descriptors. We call the selected verbs *extracted verbs by subcategorization* or simply *extracted verbs*. For example, the verbs "use" and "sit" are extracted verbs related to "chair." We collect a total of 1,732 extracted verbs by subcategorization.

We try to connect each of the extracted verbs to one of the 101 verbs associated with event descriptors that the present system can directly detect without a location detector. That is, for each extracted verb related to an object class, we use WordNet again to search for its highest-frequency synonym, which is one of the 101 associated verbs, and connect it to the synonym. For example, we connect the associated word "turn" to the extracted verb "open" related to "door." This method enables us to connect 743 verbs to their synonyms (associated verbs) among the 1,732 extracted verbs.

The connection procedure ignores the relation of a verb to an object class, although we use the relation when selecting extracted verbs. For example, it connects the extracted verb "close" with the associated verb "stop." The verb "break" is also associated with "stop." To improve the search accuracy, we construct another correspondence between a verb and its synonym (an associated verb) using a noun that denotes an object class. That is, for a pair consisting of a noun n and a verb v, we try to find an associated verb expressing the event that is most likely to occur when an event denoted by v with an object denoted by n happens. Therefore, we assign "drop" to the pair ("cup," "break"), because dropping a cup causes it to break. Also we assign "move" to the pair ("door," "close") because a door always moves

whenever it closes. The pairs of nouns and verbs serve to search events when a query includes a noun in addition to a verb.

When a verb v in a query is not a word associated with an event descriptor, (1) the query module first tries to find a verb v' connected to a pair (n, v) when the query also includes a noun n, or (2) if it fails to find it or if the query includes no noun, it tries to find an extracted verb v' connected to an associated word. If it is successful, it replaces v with v'. For example, the query module replaces "close" with "move," if a query has the noun "door." Otherwise, it replaces "close" with "stop," which is associated with the event descriptors stop and cause-to-stop$_{(a,o)}$.

Overall Process of Event Search

Figure 2 summarizes the overall process of searching for an event from a query to an answer. Let "when cup break" be an input set of words. Because "break" is not associated with an event descriptor, the query module tries to find it in the set of extracted words by subcategorization; it finds that "break" in the set is connected to "drop." The query module thus extracts the event descriptor drop-to-lower-place$_{(o)}$ with which "drop" is associated; Then binding cup to the argument of drop-to-lower-place$_{(o)}$, it constructs the event description drop-to-lower-place$_{(cup)}$. The query module also extracts the physical quantity expression, and it transmits the pair consisting of the event description and the physical quantity expression.

The sensor data grounder tries to find a data segment that is compatible with two conditions: the vertical (downward) component of the velocity is positive and the acceleration coincides with that of gravity. If it finds a data segment, it returns the start and finish times of the data segment to the search engine, which passes them to the query module. Finally, the query module displays the times, because the query includes "when."

Figure 2. Overall process of searching for an event

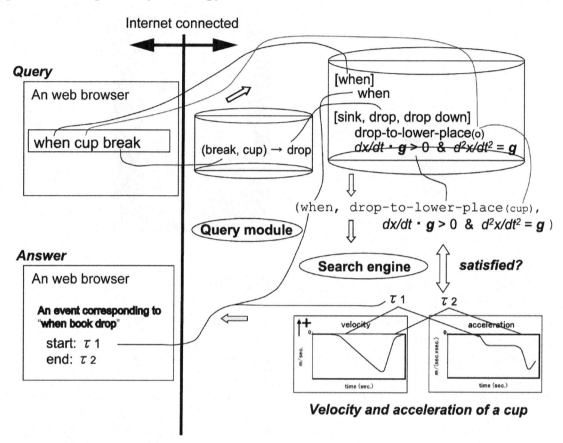

Velocity and acceleration of a cup

EVALUATION

To evaluate the event search system, we conducted two experiments in a sensor networked office environment and we assessed the precision and recall that are used to evaluate Web search engines (Oppenheiem et al., 2000). We also discuss the coverage of the words that the system can deal with against a set of 'common words.'

Experiment I

Experimental Setting

We have developed sensor nodes, a sensor data management system and an object database, and an experimental room equipped with a sensor network. Figure 3 shows a sensor node equipped with a triaxial accelerometer, a dual-axis magnetic field sensor that enables us to determine direction, a thermometer, an illuminometer, and a human detector that senses infrared light. The sensor node also has an embedded CPU and a wireless communication module. In the sensor networked environment, we installed a desk, a table, chairs, bookshelves, and many objects such as books, laptops, and teacups, at various places around the office. In Experiments I and II, we attached the sensor nodes to eight of these movable objects, namely, two books, two files, a suitcase, a chair, a door, and a teacup, and recorded the sensor data captured through the sensor network system with time stamps.

Experiment I consisted of five sessions. For each session, we prepared a list of twenty pairs consisting of a noun and a verb randomly selected from the nouns that denote the eight objects

Figure 3. A sensor node we developed and the node attached to a file

 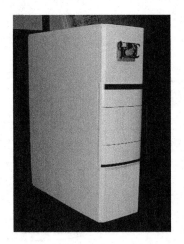

and the 844 associated and extracted verbs. In each session, we first initiated twenty events corresponding to the twenty noun-verb pairs. That is, for each pair, we initiated an event that denoted the verb using an object denoted by the noun. We then input the twenty noun-verb pairs as a query and searched for the events using the system.

Results

Table 1 shows the precision and recall for each session. The precision values for the sessions vary from 0.55 to 0.75 and the average is 0.68; the recall values range from 0.91 to 0.97 and the average is 0.95. The high recall scores indicate that the system can successfully find data segments that correspond to observable events. In contrast, the precision scores of 0.55 to 0.75 reflect the limitation of the resolving power of different word meanings introduced by the vocabulary expanding techniques described in Section 3.3.

Experiment II

Experimental Setting

Experiment II consisted of a fifteen-minute trial, where each of seven subjects (four men and three women) tried to freely induce events using the eight objects. Then we searched for the events by submitting a query to the system. In the experimental setting, we restricted the data search range to data obtained during the two minutes just prior to posing the query. We obtained 162 events in total in the experiment.

Results

Table 2 shows the precision and recall for each subject. The precision values for the subjects vary from 0.33 to 0.67 and the average is 0.44; the recall values range from 0.85 to 0.96 and the average is 0.89. Again, the high recall scores indicate that the system can successfully find data segments

Table 1. Precision and recall for each session

	b1	b2	b3	b4	b5
precision	0.70	0.75	0.55	0.75	0.65
recall	0.97	0.96	0.91	0.97	0.95

Table 2. Precision and recall for each subject

	s1	s2	s3	s4	s5	s6	s7
precision	0.39	0.50	0.33	0.67	0.50	0.34	0.38
recall	0.89	0.96	0.85	0.88	0.89	0.87	0.91

that correspond to observable events. In contrast, the precision scores of 0.33 to 0.67 suggest that in the search range in the experimental setting, the subjects induce about two to three events including a relevant event.

Search failures are classified into the following types: (1) the system fails to find data segments that match physical quantity expressions and (2) it does not have an associated or extracted verb for a query. Examples of the former type of failure are (a) searching for "knock door" because the vibration that occurred when knocking on the door did not result is a "move" that connects with "knock" and (b) detecting an event corresponding to "cup raise" because the subject had input the query before the outer temperature of the cup had begun to increase. This is because the thermometer on the sensor node attached to the outside of the cup detects the outer temperature of the cup. Therefore, we must delay the sensor response by about 20 or 30 seconds after pouring hot water into the cup. The latter is exemplified by a case where a subject rolled up a book (paperback) and she submitted the query "roll book," but the system does not have the verb "roll."

Word Coverage

As the last part of our evaluation, we comment on the coverage of the words that the system can deal with compared with a set of 'common words.' The system deals with a total of 844 verbs, namely the 101 associated verbs with event descriptors and the 743 verbs extracted by subcategorization that are connected with associated verbs. Here let us call the 844 associated or extracted verbs *manageable verbs*.

Using a defining vocabulary called the Oxford 3000™, the Oxford Advanced Learner's Dictionary (Wehmeier, 2005) explains the meaning of English words. The Oxford 3000 contains familiar high-frequency words that occur across a wide range of usage. Choosing the verbs listed in the Oxford 3000 as our set of common verbs, we tested the word coverage of the manageable verbs against the verbs in the Oxford 3000. The result shows that the manageable words cover 392 of the 862 verbs in the Oxford 3000 (coverage rate: 45.5%). Note that the Oxford 3000 necessarily includes about 200 cognitive verbs such as "think," "see," and "listen to." The coverage rate thus increases to more than 60% if we exclude the cognitive verbs found in the Oxford 3000.

RELATED WORK

Yap, Srinivasan, and Motani (2005) proposed a system that allows people to search for and locate physical objects as and when they need them. Under the assumption that all physical objects can be tagged with small devices that possess certain limited processing and communication capabilities, the system provides location information in NL sentences that offer references to identifiable landmarks rather than precise coordinates such as "my notebook is on my desk" or "the keys are on the dining room table."

The event-driven distributed model of the context-aware system proposed by Tan et al., (2005) is based on the event specification language and composite event detection algorithm. They classify events into primitive events and composite events that are constructed recursively by applying certain operators to primitive and composite events. Primitive events are low-level events that can be directly detected by sensors or other mechanisms embedded in the computing entities in the system. Composite events are events that are formed by applying a set of event operators such as "or," "and," or "seq(;)" to primitive and composite events. They also extend the context model with an event ontology so that event information can be retrieved from the infrastructure in a consistent and semantic way using SQL-like, not NL-like, semantic queries such as SELECT ?X WHERE (?X owl:hasTimeOfOccurrence>, "20.05.04 13:00:41"). Furthermore, to answer semantic queries, their system must infer events from sensor data in advance.

To create a smart environment controlled via an NL interface, Monntoro, Alaman, and Haya (2004) developed a system that automatically creates and manages the dialogue. It is based on an environment description and its state stored on a domain ontology. The ontology is formed by entities that represent real-world contextual information and abstract concepts. This information is complemented with linguistic parts that make it possible to create a spoken interface for the environment automatically. Users may interact with and modify the physical state of a living room environment by using the spoken dialogue interface.

CONCLUSION

This article described an engine that searches for sensor data that corresponds to real-world events using natural language (NL) words in a query. The engine exemplifies the concept of symbiosis that provides a bridge over a gap between the real space and the digital space. Many studies of event detection for context-aware applications address the inverse problem of inferring an event from sensor data. Generally, approaches to the inverse problem require uncertain assumptions about the

world and a powerful inference method. For example, in relation to tagging objects using RFID tags and storing the data, Philipose et al. (2004) represent people's daily activities as probabilistic sequences of used objects, and infer twenty preselected activities that relate to daily living, such as "washing," "using the toilet," and "heating use." Instead of employing probability obtained from the real world, they must use word associations on the Web to determine the involvement probability for an object in an activity while relying on certain assumptions; if an activity name often coincides with some object name in human discourse, then the activity will likely involve the object in the physical world.

In contrast, the system presented here deals with the forward problem of searching for a corresponding sensor data segment from an event represented by a set of NL words. The introduction of the physical quantity representation of events offers us an effective and feasible solution to the current problem. Physical quantity representation, which does not depend on sensor type, also offers us a highly portable system.

Note that the vocabulary expanding techniques described in Section 3.3 give rise to the problem of the resolving power of different word meanings. For example, the system cannot discriminate between the two events "sit on a chair" and "stand from a chair," because both the verbs "sit" and "stand" related to "chair" are associated with "move." Nevertheless, searching the results of the system allows us to obtain information about events because they almost always include relevant event information.

The event search engine presented here has a problem with scalability. The average search time of the engine is linearly related to the number of physical objects that sensor nodes are attached to. One of the methods that solve the problem is an automatic labeling for sensor data and indexing to labeled sensor data. That is, we can label a sensor data segment with one of the 101 verbs associated with event descriptors that have respective physical quantity expressions and create an index in saved sensor data. The labeling and indexing method improves the speed of event search.

Our own future research directions include extending our system in the following ways. (1) We plan to increase the number of event descriptors by introducing other seeds such as "change" and some adjectives that represent the physical states of objects. (2) In NL, properties can be modified by using such words as slightly, fairly, and very. We can deal with vague properties in fuzzy modeling by introducing modifiers, which are also called linguistic hedges and are defined as function mappings between fuzzy sets (Zadeh, 1972). (3) We will deal with events related to physical objects such as "air," "water," and small objects to which we cannot attach our sensors. We will address the last item using a function ontology that describes the functions of these artifacts, such as "cup: a cup holds water" or "cup: a cup transports water." If a sensor node is attached to a cup, we can reply to a query "who carries water" by specifying the data segment that corresponds to "carry cup" that is inferred from the description of a cup's function in the ontology.

ACKNOWLEDGMENT

This research is partly supported by JST, CREST.

REFERENCES

Bonnet, P., Gehrke, J., & Seshadri, P. (2000). Querying the physical world. *IEEE Pervasive Communication*, 7, 10–15. doi:10.1109/98.878531

Briscoe, T., & Carroll, J. (1997). Automatic extraction of subcategorization from corpora. In *Proceedings of the 5th Conference on Applied Natural Language Processing* (pp. 356-363).

Fellbaum, C. (Ed.). (1998). *WordNet: An Electronic Lexical Database*. Cambridge, MA: MIT Press.

Griffith, D. G., & Greitzer, F. (2007). Neo-symbiosis: the next stage in the evolution of human information interaction. *International Journal of Cognitive Informatics and Natural Intelligence*, *1*(1), 39–52.

Jiao, B., Son, S. H., & Stankovic, J. A. (2005). *Gem: Generic event service middleware for wireless sensor networks*. Paper presented at the Second International Workshop on Networked Sensing Systems (INSS05).

Kitagawa, G., & Gersh, W. (1984). A smoothness priors-state space modeling of time series with trend and seasonality. *Journal of the American Statistical Association*, *79*, 378–389. doi:10.2307/2288279

Li, X., Kim, Y. J., Govindan, R., & Hong, W. (2002). Multi-dimensional range queries in sensor networks. In *Proceedings of the ACM Conference on Embedded Networked Sensor Systems (SenSys '03)* (pp. 63-73).

Madden, S., Franklin, M. J., Hellerstein, J. M., & Hong, W. (2003). The design of an acquisitional query processor for sensor networks. In *Proceedings of the ACM SIGMOD Conference (SIGMOD2003)* (pp. 491-502).

Montoro, G., Alaman, X., & Haya, P. A. (2004). A plug and play spoken dialogue interface for smart environments. In *CICLing (*LNCS 2945, pp. 360-370).

Okadome, T. (2006). Event representation for sensor data grounding. *International Journal of Computer Science and Network Security*, *6*, 187–193.

Oppenheiem, C., Moris, A., Mcknight, C., & Lowley, S. (2000). The evaluation of www search engines. *The Journal of Documentation*, *56*, 190–211. doi:10.1108/00220410010803810

Philipose, M., Fishkin, K. P., Perkowitz, M., Patterson, D. J., Fox, D., & Kautz, H. (2004). Inferring activities from interactions with objects. *IEEE Pervasive Computing / IEEE Computer Society [and] IEEE Communications Society, 3*, 50–57. doi:10.1109/MPRV.2004.7

Rabiner, L. R., & Sambur, M. R. (1975). An algorithm for determining the endpoints of isolated utterances. *The Bell System Technical Journal, 54*, 297–315.

Tan, J. G., Zhang, D., Wang, X., & Cheng, H. S. (2005). Enhancing semantics spaces with event-driven cotnext interpretation. In *PERVASIVE2005* (LNCS 3468, pp. 80-97).

Wang, Y. (2008a). On Concept Algebra: A denotational mathematical structure for knowledge and software modeling. *International Journal of Cognitive Informatics and Natural Intelligence, 2*(2), 1–19.

Wang, Y. (2008b). On system algebra: A denotational mathematical structure for abstract systems, modeling. *International Journal of Cognitive Informatics and Natural Intelligence, 2*(2), 20–43.

Wehmeier, S. (Ed.). (2005). *Oxford Advanced Learner's Dictionary of Current English* (7th ed.). Oxford, UK: Oxford University Press.

Xue, W., & Luo, Q. (2005). Action-oriented query processing for pervasive computing. In *Proceedings of the Second Biennaial Conference on Innovative Data Systems Research (CIDR2005)* (pp. 305-316).

Yap, K. K., Srinivasan, V., & Motani, M. (2005). Max: Human-centric search of the physical world. In *Proceedings of the 3rd ACM Conference on Embedded Networked Sensor Systems (Sen-Sys'05)* (pp.166-179).

Zadeh, L. (1972). A fuzzy-set-theoretical interpretation of linguistic hedges. *Journal of Cybernetics, 2*, 4–34. doi:10.1080/01969727208542910

This work was previously published in volume 4, issue 1 of the International Journal of Cognitive Informatics and Natural Intelligence, edited by Yingxu Wang, pp. 30-44, copyright 2010 by IGI Publishing (an imprint of IGI Global).

Chapter 6
Incremental Knowledge Construction for Real–World Event Understanding

Koji Kamei
ATR Intelligent Robotics and Communication Laboratories, Japan

Yasue Kishino
NTT Communication Science Laboratories, Japan

Yutaka Yanagisawa
NTT Communication Science Laboratories, Japan

Yasushi Sakurai
NTT Communication Science Laboratories, Japan

Takuya Maekawa
NTT Communication Science Laboratories, Japan

Takeshi Okadome
Kwansei Gakuin University, Japan

ABSTRACT

The construction of real-world knowledge is required if we are to understand real-world events that occur in a networked sensor environment. Since it is difficult to select suitable 'events' for recognition in a sensor environment a priori, we propose an incremental model for constructing real-world knowledge. Labeling is the central plank of the proposed model because the model simultaneously improves both the ontology of real-world events and the implementation of a sensor system based on a manually labeled event corpus. A labeling tool is developed in accordance with the model and is evaluated in a practical labeling experiment.

INTRODUCTION

Once a computing environment becomes capable of understanding real-world events, it will be able to provide services in response to a given situation. In addition, users will be able to exchange and share real-world situations. The former application is well known as context aware services and the latter has recently been called environment-generated media (Maekawa, 2007). These applications observe the real world by using sensors, detect real-world changes as events and then drive various kinds of services according to the events occurring in the environment.

DOI: 10.4018/978-1-4666-1743-8.ch006

If the objectives of services and their environment are clearly defined, it is possible to determine the kind of information that the services require and also how to obtain them depending on the problems to be solved. For example, the e-Nightingale project (Noma et al., 2004) is targeting event recording related to medical nursing and to this end they developed a small wireless accelerometer.

In contrast, when activities of daily life are targeted, a problem arises, namely the difficulty of defining target events a priori. This requires the construction of knowledge about real-world events. In this field, Philipose (2004) and Wyatt (2005) extracted 26 activities of daily life and made it possible for them to be recognized by attaching RF-ID tags to the objects in the environment and having participants wear RF-ID readers on their hands. Perkowitz (2004) aggregated knowledge about activities and related objects and then recognized the activities from the sequences in which the objects were used.

In addition to RF-ID tags, we assume that small wireless sensor nodes containing, for example, accelerometers, magnetic compasses, and illuminometers will be attached to objects in the environment. Various events will be detected by these sensor nodes, and they will then provide various services. However, the problem of defining appropriate events will become more difficult.

In this article, we describe an incremental method for constructing an event ontology, namely the knowledge needed to understand real-world events, on the assumption that such sensor nodes are attached to various objects in the environment. Although the method mainly targets knowledge construction, it also simultaneously targets the development of a sensor networked environment. The method focuses on *labeling*, that is, constructing an event corpus in which the observed sensor data streams are annotated manually by human operators with reference to the event ontology being constructed. In the proposed method, the event ontology, event corpus

and implementation of the sensor environment are incrementally constructed during the iterative labeling process.

This article is structured as follows. We first propose a knowledge construction model. We then discuss the elements of the proposed model, and introduce a labeling tool developed in accordance with the model. We finally describe the result of a practical labeling experiment conducted in a developing sensor networked environment.

EVENT DETECTION IN SENSOR NETWORKED ENVIRONMENT

Obtaining Real-World Events

What kind of real-world events should be obtained from a sensor networked environment? When we focus on activities of daily life, we can find both human movement in the environment and changes in the status of objects, which are observed as independent events by multiple sensors. However, the observed events must be mutually related.

As an example of a daily event, assume that a person turns a light on. From the perspective of describing human activities, the event can be described as "(someone) turned the light on." In terms of describing changes in the status of a device, the status of the light changed from "off" to "on." As regards describing detected changes in the outputs of sensors attached other objects in the room, the event would be described as "the illuminometer output increased." Thus, the description of an event varies depending on the perspective. These differences arise from the way in which sensors are distributed and how they detect changes in the environment.

Returning to the example of "turning a light on", there are several ways to detect a real-world event. The simplest and most certain approach is to focus on the status of the light, and this can be detected by observing its electricity consumption. When focusing on human activities instead, a touch sensor attached to the light may detect the actions of people trying to turn the light on or off. Such actions can also be detected by attaching accelerometers to people's arms and legs, or by equipping the floor with pressure sensors. In this example, the event may also be detected indirectly, that is, if we assume a room equipped with many sensor nodes with illuminometers, most of the sensor nodes may detect changes in the room light. Video cameras are other possible sensors for use in detecting changes in illumination.

As described above, since a real-world event can be detected in various ways, various kinds of changes will be observed in sensor data streams. To understand a real-world event, the sensor networked environment must be able to detect changes in each observed data stream, and then integrate the detected changes.

Structure of Event Detection

To detect changes in event streams, the observed sensor data streams are processed and integrated structurally (Figure 1). Each layer extracts typical patterns in the streams with different levels of granularity. Those detection modules work concurrently and autonomously by monitoring both sensor readings and detected events as well as symbiotic agent (Sugawara 2008).

Layer 1 receives sensor data streams that reflect physical events, and processes them as signal streams. This layer reduces the noise on the signal streams and detects significant changes in the sensor data. Layer 2 receives the output of layer 1, namely the temporal intervals where the sensor output is changing significantly. The output of this layer is a sequence of *primitive events*. In the field of real-world event detection, an event could be either a *primitive event* or a *complex event* (Wang 2006). The words *primitive events* and *complex event* are originally used in the field of active databases with ECA rules. *Primitive events* describe physical events that can be extracted directly from the sensor output

stream. For example, the output stream of an accelerometer includes primitive physical events, such as, "falling down," "going forward horizontally," "moving in a circle (rotating around a point)" or "stopping." An increase in an illuminometer's output is also detected as a primitive event by this layer.

Unlike the primitive layers described above, layer 3 integrates a sequence or sequences of primitive events extracted from multiple sensors, and then provides a high level event that describes the kind of activities that occurred around the objects. These high level events are called *complex events* in contrast to *primitive events*. In this article, we assign an *object* (noun) – *activity* (verb) pair to a *complex event*, to describe an event that corresponds to an object. For example, when we focus on a "drawer," we describe such events as "(someone) opened the drawer," or "(someone) closed the drawer." The real-world knowledge required by this layer is, in other words, "how an object is used."

At the top of the structure, layer 4 estimates human activities in the environment. For example, an activity "having a cup of tea" may consist of multiple complex events that occur with multiple

Figure 1. Layered structure of event recognition

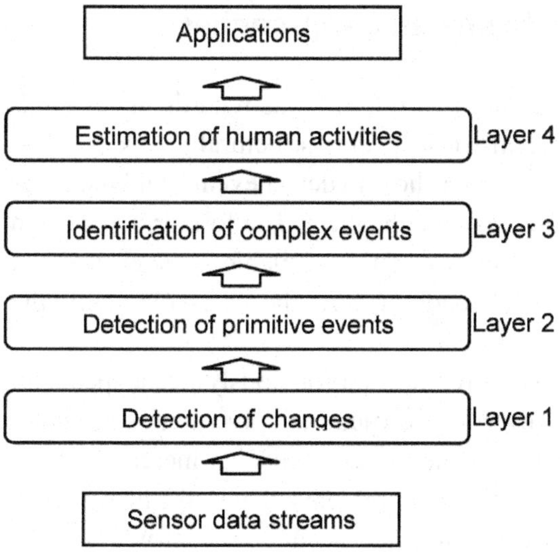

Applications
⇧
Estimation of human activities — Layer 4
⇧
Identification of complex events — Layer 3
⇧
Detection of primitive events — Layer 2
⇧
Detection of changes — Layer 1
⇧
Sensor data streams

Figure 2. Knowledge construction model for concurrent improvement of event ontology definitions and sensor implementation based on manually labeled event corpus

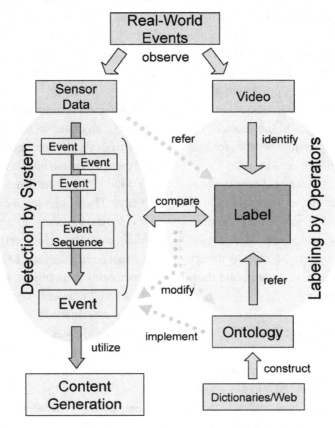

objects, such as: "(someone) stood up from a chair," "(someone) opened a drawer," and "(someone) picked a cup up from a drawer".

Problems and Approaches

There are two problems as regards understanding real-world events structurally as described above; one is how to detect events, and the other is how to describe them. The former depends on the functions of the available sensors, and the latter depends on how the users recognize the environment.

These problems are obviously not independent; however, it is difficult to solve them simultaneously. We therefore propose an incremental approach to these problems; that is, the incremental construction of knowledge for real-world event understanding. We first provide an initial solution for each problem, and then modify and extend the solution in accordance with manually annotated *labels*. Figure 2 shows a knowledge construction model based on a manually labeled event corpus.

The problems and outline of the model are described in the remaining part of this section, and the construction of an event ontology is described in the following section.

Problems in Event Definition

The definition of real-world events depends on human recognition in that the events to be detected are defined by what people want to recognize. Sensors are usually developed to detect such events. It is also assumed that a sensor networked environment will notify interested parties of such events.

The primary problem with respect to a sensor networked environment is to define the set of events to be detected. The set is defined within the constraints of sensor function and peoples' interest. The former is derived from the sensor specifications. For example, an accelerometer can detect acceleration and so can detect the movement of an object. The detection of "movement" may be of interest; however it appears to be insufficient. People may describe their interests in other words such as "pick up," "rotate," or "fall down." To cope with these differences requires knowledge about real-world events, namely, what kind of events should be detected, how the events are detected and how the events are described.

Focusing on a "door", for example, we can assume that two particular event descriptions are often used, namely, "opened" and "closed." "Knocked" may also be used frequently; however, "fall down" may not. We can therefore restrict the vocabularies used for describing events related to "doors," that is, the system does not have to detect the "fall down" of "doors."

The implementation of event detection is also facilitated by using this kind of knowledge. The sensors attached to the door can assume that a detected "movement" is possibly an instance of "rotate" or "slide (horizontal movement)" because of the restriction.

The construction of this kind of knowledge will require a lot of work; we therefore have to focus on important events that we assume will be detected and that can feasibly be detected. We first construct initial vocabularies from resources used in natural language research. The methods are described in detail in the next section.

Incremental Knowledge Construction Model

Labeling is a task that involves determining the temporal intervals at which certain events occur and describing the event details as annotations. The precision of the labels depends on the stability of the knowledge about real-world events, especially when plural operators annotate the labels. On the other hand, when the knowledge is finely defined but becomes complicated, and the sensor output contains noise, the annotation task will be difficult in deciding appropriate labels and so possibly become inconsistent. Consequently, label precision depends on both the sensor implementation and the definition of the event ontology. We therefore require a strategy for defining ontology incrementally that takes sensor implementation into consideration.

Figure 2 illustrates our approach for the incremental construction of real-world knowledge. The illustrated model focuses on the labeling and incremental modification of the event ontology. The model has three main functions: event detection from sensor data streams, manual labeling of the stored data streams and the comparison of those results to extend the event ontology.

We assume that the real-world events are observed by both sensors and video cameras.

The network of sensors observes real-world events as the output values of sensors. The system detects changes in the data streams and identifies them as primitive events such as movement or status changes. It then guesses what has actually happened from the sequences of primitive events. The extracted complex events are used by applications. The extraction or detection of each level of events should be implemented as system modules. The event ontology provides the requirements for implementation.

On the other hand, labeling is undertaken manually by human operators to construct an event corpus. The operators extract events from video streams and occasionally from sensor data streams. They have to understand what kind of events should be extracted by referring to the event ontology.

The results of automatic event detection are evaluated by comparing them with the manually annotated labels. The comparison provides cues for improving the sensor system when appropriate events are not extracted. The descriptive power of the ontology is also evaluated by the comparison, that is, the result also indicates the incompleteness of the event ontology when there are inconsistencies between labels and detected results. In the latter case, the event ontology should be modified. Therefore manual labeling should be performed repeatedly when the event ontology is modified or extended. In this way, the knowledge of real-world events is constructed incrementally during practical labeling iterations.

EVENT ONTOLOGY FOR INTERPRETING REAL-WORLD EVENTS

In this section, we describe the characteristics of the knowledge for interpreting real-world. We first show how the knowledge is used for event detection. We then describe how to obtain vocabularies for the initial version of the event ontology before embarking on practical labeling iteration. The last part of this section discusses the relationships defined between vocabularies.

Ontology for Real-World Event Detection

The fundamental question in event detection is "What kind of event can the system detect?" This question can be divided into two questions: one from the user side namely, "What kind of event should the system detect?", the other from the system side namely, "How does the system detect the event?"

We assume that many sensors are attached to many objects in a room. These sensors are expected to detect activities in the room from the pattern of object usage. To implement a sensor system for real-world event detection, the target events should be selected in advance so that the system will detect the required set of events. The detection results will be evaluated by comparison with

event occurrence answer sets, known as an event corpus, which are constructed manually for the evaluation by human operators. Operators also refer to the target set of events when constructing the corpus.

System implementation and system evaluation both require a set of real-world event definitions. In this study, the set of event definitions is called the *event ontology*, and it describes 1) relationships between objects and events; 2) relationships among events such as relationships of semantic inclusion or sequential patterns of occurrence; and 3) event descriptions in physical quantities used to detect them.

When targeting the recognition of general activities, no particular event set is defined a priori. Therefore, we propose an extensive method for constructing an event ontology based on a manually labeled event corpus.

Acquisition of Initial Vocabularies

The initial version of the event ontology is constructed by referring to resources used in natural language research including dictionaries and corpuses compiled from web texts. We first extracted typical events from those general resources, and then selected initial vocabularies that appeared to be observable by sensors. Finally, we defined the relationships between vocabularies.

WordNet is a semantic lexicon for the English language (Fellbaum, 1998). For searching real-world events, Okadome (2006) extracted a set of synonyms from WordNet that are related to movement and evaluated those words in terms of whether they were observable by sensor nodes equipped with accelerometers. We can adopt their event descriptors as a start point for basic verbs used for labeling.

In contrast, by focusing on each object in the environment, we can define a set of verbs that are often used for describing events that are connected with the object. By focusing on a "door", for example, "open" and "close" are typical verbs that describe events related to a door, rather than "fall down." Such relationships are extracted as a case frame dictionary. Kawahara and Kurohashi constructed a large case frame dictionary for the Japanese language by analyzing more than 500 million sentences aggregated from the Web (Kawahara & Kurohashi, 2006).

As a start point for defining vocabularies for the objects in the sensor networked environment, we first eliminated general verbs, such as "pick up," "carry" and "fall down", for moveable objects from Okadome's event descriptors. We then eliminated several verbs frequently used for each object according to the case frame dictionary in addition to the general verbs. Since the vocabularies obtained here are merely a start point, they should be modified and extended based on the results of labeling practice.

Relationships between Vocabularies

Relationships between vocabularies are also useful for understanding real-world events. We focus on two kinds of relationships: 1) semantic hierarchies among vocabularies, and 2) constraints in event occurrence. The event detection modules are structured according to the relationships. In addition, they control the incremental labeling procedure pointing terms of label granularity.

The semantic hierarchies are basically obtained from WordNet. For example, the "fall down" event is considered to be a subset of "move to lower place," and consequently a subset of "move." From the viewpoint of sensor implementation, "move" and "fall down" are firmly observable according to the sensors' functionalities. The former is detected when there are any changes in the outputs of accelerometers; the latter is detected when the acceleration becomes zero. On the other hand, there is no simple definition for "move to lower place" although the semantics of the event is considered between two observable events. To search for a "move to lower place" event, the hierarchy enables users to find "fall down" instead.

The constraints of event occurrence are used to detect complex events by integrating the detection result of other events including primitive events and other complex events. We consider four types of constraints: concurrence, consequence, inclusion and exclusion. For example, when a person sits down on a chair there would be a sequence of events such as 1) the chair was rotated, 2) the chair vibrated and then 3) the chair was moved horizontally. Figure 3 shows an example of real-world event and related vocabularies.

The sequence of primitive events described above is assumed to be understood as a "sit down" complex event, however, the mapping between

Figure 3. An example of event ontology for both event detection and labeling. (a person sits on a chair)

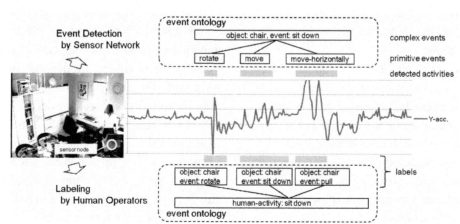

primitive events and complex events is not always one-to-one correspondence. One can "sit down," for example, without drawing the chair. The definition of vocabularies should manage these kinds of many-to-many mappings. We therefore focus on the construction of real-world knowledge through labeling practice described in the next section.

CONSTRUCTION OF REAL-WORLD KNOWLEDGE THROUGH LABELING PRACTICE

In the previous sections, we introduced an incremental method designed to construct the knowledge needed for understanding real-world events. The method focuses on *labeling,* which means adding annotations to observed data streams to describe what kind of real-world events have actually occurred. The labels are intended to be used for evaluating both automatically detected event streams and the vocabularies used for labeling. In this section, we first describe problems in labeling practice. We then describe the practice setup, that is, our sensor environment and labeling tool.

Problems in Practical Labeling

Labeling is an activity for adding annotations to observed data streams to describe what kind of real-world events have actually occurred. In this article, we focus on labeling by human operators, rather than that automatically extracted by computer systems.

To add annotations, a human operator has to determine a temporal interval during which some kind of event has likely occurred, determine what kind of event has occurred in the interval, and then describe what the event actually was and how it occurred. The labeling practice primarily aims at constructing an event corpus that describes the ground-truth of sensor data interpretation. In addition to the event corpus, it

aims at constructing an event ontology through incremental labeling practice as shown in Figure 2. The obtained event corpus is used to evaluate the result of sensor data interpretation and may be used to improve the system. It is also used to evaluate the descriptive power of the constructed event ontology. Consequently, the corpus and the ontology are constructed concurrently in the proposed workflow.

In the labeling practice, the labeling operators will encounter the following three problems: 1) What kind of events should be extracted? 2) How should the events be observed in the sensor data streams? What are the criteria for distinguishing events? 3) How can the operators notice and understand events in the sensor data?

To deal with the first problem, we must construct an event ontology as described in the previous section. It is impossible to add labels when the event vocabularies are undefined. To construct the initial event ontology, we focus on the constraints related to both the objects in the environment and the functions of the sensor devices.

The criteria for distinguishing events are defined as a part of the event ontology. They are described as constraints such as signal patterns in the sensor data stream or patterns of event sequences. These definitions are also used to implement automatic event extraction in addition to labeling.

The granularity of event vocabulary should also be addressed with regard to manual annotation, that is, the labeling operators should first add annotations with coarse vocabularies, and then annotate with finer vocabularies incrementally.

Since manual labeling depends on an operator's decision, ambiguity remains even though the ontology and criteria are defined and shown to him/her. To evaluate the ambiguity, we decided to assign more than two labeling operators to the same data. This approach is expected to improve the precision of the labeling results. Moreover it can indicate the ambiguity in the definitions of the vocabularies and their criteria.

Figure 4. (Left) Experimental office in which small sensor nodes are attached to objects. (Right) Small sensor node for attaching to various objects in sensor networked environment

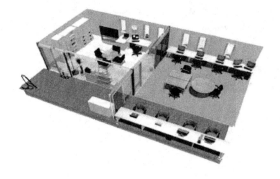

The last problem is the difficulty human operators have in understanding raw sensor data streams. Unlike speech recognition or image understanding, it is difficult for operators to understand sensor data streams because they cannot listen to or see these data directly. Moreover, since a real-world event is possibly sensed by multiple sensor nodes and each node can accommodate multiple sensors, the operators face the problem that they have to determine possible activities from a lot of data streams. To cope with this problem, we designed a labeling tool with which the operators can refer to both the video streams that are synchronized to the sensor data streams and the automatically detected event candidates. This labeling tool is described in detail later in this section.

Sensor Environment for Practice

As part of our research project, we built the sensor networked environment shown in Figure 3. This is an office environment in which our research staff is actually working every day. Small sensor nodes (shown in Figure 4) are attached to various *objects* in this office. The office contains both portable and non-portable objects: cups and books are examples of the former and the doors of the room, the doors of cabinets, and drawers are examples of the latter. Four video cameras are attached to the ceiling of the room to record all the events that occur in the room. The floor is

covered with pressure sensors to capture human movement.

Our project focuses on understanding real-world events from information obtained from objects. As well as RF-ID tags, we assume that small sensor nodes are attached to or embedded in various objects in the environment. We do not attach sensors to the human body to avoid unnecessary inconvenience to the participants. Moreover, we do not focus on automatic recognition from video streams; we use the video streams only for labeling.

We built a general-purpose sensor node for attaching to various objects in the environment. The sensor node is equipped with a 3-axis accelerometer, a 3-axis magnetic compass and an illuminometer. It also has 2.4 GHz wireless communication modules and a microprocessor that controls the sensors and communication modules. About 40 sensor nodes are attached to the objects in the sensor room, and these are used to observe changes in the environment.

Labeling Tool for Annotating Real-World Events

We have designed a labeling tool to support the proposed knowledge construction model. The labeling tool requirements can be summarized as follows: 1) operators can browse both video and sensor data streams, 2) operators can refer to

Figure 5. Screenshot of labeling tool developed in accordance with proposed knowledge construction model

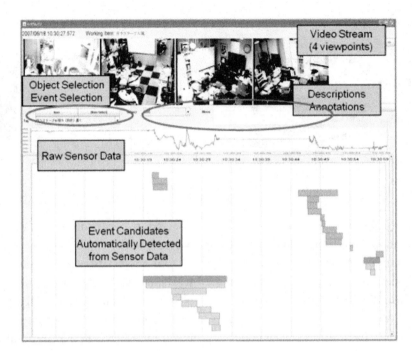

the event ontology, more specifically, the system enumerates objects in the environment and then focuses on possible event tags for the selected object, and 3) operators can browse event candidates detected by the sensor system.

Certain labeling tools are already used in dialogue understanding research. Anvil (Kipp, 2004) is a well-known example of such a tool. Unlike those labeling tools, the proposed tool focuses on knowledge construction in addition to the labeling function. The tool is implemented in accordance with the proposed construction model. Therefore, the tool can be used to compare both manually added labels and automatically detected events. Figure 5 shows a screenshot of the labeling tool.

The upper part of the user interface shows images captured by the four cameras attached to the ceiling of the room. The labeling operators mainly browse the multiple video streams to detect events occurring in the environment. The operators then refer to the automatic event detec-

tion result or inspect the raw sensor data to describe annotations about the events.

The labeling tool provides the operators with possible vocabularies in two ways: one is as the results of automatic event detection described above, and the other is as a selection user interface. Immediately below the video images, the labeling tool provides a user interface for describing events. This interface offers two selection boxes; one provides nouns that describe *objects* to which sensor nodes are attached, and the other provides verbs that describe possible *events*. When an operator selects an *object* from the selection box, the set of possible *activities* in the other selection box is modified according to the noun-verb pairs defined in the event ontology. The operators therefore receive possible event candidates from the labeling tool.

In accordance with the noun-verb selection, a raw sensor data stream is automatically selected and displayed. The operators are also allowed to select another data stream manually.

A selection box and a large text field are aligned to the right of the selection boxes. By using the selection box, the operators can provide information about the actors in the event. The text field is for additional information.

More than half of the screen is occupied by diagrams of possible events detected by the system and manual labels that have already been registered. Operators can browse the results of automatically detected events as a reference, because the results of low-level event detection, such as the temporal intervals during which the signal level changes, will notify them of possible events. Operators can also refer to labels attached by others or themselves for comparison.

LABELING PRACTICE AND EVALUATION

A practical evaluation is being conducted in an experimental sensor room where more than 40 sensors are currently attached to various objects. The sensor data streams are recorded for about four hours a day, that is, each node continues sending as long as its battery still retains a charge. Each sensor node sends the observed results every 30 ms and the data size is 125 bytes. Therefore, each node sends 60 MB of data a day and a total of 2.4 GB of data are stored.

Six operators are employed for labeling, and two of them are assigned to the same data set. This combination is varied to minimize differences between operators. About 20 minutes of observed data was processed in one day of labeling operation. A total of more than 4000 minutes of observed data was labeled in three months of labeling practice.

We analyzed the labeled data and the record of the labeling operation from four standpoints. We first describe the vocabulary modification that occurred in the early phase of labeling practice. We then analyze the result in terms of the progress of the labeling operation and the use of vocabularies. We finally compare the labels and the detected activities.

Vocabulary Modification

In the early stage of labeling practice, there were ambiguities as regards using the initial vocabularies among the labeling operators. We inspected these vocabularies to specify their exact meaning and then immediately explained the criteria to the labeling operators. Two examples of vocabulary modification are described below.

In the initial ontology, we assumed that when a person sits down on a chair, he "pulls the chair" and then occasionally "rotates the chair." These verbs, that is, "*pull*" and "*rotate*," are incorporated into the ontology as basic verbs used with *chair* since they were extracted from the case frame dictionary. According to the observation from the video stream, it seemed that both *pull* and *rotate* actually occurred. However, it was difficult for the operators to separate these events from "*sit down*" events when these actions were performed continuously.

We expect to be able to separate these events by analyzing sensor data although the system has not yet been realized. In the current phase of development, we decided not to label these events manually but just to label "sit down on the chair." Labeling with those vocabularies is planned for the next iteration of labeling practice.

Another example of vocabulary modification was "moving the sliding door of a cabinet." This vocabulary was divided into two actions as a result of labeling experience. In the initial ontology, we assigned "move to right" and "move to left" to the sliding doors. However, we noticed from the labeling results that two types of movement should be distinguished. These movements constitute a movement stopped by the actor and a movement that stopped by itself when the sliding door reached the end. Although the output of an accelerometer decreases slowly in the former case, the latter indicates a severe variation because of the collision that occurs. Those two types of movement are easily distinguished by analyzing sensor data. We decided that these events should

Figure 6. Distribution of average progress speed of one day of labeling operation, aggregated by amount of sensor data (in minutes) annotated in one hour of labeling operation

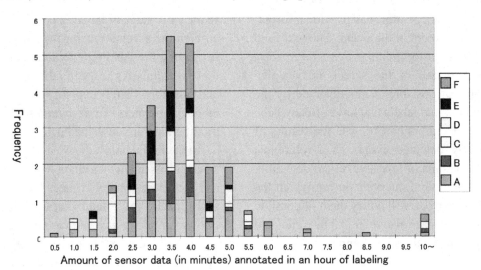

be distinguished in the labeling process. However, it requires labeling operators to inspect the output of accelerometers to confirm whether or not there were collisions.

Progress of Labeling Operation

Figure 6 shows the distribution of the operator labeling speed. It shows the number of minutes of observed data labeled in one hour by each operator (operator A to F). The average progress of the labeling operation reveals that each operator can annotate 3.5 minutes of observed data per hour of labeling operation. This means that each operator could annotate from 20 to 25 minutes of data a day. This indicates that ten days of labeling was required to annotate one day (210 minutes) of activities.

We analyzed 14 days of labeled data. For each day, 210 minutes of observed data were recorded and two operators were assigned to labeling. The maximum, minimum and average number of annotated labels was 2220, 674 and 1388.5, respectively.

The number of labels varied for each day, however, the ratio of the number of labels annotated by two operators for the same day may indicate

anomalies between operators or vocabularies. The ratios of the number of labels (obtained by dividing the smaller number of labels by the larger one for the same day) had maximum and minimum values of 0.94 and 0.51, respectively. The average was 0.76 and the deviation was 0.017. Focusing on the day when the number of labels was the fewest (674 labels were annotated to the data on that day), the ratio of the number of labels registered by two operators was 0.86. On the other hand, on the day when the number of labels was at its maximum (2220 labels were registered), the ratio was 0.67 and this was smaller than those of the other days.

These results indicate that the number of labels added by an operator who tends to annotate in detail influences both the number of labels and the ratio of the numbers of labels. Although the collected data were insufficient, it implies that the criteria were different for different labeling operators and so the number of labels varies.

Vocabularies Used in Labeling

In the initial vocabulary, an average of about 20 events were defined for each of 59 objects. More precisely, 1292 noun-verb pairs were defined in the event ontology. The maximum, minimum and average numbers of noun-verb pairs actually used in one day's annotated data were 214, 139, and 171.4, respectively. 389 types of noun-verb pairs were used in total. A group of verbs in the "movable" category expected in the annotation did not appear. The changes of illumination were also infrequently used because of the positioning of the objects.

The label most often annotated was targeted at the "white desk" and the event was "moved a mouse on it." This label was used 6766 times and it accounted for 13.9% of all annotations. Obviously the actions of a particular person who was usually working in the environment were often labeled. The top 10th of the frequently annotated labels related to "white desk", "chair", "chair 2" and "the door of the laboratory." They accounted for 49.7% of all labels.

Comparison of Labels and Detection Result

We performed a preliminary evaluation of the temporal intervals during which changes in sensor output streams were detected automatically by the system. The aim of this comparison is to determine the threshold values for change detection.

Two days worth of labeled data were evaluated. Two operators added labels for each day. We evaluated the matching of the automatic detection and the manual labels. There were 872 labels annotated manually by the labeling operators. 468 of them had a one-to-one correspondence with one of detection results. 73 of them were matched with more than two detection results. In total, 62% of the labels corresponded with detected changes. By contrast, the detected changes were found as 475 temporal intervals. However, 63% of them were related with none of the manual labels.

The latter result indicates that the threshold values used in the experiment were too small so that more changes were extracted than should have been. On the other hand, the former result

indicates there were intervals where the system could not detect changes. Two possible interpretations of the former result are as follows: 1) unlike with the latter result, the threshold values were too large to detect changes, or 2) there was data loss in the sensor nodes caused by sensors or wireless communication.

To resolve the contradiction in deciding the threshold values, we assumed that the threshold values should be raised and that there was occasional data loss. By examining data based on these assumptions, we actually found two types of irregular behavior in the sensor nodes. One was periodic data loss. There were periodically labels that could not be associated with any detection results. Another was activities with a long duration. Some of the detected intervals lasted so long that they were matched with many manual labels. The former resulted from the data correction sequence; the latter was caused by the noise from the sensor node power source when its battery level decreased.

CONCLUSION

This article proposed an incremental knowledge construction model for understanding real-world events from a sensor networked environment. The proposed model focused on three components: 1) an event ontology that contains knowledge about real-world events, 2) an event corpus that contains manually annotated labels for the sensor data streams, and 3) the result of automatic event detection. Although the components should apparently be constructed in this order, especially from the viewpoint of sensor system construction, we addressed the difficulty of defining the event ontology a priori, and then we proposed an incremental construction model that focuses on manual labeling. We also introduced a labeling tool that was developed according to the proposed model and a practical labeling experiment in a sensor networked environment.

Practice and evaluation provides a methodology for processing the proposed construction model. We experienced modification of both the ontology and the system though we have conducted only a small fraction of labeling iteration, that is, the automatically detected events are limited. The primitive event detection modules defined in the current event ontology are under construction. As the next step towards confirming the proposed model, a statistical analysis of the events detected with those modules is expected to reveal the incompleteness of the ontology.

REFERENCES

Fellbaum, C. (Ed.). (1998). *WordNet: An Electronic Lexical Database*. Cambridge, MA: Bradford Books.

Kawahara, D., & Kurohashi, S. (2006). Case frame compilation from the web using high-performance computing. In *Proceedings of the 5th International Conference on Language Resources and Evaluation (LREC2006)* (pp. 1344-1347).

Kipp, M. (2001). Anvil – a generic annotation tool for multimodal dialogue. In *Proceedings of the 7th European Conference on Speech Communication and Technology (Eurospeech)* (pp. 1367-1370).

Maekawa, T., Yanagisawa, Y., & Okadome, T. (2007). Towards environment generated media: object-participation-type weblog in home sensor network. In *Proceedings of the 16th International Conference on World Wide Web (WWW2008)* (pp. 1267-1268).

Noma, H., Ohmura, A., Kuwahara, N., & Kogure, K. (2004). Wearable sensors for auto-event-recording on medical nursing – user study of ergonomic design. In *Proceedings of the 8th IEEE Intl. Symposium on Wearable Computers (ISWC'04)* (pp. 8-15).

Okadome, T. (2006). Event representation for sensor data grounding. *International Journal of Computer Science and Network Security, 6,* 187–193.

Perkowitz, M., Philipose, M., Fishkin, K. P., & Patterson, D. (2004). Mining models of human activities from the web. In *Proceedings of the 13th International Conference on World Wide Web (WWW2004)* (pp. 573-582).

Philipose, M., Fishkin, K. P., Perkowitz, M., Patterson, D., Fox, D., & Kautz, H. (2004). Inferring activities from interactions with objects. *Pervasive Computing, 3,* 50–57. doi:10.1109/MPRV.2004.7

Sugawara, K., Fujita, S., Kinoshita, T., & Shiratori, N. (2008). A design of cognitive agents for recognizing real space — towards symbiotic computing. In *Proceedings of the 7th International Conference on Cognitive Informatics (ICCI '08)* (pp. 277-285).

Wang, F., Liu, S., Liu, P., & Bai, Y. (2006). Bridging physical and virtual worlds: complex event processing for RFID data stream. In *Proceedings of the 10th International Conference on Extending Database Technology (EDBT2006)* (pp. 588-607).

Wyatt, D., Philipose, M., & Choudhury, T. (2005). Unsupervised activity recognition using automatically mined common sense. In . *Proceedings of AAAI, 2005,* 21–27.

This work was previously published in volume 4, issue 1 of the International Journal of Cognitive Informatics and Natural Intelligence, edited by Yingxu Wang, pp. 65-79, copyright 2010 by IGI Publishing (an imprint of IGI Global).

Chapter 7
Autonomic Computing for a Complex Problem of Experimental Physics

Tadeusz Wibig
University of Lodz and the A. Soltan Institute for Nuclear Studies, Poland

ABSTRACT

Standard experimental data analysis is based mainly on conventional, deterministic inference. The complexity of modern physics problems has become so large that new ideas in the field are received with the highest of appreciation. In this paper, the author has analyzed the problem of contemporary high-energy physics concerning the estimation of some parameters of the observed complex phenomenon. This article confronts the Natural and Artificial Networks performance with the standard statistical method of the data analysis and minimization. The general concept of the relations between CI and standard (external) classical and modern informatics was realized and studied by utilizing of Natural Neural Networks (NNN), Artificial Neural Networks (ANN) and MINUIT minimization package from CERN. The idea of Autonomic Computing was followed by using brains of high school students involved in the Roland Maze Project. Some preliminary results of the comparison are given and discussed.

INTRODUCTION

The analysis of the surrounding physical reality, for last at least three thousand years, as we know it, follow the line of building simplified models and solving problems using specific tools developed

with applied approximations making them easy or relatively easy to maintain. The unquestioned successes of such, scientific, way of thinking allow us to create so-called civilization. However, this method, which we can call (Wang, 2007b) the Imperative Computing have limitations. Some problems can not be treated this way, at least at present. There is a belief that, e.g., mathematical

DOI: 10.4018/978-1-4666-1743-8.ch007

tools needed to solve some problems in quantum field theory or hydro- or thermodynamic will be developed in the future. Some see a hope in 'analog' quantum computations. However, at the moment there are much common problems where the usual methods of 'standard analysis' sometimes fail (the general problem of 'pattern' recognition is the perfect example). Quite recently the Cognitive Informatics (CI) theory shows other possible solution. It is the Autonomic Computations (AC). By definition (Wang, 2007b) the AC is not a passive system and uses among others the inference-driven mechanisms to get a (nondeterministic!) result. The realization is not obvious, but we propose that usage of untrained children brains just follows a general concept described in the Layered Reference Model of the Brain (Wang et al., 2006). The word 'untrained' here is important. The preliminary comparison with the 'professional' brain is discussed in the present work. The role of *a prior* knowledge is expected and seen, but it seems to be surprisingly small.

We would like to discuss here a particular problem of the describing of the data registered by some cosmic ray physics experimental device. The standard analysis involves extensive Monte Carlo studies (and there are still discrepancies between different groups of experimentalists and theoreticians). Situations reach the level described very well in the web 'intro' to IBM Autonomic Computing Manifesto (IBM, 2001): "Computing is too hard. It's time we stop our preoccupation with faster and more powerful and start making them smarter."

Our statement is that some extremely complex problems can be solved not only qualitatively but also quantitatively on the same level as this of the standard statistical method precision not only by ANN trained for this particular problem but also with the (over-sized, redundant) NNN using their 'natural' meta and higher cognitive functions acquired in the past, as a part of natural intelligent (NI) system category of conscious life functions known as the NI applications layers not obviously (obviously not) related to the particular problem.

Methods of the analyzing the NNN and ANN performance is shown and some first results are given in this paper. We would like to emphasize here that the present analysis is the interesting particular example of the domination of Artificial Intelligence by the Natural Intelligence (Wang, 2007a).

The Physical Problem and The Standard, Imperative Computing, Solution

The ultra high-energy cosmic ray particles, its origin and nature are one of the most intriguing questions on general interest among the physicists. The phenomenon of arriving from the cosmos of the elementary particle with energy of about 50 J is very rare and thus hard to investigate experimentally. Fortunately during the passage through the Earth atmosphere the cascade of smaller energy secondary particles is created and eventually the surface is momentarily bombarded by billions of particles spread over the area of squared kilometers. The experimental setups for registrations of such events consists of several to several thousand detectors separated by hundreds of meters to few kilometers equipped with the triggering and recording devices.

Such arrays sample the mentioned showers of particles in not very big number of points and this is the only information we have about the event. (We do not discuss here the experiments recording the fluorescent light which is the distinct and complementary technique of study such phenomena.) Each detector of the surface array registers actual number of particles passing the detector giving the information about particle density at the detector position. It is additionally smoothed by the physics of the detection process and electronic noises of different kinds. The transition from recorded digits to the physics in question is to estimate the shape of the distribution of cascade particles on the ground. The limited information allows us only to get the precise enough estimates of normalization constant - total number of particles, first or at last second moment of the distribution (or any other, more suitable, parameters of this distribution). For doing this one has to use some `prior' assumptions, e.g., about the radial symmetry or the expected analytically approximated functional form of the distribution. After that one has to go through the procedure of making the estimate.

The standard is to make a χ^2 or likelihood measure of the goodness of the fit, than to use known textbook methods to minimize the respective distance between the `theoretical line' and `measured points'.

In general this is all we need, but practically there are classes of multi-parameter problems and very noisy data when the minimization is not very straightforward. This is of course also the problem of the function to be minimized and its many local minima, distant and not very much different in depth. The problem of Extensive Air Shower (EAS) parameter estimation is a good example. The number of parameters is not very large. From physical point of view they are mainly: position of the shower axis and total number of particles and a parameter of the slope of theirs radial distribution. For simplicity and using `the prior' knowledge on the shower physics we use only one shape parameter (Barnhill, 2005). The large spacing between detectors makes this simplification justified. We neglect also, for the purposes of this paper, the two parameters describing shower inclination. So we have *only* four parameter space with well defined physical meaning. It also provides a kind of independence of them all which is very helpful for minimization.

The problem arises because of the sharpness of the distribution of particles when one tests the distances close to the shower axis. When the detector gets close to the axis number of registered particles goes into thousands while a little far it goes to tens being on the edge of 1 and below in most other detection points. From the point of view of minimization procedure when the axis

position is tested close to the one detection point it is the only one which controls the χ^2 or likelihood or whatsoever. This situation is caused by the physics of the process and one can't avoid it. The exclusion of close detectors is a remedy, but it is rather costly. The detector close to the shower core registered highest number of particles and thus the statistical importance of this point is the highest and in case of small number of detection points in general we can't afford to lose the most important one. We have to play with it.

Many methods and tricks were invented to get the minimization going with a number of problems as less as possible, but, as it will be shown, it is a hard task. The parameter which we will study comparing different methods of estimation is the number of lost events. We can define here the lost events as that having the χ^2 (or other studied measure) above some critical value. But to be comparable with others we defined them as the events for which the minimization moves the values of the parameter of the axis position: x and y and shower size exceeding some limits (which can be treated as defining the divergence of the minimization procedure).

ARTIFICIAL NEURAL NETWORK APPROACH

The process of estimation EAS parameters with the help of Artificial Neural Network, as it is shown in (Wibig, 1998) in the case of the hard shower component registered by the experiment KASCADE (Klages, 1997), can be quite successful. In the present work we used very similar network architecture which schematic view is shown in Figure 1. The input nodes are seeded with the registered particle densities, and the signal processing eventually gives the total number (its logarithm, to be precise) of shower particles. The particular network was build to work with the array of the Roland Maze Project being realized in Lodz (Feder, 2006). The array is based on detectors

Figure 1. Schematic layout of the ANN used for the evaluation of the total number of the EAS particles

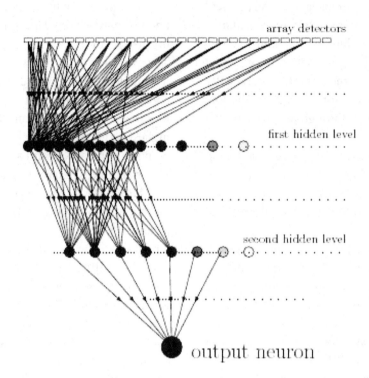

placed on the roofs of city high school. In the final phase about 30 schools will be equipped with 4 one squared meter scintillator detector each. The sum of numbers of particles registered in each school carry the same information as the four numbers from all four detectors due to the Poissonian character of the cascade. The distance of about 10 meters within each school are negligible with the kilometers between the schools and the scale of the changes of the average particle density. Thus we need the ANN with 30 input nodes. The geometry of the network we used here was not optimized for the number of neurons and its final structure analyzed here is highly redundant. We used eventually two hidden layers with 20 and 10 neurons, respectively.

During tests we check that the input values could be logarithms of the value of the input signal surface enlarged by 1.0 to avoid the zeros from detectors with no muon registered. We do not add the electronic noise here as not very big.

Each input is connected with each of the first hidden level neurons. The last hidden level neurons are connected to the single output unit. Tests done with a different number of hidden neurons show that there is no effect on network performance. Of course, we should keep this numbers with reasonable limits. The number of the network parameters to be trained was from about 5000 to 25000. As the neuron response function the common sigmoid has been used. The network was trained with the standard back-propagation algorithm using the simple `EAS generator'.

The generator works assuming particular shape of the particle distribution adopted from the measurements made by the one of the biggest arrays (in particular AGASA). The shower profile shape parameter known as "age parameter" defining the slope of the radial distribution was then smeared within physically reasonable limits. The number of particles is roughly proportional to the total energy of the primary cosmic ray particle.

The normalization, total number of particles, was generated according to the flat distribution in logarithm of particle energy scale. The cosmic ray shower spectrum is known to be of the power-law form and it is very steep with the index of about -3.0. This affects the estimated values. The generation used allows for the systematic bias, but on the other hand, too steep distribution in the training sample leads to the over-training of network with small size events while the events of energies, e.g., 100 times bigger, which are million times less abundant are practically not used for the training purposes. The uniform in $\log(E)$ is the compromise prior.

The steep spectrum makes the registered events consist mostly of events on the lower primary particle energy threshold which is defined by the trigger requirements. The 'artificial trigger' was applied to the training sample. We assumed that at least three 'schools' has to register some particles at least in two detectors each. Such trigger can be realized in the original Roland Maze Project array.

With the information limited so much, it is expected that standard minimization should fail quite often. The comparison of effectiveness of the standard and the ANN approach is one of the questions we want to answer here.

The network was trained first to estimate the most important shower parameter: the shower size (the total number of particles in the shower at the observation level). But we tested also the possibility of using network to estimate other parameters, and it was found that there is possible to train the network to estimate as well the x- and y- coordinate of the shower axis. The attempt to get the age parameter was not very successful

In Figure 2 the convergence of the training procedure is shown for the network trained with shower size a) and the axis position b). The dependence of the width of the distribution of the deviation of the estimated value from the *true* one is shown. The learning is quite a long lasting process. The first rational answers appear however already after the number of training events

comparable with the number of internal weights. Then we observe the continuous improvement. An interesting feature appeared below 1 million events on Figure 2b. There are abrupt decreases of the efficiency and then further and deeper improvements. These effects are seen for all networks we tested for both x- and y-axis position adjustments. It is seen always at the roughly some point and we suggests that it means the internal change of the network strategy of the parameter estimation. Something similar is seen also for EAS size estimation networks but at different length of training sample (around 10^4 at Figure 2a). The appearance of such unexpected, but may be obvious for the other point of view, abrupt improvement can be an evidence of at least a suggestion that the network starts (or starts to mimic) the higher (conscious!?) cognitive functions on the NI-App level Wang et al. (2006). The closer look at this phenomenon could also put some light to the process of network learning.

We ended the learning process at the 10^8 event sample. The further improvement is interesting, but of no practical importance. The final state of the trained network allows us to use it as a tool for shower size and axis position determination. Such trained network was then applied to the serial of 10000 events produced by the particles of energy generated by our event generator which build the library of the showers to be analyzed also with different methods. The ANN, when any event from the library is taken as an input, always give some answer. The accuracy of the ANN answer was studied in few 'modes'. In the Figure 3 the illustration of accuracy is presented as histograms showing the spread of the ANN guess errors. To get it easier to compare with other method some numbers should be given. Some measures of the 'goodness of the fit' are given below:

σ_N - the accuracy of size determination measured as a dispersion of the difference between decimal logarithms of the *true* and *ANN*

Figure 2. The accuracy of the ANN answer as a function of the number of events using for the training process shown as a widths of the distribution of the difference between the decimal logarithm of the estimated shower size and the `true' value a), and the difference of the respective spatial distance (in one x direction) difference b). Different lines represent different shower size samples. The solid one is for showers of the "true" size between 3 and 5 10^9 particles (the medium sizes), the dashed is for smaller showers, and the dotted one for really big showers

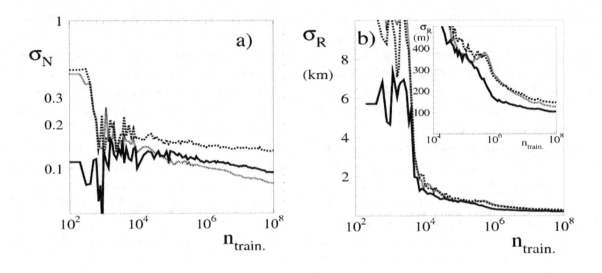

Figure 3. The spread of the trained ANN answer for the shower size a) and the spatial distance b) between guess and the true size a) and position b) of the shower axis. The result is obtained for the library showers

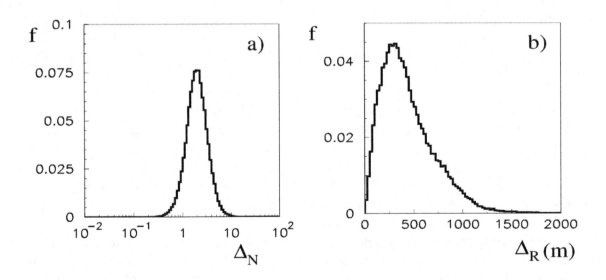

Table 1. Comparison of the performance of ANN, standard minimization and the three best NNNs found in our experiment

	ANN	MINUIT		NNN			
σ_N	0.217	0.478	0.280	0.270	0.279	0.294	0.349
Δ_N	0.29	-0.14	0.14	0.31	0.97	1.29	0.01
ξ_N	6%	17%	20%	16%	17%	12%	13%
σ_R	442	567	312	375	613	528	662
ξ_R	5%	29%	34%	33%	36%	23%	18%

reconstructed shower size (total number of particles)

Δ_N - the bias of the shower size measured as a difference of the average *true* and *ANN reconstructed* shower size

ξ_N - the fraction of *perfect* reconstructions, which we defined as these within 10% around the *true* value of the shower size (logarithm)

σ_R - the error in the localization measured as an average distance between *true* and A*NN reconstructed* shower axis position

ξ_R - the fraction of *perfect* localizations, by which we mean the *ANN reconstructed* axis closer than 100 m from the *true* one.

The values of all these five parameters obtained for our trained network are given in the Table 1 in the second column, labeled ANN.

STANDARD MINIMIZATION APPROACH

The data generated in the 10000 event shower library were also analyzed with the help of standard numerical minimization algorithms. We have used the CERN MINUIT package described in (James & Roos, 1975). The straightforward application for such, not perfectly well determined, problem as shower parameter minimization works rather bad, so some slightly improved, thus much time consuming programs reaching the minimum of the likelihood in few steps, have to be developed.

After careful adjustments of the proper divergence between 'the data' and predictions the program runs better. We have to mention here that some oversimplification was made here, because the radial distribution of shower particles used for minimization was exactly the one which was used inside the generator to calculate the averages. In the real case the particle distribution is rather unknown. This fact favours the minimization technique and the results given in this work should be treated with care, as the optimistic limit.

After applying to the library showers, the same as analyzed with the help of ANN, the results are as they are shown in the Table 1 in the columns labeled 'MINUIT'. There are two values in each case. The first on gives the average over all studied showers (we limited parameter ranges to reasonable values). Some showers due to the fluctuations cannot give the minimum within the assumed ranges of parameters of the minimum found gives the value of χ^2 too high to be accepted. If we excluded them from the averaging procedures, the results get better as they are given in the second MINUIT column. It is important to note that such 'bad' showers consist of about 1/3 of all in the 5×10^{18} eV library.

NATURAL NEURAL NETWORK APPROACH

The comparison of ANN and MINUIT methods of shower reconstruction given in the Table 1 shows

Figure 4. The layout of the graphical interface to estimate the EAS parameters using NNN (e.g., `by eye')

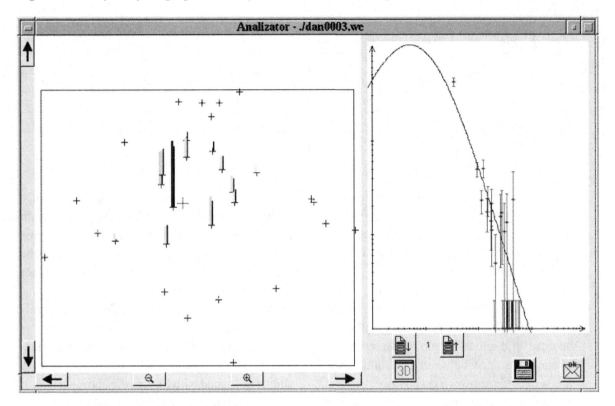

that the Neural Networks can give the competitive solutions of the complex minimization problem under study. However, the training procedure of the redundant network takes long and some systematic biases are seen. This is not very strong objections when taking into account the pros.

It would be interesting to test the performance of the extremely complex neural network one can imagine, which is, to some extend, the human brain. The training of the brain on a compound problem can be done in principle in two ways. The first one is similar to the ANN training process when the supervising teacher shows the examples of input data and told what the right answer should be. The more effective way is to use the ability of the brain collected in the whole `common' life of the neural network as it is.

One can bet that in most cases the `usual people' can react properly seeing the elephant running in their direction (whatever this reaction should be)

even if they never met an elephant before. The brain (especially human) is so redundant that it can easy adapt the past solution to the new problem. The only requirement needed is that that the new situation must be similar to something seen before. If the similarity is closer than the probability of reaction is expected to be the right one is higher.

We want to use NNN to perform the estimations of the EAS parameters. The problem has to be transformed first to the form which can be understood by the `common people'. The knowledge on the elementary particle passing through the atmosphere is helpful - in principle, but is useless - in fact, in our case. We would like the NNNs to use their natural abilities.

We have built the graphical interface shown in Figure 4 which contains all what we know and all we should get.

On the left big panel the map of the city is shown in the scale, but without any unimportant information. The map shows position of the detectors (schools) in the Roland Maze Project shower array (the crosses). Next to some schools are the vertical lines (lighter and darker - blue and red). The red shows the particle density registered by the detectors (its logarithm, but it is not relevant to the NNNs, and it hasn't been even told to them). The blue lines show `the just proposed' solution.

The right panel shows, what can be told, the radial distribution of the particle density; horizontally: the distant to the shower axis is given, vertically: the particle density. Points (in red) show the same values as they are on the left plot but `the just proposed' solution is given now by the line (blue).

The interface allows one to manipulate the shower parameter. The axis can be dragged usually using a computer mouse, or moves slightly with the batons with respective arrows next to the map side. The shower size (normalization of densities) can be changed on the left plot dragging the blue line vertically with the mouse. The horizontal movement of the clicked mouse increases the age parameter making the radial density curve wider or narrower. With this interface all the parameters can be adjusted comparing by eye the sizes of the bars of the right plot or/and, what is equivalent, controlling the positions of the points with respect to the curve on the left plot. The `user manual' describing the interface is rather short and simple. The package was supplied with the set of examples showing how the *true* (known from the simulation) line should looks like. This explains additionally the task.

As the NNN donors we used pupils from the schools collaborating with the Roland Maze Project. They were a little familiar with the problem of EAS, but it was not a requirement, some of them were not. We assumed that each one of our volunteers perform the minimization of 100 showers. The practice shows that after the initial phase one shower takes about 2-5 minutes to be fitted. This gives few hours of the hard work. All NNNs were working on their free time, so we could not motivate them very strongly and there were a number of people which started and never finished the whole task. To avoid boring students we transferred the data to them in packages of 10 and the next 10 can be sent only after receiving the adjusted previous set. So the whole examining takes usually weeks of work.

The initial position of the shower axis, normalization and age parameters were taken randomly for each new event on display to avoid any unphysical guesses. Results were sent back by e-mail, but the program coded them. It was not possible to see what the numerical value was obtained and to correct them `by hand'. The results once sent were put to the database and they couldn't be changed later on. The error once made remain what sometimes gives strong contribution to overall performance of the particular NNN.

DISCUSSION ON THE NNN RESULTS

Anyway, we get some pupils completed their work. We (TW) did it also to be compared with high school student's performance results. In the Table 1 results of TW followed by three (the best) student's NNNs are given in last four columns.

As it is seen the NNN accuracy is comparable with ANN concerning the shower size estimation (width and the bias), there are also no big differences concerning the axis position. Taking into account that NNN as well as ANN get an answer for each shower it should be compared with the `all MINUIT' (third column in the Table 1).

It is interesting to compare results obtained by high school students and TW who can be called a specialist in the field, if not in the shower parameter estimation in general, then at least some specialist, because of building and testing the system of graphic interface *etc*. In fact there is no big difference (the sample of only 100 events was used to get the numbers). One can conclude that there is not experience needed.

Table 2. The improvement (or disimprovement) of the NNN performances concerning the parameter of σ_N in the course of the EAS analysis

	number of analyzed events									
	10	20	30	40	50	60	70	80	90	100
TW	0.142	0.203	0.199	0.210	0.220	0.239	0.250	0.264	0.261	0.270
NNN 1	0.257	0.237	0.244	0.233	0.235	0.312	0.302	0.291	0.286	0.279
NNN 2	0.379	0.374	0.324	0.307	0.287	0.322	0.305	0.308	0.295	0.294
NNN 3	0.551	0.427	0.390	0.389	0.368	0.363	0.358	0.349	0.335	0.349

Insights that the statistics education community badly needs to have, even though it may not know it yet.

It is not obvious, however, when we look how the individual NNN was improving its performance during the process. After analyzing the set of 10 events the results of the accuracy of their estimations were published in the web, and each participant can check how it has gone and what kind of error he made (specially the biases were easy to identify). The ability of the work with the interface could also get better during the process of using it. Table 2 shows details in the case of the parameter describing the spread of the estimated shower size with respect to the *true* one. In some cases the improvement (NNN 3) is seen clearly, while for others (TW) the accuracy is diminishing with number of analyzed showers. This last is understood, because, in spite of the students, TW has not been limited to analyze only 10 events per day and the last 50 was taken just one by one continuously. The result is surprisingly big. If the constant care could be achieved during all the analysis process it is possible that the result of σ_N around 0.2. This value is exactly what has been achieved by the trained artificial neural network and significantly better than the standard statistical analysis.

SUMMARY

We have used, in a sense, the theoretical principia of the Cognitive Informatics to try to solve the particular complex minimization problem of contemporary physics. The general concept of the relations between CI and standard (external): classical and modern informatics (Wang, 2003) was realized and studied by utilizing of NNN, ANN and MINUIT. With the help of number of enthusiastic young people we have shown that the redundant Neural Network, Artificial or Natural may work well and in fact in some cases even better than classical statistical tools of minimization. There is the evidence that NNN analyzed in the present work gone even better than the trained ANN. We have observed an interesting feature in redundant ANN learning process. When the network reach the first looks quite stable state of efficient performance, we have seen abrupt decreases of the efficiency and then further and deeper improvements. It could looks like the internal change of the network strategy. The appearance of such unexpected (?) abrupt improvement can be an evidence of at least a suggestion that the network starts, or starts to mimic, the higher lever (conscious!?) cognitive functions. The closer look at this exciting phenomenon could also put some light to the process of network learning but it is beyond of the scope of this paper.

This also suggests that the further studies of the over-sized networks and their performance are important and the minimization of the network size should not be taken on too early steps of the network arrangement, at least in some cases.

REFERENCES

Barnhill, D., et al. (2005). Measurement of the lateral distribution function of UHECR air showers with the Pierre Auger observatory. In *Proceedings of the 29th International Cosmic Ray Conference*, Pune, India (pp. 101-104).

Feder, J. (2006). The Roland Maze project: School-based extensive air shower network. *Nucl. Phys. Proc.*, *151*(Suppl.), 430–433. doi:10.1016/j.nuclphysbps.2005.07.078

IBM. (2001). *Autonomic Computing Manifesto.* Retrieved from http://www.research.ibm.com/autonomic/

James, F., & Roos, M. (1975). MINUIT: A System for Function Minimization and Analysis of the Parameter Errors and Correlations. *Computer Physics Communications*, *10*, 343–367. doi:10.1016/0010-4655(75)90039-9

Klages, H. O. (1997). The KASCADE Experiment. *Nucl. Phys. Proc.*, *52B*(Suppl.), 92–102. doi:10.1016/S0920-5632(96)00852-3

Wang, Y. (2003). On Cognitive Informatics. *Brain and Mind*, *4*, 151–167. doi:10.1023/A:1025401527570

Wang, Y. (2007a). The Theoretical Framework of Cognitive Informatics. *International Journal of Cognitive Informatics and Natural Intelligence*, *1*(1), 1–27.

Wang, Y. (2007b). Toward Theoretical Foundations of Autonomic Computing. *International Journal of Cognitive Informatics and Natural Intelligence*, *1*(3), 1–13.

Wang, Y., Wang, Y., Patel, S., & Patel, D. (2006). A Layer reference Modes of the Brain. [Part C]. *IEEE Transactions on Systems, Man, and Cybernetics*, *36*(2), 124–133. doi:10.1109/TSMCC.2006.871126

Wibig, T. (1998). The Artificial Neural Networks in Cosmic Ray Physics Experiment; I. Total Muon Number Estimation. In A. P. del Pobil & J. Mira (Eds.), *Tasks and Methods in Applied Artificial Intelligence* (LNAI 2, p. 867). Berlin: Springer Verlag.

This work was previously published in volume 4, issue 3 of the International Journal of Cognitive Informatics and Natural Intelligence, edited by Yingxu Wang, pp. 18-28, copyright 2010 by IGI Publishing (an imprint of IGI Global).

Chapter 8
On Hierarchical Content–Based Image Retrieval by Dynamic Indexing and Guided Search

Jane You
The Hong Kong Polytechnic University, China

Qin Li
The Hong Kong Polytechnic University, China

Jinghua Wang
The Hong Kong Polytechnic University, China

ABSTRACT

This paper presents a new approach to content-based image retrieval by using dynamic indexing and guided search in a hierarchical structure, and extending data mining and data warehousing techniques. The proposed algorithms include a wavelet-based scheme for multiple image feature extraction, the extension of a conventional data warehouse and an image database to an image data warehouse for dynamic image indexing. It also provides an image data schema for hierarchical image representation and dynamic image indexing, a statistically based feature selection scheme to achieve flexible similarity measures, and a feature component code to facilitate query processing and guide the search for the best matching. A series of case studies are reported, which include a wavelet-based image color hierarchy, classification of satellite images, tropical cyclone pattern recognition, and personal identification using multi-level palmprint and face features. Experimental results confirm that the new approach is feasible for content-based image retrieval.

INTRODUCTION

Cognitive informatics is a multidisciplinary research area, which studies not only how human brains and minds internally process information but also their engineering applications. It covers

DOI: 10.4018/978-1-4666-1743-8.ch008

the Object-Attribute-Relation (OAR) model of information representation in the brain (Wang, 2007b; Wang & Wang, 2006), the cognitive processes of formal inferences (Wang, 2007a), the formal knowledge system (Wang, 2006a), and so on.

Image retrieval is an important part of multimedia systems and requires an integration of research in image understanding, artificial intelligence and databases to address the problem of information retrieval from large collections of images and video frames. The developments in this area are summarized in Antani, Kasturi, and Jain (2002) and Rui, Huang, and Chang (1999). In general, image retrieval approaches fall into two categories: attribute-based methods and content-based methods. Examples of such methods include the Kodak Picture Exchange System (KPX) (Larish, 1995) and the PressLink library (Martucci, 1995). Examples of content-based image retrieval systems include QBIC (Flickner et al., 1995), Virage, Photobook (Pentland, Picard, & Sclaroff, 1996), CANDID (Kelley, Cannon, & Hush, 1995) and Garlic (Cody et al., 1995). The current content-based and object-oriented methods cannot process abstract queries, and multiple image features are not integrated for similarity measures. In addition, they are computationally expensive and somewhat domain dependent.

Applications on the World-Wide Web require a multimedia system with scalability, flexibility and efficiency. Although some existing systems, such as WebSeek and C-BIRD (Smith & Chang, 1997), support both attribute-based queries and content-based queries, they employ limited visual features for retrieval and they lack a general approach to deal with multiple features for indexing and query. Moreover, these systems cannot handle audio data for a comprehensive multimedia system. The MARS (Multimedia Analysis and Retrieval System) project (Huang & Naphade, 2000) aims to bridge the gap between the low-level features and the high-level semantic concepts. However, the challenges faced by new techniques for processing and analyzing multimedia information remain untackled, and the traditional analysis of image data alone cannot provide satisfactory solutions to these problems. Most of the existing techniques for multimedia information retrieval are based on the use of conventional database structures to handle large collections of high-dimensional multimedia data. Although the research on multimedia database systems (Flickner et al., 1995; Antani,

Kasturi, & Jain, 2002) has made advances in the creation of large multimedia databases with effective facilities for query processing, that work has mainly focused on data modeling and structuring.

The main contributions of this paper may be summarized as follows: this paper proposed an image data warehouse structure and a new image data model to support multiple image feature extraction and integration, which allows dynamic query processing and hierarchical content-based image retrieval. The proposed data warehousing model will allow users to combine multiple image features in a top-down manner to facilitate image representation, indexing and search. Instead of using a fixed similarity measurement to search for the best matching, this paper adopted a statistically based feature selection scheme that generates the matching criteria in accordance with the type of query and the level of search. In addition, this paper introduced a feature component code to guide the coarse-to-fine search in a hierarchical structure. To demonstrate the feasibility and the advantages of our approach, the proposed algorithms are applied to several case studies.

This paper is organized by outlining the proposed concept of an image data warehouse for dynamic image indexing and compares it with the traditional image database structure. Next the authors summarize a general approach to multiple image feature extraction and representation, which is based on the wavelet transform. Then, a flexible scheme for feature selection and integration is introduced. The strategy for hierarchical search is described in following that, and then a series of case studies are reported. Finally, the conclusion is presented.

IMAGE DATA WAREHOUSE

Background

In general, the three key issues in multimedia information retrieval are feature representation and indexing, similarity measures, and searching

Figure 1. A general system structure of the multimedia data warehouse

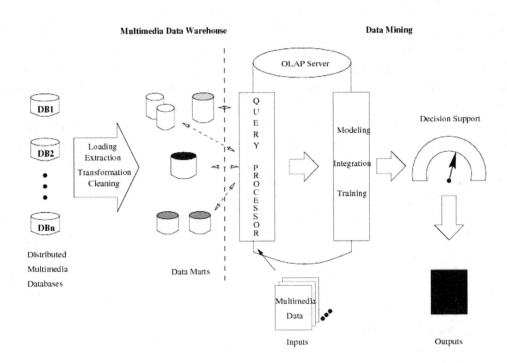

methods. To tackle the first of these issues, most of the existing systems and research are focused on representing and indexing multimedia data within a conventional database structure (Smith & Chang, 1997; Huang & Naphade, 2000; Antani, Kasturi, & Jain, 2002).

MediaHouse: A Proposed Multimedia System

The data warehousing techniques is applied to develop a so-called MediaHouse multimedia system in this subsection. A star schema is used to represent the basic data streams of media content. In such a data warehouse, detailed data concerning multimedia information is stored within a central fact table, which may be partitioned horizontally or vertically. To facilitate the management and decision support functions of the data warehouse, a starflake schema is adopted that uses a combination of denormalized star and normalized snowflake schemas (Anahory & Mur-

ray, 1997). A series of combined database views is created to allow the user access tools to treat the fact table partitions as one large table for fast information retrieval. In addition, key reference data is structured into a set of dimensions that are referenced from the fact table. Each dimension is stored in a series of normalized tables (snowflake), with an additional denormalized star dimension table. With the starflake schema, this paper structures the data and utilizes an existing data warehouse tool. Figure 1 shows the general structure for the proposed multimedia data warehouse.

It is essential to develop a general mechanism which integrates multiple features for flexible indexing and search. The development of a multimedia data warehouse turns out to be a better solution for this problem. Another factor to consider is the large amount of data arising from different media, which needs to be handled in these multimedia databases. Again, a data warehouse with its summarization, aggregation and partitioning capacity provides a better approach than using a traditional database. Table 1 summarizes a comparison of the proposed multimedia data warehouse with the existing multimedia systems. Figure 2 illustrates the proposed hierarchical structure of multidimensional data cubes for the representation of multimedia information and the major items for image feature description is listed in Table 2.

WAVELET-BASED MULTIPLE IMAGE FEATURE EXTRACTION

There are a variety of features that can be used in image representation. This section describes the extraction of three kinds of features: color features, texture features, and shape features.

Color Feature Extraction and Representation

Within the framework of a color image warehouse, which is described previously, this section proposes a wavelet-based image color hierarchy, and multiple feature integration schemes, to facilitate dynamic color indexing associated with data summarization. The proposed approach is characterized as follows: (1) wavelet transforms is applied to decompose a given image into three layers of 10 sub-images. (2) Because the mean of the wavelet is the most representative among all of its representations, it is used at three layers as a global color measurement, and it is indexed as tabular data in a global color summary table. (3) The mean of the wavelet coefficients of sub-band images (horizontal, vertical and diagonal) is calculated at different layers, as local color information, and index them as tabular data in a local color summary table. (4) the interesting points (Noble, 1988) of objects are detected in the original image and store them in a table used for fine matching.

Texture Features

Historically, structural and statistical approaches have been adopted for texture feature extraction (Haralick, 1979). Here a wavelet based approach is adopted to represent texture features (Rui, Huang, & Chang, 1999). When an image is decomposed into decorrelated sub-images through a wavelet filter bank, each sub-image represents the feature of some scale and orientation of the original image. Thus, the related wavelet coefficients can be used for texture feature representation. If an image is decomposed into three wavelet layers, there will be ten sub-images. For each sub-image, the standard deviation of the wavelet coefficients is calculated to represent its texture feature component. Consequently, ten standard deviations corresponding to ten sub-images are used as the texture representation for the image.

Shape Features

The Active Contour Model (ACM) (Kass, Witkin, & Terzopoulos, 1987), (the so-called "snake"), detects object boundaries by linking salient image feature points into a continuous curve with the optimization of a given criterion. In contrast to the existing techniques, the spline snake (Cohen, Huang, & Yang, 1995) is extended in a hierarchical fashion. The original image is decomposed into a series of sub-band images via wavelet transform. At each level, a B-spline curve, the so-called spline snake, is determined to link image boundary feature points. This snake will position itself along the feature points in a robust manner by stretching and bending, which is controlled by the parameters in its energy expression given below:

$$E_{\text{int}}\left(u(s)\right) = \alpha\left(s\right)\left|u_s\left(s\right)\right|^2 + \beta\left(s\right)\left|u_{ss}\left(s\right)\right|^2 \qquad (1)$$

where $u\left(s\right) = \left(x\left(s\right), y\left(s\right)\right)$ is the snake curve and s is the arc-length of the curve. The parameters

Figure 2. A hierarchy of multi-dimensional data cube

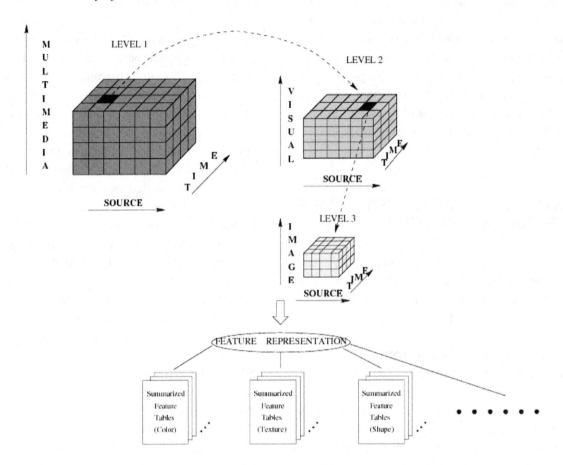

Table 1. Comparison of different multimedia information system

Name of the system	System Structure	Data Representation	Similarity Measurement	Search Method	Query Process
QBIC (Flickner et al., 1995)	Single database	Image modeling	Pre-defined measures	One-to-on comparison	User interactive
Garlic (Cody et al., 1995)	Multiple database	Image & texture features	Fuzzy set technique	Object oriented	User interactive
MARS (Huang & Naphade, 2000)	Traditional database	Image/video features	Fixed measurement	Hierarchical structure	User interactive
MediaHouse (proposed approach)	Data warehouse	Multiple features	Flexible measurement	Hierarchical search	User interactive

Table 2. The major items for image feature description

Color	Texture	Shape	Line & Points	Others
Histogram Moments wavelets ….	Structural description Statistical description Wavelets …	Moments B-spline Wavelets …	Line segments Arcs Feature points …	Frequency domain …

of elasticity α and β control the smoothness of the snake curves.

A wavelet transform is applied to decompose the original image into a collection of sub-bands ranging from low to high resolutions. The related first-, second- and third-normalized central moments for each subimage are computed and the average values (of the same moment category) for all sub-bands are used as individual shape feature components. Thus, the image shape feature vector consists of nine components that represent the average value of first-, second- and third-order moments for three different layers, respectively.

For a given set of n ordered corner points, it is aimed to fit a real-valued B-spline to the observed curve data. For a closed cubic B-spline with $m+1$ parameters (control points) $C_1, C_2, \cdots, C_m$, the curve can be modeled as a linear combination of four cubic polynomials in the parameter t, where t is normalized for each segment between 0 and 1 ($0 \leq t \leq 1$). In order to determine the error distance between the curve data and their corresponding B-spline points, the minimum mean square error estimation (MMSE) is used. This determines the final B-spline representation of the given curve data by iterative B-spline parameter estimation.

DYNAMIC IMAGE FEATURE SELECTION AND INDEXING

In the context of similarity matching for visual images, the traditional indexing methods may not be appropriate because of the diversity of image content, which cannot be accurately represented by the pre-defined numeric data in a fixed data structure. Consequently, data structures suitable for fast access of high-dimensional features for spatial relationships have to be developed. This section combines a statistically based feature selection scheme, which uses a proposed feature component code to achieve dynamic indexing in an image data warehouse structure.

Feature Component Code

To organize the index structure with these features and facilitate image query, this section proposes a three-bit feature component code to characterize the status of each individual image, according to the following specifications:

- The left bit C represents color status: 1 - a color image, 0 - a black and white image.
- The middle bit T represents texture status: 1 - a texture image, 0 - a non-texture image.
- The right bit S represents shape status: 1 - an image with clear object(s), 0 - an image without any objects.

Figure 3 shows four image samples representing an outdoor scene, a texture, a sketch, and a textured object, from left to right, respectively. The component code will facilitate the hierarchical structure used for indexing and searching. Each individual image is classified into different image groups according to its component code. Within each group, images are further ranked with respect to their individual feature vectors or measurements. The relevant data is pre-processed and stored in the corresponding summary tables in the warehouse structure. The search process will start with the image group which has the same component code as the query image, which speeds up the processing by filtering out irrelevant images from the image collection.

Statistically Based Feature Selection and Multiple Feature Integration

Feature selection criteria based on statistical measures have been extensively studied. These criteria include the Chi-square criterion, Asymmetrical Tau and Symmetrical Tau (Zhou & Dillon, 1991). This paper extends the use of the Symmetrical Tau criterion to provide guidance when combining multiple media features for content-based image

Figure 3. Image feature component coding

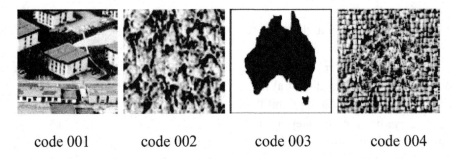

code 001   code 002   code 003   code 004

retrieval. Combination involves the normalization of feature components in each feature vector and the adjustment of weights for each component. In addition, the Symmetrical Tau is applied to determine the most appropriate weights for multiple feature integration. Instead of using individual features to calculate the corresponding Tau as initially defined, the combined feature vector is used to obtain the relevant Tau. Such a process is iteratively repeated by dynamically adjusting the weights associated with each feature component. A higher weight is assigned to the component for stronger emphasis and a lower weight reflects weaker emphasis on the non-relevant component. The set of weights with the maximum Tau is used to combine multiple features for similarity measures.

HIERARCHICAL SEARCH

Our system will support two types of queries: (a) to pose a query by image sample, and (b) to use a simple sketch as a query. In the case of a query by image sample, the search follows multiple feature extraction and image similarity measurement described in the previous sections. Based on the nature of the query image, the user can add additional component weights during the combination of image features for image similarity measurement. In the case of query by a simple sketch provided a user, a B-spline based curve matching scheme will be used to identify the most suitable candidates from the image database. In the case of a query by sample image, the proposed image component code will be used to guide the search for the most appropriate candidates in terms of color, texture and shape from the data warehouse at a coarse level and apply image matching at a finer level for the final output. A fractional discrimination function is used to identify object boundaries for hierarchical matching.

A Coarse-to-Fine Curve Matching Scheme

In a conventional data warehouse (Anahory & Murray, 1997), various methods of partitioning have been developed to improve the efficiency for query processing. The idea behind this is to decompose a single entity into multiple smaller sub-entities by slicing the table into smaller pieces. Most of the existing methods fall into two major categories: horizontal partitioning and vertical partitioning. A syntactic matching of curves has been proposed in Gdalyahu and Weinshall (1999). In general, the way in which a fact table will be partitioned depends on the type of query. This paper adopted partitioning along a dimension to facilitate a coarse-to-fine curve matching scheme for similar shape retrieval. As stated, four dimensions are associated with a shape image: feature points, contour curve, invariant moments and B-Spline curve coefficients.

The initial search for the best similar shape matching starts with the dimension of invariant moments. The similarity measurement is based a comparison of the Cosine distances of the proposed shape moment feature vectors for different samples after Gaussian normalization. The candidates with small (distance) differences will be considered for fine matching based on 2D polygonal arc matching and B-spline curve matching.

2D Polygonal Arc Matching

The fine matching algorithm starts with 2D polygonal arc matching by using a subgroup of the unit quaternions. A least-squares approach developed by Parsi, Margalit, and Rosenfeld (1991) utilized a distance measure to determine the best match between two 2D polygonal arcs. This algorithm can be further simplified by finding a closed form solution to the minimum distance, based on the use of a subgroup of the unit quaternions, where a polygonal arc is defined by a set of points (the vertices) and a distance measure between two arcs is defined as the integral of the Euclidean distance between corresponding points (Heisterkamp & Bhattacharya, 1998).

2 B-Spline Curve Matching

The goal here is to match and recognize the shape curves for the final retrieval output. The curve candidates which are selected from the 2D polygonal arc match will be further compared based on their B-spline models. Traditionally the judgment is made by comparison to their control points, using the ordered corner points from boundary tracing. To find a classifier that allocates the sampled data to one of the object curves, a residual error-based matching is described in (Cohen, Huang, & Yang, 1995). The problem with this approach is that it cannot handle occluded curves although it is straightforward to estimate the residual errors for similarity measurements. An interactive spline snake model is adopted to control the snake for robust boundary tracing by using constant feedback from the current path (Cohen, Huang, & Yang, 1995). However, the performance depends on the selection of control points and the search for the best matching could be very time consuming. Based on Huttenlocher, Klanderman, and Rucklidge (1993), the Hausdorff distance algorithm can be used to search for portions, or partial, hidden objects. *For purpose of blind reviewing, we are not citing our previous work at present.* In the work reported here, our previous research is further extended by using contour corner points as a basis for curve matching in terms of the Hausdorff distance. It aims to reduce the computation required for a reliable match and discover partially hidden curves. The Hausdorff distance is a non-linear operator which measures the mismatch of the two sets. In other words, such a distance determines the degree of the mismatch between a model and an object by measuring the distance of the point in a model that is farthest from any point in an object and vice versa. Therefore, it can be used for object recognition by comparing two images which are superimposed on one another. The key points regarding this technique are summarized below.

Given two finite sets of points $A = \{a_1, a_2, \cdots, a_m\}$ and $B = \{b_1, b_2, \cdots, b_n\}$, the Hausdorff distance D_H between these two sets is defined as $D_H = \max(d_{AB}, d_{BA})$, where d_{AB} is the distance from set A to set B expressed as $d_{AB} = \max_{a_i \in A}(d_{a_i B})$ while $d_{a_i B}$ is the distance from point a_i to set B given by $d_{a_i B} = \min_{b_j \in B}(d_{a_i b_j})$. For the curve matching, set A and set B contain the contour points of the two curves, respectively; and the best matching occurs when its Hausdorff distance is minimal. To speed up the searching for the best fit between the two given curves, once again, a hierarchical scheme is adopted. The Hausdorff distance at coarse level is determined by the B-spline control points of each curve. More neighboring contour points are considered to determine the Hausdorff distance at a finer level. Figure 4 illustrates the hierarchical computation of the Hausdorff distance.

Figure 4. The multi-level Hausdorff distance measurement

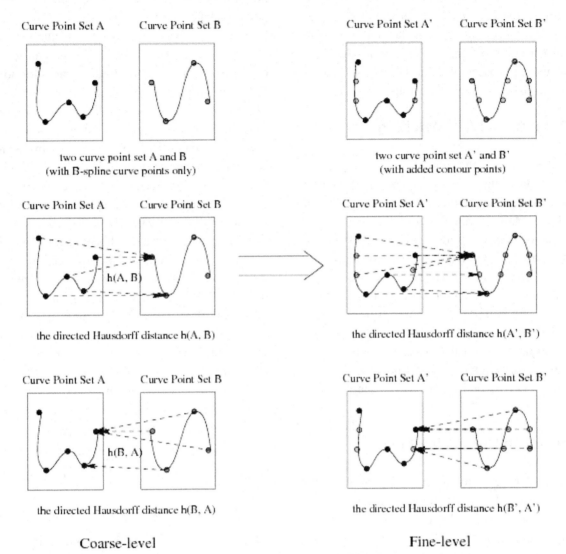

Coarse-level   Fine-level

Fractional Discrimination Function and Image Matching

Image matching plays an important role in content-based image retrieval when queries are made by image samples. The central problem is to find an effective approach to extract feature points that identify the boundaries of different regions, invariant of scales and orientations. In contrast to the traditional methods, our solution involves the introduction of fractional functions to be used as discrimination functions that perform robust (in the presence of noise), selective (band limited) and contextual feature extraction.

The generalized discrimination functions $g(\xi)$ are defined within the bounds of a multi-dimensional coordinate system ξ: in the case of one-dimensional time-domain signals, ξ represents time t; for time-invariant images, ξ refers to the spatial coordinates (x, y); and for time-dependent images, ξ means (x, y, t). Let $f(\xi)$ be a multi-dimensional periodic or aperiodic function defined over $\xi \in (-\infty, +\infty)$ in terms of its zero crossings or zero nodes (with at least one zero-crossing). The generalized discrimination function $g(\xi)$ is defined as

$$g(\xi) = \begin{cases} f(\xi) & if \; \xi \in [k_m, k_n] \\ 0 & otherwise \end{cases} \qquad (2)$$

such that

$$\int_{-\infty}^{+\infty} g(\xi) d_\xi = \int_{k_m}^{k_n} f(\xi) d_\xi = 0$$

where k represents a zero crossing (k_m and k_n refer to m^{th} and n^{th} zero crossing respectively), m and n are any integers ($m < n$).

By introducing this general form given before, the detection of feature points can be generalized with any order, size and shape or any combination of the three. Further details of this approach to detect feature points are described in our previous publications. *For purpose of blind reviewing, we are not citing our previous works at present.* A guided image matching scheme is developed to determine the degrees of similarity between the template pattern and every possible sample pattern selected throughout the previous classification procedure. Unlike the traditional image matching methods, which are based on the detection of edge points, the fractional discrimination function is applied to detect feature points for high performance. To avoid a blind search for the best fit between the given samples, a guided search strategy is essential to reduce the computational burden. A comprehensive study of hierarchical image matching is detailed in our previous publication. *For purpose of blind reviewing, once again, we are not citing our previous works at present.*

CASE STUDIES AND EXPERIMENTAL RESULTS

Five cases studies are reported in this section. First presented is the hierarchy of wavelet-based image color. Next, the cases of satellite images classification and tropical cyclone pattern recognition are presented, followed by the cases of personal identification using multi-level palmprint and face features.

Color Hierarchy and Multi-Level Color Search

In the case of content-based color image retrieval, this subsection adopted partitioning along a dimension to facilitate a coarse-to-fine color similarity measurement. Seven dimensions were associated with a color image: interesting points, global color histogram, color moments, and mean values of wavelet coefficients in four different directions (global, vertical, horizontal and diagonal).

The initial search for the most similar color composition match starts with the dimension of global mean value of wavelet coefficients. The similarity measurement is based on the difference between the query image and the image samples stored in the image warehouse. The Gaussian normalization procedure is applied before the comparison. The candidates with the smallest differences in distance will be considered for finer matching in terms of local wavelet mean values and interesting points. The color histogram and color moments are used to further narrow the selection of possible candidates for fine matching. The fine matching is conducted by using the Hausdorff distance of the interesting points associated with similar local color features. The color information represented by a star schema in an image data warehouse will facilitate the dynamic search and provide flexible similarity measurement. The color image samples used for the testing were 512×512 size, with 256 brightness levels in both RGB and YUV color space. A series of experiments have been carried out to verify the performance of the proposed algorithms. In our test, a total of 200 image samples are collected. Figure 5 shows eight samples of color images selected from the image collection to represent different color content. The mean value of wavelet coefficients for the given image at different layers is rotation invariant and can be used as the global index for color content at a coarser level, while the mean values of the wavelet coefficients for directional decomposition (horizontal, vertical and diagonal) provide a good description of local color composition which can be used to guide the search at the finer level.

Feature Guided Image Classification

To demonstrate the use of statistically based feature selection criteria to categorize images at a coarse level, the classification of the ground-cover types of satellite images was conducted. Figure 6 illustrates 8 ground cover types of remotely sensed image data used for testing.

The classification of ground-cover types of satellite images by textures can be considered as allocating an unknown input satellite image sample to one of the possible ground-cover types taken from the training set of remotely sensed image collections. The key step in any classification problem is the image feature extraction policy which reduces the dimensions of the data to a computationally tractable amount, while preserving much of the discriminant information present in the actual data. The symmetrical Tau confirms for the "texture energy", that the standard deviation of pixel gray scale, within a 15×15 window size and computed after convolution with a texture feature mask, outperforms other texture feature measurements for ground-cover type classification.

The dynamic selection of image features is further demonstrated by multi-level palmprint feature extraction for personal identification and verification. The experiment is carried out in two stages. In stage one, the global palmprint features are extracted at coarse level and candidate samples are selected for further processing. In stage two, the regional palmprint features are detected and a hierarchical image matching is performed for the final retrieval. Figure 7 illustrates the multi-level extraction of palmprint features.

Hierarchical Similar Shape Retrieval

The first test is carried out for cyclone pattern recognition in weather forecasting. The diversity of cloud patterns and their variations make it challenging to develop a reliable and efficient classification scheme for tropical cyclone pattern recognition and classification. The Dvorak technique (Dvorak, 1975) is a widely-used technique for tropical cyclone (TC) analysis. It combines pattern recognition methods and empirically-based rules to estimate TC intensity from satellite imagery. There are three parameters involved: the central features which define the cloud system center and its relation to dense overcast clouds, the outer banding features which curve around the central features, and the vertical depth of the clouds comprising these features. Intensity is measured in terms of the sum of the three parameters. The estimation of intensity precedes the following three stages: (1) model-based intensity estimation; (2) verification by cloud pattern and feature measurements; (3) adjustment of the modeled expectation. The intensity analysis and forecast is based on observation of a cyclone's progress throughout its life cycle by continually comparing its cloud features and feature changes to what is expected from the model in terms of the cyclone's past history. Although the tropical cyclones appear in a great variety of patterns in satellite images, most can be characterized by the pattern of a comma or a rotated comma configuration and this pattern configuration is very useful for the analysis of cyclone development. Figure 8 illustrates part of the TC templates used in the Dvorak technique.

Figure 5. Color image samples

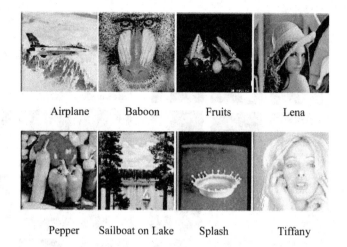

Airplane	Baboon	Fruits	Lena

Pepper	Sailboat on Lake	Splash	Tiffany

Figure 6. Samples of the ground cover types of the satellite images

forest	rocks	mountain	desert

cloud	sea	beach	residence

Figure 7. Hierarchical feature extraction

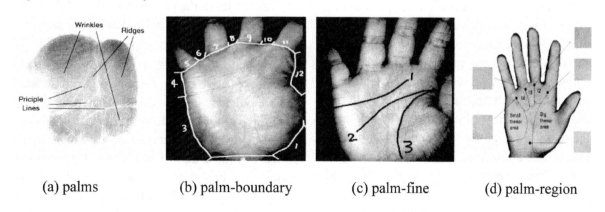

(a) palms	(b) palm-boundary	(c) palm-fine	(d) palm-region

Figure 8. Dvorak TC templates

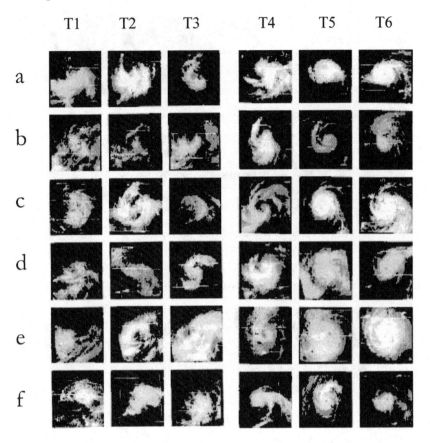

The detection of the object boundary is very important for pattern recognition by similar-shape retrieval. In contrast to the existing techniques, the spline snake (Cohen, Huang, & Yang, 1995) is extended in a hierarchical fashion. The original image is decomposed into a series of sub-band images via wavelet transform. At each level, a B-spline curve, the so-called spline snake, is determined to link image boundary feature points. Figure 9 shows the contour mapping of four tropical cyclone patterns by snake. The following lists the relevant features as dimensions for TC pattern classification: (1) list of boundary feature points, sorted in an anti-clockwise order, along the boundary of the TC pattern; (2) parameters which control the active contour 'snake' along the boundary of TC pattern; (3) measures of invariant moments, sorted

in descending order; (4) a list of coefficients of a B-spline curve; (5) the time when the TC pattern forms; (6) the location where the TC pattern forms

The proposed coarse-to-fine curve matching approach is further demonstrated in the second test of face recognition for personal identification. At coarse level, the proposed fractional discrimination function $g(\xi)$, introduced in equation (2), is used to identify the region of interest in an individual's face. At the fine curve matching level, the active contour tracing algorithm is applied to detect the boundaries of interesting face regions for the final matching. Figure 10 illustrates the tracing of face curves for face recognition. Figure 10(a) is an original image, Figure 10(b) shows the boundaries of interesting regions on the face and Figure 10(c) presents the curve seg-

Figure 9. Active contour extraction (Snake)

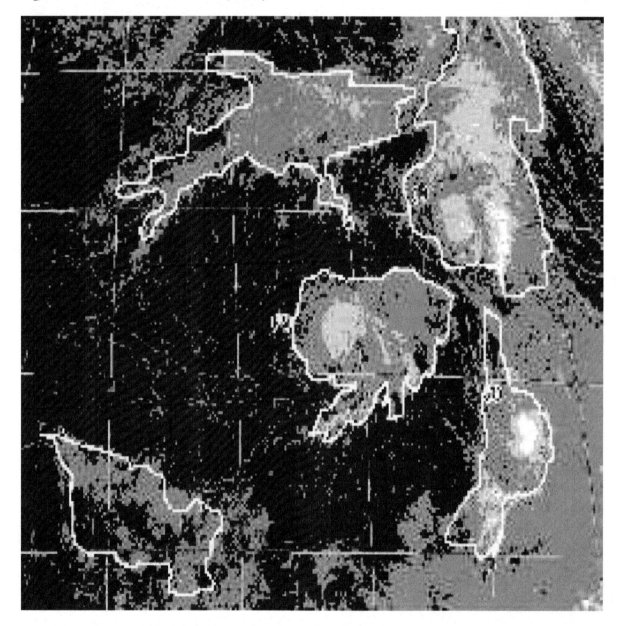

ments for hierarchical face recognition by curve matching.

To verify the effectiveness of our approach, a series of tests were carried out in a database of 200 face collections from different individuals under various conditions such as uneven lighting, moderate tilting and partial sheltering. Figure 11 shows the detected regions of different individuals that were detected using the proposed

algorithm and Table 3 lists the correctness rate of the coarse-level detection. To show the robustness of the proposed algorithm for face detection, invariant of perspective view, partial distortion and occlusion, the fine-level curve matching is applied to face images with different orientations and expressions. Figure 12 illustrates face samples for the same person at various perspective views and Table 4 summarizes the test results

Figure 10. Face curve extraction

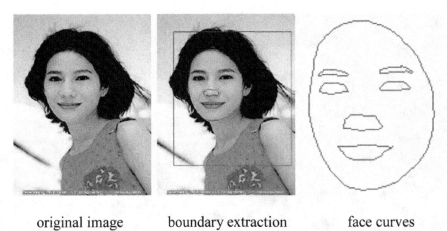

original image   boundary extraction   face curves

for 100 test cases. Figure 13 shows face samples for the same person at different conditions such as facial expression, partial occlusion and distortion. The test results for 100 cases are listed in Table 5.

CONCLUSION

To tackle the key issues such as image feature extraction, indexing and search, this paper proposes a hierarchical approach to content-based image retrieval using dynamic indexing and guided search combined with data mining and data warehousing techniques. The extension of the conventional data warehouse to a multimedia data warehouse offers a promising alternative

for effective data representation and storage. The development of a wavelet-based scheme for multiple feature extraction, and a multimedia starflake schema for image data warehouse, support multiple feature integration and dynamic image indexing. The use of a statistically based feature selection criterion and a feature component code facilitate flexible similarity measures and provides a basis to guide the search in a hierarchical structure. In addition, the introduction of a fractional discrimination function is effective for the final retrieval output by curve/image matching at the fine level. The experimental results confirm that our new approach is feasible for content-based image retrieval. It is hoped that such an approach will be useful for many other multimedia applications.

Figure 11. The detection of face region of interest

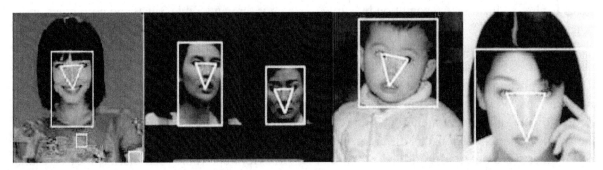

Figure 12. The face samples at different orientations

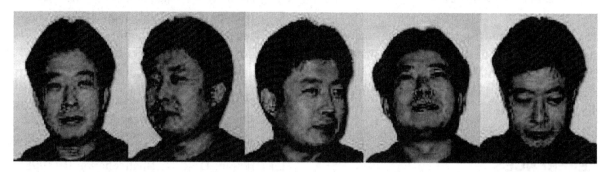

Figure 13. The face samples at different conditions

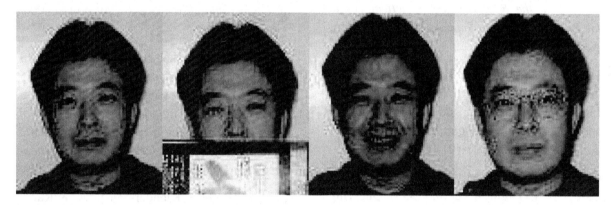

Table 3. Performance of face detection at coarse level

Face Condition	Correct Detection Rate
unevenness of lighting	98%
multiple faces	95%
moderate tilt of faces	97%
partial sheltering	85%

Table 5. Performance of face classification with different conditions

Face Condition	Correct Detection Rate
partial occlusion	77%
various expressions	81%
wearing glasses	82%

Table 4. Performance of face recognition at different orientations

Viewing Perspective	Correct Classification Rate
-20°(vertical)	84%
-10°(vertical)	86%
+10°(vertical)	86%
+20°(vertical)	83%
-20°(horizontal)	85%
-10°(horizontal)	87%
+10°(horizontal)	87%
+20°(horizontal)	84%

ACKNOWLEDGMENT

The authors are most grateful for the financial support from Hong Kong Government GRF research grant scheme and the Hong Kong Polytechnic University Research grants to carry out the relevant research.

REFERENCES

Anahory, S., & Murray, D. (1997). *Data Warehousing in the Real World-A Practical Guide for Building Decision Support Systems*. Boston: Addison-Wesley.

Antani, S., Kasturi, R., & Jain, R. (2002). A survey on the use of pattern recognition methods for abstraction, indexing and retrieval of images and video. *Pattern Recognition, 35*(4), 945–965. doi:10.1016/S0031-3203(01)00086-3

Cody, W. F., Haas, L. M., Niblack, W., Arya, M., Carey, M. J., Fagin, R., et al. (1995). Querying multimedia data from multiple repositories by content: the Garlic project. In *Proceedings of the third IFIP WG2.6 working conference on Visual database systems 3* (VDB-3) (pp. 17 - 35). New York: Lausanne, Chapman & Hall.

Cohen, F. S., Huang, Z., & Yang, Z. (1995). Invariant matching and identification of curves using B-splines curve representation. *IEEE Transactions on Image Processing, 4*(1), 1–10. doi:10.1109/83.350818

Dvorak, V. F. (1975). Tropical cyclone intensity analysis and forecasting from satellite imagery. *Monthly Weather Review, 103*, 420–430. doi:10.1175/1520-0493(1975)103<0420:TCIA AF>2.0.CO;2

Flickner, M., Sawhney, H., Niblack, W., & Ashley, J. (1995). Query by image and video content: The QBIC system. *IEEE Computer Society Press, 28*(9), 23–32.

Gdalyahu, Y., & Weinshall, D. (1999). Flexible syntactic matching of curves and its applications to automatic hierarchical classification of silhouettes. *IEEE Transactions on Pattern Analysis and Machine Intelligence, 12*(2), 1312–1328. doi:10.1109/34.817410

Haralick, R. M. (1979). Statistical and structural approaches to texture. *Proceedings of the IEEE, 67*(5), 786–804. doi:10.1109/PROC.1979.11328

Heisterkamp, D. R., & Bhattacharya, P. (1998). Matching 2D polygonal arcs by using a subgroup of the unit quaternions. *Computer Vision and Image Understanding, 69*(2), 246–249. doi:10.1006/cviu.1997.0566

Huang, T. S., & Naphade, M. R. (2000). MARS (Multimedia Analysis and Retrieval System): A test bed for video indexing, browsing, searching, filtering, and summarization. In *Proceedings of the IEEE International Workshop on Multimedia Data Storage, Retrieval, Integration and Applications*, Hong Kong, China (pp. 1-7).

Huttenlocher, D. P., Klanderman, G. A., & Rucklidge, W. J. (1993). Comparing images using the Hausdorff distance. *IEEE Transactions on Pattern Analysis and Machine Intelligence, 15*(9), 850–863. doi:10.1109/34.232073

Kass, M., Witkin, A., & Terzopoulos, D. (1987). Snakes: Active contour models. In *Proceedings of the First International Conference on Computer Vision*, London (pp. 259-268).

Kelley, P. M., Cannon, T. M., & Hush, D. R. (1995). Query by example: The CANDID approach. *SPIE Storage and Retrieval for Image and Video Databases II, 2420*, 238–248.

Larish, J. (1995). Kodak's still picture exchange for print and film use. *Advanced Imaging (Woodbury, N.Y.), 10*, 38–39.

Martucci, M. (1995). Digital still marketing at PressLink. *Advanced Imaging (Woodbury, N.Y.), 10*, 34–36.

Noble, J. A. (1988). Finding corners. *Image and Vision Computing*, *6*(2), 121–128. doi:10.1016/0262-8856(88)90007-8

Parsi, B., Margalit, A., & Rosenfeld, A. (1991). Matching general polygonal arcs. *Computer Vision . Graphics and Image Processing: Image Understanding*, *53*(2), 227–234.

Pentland, A., Picard, R. W., & Sclaroff, S. (1996). Photobook: tools for content-based manipulation of image databases. *International Journal of Computer Vision*, *18*(3), 233–254. doi:10.1007/BF00123143

Rui, R., Huang, T. S., & Chang, S. F. (1999). Image retrieval: current techniques, promising directions, and open issues. *Journal of Visual Communication and Image Representation*, *10*(1), 39–62. doi:10.1006/jvci.1999.0413

Smith, J. R., & Chang, S. F. (1997). Visually searching the web for content. *IEEE MultiMedia*, *4*(3), 12–20. doi:10.1109/93.621578

Wang, Y. (2006). *Software Engineering Foundations: A Software Science Perspective* (*Vol. 2*). Boca Raton, FL: CRC Press.

Wang, Y. (2007a). The Cognitive Processes of Formal Inferences. *International Journal of Cognitive Informatics and Natural Intelligence*, *1*(4), 75–86.

Wang, Y. (2007b). The OAR Model of Neural Informatics for Internal Knowledge Representation in the Brain. *International Journal of Cognitive Informatics and Natural Intelligence*, *1*(3), 68–82.

Wang, Y., & Wang, Y. (2006, March). On cognitive informatics models of the brain. *IEEE Transactions on Systems, Man, and Cybernetics . Part C*, *36*(2), 203–207.

Zhou, X., & Dillon, T. S. (1991). A statistical-heuristic feature selection criterion for decision tree induction. *IEEE Transactions on Pattern Analysis and Machine Intelligence*, *13*(8), 834–841. doi:10.1109/34.85676

This work was previously published in volume 4, issue 4 of the International Journal of Cognitive Informatics and Natural Intelligence, edited by Yingxu Wang, pp. 18-36, copyright 2010 by IGI Publishing (an imprint of IGI Global).

Chapter 9
Robust Feature Vector Set Using Higher Order Autocorrelation Coefficients

Poonam Bansal
Guru Gobind Singh Indraprastha University, India

Amita Dev
Ambedkar Institute of Technology, India

Shail Bala Jain
GGSIP University, India

ABSTRACT

In this paper, a feature extraction method that is robust to additive background noise is proposed for automatic speech recognition. Since the background noise corrupts the autocorrelation coefficients of the speech signal mostly at the lower orders, while the higher-order autocorrelation coefficients are least affected, this method discards the lower order autocorrelation coefficients and uses only the higher-order autocorrelation coefficients for spectral estimation. The magnitude spectrum of the windowed higher-order autocorrelation sequence is used here as an estimate of the power spectrum of the speech signal. This power spectral estimate is processed further by the Mel filter bank; a log operation and the discrete cosine transform to get the cepstral coefficients. These cepstral coefficients are referred to as the Differentiated Relative Higher Order Autocorrelation Coefficient Sequence Spectrum (DRHOASS). The authors evaluate the speech recognition performance of the DRHOASS features and show that they perform as well as the MFCC features for clean speech and their recognition performance is better than the MFCC features for noisy speech.

DOI: 10.4018/978-1-4666-1743-8.ch009

INTRODUCTION

Cognitive informatics is an emerging interdisciplinary field in the cognitive and information sciences that aims to forge links between a diverse range of disciplines spanning the natural and life sciences, informatics and computer science (Wang, 2003). It has given introduction to the data-driven/machine-learning approach to building spoken language systems (in which large corpora of annotated speech recordings are used to capture the variability of speech) coupled with the relentless increase in available computing power. Any real time practical spoken language system must be robust and flexible in real-world environments (Pols, 1999; Saroka & Braida, 2005). To make it so, exact feature extraction during processing of speech signals plays a vital role. This paper discuss about that aspect of robust system.

The main approaches considered to improve the performance of automatic speech recognition (ASR) systems could be roughly divided into three main categories, namely, robust speech feature extraction, speech enhancement and model-based compensation for noise. In the case of speech enhancement, some initial information about speech and noise is needed to allow the estimation of noise and clean up of the noisy speech. Widely used methods in this category include spectral subtraction (SS) (Beh & Ko, 2003) and Wiener filtering (Lee, Soong, & Paliwal, 1996). In the framework of model-based compensation, statistical models such as Hidden Markov Models (HMMs) are usually considered. The compensation techniques try to remove the mismatch between the trained models and the noisy speech to improve the performance of ASR systems. Methods such as parallel model combination (PMC) (Gales & Young, 1995; Gales & Young, 1996), vector Taylor series (VTS) (Acero, Deng, Kristjansson, & Zhang, 2000; Kim, Un, & Kim, 1998; Moreno, 1996; Moreno, Raj, & Stern, 1996; Shen, Hung, & Lee, 1998) and weighted projection measure

(WPM) (Mansour & Jaung, 1989a) can be classified into this category.

Use of the autocorrelation domain in speech feature extraction has recently proved to be successful for robust speech recognition. Among the techniques introduced that exploit the autocorrelation properties are Short-time Modified Coherence (SMC) (Mansour & Jaung, 1989b) and One-Sided Autocorrelation LPC (OSALPC) (Herando & Nadeu, 1997). Extracting appropriate speech features is crucial in obtaining good performance in ASR systems since all of the succeeding processes in such systems are highly dependent on the quality of the extracted features. Therefore, robust feature extraction has attracted much attention in the field.

Noise-robust spectral estimation is possible with algorithms that focus on the higher order autocorrelation coefficients such as autocorrelation mel-frequency cepstral coefficient (AMFCC) method (Shannon & Paliwal, 2006). Moreover, as the autocorrelation of noise could in many cases be considered relatively constant over time, a high pass filtering of the autocorrelation sequence, as done in relative autocorrelation sequence (RAS) (You & Wang, 1999), could lead to substantial reduction of the noise effect. Furthermore, it has been shown that preserving spectral peaks is very important in obtaining a robust set of features for ASR (Padmanabhan, 2000; Srope & Alwan, 1998; Sujatha, Prasanna, Ramakrishnan, & Balakrishnan, 2003). Methods such as peak-to-valley ratio locking (Zhu, Iseli, Cui, & Alwan, 2001) and peak isolation (PKISO) (Strope & Alwan, 1997) have been found very useful in speech recognition error rate reduction. In differential power spectrum (DPS) (Chen, Paliwal, & Nakamura, 2003), as an example, differentiation in the spectral domain is used to preserve the spectral peaks while the flat parts of the spectrum, that are believed to be more vulnerable to noise, are almost removed.

In this paper we propose a novel Differentiated Relative Higher Order Autocorrelation sequence spectrum (DRHOASS) method for computing MFCC feature vector set. In this method, removal

Figure 1. Short-time analysis of the artificial white noise signal (a) Waveform of noise frame (b) Power spectrum estimate of given frame (c) Autocorrelation spectrum corresponding to power

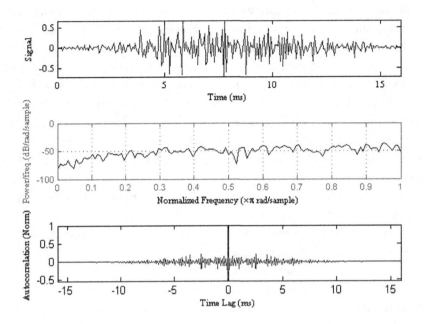

of lower orders of the autocorrelation sequence has been proposed with the additional high-pass filtering of the autocorrelation sequence to provide double fold noise suppression. In addition to this, the resultant spectral peaks are extracted as a third noise suppression step. The remainder of this paper is organized as follows. Properties of the short-time autocorrelation function are described and then an extraction of feature vector set using autocorrelation domain is explained. The proposed method will be discussed in next, followed by experiments conducted using different front-ends being discussed and compared with the proposed feature vector set. Finally, a conclusion is drawn.

PROPERTIES OF SHORT-TIME AUTOCORRELATION FUNCTION

The autocorrelation function of a signal contains the same information about the signal as its power spectrum (Kay, 1998). In the power spectrum domain, the information is presented as a function of frequency and in the autocorrelation domain it is represented as a function of time. We are proposing the DRHOASS method as a robust feature extraction procedure on the basis that the additive noise distortion has most of its autocorrelation coefficients concentrated near the lower orders and their higher order autocorrelation coefficients are zero (or, very small). Theoretically, the autocorrelation function should be zero for all the orders except for the zeroth order (Kay, 1979). We take 3s long computer-generated (artificial) white Gaussian noise and perform a short-time analysis (with Hamming window) using a frame length of 16 ms. For illustration, we take took a frame at a particular instance. The waveform of the frame, its power spectra and its autocorrelation spectra is shown in Figure 1 (a),(b) and (c). As expected, the higher order autocorrelation coefficients are smaller in magnitude than the zeroth autocorrelation coefficient, but they have non-zero values due to short-time analysis.

Furthermore, since noise spectrum is often flat and the differentiation either reduces or omits the relatively flat parts of the spectrum, it will lead to omission of the effect of noise on the signal leading to more robust features.

FEATURE VECTOR USING HIGHER ORDER AUTOCORRELATION COEFFICIENTS

If u(m,n) is the additive noise, x(m,n) noise-free speech signal and h(n) impulse response of the channel, then the noisy speech signal y(m,n) can be written as:

$$y(m,n) = [x(m,n) + u(m,n) \otimes h(n)],$$
$$0 \le m \le M-1, 0 \le n \le N-1 \qquad (1)$$

Where M denotes the number of frames in an utterance, N denotes the number of samples in a frame and $\otimes$ denotes the convolution operation. As we intend to use our method to remove or reduce additive noise from noisy speech signal, therefore the channel effect will not be considered here. We will then have

$$y(m,n) = [x(m,n) + u(m,n)],$$
$$0 \le m \le M-1, 0 \le n \le N-1 \qquad (2)$$

If the noise is uncorrelated with the speech, it follows that the autocorrelation of the noisy speech y(m,n) is the sum of autocorrelation of the clean speech x(m,n) and autocorrelation of the noise u(m,n),i.e.,

$$r_{yy}(m,k) = r_{xx}(m,k) + r_{uu}(k),$$
$$0 \le m \le M-1, 0 \le k \le N-1 \qquad (3)$$

where $r_{yy}(m,k), r_{xx}(m,k)$ and $r_{uu}(m,k)$ are the one-sided autocorrelation sequences of noisy speech, clean speech and noise respectively, and k is the autocorrelation sequence index within each frame.

If the additive noise is assumed to be stationary, the autocorrelation sequence of noise can be considered to be identical for all frames. Hence, the frame index m can be dropped out, and (3) becomes

$$r_{yy}(m,k) = r_{xx}(m,k) + r_{uu}(k),$$
$$0 \le m \le M-1, 0 \le k \le N-1 \qquad (4)$$

The N-point r_{yy}(m,k) is computed from N-point y(m,n) using the following equation,

$$r_{yy}(m,k) = \sum_{i=0}^{N-1-k} y(m,i)y(m,i+k) \qquad (5)$$

Eliminating the lower orders of the noisy speech signal autocorrelation should lead to removal of the main noise components. The maximum autocorrelation index to be removed is usually found experimentally. The resulting sequence after the removal of lower orders would be

$$r_{yy}(m,k) = r_{yy}(m,k), D \le m \le M-1$$

$$r_{yy}(m,k) = 0, \ 0 \le m \le D \qquad (6)$$

Where D is the elimination threshold (found experimentally).

Differentiating the resultant autocorrelation sequence with respect to m, will remove the noise autocorrelation and gives:

$$\frac{\partial r_{yy}(m,k)}{\partial m} = \frac{\partial r_{xx}(m,k)}{\partial m} + \frac{\partial r_{uu}(k)}{\partial m} \cong \frac{\partial r_{xx}(m,k)}{\partial m} = \frac{\sum\limits_{t=-L}^{L} t.r_{yy}(m+t,k)}{\sum\limits_{t=-L}^{L} t^2},$$
$$0 \le m \le M-1, 0 \le k \le N-1 \qquad (7)$$

The sequence,, $\left\{ \partial r_{yy}(m,k)_{k=0}^{N-1} \right\}$ is named the Relative Autocorrelation Sequence (RAS) of noisy speech at the mth frame. In order to get DRHOASS, we take differentiation of the spectrum of the filtered signal (which we get from previous step i.e. RAS). This further contributes to immunization against noise. By this approach the flat parts of the spectrum are almost removed while each spectral peak is split into two, one positive and one negative. The differential power spectrum of the filtered signal in discrete domain, can be defined as

$$Diff_{\Upsilon}(k) \approx \sum_{1=-Q}^{P} a_1 Y(k+1),$$
$$0 \leq k \leq K-1$$

(8)

where P and Q are the orders of the differential equation, al are some real-valued weighing coefficients and K is the length of FFT.

PROPOSED METHOD

In this section proposed method has been described to obtain new robust features for speech recognition. After pre-emphasis of the input speech signal using a pre-emphasis filter $Diff_{\Upsilon}(k) \approx \sum a_1 Y(k+1), 0 \leq k \leq K-1$, frame blocking of 16 ms with a frame shift of 8 ms is done. The Hamming window is applied to the pre-emphasized signal and then, the autocorrelation sequence of the framed signal is obtained. The lower orders of the autocorrelation sequence less than 1.375 ms (experimentally derived) are removed. A FIR high-pass filter is then applied to the signal autocorrelation sequence to further suppress the effect of additive noise. Then, a Hamming window is applied to the filtered signal and the short-time Fourier transform of this filtered signal is calculated. In the next step, differential

power spectrum of the filtered signal is found. Since the noise spectrum may in many occasions be considered flat, in comparison to the speech spectrum, the differentiation either reduces or omits these relatively flat parts of the spectrum, leading to even further suppression of the effect of noise. A set of cepstral coefficients (DRHOASS-MFCC) are derived from the magnitude of the differentiated high order relative autocorrelation power spectrum by applying it to a conventional mel-frequency filter-bank and passing the logarithm of the output to a DCT block. MFCC feature vector set of dimension 39 is formed by concatenating energy feature, Delta MFCC and Delta-Delta MFCC. Front-end for extraction of MFCC feature vector set by DRHOASS has been shown in Figure 2.

Experiments and Results

The proposed approach was implemented on TIFR Hindi speech database. Database of 200 Hindi words (Table 1) spoken by 30 speakers was used. The spoken samples were recorded by 15 male, 10 female and 5 child speakers in a studio environment condition using Sennheiser microphone model MD421 and a tape recorder model Philips AF6121. Each speaker uttered 5 repetitions of words. Database was divided into training set and testing set.

We evaluate the recognition performance of the proposed feature vector set in the presence of white and colored noises and compare it with other front ends. We compare it with the MFCC, AMFCC, and RAS methods. Features vector sets of size 39 are extracted using different front-ends (MFCC (for comparison purposes), RAS-MFCC, AMFCC and our method DRHOASS-MFCC). With these features vector sets, word models of training database for different front-ends are created by seven state left-right Hidden Markov model. Afterwards word recognition rates for testing database are computed with all the above front-ends and compared with the traditional MFCC.

Figure 2. Front- end for extraction of MFCC by DRHOASS

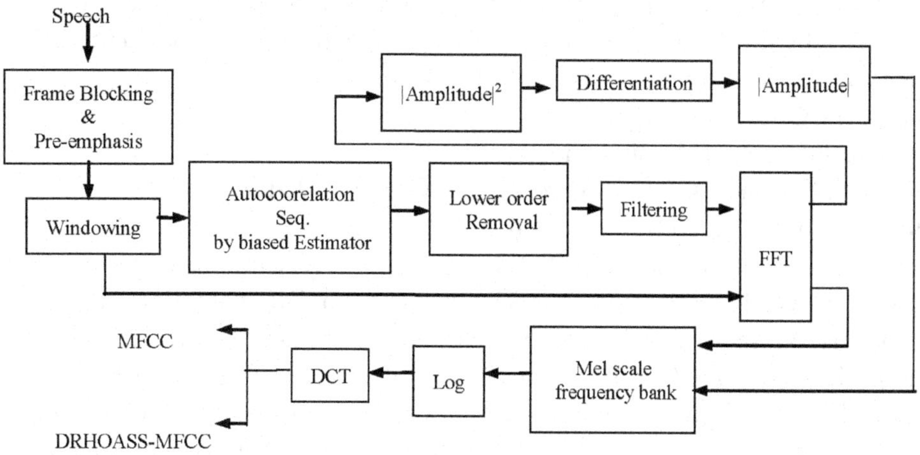

(a) Testing on clean speech

This experiment is to evaluate the performance of MFCC, RAS-MFCC, AMFCC and DRHOASS-MFCC, when training data & the testing data are in clean (40 dB) environment. The results are shown in Table 2. These are the baseline results for comparison purposes. Performance on the basis of recognition rates is observed to be more or less same if we use either MFCC, RAS-MFCC, AMFCC or DRHOASS-MFCC. This shows that the spectral information derived by DRHOASS

method captures the speech information to the same extent as that by other methods.

(b) Testing on noisy speech

The polluted testing utterances are generated by adding the artificial noises at five SNR levels. The white noise is generated by using a random number generation program, and other colored noises, i.e., factory noise, F16 noise, and babble noise, are extracted from the NATO RSG-10 corpus (Varga & Steeneken, 1993).

Table 1. TIFR database used for experiments

1. Language	Standard Hindi (Khari Boli)
2. Vocabulary Size	A set of 200 most frequently occurring Hindi words
3. Speakers	30 Speakers
4. Utterances	(15 male, 10 female and 5 children) 5 repetitions each
5. Audio Recording	Recording on a casette tape in studio S/N > 40
6. Digitization	16 kHz., Sampling 16 bit quantization.

Table 2. Comparison of clean-train and clean test recognition rates for various features

Feature Type	MFCC	AMFCC	RAS-MFCC	DRHOASS-MFCC
Recognition rate (%) at 40 dB	98.241	98.246	98.30	99.64

The noises are added to the clean speech signal at 20, 15, 10 5 and 0 dB SNRs. RAS-MFCC, AMFCC and DRHOASS-MFCC are evaluated and word recognition rates are compared with the traditional MFCC front end. Figure 3 (a)-(d) shows the results obtained using MFCC, RAS-MFCC, AMFCC and DRHOASS front-ends. For the case of white noise corruption, i.e., in Figure 3(a), the performance of MFCC degrades most significantly among all features, its performance is worse than RAS-MFCC, AMFCC and DRHOASS-MFCC. It is obvious that DRHOASS-MFCC are quite robust to the additive noises.

Figure 3(b), (c) and (d), show the performance when the testing speech is corrupted by factory, babble, and F16 noises, respectively. The figures depict that the performance of MFCC degrades significantly. The best performance comes from DRHOASS-MFCC. This is due to peak preserving property of power spectrum domain, which helps in better recognition in noisy environment.

The experiments show the better performance of the new feature vector set in comparison to the other autocorrelation based robust speech recognition parameters.

CONCLUSION

In this paper a new feature vector set is proposed based on DRHOASS to improve the performance of ASR systems. We have improved the performance of existing ASRs based on higher order autocorrelation coefficients by including additional filtering and picking the peaks in the spectral domain. Filtering stage has helped to reduce the effects of additive noises. The concept of spectral peaks has introduced a new set of cepstral features for improving the robustness of speech recognition. We note that just like the power spectrum, picking the spectral peaks can also preserve spectral information to discriminate among words.

Figure 3. Recognition rate percentages

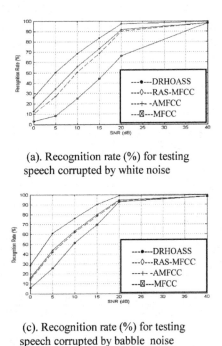

(a). Recognition rate (%) for testing speech corrupted by white noise

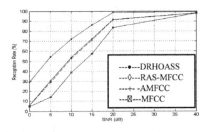

(b). Recognition rate (%) for testing speech corrupted by factory noise

(c). Recognition rate (%) for testing speech corrupted by babble noise

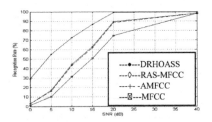

(d). Recognition rate (%) for testing speech corrupted by F16 noise

REFERENCES

Acero, A., Deng, L., Kristjansson, T., & Zhang, J. (2000). HMM adaptation using vector Taylor series for noisy speech recognition. In . *Proceedings of ICSLP, 3*, 869–872.

Beh, J., & Ko, H. (2003). A novel spectral subtraction scheme for robust speech recognition: spectral subtraction using spectral harmonics of speech. In *Proceedings of ICASSP* (pp. 648-651).

Chen, J., Paliwal, K. K., & Nakamura, S. (2003). Cepstrum derived from differentiated power spectrum for robust speech recognition. *Speech Communication, 41*, 469–484. doi:10.1016/S0167-6393(03)00016-5

Gales, M. J. F., & Young, S. J. (1995). Robust speech recognition in additive and convolutional noise using parallel model combination. *Computer Speech & Language, 9*, 289–307. doi:10.1006/csla.1995.0014

Gales, M. J. F., & Young, S. J. (1996). Robust continuous speech recognition using parallel model combination. *IEEE Transactions on Speech and Audio Processing, 4*(5), 352–359. doi:10.1109/89.536929

Hernando, J., & Nadeu, C. (1997). Linear prediction of the one-sided autocorrelation sequence for noisy speech recognition. *IEEE Transactions on Speech and Audio Processing, 5*(1), 80–84. doi:10.1109/89.554273

Kay, S. (1988). *Modern Spectral Analysis.* Upper Saddle River, NJ: Prentice Hall.

Kay, S. M. (1979). The effects of noise on the autoregressive spectral estimator. *IEEE Transactions on Acoustics, Speech, and Signal Processing, 27*(5), 478–485. doi:10.1109/TASSP.1979.1163275

Kim, D. Y., Un, C. K., & Kim, N. S. (1998). Speech recognition in noisy environments using first-order vector Taylor series. *Speech Communication, 24*(1), 39–49. doi:10.1016/S0167-6393(97)00061-7

Lee, C. H., Soong, F. K., & Paliwal, K. K. (1996). *Automatic speech and speaker recognition.* Dordrecht, The Netherlands: Kluwer Academic Publishers.

Mansour, D., & Jaung, B. H. (1989a). A family of distortion measures based upon projection operation for robust speech recognition. *IEEE Transactions on Speech and Audio Processing, 37*(11), 1659–1671.

Mansour, D., & Jaung, B. H. (1989b). The short-time modified coherence and noisy speech recognition. *IEEE Trans. Acoustics and signal processing, 37*(6), 795-804.

Moreno, P. J. (1996). *Speech recognition in noisy environment.* Unpublished doctoral dissertation, Carnegie-Mellon University, Pittsburgh, PA.

Moreno, P. J., Raj, B., & Stern, R. M. (1996). A vector Taylor series approach for environment independent speech recognition. In *Proceedings of ICASSP* (pp. 733-736).

Padmanabhan, M. (2000). Spectral peak tracking and its use in speech recognition. In *Proceedings of the ICSLP.*

Pols, L. (1999). Flexible, robust, and efficient human speech processing versus present-day speech technology. In *Proceedings of 14th Int. Congress of Phonetic Sciences (ICPhS-99)*, San Francisco, CA (pp. 9-16).

Shannon, B. J., & Paliwal, K. (2006). Feature extraction from higher-lag autocorrelation coefficients for robust speech recognition. *Speech Communication, 48*(11), 1458–1485. doi:10.1016/j.specom.2006.08.003

Shen, J. L., Hung, J. W., & Lee, L. S. (1998). Improved robust speech recognition considering signal correlation approximated by Taylor series. In *Proceedings of ICSLP.*

Sroka, J. J., & Braida, L. D. (2005). Human and machine consonant recognition. *Speech Communication, 45*(4), 401–424. doi:10.1016/j.specom.2004.11.009

Strope, B., & Alwan, A. (1997). A model of dynamic auditory perception and its application to robust word recognition. *IEEE Transactions on Speech and Audio Processing, 5*(5), 451–464. doi:10.1109/89.622569

Strope, B., & Alwan, A. (1998). Robust word recognition using threaded spectral peaks. In *Proceedings of the ICASSP* (pp. 625- 628).

Sujatha, J., Prasanna, K. R., Ramakrishnan, K. R., & Balakrishnan, N. (2003). Spectral maxima representation for robust automatic speech recognition. *In Proceedings of the Eurospeech* (pp. 3077-3080).

Varga, A., & Steeneken, H. J. M. (1993). Assessment for automatic speech recognition: II. NOISEX-92: A database and an experiment to study the effect of additive noise on speech recognition systems. *Speech Communication, 12,* 247–251. doi:10.1016/0167-6393(93)90095-3

Wang, Y. (2003). On cognitive informatics. *Brain and Mind, 4,* 151–167. doi:10.1023/A:1025401527570

You, K.-H., & Wang, H.-C. (1999). Robust features for noisy speech recognition based on temporal trajectory filtering of short-time autocorrelation sequences. *Speech Communication, 28,* 13–24. doi:10.1016/S0167-6393(99)00004-7

Zhu, Q., Iseli, M., Cui, X., & Alwan, A. (2001). Noise robust feature extraction for ASR using the AURORA2 database. *In Proceedings of Eurospeech.*

This work was previously published in volume 4, issue 4 of the International Journal of Cognitive Informatics and Natural Intelligence, edited by Yingxu Wang, pp. 37-46, copyright 2010 by IGI Publishing (an imprint of IGI Global).

Section 3
Denotational Mathematics

Chapter 10
A Web Knowledge Discovery Engine Based on Concept Algebra

Kai Hu
University of Calgary, Canada

Yingxu Wang
University of Calgary, Canada

Yousheng Tian
University of Calgary, Canada

ABSTRACT

Autonomous on-line knowledge discovery and acquisition play an important role in cognitive informatics, cognitive computing, knowledge engineering, and computational intelligence. On the basis of the latest advances in cognitive informatics and denotational mathematics, this paper develops a web knowledge discovery engine for web document restructuring and comprehension, which decodes on-line knowledge represented in informal documents into cognitive knowledge represented by concept algebra and concept networks. A visualized concept network explorer and a semantic analyzer are implemented to capture and refine queries based on concept algebra. A graphical interface is built using concept and semantic models to refine users' queries. To enable autonomous information restructuring by machines, a two-level knowledge base that mimics human lexical/syntactical and semantic cognition is introduced. The information restructuring model provides a foundation for automatic concept indexing and knowledge extraction from web documents. The web knowledge discovery engine extends machine learning capability from imperative and adaptive information processing to autonomous and cognitive knowledge processing with unstructured documents in natural languages.

DOI: 10.4018/978-1-4666-1743-8.ch010

INTRODUCTION

A central problem in web knowledge discovery, retrieval, and acquisition is how to formulate structured and effective queries on-line with a concept-oriented knowledge discovery tool. In the Internet environment, users often only submit short and incomplete queries that do not clearly express their actual needs (Spink et al., 2002). Therefore, an important issue in web knowledge mining is to improve search results by assisting users to express their information needs accurately and completely.

In order to achieve the above objectives, the following important issues must be dealt with for web-based knowledge searching engines: a) *Query Formulation:* An on-line search is preprocessed by a cognitive process to represent and formulate a query. In most information retrieval systems, this process is supposed to be an external activity and is not supported by the system. b) *Query Refinement:* When a primary query is formed with clearly identified domain, type, and attributes in an existing knowledge network, an accurate query refining process is needed to help users to efficiently formulate the query. c) *Query Expression:* There are a great variety of expression structures between the query initiator and the on-line information systems. Therefore, query expression is an important process in knowledge retrieval systems to transfer information between two heterogeneous information forms: the concept networks in the brain and the indexed databases in the web. It is the key for query expressing to effectively reduce the information leak in the transformation process from internal cognitive expressions to external formulated expressions.

A wide variety of techniques have been proposed to assist users to express a search request. Among them, an important method is *query expansion*, which adds relevant query terms to an initial query in order to improve retrieval results (Shaoira & Meirav, 2005; Na et al., 2005). *Query limitation* is another query-improvement strategy (Na et al.,

2005) opposite to query expansion, where users are provided with options to limit their search in order to receive more focused results. These methods have not got satisfactory effectiveness due to uncompleted consideration of all crucial features in query formulations.

This paper presents a web knowledge discovery and acquisition engine on the basis of a denotational mathematics known as concept algebra (Wang, 2006b, 2008a, 2008c). A formal concept-driven methodology is adopted in information restructuring for web documents. Knowledge organizations and representations are modeled by concept algebra, which represents a two-level normalized semantic space that simulates the cognitive knowledge representation inside the brain. At the lower level, concepts are formalized by a 5-tuple in concept algebra with a set of algebraic concept manipulation rules. At the higher level, knowledge is formally modeled by concept networks with nine concept associations. The web knowledge discovery engine encompasses four coherent components known as the concept network explorer, the semantic analyzer, the conceptual query editor, and the XML query generator. The concept network explorer provides a visual thinking navigator for assisting users to locate, capture, and refine a query efficiently. A graphical interface of the knowledge query engine is developed to facilitate direct expression and refinement of queries. The computer-aided knowledge retrieval system generates refined queries that best fit not only users' requirements, but also rational knowledge structures of existing information systems based on concept algebra. An information restructuring model is designed to decode and map informal texts in web documents into structured concept network represented by a concept graph. Applying WorldNet, ConceptNet, and other domain ontology, a concept-based clustering method that considers semantic relations and dependencies are proposed to index the restructured information of on-line documents.

CONCEPT ALGEBA: A DENOTATIOANL MATHEMATICAL PREPARATION

Concepts are the most fundamental unit of cognition that carries certain meanings in expression, thinking, reasoning, and system modeling (Wille, 1982). In *denotational mathematics* (Wang, 2008a, 2008b, 2009c; Wang, Zadeh & Yao, 2009), a concept is formally modeled as an abstract and dynamic mathematical structure that encapsulates attributes, objects, and relations. The formal methodology for manipulating knowledge by *concept algebra* is developed by Wang in (Wang, 2008c), which provides a generic and formal knowledge manipulation means that is capable to deal with complex knowledge and software structures as well as their algebraic operations.

Abstract Concepts

Human thinking is a cognitive process based on inferences on existing knowledge. The basic element of thinking is concepts that are the mapping of physical world objects and abstract artifacts in human brain. According to concept algebra (Wang, 2008c), human concept repository can be modeled as a concept network in which nodes express concepts and edges represent basic semantic relations between concepts.

Definition 1: *Let O denote a finite nonempty set of objects, and A be a finite nonempty set of attributes, then a semantic environment or context Θ is denoted as a triple, i.e.:*

$$\Theta \triangleq (\mathcal{O}, \mathcal{A}, \mathcal{R})$$
$$= \mathcal{R}: \mathcal{O} \to \mathcal{O} \mid \mathcal{O} \to \mathcal{A} \mid \mathcal{A} \to \mathcal{O} \mid \mathcal{A} \to \mathcal{A} \tag{1}$$

where R is a set of relations between O and A, and | demotes alternative relations.

On the basis of the semantic environment of concepts, Θ, the generic structure of abstract concepts can be modeled as follows.

Definition 2: *An abstract concept c is a 5-tuple on Θ, i.e.:*

$$c \triangleq (O, A, R^c, R^i, R^o) \tag{2}$$

where O is a nonempty set of objects of the concept, $O = \{o_1, o_2, ..., o_m\} \subseteq \text{Þ}O$ (ÞO denotes a power set of O); A is a nonempty set of attributes, $A = \{a_1, a_2, ..., a_n\} \subseteq \text{Þ}A$; $R^c = O \times A$ is a set of internal relations; $R^i \subseteq A' \times A$, $A' \sqsubseteq C' \wedge A \sqsubseteq c$, is a set of input relations, where C' is a set of external concepts, $C' \subseteq \Theta$. For convenience, $R^i = A' \times A$ may be simply denoted as $R^i = C' \times c$; and $R^o \subseteq c \times C'$ is a set of output relations.

Concept Algebra

Concept algebra is an abstract mathematical structure for the formal treatment of concepts and their algebraic relations, operations, and associative rules for composing complex concepts.

Definition 3: *A concept algebra CA on the given semantic environment Θ is a triple, i.e.:*

$$CA \triangleq (C, OP, \Theta) = (\{O, A, R^c, R^i, R^o\}, \{\bullet_r, \bullet_c\}, \Theta) \tag{3}$$

where $OP = \{\bullet_r, \bullet_c\}$ are the sets of *relational* and *compositional* operations on abstract concepts.

Definition 4: *The relational operations $\bullet_r$ of concept algebra encompass 8 comparative operators for manipulating the algebraic relations between concepts, i.e.:*

$$\bullet_r \triangleq \{\leftrightarrow, \nleftrightarrow, \prec, \succ, =, \cong, \sim, \triangleq\} \tag{4}$$

where the relational operators stand for *related, independent, subconcept, superconcept, equivalent, consistent, comparison,* and *definition,* respectively.

Definition 5: *The compositional operations $\bullet_c$ of concept algebra encompass 9 associative operators for manipulating the algebraic compositions among concepts, i.e.:*

$$\bullet_c \triangleq \{\Rightarrow, \overset{-}{\Rightarrow}, \overset{+}{\Rightarrow}, \overset{\sim}{\Rightarrow}, \uplus, \pitchfork, \Leftarrow, \vdash, \mapsto\} \qquad (5)$$

where the compositional operators stand for *inheritance, tailoring, extension, substitute, composition, decomposition, aggregation, specification,* and *instantiation*, respectively.

Details of the relational and compositional operations on concepts may be referred to (Wang, 2008c). Concept algebra provides a denotational mathematical means for algebraic manipulations of abstract concepts. Concept algebra can be used to model, specify, and manipulate generic *"to be"* type problems, particularly system architectures, knowledge bases, and detail-level system designs, in cognitive informatics, computing, software engineering, computational intelligence, and soft computing.

Concept Networks and Concept Graphs

Although concept itself is a dynamic and interlinked entity in knowledge, a higher level of human knowledge may be modeled by the interrelations and interactions among individual concepts. Such knowledge can be modeled by a formal concept network (Wang, 2008c) and illustrated by a concept graph (Wang, 2008c), which connects related concepts by relations. Complex interrelation between concept groups may be described as combinations of the fundamental relations modeled in $R = \bullet_c$, especially concept compositions (Wang, 2008c). For example, complex concept relations such as causality and behaviors can be modeled as derived relations using concept algebra. A special type of dynamic concept relations is known as actions or *"to do"* relations, which can be formally dealt

with Real-Time Process Algebra (RTPA) (Wang, 2002b, 2006a, 2007a, 2008d, 2008e).

Definition 6. *A concept network CN is a hierarchical network of concepts interlinked by the set of nine associations R defined in concept algebra, i.e.:*

$$CN = \Re : \overset{n}{\underset{i=1}{X}} C_i \to \overset{n}{\underset{i=1}{X}} C_i \qquad (6)$$

A fundamental concept network skeleton is constructed on the basis of the general cognitive taxonomy WordNet (1993), which reflect basic concept interrelation and organization of human knowledge. The nine compositional operations defined in concept algebra can be used to formally model WordNet to form different facets of the concept network.

A concept network formed by compositional operations of concept algebra can be illustrated by a concept graph as given in Example 1.

Example 1: *An abstract concept network that is formed by the composition and aggregation of a set of related concepts c_0 through c_9, as well as objects o_1 through o_3, can be illustrated by a concept graph as shown in Figure 1.*

The formal description corresponding to the above concept network can be carried out using concept algebra as given below.

$$c_0 \uplus ((c_1 \Rightarrow c_3 \overset{\sim}{\Rightarrow} c_6 \mapsto o_1) \,||\, (c_1 \overset{+}{\Rightarrow} c_4 \mapsto o_2))$$
$$||\, (c_2 \vdash c_5 \pitchfork (c_7 \,||\, (c_8 \mapsto o_3))$$

$$c_9 \Leftarrow (c_6 \,||\, c_7)$$
$$= (\, (c_1 \Rightarrow c_3 \overset{\sim}{\Rightarrow} c_6)$$
$$||\, (c_2 \vdash c_5 \pitchfork c_7)$$
$$)$$

$$(7)$$

Figure 1. An abstract concept network

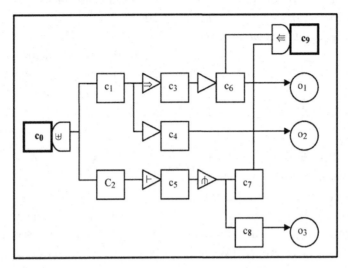

The case studies in Example 1 demonstrate that concept algebra and concept networks are a generic and formal knowledge manipulation means, which are capable to deal with complicated abstract or concrete knowledge structures and their algebraic operations. Further detailed concept operations of concept algebra may be extended into a set of inference processes, which can be formally described by RTPA (Wang, 2002b, 2006a, 2007a, 2008d, 2008e) as a set of behavioral processes.

To synthetically and efficiently express the compound relations that include multi-facet subrelations in concept networks, five *semantic relations* such as those of *causality, condition, concept-driven behavior, event-driven behavior, and comparison*, are defined based concept algebra and RTPA as given in Eqs. 8 through 11 below:

a. *Causality*: denoted by $\downarrow$, between a set of causes c_i and their effect c:

$$\bigwedge_{i=1}^{n} c_i \vdash c \qquad (8)$$

b. *Condition*: denoted by the same semantic operation as given in Eq. 8.

c. *Concept-driven behavior B_c*: denoted by $\hookrightarrow$ for expressing the semantic relations between a concept c_i and a related action or process P_i (Wang, 2002b, 2007a):

$$B_c \triangleq \mathop{R}_{i=1}^{n} c_i \hookrightarrow P_i \qquad (9)$$

d. *Event-driven behavior B_e*: denoted by $\hookrightarrow$ for expressing the semantic relations between an event e_i and a related action or process P_i (Wang, 2002b, 2008e):

$$B_e \triangleq \mathop{R}_{i=1}^{n} e_i \hookrightarrow P_i \qquad (10)$$

e. *Comparison*: denoted by $\sim$ for modeling the degree of semantic similarities and differences between two concepts (Wang, 2008c):

$$c_1 \sim c_2 = \frac{\#(A_1 \cap A_2)}{\#(A_1 \cup A_2)} * 100\% \qquad (11)$$

The semantic relations modeled above can effectively reorganize on-line information in web documents and concept networks. It also provides a solid foundation for developing an SQL-like language to accurately extract target information from concept networks and graphs.

Comparative Analyses of Concept Algebra and WordNet

A widely used electronic lexical knowledge base, WordNet (Princeton University, 1993), is adopted to build concept networks according to concept algebra. WordNet was developed by the Cognitive Science Laboratory at Princeton University since 1985. It is a general purpose knowledge base of words, which covers most English nouns, adjectives, verbs, and adverbs. The structure of WordNet is a relational semantic network. Each node in the network stands for a specific 'sense' and is expressed by a lexical unit called 'synset' that consist of several synonyms. From a cognitive view, the 'sense' in WordNet is exactly corresponding to the 'concept' in internal knowledge representation according to concept algebra (Wang, 2008c).

Parallel with WordNet, ConceptNet (Liu & Singh, 2004) is the largest commonsense knowledge base developed by the Media Laboratory at MIT. ConceptNet extends WordNet's concepts from purely lexical items (words and simple phrases) to complex concepts that composes verb with arguments. ConceptNet, also supply plenty of high order concepts such as events and processes. However, ConceptNet describes various relations between concepts in a planar way without distinguishing the difference between concept relations and attribute relations. Therefore, knowledge extracted from ConceptNet should be further identified and formalized based on the studies in concept algebra.

A comparative analysis of the relationship between concept algebra and WordNet is shown in Figure 2. Two categories of operations, those of concept formations and algebraic relations, are contrasted, which are formally defined in concept algebra and informally described in WordNet. Therefore, to a certain extent, concept algebra formalizes the informal semantics of concept structures and operations modeled in WordNet.

Concept algebra provides a formal system and denotational mathematical means for rigorously

Figure 2. Relations between Concept Algebra and WordNet

Category	Concept Algebra		WordNet		Definition
	Operation	Symbol	Operation	Symbol	
Concept formation	Definition (Identification)	$\triangleq$			$c \triangleq (O, A, R^c, R^i, R^o)\, c = (O, A, R^c, R^i, R^o \mid O \subset U, A \subset M,$ $R^c = O \times A, R^i = \varnothing, R^o = \varnothing)$
	Attribute (Qualification)	$\forall$	Meronym/ Attribute	$\%\,/\,=$	$\forall c = \forall c(O, A, R^c, R^i, R^o) = A = \{a_1, a_2, ..., a_n \mid a_i \in \underset{i=1}{\overset{m}{R}} c.o_i\}$
	Object (Elicitation)	$*$	Hyponym/ Synset	$\sim / *$	$c = c_1(O_1, A_1, R^c_1, R^i_1, R^o_1) * c_2(O_2, A_2, R^c_2, R^i_2, R^o_2)$ $= c(O, A, R^c, R^i, R^o \mid O = O_1 \cup O_2, A = A_1 \cap A_2,$ $R^c = O \times A,\ R^i = \{(c_1, c), (c_2, c)\}, R^o = \{(c, c_1), (c, c_2)\})$
Relations	Synonym (Equivalent)	$=$	Synonym/Synset	$=$	$A_1 = A_2 \wedge O_1 = O_2 \wedge R_1 = R_2 \Rightarrow c_1 = c_2$
	Antonum	$!$	Antonym	$!$	-
	Hyponym (Subconcept)	$\prec$	Hyponym	$\sim$	$A_1 \subset A_2 \Rightarrow c_1 \prec c_2$
	Holonym (Super concept)	$\succ$	Holonym	$\#$	$A_1 \supset A_2 \Rightarrow c_1 \succ c_2$
	Related	$\leftrightarrow$			$A_1 \cap A_2 \neq \varnothing \Rightarrow c_1 \leftrightarrow c_2$
	Independent	$\nleftrightarrow$			$A_1 \cap A_2 = \varnothing \Rightarrow c_1 \nleftrightarrow c_2$
	Consistent	$\cong$			a) $c_1, c_2 \in \Theta$; b) $c_1 \leftrightarrow c_2$; c) $(c_1 \succ ... \succ c_2) \vee (c_1 \prec ... \prec c_2)$

Figure 3. The architecture of the conceptual query formulator

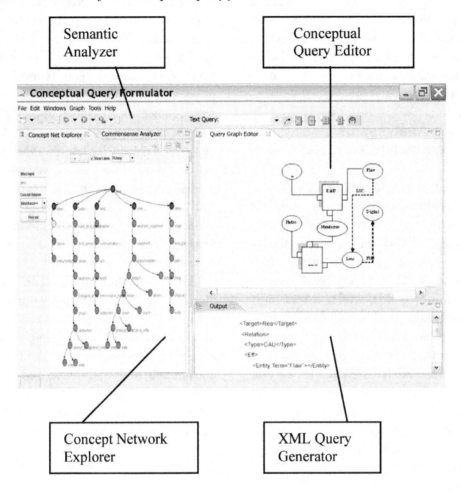

representing unstructured knowledge by concept networks using the Object-Attribute-Relation (OAR) model (Wang, 2007c). On the basis of OAR, a rigorous structure is designed for modeling concept networks of human knowledge and for integration of multiple knowledge bases in semantic analyses.

QUERY FORMULATIONS AND REFINEMENTS

The architecture of the conceptual query formulator is designed as shown in Figure 3, which possesses four coherent concepts known as the concept network explorer, the semantic analyzer,

the conceptual query editor, and the XML query generator.

The Concept Network Explorer

The concept network explorer as shown in Figure 3 visualizes a concept network to assistant user extending and exploring their thinking following semantically related concept links as a geographical map of human thinking threads. By identifying a set of concepts, users can efficiently navigate and locate the needed concept area and farther expand various related concepts in different facets and layers. Applying the visual concept network explorer, users can easily mark related concepts and key links to form a primary query.

A concept network is visualized with a well-tuned layout algorithm placing nodes and edge to make aesthetically pleasing drawings of concept graphs using an open source library of Java Universal Network/Graph (JUNG) framework (JUNG, 2007). To clearly simulate and trace the thread and skeleton of thinking, the concept network explorer can adaptively filter out a detailed concept layer and branches and dynamically deploy and spread the deep-seated micro network in the way that is similar to the cognitive processes of human thinking (Wang, 2002a, 2003, 2007b, 2007d, 2009a, 2009b, 2009d; Wang, Kinsner, & Du, 2009).

The Semantic Analyzer

Human knowledge in the form of concept networks is a latent semantic hierarchy according to concept algebra. To fully formulate queries toward machinable usages, the implied semantics should be explicitly expressed based on the given knowledge bases such as ConceptNet (Liu & Singh, 2004). With the support of ConceptNet, higher-order concepts can be extracted to build the semantic base that is useful for analyzing and extending complex concepts such as event-driven and concept-driven behaviors (Wang, 2007a, 2008c).

The Conceptual Query Editor

Query formulation in the web knowledge discovery engine consists of two processes: the graphical user query expression process and the structured query composition process. After a primary query via navigating the given concept network, users can graphically express the query prototype by creating core concept nodes and drawing relational connections between them using the graphical query editor.

The conceptual query editor provides a graphical interface for implementing the following functions:

- *Concept node modeling*: By choosing the node tool in the query editor, users can directly create a core concept node. In a popup window, users may then input the name, attributes, modifier, and constraints to model the given concept. When any of the configuration parameters need to be modified, a popup configuring interface can be activated for help.

- *Multi-link semantic connections*: In order to express complicated relations between concepts, semantic relations are formalized into 5 structured relational operations known as *related, independent, subconcept (hyponym), superconcept (holonym),* and *equivalent (synonym)* in concept algebra (Wang, 2008c). By clicking a relation button in the toolset, a semantic relation between two or more concepts can be created.

- *Concept nest and expansion*: To clearly organize their queries, users can nest and expand a set of chosen nodes and their relations by clicking the item in a popup menu.

- *Interaction with the visual inference explorer*: When clicking a node of the concept query graph in the input interface, the concept network explorer is invoked to enable users to implement query expansions and limitations by marking related concepts and links in concept networks.

- *Semantic analysis*: Using the semantic analyzer, the phrases, events, processes, and the whole conceptual query graph can be analyzed by choosing a given semantics.

- *Text query parser*: To farther facilitate the query formulation, a built-in query parser is developed based on the text restructuring technique (Hu & Wang, 2007; Tian, Wang, & Hu, 2009). Using the text query input tool in the sketch toolset, users can directly input their query in natural languages. When users push the "build" but-

Figure 4. A sample concept query graph

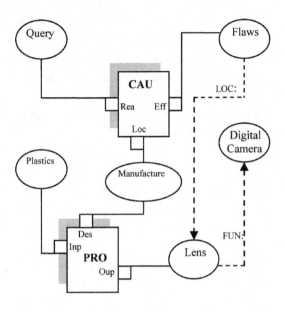

ton, the text query parser automatically generate a conceptual query graph in the graphical query editor.

The Structured Query Generator

After using the conceptual query graph to analyze and refine a query, the next process is to translate the conceptual query graph into a structured query that is machine oriented. For example, a query may state: "What are the possible quality flaws in producing lens of digital cameras?" A concept graph corresponding to the query can be generated by the graphical query expression tool as shown in Figure 4.

In the concept query graph, the attribute relations are expressed by dotted lines. Such a conceptual query graph can be translated into a structured XML expression as shown in Figure 5. The lexical, dominical, and other related information captured by the concept network explorer and semantic analyzer can also be formulated in the XML query kit. Using the designed extracting

Figure 5. XML representation of the concept query graph

```
<ConceptGraph>
    <Target>
        <Port>Rea</Port>
            <Relation IDREF="R1"/>
    </Target>
    <RelationList>
        <Relation ID="R1">
            <Type>CAU</Type>
            <Effect IDREF="E1"/>
            <Location IDREF="E2"/>
        </Relation>
            <Relation ID="R2">
            <Type>PRO</Type>
            <Description IDREF="E2"/>
            <Input IDREF="E3"/>
            <Output IDREF="E4"/>
        </Relation>
    </RelationList>
    <EntityList>
        <Entity ID="E1">
            <Term>Flaw</Term>
            <Type>State</Type>
            <LOC IDREF="E4"/>
        </Entity>
        <Entity ID="E2">
            <Term>Manufacture</Term>
            <Type>Process</Type>
        </Entity>
        <Entity ID="E3">
            <Term>Plastics</Term>
            <Type>Material</Type>
        </Entity>
        <Entity ID="E4">
            <Term>Lens</Term>
            <Type>Artifact</Type>
            <FUN IDREF="E5"/>
        </Entity>
        <Entity ID="E5">
            <Term>Digital Camera</Term>
            <Type>Artifact</Type>
        </Entity>
    </EntityList>
</ConceptGraph>
```

algorithm, the query kit can be formalized with the following elements:

- Objective concept: Entity
- Expansion term set: TSet
- Semantic type: SType
- Semantic chain: Hyponym, holonym, etc.
- Entity category: TOPC
- Near phase: PTerm

• Extension inference: ExInf

Combining the translated XML query with the conceptual query graph and the related query kit, the query generator can generate a structured intermediate query, which possesses the same conceptual structure as the restructured information from the target document by the concept-driven text formalizing technique (Wang, 2008c; Hu & Wang, 2007; Tian, Wang, & Hu, 2009). The refined conceptual query represented in XML as shown in Figure 5 can be applied by a specially designed extractor to call a traditional keyword-based search engine such as Google or IE to complete an enhanced on-line search.

INFORMATION RESTRUCTURING FOR WEB DOCUMENTS

A major obstacle in web-based knowledge acquisition is how knowledge is extracted from a huge amount of text documents. It is also a key problem in knowledge discovery affecting the efficiency, accuracy, and scalability of the implementation of knowledge discovery systems. A lot of efforts have been made to process unstructured texts by artificial intelligence, computational linguistics, data mining, and data warehousing techniques. However, due to the inherent complexity and diversity in such a task, the current knowledge discovery technologies are still far immature.

Properties of Unstructured Documents in Natural Languages

It is recognized that the basic unit of both natural language representation and human cognitive processes is concepts (Wille, 1982), which is a cognitive unit by which the meanings and semantics of a real-world or abstract entity may be represented and embodied (Wang, 2008c). In order to build a formal model for information restructuring on the basis of concept algebra as given in previous sections, major properties of text documents in natural languages are identified below:

a. *Concept networks for knowledge representation:* Web documents are usually written in natural languages for human reading. Therefore, machine cognition of the knowledge and information structures by concept networks plays an important role in knowledge discovery systems to mimic human reading, cognition, and comprehension.

b. *Rational structure of documents:* A variety of syntactic structures, composition styles, and statistical rules exist in web documents. In order to recognize such structural information, pattern-based extraction rules and machine learning techniques should be adopted in information restructuring.

c. *Latent semantics of documents:* Information and knowledge in unstructured texts should be cognized and consumed in term of their semantics, before information may be restructured and any new knowledge may be generated. Therefore, in order to enable machines to deal with web documents, the latent semantics of web documents in natural languages should be elicited based on related knowledge bases.

Formal concept analysis (Carpineto & Romano, 2004; Wang, 2008c) and ontology-based annotation system (Alani et al., 2003; Anderasen et al., 2004; Reeve & Han, 2005) have been proposed for building conceptual structures of documents by different knowledge representation techniques. However, both approaches have more or less neglected the understanding of human knowledge representation inside the brain rather than stressed the outside expression of knowledge. ConceptNet (Liu & Singh, 2004) provides an informal solution by building a static semantic network of natural languages. In addition, information extraction techniques (Chang et al., 2006) propose an integration of computational linguistic treatment, pattern recognition, and document indexing methods.

It is recognized that knowledge representation is the foundation in knowledge engineering, which can be categorized into *external* and *internal* representations (Wang, 2002a, 2003). The former refers to the forms of knowledge representation in machines and media, which may be structured or unstructured in either natural languages or formal notation systems. The latter refers to the forms of knowledge representation in the brain as a cognitive model. Conventional knowledge representation techniques focus on external knowledge representation to facilitate automatic knowledge treatment. However, internal knowledge representation and modeling was overlooked.

Multidimensional Semantic Space Modeling

The Object-Attribute-Relation (OAR) model developed by Wang is a generic internal knowledge modeling methodology (Wang, 2007c). Knowledge represented in the brain as a dynamic OAR during knowledge acquisition reveals the fundamental mechanisms of internal knowledge representation for both human and machine learning. Knowledge represented in the form of OAR can be formally treated and manipulated by concept algebra at both concept and knowledge levels (Wang, 2008c, 2009d, 2009e). In this approach, knowledge is treated as a hierarchical concept network on the basis of the logical OAR model.

The internal semantic knowledge can be decomposed into two levels: the *concept* level that describes the basic constitution of concepts and the *interrelation* levels that reflect the complicated interaction and interrelation between concepts. At the concept level, the description of a concept involves the intention (attributes) and extension (objects) (Wille, 1982; Wang, 2008c). The set of attributes of a given concept as the intension of the concept can effectively distinct the concept from others. More rigorously, the attributes of

a concept can be described as the projection of the concept on some special concept dimensions such as function, location, shape, size, state, and psychological feature etc. Therefore, by choosing these general properties as dimensions (metadata), a formalized multidimensional concept space can be constructed to model a concept with the following properties:

a. A concept *c* can be expressed as a vector by its attributes *A* in the multidimensional semantic space as follows:

$$A = \{a_1, a_2, ..., a_n \mid a_i \in \mathop{R}\limits_{i=1}^{m} c.o_i\} \qquad (12)$$

where, according to statistics based on WordNet, $n = 3$ in average, but it can be as large as 666, e.g., for the concept '*city*' according to WordNet.

b. Some special concepts may be identified as *primitive* concepts for quantifying other concepts. The primitive concepts can be used to facilitate the modification, combination, and manipulation of complex concepts according to concept algebra.

Therefore, all concepts can be classified into three types: the *entity*, *property*, and *quantification* concepts. In web documents, the property concepts act as metadata to describe different attribute dimensions such as name, color, shape, and size. The quantification concepts express values of corresponding attributes, such as blue, triangle, and small. Such distinction is useful to map a related concept of document into the structured concept space. Using existing linguistic knowledge bases such as WordNet, the property concepts and quantification concepts can be effectively identified.

Knowledge Base Modeling

Knowledge bases provide a foundation for external knowledge representation in knowledge modeling and discovery. By mimicking the knowledge repository in the brain, knowledge bases may also be modeled at two levels (concepts and concept networks). A concept network possesses basic attributes linked by the *equivalence* relation as modeled in concept algebra. The concept network is built based on the knowledge base, WordNet (1993), which has following function in information restructuring of web documents:

a. With the hierarchical concept network, attributes and links to related concepts in a document under processing can be easily identified.
b. The transformation of coordinates and mapping between coordinates (intentions) and concept objects (extensions) can be implemented.
c. The coordinate values of a concept in the semantic space can be used to calculate the concept distance that will play an important role in information indexing.

The knowledge base built on ConceptNet supports necessary semantic analyses on meanings, compound concepts, and complicated relations of web documents. With the conceptual graphs generated from a web document, the needed expansion, evolution, and population can be implemented by the semantic base built in the web knowledge discovery engine.

DESIGN OF THE KNOWLEDGE DISCOVERY AND INFORMATION RESTRUCTURING ENGINE

As a coherent component of the web knowledge discovery engine, the information restructuring subsystem is a machine cognition system to re-cursively decode and map the external knowledge contained in a web document in natural languages into structured internal knowledge in the form of concept networks. The result of information restructuring is a set of concept graphs based on concept algebra in which a concept node is described in the multi-dimensional semantic space and the relations of concepts are formulized by relational associations.

A concept-driven information restructuring framework for web document processing is designed as shown in Figure 6. The framework of the automatic information restructuring tool encompasses the following four components:

The *parser and linguistic processer:* In this component, format information and unambiguous data are extracted from an input web-document by natural language analyzing techniques such as named entity recognition, reference resolution, template element construction, template relation construction, and scenario template production.

The *concept restructurer*: Concepts are elicited by this component using the extracted information produced in the above process on the support of the knowledge bases with concept networks and semantic base. A concept graph will be generated by the tool in this process.

The *concept graph processer*: This component refines the concept model and graph in order to generate a machine cognized knowledge representation for human users for the target web document.

The *indexer and storage*: The formalized conceptual graph for a given web document is further processed in this component in order to generate detailed semantic analysis results such as concept distances and highlights of semantic evaluations. This process uses a conceptual-clustering-based indexing approach (Madhyastha, 2003), which adopts a relational semantic weight in document vector modeling where highly related semantic index of the restructured information can be extracted. As a byproduct, the formalized concept

Figure 6. Architecture of information restructuring model

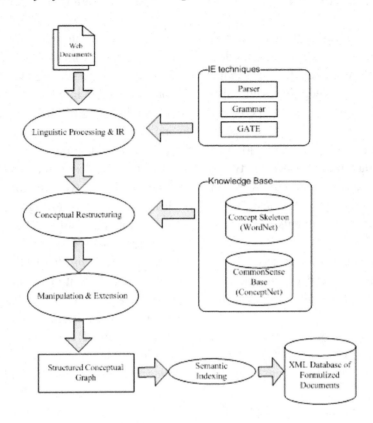

graph may be easily transformed into XML format and stored in an XML database for further query applications and analyses.

CONCLUSION

It is recognized that knowledge discovery involves the interaction of two completely heterogeneous information systems: Human brain (neutral networks) and the web (computer networks). In the former the basic element is concepts that are the mapping of physical world in human brain, while in the latter the information unit is terms or symbols that are a representation of a concept. There is a great structural gap between concept-based knowledge representation in human brain and the term-based knowledge representation in computers. The classical knowledge discovery system usually uses a term (a keyword and its constraints) based interface to convey the information from human brains to computer systems. Because of the ambiguity in expressions and implied latent relations in concept networks of human knowledge, the term-based human-computer interface will directly result in a great information leak in queries capturing and finally lead to the deficiency in knowledge discovery.

This paper has presented a query formulator based on concept algebra. The query engine is not only capable to assist users to generate rational and refined queries for any information systems, but also enables users to accurately organize and express their query in a concept based graphical query editor. A set of formal methodologies for internal and external knowledge representation and modeling has been developed on the basis of concept algebra. The formal models for information restructuring of web documents have been described, and methodologies for decoding external knowledge representations into internal knowledge representation with concept networks and concept graphs have been demonstrated. The models and methodologies developed in this paper have been applied in the design and implementation of an autonomous machine learning system known as AutoLearner (Hu & Wang, 2007).

ACKNOWLEDGMENT

The authors would like to acknowledge the Natural Science and Engineering Council of Canada (NSERC) for its partial support to this work. The author would like to thank the anonymous reviewers for their valuable comments and suggestions.

REFERENCES

Alani, H., Kim, S., Millard, D. E., Weal, M., Hall, W., & Lewis, P. H. (2003). Automatic Ontology-based Knowledge Extraction from Web Documents. *IEEE Intelligent Systems*, *18*(1), 14–21. doi:10.1109/MIS.2003.1179189

Anderasen, T., Jensen, P. A., Nilsson, J. F., Paggio, P., Pederson, B. S., & Thomsen, H. E. (2004). Content-based text querying with ontological descriptors. *Data & Knowledge Engineering*, *48*, 199–219. doi:10.1016/S0169-023X(03)00105-8

Carpineto, C., & Romano, G. (2004). *Concept Data Analysis: Theory and Applications*. New York: John Wiley & Sons.

Chang, C.-H., Kayed, M., Girgis, M. R., & Shaalan, K. (2006). A Survey of Web Information Extraction System. *IEEE Transactions on Knowledge and Data Engineering*, *18*(10), 1411–1428. doi:10.1109/TKDE.2006.152

Gleason, J. B. (1997). *The Development of Language, Introduction to Descriptive Linguistics* (4th ed.). Boston: Allyn and Bacon.

Hu, K., & Wang, Y. (2007). Autolearner: An Autonomic Machine Learning System Based on Concept Algebra. In *Proceedings of the 6th International Conference on Cognitive Informatics (ICCI'07)*, Lake Tahoe, CA (pp. 502-512).

JUNG. (2007). *Java Universal Network/Graph Framework*. Retrieved from http://jung.sourceforge.net/

Liu, H., & Singh, P. (2004). ConceptNet - A Practical Commonsense Reasoning Toolkit. *BT Technology Journal*, *22*(4), 211–225. doi:10.1023/B:BTTJ.0000047600.45421.6d

Madhyastha, H. V., Balakrishnan, N., & Ramakrishnan, K. R. (2003). *Event Information Extraction Using Link Grammar*. Paper presented at the 13th International Workshop on Research Issues in Data Engineering: Multi-lingual Information Management (RIDE'03).

Na, S. H., Kang, I. S., Roh, J. E., & Lee, J. H. (2005). An Empirical Study of Query Expansion and Cluster-Based Retrieval in Language Modeling Approach. In *Information Retrieval Technology* (LNCS 3689, pp. 274-287).

Reeve, L., & Han, H. (2005). Survey of semantic Annotation Platforms. In *Proceedings of the ACM Symposium on Applied Computing* (pp. 1634-1638).

Shapira, B., & Meirav, T. M. (2005). Subjective and Objective Evaluation of Interactive and Automatic Query Expansion. *Online Information Review*, *29*(4), 374–390. doi:10.1108/14684520510617820

Spink, A., Wolfram, D., Jansen, M. B. J., & Saracevic, T. (2002). From E-sex to E-commerce: Web search changes. *IEEE Computer*, *35*(3), 107–109.

Tian, Y., Wang, Y., & Hu, K. (2009). A Knowledge Representation Tool for Autonomous Machine Learning Based on Concept Algebra. *Transactions of Computational Science, 5*, 143–160. doi:10.1007/978-3-642-02097-1_8

Wang, Y. (2002a, August). Keynote: On Cognitive Informatics. In *Proceedings of the 1st IEEE International Conference on Cognitive Informatics (ICCI'02)*, Calgary, Alberta, Canada (pp. 34-42). IEEE CS Press.

Wang, Y. (2002b). The Real-Time Process Algebra (RTPA). *Annals of Software Engineering . International Journal (Toronto, Ont.), 14*, 235–274.

Wang, Y. (2003). On Cognitive Informatics. *Brain and Mind: A Transdisciplinary Journal of Neuroscience and Neurophilosophy, 4*(3), 151-167.

Wang, Y. (2006a). On the Informatics Laws and Deductive Semantics of Software. *IEEE Transactions on Systems, Man, and Cybernetics . Part C, 36*(2), 161–171.

Wang, Y. (2006b, July). Cognitive Informatics and Contemporary Mathematics for Knowledge Representation and Manipulation, Invited Plenary Talk. In *Proceedings of the 1st International Conference on Rough Set and Knowledge Technology (RSKT'06)*, Chongqing, China (LNAI 4062, pp. 69-78).

Wang, Y. (2007a). *Software Engineering Foundations: A Software Science Perspective, CRC Series in Software Engineering, Vol. II.* Boca Raton, FL: Auerbach Publications.

Wang, Y. (2007b). The Theoretical Framework of Cognitive Informatics. *International Journal of Cognitive Informatics and Natural Intelligence, 1*(1), 1–27.

Wang, Y. (2007c). The OAR Model of Neural Informatics for Internal Knowledge Representation in the Brain. *International Journal of Cognitive Informatics and Natural Intelligence, 1*(3), 64–75.

Wang, Y. (2007d). The Theoretical Framework and Cognitive Process of Learning. *Proc. 6th International Conference on Cognitive Informatics* (ICCI'07), IEEE CS Press, Lake Tahoe, CA., Aug., 470-479.

Wang, Y. (2008a). On Contemporary Denotational Mathematics for Computational Intelligence. *Transactions of Computational Science, 2*, 6–29. doi:10.1007/978-3-540-87563-5_2

Wang, Y. (2008b). Mathematical Laws of Software. *Transactions of Computational Science, 2*, 46–83. doi:10.1007/978-3-540-87563-5_4

Wang, Y. (2008c). On Concept Algebra: A Denotational Mathematical Structure for Knowledge and Software Modeling. *International Journal of Cognitive Informatics and Natural Intelligence, 2*(2), 1–19.

Wang, Y. (2008d). Deductive Semantics of RTPA. *International Journal of Cognitive Informatics and Natural Intelligence, 2*(2), 95–121.

Wang, Y. (2008e). RTPA: A Denotational Mathematics for Manipulating Intelligent and Computational Behaviors. *International Journal of Cognitive Informatics and Natural Intelligence, 2*(2), 44–62.

Wang, Y. (2009a). On Abstract Intelligence: Toward a Unified Theory of Natural, Artificial, Machinable, and Computational Intelligence. *International Journal of Software Science and Computational Intelligence, 1*(1), 1–17.

Wang, Y. (2009b). On Cognitive Computing. *International Journal of Software Science and Computational Intelligence, 1*(3), 1–15.

Wang, Y. (2009c). Paradigms of Denotational Mathematics for Cognitive Informatics and Cognitive Computing. *Fundamenta Informaticae*, *90*(3), 282–303.

Wang, Y. (2009d). Toward a Formal Knowledge System Theory and Its Cognitive Informatics Foundations. *Transactions of Computational Science*, *5*, 1–19. doi:10.1007/978-3-642-02097-1_1

Wang, Y. (2009e). A Formal Syntax of Natural Languages and the Deductive Grammar. *Fundamenta Informaticae*, *90*(4), 353–368.

Wang, Y., Kinsner, W., & Zhang, D. (2009). Contemporary Cybernetics and its Faces of Cognitive Informatics and Computational Intelligence. *IEEE Trans. on System, Man, and Cybernetics (B)*, *39*(4), 823–833. doi:10.1109/TSMCB.2009.2013721

Wang, Y., Zadeh, L. A., & Yao, Y. (2009). On the System Algebra Foundations for Granular Computing. *International Journal of Software Science and Computational Intelligence*, *1*(1), 64–86.

Wille, R. (1982). Restructuring Lattice Theory: An Approach Based on Hierarchies of Concepts. In I. Rival (Ed.), *Ordered Sets* (pp. 445-470). Dordrecht, The Netherlands: Reidel.

WordNet. (1993). *About WordNet*. http://wordnet.princeton.edu/

This work was previously published in volume 4, issue 1 of the International Journal of Cognitive Informatics and Natural Intelligence, edited by Yingxu Wang, pp. 80-97, copyright 2010 by IGI Publishing (an imprint of IGI Global).

Chapter 11
Approximations in Rough Sets vs Granular Computing for Coverings

Guilong Liu
Beijing Language and Culture University, China

William Zhu
University of Electronic Science and Technology of China, China

ABSTRACT

Rough set theory is an important technique in knowledge discovery in databases. Classical rough set theory proposed by Pawlak is based on equivalence relations, but many interesting and meaningful extensions have been made based on binary relations and coverings, respectively. This paper makes a comparison between covering rough sets and rough sets based on binary relations. This paper also focuses on the authors' study of the condition under which the covering rough set can be generated by a binary relation and the binary relation based rough set can be generated by a covering.

INTRODUCTION

The rough set theory, proposed by Pawlak (Pawlak, 1982, 1991) in 1982, is a recent approach for reasoning about data. This theory depends basically on a certain topological structure and has achieved a great success in many fields of real life applications (Lashin, Kozae, Khadra, & Medhat, 2005; Pawlak, 1991; Polkowski & Skow-

DOI: 10.4018/978-1-4666-1743-8.ch011

ron, 1998). Combined with other complementary concepts such as fuzzy sets, statistics, and logical data analysis, rough sets have been exploited in hybrid approaches to improve the performance of data analysis tools (Masulli & Petrosino, 2006).

A key notion in Pawlak rough set theory is an equivalence relation. An equivalence relation, i.e., a partition, is the simplest formulation of the lower and upper approximation. However, the requirement of an equivalence relation in Pawlak rough set model seems to be a very restrictive condition that may limit the applications of the rough set model. Thus one of the main directions of research in rough set theory is naturally the generalization of the Pawlak rough set approximations. For example, general binary relations were used in the neighborhood systems introduced by Lin (Lin, 1989). Lin also suggested that one may use the neighborhood systems in stead of the equivalence classes. Moreover, many interesting and meaningful extensions have been made based on binary relations (Chen, Zhang, Yeung, & Tsang, 2006; Kondo, 2005, 2006; Lin, 1989, 1992; Lin, Huang, Liu, & Chen, 1990; Lin & Liu, 1994; Liu, 2006, 2008) and coverings (Bonikowski, Bryniarski, & Wybraniec, 1998; Yeung, Chen, Tsang, Lee, & Wang, 2005; Zhu, 2007; Zhu & Wang, 2006, 2007) respectively, but they did not study the relationships between these two types of rough sets. In this paper we make a comparison between covering rough sets and rough sets based on binary relations. The paper aims to study the mathematical structure of covering-based rough sets. We show that the second, third and fifth type of upper approximations can be generated by some binary relations. Under additional assumption, the first, fourth type of upper approximations and covering lower approximation can also be generated by some binary relations. Through this study, we can have a clearer vision of rough sets and a deeper insight of possible applications of rough sets. Furthermore, our study simplifies the reasoning in covering-based rough sets.

The paper is organized as follows. In Section 2 we extend the definition of rough sets to any relation and study the uniqueness of binary relations to generate rough sets. In Section 3 and Section 4 we show that covering lower and upper approximations can be generated by a reflexive and transitive relation under additional assumption. Section 5 and Section 6 make a comparison between covering upper approximations and rough sets upper approximations based on binary relations. We show that the second and third type of upper approximations can be generated by some

binary relation. In Section 7 we study the condition under which the fourth covering upper approximation coincides with the upper approximation generated by a reflexive and transitive relation. Section 8 considers the relationships between the fifth covering upper approximation and the upper approximation generated by a reflexive and transitive relation. Section 9 concludes the paper.

ROUGH SETS BASED ON BINARY RELATIONS

Let U be a non-empty finite set of objects called the universe and $P(U)$ be the power set of U. Recall that a binary relation R on U is referred to as reflexive if for all $x \in U$, xRx; R is referred to as symmetric if for all $x, y \in U$, xRy implies yRx; R is referred to as transitive if for all $x, y, z \in U$, xRy and yRz imply xRz. R is an equivalence relation if it is reflexive, symmetric and transitive.

Several researches had pointed out the necessity to introduce a more general approach by considering an arbitrary binary relation (or even an arbitrary fuzzy relation in two universes) $R \subseteq U \times U$ in the set U of objects instead of an equivalence relation (Bonikowski, Bryniarski, & Wybraniec, 1998; Chen, Zhang, Yeung, & Tsang, 2006; Kondo, 2005, 2006).

Suppose R is an arbitrary relation on U. With respect to R, we can define the left and right neighborhoods of an element x in U as follows:

$$l(x) = \{y \mid y \in U, yRx\} \text{ and}$$
$$r(x) = \{y \mid y \in U, xRy\},$$

respectively. Clearly, if R is symmetric, then $l(x) = r(x)$. The left (or right) neighborhood $l(x)$ (or $r(x)$) becomes an equivalence class containing x if R is an equivalence relation. For an arbitrary relation R, by substituting equivalence class $[x]_R$ with right neighborhood $r(x)$, we define the operators $\underline{R}$ and $\overline{R}$ (Lin, 1992) from $P(U)$ to itself by

$\underline{R}X = \{x \mid r(x) \subseteq X\}$ and
$\overline{R}X = \{x \mid r(x) \cap X \neq \varnothing\}$.

$\underline{R}X$ is called a lower approximation of X and $\overline{R}X$ an upper approximation of X. The pair $(\underline{R}X, \overline{R}X)$ is referred to as a rough set based on R. The set $\underline{R}X$ consists of those elements whose right neighborhoods are contained in X, and $\overline{R}X$ consists of those elements whose right neighborhoods have a nonempty intersection with X. Obviously, if R is an equivalence relation, $l(x) = r(x) = [x]_R$ and these definitions are equivalent to the original definitions of Pawlak.

We list the basic properties of rough set based on a binary relation, which can be found in (Liu & Zhu, 2008).

Proposition 1. Let U be a universal set and R be an arbitrary binary relation on U. Then $\forall X, Y \in P(U)$ and $\forall x \in U$,

(1) $\underline{R}U = U$, $\overline{R}\varnothing = \varnothing$;

(2) $\overline{R}(X \cup Y) = \overline{R}X \cup \overline{R}Y$,
$\underline{R}(X \cap Y) = \underline{R}X \cap \underline{R}Y$;

(3) If $X \subseteq Y$, then $\underline{R}X \subseteq \underline{R}Y$ and $\overline{R}X \subseteq \overline{R}Y$;

(4) $\underline{R}(-X) = -\overline{R}X$ and $\overline{R}(-X) = -\underline{R}X$, where $-X$ denotes the complement of X;

(5) $\overline{R}\{x\} = l(x)$ and $\overline{R}X = \bigcup_{x \in X} l(x)$;

(6) If S is another binary relation on U and $\underline{R}X = \underline{S}X$ for all $X \in P(U)$, then $R = S$.

(7) If S is another binary relation on U and $\overline{R}X = \overline{S}X$ for all $X \in P(U)$, then $R = S$.

COVERING LOWER APPROXIMATION OPERATIONS

Extensive research on the covering rough set theory can be found in (Bonikowski, Bryniarski, & Wybraniec, 1998) and (Zhu & Wang, 2007).

Definition 1. Let U be a universal set and C be a family of subset of U. C is called a covering of U if none subsets in C is empty, and $\bigcup_{K \in C} K = U$. The order pair $\langle U, C \rangle$ is called a covering approximation space if C is a covering of U.

Definition 2. Let $\langle U, C \rangle$ be a covering approximation space, $x \in U$, the minimal description of x is defined as

$$Md(x) = \{K \mid x \in K \in C \land (\forall S \in C \land x \in S \subseteq K \Rightarrow K = S)\}$$

Definition 3. Let $\langle U, C \rangle$ be a covering approximation space. For a subset $X \subseteq U$, the set $X_* = \bigcup \{K \in C \mid K \subseteq X\}$ is called the covering lower approximation of X.

Generally, covering lower approximations cannot be represented as the lower approximations based on binary relations, but, with some additional assumptions, they are a kind of lower approximations based on binary relation.

As we know, $(X \cap Y)_* = X_* \cap Y_*$ do not hold in general (Zhu & Wang, 2007). However, if $(X \cap Y)_* = X_* \cap Y_*$ holds for all $X, Y \subseteq U$, we have the following proposition.

Proposition 2. Let $\langle U, C \rangle$ be a covering approximation space. If $(X \cap Y)_* = X_* \cap Y_*$ holds for all $X, Y \subseteq U$, then there exists a unique reflexive and transitive relation R on U such that $X_* = \underline{R}X$. On the other hand, for a reflexive and transitive relation R on U, there exists a covering C of U such that $\underline{R}X = X_*$, and $(X \cap Y)_* = X_* \cap Y_*$.

Proof. We note that any subset X of U can be written as

$$X = \bigcap_{x \notin X} (U - \{x\}) .$$

Using covering C of U, via left neighborhood of an element $x \in U$, we can construct a binary relation R on U as follows:

$$l(x) = \cap \{U - K \mid K \in C, x \notin K\}.$$

We note that

$$xRy \Leftrightarrow x \in \cap\{U - K \mid K \in C, x \notin K\}$$

$$\Leftrightarrow \forall K \in C, y \notin K \Rightarrow x \notin K$$

$$\Leftrightarrow \forall K \in C, x \in K \Rightarrow y \in K$$

$$\Leftrightarrow y \in \cap\{K \in C \mid x \in K\}.$$

Thus $r(x) = \cap\{K \in C \mid x \in K\}$.

Since

$$(U - \{x\})_* = \cup\{K \in C \mid x \notin K\}$$

$$= U - \cap\{U - K \mid K \in C, x \notin K\}$$

$$= U - l(x)$$

$$= \underline{R}(U - \{x\}).$$

We obtain

$$X_* = (\cap_{x \notin X}(U - \{x\}))_*$$

$$= \cap_{x \notin X}(U - \{x\})_*$$

$$= \cap_{x \notin X}\underline{R}(U - \{x\})$$

$$= \underline{R}(\cap_{x \notin X}(U - \{x\}))$$

$$= \underline{R}X$$

Moreover, $X_* \subseteq X$ (Zhu & Wang, 2007) implies R is reflexive and $(X_*)_* = X_*$ implies R is transitive. The uniqueness of R comes from Proposition 1 (6).

Conversely, for a reflexive and transitive relation R on U, we define C as follows:

$$C = \{r(x) \mid x \in U\},$$

where $r(x)$ is the right neighborhood of x for R.

Since R is reflexive, $\forall x \in U, x \in r(x)$, so $\cup\{r(x) \mid x \in U\} = U$. Thus, C is a covering of U.

We start to prove $\underline{R}X = X_*$. On one hand, we prove $X_* \subseteq \underline{R}X$. In fact, $\forall x \in X_*$, there exists some $y \in U$ such that $x \in r(y) \subseteq X$. Since R is transitive, from $x \in r(y)$, we have $r(x) \subseteq r(y)$. Thus $r(x) \subseteq X$. By the definition of $\underline{R}X, x \in \underline{R}X$. We proved that $X_* \subseteq \underline{R}X$.

On the other hand, we prove $\underline{R}X \subseteq X_*$. $\forall x \in \underline{R}X$, we have $r(x) \subseteq X$. By the definition of X_*, $r(x) \subseteq X_*$. Since R is reflexive, $x \in r(x)$, so $x \in X_*$. Thus $\underline{R}X \subseteq X_*$.

By the property of $\underline{R}$, we have $(X \cap Y)_* = \underline{R}(X \cap Y) = \underline{R}X \cap \underline{R}Y = X_* \cap Y_*$.

FIRST TYPE OF UPPER APPROXIMATIONS

There are several possibilities to define covering upper approximations (Zhu & Wang, 2007). The first type of covering upper approximations were defined in (Bonikowski, Bryniarski, & Wybraniec, 1998).

Definition 4. Let $\langle U, C \rangle$ be a covering approximation space. The first type of upper approximation H_1 of subset X of U is defined as

$$H_1X = X_* \cup (\cup\{Md(x) \mid x \in X - X_*\}).$$

Generally, H_1 cannot be represented as $\overline{R}$ for a binary relation, since $H_1(X \cup Y) = H_1X \cup H_1Y$ do not hold (Zhu and Wang, 2007). The next proposition shows that there is a close relationship between the condition $H_1(X \cup Y) = H_1X \cup H_1Y$ and the upper approximation generated by a reflexive and transitive relation.

Proposition 3. Let $\langle U, C \rangle$ be a covering approximation space. If $H_1(X \cup Y) = H_1X \cup H_1Y$ for all $X, Y \in P(U)$, then there exists a unique reflexive and transitive relation R on U such that $H_1X = \overline{R}X$ for all $X \subseteq U$.

Proof. Using covering C of U, via left neighborhood of an element $x \in U$, we construct the binary R on U as follows.

$$l(x) = \{y \mid y \in K \in Md(x)\}.$$

It is clear that R is a reflexive relation. Since $H_1\{x\} = l(x)$, we have

$$H_1X = \bigcup_{x \in X} H_1\{x\} = \bigcup_{x \in X} l(x) = \overline{R}X.$$

Since $H_1(H_1X) = H_1X$ (Zhu & Wang, 2007), this means that $\overline{R}(\overline{R}X) = \overline{R}X$. This implies R is transitive. Thus R is a reflexive and transitive relation.

From a result in (Zhu & Wang, 2007), we have the following equivalent conditions:

Proposition 4. Let $\langle U, C \rangle$ be a covering approximation space. The following conditions are equivalent:
(1) $H_1(X \cup Y) = H_1X \cup H_1Y$ for all $X, Y \in P(U)$;
(2) $X \subseteq Y \Rightarrow H_1X \subseteq H_1Y$ for $X, Y \in P(U)$
(3) $(X \cap Y)_* = X_* \cap Y_*$ for all $X, Y \in P(U)$
(4) There exists a unique reflexive and transitive relation R on U such that $X_* = \underline{R}X$ for all $X \in P(U)$;
(5) There exists a unique reflexive and transitive relation S on U such that $H_1X = \overline{S}X$ for all $X \in P(U)$.

Proof. The equivalence of (1), (2), and (3) comes from (Zhu & Wang, 2007). From Proposition 3, (1) and (5) are equivalent. The equivalence of (3) and (4) comes from Proposition 2.

In the above proposition, for a covering, the corresponding lower covering approximation and the first type of upper covering approximation are generally represented by two different binary relations. The following proposition presents the conditions under which they are represented by one binary relation.

Proposition 5. Let $\langle U, C \rangle$ be a covering approximation space. The following conditions are equivalent:
(1) There exists a binary relation R on U such that $H_1X = \overline{R}X$ and $X_* = \underline{R}X$ for all $X \subseteq U$;
(2) $(X \cap Y)_* = X_* \cap Y_*$ and $H_1(-X) = -X_*$ for all $X, Y \subseteq U$;
(3) $H_1(X \cup Y) = H_1X \cup H_1Y$ and $H_1(-X) = -X_*$ for all $X, Y \subseteq U$;
(4) H_1 is monotone and $H_1(-X) = -X_*$ for all $X \subseteq U$.

SECOND TYPE OF UPPER APPROXIMATIONS

In this section we will show that there is a close relationship between the second type of upper approximations and upper approximations based on binary relations.

Definition 5. Let $\langle U, C \rangle$ be a covering approximation space. The second type of upper approximation H_2 of subset X of U is defined as (Zhu & Wang, 2007)

$$H_2X = \bigcup\{K \in C \mid K \cap X \neq \varnothing\}.$$

Proposition 6. Let $\langle U, C \rangle$ be a covering approximation space. Then there exists a unique reflexive and symmetric relation R on U such that $H_2X = \overline{R}X$ for all $X \subseteq U$.

Proof. Using covering C of U, via right neighborhood of an element $x \in U$, we can construct a binary relation R on U as follows:

$$r(x) = \bigcup \{K \mid x \in K \in C\}.$$

Note that R is a reflexive and symmetric relation on U. Now we prove that $H_2X = \overline{R}X$.

Indeed, suppose that $x \in H_2X$, by definition of the second type of upper approximation, $\exists K \in C$ such that $x \in K$ and $K \cap X \neq \varnothing$. Since $\varnothing \neq K \cap X \subseteq r(x) \cap X$ implies

$$r(x) \cap X \neq \varnothing. \text{ Thus } x \in \overline{R}X \text{ and } H_2X \subseteq \overline{R}X.$$

Conversely, if $x \in \overline{R}X$, then $r(x) \cap X \neq \varnothing$. This means that $\exists K \in C$, $K \subseteq r(x)$ such that $K \cap X \neq \varnothing$. $K \subseteq r(x)$ implies $x \in K$ and $x \in H_2X$. Therefore $\overline{R}X \subseteq H_2X$ and $\overline{R}X = H_2X$. The uniqueness of R comes from Proposition 1(7).

Corollary 1. Let $\langle U, C \rangle$ be a covering approximation space. Then $H_2X = \bigcup_{x \in X} r(x)$, where $r(x) = \bigcup \{K \mid x \in K \in C\}$.

Proposition 7. Let $\langle U, C \rangle$ be a covering approximation space. If $H_2(H_2X) = H_2X$ holds for all $X \subseteq U$, then there exists a unique equivalence relation R on U such that $H_2X = \overline{R}X$ for all $X \subseteq U$. That is, H_2 is Pawlak upper approximation. Moreover, $\{r(x) \mid x \in U\}$ is a partition of U, where $r(x) = \bigcup \{K \mid x \in K \in C\}$.

Proof. By proposition 6, there exists a unique reflexive and symmetric relation R on U such that $H_2X = \overline{R}X$. Note that $H_2(H_2X) = H_2X$ implies $R^2 = R$. Since $R^2 = R$, R is a transitive relation and R is an equivalence relation on U. For every $x \in U$, $r(x)$ becomes an

equivalence class containing x and $\{r(x) \mid x \in U\}$ forms a partition of U.

Proposition 8. Let $\langle U, C \rangle$ be a covering approximation space. If $H_2(-H_2X) = -H_2X$ holds for all $X \subseteq U$, then there exists a unique equivalence relation R on U such that $H_2X = \overline{R}X$ for all $X \subseteq U$. That is, H_2 is Pawlak upper approximation. Moreover, $\{r(x) \mid x \in U\}$ is a partition of U, where $r(x) = \bigcup \{K \mid x \in K \in C\}$.

Proof. By using Proposition 6, there exists a reflexive and symmetric binary relation R on U such that $H_2X = \overline{R}X$ for all $X \subseteq U$. Since $H_2(-H_2X) = -H_2X$, we have $\overline{R}\underline{R}(-X) = \underline{R}(-X)$. Note that $\overline{R}\underline{R}(-X) = \underline{R}(-X)$ implies $\overline{R}\underline{R} = \underline{R}$ and $\underline{R}\overline{R} = \overline{R}$. For all $x \in U$, $\overline{R}\{x\} = r(x)$. This means that $\underline{R}r(x) = r(x) = \overline{R}r(x)$. If $r(x) \cap r(y) \neq \varnothing$, then $x \in \overline{R}r(y)$, so $x \in \underline{R}r(y)$ and $r(x) \subseteq r(y)$. Similarly, $r(y) \subseteq r(x)$ and $r(x) = r(y)$. Thus $\{r(x) \mid x \in U\}$ is a partition of U and R is an equivalence relation on U.

Proposition 9. Let $\langle U, C \rangle$ be a covering approximation space. If $H_2(-X) = -X_*$ holds for all $X \subseteq U$, then the covering C of U is a partition of U.

Proof. By Proposition 2, 6, there exists a unique reflexive and symmetric binary relation R on U such that $H_2X = \overline{R}X$, $X_* = -(H_2(-X)) = -(\overline{R}(-X)) = \underline{R}X$ for all $X \subseteq U$. By Proposition 2, R is transitive, so R is an equivalence relation on U. By Proposition 6, $r(x) = \bigcup \{K \mid x \in K \in C\}$, that is, xRy if and only if there exists some $K \in C$ such that $x, y \in K$. By Proposition 2, $r(x) = \bigcap \{K \mid x \in K \in C\}$. Thus $r(x) \in C$ and C is a partition of U.

As we can see from Proposition 2 and Corollary 5, for a covering C, if $(X \cap Y)_* = X_* \cap Y_*$, there exist two reflexive and transitive relations R_1 and R_2 on U such that $H_2X = \overline{R_1}X$ and $X_* = \underline{R_2}X$ for all $X \subseteq U$. Then we want to know when R_1 and R_2 are identical for a covering C. We have the following conclusion about the above issue.

Proposition 10. Let $\langle U, C \rangle$ be a covering approximation space. If there exists a relation R on U such that $H_2 X = \overline{R}X$ and $X_* = \underline{R}X$ for all $X \subseteq U$, then C is a partition.

Proof. By duality of $\underline{R}$ and $\overline{R}$, $H_2(-X) = -X_*$. By Proposition 9, C is a partition of U.

THIRD TYPE OF UPPER APPROXIMATIONS

A third type of covering rough sets has been introduced in (Tsang, Chen, Lee, & Wang, 2004). The proposed third definition of upper approximations is considered to be more reasonable than those of the first and second types in certain environments.

Definition 6. Let $\langle U, C \rangle$ be a covering approximation space. The third type of covering upper approximation operation H_3 of subset X of U is defined as follows:

$$H_3 X = \bigcup \{ Md(x) \mid x \in X \}.$$

In this section we will show that there is also a close relationship between the third type of upper approximations and upper approximations based on binary relations.

Proposition 11. Let $\langle U, C \rangle$ be a covering approximation space. Then there exists a unique reflexive relation R on U such that $H_3 X = \overline{R}X$, for all $X \subseteq U$.

Proof. Using covering C, via left neighborhood of an element $x \in U$, we can construct a binary relation R on U as follows:

$$l(x) = \{ y \mid y \in K \in Md(x) \}$$

Note that R is a reflexive relation on U. By Proposition 1, we have $H_3 X = \overline{R}X$ and R is unique.

Proposition 12. (1) If $\langle U, C \rangle$ is a covering approximation space and $H_3(H_3 X) = H_3 X$ holds for all $X \subseteq U$, then there exists a unique reflexive and transitive relation R on U such that $H_3 X = \overline{R}X$ for all $X \subseteq U$.

(2) For each reflexive and transitive binary relation R on U, there exists a covering C of U such that $\overline{R}X = H_3 X$ for all $X \subseteq U$ and $H_3(H_3 X) = H_3 X$.

Proof. (1) From Proposition 11, there exists a unique reflexive relation R on U such that $H_3 X = \overline{R}X$ for all $X \subseteq U$. By $H_3(H_3 X) = H_3 X$, R is transitive.

(2) By using the reflexive and transitive binary relation R on U, we define $C = \{ l(x) \mid x \in U \}$, where $l(x)$ is the left neighborhood of $x \in U$. Since R is reflexive, we have $\bigcup_{x \in U} l(x) = U$, thus C is a covering of U. Since R is transitive, we obtain that if $x \in l(y)$, then $l(x) \subseteq l(y)$. Thus $Md(x) = l(x)$.

By definitions,

$$H_3 X = \bigcup_{x \in X} Md(x) = \bigcup_{x \in X} l(x) = \bigcup_{x \in X} \overline{R}\{x\} = \overline{R}(\bigcup_{x \in X} \{x\}) = \overline{R}X$$

Since R is reflexive and transitive, we obtain $H_3(H_3 X) = \overline{R}(\overline{R}X) = \overline{R}X = H_3 X$.

Proposition 13. Let $\langle U, C \rangle$ be a covering approximation space. If $H_3(-H_3 X) = -H_3 X$ holds for all $X \subseteq U$, then there exists a unique equivalence relation R on U such that $\overline{R}X = H_3 X$ for all $X \subseteq U$. That is, H_3 is Pawlak upper approximation. Moreover, $\{ l(x) \mid x \in U \}$ is a partition of U, where $l(x) = \{ y \mid y \in K \in Md(x) \}$.

Proof. By using Proposition 11, there exists a unique reflexive binary relation R on U such that $\overline{R}X = H_3X$ for all $X \subseteq U$. Since $H_3(-H_3X) = -H_3X$, we have $\overline{R}(-\overline{R}X) = -\overline{R}X$ and $\overline{R}\underline{R}(-X) = \underline{R}(-X)$. Note that $\overline{R}\underline{R}(-X) = \underline{R}(-X)$ implies $\overline{R}\underline{R} = \underline{R}$. Again from $\overline{R}\underline{R}(-X) = \underline{R}(-X)$, we have $\underline{R}\,\overline{R} = \overline{R}$.

Firstly, we prove that R is symmetric. If xRy, then $y \in r(x) \cap \underline{R}r(y)$. This means that $x \in \overline{R}(\underline{R}r(y)) = \underline{R}r(y) \subseteq r(y)$. Thus yRx and we have proved that R is symmetric. From the symmetric property of R, we have $l(x) = r(x)$ for all $x \in U$. Then we prove that $\overline{R}r(x) = \underline{R}r(x)$. By $\underline{R}\,\overline{R} = \overline{R}$, we have $\underline{R}r(x) = r(x)$, so $\overline{R}\underline{R}r(x) = \overline{R}r(x)$. By $\overline{R}\underline{R} = \underline{R}$, we have $\overline{R}r(x) = \underline{R}r(x)$.

At last, we prove that $\{l(x) \mid x \in U\}$ is a partition of U. If $r(x) \cap r(y) \neq \varnothing$, then $x \in \overline{R}r(x) = \underline{R}r(y)$, so $r(x) \subseteq r(y)$. Similarly, $r(y) \subseteq r(x)$ and $r(x) = r(y)$. Thus $\{l(x) \mid x \in U\}$ is a partition of U and R is an equivalence relation on U.

If the third covering upper and covering lower approximations are dual to each other, then we have the following conclusion.

Proposition 14. Let $\langle U, C\rangle$ be a covering approximation space. If $H_3(-X) = -X_*$ holds for all $X \subseteq U$, then there exists a unique reflexive and transitive relation R on U such that $X_* = \underline{R}X$ and $H_3X = \overline{R}X$ for all $X \subseteq U$.

Proof. By Proposition 11, there exists a unique reflexive relation R on U such that $H_3X = \overline{R}X$ for all $X \subseteq U$. Condition $H_3(-X) = -X_*$ implies $X_* = \underline{R}X$. $(X_*)_* = X_*$ guarantees that R is transitive.

FORTH TYPE OF UPPER APPROXIMATIONS

The fourth type of covering rough set was first introduced in (Zhu & Wang, 2006). In their paper, Zhu and Wang presented the basic properties, explored the interdependency between the lower and the upper approximation operations, and established the conditions under which two coverings generate the same upper approximation operation.

Definition 7. (Zhu and Wang, 2006) Let $\langle U, C\rangle$ be covering approximation space. For any given $X \in P(U)$, the set $H_4X = X_* \cup \{K \in C \mid K \cap (X - X_*) \neq \varnothing\}$ is called the fourth type of covering upper approximation of X.

Since Property $H_4(X \cup Y) = H_4X \cup H_4Y$ does not hold for the fourth type of covering upper approximation (Zhu and Wang, 2007), H_4 cannot be represented as R for a binary relation. However, if $H_4(X \cup Y) = H_4X \cup H_4Y$ holds for all $X \in P(U)$, we have the following result:

Proposition 15. Let $\langle U, C\rangle$ be covering approximation space. If $H_4(X \cup Y) = H_4X \cup H_4Y$ holds for all $X \in P(U)$, then there exists a unique reflexive and transitive relation R on U such that $H_4X = \overline{R}X$ for all $X \in P(U)$.

Proof. Using the covering C of U, via left neighborhood, we can construct a relation R on U as follows.

$$l(x) = \begin{cases} \{x\}, & \{x\} \in C \\ \bigcup\{K \in C \mid x \in K\}, & \{x\} \notin C \end{cases}.$$

Computing $H_4\{x\}$ directly from the definition, we obtain the $H_4\{x\} = l(x)$. Thus

$$H_4\{x\} = H_4(\cup_{x \in X}\{x\}) = \cup_{x \in X}H_4\{x\} = \cup_{x \in X}l(x) = \cup_{x \in X}\overline{R}\{x\} = \overline{R}(\cup_{x \in X}\{x\}) = \overline{R}X$$

.

$X \subseteq H_4X$ (Zhu and Wang, 2007) guarantees that R is reflexive and $H_4(H_4X) = H_4X$ (Zhu & Wang, 2007) guarantees that R is transitive.

Similar to results in Section 4, we have the following results:

Corollary 2. Let $\langle U, C \rangle$ be a covering approximation space. The following conditions are equivalent:

(1) $H_4(X \cup Y) = H_4X \cup H_4Y$ holds for all $X, Y \in P(U)$;

(2) $X \subseteq Y \Rightarrow H_4X \subseteq H_4Y$;

(3) $(X \cap Y)_* = X_* \cap Y_*$ holds for all $X, Y \in P(U)$;

(4) There exists a unique reflexive and transitive relation R on U such that $X_* = \underline{R}X$ for all $X \in P(U)$;

(5) There exists a unique reflexive and transitive relation S on U such that $H_4X = \overline{S}X$ for all $X \in P(U)$.

Proposition 16. Let $\langle U, C \rangle$ be a covering approximation space. There exists a binary relation R_1 on U such that $H_4X = \overline{R_1}X$ for all $X \in P(U)$ if and only if there exists a binary relation R_2 on U such that $X_* = \underline{R_2}X$ for all $X \in P(U)$.

Proposition 17. Let $\langle U, C \rangle$ be a covering approximation space. The following conditions are equivalent:

(1) There exists a binary relation R on U such that $H_4X = \overline{R}X$ and $X_* = \underline{R}X$ for all $X \in P(U)$;

(2) $(X \cap Y)_* = X_* \cap Y_*$ and $H_4(-X) = -X_*$ for all $X, Y \in P(U)$;

(3) $H_4(X \cup Y) = H_4X \cup H_4Y$ and $H_4(-X) = -X_*$ for all $X, Y \in P(U)$;

(4) H_4 is monotone and $H_4(-X) = -X_*$ for all $X \in P(U)$.

FIFTH TYPE OF UPPER APPROXIMATIONS

The fifth type of covering rough set was first introduced by (Zhu, 2007) from the topological point of view. Because the core concept for topology is the neighborhood of a point, we introduce the neighborhood concept into covering rough sets.

Definition 8. Let $\langle U, C \rangle$ be a covering approximation space. For any $x \in U$, we define the neighborhood of x as follows:

$$N(x) = \bigcap \{K \mid x \in K \in C\}.$$

Definition 9. Let $\langle U, C \rangle$ be a covering approximation space. The fifth type of upper approximation operation H_5 of subset X of U is defined as follows:

$$H_5X = X_* \cup \left(\bigcup_{x \in X - X_*} N(x) \right).$$

Zhu has proved the following proposition in (Zhu, 2007).

Proposition 18. (Zhu, 2007) Let $\langle U, C \rangle$ be a covering approximation space. For any $X \in P(U)$, $H_5X = \bigcup_{x \in X} N(x)$.

Proposition 19. Let $\langle U, C \rangle$ be a covering approximation space. Then there exists a unique reflexive and transitive binary relation R on U such that $H_5X = \overline{R}X$ for all $X \in P(U)$. Conversely, for each reflexive and transitive binary relation R on U, there exists a covering approximation space $\langle U, C \rangle$ such that $\overline{R}X = H_5X$ for all c.

Proof. By using covering C of U, we define the binary relation R on U as follows.

$$xRy \Leftrightarrow x \in N(y).$$

It is clear that R is reflexive. By Proposition 1 and Proposition 18, we have $H_5 X = \overline{R}X$ for all $X \in P(U)$. $H_5(H_5 X) = H_5 X$ implies $\overline{R}(\overline{R}X) = \overline{R}X$, and $\overline{R}(\overline{R}X) = \overline{R}X$ guarantees that R is transitive. The uniqueness of R comes directly from Proposition 1 (7).

Conversely, by using the reflexive and transitive binary relation R on U, we define $C = \{l(x) \mid x \in U\}$, where $l(x)$ is the left neighborhood of $x \in U$. Since R is reflexive, we have $\bigcup_{x \in X} l(x) = U$, thus C is a covering of U. Now we prove that $x \in U, N(x) = l(x)$.

Since R is transitive, we obtain that if $x \in l(y)$, then $l(x) \subseteq l(y)$. Since R is reflexive, we have

$$N(x) = \bigcap\{K \mid x \in K \in C\} = \bigcap\{l(y) \mid x \in l(y)\} = l(x)$$

this means that $H_5\{x\} = N(x) = l(x) = \overline{R}\{x\}$. Therefore

$$H_5 X = \bigcup_{x \in X} N(x) = \bigcup_{x \in X} \overline{R}\{x\} = \overline{R}(\bigcup_{x \in X}\{x\}) = \overline{R}X$$

Remark. In Proposition 19, the covering generated by a reflexive and transitive relation is not unique as shown in the following example.

Example 1. Let $U = \{a, b, c, d, e\}$, $K_1 = \{a, b\}$, $K_2 = \{c, d\}$, $K_3 = \{e\}$, $K_4 = \{a, b, e\}$, $C_1 = \{K_1, K_2, K_3\}$ and $C_2 = \{K_1, K_2, K_3, K_4\}$. Clearly, C_1, C_2 are different coverings of U, but C_1, C_2 generate the same binary relation.

Unlike Pawlak rough sets, the covering lower approximations and the fifth type of upper approximations are not dual in general as we can see from the counterexample in (Zhu, 2007). If the covering lower approximations and the fourth type of upper approximations are dual to each other, we have the following proposition.

Proposition 20. Let $\langle U, C \rangle$ be a covering approximation space. If the covering lower approximation X_* of $X \in P(U)$ and the fifth type of upper approximation $H_5 X$ of $X \in P(U)$ are dual to each other, then $(X_*, H_5 X)$ is the rough set in the sense of Pawlak. That is, there exists a unique equivalence relation R on U such that $X_* = \underline{R}X$ and $H_5 X = \overline{R}X$ for all $X \in P(U)$ and $\{N(x) \mid x \in U\}$ is a partition of U.

Proof. By Proposition 19, there exists a unique reflexive and transitive relation R on U such that $H_5 X = \overline{R}X$, where the relation R on U is defined by left neighborhood of an element $x \in U$,

$$l(x) = \bigcap\{K \mid x \in K \in C\} = N(x).$$

Since $X_* = -H_5(-X) = -\overline{R}(-X) = \underline{R}X$ for all $X \in P(U)$, we have $(X \cap Y)_* = X_* \cap Y_*$. By Proposition 2, the relation R on U is defined by right neighborhood of an element $x \in U$,

$$r(x) = \bigcap\{K \mid x \in K \in C\}.$$

Thus $l(x) = r(x)$ holds for all $x \in U$ and R is symmetric. Therefore R is an equivalence relation on U.

CONCLUSION

The covering rough set model is an extension to Pawlak rough sets. It is more flexible in dealing with uncertainty and granularity in information systems. In this paper we have studied five types of covering rough sets. Under additional assumption we have shown that the first and fourth covering upper approximations can be generated by a binary relation. We made comparisons between the other three covering rough sets and rough sets based on binary relations. The results presented in this paper can hopefully provide more insight into and a better understanding of rough set theory.

ACKNOWLEDGMENT

This work is partially supported by the National Natural Science Foundation of China (No. 60973148 & No. 60873077) and the Key Project of the Chinese Ministry of Education (No. 108133). The authors greatly appreciate the valuable comments of Professor T.Y. Lin.

REFERENCES

Bonikowski, Z., Bryniarski, E., & Wybraniec, U. (1998). Extensions and intentions in the rough set theory. *Information Sciences, 107*, 149–167. doi:10.1016/S0020-0255(97)10046-9

Chen, D., Zhang, W., Yeung, D., & Tsang, E. (2006). Rough approximations on a complete completely distributive lattice with applications to generalized rough sets. *Information Sciences, 176*, 1829–1848. doi:10.1016/j.ins.2005.05.009

Kondo, M. (2005). *Algebraic approach to generalized rough sets (. LNAI, 3641*, 132–140.

Kondo, M. (2006). On the structure of generalized rough sets. *Information Sciences, 176*, 589–600. doi:10.1016/j.ins.2005.01.001

Lashin, E. F., Kozae, A. M., Khadra, A. A., & Medhat, T. (2005). Rough set theory for topological spaces. *International Journal of Approximate Reasoning, 40*, 35–43. doi:10.1016/j.ijar.2004.11.007

Lin, T. Y. (1989). Neighborhood Systems and approximation in database and Knowledge buse systems. In *Proceedings of the Fourth International symposium on Methodologies of intelligent systems* (pp. 75-86).

Lin, T. Y. (1992). Topological and fuzzy rough sets . In Slowinski, R. (Ed.), *Intelligent Decision support: Hand book of Applications and Advances of rough set theory* (pp. 287–304). London: Kluwer Academic Publishers.

Lin, T. Y. (1998). Granular Computing on Binary Relations I: Data Mining and Neighborhood Systems . In Skowron, A., & Polkowski, L. (Eds.), *Rough Sets In Knowledge Discovery* (pp. 107–121). Berlin: Physica Verlag.

Lin, T. Y. (1998). Granular Computing on Binary Relations II: Rough Set Representations and Belief Functions . In Skowron, A., & Polkowski, L. (Eds.), *Rough Sets In Knowledge Discovery* (pp. 121–140). Berlin: Physica Verlag.

Lin, T. Y., Huang, K. J., Liu, Q., & Chen, W. (1990). Rough sets, neighborhood systems and approximation. In *Proceedings of the Fifth International Symposium on Methodologies of Intelligent Systems*, Knoxville, Tennessee (pp. 130-141).

Lin, T. Y., & Liu, Q. (1994). Rough approximate operators-Axiomatic Rough Set Theory . In Ziarko, W. P. (Ed.), *Rough sets, fuzzy sets and knowledge Discovery* (pp. 256–260). London: Springer Verlag.

Liu, G. L. (2006). The axiomatization of the rough set upper approximation operations. *Fundamenta Informaticae, 69*, 331–342.

Liu, G. L. (2008). Generalized rough sets over fuzzy lattices. *Information Sciences, 178*, 1651–1662. doi:10.1016/j.ins.2007.11.010

Liu, G. L., & Zhu, W. (2008). The algebraic structures of generalized rough set theory. *Information Sciences, 178*(21), 4105–4113. doi:10.1016/j.ins.2008.06.021

Masulli, F., & Petrosino, A. (2006). Advances in fuzzy sets and rough sets. *International Journal of Approximate Reasoning, 41,* 75–76. doi:10.1016/j.ijar.2005.06.010

Pawlak, Z. (1982). Rough sets. *International Journal of Computer and Information Sciences, 11,* 341–356. doi:10.1007/BF01001956

Pawlak, Z. (1991). *Rough sets: Theoretical aspects of reasoning about data.* Boston: Kluwer Academic Publishers.

Pei, D. (2005). A generalized model of fuzzy rough sets. *International Journal of General Systems, 34*(5), 603–613. doi:10.1080/03081070500096010

Polkowski, L., & Skowron, A. (Eds.). (1998). *Rough sets in knowledge discovery (Vol. 1).* Heidelberg, Germany: Physica Verlag.

Polkowski, L., & Skowron, A. (Eds.). (1998). *Rough sets in knowledge discovery (Vol. 2).* Heidelberg, Germany: Physica Verlag.

Qi, G., & Liu, W. (2004). Rough operations on Boolean algebras. *Information Sciences, 173,* 49–63. doi:10.1016/j.ins.2004.06.006

Radzikowska, A. M., & Kerre, E. E. (2004). Fuzzy rough sets based on residuated lattices. In *Transactions on Rough Sets* (LNCS 3135, pp. 278-296).

Tsang, E., Cheng, D., Lee, J., & Yeung, D. (2004). On the upper approximations of covering generalized rough sets. In *Proceedings of the Third International Conference on Machine Learning and Cybernetics* (pp. 4200-4203).

Yeung, D., Chen, D., Tsang, E., Lee, J., & Xizhao, W. (2005). On the generalization of fuzzy rough sets. *IEEE Transactions on Fuzzy Systems, 13*(3), 343–361. doi:10.1109/TFUZZ.2004.841734

Zhu, W. (2007). Topological approaches to covering rough sets. *Information Sciences, 177*(6), 1499–1508. doi:10.1016/j.ins.2006.06.009

Zhu, W. (2007). Generalized rough sets based on relations. *Information Sciences, 177*(22), 4997–5011. doi:10.1016/j.ins.2007.05.037

Zhu, W., & Wang, F. Y. (2006). A new type of covering rough sets. In *Proceedings of the Third IEEE International Conference on Intelligent System* (pp. 444-449).

Zhu, W., & Wang, F. Y. (2007). On three types of covering rough sets. *IEEE Transactions on Knowledge and Data Engineering, 19*(8), 1131–1144. doi:10.1109/TKDE.2007.1044

This work was previously published in volume 4, issue 2 of the International Journal of Cognitive Informatics and Natural Intelligence, edited by Yingxu Wang, pp. 61-74, copyright 2010 by IGI Publishing (an imprint of IGI Global).

Chapter 12
Further Considerations of Classification–Oriented and Approximation–Oriented Rough Sets in Generalized Settings

Masahiro Inuiguchi
Osaka University, Japan

ABSTRACT

Rough sets can be interpreted in two ways: classification of objects and approximation of a set. From this point of view, classification-oriented and approximation-oriented rough sets have been proposed. In this paper, the author reconsiders those two kinds of rough sets with reviewing their definitions, properties and relations. The author describes that rough sets based on positive and negative extensive relations are mathematically equivalent but it is important to consider both because they obtained positive and negative extensive relations are not always in inverse relation in the real world. The difference in size of granules between union-based and intersection-based approximations is emphasized. Moreover, the types of decision rules associated with those rough sets are shown.

INTRODUCTION

The usefulness and efficiency of rough sets in analyses of data, information, decision and conflict have been demonstrated in the literatures (Lin, 1989a; Pawlak, 1991; Alpigini et al., 2002;

Inuiguchi et al., 2003a; Wang et al., 2003). Rough set approaches have been developed mainly under equivalence relations. In order to enhance the ability of the analysis, as well as from the mathematical interests, rough sets have been generalized by many researchers (for example, (Lin, 1989a; Lin, 1989b; Dubois et al., 1990; Dubois et al., 1992; Lin, 1992; Ziarko, 1993; Yao et al., 1996;

DOI: 10.4018/978-1-4666-1743-8.ch012

Bonikowski, 1998; Greco et al., 1999; Słowiński et al., 2000; Greco et al., 2003; Inuiguchi et al., 2003b; Inuiguchi et al., 2003c)). Among listed references, Ziarko (1993) generalized rough sets by parameterizing the accuracy while the others generalized rough sets by extending the equivalence relation of approximation space. In this paper, we concentrate on the latter generalizations.

Rough sets are often applied to analysis of decision tables, a collection of examples about object classifications by means of condition attributes. Considering classical rough set approaches to analysis of decision tables, the equivalence relation induced from the equality of condition attribute values implies that attributes are all nominal. Because of this assumption, unreasonable results for human intuition have been exemplified when some attributes are ordinal (Greco et al., 1999). To overcome the unreasonableness caused by the ordinal property, the dominance-based rough set approach has been proposed by Greco et al. (1999). Moreover, when the decision table includes missing values, the classical rough set approach does not work sufficiently. The generalization of rough sets is an interesting topic not only in practical point of view but also in mathematical point of view. Along this direction, rough sets have been generalized under neighborhood systems (Lin, 1989a; Lin, 1989b; Lin, 1992), similarity relations (Słowiński et al., 2000; Inuiguchi et al., 2003b), covers (Bonikowski, 1998; Inuiguchi et al., 2003b) and general relations (Yao et al., 1996). The neighborhood systems (Lin, 1989a; Lin, 1989b; Lin, 1992) are the most general case that includes all these generalizations. Those results demonstrate a very far reaching generalization.

Considering applications of rough sets in the generalized setting, the interpretation of rough sets plays an important role. This is because any mathematical model cannot be properly applied without its interpretation. Two interpretations have been implicitly considered in the classical rough sets. One is rough set as classification of objects into positive, negative and boundary regions of a given concept. The other is rough set as approximation of a set by means of elementary sets. Those different interpretations are found in names 'positive region' (resp. 'possible region') and 'lower approximation' (resp. upper approximation') in the classical rough sets. The former rough sets are called *classification-oriented* while the latter rough sets are called *approximation-oriented*. The generalizations of rough sets under those interpretations have been proposed by Inuiguchi (Inuiguchi, 2004).

In this paper, these two kinds of rough sets are reconsidered. Reviewing the definitions and fundamental properties, we remark a connection between positively and negatively extensive relationships and the difference of the sizes of granules in union-based and intersection-based approximations. Moreover, we investigate the types of decision rules corresponding to two kinds of rough sets. We newly give the decision rules corresponding to possible and conceivable regions and upper approximations. We demonstrate the differences and similarities of classification- and approximation-oriented rough sets by a numerical example.

Classical rough sets are briefly introduced. Then define classification- and approximation-oriented rough sets and give the fundamental properties. The relationships between those two kinds of rough sets are shown. We also discuss the types of decision rules corresponding to the two kinds of rough sets. The differences of those rough sets are illustrated by a numerical example. Finally, we give the concluding remarks.

THE CLASSICAL ROUGH SETS

Let R be an equivalence relation in the finite universe U, i.e., $R \subseteq U \times U$. In rough set literature, R is referred to as an indiscernibility relation and a pair (U, R) is called an approximation space. By the equivalence relation R, U can be partitioned into a collection of equivalence classes or elementary sets, $U \mid R = \{E_1, E_2, \&, E_p\}$. Define $R(x) = \{y \in U \mid (y,x) \in R\}$. Then we have $x \in E_i$ if and only if $E_i = R(x)$. Note that $U \mid R = \{R(x) \mid x \in U\}$.

Let X be a subset of U. Using $R(x)$, a rough set of X is defined by a pair of the following lower and upper approximations:

$$R_*(X) = \{x \in X \mid R(x) \subseteq X\} = U - \bigcup\{R(y) \mid y \in U - X\}$$
$$= \bigcup\{E_i \mid E_i \subseteq X, \ i = 1,2,...,p\}$$
$$= \bigcup\left\{\bigcap_{i \in I}(U - E_i)\Big|\bigcap_{i \in I}(U - E_i) \subseteq X, \ I \subseteq \{1,2,...,p\}\right\},$$
$$(1)$$

$$R^*(X) = \bigcup\{R(x) \mid x \in X\} = U - \bigcup\{y \in U - X \mid R(y) \subseteq U - X\}$$
$$= \bigcap\left\{\bigcup_{i \in I}E_i\Big|\bigcup_{i \in I}E_i \supseteq X, \ I \subseteq \{1,2,...,p\}\right\}$$
$$= \bigcap\{U - E_i \mid U - E_i \supseteq X\}.$$
$$(2)$$

Let us interpret $R(x)$ as a set of objects we intuitively expect as members of X from the fact $x \in X$. Then, from the first expression of $R_*(X)$ in (1), $R_*(X)$ is interpreted as a set of objects which are consistent with our intuition that $R(x) \subseteq X$ if $x \in X$. Under the same interpretation of $R(x)$, $R^*(X)$ is interpreted as a set of objects which can be intuitively expected as members of X from the first expression of $R^*(X)$ in (2). In other words, $R_*(X)$ and $R^*(X)$ show positive (consistent) and possible members of X. Moreover, $R^*(X) - R_*(X)$ and $U - R^*(X)$ show ambiguous (boundary) and negative members of X. In this way, a rough set classifies objects of U into three classes, i.e., positive, negative and boundary regions.

On the contrary let us interpret $R(x)$ as a set of objects we intuitively expect as members of $U - X$ from the fact $x \in U - X$. In the same way as previous discussion, $\bigcup\{R(y) \mid y \in U - X\}$ and $\{y \in U - X \mid R(y) \subseteq U - X\}$ show possible and positive members of $U - X$, respectively. From

the second expression of $R_*(X)$ in (1), $R_*(X)$ can be regarded as a set of impossible members of $U - X$. In other words, $R_*(X)$ show certain members of X. Similarly, from the second expression of $R^*(X)$ in (2), $R^*(X)$ can be regarded as a set of non-positive members of $U - X$. Namely, $R^*(X)$ show conceivable members of X. $R^*(X) - R_*(X)$ and $U - R^*(X)$ show border and inconceivable members of X. In this case, a rough set again classifies objects of U into three classes, i.e., certain, inconceivable and border regions.

From the third expression of $R_*(X)$ in (1), $R_*(X)$ is the best approximation of X by means of the union of elementary sets E_i such that $E_i \subseteq X$. On the other hand, from the third expression of $R^*(X)$ in (2), $R^*(X)$ is the minimal superset of X by means of the union of elementary sets E_i.

Finally, from the fourth expression of $R_*(X)$ in (1), $R_*(X)$ is the maximal subset of X by means of the intersection of complements of elementary sets $U - E_i$. From the fourth expression of $R^*(X)$ in (2), $R^*(X)$ is the best approximation of X by means of the intersection of complements of elementary sets $U - E_i$ such that $U - E_i \supseteq X$.

We introduced only four kinds of expressions of lower and upper approximations but there are other many expressions (Lin, 1992; Yao et al., 1996; Słowiński, 2000; Inuiguchi et al., 2003b). The interpretation of rough sets depends on the expression of lower and upper approximations. Thus we may have more interpretations by adopting the other expressions. However the interpretations described above seem appropriate for applications of rough sets. Those interpretations can be divided into two categories: interpretation of rough sets as classification of objects and interpretation of rough sets as approximation of a set.

The fundamental properties listed in Table 1 are satisfied with the lower and upper approximations in the classical rough sets.

Table 1. Fundamental properties of rough sets

(i)	$R_*(X) \subseteq X \subseteq R^*(X)$.
(ii)	$R_*(\varnothing) = R^*(\varnothing) = \varnothing$, $R_*(U) = R^*(U) = U$.
(iii)	$R_*(X \cap Y) = R_*(X) \cap R_*(Y)$, $R^*(X \cup Y) = R^*(X) \cup R^*(Y)$.
(iv)	$X \subseteq Y$ implies $R_*(X) \subseteq R_*(Y)$, $X \subseteq Y$ implies $R^*(X) \subseteq R^*(Y)$.
(v)	$R_*(X \cup Y) \supseteq R_*(X) \cup R_*(Y)$, $R^*(X \cap Y) \subseteq R^*(X) \cap R^*(Y)$.
(vi)	$R_*(U - X) = U - R^*(X)$, $R^*(U - X) = U - R_*(X)$.
(vii)	$R_*(R_*(X)) = R^*(R_*(X)) = R_*(X)$, $R^*(R^*(X)) = R_*(R^*(X)) = R^*(X)$.

CLASSIFICATION-ORIENTED GENERALIZATION

In this generalization, we assume that there exists a relation $P \subseteq U \times U$ such that $P(x) = \{y \in U \mid (y,x) \in P\}$ means a set of objects we intuitively expect as members of $X \subseteq U$ from the fact $x \in X$. Then if $P(x) \subseteq X$ for an object $x \in X$ then there is no objection against $x \in X$. In this case, $x \in X$ is consistent with the intuition obtained from the relation P. Such an object $x \in X$ can be considered as a positive member of X. Hence the positive region of X can be defined as

$$P_*(X) = \{x \in X \mid P(x) \subseteq X\}. \qquad (3)$$

On the other hand, by the intuition from the relation P, an object $y \in P(x)$ for $x \in X$ can be a member of X. Namely, such an object $y \in U$ is a possible member of X. Moreover, every object $x \in X$ is evidently a possible member of X. Hence the possible region of X can be defined as

$$P^*(X) = X \cup \bigcup \{P(x) \mid x \in X\}. \qquad (4)$$

Using the positive region $P_*(X)$ and the possible region $P^*(X)$, we can define a rough set of X as a pair $(P_*(X), P^*(X))$. We call such rough sets as *classification-oriented rough sets under a positively extensive relation* P of X (for short *CP-rough sets*).

Since the relation P depends on the meaning of a set X, to define a CP-rough set of $U - X$, we should introduce another relation $Q \subseteq U \times U$ such that $Q(x) = \{y \in U \mid (y,x) \in Q\}$ means a set of objects we intuitively identify as members of $U - X$ from the fact $x \in U - X$. Using Q we have positive and possible regions of $U - X$ by

$$Q_*(U - X) = \{x \in U - X \mid Q(x) \subseteq U - X\}, \qquad (5)$$

$$Q^*(U - X) = (U - X) \cup \bigcup \{Q(x) \mid x \in U - X\}. \qquad (6)$$

Using $Q_*(X)$ and $Q^*(X)$, we can define certain and conceivable regions of X by

$$\bar{Q}_*(X) = U - Q^*(U - X) = X \cap \left(U - \bigcup \{Q(x) \mid x \in U - X\}\right), \qquad (7)$$

$$\bar{Q}^*(X) = U - Q_*(U - X) = U - \{x \in U - X \mid Q(x) \subseteq U - X\}.$$

$$(8)$$

We can define another rough set of X as a pair $(\bar{Q}_*(X), \bar{Q}^*(X))$ with the certain region $\bar{Q}_*(X)$ and the conceivable region $\bar{Q}^*(X)$. We call this type of rough sets as *classification-oriented rough sets under a negatively extensive relation Q of X* (for short *CN-rough sets*).

Similar definitions to CP- and CN-rough sets can be found in (Lin, 1992; Yao et al., 1996; Greco et al., 1999; Słowiński et al., 2000; Inuiguchi et al., 2003b). In the definitions we take intersection and union with X, then it looks different from the previous definitions (Greco et al., 1999; Słowiński et al., 2000; Inuiguchi et al., 2003b). However, they are essentially same as those if we reflexivize the given relations. Namely, if we define $\hat{P} = P \cup \{(x,x) \mid x \in X\}$, we have $P_*(X) = \{x \in X \mid \hat{P}(x) \subseteq X\}$ and $P^*(X) = \bigcup \{\hat{P}(x) \mid x \in X\}$, i.e., $P_*(X)$ and $P^*(X)$ are the same as lower and upper approximations with respect to $\hat{P}$ in (Greco et al., 1999).

The fundamental properties of CP- and CN-rough sets are shown in Table 2 (see Inuiguchi (2004) for the proof).

Remark 1. In the real world problems, we may obtain only partial information about positively extensive relation or a negatively extensive relation. However, having a positively extensive relation is equivalent to having a negatively extensive relation. This can be explained as follows. Let $x \in X$ and Q be a negatively extensive relation of X. Then we cannot expect there exists $y \notin X$ such that $(x,y) \in Q$, because if there exists such y, $x \in X$ has a conflict with the negatively extensive relation. In other words, the inverse of Q is a positively extensive relation. Indeed, this fact is reflected on the fundamental property (vi) in Table 2.

We may find a positively extensive relation and a negatively extensive relation, independently, in the real world, where 'independence' means that the positively extensive relation is not the inverse of the negatively extensive relation. For example, let us consider the judgment of acceptance based on two independent test scores x and y under the following two published rules: (1) the larger x and y, the more it is preferred and (2) if sums of scores of two candidates are same and if the orders between scores x and y are not reversed, the better balanced one is preferred. Those two rules imply that the boundary curve will be selected between L-shaped curve $\{(x,y) \in \mathbf{R}^2 \mid \min(x,y) = r\}$ and a line $\{(x,y) \in \mathbf{R}^2 \mid x + y = 2r\}$ with an unknown real number r (see Figure 1). Under the information we may directly find a positively extensive relation P as

$$\begin{aligned} P = \{&(u_1, u_2) \in U \times U \mid x(u_1) \geq x(u_2), y(u_1) \geq y(u_2)\} \\ &\cup \{(u_1, u_2) \in U \times U \mid x(u_1) + y(u_1) = x(u_2) + y(u_2), \\ &\quad (x(u_1) - y(u_1))(x(u_2) - y(u_2)) \geq 0, \mid x(u_1) - y(u_1) \mid \leq \mid x(u_2) - y(u_2) \mid\} \end{aligned}$$

and a negatively extensive relation Q as

$$\begin{aligned} Q = \{&(u_1, u_2) \in U \times U \mid x(u_1) \leq x(u_2), y(u_1) \leq y(u_2)\} \\ &\cup \{(u_1, u_2) \in U \times U \mid x(u_1) + y(u_1) \leq 2\min(x(u_2), y(u_2))\} \\ &\cup \{(u_1, u_2) \in U \times U \mid x(u_1) + y(u_1) = x(u_2) + y(u_2), \\ &\quad (x(u_1) - y(u_1))(x(u_2) - y(u_2)) \geq 0, \mid x(u_1) - y(u_1) \mid \geq \mid x(u_2) - y(u_2) \mid\}. \end{aligned}$$

In this case, we have $P \neq Q^{-1}$ and then they are independent. Note that P and Q described above are not transitive, Under the information (1) and (2), we easily accept that even if $\mid x(u_1) - y(u_1) \mid > \mid x(u_2) - y(u_2) \mid$, if there exists s and t such that $x(u_1) \geq x$, $y(u_1) \geq t$, $s + t = x(u_2) + y(u_2)$, $(s - t)(x(u_2) - y(u_2)) \geq 0$ and $\mid s - t \mid \leq \mid x(u_2) - y(u_2) \mid$ then u_1 is preferred to u_2. Considering this the transitive closure of P could be also considered as positively extensive relation. Similar assertion is valid for the negatively extensive relation.

Table 2. Fundamental properties of CP- and CN-rough sets

(i)	$P_*(X) \subseteq X \subseteq P^*(X)$, $\bar{Q}_*(X) \subseteq X \subseteq \bar{Q}^*(X)$.
(ii)	$P_*(\varnothing) = P^*(\varnothing) = \varnothing$, $P_*(U) = P^*(U) = U$, $\bar{Q}_*(\varnothing) = \bar{Q}^*(\varnothing) = \varnothing$, $\bar{Q}_*(U) = \bar{Q}^*(U) = U$.
(iii)	$P_*(X \cap Y) = P_*(X) \cap P_*(Y)$, $P^*(X \cup Y) = P^*(X) \cup P^*(Y)$, $\bar{Q}_*(X \cap Y) = \bar{Q}_*(X) \cap \bar{Q}_*(Y)$, $\bar{Q}^*(X \cup Y) = \bar{Q}^*(X) \cup \bar{Q}^*(Y)$.
(iv)	$X \subseteq Y$ implies $P_*(X) \subseteq P_*(Y)$, $X \subseteq Y$ implies $P^*(X) \subseteq P^*(Y)$, $X \subseteq Y$ implies $\bar{Q}_*(X) \subseteq \bar{Q}_*(Y)$, $X \subseteq Y$ implies $\bar{Q}^*(X) \subseteq \bar{Q}^*(Y)$.
(v)	$P_*(X \cup Y) \supseteq P_*(X) \cup P_*(Y)$, $P^*(X \cap Y) \subseteq P^*(X) \cap P^*(Y)$, $\bar{Q}_*(X \cup Y) \supseteq \bar{Q}_*(X) \cup \bar{Q}_*(Y)$, $\bar{Q}^*(X \cap Y) \subseteq \bar{Q}^*(X) \cap \bar{Q}^*(Y)$
(vi)	When Q is the inverse of P, i.e., $(x, y) \in P$ if and only if $(y, x) \in Q$, $P^*(X) = U - Q_*(U - X) = \bar{Q}^*(X)$, $P_*(X) = U - Q^*(U - X) = \bar{Q}_*(X)$.
(vii)	$X \supseteq P^*(P_*(X)) \supseteq P_*(X) \supseteq P_*(P_*(X))$, $X \subseteq P_*(P^*(X)) \subseteq P^*(X) \subseteq P^*(P^*(X))$, $X \supseteq \bar{Q}^*(\bar{Q}_*(X)) \supseteq \bar{Q}_*(X) \supseteq \bar{Q}_*(\bar{Q}_*(X))$, $X \subseteq \bar{Q}_*(\bar{Q}^*(X)) \subseteq \bar{Q}^*(X) \subseteq \bar{Q}^*(\bar{Q}^*(X))$. When P is transitive, $P_*(P_*(X)) = P_*(X)$, $P^*(P^*(X)) = P^*(X)$. When Q is transitive, $\bar{Q}_*(\bar{Q}_*(X)) = \bar{Q}_*(X)$, $\bar{Q}^*(\bar{Q}^*(X)) = \bar{Q}^*(X)$. When P is reflexive and transitive, $P^*(P_*(X)) = P_*(X) = P_*(P_*(X))$, $P_*(P^*(X)) = P^*(X) = P^*(P^*(X))$. When Q is reflexive and transitive, $\bar{Q}^*(\bar{Q}_*(X)) = \bar{Q}_*(X) = \bar{Q}_*(\bar{Q}_*(X))$, $\bar{Q}_*(\bar{Q}^*(X)) = \bar{Q}^*(X) = \bar{Q}^*(\bar{Q}^*(X))$.

In cases such that a positively extensive relation and a negatively extensive relation are obtained independently, using both relations to define positive/certain and possible/conceivable regions would be advantageous in finding inconsistency. Concerning on this, we have the following useful properties:

$$(P \cup Q^{-1})_*(X) = \overline{(P^{-1} \cup Q)}_*(X) = P_*(X) \cap \bar{Q}_*(X), \tag{9}$$

$$(P \cup Q^{-1})^*(X) = \overline{(P^{-1} \cup Q)}^*(X) = P^*(X) \cup \bar{Q}^*(X), \tag{10}$$

Figure 1. The boundary curve

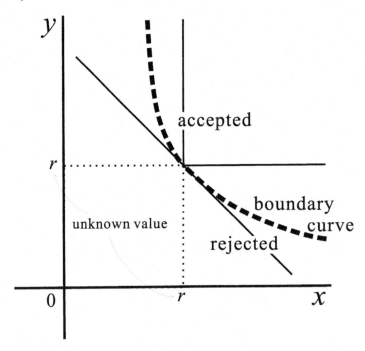

where P^{-1} and Q^{-1} are inverse relations of P and Q, respectively. Those equations imply that the positive/ certain and possible/conceivable regions defined by using both positively and negatively extensive relations can be obtained from positive, certain, possible and conceivable regions defined independently. Those equations show that positive and certain regions become smaller while possible and conceivable regions become larger by using both relations.

In the example depicted by Figure 1, we have

$$P^{-1} = \{(u_1, u_2) \in U \times U \mid x(u_1) \leq x(u_2), y(u_1) \leq y(u_2)\}$$
$$\cup \{(u_1, u_2) \in U \times U \mid x(u_1) + y(u_1) = x(u_2) + y(u_2),$$
$$(x(u_1) - y(u_1))(x(u_2) - y(u_2)) \geq 0, \mid x(u_1) - y(u_1) \mid \geq \mid x(u_2) - y(u_2) \mid\}$$

and

$$Q^{-1} = \{(u_1, u_2) \in U \times U \mid x(u_1) \geq x(u_2), y(u_1) \geq y(u_2)\}$$
$$\cup \{(u_1, u_2) \in U \times U \mid (x(u_1) \geq \tfrac{1}{2}(x(u_2) + y(u_2)), y(u_1) \geq \tfrac{1}{2}(x(u_2) + y(u_2)))\}$$
$$\cup \{(u_1, u_2) \in U \times U \mid x(u_1) + y(u_1) = x(u_2) + y(u_2),$$
$$(x(u_1) - y(u_1))(x(u_2) - y(u_2)) \geq 0, \mid x(u_1) - y(u_1) \mid \leq \mid x(u_2) - y(u_2) \mid\}$$

Thus, in this case, we obtain $P \cup Q^{-1} = Q^{-1}$ and $P^{-1} \cup Q = Q$.

Example 1. Let us consider a decision table of Table 3 which shows scores of mathematics and physics and pass-fail grades of several students of a virtual examination. In Table 3, "P" and "F" are abbreviations of Pass and Fail. The students are evaluated not only by scores of mathematics and physics but also by an interview. The scores of interview are not known because, during the interview, the interviewer directly assigned the pass-fail grade of each student considering the scores of mathematics and physics as well as the interview. Without consideration of interview, we know (1) the higher scores of both in mathematics and physics a student has, the more he/she is preferred and (2) if the order between scores of mathematics and physics is not reversed and the sum of scores of mathematics and physics is not different, the more balanced score between mathematics and physics is preferred. Moreover, in connection to the interview, (3) the interviewer never rejects a student who takes

Table 3. Scores and pass-fail grades

student	x_1	x_2	x_3	x_4	x_5	x_6	x_7	x_8	x_9	x_{10}
math.	65	70	85	35	30	48	30	45	54	60
physics	64	75	66	75	70	63	55	54	60	65
pass/fail	P	P	P	P	F	F	F	F	F	F

5 point more sores both in mathematics and physics than a passed student.

Let $m(x)$ be the score of mathematics of student x and $p(x)$ the score of physics of student x. Then we may obtain the following positively and negatively extensive relations P and Q from the knowledge:

$$P = \{(y,x) \in U \times U \mid m(y) \ge m(x) + 5, p(y) \ge p(x) + 5\}$$
$$, \tag{11}$$

$$Q = \{(y,x) \in U \times U \mid m(y) \le m(x) - 5, p(y) \le p(x) - 5\}$$
$$\cup \{(y,x) \in U \times U \mid m(y) + p(y) \le 2\min(m(x) - 5, p(x) - 5)\}. \tag{12}$$

According to Remark 1, we may obtain more complex positively and negatively extensive relations but in this example, we simply assume (11) and (12).

Then, we obtain $P(x_1) = \{x_2\}$, $P(x_2) = \varnothing$, $P(x_3) = \varnothing$, $P(x_4) = \varnothing$, $P(x_5) = \{x_2, x_4\}$, $P(x_6) = \{x_2\}$, $P(x_7) = \{x_1, x_2, x_3, x_4, x_6, x_{10}\}$, $P(x_8) = \{x_1, x_2, x_3, x_9, x_{10}\}$, $P(x_9) = \{x_2, x_3, x_{10}\}$ and $P(x_{10}) = \{x_2, x_3\}$. Similarly, we obtain $Q(x_1) = \{x_4, x_5, x_6, x_7, x_8\}$, $Q(x_2) = \{x_1, x_4, x_5, x_6, x_7, x_8, x_9, x_{10}\}$, $Q(x_3) = \{x_4, x_5, x_6, x_7, x_8, x_9\}$, $Q(x_4) = \{x_5, x_7\}$, $Q(x_5) = \varnothing$, $Q(x_6) = \{x_7, x_8\}$, $Q(x_7) = \varnothing$, $Q(x_8) = \varnothing$, $Q(x_9) = \{x_8\}$ and $Q(x_{10}) = \{x_4, x_5, x_7, x_8, x_9\}$.

Let X be a set of passed students, i.e., $X = \{x_1, x_2, x_3, x_4\}$ and $Y = U - X$ be a set of failed students. We obtain the following positive, certain, possible and conceivable regions of CP- and CN-rough sets:

$$P_*(X) = \{x_1, x_2, x_3, x_4\}, \ \overline{Q}_*(X) = \{x_1, x_2, x_3\} \tag{13}$$

$$P^*(X) = \{x_1, x_2, x_3, x_4\},$$
$$\overline{Q}^*(X) = \{x_1, x_2, x_3, x_4, x_{10}\} \tag{14}$$

We obtain

$$Q^{-1} = \{(y,x) \in U \times U \mid m(y) \ge m(x) + 5, p(y) \ge p(y) + 5\}$$
$$\cup \left\{(y,x) \in U \times U \mid m(y) \ge \frac{1}{2}(m(x) + p(x)) + 5, p(y) \ge \frac{1}{2}(m(x) + p(x)) + 5\right\}$$
$$\supseteq P. \tag{15}$$

Then we have $(P \cup Q^{-1})_*(X) = \overline{(P^{-1} \cup Q)}_*(X) = (Q^{-1})_*(X) = \overline{Q}_*(X)$ and $(P \cup Q^{-1})^*(X) = \overline{(P^{-1} \cup Q)}^*(X) = (Q^{-1})^*(X) = \overline{Q}^*(X)$. Therefore, the negatively extensive relation Q finds more inconsistency than the positively extensive relation P. Indeed, we have $P_*(X) \supseteq \overline{Q}_*(X)$ and $P^*(X) \subseteq \overline{Q}^*(X)$.

APPROXIMATION-ORIENTED GENERALIZATION

In order to generalize the classical rough sets under the interpretation of rough sets as approximation of a set by means of elementary sets, we introduce a family with a finite number of elementary sets on U, $F = \{F_1, F_2, \&, F_p\}$. Each

F_i is a group of objects collected according to some specific meaning.

There are two ways to define lower and upper approximations of a set X under a family F : one way is to define approximations by means of the union of elementary sets F_i and the other is to define approximations by means of the intersection of complements of elementary sets $U - F_i$. Lower and upper approximations of a set X under F are defined in the following two ways:

$$F_*^\cup(X) = \bigcup \{F_i \mid F_i \subseteq X, i = 0, 1, \&, p\}, \qquad (16)$$

$$F_*^\cap(X) = \bigcup \left\{ \bigcap_{i \in I} (U - F_i) \middle| \bigcap_{i \in I} (U - F_i) \subseteq X, I \subseteq \{1, 2, \&, p+1\} \right\}, \qquad (17)$$

$$F_\cup^*(X) = \bigcap \left\{ \bigcup_{i \in I} F_i \middle| \bigcup_{i \in I} F_i \supseteq X, I \subseteq \{1, 2, \&, p+1\} \right\}, \qquad (18)$$

$$\mathcal{F}_\cap^*(X) = \bigcap \{U - F_i \mid U - F_i \supseteq X, i = 0, 1, \&, p\}, \qquad (19)$$

where, for convenience, we define $F_0 = \varnothing$ and $F_{p+1} = U$. Because we do not assume $F_i \cap F_j \neq \varnothing$ for $i \neq j$, we do not always have a unique maximal intersection $\bigcap_{i \in I} (U - F_i)$ determining $\mathcal{F}_*^\cap(X)$. We usually have several maximal intersections $\mathcal{F}_j^\cap(X) = \bigcap_{i \in I_j} (U - F_i)$, $j = 1, 2, \&, t^\cap$ such that $\mathcal{F}_*^\cap(X) = \bigcup_{j=1,2,\&,t^\cap} \mathcal{F}_j^\cap(X)$. Similarly, $\mathcal{F}_\cup^*(X)$ is usually expressed by an intersection of several minimal unions $\mathcal{F}_j^\cup(X) = \bigcup_{i \in J_j} F_i$, $j = 1, 2, \&, t^\cup$, i.e., $\mathcal{F}_\cup^*(X) = \bigcap_{j=1,2,\&,t^\cup} \mathcal{F}_j^\cup(X)$. We call a pair $(\mathcal{F}_*^\cup(X), \mathcal{F}_\cup^*(X))$ an *approximation-oriented rough set by means of the union of elementary sets F_i under a family $\mathcal{F}$ (for short, an AU-rough set)* or *a union-based approximation-oriented rough set* and a pair $(\mathcal{F}_*^\cap(X), \mathcal{F}_\cap^*(X))$ an *approximation-oriented rough*

set by means of the intersection of complements of elementary sets $U - F_i$ under a family $\mathcal{F}$ (for short, an AI-rough set) or *an intersection-based approximation-oriented rough set.*

Similar definitions to those can be found in (Lin, 1989a; Lin, 1989b; Lin, 1992; Bonikowski et al., 1998; Inuiguchi et al., 2003b). In (Bonikowski et al., 1998; Inuiguchi et al., 2003b), the family is assumed a cover. Moreover the definition of upper approximations of (Bonikowski et al., 1998) is different from (18) and (19).

The fundamental properties of AU- and AI-rough sets are shown in Table 4 (see Inuiguchi (2004) for the proof).

Remark 2. In rough sets, an elementary set F_i (i.e., E_i in the classical rough set) is implicitly assumed to be a small subset so that we approximate a subset X by means of the union of F_i's (E_i's in the classical rough set). Consider a data table given in Table 5. In rough sets, we often build F_i's by combinations of (attribute, value) pairs. For example. F_1 can be a set of fruits whose color, shape and season are red, round and autumn–winter, respectively, while F_2 can be a set of fruits whose color, shape and season are yellow, crescent and all season, respectively. Then we approximate a subset of fruits by means of unions of those F_i's. $\mathcal{F}_*^\cup(X)$ and $\mathcal{F}_\cup^*(X)$ are defined in this perspective.

However, we may approximate a subset of fruits by means of intersections of large elementary sets. We may build each elementary set by a (attribute, value) pair when a data table is given. For example, in Table 5, we may define G_1 by a set of red fruits, G_2 by a set of winter fruits, G_3 by a set of ellipsoid shaped fruits, and so on. Regarding $U - F_i$ as G_i, $\mathcal{F}_*^\cap(X)$ and $\mathcal{F}_\cap^*(X)$ are defined in this perspective.

Table 4. Fundamental properties of AU- and AI-rough sets

(i)	$\mathcal{F}_*^{\cup}(X) \subseteq X \subseteq \mathcal{F}_{\cup}^*(X)$, $\mathcal{F}_*^{\cap}(X) \subseteq X \subseteq \mathcal{F}_{\cap}^*(X)$, $\mathcal{F}_*^{\cup}(\varnothing) = \mathcal{F}_*^{\cap}(\varnothing) = \varnothing$, $\mathcal{F}_{\cup}^*(U) = \mathcal{F}_{\cap}^*(U) = U$.
(ii)	When $\bigcup \mathcal{F} = \bigcup_{i=1,\&,p} F_i = U$, $\mathcal{F}_{\cap}^*(\varnothing) = \varnothing$, $\mathcal{F}_*^{\cup}(U) = U$. When $\bigcap \mathcal{F} = \bigcap_{i=1,\&,p} F_i = \varnothing$, $\mathcal{F}_{\cup}^*(\varnothing) = \varnothing$, $\mathcal{F}_*^{\cap}(U) = U$.
(iii)	$\mathcal{F}_*^{\cup}(X \cap Y) \subseteq \mathcal{F}_*^{\cup}(X) \cap \mathcal{F}_*^{\cup}(Y)$, $\mathcal{F}_*^{\cap}(X \cap Y) = \mathcal{F}_*^{\cap}(X) \cap \mathcal{F}_*^{\cap}(Y)$, $\mathcal{F}_{\cup}^*(X \cup Y) = \mathcal{F}_{\cup}^*(X) \cup \mathcal{F}_{\cup}^*(Y)$, $\mathcal{F}_{\cap}^*(X \cup Y) \supseteq \mathcal{F}_{\cap}^*(X) \cup \mathcal{F}_{\cap}^*(Y)$. When $F_i \cap F_j = \varnothing$, for any $i \neq j$, $\mathcal{F}_*^{\cup}(X \cap Y) = \mathcal{F}_*^{\cup}(X) \cap \mathcal{F}_*^{\cup}(Y)$, $\mathcal{F}_{\cap}^*(X \cup Y) = \mathcal{F}_{\cap}^*(X) \cup \mathcal{F}_{\cap}^*(Y)$.
(iv)	$X \subseteq Y$ implies $\mathcal{F}_*^{\cup}(X) \subseteq \mathcal{F}_*^{\cup}(Y)$, $X \subseteq Y$ implies $\mathcal{F}_*^{\cap}(X) \subseteq \mathcal{F}_*^{\cap}(Y)$, $X \subseteq Y$ implies $\mathcal{F}_{\cup}^*(X) \subseteq \mathcal{F}_{\cup}^*(Y)$, $X \subseteq Y$ implies $\mathcal{F}_{\cap}^*(X) \subseteq \mathcal{F}_{\cap}^*(Y)$.
(v)	$\mathcal{F}_*^{\cup}(X \cup Y) \supseteq \mathcal{F}_*^{\cup}(X) \cup \mathcal{F}_*^{\cup}(Y)$, $\mathcal{F}_*^{\cap}(X \cup Y) \supseteq \mathcal{F}_*^{\cap}(X) \cup \mathcal{F}_*^{\cap}(Y)$, $\mathcal{F}_{\cup}^*(X \cap Y) \subseteq \mathcal{F}_{\cup}^*(X) \cap \mathcal{F}_{\cup}^*(Y)$, $\mathcal{F}_{\cap}^*(X \cap Y) \subseteq \mathcal{F}_{\cap}^*(X) \cap \mathcal{F}_{\cap}^*(Y)$.
(vi)	$\mathcal{F}_*^{\cup}(U - X) = U - \mathcal{F}_{\cap}^*(X)$, $\mathcal{F}_*^{\cap}(U - X) = U - \mathcal{F}_{\cup}^*(X)$, $\mathcal{F}_{\cup}^*(U - X) = U - \mathcal{F}_*^{\cap}(X)$, $\mathcal{F}_{\cap}^*(U - X) = U - \mathcal{F}_*^{\cup}(X)$.
(vii)	$\mathcal{F}_*^{\cup}(\mathcal{F}_*^{\cup}(X)) = \mathcal{F}_*^{\cup}(X)$, $\mathcal{F}_*^{\cap}(\mathcal{F}_*^{\cap}(X)) = \mathcal{F}_*^{\cap}(X)$, $\mathcal{F}_{\cup}^*(\mathcal{F}_{\cup}^*(X)) = \mathcal{F}_{\cup}^*(X)$, $\mathcal{F}_{\cap}^*(\mathcal{F}_{\cap}^*(X)) = \mathcal{F}_{\cap}^*(X)$, $\mathcal{F}_{\cup}^*(\mathcal{F}_*^{\cup}(X)) = \mathcal{F}_*^{\cup}(X)$, $\mathcal{F}_{\cap}^*(\mathcal{F}_*^{\cap}(X)) = \mathcal{F}_{\cap}^*(X)$, $\mathcal{F}_{\cap}^*(\mathcal{F}_*^{\cap}(X)) \supseteq \mathcal{F}_*^{\cap}(X)$, $\mathcal{F}_*^{\cup}(\mathcal{F}_{\cup}^*(X)) \subseteq \mathcal{F}_{\cup}^*(X)$. When $F_i \cap F_j = \varnothing$, for any $i \neq j$, $\mathcal{F}_{\cap}^*(\mathcal{F}_*^{\cap}(X)) = \mathcal{F}_*^{\cap}(X)$, $\mathcal{F}_*^{\cup}(\mathcal{F}_{\cup}^*(X)) = \mathcal{F}_{\cup}^*(X)$.

Example 2. Let us consider the same decision table discussed in Example 1, i.e., Table 3. Using relation P defined by (11), we define two families as

$$\mathcal{P} = \{P(x_i), i = 1, 2, \&, 10\} \cup \{\varnothing, U\}, \tag{20}$$

$$\mathcal{F} = \{M(x_i) = \{x \in U \mid m(x) < m(x_i)\}, i = 1, 2, \&, 10\}$$
$$\cup \{Ph(x_i) = \{x \in U \mid p(x) < p(x_i)\}, i = 1, 2, \&, 10\} \cup \{\varnothing, U\}. \tag{21}$$

Table 5. A data table of fruits

fruits	color	shape	season
apple	red	round	autumn–winter
orange	orange	round	autumn–winter
lemon	yellow	ellipsoidal	autumn–winter
banana	yellow	crescent	all season
strawberry	red	conic	winter–spring

$\mathcal{P}$ is applied to the approximation-oriented rough set of $X = \{x_1, x_2, x_3, x_4\}$ (the set of passed students) by means of the union of elementary sets while $\mathcal{F}$ is applied to the approximation-oriented rough set of X by means of the intersection of elementary sets.

Because we calculated $P(x_i)$, $i = 1, 2, \& , 10$ in Example 1, we obtain

$$\mathcal{P}_*^{\cup}(X) = P(x_1) \cup P(x_2) \cup P(x_3) \cup P(x_4) \cup P(x_5) \cup P(x_6) = \{x_2, x_4\}, \tag{22}$$

$$\mathcal{P}_{\cup}^*(X) = P(x_7) \cap (P(x_5) \cup P(x_8)) = \{x_1, x_2, x_3, x_4, x_{10}\}. \tag{23}$$

On the other hand, $M(x_i)$ and $Ph(x_i)$ are obtained as $M(x_1) = \{x_4, x_5, x_6, x_7, x_8, x_9, x_{10}\}$, $M(x_2) = \{x_1, x_4, x_5, x_6, x_7, x_8, x_9, x_{10}\}$, $M(x_3) = U$, $M(x_4) = \{x_5, x_8\}$, $M(x_5) = \varnothing$, $M(x_6) = \{x_4, x_5, x_7, x_8\}$, $M(x_7) = \varnothing$, $M(x_8) = \{x_4, x_5, x_7\}$, $M(x_9) = \{x_4, x_5, x_6, x_7, x_8\}$, $M(x_{10}) = \{x_4, x_5, x_6, x_7, x_8, x_9\}$, $Ph(x_1) = \{x_6, x_7, x_8, x_9\}, Ph(x_2) = \{x_1, x_3, x_5, x_6, x_7, x_8, x_9, x_{10}\}$, $Ph(x_3) = \{x_1, x_6, x_7, x_8, x_9, x_{10}\}$, $Ph(x_4) = \{x_1, x_3, x_5, x_6, x_7, x_8, x_9, x_{10}\}$, $Ph(x_5) = \{x_1, x_3, x_6, x_7, x_8, x_9, x_{10}\}$, $Ph(x_6) = \{x_7, x_8, x_9\}$, $Ph(x_7) = \{x_8\}$, $Ph(x_8) = \varnothing$, $Ph(x_9) = \{x_7, x_8\}$ and $M(x_{10}) = \{x_1, x_6, x_7, x_8, x_9\}$. Then we obtain

$$\mathcal{F}_*^{\cap}(X) = (U - M(x_1)) \cup (U - Ph(x_2)) \cup ((U - M(x_6)) \cap (U - Ph(x_3))) = \{x_1, x_2, x_3, x_4\} \tag{24}$$

$$\mathcal{F}_{\cap}^*(X) = ((U - M(x_4)) \cap (U - Ph(x_1))) = \{x_1, x_2, x_3, x_4, x_{10}\}. \tag{25}$$

RELATIONSHIPS AMONG CP-, CN-, AU- AND AI-ROUGH SETS

Given a relation P, we may define a family by $\mathcal{P} = \{P(x) \mid x \in U\} \cup \{\varnothing, U\}$. Therefore, under a positively extensive relation P, we obtain not only CP-rough sets but also AU- and AI-rough sets. This is the same for a negatively extensive relation Q. Namely, by a family $\mathcal{Q} = \{Q(x) \mid x \in U\} \cup \{\varnothing, U\}$, we obtain AU- and AI-rough sets. Under those settings, relations between CP-/CN-rough sets and AU/AI-rough sets are shown in Table 6 (see [Inuiguchi04] for the proof).

Example 3. Let us consider again the decision table given in Table 3. We calculate $\mathcal{Q}_*^{\cap}(X)$ and $\mathcal{Q}_{\cap}^*(X)$ for $X = \{x_1, x_2, x_3, x_4\}$ with

$$\mathcal{Q} = \{Q(x_i), i = 1, 2, \& , 10\} \cup \{\varnothing, U\}, \tag{26}$$

where $Q(x_i)$, $i = 1, 2, \& , 10$ are defined in Example 1. We obtain

$$\mathcal{Q}_*^{\cap}(X) = U - Q(x_2) = \{x_2, x_3\}, \tag{27}$$

$$\mathcal{Q}_{\cap}^*(X) = (U - Q(x_4)) \cap (U - Q(x_6)) = \{x_1, x_2, x_3, x_4, x_6, x_9, x_{10}\}. \tag{28}$$

Because P and Q in Example 1 are not reflexive but transitive, from (13), (14), (22), (23), (27) and (28), we observe $\mathcal{P}_{\cup}^*(X) \supseteq P^*(X) = X = P_*(X) \supseteq \mathcal{P}_*^{\cup}(X)$ and $\mathcal{Q}_*^{\cap}(X) \subseteq \bar{Q}_*(X) \subseteq X \subseteq \bar{Q}^*(X) \subseteq \mathcal{Q}_{\cap}^*(X)$.

Table 6. Relationships between two kinds of rough sets

(a)	When P is reflexive, $P_*(X) \subseteq \mathscr{P}_*^{\cup}(X) \subseteq X \subseteq \mathscr{P}_{\cup}^*(X) \subseteq P^*(X)$. When Q is reflexive, $\bar{Q}^*(X) \supseteq \mathscr{Q}_{\cap}^*(X) \supseteq X \supseteq \mathscr{Q}_*^{\cap}(X) \supseteq \bar{Q}_*(X)$.
(b)	When P is transitive, $\mathscr{P}_{\cup}^*(X) \supseteq P^*(X) \supseteq X \supseteq P_*(X) \supseteq \mathscr{P}_*^{\cup}(X)$. When Q is transitive, $\mathscr{Q}_*^{\cap}(X) \subseteq \bar{Q}_*(X) \subseteq X \subseteq \bar{Q}^*(X) \subseteq \mathscr{Q}_{\cap}^*(X)$.
(c)	When P is reflexive and transitive, $P_*(X) = \mathscr{P}_*^{\cup}(X) \subseteq X \subseteq \mathscr{P}_{\cup}^*(X) = P^*(X)$ When Q is reflexive and transitive, $\bar{Q}^*(X) = \mathscr{Q}_{\cap}^*(X) \supseteq X \supseteq \mathscr{Q}_*^{\cap}(X) = \bar{Q}_*(X)$

TYPES OF DECISION RULES

Decision Rules Corresponding to CP- and CN-Rough Sets

First, let us discuss the type of decision rule corresponding to positive and certain regions of CP- and CN-rough sets. Considering the inverse relation $Q^{-1} = \{(x,y) \mid (y,x) \in Q\}$, a certain region $\bar{Q}_*(X)$ and a conceivable region $\bar{Q}^*(X)$ can be represented by $\bar{Q}_*(X) = \{x \in X \mid Q^{-1}(x) \subseteq X\}$ and $\bar{Q}^*(X) = X \cup \bigcup \{P(x) \mid x \in U\}$, respectively. Therefore the type of extracted decision rules are same but the difference is only in P versus Q^{-1}.

From the definition of positive region $P_*(X)$ of (3), any object $y \in U$ satisfying the condition of the decision rules with respect to $P_*(X)$ should fulfill $y \in X$ and $P(y) \subseteq X$. Considering this requirement, we should explore suitable conditions of the decision rules. When we confirm $y = x$ for an object $x \in P_*(X)$, we may obviously conclude $y \in P_*(X)$. Therefore for $x \in P_*(X)$, we obtain a rule,

if $y = x$ then $y \in X$.

Let us call this type of the decision rule, an *identity if-then rule* (for short, *id-rule*). The difficulty of the id-rule is how we recognize y to be same as x. In a way, we identify y as x when all attribute values which characterize y and x are same and there is no possibility to have other object z whose all attribute values are same as y.

When the relation P is transitive, we may conclude $y \in P_*(X)$ from the fact that $(y,x) \in P$ and $x \in P_*(X)$. This is because we have $P(y) \subseteq P(x) \subseteq X$ and $y \in P(x) \subseteq X$ from transitivity and from the fact $x \in P_*(X)$. In this case, we may have the following type of decision rule for $x \in P_*(X)$,

if $(y,x) \in P$ then $y \in X$.

This type of if-then rule is called a *relational if-then rule* (for short, *R-rule*). When the relation P is reflexive and transitive, the R-rule includes the corresponding id-rule.

Even in a case when the relation P is not transitive, if we find a relation $\underline{P} \subseteq P$ such that $P(y) \subseteq P(x)$ for any $y \in \underline{P}(x)$ and for any $x \in P_*(X)$, we may conclude $y \in P_*(X)$ from the fact that $(y,x) \in \underline{P}$ and $x \in P_*(X)$. This is because we know $y \in \underline{P}(x) \subseteq P(x) \subseteq X$ and $P(y) \subseteq P(x) \subseteq X$ for any $y \in \underline{P}(x)$. In this case, we may have the following relational if-then rule for $x \in P_*(X)$:

Figure 2. An example of $\underline{P}$

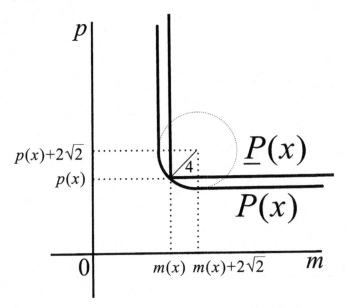

if $(y, x) \in \underline{P}$ then $y \in X$.

For example, let

$$P = \{(y, x) \in U \times U \mid (m(y) - m(x) - 2\sqrt{2})^2 + (p(y) - p(x) - 2\sqrt{2})^2 \leq 16,$$
$$m(y) \geq m(x) + 2\sqrt{2} - 4, p(y) \geq p(x) + 2\sqrt{2} - 4\},$$

where $m(x)$ and $p(x)$ are two different scores of object x. Then we find $\underline{P} = \{(x, y) \in U \times U \mid m(y) \geq m(x), p(y) \geq p(x)\}$. In Figure 2, we depict this example with $P(x) = \{(m(y), p(y)) \in \mathbf{R}^2 \mid (y, x) \in P\}$ and $\underline{P}(x) = \{(m(y), p(y)) \in \mathbf{R}^2 \mid (y, x) \in \underline{P}\}$.

Now let us consider decision rules corresponding to a possible region $P^*(X)$. From its definition (4), we know if $x \in X$ or $x \in P(y)$ for some $y \in X$ then x is a possible member of X. Therefore, for each $x \in X$, we have the following decision rules:

if $y = x$ then $y \in X$ is possible,
if $(y, x) \in P$ then $y \in X$ is possible

While the former decision rule can be called an *identical possible if-then rule* (for short, *id-p-rule*) the latter decision rule a *relational possible*

if-then rule (for short, *R-p-rule*). As in the case of the identical if-then rule, the identification of y as x is not an easy task. However, considering that the conclusion parts of decision rules guarantee only the possibility of the membership to X, we may relax the condition ' $y = x$ ' to ' $y = x$ is possible'. Then the identical possible if-then rule can be extended to

if $y = x$ is possible then $y \in X$ is possible.

This decision rule is called a *possibly identical possible if-then rule* (for short, *p-id-p-rule*).

Decision Rules Corresponding to AU-Rough Sets

Let us discuss the type of decision rule corresponding to lower and upper approximations of AU-rough set. First let us discuss decision rules corresponding to the lower approximation defined by (17). From the definition, any object $y \in U$ satisfying the condition of the decision rules should fulfill $y \in F_i$ and $F_i \subseteq X$. We should explore suitable conditions of the decision rules considering this requirement. When we confirm $y \in F_i$ for an elementary set $F_i \in \mathcal{F}$ such that $F_i \subseteq X$, we can obviously conclude $y \in X$. From this fact, when $F_i \subseteq X$ we have the following type of decision rule:

if $y \in F_i$ then $y \in X$.

This type of if-then rule is called a *block if-then rule* (for short, *B-rule*). From the lower approximations of AU-rough sets, B-rules can be extracted.

Note that the extracted block if-then rules are same as relational if-then rules when we define $\mathcal{F} = \{P(x) \mid x \in U\} \cup \{\varnothing, U\}$ with a transitive positively extensive relation P.

Now let us discuss decision rules corresponding to the upper approximation defined by (4). As described in Section 4, the upper approximation can be expressed by an intersection of several minimal unions $\mathcal{F}_j^{\cup}(X) = \bigcup_{i_j \in J_j} F_{i_j}$, $j = 1, 2, \&, t^{\cup}$, i.e., $\mathcal{F}_{\cup}^*(X) = \bigcap_{j=1,2,\&,t^{\cup}} \mathcal{F}_j^{\cup}(X)$. Applying the distribution law, we obtain

$$\mathcal{F}_{\cup}^*(X) = \bigcup_{\substack{i_j \in J_j, \\ j=1,2,\&,t^{\cup}}} \bigcap_{j=1,2,\&,t^{\cup}} F_{i_j}.$$

From the discussion above, after obtaining all minimal unions $\mathcal{F}_j^{\cup}(X) = \bigcup_{i_j \in J_j} F_{i_j}$, we may extract the following type of decision rule:

if $y \in F_{i_1}$ and $\cdots$ and $y \in F_{i_{t^{\cup}}}$ then $y \in X$ is possible.

This type of decision rule is called a *block possible if-then rule* (for short, *B-p-rule*).

Decision Rules Corresponding to AI-Rough Sets

Let us discuss the type of decision rule corresponding to lower and upper approximations of AI-rough set. First let us discuss decision rules

corresponding to the lower approximation defined by (18). Consider the maximal intersections $\mathcal{F}_j^{\cap}(X)$, $j = 1, 2, \&, t^{\cap}$ such that $\mathcal{F}_*^{\cap}(X) = \bigcup_{j=1,2,\&,t^{\cap}} \mathcal{F}_j^{\cap}(X)$. By the same discussion as in the previous subsection, for each $y \in \mathcal{F}_j^{\cap}(X)$ with some $j \in \{1, 2, \&, t^{\cap}\}$, we can conclude $y \in X$. Let $\mathcal{F}_j^{\cap}(X) = \bigcap_{i=1,2,\&,s}(U - F_{j_i})$. Then we may have the following rule for each $\mathcal{F}_j^{\cap}$:

if $y \notin F_{j_1}$ and $\cdots$ and $y \notin F_{j_s}$ then $y \in X$.

This type of if-then rule is called a *reverse block if-then rule* (for short, *RB-rule*). From the lower approximations of AU-rough sets, RB-rules can be extracted.

Now we discuss decision rules corresponding to the upper approximation defined by (20). Let $\{U - F_{i_1}, U - F_{i_2}, \&, U - F_{i_t}\}$ be a family of minimal subsets of $\{U - F_i \mid U - F_i \supseteq X, i = 0, 1, \&, p\}$. By the definition, we may extract the following decision rules:

if $y \notin F_{i_1}$ and $\cdots$ and $y \notin F_{i_t}$ then $y \in X$ is possible.

This type of decision rule is called a *reverse block possible if-then rule* (for short *RB-p-rule*).

Results

The correspondence between generalized rough sets and types of decision rules is assembled in Table 4. The conditions of id-rules tend to be stronger than the B- and RB-rules. Using a similarity relation, some differences in decision rules extracted from the same decision tables were examined in (Inuiguchi et al., 2003b). Whereas id-rules and R-rules (if they exist) are safer but passive, B- and RB-rules are active but more conflictive. Since the conditions of B-rules and RB-rules are often overlapped, we may use those rules for

Table 7. Correspondence between generalized rough sets and types of decision rules

Corresponding to positive region, certain region and lower approximations		
rough sets	definition	type of decision rules
CP-rough sets	$\{x \in X \mid P(x) \subseteq X\}$	if $x = \bar{x}$ then $x \in X$, if $(x, \bar{x}) \in P$ then $x \in X$ (if P is transitive).
CN-rough sets	$X \cap (U - \bigcup \{Q(x) \mid x \in U - X\})$	if $x = \bar{x}$ then $x \in X$, if $(\bar{x}, x) \in Q$ then $x \in X$ (if Q is transitive).
AU-rough sets	$\bigcup \{F_i \in \mathcal{F} \mid F_i \subseteq X\}$	if $x \in F_i$ then $x \in X$.
AI-rough sets	$(*1)$	if $x \notin F_{j_1}$ and $\cdots$ and $x \notin F_{j_s}$ then $x \in X$.
corresponding to possible region, conceivable region and upper approximations		
CP-rough sets	$X \cup \bigcup \{P(x) \mid x \in X\}$	if $x = \bar{x}$ is possible then $x \in X$ is possible, if $(x, \bar{x}) \in P$ then $x \in X$ is possible.
CN-rough sets	$U - \{x \notin X \mid Q(x) \subseteq U - X\}$	if $x = \bar{x}$ is possible then $x \in X$ is possible, if $(\bar{x}, x) \in Q$ then $x \in X$ is possible.
AU-rough sets	$(*2)$	if $x \in F_{j_1}$ and $\cdots$ and $x \in F_{j_u}$ then $x \in X$ is possible.
AI-rough sets	$\bigcap \{U - F_i \mid U - F_i \supseteq X,\ i = 0, 1, ..., p\}$	if $x \notin F_{j_1}$ and $\cdots$ and $x \notin F_{j_t}$ then $x \in X$ is possible.

interpolative reasoning. On the other hand, because they are safer, id-rules and R-rules (if they exist) will be useful to analyze decision tables with uncertain values such as missing values, multiple possible values, and so forth. In the following section, the differences in the extracted decision rules are demonstrated using Examples 1 and 2.

$(*1)$ $\bigcup \left\{ \bigcap_{i \in I} (U - F_i) \mid \bigcap_{i \in I} (U - F_i) \subseteq X, I \subseteq \{1, 2, \&, p+1\} \right\}$

$(*2)$ $\bigcup \left\{ \bigcup_{i \in I} F_i \mid \bigcup_{i \in I} F_i \supseteq X, I \subseteq \{1, 2, \&, p+1\} \right\}$

A NUMERICAL EXAMPLE

Example 4. Consider the decision table discussed in Example 1, i.e., Table 3. Using positively and negatively extensive relations P and Q defined by (11) and (12), respectively, we calculated $P_*(X)$ and $Q^*(X)$, where $X = \{x_1, x_2, x_3, x_4\}$, passed students. First let us discuss decision rules corresponding to elements of those sets. Using positive and certain regions, we may extract identity if-then rules and relational if-then rules if the associated relation is transitive. By the nature of decision table given by Table 3, we hardly identify $x = y$ from the fact $m(x) = m(y)$ and $p(x) = p(y)$. This is because we may have two different students whose scores of mathematics and physics are both (m_0, p_0). However, since P is transitive, we may confirm $P(y) \subseteq P(x) \subseteq X$ for $x \in P_*(X)$ and $y \in P(x)$ (i.e., $(y,x) \in P$). Thus, we have relational if-then rules 'if $(y,x) \in P$ then $y \in X$' for $x \in P_*(X)$.

Applying the definitions of P and X, the extracted relational if-then rules from $P_*(X)$ are as follows:

if $m(x) \geq 70$ and $p(x) \geq 69$ then x passes the examination,
if $m(x) \geq 75$ and $p(x) \geq 80$ then x passes the examination,
if $m(x) \geq 90$ and $p(x) \geq 71$ then x passes the examination,
if $m(x) \geq 40$ and $p(x) \geq 80$ then x passes the examination.

The second and third decision rules are covered by the first one. Then those decision rules are compressed as

if $m(x) \geq 70$ and $p(x) \geq 69$ then x passes the examination,
if $m(x) \geq 40$ and $p(x) \geq 80$ then x passes the examination.

Q is also transitive. We can extract the following rules from $\bar{Q}_*(X)$:

if $(m(x) \geq 70$ and $p(x) \geq 69)$ or $(m(x) \geq 69.5$ and $p(x) \geq 69.5)$
then x passes the examination,
if $(m(x) \geq 75$ and $p(x) \geq 80)$ or $(m(x) \geq 77.5$ and $p(x) \geq 77.5)$
then x passes the examination,
if $(m(x) \geq 90$ and $p(x) \geq 71)$ or $(m(x) \geq 80.5$ and $p(x) \geq 80.5)$
then x passes the examination.

A disjunction, 'or' is included in the condition of each decision rule due to the definition of Q by (12). Dividing each decision rule into two decision rules and eliminating decision rules covered by another one, the obtained decision rules become as follows:

if $m(x) \geq 70$ and $p(x) \geq 69$ then x passes the examination,
if $m(x) \geq 69.5$ and $p(x) \geq 69.5$ then x passes the examination.

As shown in Example 1, because we have $Q^{-1} = P \cup Q^{-1}$, i.e., Q includes more information for inference from positive/negative examples than P, $\bar{Q}_*(X) \subseteq P_*(X)$. However, the obtained decision rules with respect to $\bar{Q}_*(X)$ do not have stronger conditions than the obtained decision rules with respect to $P_*(X)$. This is because we have $Q^{-1}(x) \supseteq P(x)$ for each $x \in U$.

Now, let us discuss decision rules corresponding to lower approximations $\mathscr{P}_*^{\cup}(X)$ and $\mathscr{F}_*^{\cap}(X)$ calculated in Example 2. Since $\mathscr{P}_*^{\cup}(X)$ is composed of $P(x_i)$, $i = 1, 2, \&, 6$ as shown in (23). Then we obtain the following decision rules:

if $m(x) \geq 70$ and $p(x) \geq 69$ then x passes the examination,
if $m(x) \geq 75$ and $p(x) \geq 80$ then x passes the examination,
if $m(x) \geq 90$ and $p(x) \geq 71$ then x passes the examination,
if $m(x) \geq 40$ and $p(x) \geq 80$ then x passes the examination,
if $m(x) \geq 35$ and $p(x) \geq 75$ then x passes the examination,
if $m(x) \geq 53$ and $p(x) \geq 68$ then x passes the examination.

The first, second and third rules are covered by the sixth while the fourth is covered by the fifth. Then the obtained decision rules are compressed as

if $m(x) \geq 35$ and $p(x) \geq 75$ then x passes the examination,
if $m(x) \geq 53$ and $p(x) \geq 68$ then x passes the examination.

Now let us extract the reverse block if-then rules corresponding to $\mathscr{F}_*^{\cap}(X)$. Since $\mathscr{F}_*^{\cap}(X)$ is obtained as a union of $U - M(x_4)$, $U - Ph(x_2)$ and $(U - M(x_6)) \cap (U - Ph(x_3))$, we have the following reverse block if-then rules,

if $m(x) \geq 65$ then x passes the examination,
if $p(x) \geq 75$ then x passes the examination,
if $m(x) \geq 48$ and $p(x) \geq 66$ then x passes the examination.

Those three rules are independent.

As shown above, the extracted bodies of decision rules are different depending on the definitions of rough sets. Moreover, the obtained decision rules depend also on the given positively and negatively extensive relations P and Q for classification-oriented generalizations, and on the given families $\mathscr{P}$ and $\mathscr{F}$ for approximation-oriented generalizations. We have not discussed about the simplification of conditions of decision rules. However, as demonstrated by the decision rules with respect to $\mathscr{F}_*^{\cap}$, if the complements of elementary sets $U - F_i$, $\forall F_i \in \mathscr{F}$ corresponds to simple conditions, the obtained decision rules are fairly simple.

Moreover, let us discuss decision rules corresponding to a possible region $P^*(X)$, a conceivable region $\bar{Q}^*(X)$ and upper approximations $\mathscr{P}_{\cup}^*(X)$ and $\mathscr{Q}_{\cap}^*(X)$. We directly obtain the following bodies of decision rules with regarding y such that $m(y) = m(x)$ and $p(y) = p(x)$ as possibly identified with x:

$P^*(X)$: if $m(x) = 65$ and $p(x) = 64$ then x possibly passes the examination,
  if $m(x) = 70$ and $p(x) = 75$ then x possibly passes the examination,
  if $m(x) = 85$ and $p(x) = 66$ then x possibly passes the examination,
  if $m(x) = 35$ and $p(x) = 75$ then x possibly passes the examination,
  if $m(x) \geq 70$ and $p(x) \geq 69$ then x possibly passes the examination,
  if $m(x) \geq 75$ and $p(x) \geq 80$ then x possibly passes the examination,
  if $m(x) \geq 90$ and $p(x) \geq 71$, then x possibly passes the examination,
  if $m(x) \geq 40$ and $p(x) \geq 80$, then x possibly passes the examination,

$\bar{Q}^*(X)$: if $m(x) = 65$ and $p(x) = 64$ then x possibly passes the examination,
  if $m(x) = 70$ and $p(x) = 75$ then x possibly passes the examination,
  if $m(x) = 85$ and $p(x) = 66$ then x possibly passes the examination,
  if $m(x) = 35$ and $p(x) = 75$ then x possibly passes the examination,
  if $(m(x) \geq 70$ and $p(x) \geq 69)$ or $(m(x) \geq 69.5$ and $p(x) \geq 69.5)$
    then x possibly passes the examination,
  if $(m(x) \geq 75$ and $p(x) \geq 80)$ or $(m(x) \geq 77.5$ and $p(x) \geq 77.5)$
    then x possibly passes the examination,
  if $(m(x) \geq 90$ and $p(x) \geq 71)$ or $(m(x) \geq 80.5$ and $p(x) \geq 80.5)$
    then x possibly passes the examination,
  if $(m(x) \geq 40$ and $p(x) \geq 80)$ or $(m(x) \geq 60$ and $p(x) \geq 60)$
    then x possibly passes the examination,
$P_{\cup}^*(X)$: if $m(x) \geq 35, p(x) \geq 60, m(x) \geq 35$ and $p(x) \geq 75$
    then x possibly passes the examination,
  if $m(x) \geq 35, p(x) \geq 60, m(x) \geq 50$ and $p(x) \geq 59$
    then x possibly passes the examination,
$F_{\cap}^*(X)$: if $m(x) \geq 35$ and $p(x) \geq 64$, then x possibly passes the examination.

Dividing each decision rule including 'or' in its conditions, simplifying the conditions of deci-sion rules and eliminating covered decision rules by another one, we obtain the following simpler decision rules:

$P^*(X)$: if $m(x) = 65$ and $p(x) = 64$ then x possibly passes the examination,
  if $m(x) = 85$ and $p(x) = 66$ then x possibly passes the examination,
  if $m(x) = 35$ and $p(x) = 75$ then x possibly passes the examination,
  if $m(x) \geq 70$ and $p(x) \geq 69$ then x possibly passes the examination,
  if $m(x) \geq 40$ and $p(x) \geq 80$ then x possibly passes the examination,
$\bar{Q}^*(X)$: if $m(x) = 35$ and $p(x) = 75$ then x possibly passes the examination,
  if $m(x) \geq 40$ and $p(x) \geq 80$ then x possibly passes the examination,
  if $m(x) \geq 60$ and $p(x) \geq 60$ then x possibly passes the examination,
$P_{\cup}^*(X)$: if $m(x) \geq 35$ and $p(x) \geq 75$ then x possibly passes the examination,
  if $m(x) \geq 50$ and $p(x) \geq 60$ then x possibly passes the examination,
$F_{\cap}^*(X)$: if $m(x) \geq 35$ and $p(x) \geq 64$, then x possibly passes the examination.

As demonstrated above, extracted decision rules are different by the problem setting. We should consider what languages we would like to express the target set X and what kinds of decision rules we would like to extract. The positively and negatively extensive relations in classification-oriented rough sets and families in approximation-oriented rough sets correspond to the languages. While classification-oriented rough sets extract decision rules inferring positive (certain) and possible (conceivable) regions, approximation-oriented rough sets extract decision rules inferring lower and upper approximations. Moreover, whereas classification-oriented rough set approach is more ana-lytic, approximation-oriented rough set ap-proach is more compositional. Namely, the former can be seen as an analysis of a concept (set) by means of given meaningful relations, but the latter can be seen as a composition of modules (words) given as a family so as to explain a concept (set).

Finally, we should note that for the extracted rules based on approximation-oriented rough sets, there is no guarantee that the decision rules w.r.t. lower approximations are not always in-cluded in the decision rules w.r.t. upper ap-proximations. Indeed, we can find the counter-example in decision rules based on the AI-rough set $(\mathscr{F}_*^{\cap}(X), \mathscr{F}_{\cup}^*(X))$.

CONCLUDING REMARKS

In this paper we discuss generalized rough sets under two different interpretations: rough sets as classification of objects and rough sets as approximation of a set. In each interpretation, we have more than two definitions of rough sets depending on the given relation or family. The fundamental properties and relationships of those rough sets are described. Moreover, we discussed the correspondences between types of extracted decision rules and generalized crisp rough sets. We demonstrated the differences among decision rules corresponding to two different kinds of rough sets.

For the application of classification-oriented rough sets, we need to specify a positively or negatively extensive relation which is suitable for the given set. By the application, we can find the consistent part (well-explained part) and the doubtful part (ill-explained part) of the set. Therefore, we can analyze the set by means of our knowledge on the set expressed as a relation.

On the other hand, for the application of approximation-oriented rough sets, we need to specify a family to express the given set. By the application, we can find an approximated expression of the set by means of elementary sets of the family. Therefore, we can explain the set as a composition of elementary sets of the given family.

The definition of rough sets can be different by the aim of analysis. Therefore the interpretation of rough set is important to have an analysis proper to the problem setting. Many applications and extensions of the approach proposed in this paper are future topics. Especially, the extraction of re-ducts and decision rules with minimal conditions under each kind of rough set and fuzzy extensions are highly interesting in the theoretical point of view. Moreover, we may define variable precision model (Ziarko, 1993) in each kind of rough set.

ACKNOWLEDGMENT

This Research is supported by the Grant-in-Aid for Scientific Research (B) No.17310098.

REFERENCES

Alpigini, J. J., Peters, J. F., Skowron, A., & Zhong, N. (2002). *Rough Sets and Current Trends in Computing* (LNAI 2475). Berlin: Springer Verlag.

Bonikowski, Z., Bryniarski, E., & Wybraniec-Skardowska, U. (1998). Extensions and Intensions in the Rough Set Theory. *Information Sciences*, 149–167. doi:10.1016/S0020-0255(97)10046-9

Dubois, D., & Prade, H. (1990). Rough Fuzzy Sets and Fuzzy Rough Sets. *International Journal of General Systems*, 191–209. doi:10.1080/03081079008935107

Dubois, D., & Prade, H. (1992). Putting Rough Sets and Fuzzy Sets Together . In Słowiński, R. (Ed.), *Intelligent Decision Support* (pp. 203–232). Dordrecht, The Netherlands: Kluwer.

Greco, S., Inuiguchi, M., & Słowiński, R. (2003). Rough Sets and Gradual Decision Rules . In Wang, G., (Eds.), *Rough Sets, Fuzzy Sets, Data Mining, and Granular Computing* (pp. 156–164). Berlin: Springer Verlag. doi:10.1007/3-540-39205-X_20

Greco, S., Matarazzo, B., & Słowiński, R. (1999). The Use of Rough Sets and Fuzzy Sets in MCDM . In Gal, T., Stewart, T. J., & Hanne, T. (Eds.), *Multicriteria Decision Making: Advances in MCDM Models, Algorithms, Theory, and Applications*. Boston: Kluwer Academic Publishers.

Inuiguchi, M. (2004). Generalizations of Rough Sets and Rule Extraction . In Peters, J. F., Skowron, A., Grzymała-Busse, J. W., Kostek, B., Świniarski, R., & Szczuka, M. (Eds.), *Transactions on Rough Sets I* (pp. 96–119). Berlin: Springer Verlag.

Inuiguchi, M., Hirano, S., & Tsumoto, S. (2003a). *Rough Set Theory and Granular Computing*. Berlin: Springer Verlag.

Inuiguchi, M., & Tanino, T. (2003b). Two Directions toward Generalization of Rough Sets . In Inuiguchi, M., Hirano, S., & Tsumoto, S. (Eds.), *Rough Set Theory and Granular Computing* (pp. 47–57). Berlin: Springer Verlag.

Inuiguchi, M., & Tanino, T. (2003c). New Fuzzy Rough Sets Based on Certainty Qualification . In Pal, K., Polkowski, L., & Skowron, A. (Eds.), *Rough-Neural Computing* (pp. 278–296). Berlin: Springer Verlag.

Lin, T. Y. (1989a, December 4-8). Chinese Wall Security Policy: An Aggressive Model. In *Proceedings of the Fifth Aerospace Computer Security Application Conference* (pp. 286-293).

Lin, T. Y. (1989b, October 12-15). Neighborhood Systems and Approximation in Database and Knowledge Base Systems. In *Proceedings of the Fourth International Symposium on Methodologies of Intelligent Systems* (pp. 75-86).

Lin, T. Y. (1992). Topological and Fuzzy Rough Sets. In R. Słowiński (Ed.), *Intelligent Decision Support: Handbook of Applications and Advances of the Rough Sets theory* (287-304). Dordrecht, The Netherlands: Kluwer Academic Publishers.

Pawlak, Z. (1991). *Rough Sets: Theoretical Aspects of Reasoning About Data*. Boston: Kluwer Academic Publishers.

Słowiński, R., & Vanderpooten, D. (2000). A Generalized Definition of Rough Approximations Based on Similarity. *IEEE Transactions on Data and Knowledge Engineering, 2*, 331–336. doi:10.1109/69.842271

Wang, G., Liu, Q., Yao, Y., & Skowron, A. (2003). *Rough Sets, Fuzzy Sets, Data Mining, and Granular Computing* (LNAI 2639). Berlin: Springer Verlag.

Yao, Y. Y., & Lin, T. Y. (1996). Generalization of Rough Sets Using Modal Logics. *Intelligent Automation and Soft Computing, 2*, 103–120.

Ziarko, W. (1993). Variable Precision Rough Set Model. *Journal of Computer and System Sciences, 1*, 39–59. doi:10.1016/0022-0000(93)90048-2

This work was previously published in volume 4, issue 2 of the International Journal of Cognitive Informatics and Natural Intelligence, edited by Yingxu Wang, pp. 12-33, copyright 2010 by IGI Publishing (an imprint of IGI Global).

Chapter 13
Generalized Rough Logics with Rough Algebraic Semantics

Jianhua Dai
College of Computer Science, Zhejiang University, China

ABSTRACT

The collection of the rough set pairs <lower approximation, upper approximation> of an approximation (U, R) can be made into a Stone algebra by defining two binary operators and one unary operator on the pairs. By introducing a more unary operator, one can get a regular double Stone algebra to describe the rough set pairs of an approximation space. Sequent calculi corresponding to the rough algebras, including rough Stone algebras, Stone algebras, rough double Stone algebras, and regular double Stone algebras are proposed in this paper. The sequent calculi are called rough Stone logic (RSL), Stone logic (SL), rough double Stone logic (RDSL), and double Stone Logic (DSL). The languages, axioms and rules are presented. The soundness and completeness of the logics are proved.

INTRODUCTION

Rough set theory was invented by Pawlak to account for the definability of a concept in terms of some elementary ones in an approximation space (U, R), where U is a set, and R is an equivalence relation on U. It captures and formalizes the basic phenomenon of information granulation. The finer the granulation is, the more concepts are definable in it. For those concepts not definable in an approximation space, the lower and upper approximations for them can be defined. These approximations construct a representation of the given concept in the approximation space.

Research on rough sets by algebraic method has gathered many researchers' attention such as (Iwinski, 1987; Pomykala et al., 1988; Gehrke, 1992; Comer, 1993; Lin et al., 1994; Pagliani, 1996; Banerjee et al., 1996; Banerjee, 1997; Jarvinen, 2002; Dai, 2004; Dai, et al., 2006(a), Dai

DOI: 10.4018/978-1-4666-1743-8.ch013

et al., 2006(b); Dai, 2007; Dai, 2008). In (Lin et al., 1994), the researchers studied the approximations under the structure of set algebra. Iwinski paid more attention about the lattice properties of set algebra and proposed the method of defining of rough approximations (Iwinski, 1987). Based on atomic Boolean lattice, Jarvinen proposed a novel definition method of rough approximations (Jarvinen, 2002). Based on the molecules, Dai constructed a more general structure of rough approximations based on molecular lattices (Dai 2004). At the same time, researchers also study rough sets from the point of description of the rough set pairs i.e. <lower approximation set, upper approximation set>. Pomykala and Pomykala laid a foundation for this field (Pomykala et al., 1988). They used Stone algebra to describe rough sets. They showed that collection of the rough set pairs of an approximation (U, R) can be made into a Stone algebra. By introducing another unary operator, Comer got a regular double Stone algebra to describe the rough set pairs of an approximation space (Comer, 1993). Pagliani adopted semi-simple Nelson algebra (Pagliani, 1996). Banerjee and Chakraborty defined pre-rough algebra which is more structured than topological quasi-Boolean algebra and used pre-rough algebra to describe rough sets (Banerjee et al., 1996). Some rough algebras with Brouwer-Zadeh lattices and 3-valued Lukasiewicz algebras were connected (Dai et al., 2006(a); Dai et al., 2006(b); Dai, 2007). Recently, the concept of rough 3-valued Lukasiewicz algebras was proposed and studied in (Dai, 2008).

At the same time, research in approximation reasoning has taken a new turn after the advent of rough set theory. There has been a variety of approaches for rough sets, including (Lin et al., 1996; Duentsch, 1997; Liau, 2000; Sen et al., 2002; Fan et al., 2002; Dai, 2005; Dai et al., 2005). Pawlak proposed a logic based on decision system, called decision logic (Pawlak, 1991), which is a special kind of classical two-valued logic. Lin and Liu introduced two operators similar to the "possiblity" and "necessity" operators in modal logic and

constructed a first order rough logic in (Lin et al., 1996). Fan, Liau and Yao modified the decision logic by the method of modal logic and fuzzy logic in (Fan et al., 2002(a); Fan et al., 2002(b)). As a matter of fact, majority of studies about logics for rough set theory have great relations with all kinds of modal logics. Readers who want to check the preceding judgment can refer to (Liau, 2000).

It is well known that the search for relationship between logic and algebra goes back to the inventions of Boolean and his follows (Rasiowz, 1974). Those investigations yielded what we now call Boolean algebra. The close links between classical logic and the theory of Boolean algebras has been known for a long time. Consequently, a question naturally arose: what are the logics that correspond to the rough algebras? Unfortunately, there are few studies about logics for rough set theory by algebraic approach. Duentsch presents a logic corresponding to regular double Stone algebras (Duentsch, 1997). The interconnections between the logic and regular double Stone algebras was discussed, but the logic itself including axioms, inference rules, soundness and completeness were not discussed. Banerjee and Chakraborty proposed an infinite propositional logic corresponding to pre-rough algebras in (Banerjee et al., 1996). In a subsequent paper, Banerjee has established a relationship between the finite fragment of the logic and 3-valued Lukasiewicz logic (Banerjee, 1997). They are Hilbert-type formulations with axioms and rules of inference. The implication operator in the logics is interpreted as "rough inclusion" and so the bi-implication turns out to be "rough equality". But, no suitable implication could be obtained to develop a Hilbert-type system that would be sound and complete relative to the class of all topological quasi-Boolean algebras which are more initial structures. Sen and Chakraborty proposed sequent calculi for topological quasi-Boolean algebra and pre-rough algebras (Sen et al., 2002). We tried to study the logics with rough Stone algebraic semantics and rough double Stone algebraic semantics (Dai, 2005; Dai et al., 2005).

As mentioned above, the work of Pomykala (1988) and the work of Comer (1993) are found to be quite significant in the studies of rough set theory. Based on their works, we intend to propose sequent calculi for their algebras, including rough Stone algebras, Stone algebras, rough double Stone algebras, and regular double Stone algebras. The sequent calculi are called rough Stone logic (RSL), Stone logic (SL), rough double Stone logic (RDSL), and double Stone Logic (DSL). The languages, axioms and rules are presented. The soundness and completeness of the logics are proved.

SEQUENT CALCULUS FOR ROUGH STONE ALGEBRA

Rough Stone Algebra

Let (U, R) be an approximation space, where U is the universe and R is an equivalence relation on U. With each approximation space (U, R), two operators on power set of U $\rho(U)$ can be defined. For any $X \subseteq U$, then the lower approximation of X and the upper approximation of X are defined as:

$$R_-(X) = \bigcup \{[x]_R \mid [x]_R \subseteq X\} \qquad (1)$$

$$R^-(X) = \bigcup \{[x]_R \mid [x]_R \cap X \neq \varphi\} \qquad (2)$$

The lower approximation $R_-(X)$ of X in the approximation (U, R) is the union of equivalence classes contained in X, while its upper approximation $R^-(X)$ in the approximation (U, R) is the union of equivalence classes properly intersecting X. $R_-(X)$ is interpreted as the collection of those objects of the domain U that definitely belong to X, while $R^-(X)$ is interpreted as the collection of those objects of the domain U that possibly belong to X.

We call each $X \subseteq U$ a rough set in the approximation space (U, R). And we can represent a rough set X as a pair $< R_-(X),\ R^-(X) >$. Therefore, the pair $< R_-(X),\ R^-(X) >$ is also called a rough set. X is termed definable (also termed exact) in (U, R) if and only if $R_-(X) = R^-(X)$.

Definition 1. A structure $\boldsymbol{L} = (L, \overline{\vee}, \overline{\wedge}, \,^{\circ}, 0, 1)$ is a pseudo-complemented lattice if

(a) $(L, \overline{\vee}, \overline{\wedge}, 0, 1)$ is a lattice with least element 0 and greatest element 1;
if $\forall x \in L$ there is an element x°, for any $y \in L$ satisfying

$$x \overline{\wedge} y = 0 \text{ iff } y \leq x^{\circ}.$$

The element x° is termed pseudo-complement of x. And $^{\circ}$ is called pseudo-complement operator.

Definition 2. (Pomykala et al., 1988) Let $\boldsymbol{L} = (L, \overline{\vee}, \overline{\wedge}, \,^{\circ}, 0, 1)$ be a bound distributive pseudo-complemented lattice, where $^{\circ}$ is the pseudo-complement and 0, 1 are least and greatest element respectively. $\boldsymbol{L}$ is a Stone algebra if

$$\forall x \in L \Rightarrow x^{\circ} \overline{\vee} x^{\circ\circ} = 1$$

And $x^{\circ} \overline{\vee} x^{\circ\circ} = 1$ is called Stone equation.

It was shown by in (Pomykala et al., 1988) that the collection of $\wp(U)$ of rough sets of (U, R) can be made into a Stone algebra expressed as:

$$(\wp(U), \oplus, \otimes, *, <\varphi, \varphi>, <U, U>),$$

where $<\varphi, \varphi>$ is the least element and $<U, U>$ is the greatest element. And the union operator $\oplus$, join operator $\otimes$ and pseudo-complement operator $*$ are defined as following:

$$< R_{\_}(X), R^{-}(X)> \oplus < R_{\_}(Y), R^{-}(Y)> = < R_{\_}(X)$$
$$\cup R_{\_}(Y), R^{-}(X) \cup R^{-}(X)> \qquad (3)$$

$$< R_{\_}(X), R^{-}(X)> \otimes < R_{\_}(Y), R^{-}(Y)> = < R_{\_}(X)$$
$$\cap R_{\_}(Y), R^{-}(X) \cap R^{-}(X)> \qquad (4)$$

$$< R_{\_}(X), R^{-}(X)> * = < U - R^{-}(X), U - R^{-}(X)> \qquad (5)$$

We call the algebra $(\wp(U), \oplus, \otimes, *, <\varphi, \varphi>, <U,U>)$ Rough Stone Algebra in this paper. In fact, rough Stone algebra can be constructed in the following way.

Let DS denotes the collection of all definable sets in (U, R), and consider the following algebra

$$\mathbf{D} = (DS, \cup, \cap, {}^{c}, \varphi, U),$$

where $\cup, \cap, {}^{c}$ are the union, join and complement operators in ordinary set theory. Then $\mathbf{D}$ can be embedded in the rough Stone algebra $(\wp(U), \oplus, \otimes, *, <\varphi, \varphi>, <U,U>)$, where

$$\wp(U) = \{<D, D'> \in DS \times DS : D \subseteq D'\}$$

and for any $<D, D'>, <D_1, D_1'>, <D_2, D_2'> \in \wp(U)$, we have

$$< D_1, D_1'> \oplus < D_2, D_2'> = < D_1 \cup D_2, D_1' \cup D_2'> \qquad (6)$$

$$< D_1, D_1'> \otimes < D_2, D_2'> = < D_1 \cap D_2, D_1' \cap D_2'> \qquad (7)$$

$$< D, D'> * = < D'^{c}, D'^{c}> \qquad (8)$$

Logic with Rough Stone Algebraic Semantics

Motivated by the background described in the preceding section, we propose here a Logic for Rough sets with Stone algebraic semantics. We denote this logic with **RSL**.

Expressions of the language of the logic **RSL** are built from the symbols of the following disjoint sets:

- VAR: prepositional variables ϕ, ψ, ...
- Connectives: two binary connectives $\wedge, \vee$, which represent join and union; one unary connective $\sim$, which represents negation.
- Constants: T, $\perp$ mean true and false.
- Brackets: (,)

The set WFF of all well-formed formulas of the language of **RSL** is defined as follows:

Definition 3. The set WFF of all well-formed formulas (wffs) is the least set satisfying the following conditions:
  ○ VAR $\subseteq$ WFF,
  ○ ϕ, $\psi \in$ WFF implies $\sim\phi$, $(\phi) \wedge (\psi)$, $(\phi) \vee (\psi) \in$ WFF.

The brackets are omitted by the familiar rules. The semantics of the logic is defined as follows:

Definition 4. A rough Stone algebra model or rS-model means the following system

$$\mathbf{M} = (\wp(U), \oplus, \otimes, *, <\varphi, \varphi>, <U,U>, m) \qquad (9)$$

where $\wp(U), \oplus, \otimes, *, <\varphi, \varphi>, <U,U>$ are discussed in the preceding section and the meaning function m **is defined based on** v which is a mapping $v : \text{VAR} \rightarrow \wp(U)$, called the valuation function, for which for all $\phi \in \text{VAR}$,

$$v(\phi) = < A, B > \in \wp(U) \qquad (10)$$

And the meaning function $m : \text{WFF} \rightarrow \wp(U)$ as an extension of the valuation v as follows:

$$m(T) = < U, U > \qquad (11)$$

$$m(\perp) = <\varphi, \varphi> \qquad (12)$$

For each $\phi \in$ VAR,

$$m(\phi) = v(\phi) \qquad (13)$$

For ϕ, $\psi \in$ WFF, we have

a) $m(\phi \wedge \psi) = m(\phi) \otimes m(\psi)$
b) $m(\phi \vee \psi) = m(\phi) \oplus m(\psi)$
c) $m(\sim \phi) = m(\phi)^*$

Definition 5. By a sequent we mean an expression of the form $\Gamma \Rightarrow \Delta$, where Γ and Δ are sequences of wffs.

In this paper, we use same notations as (Sen et al., 2002) (the notations were first used by Troelstra) to present a sequent.

Definition 6. Let Γ is φ_1, φ_2,......, φ_m and Δ is Ψ_1, Ψ_2,......, ψ_n then the sequent $\Gamma \Rightarrow \Delta$ is said to be valid in a rough Stone algebra or rS-model $\mathbf{M} = (\wp(U), \oplus, \otimes, *, <\varphi, \varphi>, <U,U>, m)$, denoted as $\models_{\mathbf{M}} \Gamma \Rightarrow \Delta$, if and only if

$$m(\phi_1) \otimes ... \otimes m(\phi_m) \leq m(\psi_1) \oplus ... \oplus m(\psi_n)$$

which can be written as $m(\Gamma) \leq m(\Delta)$. $\Gamma \Rightarrow \Delta$ is said to be valid, denoted as $\models \Gamma \Rightarrow \Delta$, if $\Gamma \Rightarrow \Delta$ is valid in every rough Stone algebra or rS-model $\mathbf{M}$.

Lemma 1. Let $\phi, \psi \in$ wffs, $m(\phi) = <A, B>$, $m(\psi) = <C, D>$, then the sequent $\phi \Rightarrow \psi$ is said to be valid if and only if $A \subseteq C$ and $B \subseteq D$.

Now, we state the axioms and rules of **RSL** in the following.

Axiom schemes:

(A1) $p \Rightarrow p$

(A2) $\phi \Rightarrow \sim\sim \phi$

(A3) $\sim \phi \Rightarrow \sim\sim\sim \phi$

It is interesting to note that the standard axiom $\sim\sim p \Rightarrow p$ is not included in the axiom schemes. We should notice that $\sim$ is not the standard negation connective. It can be called pseudo-negation connective.

Rules of inference:

$$(\text{Cut}) \frac{\Gamma \Rightarrow \phi, \Delta \quad \Gamma', \phi \Rightarrow \Delta'}{\Gamma, \Gamma' \Rightarrow \Delta, \Delta'}$$

$$(\text{Rule}\sim) \frac{\Gamma \Rightarrow \Delta}{\sim \Delta \Rightarrow \sim \Gamma}$$

$$(\text{LW}) \frac{\Gamma \Rightarrow \Delta}{\Gamma, \phi \Rightarrow \Delta} \quad (\text{RW}) \frac{\Gamma \Rightarrow \Delta}{\Gamma \Rightarrow \phi, \Delta}$$

$$(\text{LC}) \frac{\Gamma, \phi, \phi \Rightarrow \Delta}{\Gamma, \phi \Rightarrow \Delta} \quad (\text{RC}) \frac{\Gamma \Rightarrow \phi, \phi, \Delta}{\Gamma \Rightarrow \phi, \Delta}$$

$$(L\vee) \frac{\Gamma, \varphi \Rightarrow \Delta \quad \Gamma', \psi \Rightarrow \Delta'}{\Gamma, \Gamma', \varphi \vee \psi \Rightarrow \Delta, \Delta'}$$

$$(R\vee) \frac{\Gamma \Rightarrow \phi, \psi, \Delta}{\Gamma \Rightarrow \phi \vee \psi, \Delta}$$

$$(L\wedge) \frac{\Gamma, \phi, \psi \Rightarrow \Delta}{\Gamma, \phi \wedge \psi \Rightarrow \Delta}$$

$$(R\wedge) \frac{\Gamma \Rightarrow \phi, \Delta \quad \Gamma' \Rightarrow \psi, \Delta'}{\Gamma, \Gamma' \Rightarrow \phi \wedge \psi, \Delta, \Delta'}$$

$$(L\perp) \Gamma, \perp \Rightarrow \Delta \quad (\text{RT}) \Gamma \Rightarrow \text{T}, \Delta$$

$\sim \Gamma$ is $\sim \phi_1, \sim \phi_2, \ldots\ldots, \sim \phi_m$, when Γ is ϕ_1, $\phi_2, \ldots\ldots, \phi_m$. Similar convention is adopted for Δ.

Definition 7. $\vdash_{RSL} \Gamma \Rightarrow \Delta$ will denote that $\Gamma \Rightarrow \Delta$ is a theorem of **RSL**. Without confusing, the $\vdash_{RSL} \Gamma \Rightarrow \Delta$ is written as $\vdash \Gamma \Rightarrow \Delta$.

Theorem 1. (Soundness) If $\vdash \Gamma \Rightarrow \Delta$ in **RSL**, then $\Gamma \Rightarrow \Delta$ is valid in every rS-model, i.e., $\models_M \Gamma \Rightarrow \Delta$.

Proof. In order to prove soundness of a logical system, it is necessary to prove validity of the axioms and that the rules preserve validity. Here, we just prove the validity of axiom (A2) and that the rule(R1), (R2) preserves validity. Other axioms and rules can be proved similarly.

(A2). Let $m(\phi) = <A, B>$, then we can get the following by the definition of meaning function $m(\sim\sim \phi) = <A, B>^{**} = <B, B>$. Then (A2) is easy to get by lemma 1.

(R1). Let $\Gamma \Rightarrow \phi, \Delta$ and $\Gamma', \phi \Rightarrow \Delta'$ be valid, and we now prove that $\Gamma, \Gamma' \Rightarrow \Delta, \Delta'$ is valid. The validity of $\Gamma \Rightarrow \phi, \Delta$ means $m(\Gamma) \le m(\Delta) \oplus m(\phi)$. Let $m(\Gamma) = <E,F>$, $m(\phi) = <A,B>$, $m(\Delta) = <G,H>$, then we know $E \subseteq A \cup G$. It means $E \cap E' \subseteq (E' \cap A) \cup (G \cap E')$. From the validity of $\Gamma', \phi \Rightarrow \Delta'$, we can get $E' \cap A \subseteq G'$. It is obvious that $E \cap E' \subseteq G \cup G'$. Similarly, we can prove $F \cap F' \subseteq H \cup H'$. Consequently, $m(\Gamma) \otimes m(\Gamma') \le m(\Delta) \oplus m(\Delta')$ which means $\Gamma, \Gamma' \Rightarrow \Delta, \Delta'$.

(R2). Let $\Gamma \Rightarrow \Delta$ be valid, and we now prove that $\sim \Delta \Rightarrow \sim \Gamma$ is valid. The validity of $\Gamma \Rightarrow \Delta$ means $m(\Gamma) \le m(\Delta)$. Let $m(\Gamma) = <E,F>$, $m(\Delta) = <G,H>$, then we know $E \subseteq G$, $F \subseteq H$. It is obvious that $G^c \subseteq E^c$, $H^c \subseteq F^c$. Consequently, $m(\sim \Delta) \le m(\sim \Gamma)$ which means $\sim \Delta \Rightarrow \sim \Gamma$.

By the validity of axioms and preserving validity of rules, mathematical induction is used on the depth of derivation of the sequent, then the soundness can be proved.

Theorem 2. (Completeness) If $\Gamma \Rightarrow \Delta$ is valid in every rS-model, i.e., $\models_M \Gamma \Rightarrow \Delta$, then $\vdash \Gamma \Rightarrow \Delta$ in **RSL**.

Proof. In order to prove completeness of a system, we first construct the corresponding Lindenbaum algebra. A relation $\approx$ is defined on the set WFF by the following:

$$\phi \approx \psi \text{ if and only if } \vdash \phi \Rightarrow \psi \text{ and } \vdash \psi \Rightarrow \phi$$

We can prove that $\approx$ is a congruence relation. The quotient algebra is then formed in the usual way with the equivalence classes $[\phi]$ for each well-formed formula ϕ. That the compositions in $\text{WFF}\big/_{\approx}$ become independent of the choice of representatives of the equivalence classes has to be checked. Moreover, the relation $\le$ on $\text{WFF}\big/_{\approx}$ defined by the equivalence $[\phi] \le [\psi]$ if and only if $\vdash \phi \Rightarrow \psi$ in **RSL**, is an ordering on $\text{WFF}\big/_{\approx}$.

Then it is shown that the Lindenbaum algebra along with the canonical valuation i.e. when ϕ is mapped to its equivalence class $[\phi]$ is one model for **RSL**. This proves completeness, since if $\models \Gamma \Rightarrow \Delta$, it holds in $\big(\text{WFF}\big/_{\approx}, \le\big)$ with the canonical valuation. Thus $[\Gamma] \le [\Delta]$ which implies $\vdash \Gamma \Rightarrow \Delta$ in **RSL**.

Generalized to General Stone Algebraic Semantics

If fact, the model of **RSL** can be generalized to general Stone algebras with meaning function. The generalized logic is called Stone logic (**SL**).

Definition 8. A Stone algebra model or S-model means the following system

$$\mathbf{M'} = (L, \overline{\vee}, \overline{\wedge}, °, 0, 1, m') \tag{14}$$

where $(L, \vee, \wedge, °, 0, 1)$ is a Stone algebra discussed in the preceding section and the meaning function $m' : \mathrm{WFF} \to L$ is defined as follows:

a) $m'(\mathrm{T}) = 0$
b) $m'(\perp) = 1$
c) $m'(\phi) = l \in L, \forall \phi \in \mathrm{VAR}$

For $\phi, \psi \in \mathrm{WFF}$, we have

d) $m'(\phi \wedge \psi) = m'(\phi) \overline{\wedge} m'(\psi)$
e) $m'(\phi \vee \psi) = m'(\phi) \overline{\vee} m'(\psi)$
f) $m'(\sim \phi) = (m'(\phi))°$

Definition 9. Let Γ is $\phi_1, \phi_2, \ldots\ldots, \phi_m$ and Δ is $\psi_1, \psi_2, \ldots\ldots, \psi_n$, then the sequent $\Gamma \Rightarrow \Delta$ is said to be valid in a Stone algebra or S-model $\mathbf{M'} = (L, \vee, \wedge, °, 0, 1, m')$, denoted as $\models_{\mathbf{M'}} \Gamma \Rightarrow \Delta$, if and only if

$$m'(\phi_1) \overline{\wedge} \ldots \overline{\wedge} m'(\phi_m) \le m'(\psi_1) \overline{\vee} \ldots \overline{\vee} m'(\psi_n)$$

which can be written as $m'(\Gamma) \le m'(\Delta)$. $\Gamma \Rightarrow \Delta$ is said to be valid, denoted as $\models \Gamma \Rightarrow \Delta$, if $\Gamma \Rightarrow \Delta$ is valid in every rough Stone algebra or rS-model $\mathbf{M'}$.

Theorem 3. (Soundness) If $\vdash \Gamma \Rightarrow \Delta$ in $\mathbf{SL}$, then $\Gamma \Rightarrow \Delta$ is valid in every S-model, i.e., $\models_{\mathbf{M'}} \Gamma \Rightarrow \Delta$.
Proof. It can be proved in the same way as Theorem 1.
Theorem 4. (Completeness) If $\Gamma \Rightarrow \Delta$ is valid in every S-model, i.e., $\models_{\mathbf{M'}} \Gamma \Rightarrow \Delta$, then $\vdash \Gamma \Rightarrow \Delta$ in $\mathbf{SL}$.
Proof. It can be proved in the same way as Theorem 2.

SEQUENT CALCULUS FOR ROUGH DOUBLE STONE ALGEBRA

Rough Double Stone Algebra

Definition 10: A structure $\boldsymbol{L} = (L, \overline{\vee}, \overline{\wedge}, °, {}^{\bullet}, 0, 1)$ is a double Stone algebra if

(a) $(L, \overline{\vee}, \overline{\wedge}, 0, 1)$ is a lattice with least element 0 and greatest element 1;
$\forall x \in L$ there is an element $x°$, for any $y \in L$ satisfying

$$x \overline{\wedge} y = 0 \text{ iff } y \le x°,$$

$\forall x \in L$ there is an element $x^{\bullet}$, for any $y \in L$ satisfying

$$x \overline{\vee} y = 1 \text{ iff } x^{\bullet} \le y,$$

(d) $x° \overline{\vee} x°° = 1$, $x^{\bullet} \overline{\wedge} x^{\bullet\bullet} = 0$, $\forall x \in L$.

The element $x°$ is termed pseudo-complement of x, $x^{\bullet}$ is termed dual pseudo-complement of x. L is called regular, if it additionally satisfies the equation

(e) $x° = y°$ and $x^{\bullet} = y^{\bullet}$ imply $x = y$.

This is equivalent to

$$x \overline{\wedge} x^{\bullet} \le x \overline{\vee} x°.$$

The work of J. Pomykala and J. A. Pomykala was improved by Comer (Comer, 1993) who noticed that the collection of $\wp(U)$ of rough sets of (U, R) is in fact a regular double Stone algebra expressed as:

$$(\wp(U), \oplus, \otimes, *, ^+, <\varphi, \varphi>, <U,U>),$$

when one defines the dual pseudo-complement + by:

$$< R_-(X), R^-(X) >^+ = < U - R_-(X), U - R_-(X) > \tag{15}$$

where $<\varphi, \varphi>$ is the least element and $<U,U>$ is the greatest element. And we call $(\wp(U), \oplus, \otimes, *, ^+, <\varphi, \varphi>, <U,U>)$ rough double Stone algebra.

D can be embedded in the rough double Stone algebra with (6),(7),(8), together with

$$< D, D' >^+ = < D^c, D^c > \tag{16}$$

Logic with Rough Double Stone Algebraic Semantics

To form the corresponding sequent calculus, i.e., Rough Double Stone Logic (**RDSL**), we add one unary connective $\neg$ in the language of **RSL**.

Definition 11. The set WFF of all well-formed formulas (wffs) is the least set satisfying the following conditions:
- VAR $\subseteq$ WFF,
- $\phi, \psi \in$ WFF implies $\sim\phi, \neg\phi, (\phi) \wedge (\psi), (\phi) \vee (\psi) \in$ WFF.

The brackets are omitted by the familiar rules. The semantics of the logic **RDSL** is defined as follows:

Definition 12. A model of **RDSL** means the following system

$$\mathbf{M2} = (\wp(U), \oplus, \otimes, *, ^+, <\varphi, \varphi>, <U,U>, m) \tag{17}$$

where $\wp(U), \oplus, \otimes, *, ^+, <\varphi, \varphi>, <U,U>, m$ are discussed in the above. Given a model $\mathbf{M2} = (\wp(U), \oplus, \otimes, *, <\varphi, \varphi>, <U,U>, m)$, we define its meaning function $m : \text{WFF} \rightarrow \wp(U)$ as an extension of the valuation v in the same way as **RSL** as follows. For $\phi, \psi \in$ WFF, we have

a) $m(\phi \wedge \psi) = m(\phi) \otimes m(\psi)$

b) $m(\phi \vee \psi) = m(\phi) \oplus m(\psi)$

c) $m(\sim\phi) = m(\phi)*$

d) $m(\neg\psi) = m(\psi)^+$

Definition 13. Let Γ is $\phi_1, \phi_2, \ldots, \phi_m$ and Δ is $\psi_1, \psi_2, \ldots, \psi_n$, then the sequent $\Gamma \Rightarrow \Delta$ is said to be valid in a rough double Stone algebra or r2S-model $\mathbf{M2} = (\wp(U), \oplus, \otimes, *, <\varphi, \varphi>, <U,U>, m)$, denoted as $\models_{\mathbf{M2}} \Gamma \Rightarrow \Delta$, if and only if

$$m(\phi_1) \otimes \ldots \otimes m(\phi_m) \leq m(\psi_1) \oplus \ldots \oplus m(\psi_n)$$

which can be written as $m(\Gamma) \leq m(\Delta)$. $\Gamma \Rightarrow \Delta$ is said to be valid, denoted as $\models \Gamma \Rightarrow \Delta$, if $\Gamma \Rightarrow \Delta$ is valid in every rough Stone algebra or r2S-model **M2**.

Now, we state the axioms and rules of **RDSL**. In the logic for rough double Stone algebra, two more axioms are taken:

$$(A4) \neg\neg\phi \Rightarrow \phi$$

$$(A5) \neg\neg\neg\phi \Rightarrow \neg\phi$$

It is interesting to note that the standard axiom $\phi \Rightarrow \neg\neg\phi$ is not included in the axiom schemes. We should notice that $\neg$ is not the standard negation connective too. It can be called dual pseudo-negation connective.

As far as the rules of inference are concerned, one more rule is taken:

$$(R10) \frac{\Gamma \Rightarrow \Delta}{\neg \Delta \Rightarrow \neg \Gamma}$$

$\neg \Gamma$ is $\neg \phi_1$, $\neg \phi_2$,......, $\vee \phi_m$, when Γ is ϕ_1, ϕ_2,......, ϕ_m. Similar convention is adopted for Δ.

Definition 14. $\vdash_{RDSL} \Gamma \Rightarrow \Delta$ will denote that $\Gamma \Rightarrow \Delta$ is a theorem of **RDSL** . Without confusing, the $\vdash_{RDSL} \Gamma \Rightarrow \Delta$ is written as $\vdash \Gamma \Rightarrow \Delta$.

Theorem 5. (Soundness) If $\vdash \Gamma \Rightarrow \Delta$ in **RDSL**, then $\Gamma \Rightarrow \Delta$ is valid in every r2S-model, i.e., $\models \Gamma \Rightarrow \Delta$.

Proof. Based on theorem 1, here we just need to prove the validity of axiom (A4), (A5) and the preserving validity of rule (R10).

(A4). Let $m(\phi) = < A, B >$, then we can get the following by the definition of meaning function $m(\neg\neg p) = < A, B >^{++} = < A, A >$. Then (A4) is easy to get by lemma 1.

(A5). Let $m(\phi) = < A, B >$, then we can get the following by the definition of meaning function $m(\neg\neg\neg\phi) = < A, B >^{+++} = < A^c, A^c >$, $m(\neg\phi) = < A^c, A^c >$. Then (A4) is easy to get by lemma 1.

(R10). Let $\Gamma \Rightarrow \Delta$ be valid, and we now prove that $\neg \Delta \Rightarrow \neg \Gamma$ is valid. The validity of $\Gamma \Rightarrow \Delta$ means $m(\Gamma) \leq m(\Delta)$. Let $m(\Gamma) = <E,F>$, $m(\Delta) = <G,H>$, then we know $E \subseteq G, F \subseteq H$. It is obvious that $H^c \subseteq F^c$, i.e., $m(\neg\Delta) \leq m(\neg\Gamma)$ which means $\neg \Delta \Rightarrow \neg \Gamma$.

By the validity of axioms and preserving validity of rules, mathematical induction is used on the depth of derivation of the sequent, then the soundness can be proved.

Theorem 6. (Completeness) If $\Gamma \Rightarrow \Delta$ is valid in every r2S-model, i.e., $\models \Gamma \Rightarrow \Delta$, then $\vdash \Gamma \Rightarrow \Delta$ in **RDSL**.

Proof. The theorem can be proved in the similar way as theorem 2.

Generalized to General Regular Double Stone Algebraic Semantics

If fact, the model of **RDSL** can be generalized to general regular double Stone algebras with meaning function. The generalized logic is called double Stone logic (**DSL**).

Definition 15. A regular double Stone algebra model or 2S-model means the following system

$$\textbf{M2'} = (L, \vee, \wedge, ^\circ, ^*, 0, 1, m') \tag{18}$$

where $(L, \vee, \wedge, ^\circ, ^*, 0, 1)$ is a regular double Stone algebra discussed in the preceding section and the meaning function $m' : \text{WFF} \rightarrow L$ is defined as follows:

a) $m'(\text{T}) = 0$

b) $m'(\perp) = 1$

c) $m'(\phi) = l \in L, \forall \phi \in \text{VAR}$

For ϕ, $\psi \in \text{WFF}$, we have

d) $m'(\phi \wedge \psi) = m'(\phi) \overline{\wedge} m'(\psi)$

e) $m'(\phi \vee \psi) = m'(\phi) \overline{\vee} m'(\psi)$

f) $m'(\sim \phi) = (m'(\phi))^\circ$

g) $m'(\neg\phi) = (m'(\phi))^*$

Definition 16. Let Γ is ϕ_1, ϕ_2,......, ϕ_m and Δ is ψ_1, ψ_2,......, ψ_n, then the sequent $\Gamma \Rightarrow \Delta$ is said to be valid in a Stone algebra or S-model $\textbf{M2'} = (L, \vee, \wedge, ^\circ, ^*, 0, 1, m')$, denoted as $\models_{M'} \Gamma \Rightarrow \Delta$, if and only if

$$m'(\bar{\phi_1})\bar{\wedge}...\bar{\wedge}m'(\phi_m) \leq m'(\bar{\psi_1})\bar{\vee}...\bar{\vee}m'(\psi_n)$$

which can be written as $m'(\Gamma) \leq m'(\Delta)$. $\Gamma \Rightarrow \Delta$ is said to be valid, denoted as $\models \Gamma \Rightarrow \Delta$, if $\Gamma \Rightarrow \Delta$ is valid in every rough Stone algebra or 2S-model **M2'**.

Theorem 7. (Soundness) If $\vdash \Gamma \Rightarrow \Delta$ in *DSL*, then $\Gamma \Rightarrow \Delta$ is valid in every 2S-model, i.e., $\models \Gamma \Rightarrow \Delta$.

Proof. It can be proved in the same way as Theorem 1.

Theorem 8. (Completeness) If $\Gamma \Rightarrow \Delta$ is valid in every 2S-model, i.e., $\models \Gamma \Rightarrow \Delta$, then $\vdash \Gamma \Rightarrow \Delta$ in *DSL*.

Proof. It can be proved in the same way as Theorem 2.

CONCLUSION

This paper has proposed some logics for rough sets, i.e., sequent calculi for rough Stone algebras, Stone algebras, rough double Stone algebras, and regular double Stone algebras. The sequent calculi are called rough Stone logic (*RSL*), Stone logic (*SL*), rough double Stone logic (*RDSL*), and double Stone Logic (*DSL*). The languages, axioms and rules are presented. The soundness and completeness of the logics are proved.

ACKNOWLEDGMENT

The work is supported by the National Natural Science Foundation of China (No.60703038), the Excellent Young Teachers Program of Zhejiang University and the Research Foundation of Center for the Study of Language and Cognition of Zhejiang University.

REFERENCES

Banerjee, M. (1997). Rough sets and 3-valued Lukasiewicz logic. *Fundamenta Informaticae, 31*, 213–220.

Banerjee, M., & Chakraborty, M. K. (1996). Rough sets through algebraic logic. *Fundamenta Informaticae, 28*(3-4), 211–221.

Comer, S. (1993). On connections between information systems, rough sets and algebraic logic . In *Algebraic methods in logic and computer science* (pp. 117–124). Warszawa, Poland: Banach Center Publications.

Dai, J. H. (2004). Structure of rough approximations based on molecular lattices. In *Proceedings of 4th International Conference on Rough Sets and Current Trends in Computing (RSCTC2004)* (LNAI 3066, pp. 69-77). Berlin: Springer Verlag.

Dai, J. H. (2005). Logic for rough sets with rough double Stone algebraic semantics. In *Proceedings of the 10th International Conference on Rough Sets, Fuzzy Sets, Data Mining, and Granular Computing (RSFDGrC 2005)* (LNAI 3641, pp. 141-148). Berlin: Springer Verlag.

Dai, J. H. (2007). Rough algebras and 3-valued Lukasiewicz algebras. *Chinese Journal of Computers, 30*(2), 161–167.

Dai, J. H. (2008). Rough 3-valued algebras. *Information Sciences, 179*(8), 1986–1996. doi:10.1016/j.ins.2007.11.011

Dai, J. H., Chen, W. D., & Pan, Y. H. (2005). Sequent calculus system for rough sets based on rough Stone algebras. In *Proceedings of the IEEE International Conference on Granular Computing (IEEE GrC2005)* (pp. 423-426). Washington, DC: IEEE Press.

Dai, J. H., Chen, W. D., & Pan, Y. H. (2006a). Rough sets and Brouwer-Zadeh lattices. In *Proceedings of First International Conference on Rough Sets and Knowledge Technology* (pp. 200-207). Berlin: Springer Verlag.

Dai, J. H., Lv, H. F., Chen, W. D., & Pan, Y. H. (2006b). Two kinds of rough algebras and Brouwer-Zadeh lattices. In *Proceedings of 5th International Conference on Rough Sets and Current Trends in Computing (RSCTC2006)* (pp. 99-106). Berlin: Springer Verlag.

Duentsch, I. (1997). A logic for rough sets. *Theoretical Computer Science, 179*(1-2), 427–436. doi:10.1016/S0304-3975(96)00334-9

Fan, T. F., Liau, C. J., & Yao, Y. Y. (2002). On modal decision logics. *Communications of Institute of Information and Computing Machinery, 5*(2), 21–26.

Fan, T. F., Liau, C. J., & Yao, Y. Y. (2002). On modal and fuzzy decision logics based on rough set theory. *Fundamenta Informaticae, 52*(4), 325–344.

Gehrke, M., & Walker, E. (1992). On the structure of rough sets. *Bulletin of the Polish Academy of Sciences: Mathematics, 40*(3), 235–255.

Iwinski, T. B. (1987). Algebraic approach to rough sets. *Bulletin of the Polish Academy of Sciences: Mathematics, 35*(9-10), 673–683.

Jarvinen, J. (2002). On the structure of rough approximations. In *Proceedings of 3rd International Conference on Rough Sets and Current Trends in Computing (RSCTC2002)* (LNAI 2475, pp. 123-130). Berlin: Springer Verlag.

Liau, C. J. (2000). An overview of rough set semantics for modal and quantifier logics. *International Journal of Uncertainty, Fuzziness and Knowledge-based Systems, 8*(1), 93–118. doi:10.1016/S0218-4885(00)00007-1

Lin, T. Y., & Liu, Q. (1994). Rough approximate operators: Axiomatic rough set theory. In Ziarko, W. P. (Ed.), *Rough Sets, Fuzzy Sets and Knowledge Discovery* (pp. 256–260). Berlin: Springer Verlag.

Lin, T. Y., & Liu, Q. (1996). First-order rough logic I: approximate reasoning via rough sets. *Fundamenta Informaticae, 27*(2-3), 137–144.

Pagliani, P. (1996). Rough sets and Nelson algebras. *Fundamenta Informaticae, 27*(2-3), 205–219.

Pawlak, Z. (1991). *Rough Sets–Theoretical Aspects of Reasoning about Data*. Dordrecht, The Netherlands: Kluwer Academic Publishers.

Pomykala, J., & Pomykala, J. A. (1988). The Stone algebra of rough sets. *Bulletin of the Polish Academy of Sciences: Mathematics, 36*(7-8), 495–508.

Rasiowz, H. (1974). *An algebraic approach to non-classical logics*. Amsterdam: North Holland.

Sen, J., & Chakraborty, M. K. (2002). A study of interconnections between rough and 3-valued Lukasiewicz logics. *Fundamenta Informaticae, 51*, 311–324. doi:10.1046/j.1472-8206.2002.00092.x

This work was previously published in volume 4, issue 2 of the International Journal of Cognitive Informatics and Natural Intelligence, edited by Yingxu Wang, pp. 34-47, copyright 2010 by IGI Publishing (an imprint of IGI Global).

Section 4
Computational Intelligence

Chapter 14
Feature Reduction with Inconsistency

Yong Liu
Institute of Cyber-Systems and Control of Zhejiang University, China

Yunliang Jiang
Huzhou Teachers College, China

Jianhua Yang
SCI-Tech Academy of Zhejiang University, China

ABSTRACT

Feature selection is a classical problem in machine learning, and how to design a method to select the features that can contain all the internal semantic correlation of the original feature set is a challenge. The authors present a general approach to select features via rough set based reduction, which can keep the selected features with the same semantic correlation as the original feature set. A new concept named inconsistency is proposed, which can be used to calculate the positive region easily and quickly with only linear temporal complexity. Some properties of inconsistency are also given, such as the monotonicity of inconsistency and so forth. The authors also propose three inconsistency based attribute reduction generation algorithms with different search policies. Finally, a "mini-saturation" bias is presented to choose the proper reduction for further predictive designing.

Feature selection is to find the "useful" feature subset from the original features. It is similar to a dimension reduction problem, and normally, after the feature selection, the selected feature set may achieve a superior classifier.

The main solutions of feature selection always try to project the large and high dimensional feature set into a small dimension with a certain constraint, and remove the irrelevant features. From the viewpoint of granular computing (Lin, 1989; Lin, 1997; Lin, 1998a; Lin, 1998b), the high dimensional feature set is a thin granular structure and the feature selection is to find a proper granular structure that can reflect the original feature set.

Many previous feature selection approaches (Bell & Wang, 2000; Koller & Sahami, 1996; Dash & Liu, 2003; Kononenko, 1994; Segen, 1984; Cardie, 1993; Sheinvald, Dom, & Niblack,

DOI: 10.4018/978-1-4666-1743-8.ch014

1990; Blum & Langley, 1997) can be classified into two categories: one is to use a related approximate measure to evaluate the features one by one and adds the features with positive value into the selected feature set, and the other one is to evaluate the subsets of features directly.

There are two disadvantages for the above approaches. The method, which evaluates the feature set one by one, will destroy the internal semantic relation of the original feature set. And the evaluation for the whole subset of features will lead to low efficiency both in temporal complexity and spatial complexity.

To overcome these two problems, many researchers introduce the rough set based reduction into feature selection (Hu, Zhao, Xie, & Yu, 2007; Jelonek, Krawiec, & Slowinski, 1995; Lin & Yin, 2004; Zhong, Dong, & Ohsuga, 2001; Swiniarski & Skowron, 2003). The reduction could preserve the semantic correlation of original features (Jensen & Shen, 2004).

In this paper, we address the two weaknesses in traditional feature selection and introduce a new feature selection approach with rough set based reduction. We propose a new concept named inconsistency which is easy to calculate and can evaluate whether the attribute set is a reduct quickly.

The rest of this paper is organized as follow: Section 2 presents the definitions and concepts related with inconsistency, some properties of inconsistency are also given in this section; Section 3 proposes three inconsistency based reduction algorithms with different search policies; Section 4 presents the "mini-saturation" bias based reduct selection policy to choose the "optimal" one from multiple reducts for further predictive modeling; and finally we conclude this paper in section 5.

1. RELATED DEFFINITIONS AND CONCEPTS

Some related definitions and concepts are presented as follow:

Definition 1 Positive region, P and Q are two sets in the information system $U(C, D)$, $P, Q \subseteq C \cup D$, then the positive region of Q in P, denoted as $POS_P(Q)$, can be calculated as:

$$POS_P(Q) = \bigcup_{X \in U / IND(Q)} \underline{P}X$$

Definition 2 Attribute dependency, P and Q are two sets in the information system $U(C, D)$, $\forall P, Q \subseteq C \cup D$, then the attribute dependency of attribute set Q on attribute set P, denoted as $\gamma_P(Q)$, can be calculated as:

$$\gamma_P(Q) = \frac{|POS_P(Q)|}{|U|}$$

The attribute dependency can describe which variables are strongly related to which other variables, for example, if $P \subset C$, then $\gamma_P(D)$ can be viewed as the measure between the decision attributes and the condition attributes, which can be implemented in further predictive modeling.

With the definition of attribute dependency, the attribute reduct can be defined as follow:

Definition 3 Attribute reduct, In information system $U(C, D)$, $R \subseteq C$, R is the reduct of C if and only if

$$POS_R(D) = POS_C(D) \text{ and}$$
$$\forall a \in R, \ POS_{R-\{a\}}(D) \neq POS_R(D)$$

or equivalently $\gamma_R(D) = \gamma_C(D)$ and $\forall a \in R, \ \gamma_{R-\{a\}}(D) \neq \gamma_R(D)$

The essence of attribute reduct is to find a subset P from condition set, and the subset P can maintain the same discriminability under the instance space. So we can judge whether the set is a reduct by its discriminability under the instance space. So the positive region, which calculates the number of instances that can be discriminable with the attribute set, can be used to find the reduct.

From the definition of attribute reduct, we can see the reduct could keep the internal correlation of the attributes. Here we introduce the reduction into the feature selection, as the reduct can maintain the same discriminability as the original data set (Jensen & Shen, 2004).

Definition 4 Inconsistent condition, in information system $U(C, D)$, C is the condition attribute set, D is the decision attribute set, $x_1, x_2 \in U$, if $\forall a \in C, a(x_1) = a(x_2)$ and $\exists d \in D, d(x_1) \neq d(x_2)$, then there are inconsistent condition between instance x_1 and instance x_2.

Definition 5 Inconsistent instance number, in information system $U(C, D)$, C is the condition attribute set, D is the decision attribute set, if $P \subseteq C$, $E_i \in U / IND(P)$, $i = 1, 2, 3, ..., | U / IND(P) |$, the inconsistent instance number of set P is denoted as $IN(P)$, and calculated as follow:

$$IN(P) = \sum | E_k |, \quad E_k \text{ is the equivalent class}$$

with inconsistent condition.

Definition 6 Inconsistency, in information system $U(C, D)$, C is the condition attribute set, D is the decision attribute set, if $P \subseteq C$, the inconsistency of attribute set P is κ_p, given as

$$\kappa_p = \frac{| U | - IN(P)}{| U | - IN(C)}$$

Obviously, $0 \leq \kappa_p \leq 1$.

After given the definition of inconsistency, we can present several properties of inconsistency,

Lemma 1 In information system $U(C, D)$, C is the condition attribute set, D is the decision attribute set, $\forall Q \subseteq C$, information system $U(Q, D)$ is consistent if and if only $IN(Q) = 0$.

The proof of Lemma 1 is obviously based on the definition 5, so we omit it here.

Lemma 2 In information system $U(C, D)$, C is the condition attribute set, D is the decision attribute set, there is

$$\forall Q \subset R \Rightarrow IN(R) \leq IN(Q)$$

Proof, we first assume $Q = R - \{a\}$, and the inconsistent instances in $IN(R)$ are $x_1, x_2, ...x_{IN(R)}$ respectively, and then consider the $IN(Q)$ of attribute set Q, obviously all the inconsistent instance $x_1, x_2, ...x_{IN(R)}$ of R are also belonging to the inconsistent instance set of Q, that is the number of $IN(Q)$ will not less than $IN(R)$, and for the conditions that Q is the subset of $R - \{a\}$, the proof can be similar to the above, so we have $IN(R) \leq IN(Q)$.

Lemma 3 In information system $U(C, D)$, C is the condition attribute set, D is the decision attribute set, $\forall Q \subset C$, $POS_Q(D) = POS_C(D)$ if and only if $IN(Q) = IN(C)$.

Proof, based on the definition of positive region $POS_Q(D) = \bigcup_{X \in U / IND(D)} \underline{P}X$, that is in information system $U(C, D)$,

$$\underline{P}X = \{E_i \mid E_i \in U / IND(Q) \& E_i \subseteq X_j, X_j \in U / IND(D)\}$$

Here $i = 1, 2, 3, ..., | U / IND(Q) |, j = 1, 2, .., | U / IND(D) |$ $E_i \subseteq X_j$, then to any $x_m, x_n \in E_i$ we have $\forall a \in Q, a(x_m) = a(x_n)$ and $\forall d \in D, d(x_m) = d(x_n)$. Considering the equivalent class $E \notin \underline{P}X$, there are inconsistent condition in these equivalent classes, so the equivalent classes in U/IND(Q) can be classified into two categories, one belongs to $\underline{P}X$ and without inconsistent condition, and the other one does not belong to $\underline{P}X$ and with inconsistent condition, then

$$card(\bigcup_{X \in U / IND(D)} \underline{P}X) = | U | - IN(Q)$$

That is

$$POS_Q(D) = | U | - IN(Q)$$

Figure 1. Attribute reduction+ feature selection workflow

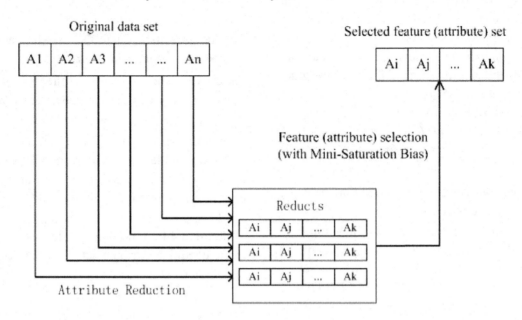

Similarly, we have

$$POS_C(D) = |U| - IN(C)$$

If $POS_Q(D) = POS_C(D)$, then obviously $IN(Q) = IN(C)$.

Based on the above lemmas, we can propose the theorem 1.

Theorem 1 In information system $U(C, D)$, C is the condition attribute set, D is the decision attribute set, R is a reduct of C, if and only if $\kappa_R = 1$ and $\forall Q \subset R, \kappa_Q \neq 1$.

Proof,

$$\kappa_R = 1 \Leftrightarrow \frac{|U| - IN(R)}{|U| - IN(C)} = 1 \Leftrightarrow IN(R) = IN(C)$$

Based on the Lemma 3, $POS_R(D) = POS_C(D)$, that is $\gamma_R(D) = \gamma_c(D)$, then R is a reduct of C.

2. REDUCTION ALGORITHMS BASED ON THE INCONSISTENCY

The feature reduction can be used as the pre-selection in feature selection shown in figure 1.

We first generate multiple reducts which could preserve the semantic and discriminability as the same as the original attribute set, and then choose one of the attribute reduct set for further predictive modeling.

The traditional reduct algorithm normally required the data set is consistent (Han, Hu, & Lin, 2004), which will constraint its implementation in practice cases.

In this paper, we propose several reduction algorithms that can generate reducts with the new measure, inconsistency, and there are three advantages for our approach:

1. The reduction algorithms can well support the inconsistent data sets, which are quite normal in practice or the data set with noises or partly absence.
2. The algorithms can remove the redundant attributes effectively and keep the same semantic correlation and discriminability as the same as the original data set.
3. The temporal complexity of calculate the inconsistency is only O(|U|) (Liu, Xiong, & Chu, 2009), and the total computation

time will be reduced significantly. With the hash method (Liu, Xiong, & Chu, 2009), the temporal complexity of reduction is $O(|C|^2|U/C|)$, which is the one of the fastest reduction algorithm.

2.1 Main Idea for Inconsistency Reduction

Normally, the reduction algorithms need to compute the positive region (Hu, 1995) frequently or even compute the discernibility matrix (Pawlak, 1991). As the computation for positive region and discernibility matrix is quite complex both in temporal complexity and spatial complexity, here we switch the reduction measure from positive region to inconsistency which is much easy to compute.

2.2 Monotonicity of Inconsistency

Before proposing our algorithms based on the inconsistency, the *monotonicity of inconsistency* should be presented firstly.

Monotonicity of inconsistency, In information system *U(C, D)*, *C* is the condition attribute set, *D* is the decision attribute set, there are n attributes sets $Q_1, Q_2, ..., Q_n \subseteq C$, the *monotonicity of inconsistency* is

$$Q_1 \supset Q_2 \supset ... \supset Q_n \Rightarrow \kappa_{Q_1} \geq \kappa_{Q_2} \geq ... \geq \kappa_{Q_n}$$

Theorem 2 In information system, the inconsistency is *monotonicity*.

Proof, if $Q_i \subset Q_j$, based on the Lemma 2, we have $IN(Q_i) \geq IN(Q_j)$, and from the definition of inconsistency, $\kappa_{Q_i} = \dfrac{|U| - IN(Q_i)}{|U| - IN(C)}$, $\kappa_{Q_j} = \dfrac{|U| - IN(Q_j)}{|U| - IN(C)}$, then we obtain $\kappa_{Q_i} \leq \kappa_{Q_j}$.

2.3 Attribute Reduction Algorithms with Inconsistency

According to Theorem 1, when an attribute set R satisfied $\kappa_R = 1$, and $\kappa_{R-\{a\}} \neq 1$, then we can say R is a reduct of C. So the following reduction algorithms are designed based on the property of inconsistency.

To find the reducts from all the attribute subsets is a search problem with very highly complexity, the search space could reach $O(2^{|C|})$. So we propose three attribute reduction algorithms based on different search polices, they are Exhaustive Search algorithm (ESA), Recursive Subset Search Algorithm(RSSA) and Heuristic Reduct Search Algorithm (HRSA). The above two algorithms are used to generate all the reducts of condition attribute set and the last one is used to generate a reduct quickly.

2.3.1 Exhaustive Search Algorithm (ESA)

The exhaustive search policy (Dash & Liu, 2003) is widely used in machine learning problem. In this policy, the search starts from an empty set, and constructs a target set to test whether the target set is the desired one. Then the search is processed with a breadth-first policy until the best result is obtained. Here in ESA, we need to find all the reducts, so we design our exhaustive search algorithm with a minor revising. It starts from empty set, constructs the target sets and searches all the target space by the breadth-first policy, stops until all the subsets are tested. The details are shown in algorithm 1.

ESA constructs the reduct from empty set, and then calculate the inconsistency of target set *R*, if $\kappa_R = 1$, then R may be a candidate of reduct. For the condition that $Q \supset R$ and $\kappa_Q = 1$, in this case, R is not a reduct. So in algorithm1, we should check whether there is a subset of current set that can satisfy $\kappa = 1$ (see step 6 in algorithm1).

Algorithm 1. Exhaustive Search Algorithm (ESA)

```
Input: U(C, D)
Output: all the reducts set, O
1.      S ← C
2.      O ← φ
3.          for   size = 0 to |S|
4.                      for all subsets S' with |S'|= size
5.                          if κ_{S'} = 1
6.                              if ∀S" ∈ O having S" ⊄ S'
7.
O ← O ∪ {S'}
8.                      end for
9.          end for
10.             return O
```

2.3.2 Recursive Subset Search Algorithm (RSSA)

The advantages of ESA is easy to implement and can obtain all the reducts without missing. However, it is low efficiency in computation and with very high temporal complexity and especially the number of condition attributes is large. So we present RSSA with better temporal efficiency.

RSSA can obtain all the reducts of condition attribute set and also can search the reducts from a specific attribute set, and obtain all the reducts of that specific attribute set. RSSA removes the irrelevant attributes one by one until the reducts are obtained. The details are given in algorithm 2.

As we can see from algorithm 2, RSSA will not processing further search in subsets for those sets with inconsistency less than one. This can be guaranteed by the *monotonicity of inconsistency*. That is if the inconsistency of a set is less than 1(not equal 1), then the inconsistencies of that set's subsets can not equal 1. With the *monotonicity of inconsistency*, we can avoid search the full attribute subset space, and reduce the search iterations. This algorithm can be viewed as a bound

pruning method with constraint, which uses the constraint to prune the search brunch without solutions and switch to the search brunch with solutions recursively.

2.3.3 Heuristic Reduct Search Algorithm (HRSA)

The above two algorithms are designed to obtain all the reducts from information system, and the temporal computation is very high (it is normally a NP problem to get all the reducts.). So we propose a quick reduction algorithm with heuristic, HRSA. The temporal complexity of HRSA is much lower than the above twos, for it only needs to generate one reduct from condition attribute set.

HRSA uses the *monotonicity of inconsistency* as the heuristic condition. It also starts from empty set and choose an attribute with largest inconsistency into the candidate attribute set until the inconsistency of current candidate attribute set equal 1, and then output the reduct.

Although HRSA can generate a reduct quickly, it can not guarantee the output reduct is the shortest one. The HRSA is detailed as follow:

Algorithm 2. Recursive Subset Search Algorithm (RSSA)

```
Input: U(C, D), target search set Q, Q ⊆ C
Output: all the reducts set, O
```

1. $\quad R \leftarrow Q$
2. $\quad O \leftarrow \phi$
3. $\qquad$ **if** $\kappa_R = 1$ & $\forall x \in R$, having $\kappa_R < 1$
4. $\qquad O \leftarrow O \cup \{R\}$
5. $\quad$ **else**
6. $\qquad$ **for** each $q \in R$
7. $\qquad\qquad$ **if** $\kappa_{R-\{q\}} = 1$
8. $\qquad\qquad\qquad O \leftarrow O \cup RSSA(U(C,D), R - \{q\})$ /* **Recursive** */
9. $\qquad$ **end for**
10. $\quad$ **return** O

3. "MINI-SATURATION" BIAS FOR REDUCTION SELECTION

Review the feature selection process in Figure 1, after obtaining multiple reducts by inconsistency methods, a further reduction selection should be adopted to choose an optimal reduct for further predictive designing.

Normally, the reduction selection processing prefers a shortest bias with the classical Occam's razor (Prefer the simplest hypothesis that fits the data), that is to choose the $\min[card(S_1), card(S_2), ..., card(S_n)]$ as the optimal output, here S_i is the reduct set[1].

The typical sample is the "Mini-features" presented by Almuallim in (Hussein & Thomas, 1994). And Almuallim proofed that the consistent classifiers with "Mini-features" will achieve superior performance both in theoretical and experiments. Here consistent classifiers refer to those classifiers that can discriminate all the training data set. Similarly, we can implement Almuallim's bias in our approach. However, our condition is slightly different with Almuallim's shortest bias.

Algorithm 3. Heuristic Reduct Search Algorithm (HRSA)

```
Input: U(C, D)
Output: Reduct R
```

1. $\quad R \leftarrow \phi$
2. $\quad$ **do**
3. $\qquad\qquad O \leftarrow \phi$
3. $\qquad$ **for** each $q \in C - R$
4. $\qquad\qquad$ **if** $\kappa_{R \cup \{Q\}} > \kappa_R$ (or **if** $IN(R \cup \{q\}) < IN(R)$)
5. $\qquad\qquad O \leftarrow O \cup \{R\}$
6. $\qquad$ **end for**
7. $\quad R \leftarrow O$
8. $\quad$ **until** $\kappa_R = 1$
9. $\quad$ **return** R

As his mini-feature bias is established under boolean attribute set (that is each attribute's values is either 0 or 1), it will not be true when switching to multiple value attribute set. A special example is that if we choose a reduct (with the mini-features bias) that only contain one attribute which is the sequence of each instance, in this case, obviously this reduct can not be a good predictor in classification models, it can not construct classifier with good generalization.

So we need an improvement on Almuallim's bias, here we present a "Mini-Saturation" bias.

The data saturation is defined as follow:

Definition 7. Data Saturation In information system $U(C, D)$, C is the condition attribute set, D is the decision attribute set, $P \subseteq (C \cup D)$, and $P = \{p_1, p_2, p_3, ..., p_n\}$, the data saturation of set P, denoted as ξ_P, calculated as follow:

$$\xi_P = \prod_{i=1}^{n} N_{P_i}$$

Here N_{P_i} is the number of attribute p_i's value, if $P = \phi$, then $\xi_P = 1$.

According to the definition, the indiscernibility relation could represent the discriminability of the attribute set P, and the data saturation could represent the number of the maximal instances contained by attribute set P without redundancy. So the data saturation can be viewed as a maximal boundary measure for attribute set in granular computing.

The "Mini-Saturation" bias is presented as follow:

There are two classifiers $f(x_1, x_2, ..., x_n)$ and $f(x_1, x_2, ..., x_m)$, which are consistent in their training data set, here x_i is the input feature parameters. When choosing the feature set as the predictor, it prefers the feature set with minimal data saturation, that is

$$f = \arg\min(\xi_{\{x_1, x_2, ..., x_m\}}, \xi_{\{x_1, x_2, ..., x_n\}})$$

4. CONCLUSION

This paper proposes a feature reduction approach which can integrate the advantages of attribute reduct and feature selection. That is first calculate the multiple reducts with inconsistency and then choose an optimal reduct with mini-bias for further predictive designing. The feature set selected with our approach can keep the same semantic and self-contained properties as the original data set. Besides, the inconsistency introduced in this paper is especially suit for huge data set condition for its calculation is easy and efficient; it only needs to scan the whole data set one time with the hash method (Liu, Xiong, & Chu, 2009).

The further work can be carried out to evaluate the correlation of the attribute sets within different granula and find a better granular structure which may be easy to calculate and more discriminable in feature set. Also the theoretical explorations for the self-containing in correlation and integration in semantic are challenge problems in our future works.

ACKNOWLEDGEMENTS

This work was supported by the National Natural Science Foundation of China (60803053, 60872057), Natural Science Foundation of Zhejiang Province (Y1080212, R1090244, Y1090449), Science Foundation of Chinese University(2009QNA5004), Astronautical Supporting Technology Foundation of China (Grant No. No. 08-3.4), the Ph.D. Programs Foundation of Ministry of Education of China (Grant No. 200803351129), Defense Advanced Research Foundation of the General Armaments Department of the PLA (9140A06060307JW0403, 9140A06050208JW0414, 9140A06050509JW0401, 9140A16070409JW0403, 9140A06050609JW0402, 9140A06050610JW0409, 9140A06070210JW0408).

REFERENCES

Bell, D. A., & Wang, H. (2000). A formalism for relevance and its application in feature subset selection. *Machine Learning, 41*(2), 175–195. doi:10.1023/A:1007612503587

Blum, A., & Langley, P. (1997). Selection of relevant features and examples in machine learning. *Artificial Intelligence, 97*(1-2), 245–271. doi:10.1016/S0004-3702(97)00063-5

Cardie, C. (1993). Using Decision Trees to Improve Case-based Learning. In *Proceedings of Tenth International Conference on Machine Learning* (pp. 25-32).

Dash, M., & Liu, H. (2003). Consistency-based Search in Feature Selection. *Artificial Intelligence, 151*, 155–176. doi:10.1016/S0004-3702(03)00079-1

Han, J. K., Hu, X. H., & Lin, T. Y. (2004). *Feature Subset Selection Based on Relative Dependency between Attributes* (pp. 176–185). Rough Sets and Current Trends in Computing.

Hu, Q. H., Zhao, H., Xie, Z. X., & Yu, D. R. (2007). Consistency Based Attribute Reduction. In . *Proceedings of PAKDD, 2007*, 96–107.

Hu, X. H. (1995). Knowledge discovery in database: an attribute-oriented rough set approach. Unpublished doctoral dissertation, Regina.

Hussein, A., & Thomas, G. D. (1994). Learning Boolean Concepts in the Presence of Many Irrelevant Features. *Artificial Intelligence, 69*(1-2), 279–305. doi:10.1016/0004-3702(94)90084-1

Jelonek, J., Krawiec, K., & Slowinski, R. (1995). Rough set reduction of attributes and their domains for neural networks. *Computational Intelligence, 11*, 339–347. doi:10.1111/j.1467-8640.1995.tb00036.x

Jensen, R., & Shen, Q. (2004). Semantics-preserving dimensionality reduction: rough and fuzzy-rough-based approaches. *IEEE Transactions on Knowledge and Data Engineering, 16*(12), 1457–1471. doi:10.1109/TKDE.2004.96

Koller, D., & Sahami, M. (1996). Towards Optimal Feature Selection. In *Proceedings of the Thirteenth International Conference on Machine Learning*. San Francisco, CA: Morgan Kaufumann.

Kononenko, I. (1994). Estimating Attributes: Analysis and Extension of RELIEF. In *Proceedings of the Sixth European Conf. Machine Learning* (pp. 171-182).

Lin, T. Y. (1989). Neighborhood Systems and Approximation in Database and Knowledge Base Systems. In *Proceedings of the Fourth International Symposium on Methodologies of Intelligent Systems* (pp. 75-86).

Lin, T. Y. (1997). Neighborhood Systems-A Qualitative Theory for Fuzzy and Rough Sets . In Wang, P. (Ed.), *Advances in Machine Intelligence and Soft Computing* (*Vol. 4*, pp. 132–155). Durham, NC: Duke University.

Lin, T. Y. (1998a). Granular Computing on Binary Relations I: Data Mining and Neighborhood Systems . In Skowron, A., & Polkowski, L. (Eds.), *Rough Sets In Knowledge Discovery* (pp. 107–121). Berlin: Physica Verlag.

Lin, T. Y. (1998b). Granular Computing on Binary Relations II: Rough Set Representations and Belief Functions . In Skowron, A., & Polkowski, L. (Eds.), *Rough Sets In Knowledge Discovery* (pp. 121–140). Berlin: Physica Verlag.

Lin, T. Y., & Yin, P. (2004). Heuristically Fast Finding of the Shortest Reducts. *Rough Sets and Current Trends in Computing*, 465-470.

Liu, Y., Xiong, R., & Chu, J. (2009). Quick Hash based Attribute Reduction. *Chinese Journal of Computers, 32*(8), 1493–1499.

Pawlak, Z. (1991). *Rough sets: theoretical aspects and reasoning about data*. Boston: Kluwer Academic Publishers.

Segen, J. (1984). Feature Selection and Constructive Inference. In *Proceedings of the Seventh Int'l Conf. Pattern Recognition* (pp. 1344-1346).

Sheinvald, J., Dom, B., & Niblack, W. (1990). A Modelling Approach to Feature Selection. In *Proceedings of Tenth International Conference on Pattern Recognition* (Vol. 1, pp. 535-539).

Swiniarski, R. W., & Skowron, A. (2003). Rough set methods in feature selection and recognition. *Pattern Recognition Letters, 24*(6), 833–849. doi:10.1016/S0167-8655(02)00196-4

Zhong, N., Dong, J., & Ohsuga, S. (2001). Using rough sets with heuristics for feature selection. *Journal of Intelligent Information Systems, 16*(3), 199–214. doi:10.1023/A:1011219601502

ENDNOTE

[1] From this viewpoint, this problem can be equivalent to find the shortest reduct.

This work was previously published in volume 4, issue 2 of the International Journal of Cognitive Informatics and Natural Intelligence, edited by Yingxu Wang, pp. 75-84, copyright 2010 by IGI Publishing (an imprint of IGI Global).

Chapter 15
Learning Hierarchical Lexical Hyponymy

Jiayu Zhou
Arizona State University, USA

Shi Wang
Chinese Academy of Sciences, China

Cungen Cao
Chinese Academy of Sciences, China

ABSTRACT

Chinese information processing is a critical step toward cognitive linguistic applications like machine translation. Lexical hyponymy relation, which exists in some Eastern languages like Chinese, is a kind of hyponymy that can be directly inferred from the lexical compositions of concepts, and of great importance in ontology learning. However, a key problem is that the lexical hyponymy is so commonsense that it cannot be discovered by any existing acquisition methods. In this paper, we systematically define lexical hyponymy relationship, its linguistic features and propose a computational approach to semi-automatically learn hierarchical lexical hyponymy relations from a large-scale concept set, instead of analyzing lexical structures of concepts. Our novel approach discovered lexical hyponymy relation by examining statistic features in a Common Suffix Tree. The experimental results show that our approach can correctly discover most lexical hyponymy relations in a given large-scale concept set.

1. INTRODUCTION

With the advancement of modern information technology, we are facing the increasing need of language processing technologies in Eastern languages like Chinese. During past centuries, ontology building becomes an important part in

DOI: 10.4018/978-1-4666-1743-8.ch015

semantic-level linguistic and knowledge processing, and meanwhile, since most of our knowledge is incarnated within free text as the form of natural language, development of linguistic processing is helping to better ontology learning. Hyponymy relations play an important role in knowledge engineering and the acquisition of which becomes an essential and crucial problem. The hierarchy structure of hyponymy relations composes the skeleton of knowledge bases and application of which ranges natural language processing, information retrieval, machine translation to other related domains.

Several knowledge sources are used in hyponymy acquisition, three primary types of which are: structured corpus (De Meo, Terracina, Quattrone & Ursino, 2004), semi-structured corpus (Dolan, Vanderwende & Richardson, 1993) and unstructured corpus (Cao & Shi, 2001). The largest among the three is unstructured text, the research of which has attracted a lot of researchers and has become a key research area. Thanks to recent research effort on knowledge engineering, new knowledge sources, such as large scale Chinese concept set extracted from unstructured corpus (Wang, Cao, Cao and Cao, 2007; Zhou, Wang & Cao, 2007), are available and have provided rich information.

There are three mainstream approaches—the *Symbolic* approach, the *Statistical* approach and the *Hierarchical* approach—to discovery general hyponymy relations automatically or semi automatically (Du & Li, 2006). The Symbolic approach, depending on lexicon-syntactic patterns, is currently the most popular technique (Hearst, 1992; Liu, Cao, Wang & Chen, 2006; Liu, Cao & Wang, 2005; Ando, Sekine & Ishizaki, 2003). Hearst (1992) was one of the early researchers to extract hyponymy relations from Grolier's Encyclopedia by matching 4 given lexicon-syntactic patterns, and more importantly, she discussed about extracting lexicon-syntactic patterns by existing hyponymy relations. Liu (2005, 2006) used the "isa" pattern to extract Chinese hyponymy relations from unstructured Web corpus, and have been proven to have a promising performance. Zhang (2007) proposed a method to automatically extract hyponymy from Chinese domain-specific free text by three symbolic learning methods. The statistical approach usually adopts clustering and associative rules. Zelenko, Aone and Richardella (2003) introduced an application of kernel methods to extract two certain kinds of hyponymy rela-

tions with promising results, combining Support Vector Machine and Voted Perception learning algorithms. The hierarchical approach is trying to build a hierarchical structure of hyponymy relations. Caraballo (1999) built a hypernymy hierarchy of nouns via a bottom-up hierarchical clustering technique, which was akin to manually constructed hierarchy in WordNet.

In this study, we have found a special kind of Chinese hyponymy relationship, called *lexical hyponymy*, which is of great importance in ontology learning. To the best of our knowledge, no existing method can extract these hyponym relations. We propose a semi-automatic lexical hyponymy acquisition approach within a large-scale concept set, which integrates symbolic, statistical and hierarchical techniques. The fundamental process of our method is that we firstly hierarchically cluster the large-scale concept set according to our *common suffix tree clustering* algorithm, we then use some crucial statistics of concept set to construct *suffix concept identification rules*, which are used to extract *class concept candidates*. Then we apply a Google-based *class concept verification* on the candidates. After that, we use a prefix clustering in order to improve the efficiency of the human-involved judgment. Finally, we can export hierarchical lexical hyponymy relations from the common suffix tree. Experimental results prove that our approach can find lexical hyponymy with a promising result.

Recent advances in cognitive informatics and computing witness the growing demand of concepts, and abstract computation on concepts becomes the focuses of current researches in various fields. Concept algebra has been a fundamental part of the Denotational Mathematics framework (Wang, 2008), where concepts serve as a type of new mathematical entities. Success applications of concept algebra include internal knowledge representation, autonomous machine learning, intelligent search engines, etc. (Wang, 2009). Lexical hyponymy described in this paper can be used to extend the relationships of current knowledge base and more important, to facilitate the concept computation and related algebraic operations in the Denotational Mathematics framework.

The structure of the paper is as follows: In Section 2 we explain some basic concepts related. In Section 3 we describe our lexical hyponymy acquisition framework. The common suffix clustering is described in Section 4. In Section 5, we analyze the suffix with empirical rules we discovered. Moreover, baseline comparisons of such rules are provided. In Section 6 and 7 we propose a Google-based class concept verification method and an idea of Prefix Clustering, respectively. In Section 8 we illustrate the hierarchical hyponymy acquisition process. Experimental results and discussions are provided in Section 9. Finally, in Section 10 we conclude the paper and point out the direction of future research.

2. TERMINOLOGY

2.1 Hyponymy Relation

We introduce the definition of hyponymy relation in WordNet (Miller, Beckwith, Felbaum, Gross & Miller 1990). A concept represented by a synset {*x, x', ...*} is said to be a hyponym of the concept represented by the synset {*y, y', ...*} if native speakers accept sentences constructed from such frames as "*An x is a (kind of) y*", in which the *x* is the hyponymy concept (hyponymy for short) of *y*, and *y* is the hypernymy concept (hypernymy for short) of *x*. Hyponymy is transitive and asymmetrical, denoted by *ISA(x, y)*.

2.2 Transparent Noun Compound, Endocentric and Exocentric Compound

Transparent noun compounds, composing the majority of lexical concepts, can be derived from the meaning of its elements. For instance, concept '中国公民(Chinese citizen)' means a kind of

people owing loyalty to and entitled by birth or naturalization to the protection of China. Transparent noun compounds can be further divided into *endocentric* compound and *exocentric* compound. The endocentric compound is a hyponymy of its head (Barker & Szpakowicz, 1998). Term '大学校园(University Campus)' is endocentric because it is a kind of campus. Term '改革开放(Reform and Opening up)' is exocentric because it does not refer to a kind of "Opening up", but rather a parallel pair.

2.3 Lexical Hyponymy Relation

Lexical hyponymy relation is a kind of hyponymy relation we defined, which can be directly inferred from lexical composition of endocentric compounds.

For a n-gram lexical concept $<cpt>=<w_m><w_{m-1}>..<w_1>$ of endocentric noun compounds, where each $<w_i>$ denotes a single gram, if a hypernymy concept $<hyper>$ appears lexically in its suffix (i.e. $<hyper>=<w_j>...<w_1>$, $j<m$), we call the relation between $<cpt>$ and $<hyper>$ a lexical hyponymy relation. The concept *prefix* of a hyponymy concept is defined as $<pref>=<w_m>...<w_{j+1}>$ when it takes a suffix $<w_j>...<w_1>$. The lexical hyponymy relation in concept $<cpt>=<pref><hyper>$ is denoted as *HISA($<cpt>,<hyper>$)*.

One lexical concept may have multiple lexical hypernymy concepts, and lexical hyponymy relations may also occur among them, in which the concept of fewer grams is the hypernymy of the longer one. For instance, given a concept "北京人民政府(People's Government of Beijing)", we have:*(1)*<北京人民政府> =<北京*(Beijing)*><人民政府*(People's Government)*>. Further, we have: *(2)*. <人民政府>= <人民*(People)*><政府*(Government)*>

In (1), the lexical hypernymy of <北京人民政府> is <人民政府>, denoted by *HISA(<北京人民政府>, <人民政府>)*. Accordingly, we have *HISA(<人民政府>,<政府>)*. Through transitive attribute, we further have *HISA(<北京人民政府>, <政府>)*.

Notablely, lexical hyponymy relations in endocentric noun compounds are so commonsense that they rarely appear as lexical terms in corpus. For example, lexical term '大学校园是校园(university campus is a kind of campus)' is unlikely to be found in corpus. Therefore, popular corpus-based hyponymy acquisition methods are not viable to obtain this kind of hyponymy relations.

2.4 Class Concept

Class concept is a kind of concept that can be the hypernymy concept $<hyper>$ in $HISA(<cpt>, <hyper>)$. In the case above, $<$人民政府$(People's Government)>$ and $<$政府$(Government)>$ are both class concept. However, not all concepts are class concepts. Given a concept $<$吃在南京$(Food in Nanjing)>$, for example, the suffix concept $<$南京$(Nanjing)>$ is not a class concept, since there is no lexical hyponymy relation $HISA(<$吃在南京$(Food in Nanjing)>, <$南京$(Nanjing)>)$.

3. LEARNING FRAMEWORK

In a large-scale concept set C, if a subset $S=\{<cpt_1>,<cpt_2>,...,<cpt_n>\}$ exists, where

```
<cpt₁>=<pref₁><suf>,
<cpt₂>=<pref₂><suf>,
…
<cptₙ>=<prefₙ><suf>.
```

The $<suf>$ here denotes a *common suffix* of all concepts. We may think the $<suf>$ *could* be a hypernymy concept and following relations *may* exist:

```
HISA(<cpt₁>, <suf>),
HISA(<cpt₂>,<suf>),…,
HISA(<cptₙ>,<suf>)
```

For instance, given $S=\{$炭疽活菌苗$(Live Anthrax Vaccine),$ 冻干鼠疫活菌苗$(Freeze Dried$

$Plague Vaccine),$ 结核活菌苗$(Bacille Calmette Guerin),$ 自身菌苗$(Autovaccine),$ 外毒素菌苗$(Exotoxin vaccine)\}$, we can segment the concepts as follows,

$<$自身菌苗$>=<$自身$><$菌苗$>,$
$<$外毒素菌苗$>=<$外毒素$><$菌苗$>,$
$<$结核活菌苗$>=<$结核活$><$菌苗$>,$
$<$炭疽活菌苗$>=<$炭疽活$><$菌苗$>,$
$<$冻干鼠疫活菌苗$>=<$冻干鼠疫活$><$菌苗$>,$

where the corresponding hypernymy concept suffix $<suf>$ is $<$菌苗$(vaccine)>$ and all $HISA$ relations come into existence. However, if we consider the suffix chunk $<$苗$>$ to be $<suf>$ instead of $<$菌苗$>$ (i.e. we segment the concept $<$外毒素菌苗$>:=<$外毒素菌$><$苗$>$), all $HISA$ relations do not exist. Moreover, the suffix $<$苗$>$ can not even be considered as a concept. We notice that a subset $S'=\{$结核活菌苗, 炭疽活菌苗, 冻干鼠疫活菌苗$\}$ of S contains a longer common hyponymy $<$活菌苗$(live vaccine)>$, lexical hyponymy relations $HISA($结核活菌苗, 活菌苗$), HISA($炭疽活菌苗, 活菌苗$)$ and $HISA($冻干鼠疫活菌苗, 活菌苗$)$.

We will investigate into such common suffix in a concept set and mine lexical hyponymy taking advantage of the common suffix features. There is a limitation in this approach: the size of the concept set should be *very large* in order to find such common chunks. In an extreme case, we can extract nothing if there is only one concept in the concept set, even if the only concept in the set contains rich lexical hyponymy relations. However, there is no definition how large can be thought to be very large and we will analysis this factor in the experiment section.

Figure 1 describes our framework of lexical hyponymy acquisition. We use a Google-based statistical acquisition model (Zhou, Wang & Cao, 2007) to extract concepts from web corpus, which results in a large-scale concept set and then clustered them into a common suffix tree according to suffixes of concepts. The suffix analysis module uses a set of statistical-based

Figure 1. Lexical hyponymy learning framework

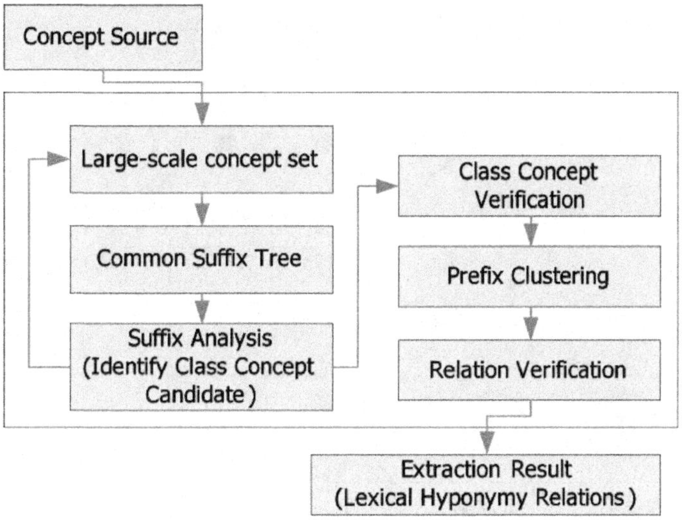

rules to analyze suffix nodes. Class concept candidates, which are concepts, are identified by our Google-base verification module and used to enlarge the original concept set. A class concept verification process was taken to verify class concept candidates. Human judgment-based relation verification is taken after a prefix clustering process dedicating to reduce the verification cost is done. Finally we got extracted hyponymy relations from the common suffix tree with a hierarchical structure.

4. COMMON SUFFIX TREE CLUSTERING

To find and analyze the common suffix, we propose a data structure called *common suffix tree (CST)*, inspired by suffix tree clustering (Gusfield, 1997).

Definition 1: *A common suffix tree containing m concepts is a tree with exactly m leaves. Each inner node, other than leaf, has more than two children, and contains a single Chinese gram. Each leaf indicates a concept with a longest shared suffix that equals the string leading from the leaf to root. Along with the path, the string from each inner node to root is a shared suffix of the concept indicated by leaves it can reach.*

With CST, not only are we able to find what is the longest shared suffix, we can also find which concepts share a certain common suffix. Following CST clustering algorithm will help us construct a CST in linear time complexity (Box 1).

The convergence condition of algorithm above is when the all clusters leave one leaf. For instance, in a given concept-set *S*={北京第六中学, 南京第十六中学, 天津第二十六中学, 经济学, 生物

Box 1.

CST Clustering Algorithm:
Use the suffix-based clustering, and compute big 1-gram concept clusters.
Until(convergence) {
    From each n-gram cluster, iterate the algorithm to get finer, hierarchy n+1 gram clusters.
}

Figure 2. Common Suffix Tree of {学}-cluster

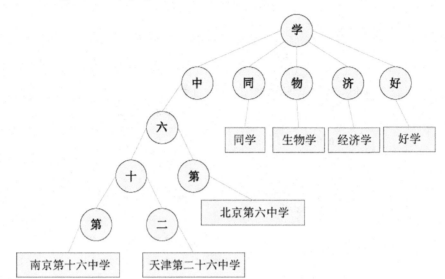

学, 好学, 同学, 木鱼, 黄花鱼, 烧黄花鱼, 鲤鱼}, The CST algorithm can be described as following steps:

1. Using the suffix-based clustering, we get big 1-gram clusters ({*} represents the least common suffix):

[北京第六中, 南京第十六中, 天津第二十六中, 经济, 生物, 好, 同] {学} [木, 黄花, 烧黄花, 鲤] {鱼},

2. From each 1-gram cluster, we iterate the algorithm to get finer, hierarchical clusters until convergence:

[[[北京第, [南京第, 天津第二] {十}] {六}] {中}, 经济, 生物, 好, 同] {学} [木, [#, 烧] {黄花}, 鲤] {鱼},

where # represents an empty entry.

Figure 2 visualized the CST structure of {学}-cluster. The rest parts of our framework are built on the computing and analysis on suffixes of CST.

5. SUFFIX ANALYSIS

Given the "学" cluster in the example above, the suffix collection **S**={第十六中学, 十六中学, 六中学, 中学} may all hypernymy concepts we interested in, without any other information supporting (1-gram suffix causes great ambiguous, therefore we leave it alone in our system).

Some suffix concepts may be extracted by some Chinese word segment systems, however, there is no word segment system adopted in our system, because the segment system performs poor in a large scale general-purposed concept set, where many suffixes cannot be correctly segmented and thus lowered the performance of the entire system.

However, some useful statistic features can be obtained in a concept-set to identify class concepts. For a suffix chunk $<ck>$ in concept-set, we may have patterns such as $CNT[<ck><*>]$, $CNT[<*><ck>]$, $CNT[<*><ck><*>]$ and etc., where $CNT[<pattern>]$ means the frequency of $<pattern>$ in concept set. A list of examples of such patterns was listed in Table 1.

Pattern (1) is not a real statistic. The pattern, once appears in the given concept set, prove that indicated suffix $<ck>$ is a class concept candidate.

If the concept set is *large enough* (i.e. for any *<cpt>*, always exists *<cpt>*∈*S*), this single rule can be used to identify all class concept candidates. Actually, our concept set can never achieve that large.

The emergence of pattern (2) and (3) is a strong indication of class concept, which usually can be some components of other words. Class concept *<大学(university)>* can be used as *limitation* of other concept, such as *<大学校区(university campus)>*, which indicates a special kind of *<校区(campus)>*. Experiment in following content shows that once the pattern (2) or (3) appears, the empirical probability of *<ck>* to be a concept is very high.

The information embedded in the pattern (4) is richer. We rewrite the *CNT[<*><ck>]* as $f_{suf}(<ck>)$, called *suffix frequency*. The *i*th suffix of concept *<cpt>* = *<x_m>*...*<x_1>* (i.e. *<x_i>*... *<x_1>*), where *<x_i>* a is single gram, is denoted as *Suf(<cpt>, i)* and *m* is the length of *<cpt>*. The *suffix probability S_{suf}(<cpt>,n)* is defined as:

$$S_{suf}(<cpt>,n) = p_{suf}(<x_m>...<x_1>, <x_{n+1}><x_n>...\\ <x_1>)$$

$$= f_{suf}(Suf(<cpt>,n+1)) / f_{suf}(Suf(<cpt>,n))$$

where $n \leq Length(<cpt>)-1$. $p_{suf}(<ck_1>, <ck_2>)$ is the joint probability of chunk *<ck_1>* and *<ck_2>*, which is produced by suffix frequency of the chunk *<ck_1>* devided by that of the chunk *<ck_2>*. We

Table 1. Statistical patterns and examples

Pattern	Example
(1) *ISCpt[<ck>]*	〈大学〉∈S
(2) *CNT[<ck><*>]*	〈大学〉学生服务部, 〈大学〉校区,…
(3) *CNT[<*><ck>]*	理工〈大学〉, 科技〈大学〉, …
(4) *CNT[<*><ck><*>]*	北京〈大学〉学生会, 中国〈大学〉评估组, …

define that single-gram concepts have no suffix probability.

Figure 3 shows some cases of suffix probability whose numbers of -grams composed are ranging from 4 to 9. Such cases illustrate how suffix probability changes with varying number of -grams.

Figure 3 (V) shows the change of suffix frequency of concept *<cpt>:= "混合型证券投资基金"* in a concept set with a size of 800,000. Figure 3 (U) shows the situation when *<cpt>:= "流行性感冒病毒感染"*. For instance,

S("混合型证券投资基金", 2)=P("基金", "资基金")=F("资基金")/F("基金")= 300/498 = 0.60241

From the case (S) we observe that *S(<cpt>, 3)=0.99667* is the maximum among *S(<cpt>, 2)*, *S(<cpt>, 3)* and *S(<cpt>, 4)*. At the same time *Suf(<cpt>, 4)* (i.e. 投资基金) is a class concept. Same situation could be found in maximum point *S(<cpt>, 5)* and *S(<cpt>, 8)*, while *Suf(<cpt>, 6)* and *Suf(<cpt>, 8)* are both class concepts. In another case when <cpt>="流行性感冒病毒感染", we find the same phenomenon that class concept happened to appear in inflexions, which makes us believe it to be a useful rule. The rule is proved to be very effective in later experiment and is defined as follows:

Definition 2: *(Suffix Probability Inflexion Rule) In a large-scale concept set, whenever the suffix probability S(<cpt>,n) encounters an inflexion, the suffix Suf(<cpt>,n+1) =<w_{n+1}><w_n>...<w_1> is considered to be a class concept candidate, which is called Inflexion Rule.*

The suffix probability inflexion rule is exported from empirical study, and the hidden theoretical support of this rule is based on *mutual information*. The higher the *S(<cpt>,n)*, then the suffix *<w_n>*... *<w_1>* and *<w_{n+1}><w_n>...<w_1>* has higher mutual information, which may lead to a close correlation, the sudden reduce of mutual information means differentiation in linguistic usage.

Figure 3. Case study: suffix probability of 4, 5, 6, 8, 9-gram concepts respectively

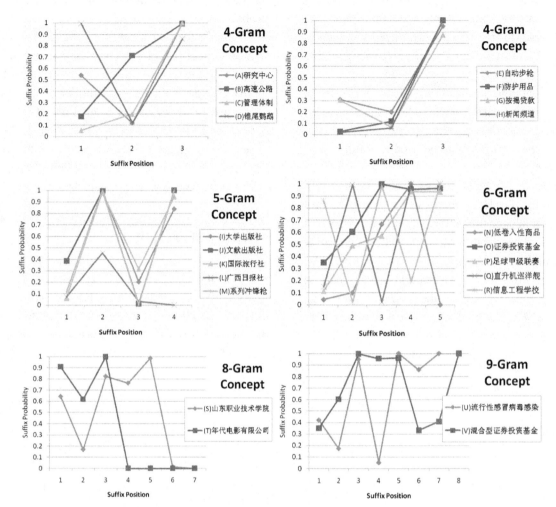

Based on the discussions above, we summarize three *Suffix Concept Identification (SCI)* Rules:

1. Pattern ISCpt[<wx>] appears, then <wx> must be a concept.
2. Pattern CNT[<wx><*>] or CNT[<*><wx><*>] appears, then <wx> can be a concept.
3. Suffix Probability Inflexion Rule.

SCI Rules is practical when we are trying to extract and identify potential concepts from concept set. It is, of course, easy for people to identify such concepts from text based on our perception and cognition, but there are no existing methods for machine to do such task. SCI rules take advantage of empirical and statistical features of patterns in the concept set to find concepts. The experimental baseline comparisons among three rules are listed in Table 2. We use SCI rules in an 800,000 concept set and 300 test cases and manually extract all the class concept candidates in test cases, denoted by *cm*. Then we use SCI rules to extract class concepts, denoted by *ca*. We adopt following evaluation measurements in baseline experiment:

Precision = | ca ∩ cm | / | ca |

Table 2. SCI Rules Baseline Comparison (- mean the value is lower than 5%)

	Precision		Recall	
	Average	Std. Dev	Average	Std. Dev
Rule(1)	100%	0	-	n/a
Rule(2)	95.753%	0.4603	-	n/a
Rule(3)	98.641%	0.1960	65.125%	2.393
Rule(1,2)	96.561%	0.5133	-	n/a
Rule(1,2,3)	98.145%	0.5029	66.469%	2.792

Recall = | ca ∩ cm | / | cm |

The average value and standard deviation of precisions and recalls are computed in 5 baseline scheme. Rules based on (1), (2) or the combinations of which have a low recall although with a high precision, as a result of the data sparsity. However, rule (3) holds a high precision and at the same time has a promising recall once combined with the other two rules.

6. CLASS CONCEPT VERIFICATION

In previous section we mentioned that not every concept could be a class concept. In this section, we proposed a lexicon-syntactic approach to verify class concept by scoring concepts via Googling web corpus.

Through our investigation over large free-text corpus, class concepts primarily appear in three kinds of lexicon-syntactic patterns which have different semantic meanings: Class I patterns appear when people are trying to give examples. Class II patterns are used when people construct question sentences. Class III patterns are, on the other hand, commonly used when we give definitions. The generic type of Class II is $<Which><*>$, where $<Which>$ is one of the interrogatives. The generic type of Class II is $<是> <Unit><*>$, and here $<Unit>$ is one of the unit quantifiers. Therefore, the pattern II and III includes a number of patterns. All three types of pattern with examples are summarized as shown in Table 3.

Definition 3: *Google provides statistical information in web corpus, probability framework based on which has been built by (Zhou, Wang & Cao, 2007; Cilibrasi & Vitanyi, 2007). Given a lexical*

Table 3. Patterns and examples in three classes

Pattern Type	Pattern Examples	Examples
Class I *<Such as><*>*	<ClassCpt>例如	一些水果例如香蕉, 它如何繁衍后代
	等<ClassCpt>	76%预期深圳等城市的房价将下跌
Class II *<Which><*>*	什么<ClassCpt>	福威镖局在福州府的什么大街
	哪些<ClassCpt>	中国哪些城市适宜工作?
	那种<ClassCpt>	青苹果和红苹果哪种苹果有营养
Class III *<是><Unit><*>*	是一个<ClassCpt>	法国夏特瑞城是一个小镇
	是一种<ClassCpt>	宪政是一种文化
	是一类<ClassCpt>	他和你是一类人

chunk <ck>, the frequency of this term is defined as number of pages containing such term, denoted by f(<ck>).

Definition 4: *For a concept <cpt>, the pattern frequency is defined as f(Pattern(<cpt>)), where Pattern(<cpt>) is applying the concept to a certain pattern. Pattern association is defined as the pattern frequency of the concept dividing its frequency, denoted by p(Pattern(<cpt>)).*

$$p(Pattern(<cpt>)) = \\ f(Pattern(<cpt>)) \, / \, f(<cpt>)$$

To verify class concepts, pattern associations can be used as attributes to train a classifier by machine learning algorithms. However, according to the linguistic property of the three classes, the pattern associations of a certain concept are likely to associate well with only one pattern in each class. Therefore we only use the patterns that can have the maximum pattern association in each class. We use the liner combination to sum pattern associations of all three classes into a scoring function, which is proved to be more effective than adopting three separate attributes.

Three classes of patterns are assigned with different *class weights* w_I, w_{II}, w_{III}, which can be used to adjust score according to liner analysis methods. Besides, we take the frequency of concept as a coefficient of the score, which indicates that a concept with a higher frequency is more likely to be a class concept. To sum all effects above, the expression of scoring a concept <cpt> is:

$$Score(<cpt>) = Log(f(<cpt>)) \times \\ \sum_{i \in (I,II,III)} (w_i \times \underset{j \in Class_i}{Max}(p(Pattern_j(<cpt>))))$$

To obtain a score threshold identifying class concept, we firstly annotate a training set of 3000 concepts, including 1500 class concept and 1500

non-class concept. We then use Google to retrieve pattern associations of training set. So the pattern associations are calculated into a score. And we use a linear analysis method to adjust the class weighs that can maximize the scoring function, and finally we get a score threshold. Concepts that exceed the given threshold are classified as class concept and vice versa. In our experiment, the class concept classifier we built is proved to achieve a remarkable high accuracy at 95.52%.

7. PREFIX CLUSTERING

Due to the property of lexical hyponymy relations, they hardly appear in other sources such as text corpus and web corpus, which makes human judgment a compulsory step in the relation verification process. In a large-scale concept set, the number of lexical hyponymy relations is huge, and thus it becomes a misery if we need to manually verify each relation.

In a concept sub-set S={〈京津塘高速公路〉, 〈长株潭高速公路〉, 〈京石高速公路〉, 〈京承高速公路〉, 〈信息高速公路〉} with the suffix Suf={<*>, 4} and Suf={<*>, 2}, where <*> denotes the wildcard of concepts, but the hyponymy relation within term <信息高速公路 *(Information High-Way)*> is different from others. Since the concept is a kind of metaphor, there is not a real lexical hyponymy relation. If we can cluster the relations into meaningful groups, such as, metaphor group and non-metaphor group, it is possible for us to verify parts of the relation group instead of all relations.

We notice that a prefix <*pref*> of a concept <*cpt*>=<*pref*><*suf*> is typically a term that forms parts of other concepts in our concept set. Given a <*pref*>, $H(<pref>)$ denotes all chunks that appears before <*pref*> in other concepts and $T(<pref>)$ denotes all chunks that appears after <*pref*> in other concepts. The two statistical information, that provided by *concept set context*, can be used to define the similarity of two prefixes.

Figure 4. Judging cases and accuracy in prefix clustering

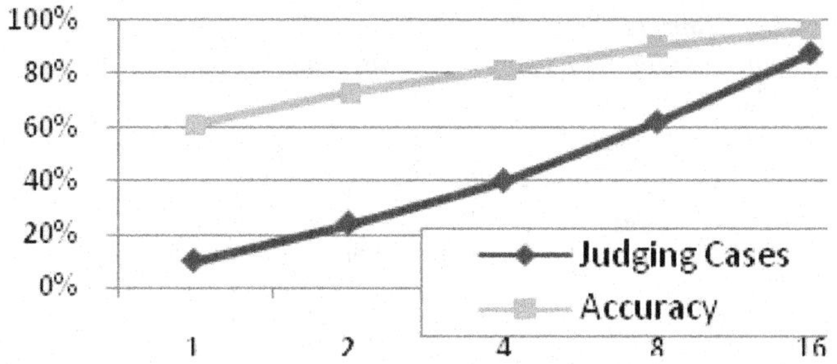

Definition 5: *Prefix Similarity is a quantity for measuring the similarity of two prefixes within a concept-set context. It is the average of Crossover Coefficients of Head Similarity and Tail Similarity.*

$$Sim(<x>,<y>) =$$
$$(\frac{|H(<x>) \cap H(<y>)|}{\min(|H(<x>)|,|H(<y>)|)} + \frac{|T(<x>) \cap T(<y>)|}{\min(|T(<x>)|,|T(<y>)|)})$$

K-cluster technique, which is the simplest unsupervised learning algorithm, enables us to cluster data according to a given number of clusters *k* (MacQueen, 1967). With the ease to control cluster number, we can then flexibly choose a specific grain to cluster our relations. We perform a k-cluster algorithm on concept set using prefix similarity. In the case above, there are 1210 concepts containing "信息" in our 800,000 concept set. Other prefix terms rarely appear and share some terms such as <*><收费站>. Given *k=2*, the prefix <信息> will be placed in a separate group through clustering, while the rest four prefixes are grouped into one cluster. Hence, we only need to judge two hyponymy relations respectively from each cluster. From the empirical study, the best k-value is a median proportion of the size of the target concept sub-set.

This step is optional comparing to other modules employed in our framework, and sometimes it may lower the precision of the system. Figure 4 describes our judging cases and accuracy in a 1000-sized sub tree of a CST built by an 800,000 concept set. When setting the K-value to be 8,

we will have an accuracy of 90.4% by judging 62% relation cases. Remarkably, not only does the percentage of judging cases depend on K-value, it also relates to the structure of targeting CST. However, prefix clustering will significantly improve the efficiency of human judgment during verification phase.

8. ACQUIRING HIERARCHICAL LEXICAL HYPONYMY

Given a concept set *C*, we use the CST clustering technique in Sect.4 to build a CST. Then we compute the statistics of patterns described in Sect. 5 and store them in each CST node. We apply the SCI rules to extract class concept candidates *T'*, and add them to *C*, enlarging our original concept set. We verify the unverified candidates in *T'* with the Google-base verification described in Sect. 6, and get a class concept set *T*. In lexical hyponymy relation candidate set *H'*, we remove all the relations that have hypernymy concepts in *T-T'*.

Lexical hyponymy relations are generated as follows: For a given concept node *<cpt>*, set *{<s-cpt_i> ... <s-cpt_n>}* is used to denote all the verified class concept nodes it goes through in CST, and we have *HISA(<s-cpt_i>, <s-cpt_j>)* (*i<j*). Put all generated relations to *H'*. As the original concept set changed, we update statistical information of each node, and keep performing steps above until the status of each node remains unchanged.

Figure 5. Acquiring hierarchical lexical hyponymy relations

> *Acquiring a large-scale concept set **C**.*
> *Constructing CST using CST clustering.*
> *While(Convergence){*
>   *Compute statistical information of inner nodes.*
>   *For each concept node <cpt> in CST {*
>   *Apply SCI rules.*
>   *Get all class concept candidates **T'***
>   ***C ←T'***
>   ***T ←** Verify unverified candidates in **T'***
>   *Remove hyponymy of invalid candidates*
>   ***H' ←**All relation candidates in **T***
>   *}*
> *}*
> *Perform Prefix Clustering in **H'***
> *Judging Relations in **H'**, resulting **H***

Finally we cluster the prefix according to Sect.7 and judge one relation candidate in each cluster in ***H'***, resulting our final *hierarchical* lexical hyponymy relation set ***H***. The pseudo code of acquiring process is given in Figure 5.

To better illustrate this acquisition process, an example is given in Figure 6. Nodes {*a, b, c, d, e, f*} are *suffix chunk nodes* in a Common Suffix Tree. A suffix chunk node represents a lexical chunk of string starting from the corresponding CST node leading to the root. In (I), we have already known that *b, d, e* are class concept nodes and the rest are unknown nodes. Through suffix analysis, *a* is proved to be a non-concept and *b, c* are identified to be class concept candidates, as shown in (II).

The candidates are then verified by the class concept classifier. In (III), *c* is classified as class concept and *d* is classified as non-class concept. Hyponymy relation candidates are *HISA(d, c)*, *HISA(e, c)*, *HISA(d, b)*, *HISA(e, b)*, *HISA(f, b)*, where *HISA(d, b)* and *HISA(e, b)* are derived from *transitivity* of hyponymy relation. *HISA(e, c)* is judged as a non-hyponymy relation, leading that *HISA(e, b)* to be removed, as shown in (IV).

9. EXPERIMENTAL RESULT

Our lexical hyponymy relation acquisition is being evaluated through 5 concept sets of the size

Figure 6. An example of hierarchical acquisition process

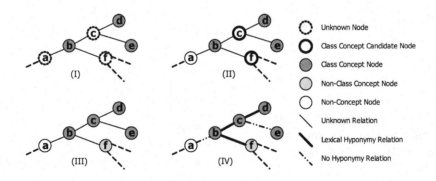

Figure 7. System performance with different concept set size

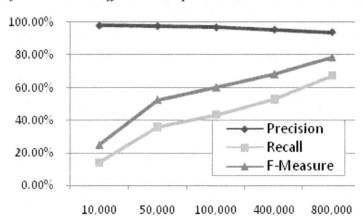

of 10000, 50000, 100000, 400000, and 800000, respectively. To compare their performances under different settings, we use the resulting lexical hyponymy relations acquired, followed by a human judgment with a k=10 prefix clustering. Following commonly used formulas are used to evaluate the performance of our system:

Precision = Correct Relations Acquired / Relations Acquired,

Recall = Correct Relations Acquired / Total Relations Exist,

F-Measure = 2 * Precision * Recall / (Precision + Recall).

From the acquisition result shown in Figure 7, we can discover that F-measure incrementally increases coincides the larger concept-set size, from 24.93 in 10000-sized concept set, climbing to 78.34 in 800000 one. Precision lower slightly and recall increase significantly with a larger concept set. As the size of concept set enlarges, more statistical information emerges, and at the same time more suffix concepts are extracted as class concepts, some of which form lexical hyponymy relations, causing a higher recall, while some other relations are invalid, leading to a lower precision.

Under the concept-set with a size of 800000, the precision is 93.8% and recall reaches to 67.24%. The recall can be even higher when given a larger concept set.

In our concept set, we discover noise due to exocentric compounds, in which the suffix concepts are not hypernymy concepts. So far, no effort has been done to verify Chinese exocentric structures and the difficulty of linguistic usage makes it hard to analyze semantic relation within Chinese lexical concepts, which inevitably lower the precision of our framework.

Single-gram hypernymy concepts, such as '计', are likely to cause ambiguity. In our concept set, we find a large number of concepts ended with suffixes like {"硬度计","光度计", "温度计", "速度计", "长度计", "高度计"}. The mutual information between "度" and "计" is very high, leading the algorithm adopting SPI rule to wrongly mark the chunk "度计", rather than "计", as a class concept candidate. This problem might be solved if we could avoid the information sparsity by further enlarging the concept set.

The precision of class concept verification module is an important factor to the performance of whole system. We can further obtain a larger feature space and enhance the performance by employing advanced learning techniques such as SVM and Naïve Bayes Network.

Final precision of the framework is affected by our prefix clustering judgment, however, when the concept set becomes larger and thus more relations are extracted, it is inevitable for us to adopt that judgment.

10. CONCLUSION

We propose a novel approach to discover lexical hyponymy relations in a large-scale concept set and make the acquisition of lexical hyponymy relations possible. In this method we cluster a concept set into a common suffix tree firstly, and then use the proposed statistical suffix identification rules to extract class concept candidates in the inner nodes of the common suffix tree. We then design a Google-base symbolic class concept verifier. Finally we extract Lexical hyponymy relations and judge them after the prefix clustering process. Experimental result has shown that our approach is efficient and can correctly acquire most lexical hyponymy relations in a large-scale concept set.

Future work will be concentrated on the extraction of single-gram suffixes, which covers a large part of lexical hyponymy relations. On the other hand, through inner cross verification within a concept set, an approach that automatically verifies hyponymy relation is coming soon.

ACKNOWLEDGMENT

This work is supported by the National Natural Science Foundation of China under Grant No. 60496326, 60573063, and 60573064; the National 863 Program under Grant No.2007AA01Z325. The authors would like to thank anonymous reviewers for their valuable comments and suggestions.

REFERENCES

Ando, M., Sekine, S., & Ishizaki, S. (2003). *Automatic Extraction of Hyponyms from Newspaper Using Lexicon-syntactic Patterns* (IPSJ SIG Technical Report 2003-NL-157). Tokyo: Information Processing Society in Japan.

Barker, K., & Szpakowicz, S. (1998). Semi-automatic recognition of noun modifier relationships. In *Proceedings of the 36th Annual Meeting of the Association for Computational Linguistics, 17th International Conference on Computational Linguistics* (Vol. 1, pp. 96-102). ACL/ Morgan Kaufmann Publishers.

Beeferman, D. (1998). Lexical discovery with an enriched semantic network. In *Proceedings of the ACL/COLING Workshop on Applications of WordNet in Natural Language Processing Systems* (pp. 135-141). Association of Computational Linguistics.

Cao, C., & Shi, Q. (2001). Acquiring Chinese Historical Knowledge from Encyclopedic Texts. In *Proceedings of the International Conference for Young Computer Scientists* (pp. 1194-1198). IEEE Computer Society Press.

Caraballo, A. S. (1999). Automatic construction of a hypernym-labeled noun hierarchy from text. In *Proceedings of 37th Annual Meeting of the Association for Computational Linguistics* (pp. 120-126). Association for Computational Linguistics.

Cilibrasi, R. L., & Vitanyi, P. (2007). The Google Similarity Distance. *IEEE Transactions on Knowledge and Data Engineering, 19*(3), 370–383. doi:10.1109/TKDE.2007.48

De Meo, P., Terracina, G., Quattrone, G., & Ursino, D. (2004). Extraction of synonymies, hyponymies, overlappings and homonymies from XML schemas at various "severity" levels. In *Proceedings of the International Conference on Database Engineering and Application Symposium* (pp. 389-394). IEEE Computer Society Press.

Dolan, W., Vanderwende, L., & Richardson, S. D. (1993). Automatically Deriving Structured Knowledge Bases from Online Dictionaries. In *Proceedings of the 1993 Pacific Association for Computational Linguistics* (pp. 5-14). Pacific Association for Computational Linguistics.

Du, X., & Li, M. (2006). A Survey of Ontology Learning Research. *Journal of Software, 17*(9), 1837–1847. doi:10.1360/jos171837

Gusfield, D. (1997). *Algorithms on Strings, Trees and Sequences: Computer Science and Computational Biology*. Cambridge, UK: Cambridge University Press.

Hearst, A. M. (1992). Automatic acquisition of hyponyms from large text corpora. In *Proceedings of the 14th International Conference on Computational Linguistics* (pp. 539-545). Association of Computational Linguistics.

Liu, L., Cao, C., & Wang, H. (2005). Acquiring Hyponymy Relations from Large Chinese Corpus. *WSEAS Transactions on Business and Economics, 2*(4), 211–218.

Liu, L., Cao, C., Wang, H., & Chen, W. (2006). A Method of Hyponym Acquisition Based on "isa" Pattern. *Journal of Computer Science,* 146-151.

MacQueen, J. (1967). Some Methods for classification and Analysis of Multivariate Observations. In *Proceedings of the 5th Berkeley Symposium on Mathematical Statistics and Probability* (pp. 281-297). Berkeley, CA: University of California Press.

Miller, G. A., Beckwith, R., Felbaum, C., Gross, D., & Miller, K. J. (1990). Introduction to WordNet: An On-line Lexical Database. *International Journal of Lexicography, 3*(4), 235–244. doi:10.1093/ijl/3.4.235

Rydin, S. (2002). Building a hyponymy lexicon with hierarchical structures. In *Proceedings of the ACL-02 Workshop on Unsupervised Lexical Acquisition* (Vol. 9, pp. 26-33). Association of Computational Linguistics.

Wang, S., Cao, Y., Cao, X., & Cao, C. (2007). Learning concepts from text based on the inner-constructive model. In Z. Zhang & J. Siekmann (Eds.), *2nd International Conference on Knowledge Science, Engineering, and Management* (pp. 255-266). Springer.

Wang, Y. (2008). On Concept Algebra: A Denotational Mathematical Structure for Knowledge and Software Modeling. *International Journal of Cognitive Informatics and Natural Intelligence, 2*(2), 1–19.

Wang, Y. (2009). On Abstract Intelligence: Toward A Unified Theory of Natural, Artificial, Machinable, and Computational Intelligence. *International Journal of Software Science and Computational Intelligence, 1*(1), 1–17.

Zelenko, D., Aone, C., & Richardella, A. (2003). Kernel Methods for Relation Extraction. *Journal of Machine Learning Research, 3*, 1083–1106. doi:10.1162/153244303322533205

Zhang, C. (2005). The State of the Art and Difficulties in Automatic Chinese Word Segmentation. *Journal of System and Simulation, 17*(1), 138–143.

Zhang, C., Cao, C., Liu, L., Niu, Z., & Lin, J. (2007). Extracting hyponymy relations from domain-specific free texts. In *Proceedings of the 9th International Conference on Machine Learning and Cybernetics* (pp. 3360-3365). IEEE Computer Society Press.

Zhou, J., Wang, S., & Cao, C. (2007). A Google-based statistical acquisition model of Chinese lexical concepts. In Z. Zhang & J. Siekmann (Eds.), *2nd International Conference on Knowledge Science, Engineering, and Management* (pp. 243-254). Springer.

This work was previously published in volume 4, issue 1 of the International Journal of Cognitive Informatics and Natural Intelligence, edited by Yingxu Wang, pp. 98-114, copyright 2010 by IGI Publishing (an imprint of IGI Global).

Chapter 16

A New Quantum Evolutionary Algorithm with Sifting Strategy for Binary Decision Diagram Ordering Problem

Abdesslem Layeb
University Mentouri of Constantine, Algeria

Djamel-Eddine Saidouni
University Mentouri of Constantine, Algeria

ABSTRACT

In this work, the authors focus on the quantum evolutionary quantum hybridization and its contribution in solving the binary decision diagram ordering problem. Therefore, a problem formulation in terms of quantum representation and evolutionary dynamic borrowing quantum operators are defined. The sifting search strategy is used in order to increase the efficiency of the exploration process, while experiments on a wide range of data sets show the effectiveness of the proposed framework and its ability to achieve good quality solutions. The proposed approach is distinguished by a reduced population size and a reasonable number of iterations to find the best order, thanks to the principles of quantum computing and to the sifting strategy.

INTRODUCTION

The checking of software and electrical circuit is crucial element to detect the errors which they contain or to show that they function well. One of the most used verification methods used is the model-checking (Clarke, 1994). However, the great difficulty encountered in the domain of formal verification is the combinatorial explosion problem. For example in the model checking, the number of states in the transition graphs can reach prohibitive level, which makes their manipulation

DOI: 10.4018/978-1-4666-1743-8.ch016

difficult or impossible. Consequently, compression methods are used in order to reduce the size of the state graph. The compression is done by using data structures in order to represent in a concise manner the set of states. In this case, the operations are done so on set of states rather than on explicit states.

The representation by the Binary Decision Diagrams BDD is among the most known symbolic notations (Akers, 1978; Drechsler & Becker, 1998). The BDD is a data structure used to efficiently represent Boolean functions. Since they offer a canonical representation and an easy manipulation, the BDD is largely used in several fields such as the logic synthesis (Hachtel & Somenzi, 2006) and the formal verification (Hu, Dill, Drexler, & Yang, 1992). However, the BDD size depends strongly on the selected variable order. Therefore it is important to find a variable order which minimizes the number of nodes in a BDD. The BDD variable order is very important especially in the symbolic model checking, employed in the formal verification of digital circuits and other finite state systems (McMillan, 1992). The exact methods used to resolve this problem are based on dynamic programming with pruning to find the optimal order (Ishiura, Sawada, & Yajima, 1991; Drechsler, Drechsler, & Slobodova, 1998; Friedman & Supowit, 1987). Unfortunately, these methods are not practicable for large instances considering the fact that there are an exponential number of possible variable orders. Indeed, the problem of variable ordering has been shown to be Np-difficult (Bollig & Wegener, 2002). For that, several heuristics were proposed to find the best BDD variable order and which can be classified in two categories. The first class tries to extract the good order by inspecting the logical circuits (Fujii, Ootomo, & Hori, 1988; Fujita, Fujisawa, & Kawato, 1988), whereas, the second class is based on the dynamic optimization of a given order (Meinel & Slobodova, 1997; Ishiura, Sawada, & Yajima, 1991). The Sifting algorithm introduced by Rudell (1993) constitutes one of the most

successful algorithms for dynamic reordering of variables. This algorithm is based on finding the best position of a variable in the order by moving the variable to all possible positions while preserving the other variables static. There are other methods based on metaheuristics like genetic algorithms (Drechsler, Becker, & Göckel, 1996; Costa, Déharbe, & Moreira, 2000), simulated annealing (Bollig, Löbbing, & Wegener, 1995), and scatter search algorithm (Hung & Song, 2001).

Quantum Computing (QC) is a new research field that encompasses investigations on quantum mechanical computers and quantum algorithms (Williams & Clearwater, 1998; Nielsen & Chuang, 2000; Jaeger, 2006). QC relies on the principles of quantum mechanics like qubit representation and superposition of states. QC is capable of processing huge numbers of quantum states simultaneously in parallel. QC brings new philosophy to optimization due to its underlying concepts. Recently, a growing theoretical and practical interest is devoted to researches on merging evolutionary computation and quantum computing (Han & Kim, 2004; Layeb, Meshoul, & Batouhe, 2006). The purpose of this combination is to get benefit from quantum computing capabilities to enhance both efficiency and speed of classical evolutionary algorithms. This has led to the design of Quantum inspired Evolutionary Algorithms (QEA) that have been proven to be better than conventional evolutionary algorithms in many areas. Unlike pure quantum computing, QEA doesn't require the presence of a quantum machine to work.

The present study was designed to investigate the use of a QEA hybridized with the Sifting technique to deal with the BDD variable ordering problem. In this context, we propose in this article, a new Quantum Evolutionary Algorithm for Binary Decision Diagram problem called QEABDD. For that, a problem formulation in terms of quantum representation and evolutionary dynamic borrowing quantum operators were defined. The quantum representation of the solutions allows the coding of all the potential orders with

Figure 1. BDD representation of the function (X1∨X3)∧(X2⇒X4)

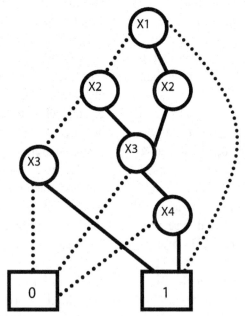

a certain probability. The optimization process consists in the application of a quantum dynamic constituted of a set of quantum operations such as interference, quantum mutation and measure. To foster the convergence to optimality, a local search based sifting technique has been embedded within the optimization process. The experiences carried out on QEABDD showed the feasibility and the effectiveness of our approach.

BINARY DECISION DIAGRAM

A BDD is a rooted directed acyclic graph $G = (V, E)$ with node set V containing two kinds of nodes, *non-terminal* and *terminal* nodes (Figure 1) (Drechsler & Becker, 1998). A non-terminal node v has as tag a variable *index* $(v) \in \{x_1, x_2, ..., x_n\}$ and two children $low(v)$, $high(v) \in V$. The final nodes are called *0-final and 1-final*. A BDD can be used to compute a Boolean function $f(x_1, x_2, .., x_n)$ in the following way. Each input $a = (a_1, a_2, ..., a_n) \in \{0,1\}^n$ defines a computation path

through the BDD that starts at the root. If the path reaches a non-terminal node v that is labelled by x_i, it follows the path *low(v)* if $a_i = 0$, and it follows the path *high(v)* if $a_i = 1$. The label of the terminal node determines the return value of the BDD on input a. the BDD is called "ordered" if the different variables appear in the same order on all the ways from the root (Figure 1). It is important to note that for a given order of variables, the minimal binary decision graph is single. A BDD can be reduced while using the two following rules (Bryant, 1986):

- Recognize and share identical sub-trees.
- Erase nodes whose left and right child nodes are identical.

It is very important to take into account the order of variables to be used when using the BDD in practice. The size of a BDD is largely affected by the choice of the variable ordering as is shown in the Figure 2. Unfortunately, there are an exponential number of possible orders (permutation).

Figure 2. The influence of variable order on BDD complexity. Two BDDs representation of the function (X1∨X3)∧(X2⇒X4), in the left the order of variable is: X1, X2, X3, X4; in the right the order is: X1, X3, X2, X4

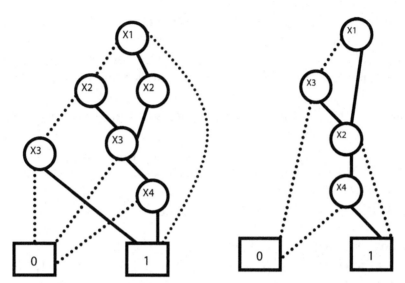

It is completely clear that finding the optimal BDD variable order is NP-difficult (Friedman & Supowit, 1987). The use of heuristics is essential to find acceptable solutions within reasonable times. Within this perspective, we are interested in applying a hybrid evolutionary approach based on quantum computing principles and sifting algorithm to solve the variable ordering problem.

QUANTUM COMPUTING

Quantum Computing (QC) is an emergent field calling upon several specialties: physics, engineering, chemistry, computer science and mathematics. QC uses the specificities of quantum mechanics for the processing and the transformation of information. The aim of this integration of knowledge is the realization of a quantum computer in order to carry out certain calculations much more quickly than with a traditional computer. This acceleration is made possible while benefiting from the quantum phenomena such as the superposition of states, the entanglement and the interference. A particle

according to principles of quantum mechanics can be in a superposition of states. By taking account of this idea, one can define a quantum bit or the qubit which can take value 0, 1 or a superposition of the two at the same time. Its state can be given by (Williams & Clearwater, 1998):

$$\Psi = \alpha \,|0\rangle + b|1\rangle \qquad (1)$$

Where $|\Psi\rangle$ denotes more than a vector $\vec{\Psi}$ in some vector space. $|0\rangle$ and $|1\rangle$ represent the classical bit values 0 and 1 respectively; α and β are complex numbers such that

$$|\alpha|^2 + |b|^2 = 1 \qquad (2)$$

The probability that the qubit collapses towards 1 (0) is $|\alpha|^2$ ($|b|^2$). This idea of superposition makes it possible to represent an exponential set of states with a small number of qubits. According to the quantum laws like interference, the linearity of quantum operations and entanglement make the quantum computing more powerful than the classical machines. Each quantum operation will deal with all the states present within the superposition in parallel. For in-depth theoretical insights on quantum information theory, one can refer to (Nielsen & Chuang, 2000; Jaeger, 2006).

A quantum algorithm consists in applying of a succession of quantum operations on quantum systems. Quantum operations are performed using quantum gates and quantum circuits. Yet, a powerful quantum machine is still under construction. By the time when a powerful quantum machine would be constructed, researches are conducted to get benefit from the quantum computing field. Since the late 1990s, merging quantum computation and evolutionary computation has been proven to be a productive issue when probing complex problems. Like any other EA, a Quantum Evolutionary Algorithm (QEA) relies on the representation of the individual, the evaluation function and the population dynamics. The particularity of QEA stems from the quantum representation they adopt which allows representing the superposition of all potential solutions for a given problem. It also stems from the quantum operators it uses to evolve the entire population through generations (Han & Kim, 2004; Layeb, Meshoul, & Batouche, 2006). QEA has been successfully applied on many problems (Draa, Meshoul, Talbi, & Batouche, 2010; Layeb & Saidouni, 2008).

THE PROPOSED APPROACH

The development of the suggested approach called QEABDD is based basically on a quantum representation of the research space associated with the problem and a quantum dynamic used to explore this space by operating on the quantum representation by using quantum operations. In order to increase intensification capabilities of search, we apply a local search algorithm.

Quantum Representation of Variable Order

The problem of variable ordering can be mathematically formulated as follows.

Given a set of variables $V=\{X_1, X_2,..., X_n\}$, the problem of BDD variable ordering can be defined by specifying implicitly a pair (Ω, SC) where Ω is the set of all possible solutions that is potentials variables order and SC is a mapping $\Omega \rightarrow IN$ called score of the variable ordering. This score is the BDD size. Each solution is viewed as permutation of the V variables. Consequently, the problem consists to define the best permutation of V that gives the minimal BDD size.

In order to easily apply quantum principles on variable ordering problem, we need to map potential solutions into a quantum representation that could be easily manipulated by quantum operators. The variable order is represented as binary matrix (Figure 3) satisfying the following criteria:

- For N variable, the size of the matrix is N*N. The columns represent the variables and the rows represent their order.
- The presence of 1 in the position *(i,j)* indicates that the rang of the variable *j* is *i* in the variable ordering.
- In each column and row there is a single 1.

Figure 3. Binary representation of the variable ordering. The binary matrix shows the binary representation of the variable order {2, 1, 4, 3}

$$\begin{bmatrix} 0 & 1 & 0 & 0 \\ 1 & 0 & 0 & 0 \\ 0 & 0 & 0 & 1 \\ 0 & 0 & 1 & 0 \end{bmatrix}$$

In terms of quantum computing, each variable position is represented as a quantum register as shown in Figure 4. One quantum register contains a superposition of all possible variable positions. Each column $\begin{pmatrix} a_i \\ b_i \end{pmatrix}$ represents a single qubit and corresponds to the binary digit 1 or 0. The probability amplitudes a_i and b_i are real values satisfying $|a_i|^2 + |b_i|^2 = 1$. For each qubit, a binary value is computed according to its probabilities $|a_i|^2$ and $|b_i|^2$, which can be interpreted as the probabilities to have respectively 0 or 1. Consequently, all feasible variable orders can be represented by a quantum matrix QM (Figure 5) that contains the superposition of all possible variable permutations. This quantum matrix can be viewed as a probabilistic representation of all potential orders. When embedded within an evolutionary framework, it plays the role of the chromosome. A quantum representation offers a powerful way to represent the solution space and reduces consequently the required number of chromosomes. Only one chromosome is needed to represent the entire population.

Quantum Operators

The quantum operations used in our approach are as follows:

Measurement

This operation transforms by projection the quantum matrix into a binary matrix (Figure 6). Therefore, there will be a solution among all the solutions present in the superposition. But contrary to the pure quantum theory, this measurement does not destroy the superposition. That has the advantage of preserving the superposition for the following iterations knowing that we operate on traditional machines. The binary values for a qubit are computed according to its probabilities $|a_i|^2$ and $|b_i|^2$.

Figure 4. Quantum register encoding a row in the binary matrix

$$\begin{pmatrix} \mathbf{a_1} & \mathbf{a_2} & & \mathbf{a_m} \\ \mathbf{b_1} & \mathbf{b_2} & \cdots & \mathbf{b_m} \end{pmatrix}$$

The binary matrix is then translated into a succession of integers.

The Quantum Interference

This operation amplifies the amplitude of the best solution and decreases the amplitudes of the bad ones. It primarily consists in moving the state of each qubit in the direction of the corresponding bit value in the best solution in progress. The operation of interference is useful to intensify research around the best solution. This operation can be accomplished by using a unit transformation which achieves a rotation whose angle is a function of the amplitudes a_i, b_i and of the value of the corresponding bit in the solution reference (Figure 7).

The values of the rotation angle $\delta\theta$ is chosen so that to avoid premature convergence. It is set experimentally and its direction is determined as

Figure 5. Quantum representation of variable ordering

$$\begin{bmatrix} \begin{pmatrix} \mathbf{a_{11}} & \mathbf{a_{12}} & & \mathbf{a_{1m}} \\ \mathbf{b_{11}} & \mathbf{b_{12}} & \cdots & \mathbf{b_{1m}} \end{pmatrix} \\ \begin{pmatrix} \mathbf{a_{21}} & \mathbf{a_{22}} & & \mathbf{a_{2m}} \\ \mathbf{b_{21}} & \mathbf{b_{22}} & \cdots & \mathbf{b_{2m}} \end{pmatrix} \\ \vdots \\ \begin{pmatrix} \mathbf{a_{n1}} & \mathbf{a_{n2}} & & \mathbf{a_{nm}} \\ \mathbf{b_{n1}} & \mathbf{b_{n2}} & \cdots & \mathbf{b_{nm}} \end{pmatrix} \end{bmatrix}$$

Figure 6. Quantum measurement operator. It allows the extraction of a binary solution from the quantum chromosome.

$$
\begin{pmatrix}
\begin{pmatrix} 0.99 \\ 0.14 \end{pmatrix} & \begin{pmatrix} 0.3778 \\ -0.9259 \end{pmatrix} & \begin{pmatrix} 0.14 \\ 0.99 \end{pmatrix} & \begin{pmatrix} 0.8884 \\ -0.459 \end{pmatrix} \\
\begin{pmatrix} 0.14 \\ 0.99 \end{pmatrix} & \begin{pmatrix} 0.3778 \\ -0.9259 \end{pmatrix} & \begin{pmatrix} 0.99 \\ 0.14 \end{pmatrix} & \begin{pmatrix} 0.14 \\ 0.99 \end{pmatrix} \\
\begin{pmatrix} 0.14 \\ 0.99 \end{pmatrix} & \begin{pmatrix} 0.14 \\ 0.99 \end{pmatrix} & \begin{pmatrix} 0.3778 \\ -0.9259 \end{pmatrix} & \begin{pmatrix} 0.8884 \\ -0.459 \end{pmatrix} \\
\begin{pmatrix} 0.8884 \\ -0.459 \end{pmatrix} & \begin{pmatrix} 0.8884 \\ -0.459 \end{pmatrix} & \begin{pmatrix} 0.14 \\ 0.99 \end{pmatrix} & \begin{pmatrix} 0.99 \\ 0.14 \end{pmatrix}
\end{pmatrix}
\xrightarrow{\text{Measure}}
\begin{pmatrix}
0 & 1 & 0 & 0 \\
0 & 0 & 0 & 1 \\
1 & 0 & 0 & 0 \\
0 & 0 & 1 & 0
\end{pmatrix}
$$

a function of the values of a_i, b_i and the corresponding element's value in the binary matrix (Table 1).

Mutation Operator

This operator performs permutation between two qubits (Figure 8). It allows moving from the current solution to one of its neighbors. It consists first in selecting randomly a register in the quantum matrix. Then, pairs of qubits are chosen randomly according to a defined probability. This operator allows exploring new solutions and thus enhances the diversification capabilities of the search process.

Figure 7. Quantum interference. It allows a shift of each qubit toward the corresponding bit value in the binary solution.

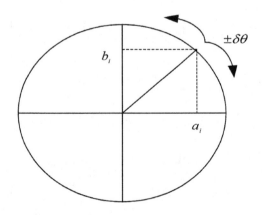

The Sifting Search Strategy

In order to improve the efficiency of the exploration process, we have introduced the local search method in the quantum dynamics. The heuristic used in our algorithm consists in seeking the best position of a variable without changing the position of the other variables. This algorithm is known under the name *Sifting* (Rudell, 1993; Panda & Somenzi, 1995). First of all, the algorithm evaluates the cost of the displacement of a variable along the order and memorizes the good position which reduces the size of the BDD. In the second stage, the Sifting algorithm moves the variable towards the best found position. This displacement can be carried out either from right to left, or the reverse as it is shown on the Figure 9. The

Table 1. Lookup table of the rotation angle

a	b	Reference bit value	Angle
> 0	> 0	1	$+\delta\theta$
> 0	> 0	0	$-\delta\theta$
> 0	< 0	1	$-\delta\theta$
> 0	< 0	0	$+\delta\theta$
< 0	> 0	1	$-\delta\theta$
< 0	> 0	0	$+\delta\theta$
< 0	< 0	1	$+\delta\theta$
< 0	< 0	0	$-\delta\theta$

Figure 8. Mutation operators. An example of qubit permutation

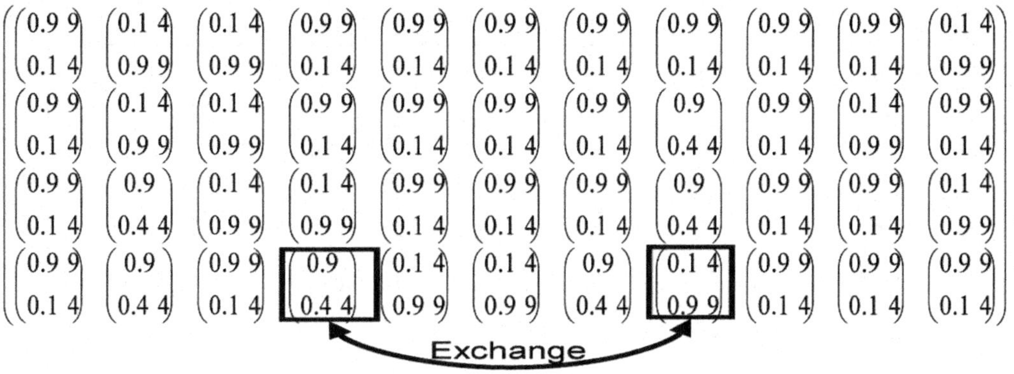

great advantage of this algorithm is to escape the local minima. Indeed, this algorithm generally gives good performances compared to the other methods of local search in the scheduling of BDD variables. Nevertheless, the major disadvantage of this method is the slowness, because it carries out several evaluation of the objective function. Several other heuristics can be used to improve the efficiency of the sifting algorithm.

Outline of the Proposed Framework

Now, we describe how the representation scheme including quantum representation and quantum operators has been embedded within an evolutionary algorithm and hybridized with sifting

Figure 9. The Sifting algorithm. The starting point is x_4

$x_1,x_2,x_3,x_4,x_5,x_6,x_7$	initial
$x_1,x_2,x_3,x_5,x_4,x_6,x_7$	swap(x_4,x_5)
$x_1,x_2,x_3,x_5,x_6,x_4,x_7$	swap(x_4,x_6)
$x_1,x_2,x_3,x_5,x_6,x_7,x_4$	swap(x_4,x_7)
$x_1,x_2,x_3,x_5,x_6,x_4,x_7$	swap(x_7,x_4)
$x_1,x_2,x_3,x_5,x_4,x_6,x_7$	swap(x_6,x_4)
$x_1,x_2,x_3,x_4,x_5,x_6,x_7$	swap(x_5,x_4)
$x_1,x_2,x_4,x_3,x_5,x_6,x_7$	swap(x_3,x_4)
$x_1,x_4,x_2,x_3,x_5,x_6,x_7$	swap(x_2,x_4)
$x_4,x_1,x_2,x_3,x_5,x_6,x_7$	swap(x_1,x_4)

technique to constitute a hybrid stochastic algorithm performing variable ordering. The proposed QEABDD is described by the Figure 10.

Given a set S of BDD variables to be ordered. Firstly, initial solutions are encoded in n chromosomes representing the initial population. Each chromosome is encoded as a quantum matrix QM which encodes all possible BDD variable orders. Each quantum chromosome gives by using the measurement operation a binary matrix BM which represents a solution. In our algorithm, all the initial solutions have been randomly generated. However, it should be noted that in order to reduce the execution time, it is recommended to start with a diverse population containing both good and bad solutions. For this example, we can use the Depth-First Search algorithm (DFS) (Malik, Wang, Brayton, & Sangiovanni-Vincentelli, 1988) to construct the initial binary matrix. The binary matrix obtained by the measurement operation is translated into variable order. This latter is used for the construction of the BDD corresponding to the input Boolean formula. After this step, we compute the fitness of the resulting BDD. The fitness in our case is the number of nodes in the resulting BDD. The best individual is one who gives a minimum number of nodes; the greater the size of the BDD is minimal, the resulting solution is optimal. The algorithm

Figure 10. The general scheme of quantum evolutionary algorithm for binary decision diagram ordering problem

```
Input: A set of variable ord
   (1) Construct  the  initial  population  of  Quantum
       Matrix QM
   (2) Generate  the  initial  Binary  Matrix  BM.  Generate
       an initial variable order ord' from BM.
Set ord_best = ord' and SC_best = SC(ord').
Repeat
Apply  an  interference  operation  on  QM  according  to
    the best solution.
Apply  a  mutation  operation  on  QM  according  to  the
    permutation probability p_m.
Apply  a  measurement  operation  on  QM  to  derive  a  new
    binary matrix BM.
Apply the sifting procedure
Evaluate the current order ord' corresponding to BM
if        SC(ord_best)         >         SC(ord')         then
    ord_best = ord' and C_best = C ( ord')
Until a termination-criterion is reached
Output: ord_best and SC(ord_best)
```

progresses through a number of generations according to a quantum based dynamics. At each iteration, the following main tasks are performed: the application of the interference operation, the application of the mutation operation and the application of the local search method based on the sifting procedure. Finally, we compute the fitness of the new population. If a better solution than that saved is found, so we keep this solution as the best current solution. The whole process is repeated until reaching a stopping criterion.

IMPLEMENTATION AND EVALUATION

QEABDD is implemented in java 1.5 and is tested on a microcomputer with a processor of 3 GHZ and 1 GB of memory. We have used the package JAVABDD (Whaley, 2007) which contains a set of tools for the creation and the manipulation of BDD. To assess the efficiency and accuracy of our approach several experiments were designed. The experiments were undertaken on a set of tests created randomly with the logic gates AND, XOR

Table 2. The results: QEABDD based Sifting compared with other heuristics

Test	Number of variables	Windows-permutation	SWAP	SIFTING	QGABDD	WIN3ITE
Test40_1	40	232	172	108	242	138
Test40_2	40	405	335	268	437	319
Test60_1	60	1016	874	437	1339	2216
Test60_2	60	873	781	883	2402	1451
Test80_1	80	359	453	320	720	1720
Test80_2	80	904	713	579	1499	1990
Test100_1	100	6719	2540	1733	8275	10777
Test100_2	100	2507	1973	1407	4315	3491
Test100_3	100	483	435	399	798	1061
Test100_4	100	6952	2451	2325	8574	8112
Test150_1	150	3301	3128	3385	15984	18330
Test150_2	150	6611	6394	4447	8699	11980
Test150_3	150	1909	1764	1290	3516	4414
Test200_1	200	8359	6059	4021	20273	21966
Test200_2	200	7114	4620	4574	11295	13310
Test200_3	200	4754	5348	4857	27730	36593
Test200_4	200	112585	124781	109760	209380	256879
Test250_1	250	447097	291626	259763	443280	483304
Test250_2	250	12311	13727	9107	21803	25043
Test250_3	250	54251	51535	48359	60451	61518

and NOT. The tests are classified according to the number of variables in each test (Table 2).

We have compared the performance of the QEABDD with sifting strategy against two local search strategies. The first is the Swap method which consists in changing the order of two variables as shown in the Figure 11. The second method is based on the window permutation algorithm (Fujita, Matsunaga, & Kakuda, 1991). The main idea of this method is firstly to select a window of constant size (typical values are 2, 3, 4) in the variable order and then tries all permutations of the variables in within this windows in order to get the best variable order as shown in the Figure 12. We have also compared our method with two programs for solving BDD ordering problem; QGABDD: a Quantum Genetic Algorithm for BDD problem (Layeb & Saidouni, 2007), and the program WIN3ITE which

is based on an iterated version of the window permutation algorithm with windows size k=3. This program is integrated in the popular BDD package *Buddy* (Lind-Nielsen, 1999). Finally, Friedman and Wilcoxon matched-pair signed-rank tests were carried out to test the significance of the difference in the accuracy of each method.

The results are summarized in Table 2. The first column shows the benchmark name, the second column show the number of variables in each test, and the others column show the results found by each method in this experiment. According to the found results (Table 2), the QEABDD with Sifting procedure is the most successful in this experiment (Figure 13). Unfortunately, it was found that QEABDD becomes slow with the procedure sifting compared to the other methods used in this experiment. On the other hand, the results of QE-

Figure 11. An example of variable Swap

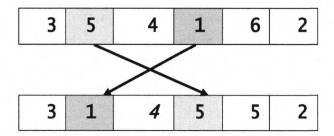

ABDD with the procedure swap are close to those of QEABDD with sifting technique than the other methods (Figure 13). However, the hybridization of QEABDD with the local search method window permutation is less powerful in the handling of BDD variable reordering problem. The obtained results agree with the common remark that window permutation is fast but not a powerful minimization heuristic. Finally, the iterated window permutation method WIN3ITE is not successful in this experiment. In most cases, WIN3ITE runs worse than the result achieved by the other methods.

CONCLUSION

In this paper, we have presented a new approach called QEABDD to deal with the BDD variable problem. QEABDD is based on a hybridizing of

quantum computing principles and the sifting algorithm. The quantum representation of the solutions allows the coding of all the potential variable orders with a certain probability. The optimization process consists of the application of a quantum dynamics constituted of quantum operations such as the interference, the quantum differential mutation and measurement. The experimental studies prove the feasibility and the effectiveness of our approach. In most cases, our approach improves the BDD size. The proposed algorithm reduces efficiently the population size and the number of iterations to have the optimal solution. Thanks to superposition, interference, mutation operators and the sifting technique, better balance between intensification and diversification of the search is achieved. There are various issues to improve our approach. In the hybridization step, we can use the group sifting technique, which depends on the same schema as

Figure 12. Example of Window permutation algorithm, the window size k = 3; Starting from the position x2

$x_1, x_2, x_3, x_4, x_5, x_6, x_7$	initial
$x_1, x_3, x_2, x_4, x_5, x_6, x_7$	swap(x_2, x_3)
$x_1, x_3, x_4, x_2, x_5, x_6, x_7$	swap(x_2, x_4)
$x_1, x_4, x_3, x_2, x_5, x_6, x_7$	swap(x_3, x_4)
$x_1, x_4, x_2, x_3, x_5, x_6, x_7$	swap(x_3, x_2)
$x_1, x_2, x_4, x_3, x_5, x_6, x_7$	swap(x_4, x_2)

Figure 13. Test of Friedman (a=0.05): comparison between QEABDD based permutation of windows (QEA_WIN), QEABDD based SWAP (QEA_SWAP), QEABDD based Sifting (QEA_SIFT), QGABDD and WIN3ITE

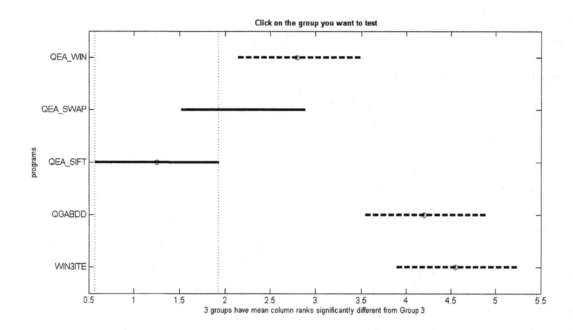

sifting, but moves groups of neighboring variables rather than single variables. In order to accelerate our approach, we may apply parallelization techniques. Finally, the performance of the algorithm may be improved by using a clever startup solution.

REFERENCES

Akers, S. B. (1978). Binary decision diagrams. *IEEE Transactions on Computers, 27*(6), 509–516. doi:10.1109/TC.1978.1675141

Bollig, B., Löbbing, M., & Wegener, I. (1995). Simulated Annealing to Improve Variable Orderings for OBDDs. In *Proceedings of the International Workshop on Logic Synthesis.*

Bollig, B., & Wegener, I. (2002). Improving the variable ordering of OBDDs is NPcomplete. *IEEE Transactions on Computers, 45*(9), 993–1002. doi:10.1109/12.537122

Bryant, R. (1986). Graph-Based Algorithms for Boolean Function Manipulation. *IEEE Transactions on Computers, 35*(8), 677–691. doi:10.1109/TC.1986.1676819

Clarke, E. M., Grumberg, O., & Long, D. E. (1994). Model checking and abstraction. *ACM Transactions on Programming Languages and Systems, 16*(5), 1512–1542. doi:10.1145/186025.186051

Costa, U. S., Déharbe, D., & Moreira, A. M. (2000). Variable ordering of BDDs with parallel genetic algorithms. In *Proceedings of the International Conference on Parallel and Distributed Processing Techniques and Applications.*

Draa, A., Meshoul, S., Talbi, H., & Batouche, M. (2010). A Quantum-Inspired Differential Evolution Algorithm for Solving the N-Queens Problem. *Int. Arab J. Inf. Technol., 7*(1), 21–27.

Drechsler, R., & Becker, B. (1998). *Binary Decision Diagrams: Theory and Implementation.* Boston: Kluwer Academic Publisher.

Drechsler, R., Becker, B., & Göckel, N. (1996). A Genetic Algorithm for Variable Ordering of OBDDs. In *Proceedings of the IEEE on Computers and Digital Techniques* (pp. 363-368).

Drechsler, R., Drechsler, N., & Slobodova, A. (1998). Fast exact minimization of BDDs. In *Proceedings of the 35th Design Automation Conference* (pp. 200-205).

Friedman, S. J., & Supowit, K. J. (1987). Finding the Optimal Variable Ordering for Binary Decision Diagrams Design. In *Proceedings of the Automation Conference* (pp. 348-356).

Fujii, H., Ootomo, G., & Hori, C. (1993). Interleaving based variable ordering methods for ordered binary decision diagrams. In *Proceedings of the International Conference on Computer-Aided Design* (pp. 38-41).

Fujita, M., Fujisawa, H., & Kawato, N. (1988). Evaluation and improvements of Boolean comparison method based on binary decision diagrams. In *Proceedings of the International Conference on Computer-Aided Design* (pp. 2-5).

Fujita, M., Matsunaga, Y., & Kakuda, T. (1991). On Variable Orderings of Binary Decision Diagrams for the Application of Multi-Level Logic Synthesis. In *Proceedings of the European Conference on Design Automation* (pp. 50-54).

Hachtel, G. D., & Somenzi, F. (2006). *Logic Synthesis and Verification Algorithms.* New York: Springer Verlag.

Han, K. H., & Kim, J. H. (2004). Quantum-inspired Evolutionary Algorithms with a New Termination Criterion, Hε Gate, and Two Phase Scheme. *IEEE Transactions on Evolutionary Computation, 8*(2), 156–169. doi:10.1109/TEVC.2004.823467

Hu, A. J., Dill, D. L., Drexler, A. G., & Yang, C. H. (1992). Higher-Level Specification and Verification With BDDs. In *Proceedings of the Workshop on Computer-Aided Verification* (pp.82-95).

Hung, W. N., & Song, X. (2001). BDD Variable Ordering By Scatter Search. In *Proceedings of the International Conference on Computer Design: VLSI in Computers & Processors* (pp. 368-373).

Ishiura, N., Sawada, H., & Yajima, S. (1991). Minimization of binary decision diagrams based on exchange of variables. In *Proceedings of the International Conference on Computer-Aided Design* (pp. 472-475).

Jaeger, G. (2006). *Quantum Information: An Overview.* Berlin: Springer.

Layeb, A., Meshoul, S., & Batouche, M. (2006). Multiple Sequence Alignment by Quantum Genetic Algorithm. In *Proceedings of the 7th International Workshop on Parallel and Distributed Scientific and Engineering Computing of the 20th IPDPS* (pp. 1-8).

Layeb, A., & Saidouni, D. E. (2007). Quantum Genetic Algorithm for Binary Decision Diagram Ordering Problem. In . *Proceedings of the International Journal of Computer Science and Network Security, 7*(9), 130–135.

Layeb, A., & Saidouni, D. E. (2008). A New Quantum Evolutionary Local Search Algorithm for Max 3-SAT Problem. In *Proceedings of the 3rd International Workshop on Hybrid Artificial Intelligence Systems* (Vol. 5271, pp. 172-179).

Lind-Nielsen, J. (1999). *BuDDy - A Binary Decision Diagram Package* (Tech. Rep. No. 1999-028). Denmark: Institute of Information Technology, Technical University.

Malik, S., Wang, A. R., Brayton, R. K., & Sangiovanni-Vincentelli, A. (1988). Logic Verification using Binary Decision Diagrams in a Logic Synthesis Environment. In *Proceedings of the International Conference on Computer-Aided Design* (pp. 6-9).

McMillan, K. L. (1992). *Symbolic Model Checking: An Approach to the State Explosion Problem.* Unpublished doctoral dissertation, Carnegie-Mellon university, School of Computer Science, Pittsburgh, PA.

Meinel, C., & Slobodova, A. (1997). Speeding up variable ordering of OBDDs. In *Proceedings of the International Conference on Computer-Aided Design* (pp. 338-343).

Nielsen, M. A., & Chuang, I. (2000). *Quantum Computation and Quantum Information.* Cambridge, UK: Cambridge University Press.

Panda, S., & Somenzi, F. (1995). Who are the variables in your neighborhood. *In Proceedings of the International Conference on Computer-Aided Design* (pp. 74-77).

Rudell, R. (1993). Dynamic variable ordering for ordered binary decision diagrams. In *Proceedings of the International Conference on Computer-Aided Design* (pp. 42-47).

Whaley, J. (2007). *JAVABDD: a Java Binary Decision Diagram Library, Stanford University.* Retrieved October 29, 2007, from http://javabdd.sourceforge.net/

Williams, C. P., & Clearwater, S. H. (1998). *Explorations in quantum computing.* Berlin: Springer.

This work was previously published in volume 4, issue 4 of the International Journal of Cognitive Informatics and Natural Intelligence, edited by Yingxu Wang, pp. 47-61, copyright 2010 by IGI Publishing (an imprint of IGI Global).

Chapter 17
A Robust Facial Feature Tracking Method Based on Optical Flow and Prior Measurement

Guoyin Wang
Chonggqing University of Posts and Telecommunications, China

Yong Yang
Chonggqing University of Posts and Telecommunications, China

Kun He
Tencent Corporation, China

ABSTRACT

Cognitive informatics (CI) is a research area including some interdisciplinary topics. Visual tracking is not only an important topic in CI, but also a hot topic in computer vision and facial expression recognition. In this paper, a novel and robust facial feature tracking method is proposed, in which Kanade-Lucas-Tomasi (KLT) optical flow is taken as basis. The prior method of measurement consisting of pupils detecting features restriction and errors and is used to improve the predictions. Simulation experiment results show that the proposed method is superior to the traditional optical flow tracking. Furthermore, the proposed method is used in a real time emotion recognition system and good recognition result is achieved.

INTRODUCTION

Cognitive Informatics (CI) is the transdisciplinary study into the internal information processing mechanisms and processes of the Natural Intel-

ligence (NI) – human brains and minds – and their engineering applications in computing, ICT, and healthcare industries. It is a cutting-edge and multidisciplinary research area that tackles the fundamental problems shared by modern informatics, computation, software engineering, AI, cybernetics, cognitive science, neuropsychology,

DOI: 10.4018/978-1-4666-1743-8.ch017

medical science, systems science, philosophy, linguistics, economics, management science, and life sciences. (Wang, 2009; Wang, 2007a; Wang & Kinsner, 2006).

As an aspect of the major cognitive processes, emotion has been studied by many researchers (Wang, 2007b; Picard, 2003). In the research works about affective and emotion, Picard proposed affective computing (AC), which handles with recognition, expressing, modeling, communicating and responding to emotion (Ahn & Picard, 2006; Picard, 2003). In the research works of AC, emotion recognition is one of the most basic and important modules in affective computing. Some progress has been achieved in emotion recognition, however, in order to recognize human emotions in real time, some foundational problems have to be dealt with, such as face detecting, feature tracking, etc.

With the increasingly development of computing technology since the last decades of 20th century, the visual tracking has become a very hot spot in computer vision (Hou & Han, 2006; Wang, Hu, & Tan; Moeslund & Granum, 2001). Visual tracking could further be classified into model-based tracking, motion-based tracking, facial feature-based tracking, neural network-based tracking and etc. Among these methods, facial feature tracking, which consists of detecting facial features, computing features' shifts, and predicting new locations, is the premise of the works, such as pattern recognition and 3D-reconstructions (Hou & Han, 2006). Meanwhile, visual tracking can be used for non-sequence images and image sequence. There are some classical facial feature tracking methods for non-sequence images, such as AAM and ASM (Cootes, Edwards & Taylor, 2001; Cootes, Taylor, Cooper, & Graham, 1995). For sequential image frames, the representative method is KLT optical flow (Lucas & Kanade, 1981; Tomasi & Kanade, 1991; Shi & Tomasi, 1994).

The KLT (Kanade-Lucas-Tomasi) algorithm was proposed for image alignment (Lucas & Kanade, 1981; Tomasi & Kanade, 1991; Shi &

Tomasi, 1994). The goal of KLT algorithm is to align a template image $T(x)$ comprising a group of points to an input image $I(x)$. The KLT algorithm uses SSD (sum of squared intensity differences) as measurement to minimize the errors for each tracking window.

Duan et al. (2004) used KLT algorithm to track facial feature points (Duan et al., 2004). They aligned all interested points on the first image of sequences, and computed the shifts of points on the next image based on KLT algorithm.

In the research work of Yan and Su (Yan & Su, 1998), 12 feature points were chosen, at the same time, restrictions were considered according to facial statistic information. However, errors estimation wasn't considered in their work. An average error of 2-3 pixels was resulted in their work.

Yu and Li proposed an expression recognition method based on optical flow (Yu & Li, 2005). In their work, 26 points were chosen as emotional feature points, and each point represented the center of a 13*13 window. Optical flow algorithm was used to track these feature points in each frame. A neural network-based classifier was trained for expression recognition. Characters of tracking method are not discussed. An average recognition rate of 88.38% is got in their paper.

Song and his colleagues combined KLT optical flow with DAM (direct appearance model) to generate a new hybrid tracking model (Song, Ai, & Xu, 2004). As for the correlation between shape and texture, the new model applied KLT algorithm to predict the rough locations of feature points at first, then uses DAM to correct matching errors of the global texture. The robustness and accuracy of the algorithm have been enhanced. However face rotation would lead to false tracking.

Although the optical flow method has an apparent merit that it can compute features' locations in the next image frame rapidly, unfortunately, it has some disadvantages: 1) there are no restrictions between separate features; 2) one feature wouldn't be refreshed if it is lost; 3) the accuracy can't be guaranteed.

In this paper, a novel and robust facial feature tracking method is proposed. Firstly, KLT optical flow is used to get the features' rough locations in the next image frame. Secondly, the rapid object detection method proposed by Paul and Michael (Paul & Michael, 2001) is applied to locate pupils. At last, the features' locations are corrected by the prior statistical facial feature restriction, and re-fixed when errors occur to a certain threshold. The proposed method is proved to be able to improve the tracking accuracy according to the experiment results. Furthermore, the facial feature tracking is used in a real time emotion recognition system. The rest of this paper is organized as follows. In the next section, KLT optical flow tracking and prior measurement are introduced, and a robust facial feature tracking method is proposed. The simulation experiment results are then discussed followed by a conclusion.

OPTICAL FLOW-BASED FACIAL FEATURE TRACKING

In this section, a prior measurement method is proposed to overcome the disadvantages of KLT. Afterwards, feature tracking result of each frame is corrected and taken as the initiation state of the next frame. A close loop-like method is gotten based on KLT and prior measurement as shown in Figure 1.

Figure 1. The close loop-like architecture

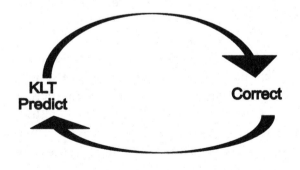

KLT OPTICAL FLOW

KLT is a classical tracking algorithm which takes SSD (sum of squared intensity differences) as the measurement of each two adjacent images (Lucas & Kanade, 1981; Tomasi & Kanade, 1991; Shi & Tomasi, 1994). Let I and J be two adjacent 2D gray-scaled images, $u=[u_x, u_y]^T$ be a point on the image I. The goal of KLT is to compute new locations $v = v + d = [u_x + d_x, u_y + d_y]^T$ on the image J, where the vector $d = [d_x, d_y]^T$ is the instantaneous velocity produced at point u, also called optical flow of u. For convenience, let $w_x = w_y$ be the size of searching window which often take values of 2, 3, 4, 5, 6, 7, 8, 9, 10 pixels. The difference function of the optical flow d is defined as follows:

$$\varepsilon(d) = \varepsilon(d_x, d_y) = \sum_{x=u_x-w_x}^{u_x+w_x} \sum_{y=u_y-w_y}^{u_y+w_y} \left(I(x,y) - J(x + d_x, y + d_y)\right)^2 \quad (1)$$

The original grey-scale image I could be marked as I^0, I^L is defined as the Lth level of image I. In order to compute the optical flow more quickly than the original Lucas-Kanade method (Lucas & Kanade, 1981), we can define the recursive form as follows,

$$\begin{aligned} I^L(x,y) &= \frac{1}{4} I^{L-1}(2x, 2y) + \frac{1}{8}(I^{L-1}(2x-1, 2y) \\ &+ I^{L-1}(2x+1, 2y) + I^{L-1}(2x, 2y-1) \\ &+ I^{L-1}(2x, 2y-1)) + \frac{1}{16}(I^{L-1}(2x-1, 2y-1) \\ &+ I^{L-1}(2x+1, 2y+1) + I^{L-1}(2x-1, 2y+1) \\ &+ I^{L-1}(2x+1.2y+1)) \end{aligned} \quad (2)$$

Therefore, the difference function could be redefined as follows.

$$\varepsilon(\bar{v}) = \varepsilon(v_x, v_y) = \sum_{x=p_x-w_x}^{p_x+w_x} \sum_{y=p_y-w_y}^{p_y+w_y} \left(A(x,y) - B(x + v_x, y + v_y)\right)^2 \quad (3.1)$$

Where, v is the optical flow of image I,

$$A(x,y) = I^L(x,y),$$
$$B(x + v_x, y + v_y) = J^L(x + v_x, y + v_y). \qquad (3.2)$$

In order to minimize the SSD of $\varepsilon(\bar{v})$ with subject to the following equation,

$$\left. \frac{\partial \varepsilon(\bar{v})}{\partial \bar{v}} \right|_{\bar{v} = \bar{v}_{opt}} = [00], \qquad (4)$$

$\bar{v}_{opt}$ will be the solution of the whole algorithm. Finally, a new location

$$v = v + d = [u_x + d_x, \ u_y + d_y]^T$$

is gotten.

Some disadvantages of KLT are discussed by Paul and Michael (Paul & Michael, 2001). The most crucial shortcoming of KLT is that it is not robust. To overcome the defect of the original KLT, face prior measurement is proposed in this paper and listed in detail as follows.

PRIOR MEASUREMENT

Firstly, pupils detection is taken and the points of both pupils are taken as the key features. Secondly, the methods of facial feature restriction (Yan & Su, 1998; Yu & Li, 2005) is used to correct KLT tracking results. Thirdly, the errors between two adjacent images are measured and the features were refreshed if errors occur to a predefined threshold.

Pupils Detection

Pupils detection is to determine whether there are pupils in a single face image and find their locations. In this paper, boosted cascade of simple features are used to detect pupils (Duan, Cheng, Wang, & Cai, 2004) and listed as follows.

Step 1: Three kinds of basic features are defined and shown in Figure 2. The rectangle regions have the same size, same shape, and are horizontally or vertically adjacent. The sum of the pixels which lie within the white rectangles subtracted from the sum of pixels in the grey rectangles is taken as the feature value in Figure 2.

Step 2: Rectangle features are computed using an intermediate representation for the image called the integral image. The integral image at the location *[x, y]* contains the sum of pixels above and to the left of *[x, y]*. Let's look at the example shown in Figure 3. The image is divided into 4 regions. The value at location 1 contains the sum of region A, location 2 is A+B, location 3 is A+C, and location 4 is A+B+C+D.

Step 3: It is obvious that computing the complete feature set is prohibitively expensive. Therefore, a small group of features are selected to train pupil detector according to the Adaboost algorithm (Freund, 1995). As a result, 200 features out of 180,000 are selected.

Step 4: All detectors(classifiers) construct a cascade model (Paul & Michael, 2001) like degenerate decision tree. Each classifier of the cascade excludes one region that doesn't contain the pupils, and so on. At last, the rest region of image contains the pupils.

Feature Restriction

It is a pity that the restriction of feature tracking between adjacent images is not considered in KLT algorithm. Yu and Li defined a series of experienced restrictions to guarantee the right locations of tracking results (Yu & Li, 2005). In this work, restrictions of domain-oriented applications were taken into consideration, a novel restrictions based on statistical information and the work of Yan and

Figure 2. Four basic feature definition

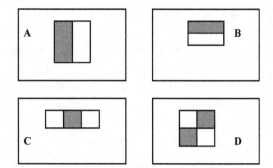

Figure 3. Integral image definition

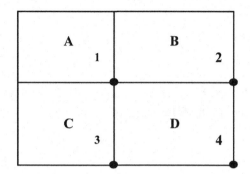

Su (Yan & Su, 1998) is designed. It is shown in Table 1. In Table 1, *dst* is the distance between left pupil and right pupil. *Wid, dist, len* means width, distance and length respectively. Furthermore, as the face profile is almost perfectly symmetry, the vertical and parallel relations of the facial features are drawn and listed in Table 2.

Using these restrictions listed in Table 1 and Table 2, we can correct the tracking results in each image frame from image sequences. It could guarantee the accuracy in an easy and efficient way.

ERROR ACCUMULATION

For estimating the error of each feature to compute the whole errors of the tracking system, a region matching method could be used to measure the

regional similarity of the same features in two adjacent images. Hu proposed a set of seven variables which were derived from the second and third moments of interested image region (Hu, 1962). Hu proved that these variables were invariant to translation, rotation, and scale changing. Thus, it could be a good judge for errors estimation. All variables are shown as follows.

$$h_1 = \eta_{20} + \eta_{02}, \quad h_2 = (\eta_{20} - \eta_{02})^2 + 4\eta_{11}^2,$$
$$h_3 = (\eta_{30} - 3\eta_{12})^2 + (3\eta_{21} - \eta_{03})^2,$$
$$h_4 = (\eta_{30} + \eta_{12})^2 + (\eta_{21} + \eta_{03})^2,$$
$$h_5 = (\eta_{30} - 3\eta_{12})(\eta_{30} + \eta_{12})[(\eta_{30} + \eta_{12})^2 - 3(\eta_{21} + \eta_{03})^2]$$
$$+ (3\eta_{21} - \eta_{03})(\eta_{21} + \eta_{03})[3(\eta_{30} + \eta_{12})^2 - (\eta_{21} + \eta_{03})^2],$$
$$h_6 = (\eta_{20} - \eta_{02})[(\eta_{30} + \eta_{12})^2 - (\eta_{21} + \eta_{03})^2]$$
$$+ 4\eta_{11}(\eta_{30} + 3\eta_{12})(\eta_{21} + \eta_{03}),$$
$$h_7 = (3\eta_{21} - \eta_{03})(\eta_{30} + \eta_{12})[(\eta_{30} + \eta_{12})^2 - 3(\eta_{21} + \eta_{03})^2]$$
$$- (\eta_{30} - 3\eta_{12})(\eta_{21} + \eta_{03})[3(\eta_{30} + \eta_{12})^2 - (\eta_{21} + \eta_{03})^2].$$

(5)

Table 1. Restrictions of facial features

Ratio to *dst*	*Wid* of eyes	*Dist* between pupil and eyebrow	*Len* of nose	Height of mouth(shut)	Width of mouth(shut)
Average	0.50	0.39	0.80	0.25	0.75
Variation	±0.01	±0.10	±0.02	±0.09	±0.09

Table 2. Vertical or parallel relations of facial features

Pupils-line	Canthus-line	Midline of nose	Midline of mouth (vertical)	Midline of mouth (Parallel)
Angle(degree)	0	90	90	0
Variation(degree)	±2	±3	±5	±10

Figure 4. Optical flow-based robust facial feature tracking algorithm framework

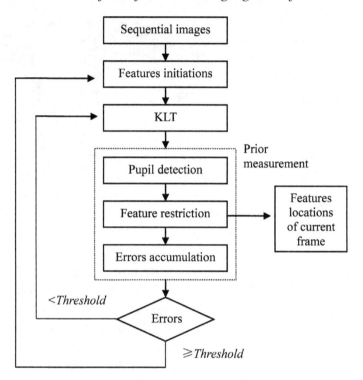

Where, $\eta_{pg}=\iint_{domain}x^{p}y^{q}\rho(x,y)dxdy$, $\rho(x,y)$ is the density distribution function of image region. We adopt *err(i)* to measure the similarity of each feature region in two adjacent image *I* and *J*. It is defined as the error of feature *k*.

$$err(k) = E(I, J) = \max | (m_k^I - m_k^J) / m_k^I | \qquad (6)$$

Where, $m_k^I=\mathrm{sgn}(h^I)\log_{10}|h_k^I|$, $m_k^J=\mathrm{sgn}(h^J)\log_{10}|h_k^J|$. Obviously, the less *err(k)*, the better feature tracking result will be got. Therefore, the whole tracking system errors can be accumulated in each image frame as follows,

$$ERR = \sum_{k=1}^{N} err\left(k\right) \qquad (7)$$

where, *N* is the number of features.

OPTICAL FLOW-BASED ROBUST FACIAL FEATURE TRACKING ALGORITHM

Based on the above discussions, an improved KLT method is proposed in this section. The whole integrated tracking method consists of several sections which form a close loop-like framework and shown in Figure 4.

Optical Flow-Based Robust Facial Feature Tracking Algorithm

Input: *M* sequential image frames, *I*=1 (1st frame).
Output: Feature locations of each frame.
Step 1: Initialize facial features using statistical information of human face.
Step 2: Apply KLT to track facial features in the *I*-th frame.
Step 3: Detect pupils, and correct features locations by restrictions.

Figure 5. Feature definition

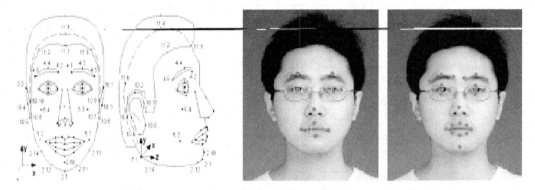

(a) FAP definition   *(b) 13 facial features*   *(c) 26 facial features*

Step 4: Compute the accumulated tracking errors.
Step 5: *I=I+1*
If (*I<=M*)
If (*ERR*>=threshold), goto Step 1.
Else, goto Step 2.
Else, end.

EXPERIMENT RESULTS AND DISCUSSION

Experiment Condition

In order to test the effectiveness of the proposed tracking method in this paper, some crucial facial features which can describe the motion of human face should be chosen firstly. The MPEG-4 standard is a popular standard for feature point selection. It extends FACS (facial action coding system) to derive FDP (facial definition parameters) and FAP (facial animation parameters). There are 68 FAP parameters, in which 66 low parameters are defined according to FDP parameters to describe the motion of a human face (Abrantes & Pereira, 1997). FAP definition is shown in Figire 5 (a). According to the FAP parameters, two sets of facial features are chosen in Figure 5 (b) and Figure 5 (c) based on our previous works (Yang, Wang, & Kong, 2009; Yang, Wang, Chen, Zhou, & He, 2007; Yang, Wang, Chen, & Zhou, 2006; Chen, Wang, Yang, & Zhou,

2006). In Figure 5 (b), 13 features are defined while 26 features in Figure 5 (c). Apparently, 26 features can present a face more precisely than 13 features, and on the other hand, tracking the 26 features should be more time consuming and slower than the other one.

Considering the practical situation, the threshold of errors accumulation is set to be 0.3.

There are two experiments taken for comparison of the proposed method with the traditional KLT method at different period *T* under the simulation configuration with P42.7G, RAM1.0G, Logitech camera of 1.3 mega pixels. Meanwhile, for the presentation, we defined *AEPI*(average errors in pixel of image) and *AEPF*(average errors in pixel of features) for the algorithm performance.

As for the two experiments, initially, all facial features are aligned on the 1st image frame and start to track these features respectively at the same time. During each period *T*, corresponding image frames with different tracked features of both methods are obtained. Therefore, a series of image frames with features will be saved.

Experiment on 13 Facial Features

In Figure 6 (a) and Figure 6 (c), T_i is set to 10 frame, 500 sequential image frames are used to test the two methods, and 50 tracking results are

Figure 6. Experiment results on the two methods (13 features)

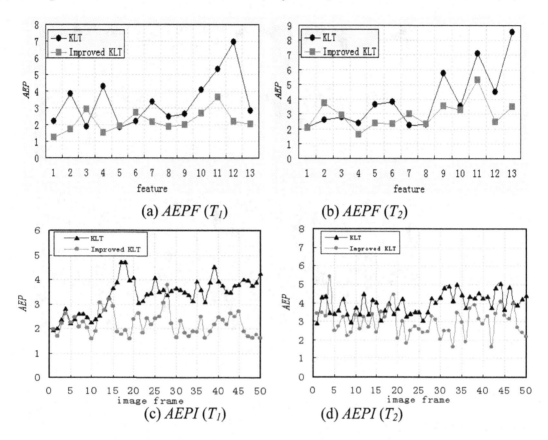

(a) *AEPF* (T_1)

(b) *AEPF* (T_2)

(c) *AEPI* (T_1)

(d) *AEPI* (T_2)

got. The total errors of KLT are 3.38 pixels while the proposed method is 2.20 pixels. In Figure 6 (b) and Figure 6 (d), T_2 is set to 30 frames, 50 tracking results are got from 1500 sequential image frames. The total errors of KLT are 3.96 pixels while the proposed method is 2.96 pixels. Furthermore, from the experiment results, we find that most facial features of the proposed method, 10 out of 13 in Figure 6 (a) and 9 out of 13 in Figure 6 (b), have less *AEPF* than KLT. Meanwhile, the errors of most frames have been decreased definitely in Figure 6 (c) and Figure 6 (d). Some tracking results are shown in Figure 7. From Figure 7, we can found that there are features on mouth are tracking lost in the frame of No.151, 181, 251, 500 in the period of T_1, meanwhile, the proposed method can track more precisely and there is no apparently feature lost. Moreover, in the period of

T_2, there are features tracking lost in all the listed frames, and there is no apparently feature lost for the proposed method.

Experiment on 26 Facial Features

In this experiment, 26 facial features listed in Figure 5 (c) are used for tracking. The experiment setting is the same as the last one, that is to say, T_1 is set to 10 frames and 50 tracking results are gotten from 500 sequential image, meanwhile, T_2 is set to 30 frames and 50 tracking results are got from 1500 sequential images. In Figure 8 (a) and Figure 8 (c), the total error of KLT is 3.83 pixels while the proposed method is 2.60 pixels under T_1. In Figure 8 (c) and Figure 8 (d), the total error of KLT is 2.96 pixels while the improved KLT 2.37 pixels under *T2*.

Figure 9. Tracking results of the two methods (26 features)

KLT

Proposed
method

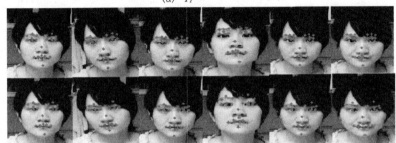

1ˢᵗ frame 101-th frame 151-th frame 181-th frame 251-th frame 500-th frame

(a) *T₁*

KLT

Proposed
method

151-th fame 241-th fame 601-th frame 931-th frame 1021-th frame 1471-th frame

(b) *T₂*

Figure 7. Tracking results on the two methods (13 features)

KLT

Proposed
method

1ˢᵗ frame   101-th frame 151-th frame 181-th frame 251-th frame 500-th frame

(a) *T₁*

KLT

Proposed
method

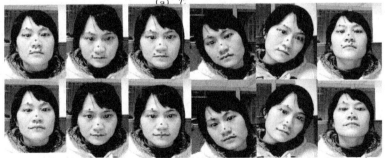

151-th fame 241-th fame 601-th frame 931-th frame 1021-th frame 1471-th frame

Figure 8. Experiment results on the two methods (26 features)

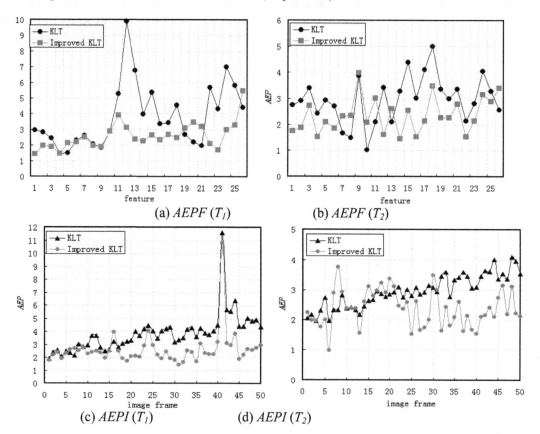

(a) *AEPF* (T_1)

(b) *AEPF* (T_2)

(c) *AEPI* (T_1)

(d) *AEPI* (T_2)

Some tracking results are shown in Figure 9. From Figure 9, we can also found that there are features on mouth which are tracking lost apparently in the frame of No.151, 181, 251, 500 in the period of T_1, meanwhile, the proposed method lost some features in the frame of No. 101 and 181. Moreover, in the period of T_2, there are features tracking lost in the frame of No. 601, 931, 1021 and 1471, and the proposed method can track more precisely and there is no apparently feature lost.

DISCUSSION

From the above two experiments, it's obvious to figure out that the proposed and improved KLT method is superior to the original KLT method in feature tracking, since the KLT method doesn't focus on the characters of mouth movement, and no measurements are considered to restrict particular flexible features, therefore, features in mouth region will lead to a false tracking. Furthermore, the amount of features has no apparent impact on the tracking capability of the proposed method. Based on these results, it can be concluded that the proposed algorithm is more robust, accurate than the traditional KLT, and thus it is suitable for real-time applications in supervision and recognition.

Real Time Face Expression Recognition

The facial feature tracking method has been used in our real time emotion recognition system. In the system, the proposed tracking method is applied as the most crucial component to track emotion features dynamically. The tracked emotion features defined in our previous works (Yang, Wang, & Kong, 2009; Yang, Wang, Chen, Zhou, & He, 2007; Yang, Wang, Chen, & Zhou, 2006) could respond to one definite kind of emotions by Ekman and Friesen (Ekman & Friesen, 1978). After tracking the pre-defined features, geometrical features of a face are gotten, based on these features, SVM is taken as the classifier, and the emotion recognition system can give the cue according to the recognized emotion state. Some recognition results of our real time emotion system are shown in Figure 10. From Figure 10, we can find that the system can recognize people's emotion state, and the system can work in many circumstances such as different illumination. The system is proved to be effective and robust.

CONCLUSION

In this paper, a robust facial feature tracking method is proposed. The method combines KLT and prior measurement to overcome the disadvantages of KLT. Pupils detection is used to find whether pupils exist in an image, feature restriction is used to initialize and correct features, errors accumulation is used to refresh features when errors occur to a threshold. Experiment results prove that the proposed method is superior to the traditional KLT. Furthermore, the proposed method is used in a real time emotion recognition system and good recognition result is achieved.

ACKNOWLEDGMENT

The paper is supported by Natural Science Foundation of China under Grant No. 60773113, Natural Science Foundation Grant of Chongqing under Grant No.2008BA2041, No.2008BA2017 and No. 2007BB2445, Science & Technology Research Program of Chongqing Education Commission under grant No.KJ090512, Chongqing Key Lab of Computer Network and Communication Technology Foundation under Grant No. CY-CNCL-2009-02, Natural Science Foundation of Chongqing University of Posts and Telecommunications under Grant A2009-26.

REFERENCES

Abrantes, G., & Pereira, F. (1997). Mpeg-4 facial animation technology: survey, implementation, and results. *IEEE Transactions on Circuits and Systems for Video Technology*, 9(2), 290–305. doi:10.1109/76.752096

Ahn, H., & Picard, R. W. (2006). Affective cognitive learning and decision making: The role of emotions. In *Proceedings of the 18th European Meeting on Cybernetics and Systems Research*, Vienna, Austria (201-207).

Chen, P. J., Wang, G. Y., Yang, Y., & Zhou, J. (2006). Facial expression recognition based on rough set theory and SVM. In G. Y. Wang (Ed.), *First International Conference on Rough Sets and Knowledge Technology*, Chongqing (pp. 772-777). New York: Springer.

Cootes, T. F., Edwards, G. J., & Taylor, C. J. (2001). Active appearance models. *IEEE Transactions on Pattern Analysis and Machine Intelligence*, 23(6), 681–685. doi:10.1109/34.927467

Cootes, T. F., Taylor, C. J., Cooper, D. H., & Graham, J. (1995). Active shape models-Their training and application. *Computer Vision and Image Understanding*, 61(1), 38–59. doi:10.1006/cviu.1995.1004

Duan, H., Cheng, Y. M., Wang, Y. X., & Cai, S. H. (2004). Tracking facial feature points using Kanade-Lucas Tomasi Approach. *Journal of Computer-aided Design & . Computer Graphics*, 16(3), 279–283.

Ekman, P., & Friesen, W. V. (1978). *Facial Action Coding System (FACS): manual*. Palo Alto, CA: Consulting Psychologist Press.

Freund, Y. (1995). Boosting a weak algorithm by majority. *Information and Computation*, 121(2), 256–285. doi:10.1006/inco.1995.1136

Hou, Z. Q., & Han, C. Z. (2006). A survey of visual tracking. *Acta Automatica Sinica*, *32*(4), 603–617.

Hu, M. K. (1962). Visual pattern recognition by moment invariants. *IEEE Transactions on Information Theory*, *8*(2), 179–187. doi:10.1109/TIT.1962.1057692

Lucas, B., & Kanade, T. (1981). An iterative image registration technique with an application to stereo vision. In P. J. Hayes (Ed.), *Proceedings of the 7th Int'l Joint Conf. on Artificial Intelligence*, Vancouver, Canada (pp. 674-679). San Francisco: Morgan Kaufmann Publishers.

Moeslund, T. B., & Granum, E. (2001). A survey of computer vision-based human motion capture. *Computer Vision and Image Understanding*, *81*(3), 231–268. doi:10.1006/cviu.2000.0897

Paul, V., & Michael, J. (2001). Rapid Object Detection using a Boosted Cascade of Simple Features. In *Computer Vision and Pattern Recognition* (pp. 511-518).

Picard, R. W. (2003). Affective Computing: Challenges. *International Journal of Human-Computer Studies*, *59*(1), 55–64. doi:10.1016/S1071-5819(03)00052-1

Shi, J. B., & Tomasi, C. (1994). Good features to track . In *Proceedings of Computer Vision and Pattern Recognition 1994, Seattle, WA* (pp. 593–600). Washington, DC: IEEE Press.

Song, G., Ai, H. Z., & Xu, G. Y. (2004). Texture Constrained Facial Feature Point Tracking. *Journal of Software*, *15*(11), 1607–1615.

Tomasi, C., & Kanade, T. (1991). *Detection and tracking of point features* (Tech. Rep. No. CMU-CS-91-132). Pittsburgh, PA: Carnegie Mellon University.

Wang, L., Hu, W. M., & Tan, T. N. (2002). A survey of visual analysis of human motion. *Chinese Journal of Computers*, *25*(3), 225–237.

Wang, Y. (2007a). The Theoretical Framework of Cognitive Informatics. *International Journal of Cognitive Informatics and Natural Intelligence*, *1*(1), 1–27.

Wang, Y. (2007b). On The Cognitive Processes of Perception with Emotions, Motivations, and Attitudes. *International Journal of Cognitive Informatics and Natural Intelligence*, *1*(4), 1–13.

Wang, Y. (2009). On Cognitive Computing. *International Journal of Software Science and Computational Intelligence*, *1*(3), 1–15.

Wang, Y., & Kinsner, W. (2006). Recent Advances in Cognitive Informatics. *IEEE Transactions on Systems, Man and Cybernetics. Part C, Applications and Reviews*, *36*(2), 121–123. doi:10.1109/TSMCC.2006.871120

Yan, C., & Su, G. D. (1998). Location and acquisition of characters of human face. *Journal of Image and Graphics*, *3*(5), 375–379.

Yang, Y., Wang, G. Y., Chen, P. J., & Zhou, J. (2006). An Emotion Recognition System Based on Rough Set Theory . In Li, Y. F. (Ed.), *Active Media Technology 2006, Sydney, Australia* (pp. 293–297). Paris: IOS Press.

Yang, Y., Wang, G. Y., Chen, P. J., Zhou, J., & He, K. (2007). Feature Selection in Audiovisual Emotional Recognition Based on Rough Set Theory. *Transactions on Rough Sets*, *7*, 283–294.

Yang, Y., Wang, G. Y., & Kong, H. (2009). Self-Learning Facial Emotional Feature Selection Based on Rough Set Theory. *Mathematical Problems in Engineering*. .doi:10.1155/2009/802932

Yu, M. S., & Li, S. F. (2005). Dynamic facial expression recognition based on optical flow. *Microelectronics & Computer*, *22*(7), 113–119.

This work was previously published in volume 4, issue 4 of the International Journal of Cognitive Informatics and Natural Intelligence, edited by Yingxu Wang, pp. 62-75, copyright 2010 by IGI Publishing (an imprint of IGI Global).

Section 5
Applications of Cognitive Informatics and Cognitive Computing

Chapter 18
Modeling a Secure Sensor Network Using an Extended Elementary Object System

Vineela Devarashetty
University of Illinois at Chicago, USA

Jeffrey J. P. Tsai
University of Illinois at Chicago, USA

Lu Ma
University of Illinois at Chicago, USA

Du Zhang
California State University at Sacramento, USA

ABSTRACT

A sensor network consists of a large number of sensor nodes, which are spread over a geographical area. Sensor networks have found their way into many applications, from military domains to traffic or environmental monitoring, and as sensor networks reach toward wide spread deployment, security becomes a major concern. In this regard, one needs to be sure about the confidentiality, authenticity and tamper-proof of data. The research thus far has focused on how to deploy sensor networks so that they can work efficiently; however, the focus of this paper is on sensor networks' security issues. In this paper, the authors propose a formal model to design and analyze the secure sensor network system. The model is based on an augmented Petri net formalism called Extended Elementary Object System. This proposed secure sensor network model has a multi-layered structure consisting of sink node layer, sensor node layer and security mechanism layer. At the security mechanism layer, a synchronous firing mechanism is utilized as a security measure to detect malicious node attacks to sensor data and information flow. In addition, the model applies SNEP protocol for authentication and confidentiality of sensor data.

DOI: 10.4018/978-1-4666-1743-8.ch018

1. INTRODUCTION

Recent advances in wireless communications and mobile computing have enabled the development of low cost, low power, and multifunctional sensor nodes that are small in size and communicate un-tethered short distances. These tiny sensor nodes, which consist of sensing, data processing, and communicating components, form sensor networks (Akyldiz et al., 2002; Levis et al., 2005; Lewis, 2004; Romer & Mattern, 2004). A sensor network can provide access to information anytime, anywhere by collecting, processing, analyzing and disseminating data. Each sensor has wireless communication capability and intelligence for signal processing and data communicating. The positions of sensor nodes can be randomly deployed which implies that the sensor networks are self-organized. They can be easily deployed because no human intervention or infrastructure is needed. Hence, sensor networks can help pave the way for autonomic computing (Wang, 2007).

Although much research has thus far focused on making sensor networks feasible and useful, security has been receiving increasing attention (Karlof & Wagner, 2003; Perrig et al., 2002; Walters et al., 2007). As sensor networks reach towards wide spread deployment in different application domains, security issues become a central concern. Power and computation constraints are often high on the agenda in sensor networks, relegating security requirements to a lesser place. Given the fact that there has not been much attention on formal modeling and analysis of the security aspects in sensor networks and that little prior work exists in this area, we recognize the need to identify potential problems and challenges in the sensor network's security and propose solution techniques.

Before delving into the specifics in sensor network security, we first examine the security requirements for a sensor network. They include:

- Data Authenticity
- Data Confidentiality
- Data Integrity
- Data Freshness

Data Authenticity: Data authenticity in general is the requirement that the sender is a valid one and not a bogus one. Data authenticity serves as a prerequisite to access the data. It requires verifying the sender. In sensor networks, data authentication requires a message recipient to verify the identity of the message source to ensure the truthfulness of data origin. It requires a party to prove its identity. Ensuring data authenticity provides protection against forgery or masquerade and prevents injecting bogus messages.

Data Confidentiality: Data confidentiality in general is the requirement to make sure that data can be accessible only to those authorized to have access. It protects the data from intentional or accidental tampering. Data confidentiality covers the data in storage, during processing, and while in transit. It is necessary that the communication between the sensor nodes be private and the intended receiver of data should have confidence that the data is not modified during its transmission. A loss of data confidentiality affects data privacy. Ensuring data confidentiality provides protection against eavesdropping.

Data Integrity: Data Integrity requires that the data should not be modified or destroyed in an unauthorized manner to provide data consistency. It covers data in storage, during processing and while in transit. In sensor networks, data integrity requires that messages are not accidentally corrupted by an imperfect communications channel and not intentionally corrupted by an attacker during transmission.

Data Freshness: Data freshness, in sensor networks, requires the messages to be current, ordered and not to duplicate (replays) a previously transmitted message. There are two types of data freshness:

- ◦ **Weak freshness:** provides partial ordering of messages but no delay information.
- ◦ **Strong freshness:** provides total ordering and allows for delay estimation.

These are the main security requirements for a sensor network to function properly and efficiently. There are other domain-specific requirements, which are necessary for the proper functioning of a particular sensor network. There are circumstances where the aforementioned security requirements of a sensor network may have conflicts among them. For the data to be available in sensor networks, certain tradeoffs need to be made between data confidentiality and integrity. It is generally the case that existing security protocols do not provide all the aforementioned security requirements because of potential conflicts among the security goals of a sensor network.

In this paper, we present a formal model to design and analyze a secure sensor network system. The model is based on an augmented Petri net formalism called *Extended Elementary Object System* (EEOS) (Ma & Tsai, 2008). This proposed secure sensor network model has a multi-layered structure consisting of sink node layer, sensor node layer and security mechanism layer. At the security mechanism layer, a synchronous firing mechanism is utilized as a security measure to detect malicious node attacks to sensor data and information flow. In addition, the model applies SNEP protocol for authentication and confidentiality of sensor data (Perrig et al, 2002).

The rest of the paper is organized as follows. In section 2, we describe the three-layered EEOS model for sensor networks. Section 3 deals with issues in the security mechanism layer. Analysis of system properties in terms of the proposed model is discussed in Section 4. Finally, in Section 5, we conclude the paper with remarks on future work.

2. FORMAL MODEL FOR SENSOR NETWORKS

Various security protocols (Akyldiz et al., 2002; Karlof & Wagner, 2003; Perrig et al., 2002) have been proposed for sensor networks with regard to the security requirements discussed earlier. However, none of them has a formal method basis. It is not easy to formally prove or analyze the characteristics, including the security features, of the sensor network using these protocols.

The formal model we propose for a generic sensor network system is based on EEOS which combines object oriented technology with Petri nets (Lakos, 2001). Petri Nets have become a widely accepted technique in mainstream software engineering, because they can be used simultaneously as a graphical representation, a mathematical description, and a simulation tool for the system under study (Murata, 1989). Using Petri Nets also eliminates errors which may occur from modeling to implementation because modeling and simulation of a system happen at the same time. EEOS (Ma & Tsai, 2008) is an extension of the Elementary Object System (EOS) in which tokens themselves are Petri nets again (Valk, 1998). EOS consists of two levels of Petri nets. The base Petri nets are called *system nets* or *environmental nets*, while the tokens in the net form are called *object nets* or *token nets*. Object nets are stored in places and moved by firing transitions in system nets like ordinary tokens. They can change their markings, but not their structures. If the change is independent from the system nets, it is called *autonomous occurrence* of the transition. If it is triggered by the system net, it is called *interaction*, in which case the relation between system net transitions and object net transitions is called *interaction relation*. Since these tokens have their own dynamic behaviours and can change their own markings both independently and dependently, system nets and object nets combined together have more powerful modeling capacity. EOS with the following five extensions forms EEOS which is appropriate for modeling a generic secure sensor network system because it can capture sensor nodes mobility and also leave space for security consideration:

1. Multiple system nets,
2. Multiple layers,
3. Token pool,
4. Two new arcs,
5. Extended interaction relation.

Next we formally define an EEOS.

Definition 1. Extended Elementary Object System (EEOS). An EEOS is defined by (SN, ON, ρ, τ) where

1. $SN = (SN_1, SN_2, \cdots, SN_i, \cdots, SN_n, TP)$ is the set of system nets $SN_i (i = 1, \cdots, n)$ and the token pool TP. Each system net SN_i is a tuple $SN_i = (SID_i, P_i, T_i, F_i, K_i, W_i, M_{0i})$ where

    (1) SID_i is a unique identifier of the system net;

    (2) P_i is a finite set of places $P_{ij} (j = 1, \cdots, J)$;

    (3) T_i is a finite set of transitions $T_{ir} (r = 1, \cdots, R)$;

    (4) F_i is a finite set of directed arcs $F_{ih} (h = 1, \cdots, H)$ between places and transitions;

    (5) K_i is a set of tokens with colors or referencing to object nets $K_{ic} (c = 1, \cdots, C)$;

    (6) W_i is a label function $W_{ih} (h = 1, \cdots, H)$ assigned on arcs $F_{ih} (h = 1, \cdots, H)$;

    (7) M_{0i} is the initial marking of SN_i, which lists the content of token(s) held in each place of SN_i in the form of $(m_{o\_P_{i1}}, m_{o\_P_{i2}}, \cdots, m_{o\_P_{ij}}, \cdots m_{o\_P_{iJ}})$ where $m_{o\_P_{ij}}$ is a multiset of K_i.

TP is a place which connects with each system net SN_i. There is only one TP in each EEOS.

2. $ON = (ON_1, ON_2, \cdots, ON_l, \cdots, ON_m)$ is the set of m object nets $ON_l (l = 1, \cdots, m)$, which can be a system net again for higher level object nets. Each object net is a tuple $ON_l = (OID_l, P_l, T_l, F_l, K_l, W_l, M_{0l})$ in which symbols have similar meanings to those above. OID_l is the unique identifier of this object net; P_l is the place set; T_l is the transition set; F_l is the arc set; K_l are the token set; W_l is the label functions set associated with F_l; and M_{0l} is the initial marking of ON_l.

3. ρ is the set of extended interaction relations $\rho \subseteq \bigcup f_{ab} : T_a \times T_b$ between transitions set T_a in system net SN_a and transitions set T_b in object net ON_b. Suppose $EIR(T_1, T_2)$ stands for the extended interaction relationship between transitions T_1 and T_2. We have $f_{ab} \subseteq \bigcup (EIR(T_{ar}, T_{br'}) \vee EIR(T_{br'}, T_{ar}))$ where $T_{ar} \in T_a$ and $T_{br'} \in T_b$.

4. τ is the set of referencing functions $\tau \subseteq \bigcup mf_x : K_x \times ON$ from tokens set K_x in system net SN_x to object nets ON. Each $mf_x \subseteq \bigcup mf_{xy} : K_{xy} \times ON_{y'}$ where $K_{xy} \in K_x$ and $ON_{y'} \in ON$.

Definition 2. A Bi-Marking of an EEOS is a pair (M, m) where $M = (M_1, ..., M_i, ..., M_n, M_{TP})$ is a marking of SN, the set of system nets and token pool. $m = (m_1, ..., m_l, ..., m_{n'})$ is a marking of the set of object nets ON.

1. A transition $t \in T_i$ is activated in a bi-marking (M, m) of EEOS if $\neg EIR(e, t)$ where $e \in T_j'$ and t is activated in M. Then the successor bi-marking (M', m') is defined by $M \xrightarrow{t} M'$ (w.r.t. SN) and

$m = m'$. We write $(M, m) \overset{[t, \lambda]}{\rightarrow} (M', m')$ in this case.

2. A transition $e \in T_j'$ is activated in a bi-marking (M, m) of EOS if $\neg EIR(t, e)$ where $t \in T_i$ and e is activated in m. Then the successor bi-marking (M', m') is defined by $m \overset{e}{\rightarrow} m'$ (w.r.t. ON) and $M = M'$. We write $(M, m) \overset{[\lambda, e]}{\rightarrow} (M', m')$ in this case.

3. A pair $[t, e] \in T \times E$ is activated in a bi-marking (M, m) of EOS if $EIR(t, e) \vee EIR(e, t)$, t and e are activated in M and m respectively. Then the successor bi-marking (M', m') is defined by $M \overset{t}{\rightarrow} M'$ (w.r.t. SN) and $m \overset{e}{\rightarrow} m'$ (w.r.t. ON). We write $(M, m) \overset{[t, e]}{\rightarrow} (M', m')$ in this case.

Before modeling the sensor networks based on EEOS, a brief description of sensor network is given. A sensor network consists of a large number of sensor nodes scattered in a geographic area to measure a phenomenon (Akyldiz et al., 2002). The sensor nodes send their services to the sink node, which is computationally powerful and provides the data accessible to the application. The sensor nodes are capable of aggregating and routing the services to the sink node. The sink node acts as an interface between sensor nodes and external applications which request for sensor data.

In our paper we assume that the sensor network consists of *mobile* sensor nodes as well as *static* sensor nodes. By mobile sensor nodes, we mean that these sensor nodes can move from one region called a *sensor area* to another, while the static sensor nodes stay at one position. Sensor networks offer many new capabilities for monitoring environments with applicability to medical, industrial, military, environmental, and experiential fields. By making the system mobile, we increase the application space for the wireless

and distributed sensor network mainly by providing context-dependent deployment, continual relocatability, automatic node recovery, and a larger area of coverage. By adding autonomous mobility to the sensor nodes, the system becomes more able to dynamically localize around areas of interest, allowing it to cover a larger total area with fewer nodes by moving nodes away from uninteresting areas. Such approaches are well suited to sampling dynamic or poorly modeled phenomena. The addition of locomotion further provides the ability to deploy the sensor network at a distance away from the area of interest, especially useful in hostile environments. Cooperative micro-robots can reach places and perform tasks that their larger cousins cannot. Mobility also allows the design of a system where nodes can seek out power sources, request the dispatch of other nodes to perform tasks that require more sensing capability, seek out repair, and locate data portals from which to report. But the creation and deployment of these mobile sensor nodes is out of scope of this paper.

Based on EEOS (Ma & Tsai, 2008), we model a generic secure sensor network which is structured into three hierarchical layers: a sink node layer, sensor node layer and security mechanism layer. The sink node layer is the base layer, in which sink nodes are modeled as system nets and sensor nodes are tokens that can be transported among sink nodes. The sink nodes are resource rich access points which perform digital signatures and maintain most of the security parameters. The next layer up is the sensor node layer. In this layer, sensor nodes are system nets while the security mechanisms equipped with sensor nodes are tokens. These sensor nodes are unable to perform public key cryptography due to limited computing resources. Instead, the security protocol SNEP is used by these nodes to perform authentication. Finally, at the top layer is the security mechanism layer that models the structure of the security mechanisms. Figure 1 gives a hierarchy

Figure 1. The hierarchy of the EEOS model for a generic secure sensor network

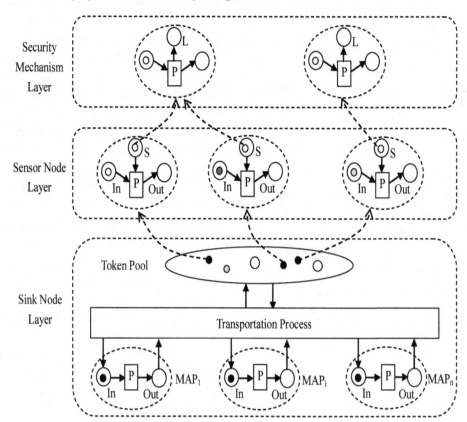

of an EEOS model for a generic secure sensor network system.

In our model, the sink node acts an interface between the sensor network and external applications. The sink node serves as a trusted server, so all the data has to pass through the sink node before reaching either the sensor nodes or an application. Sensor nodes store and process aggregation filters while the sink nodes concentrate on collecting data from sensor network and providing the data to the external applications.

We assume that sink node can perform digital signatures like RSA. There can be any number of sink nodes in a network. Also we assume that the sensor network is divided into sectors called sensor areas, where all the sensor nodes within one sensor area will send the data to the sink node which is nearest to them. All the sink nodes exchange information about the sensor nodes and

the services they provide, so that all the sink nodes in a given network contain the same information. This provides the needed robustness to attacks on a base station/sink node; because an application can access another sink node if one fails, thereby providing reliability.

The sensor network operates in three steps. Step 1 is initialization, where the sensor network topology is discovered, the sensor nodes get to know each other, and the sink nodes know all the services offered by the sensor nodes. Step 2 is interest advertisement, by which it means that the application sends an interest message, specifying its interest in a particular service to the sink node. Step 3 is data advertisement, which is issued by the sensor node sending the service which the application is interested in. So the core elements involved in our model are sink nodes and sensor nodes. We will model these elements using EEOS

Figure 2. The simplified EEOS model of a sink node

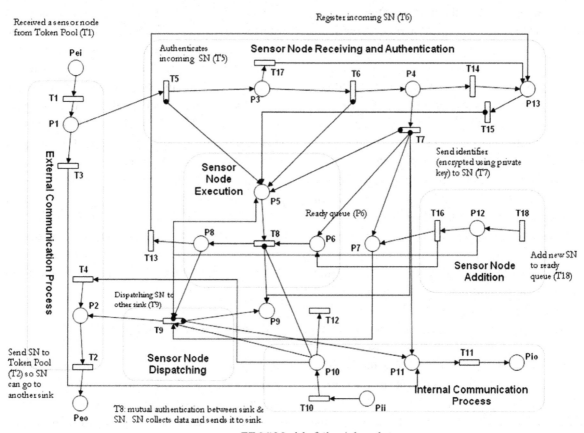

EEOS Model of the sink node

system and also model security objectives of authenticity, confidentiality and integrity.

2.1 Sink Node Layer

Sink node layer consists of two parts: sink nodes and the token pool. Token pool is a Petri net place connecting to/from all sink nodes and represents the network environment. In a generic sensor network model, each sensor node sends collected sensor data to nearby sink nodes, which in turn exchange the sensor data among themselves so that all the sink nodes have the same data. The sensor nodes can be mobile so that they can move around in a sensor network. All the sensor nodes which send data to the same nearby sink node are said to be in one area. When a sensor

node moves from one sensor area to another, it changes its sink node and sends the sensor data to the new nearby sink node. As the sensor node moves from one sensor area to another, it is assumed to be in token pool, till it acquires a new sink node. Token pool is thus a place for traveling sensor node token nets. A sink node is responsible for collecting sensor data from sensor nodes and for ensuring that the sensor nodes are functioning properly during their lifetime and have not been compromised under certain security policies. A sink node can communicate with sensor nodes residing in its sensor area and also with other sink nodes to exchange sensor data. A sink node also communicates with an external application requesting for sensor data. Figure 2 shows the simplified model of a sink node.

A sink node in the EEOS model has six functional modules: external communication process module, internal communication process module, sensor node receiving and authentication module, sensor node execution module, sensor node dispatching module and sensor node addition module.

A sink node is assumed to be secure from adversaries and is computationally robust, has the requisite processor speed, memory and power to support the cryptographic and routing requirements of a sensor network and to support proper functioning of sensor nodes. A sensor node is said to be executing when it collects the data from the environment.

A sink node receives (T1) a sensor node from token pool through its external communication channel. Then the sink node authenticates (T5) the incoming sensor node with its security mechanism (digital signatures like RSA) and registers (T6) it accordingly. Each sensor node has a unique identifier which is generated when the sensor node is created. An incoming sensor node together with its unique identifier is encrypted twice by the source sink node using the private key of the source sink node and the public key of destination sink node before it moves from the source sink node. Therefore by decrypting an incoming sensor node using the public key of the source sink node and the private key of the destination sink node, the sink node to which the sensor node is intended to migrate can authenticate the source sink node of the sensor node and can also check the sensor node's identity. Once this is done, the sink node also needs to prove its identity to the incoming sensor nodes to achieve mutual authentication.

This requires the sink node to send (T7) its unique identifier encrypted using its private key to the sensor node using internal communication channel. The sensor node, which is put into the ready queue (P6) of the sink node at that time and therefore can be executed (T8), goes ahead to decrypt the identifier using the public key of the sink node. Only after all these procedures are successfully completed, the mutual authentication between the sink node and the incoming sensor

node is achieved. Afterwards, the sink node starts executing the sensor node. By this, it means that sensor nodes start collecting the sensor data and send it to the sink node. After the sensor data is sent to the sink node, the sink node will encrypt (T9) it twice by using its own private key and the public key of the next destination sink node in the sensor node's itinerary, then send (T2) the sensor node to the token pool again so that it can go to other sink nodes or return to its home sink node via the token pool. A sink node can also add new sensor nodes (T8) and put (T16) them into ready queue for execution or dispatch them (T9) into the outside network directly. Concurrent management of sensor nodes is supported in the EEOS model of a sensor network as well as communications with these sensor nodes.

2.2 Sensor Node Layer

A sensor node should be able to migrate among sink nodes to perform its actions automatically. A sensor node does the following actions: collecting sensor data and sending the data to sink nodes, migrating to a different sensor area to be under a new sink node, and responding to a query from a sink node. These actions are in sync with the mobile senor actions: reactive actions, autonomous actions and move actions. Figure 3 shows the simplified EEOS model of a sensor node. In this model, we have integrated rules which determine an appropriate action to perform based on its current state and certain other conditions. Security base for a sensor node is place P12, where tokens represent security mechanisms. Their structure and behaviour are discussed in the security mechanism layer. SNEP protocol is embedded in the security base for authentication and confidentiality of sensor data.

A sensor node has six functional modules: communication process module, authentication and record module, reactive action module, autonomous action module, move action module and security mechanism module. A sensor node communicates

Figure 3. The simplified EEOS model of a sensor node

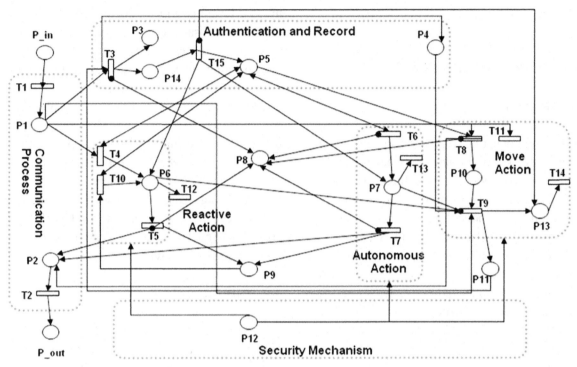

Tokens in P12 represent security mechanisms

with other sensor nodes and sink nodes using it's In and Out communication channels. These channels support both synchronous and asynchronous communications. A sensor node performs any of the three types of actions based on its goals, status, location or any request from sink node.

When a sensor node migrates to another sensor area, it removes the token to disable its functionalities and stores its current status through the integrated "remove-restore" mechanism. Afterwards the sensor node is transferred to the token pool from which it moves to destination sink node in a new sensor area. As was described in the sink node layer, after the destination sink node authenticates an incoming sensor node, the sink node sends its own identifier encrypted by its private key to the sensor node. The sensor node starts executing on the new sink node and decrypts the identifier for mutual authentication. After that, the sensor node's state is restored by the sink node (P13, T15) and

continues its execution from the point it stops its execution before migration. In this way a strong mobility is achieved in our model.

2.3 Security Mechanism Layer

The top layer in our model is the security mechanism layer. Petri nets in this layer are token nets for sink node system nets. They are carried by sensor nodes as tokens. The structure of token nets is not fixed in this layer as there may be different security objectives which require different security mechanisms. In this paper, we take authentication, confidentiality and integrity as the security objectives under consideration. For authentication and confidentiality, we use SNEP protocol of SPINS in the sensor nodes. For integrity, we use the synchronous firing mechanism used in the EEOS model for a secure mobile agent system. The details of the security mechanism layer are proposed in the following section.

3. SECURITY MECHANISMS

3.1 Integrity

For a sensor node, the integrity is concerned with possible attacks to the data it collected, resulting in a sensor node getting compromised and produces false sensor data or corrupted data. In this case a sensor node does what it is not supposed to do or does not do what it is supposed to do. When projected to our model, it boils down to a change in the structure of a sensor node. A malicious sensor node might actually corrupt the sensor data or delete the sensor data and inject its own data, in which case the structure of a sensor node is definitely changed from EEOS perspective. To deal with this type of attack, a security mechanism called *synchronous firing security* mechanism is introduced.

In the synchronous firing mechanism, an object net in the security mechanism layer does not have a security base place because it does not need extra security mechanisms. It has an additional "Firing Log" place, which records the firing sequence of transitions for later checkup. Also an object net in security mechanism layer is encrypted. Each transition in this net is encrypted separately. At the same time, each transition in a sensor node system net (*S-net*) has a special extended interaction relation with its counterpart transition in object net (*O-net*), while the S-net transition is a driving transition and the O-net transition is a driven transition. A driving transition is responsible to decrypt its driven transition. This is the key point of this mechanism, which is discussed below.

The decryption algorithms are integrated in driving transitions in S-net. Once a transition in S-net is fired, the decryption part gets executed to decrypt its driven transition in O-net. The driven transition may be fired afterwards. Correspond-

ing firing information is added as a color token into the Firing Log place. Afterwards the driven transition is disabled. In the context of a sensor network, firing the driving transition corresponds to decrypting the sensor data represented by the driven transition. The decrypted data is then stored in certain memory area of the hosting platform and is executed with execution information recorded. After execution, this data removes itself from the memory. When a sensor node finishes its execution and returns to its home sink node, the results it brings back together with its O-net will be checked. If two parts do not match with each other, the home sink node may conclude that the sensor node might have been attacked.

3.2 Authentication

Data authentication is important for many applications in sensor networks. Within a sensor network, authentication is necessary for many administrative tasks (e.g., network reprogramming or controlling sensor node duty cycle). At the same time, an adversary can easily inject messages, so the receiver needs to make sure that the data used in any decision-making process originates from the correct source. Data authentication allows a receiver to verify that the data really was sent by the claimed sender. In our model, the sink node acts as gateway for the sensor nodes to communicate with outside network. So compromising the sink node may render the sensor network useless. For this purpose, we assume that there are multiple sink nodes in a given sensor network.

In our model, we have a two-party communication between a sink node and a sensor node. But when a sink node needs to broadcast queries to sensor nodes, we need to provide authenticated broadcast. For two-party authentication, we use symmetric mechanism to achieve data authentication. The sink node and the sensor node share a secret key to compute a message authentication code (MAC) of all communicated data. When a message with a correct MAC arrives, the sink node knows that it must have been sent by the legitimate sensor node. But this style of authentication cannot be applied to a broadcast setting, without placing much stronger trust assumptions on the network nodes. If one sink node wants to send authentic data to mutually un-trusted sensor nodes, using a symmetric MAC is insecure: Any one of the sensor nodes knows the MAC key, and hence could impersonate the sink node and forge messages to other sensor nodes. Hence, we need an asymmetric mechanism to achieve authenticated broadcast. So in our model we provide authenticated broadcast from symmetric primitives only, and introduce asymmetry with delayed key disclosure and one-way function key chains. We assume that the sink nodes and sensor nodes are loosely time synchronized, and each sensor node knows an upper bound on the maximum synchronization error. To send an authenticated packet, the sink node simply computes a MAC on the packet with a key that is secret at that point in time. When a sensor node gets a packet, it can verify that the corresponding MAC key was not yet disclosed by the sink node (based on its loosely synchronized clock, its maximum synchronization error, and the time schedule at which keys are disclosed). Since a receiving sensor node is assured that the MAC key is known only by the sink node, the receiving node is assured that no adversary could have altered the packet in transit. The node stores the packet in a buffer. At the time of key disclosure, the sink node broadcasts the verification key to all receivers. When a sensor node receives the disclosed key, it can easily verify the correctness of the key. If the key is correct, the node can now use it to authenticate the packet stored in its buffer. Each MAC key is a key of a key chain, generated by a public one-way function F. To generate the one-way key chain, the sender chooses the last key K_n of the chain randomly, and repeatedly applies F to compute all other keys: $K_i = F(K_{i+1})$. Each node can easily perform

time synchronization and retrieve an authenticated key of the key chain for the commitment in a secure and authenticated manner, using the SNEP building block (Perrig, 2002).

3.3 Confidentiality

Data confidentiality is one of the most basic security primitives and it is used in almost every security protocol. A simple form of confidentiality can be achieved through encryption, but pure encryption is not sufficient. Another important security property is semantic security, which ensures that an eavesdropper has no information about the plaintext, even if it sees multiple encryptions of the same plaintext. For this purpose we use a shared counter between sink node and sensor node. We assume that both the sensor node and sink node share a counter which is used as an Initialization Vector (IV). When a sensor node sends data to sink node, it will not send the counter. But the counter value is incremented after each block of data has been sent. The counter value is never repeated. Since the counter value is incremented after each block of data has been sent, the same data is encrypted differently each time, thus achieving semantic security and data confidentiality.

4. SIMULATION AND ANALYSIS

With the EEOS model in place for sensor networks and some additional effort to convert an EEOS model into a form amenable to Design/CPN, the most widely used simulation tool for colored Petri nets, simulation and simulation-based analysis can be carried out to provide a description of the behaviors and characteristics of the sensor network system. Two kinds of simulation-based analysis can be performed. The first type of analysis is the standard analysis supported directly by the standard simulation report generated through Design/CPN, which includes boundedness and liveness properties. The advantage of this type of analysis is that it is usually easy to draw conclusions on certain features. The second type of analysis is referred to as query-based analysis that is performed based on user-defined queries about the Occurrence Graph, which is the state space, of the model. Although such queries are always complicated and not easy to write, they can provide more insights into the model and support analysis for specific features, such as security features. It should also be noted that with different initial markings, behaviors of a system under analysis could be quite different.

While tools like Design/CPN can be useful in providing valuable information with regard to the EEOS model, they can be complemented by platform-specific simulation tools such as TOS-SIM, whose primary goal is to provide a high fidelity simulation for TinyOS applications (Levis & Lee, n.d.). TOSSIM is a TinyOS simulator made exclusively to ease the development of sensor network applications. TOSSIM scales to thousands of nodes, and compiles directly from TinyOS code; developers can test not only their algorithms, but also their implementations. TOSSIM also has a Java-based GUI tool, TinyViz, which can visualize and interact with running simulations, and also inspect debug messages and radio packets. The simulation provides several mechanisms for interacting with the network; packet traffic can be monitored, packets can be statically or dynamically injected into the network. Using a simple plug-in module, users can develop new visualizations and interfaces for TinyViz.

In the rest of this section, we use TOSSIM to simulate a wireless sensor network consisting of 30 sensor nodes out of which 12 nodes are mobile. There are 3 sink nodes in the network. The TOSSIM simulator produces sensor data in the form of trace files as run-time configurable debugging output, allowing a user to examine the execution of a sensor network from different perspectives without needing to recompile. The routing protocol used in sensor network is loop-free AODV protocol (Ad-hoc On-demand Distance Vector). The radio propagation distance at the physical layer is set to $200m$ for each node. The ADC channel capacity is $1Mbps$. The communication medium is broadcast and nodes have bi-directional connectivity.

The radio links in our simulation graphically display radio message activity. When a sensor node broadcasts a message, a blue circle will be drawn around it. When a sensor node sends a message to another node, a directed arrow will be drawn between the two nodes. The location of all sensor nodes can also be set in TOSSIM. We use "Empirical" radio model which allows us to use realistic connectivity models for our simulations. For each sensor node, its connectivity to other nodes is shown including link communication cost, communication ranges between sensor nodes and distance between sensor nodes. The number shown next to each edge is the probability of a packet getting through. The overall message format for our sensor network model is as follows:

- Destination address (2 bytes)
- Active Message handler ID (1 byte)
- Group ID (1 byte)
- Message length (1 byte)
- Payload (up to 29 bytes):
- Source sink ID (2 bytes)
- Sample counter (2 bytes)
- ADC channel (2 bytes)
- ADC data readings (10 readings of 2 bytes each) (sensor data)

The sample output of our simulation is shown in Box 1.

For example, the second line of output means: (see Box 2).

We can visualize the sensor network using TinyViz. Figure 4 shows a sensor network with 30 nodes.

Figure 5 shows link communication cost, distance between the nodes in a sensor network. It also shows the connectivity between the nodes.

Box 1.

```
% java net.tinyos.tools.Listen

serial@COM1:19200: resynchronising

7e 00 0a 7d 1a 01 00 0a 00 01 00 46 03 8e 03 96 03 96 03 96 03 97 03 97 03 97 03 97 03 97 03
7e 00 0a 7d 1a 01 00 14 00 01 00 96 03 97 03 97 03 98 03 97 03 96 03 97 03 96 03 96 03 96 03
7e 00 0a 7d 1a 01 00 1e 00 01 00 98 03 98 03 96 03 97 03 97 03 98 03 96 03 97 03 97 03 97 03
7e 00 0a 7d 1a 01 00 0a 00 01 00 46 03 8e 03 96 03 96 03 96 03 97 03 97 03 97 03 97 03 97 03
7e 00 0a 7d 1a 01 00 16 00 01 00 96 03 97 03 97 03 98 03 97 03 96 03 97 03 96 03 96 03 96 03
7e 00 0a 7d 1a 01 00 1e 00 01 00 98 03 98 03 98 03 96 03 97 03 98 03 96 03 97 03 97 03 97 03
```

Box 2.

```
dest addr: 7e 00
handlerID: 0a
groupID: 7d
msg len: 1a
source addr: 01 00
counter: 14 00
channel: 01 00
readings (actual sensor data): 96 03 97 03 97 03 98 03 97 03 96 03 97 03 96 03 96 03 96 03
```

Figure 4. A sensor network with 30 nodes

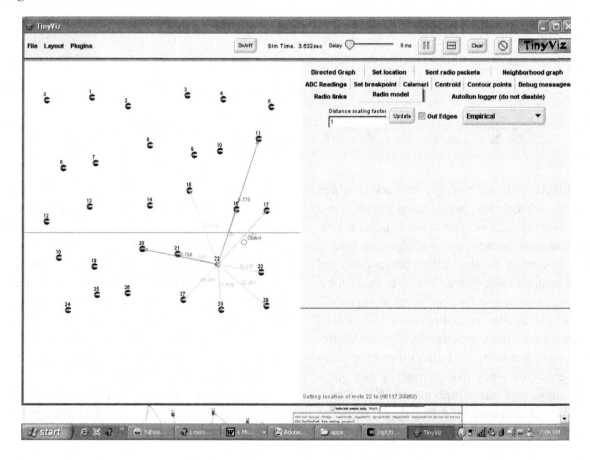

Figure 5. Communication cost, distance and connectivity between the nodes

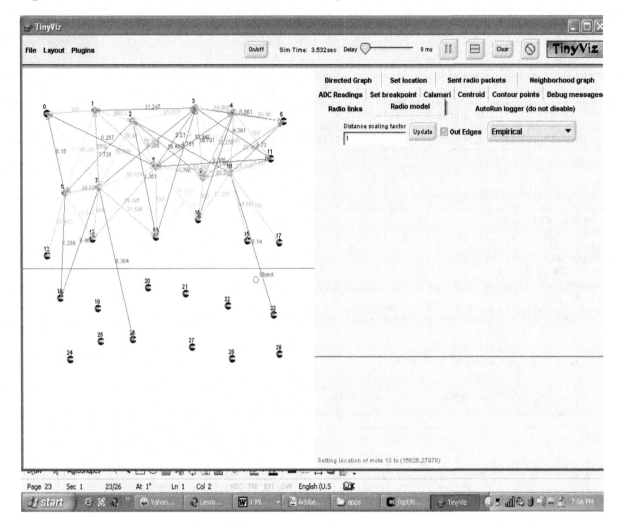

Figure 6 shows a sensor network in which mobile sensor nodes are directed to move in a particular direction. The arrows indicate how mobile nodes move to the needed sensor area. In our simulation, we show all the sensor areas and sink nodes in one plane. The debugging messages are shown on the right panel in Figure 6.

The simulated sensor network can be analyzed for security requirements of authenticity, confidentiality and also other properties of sensor network like scalability and completeness. We have implemented SNEP protocol and authenticated broadcast property. We have conducted simulation based analysis

when there are some packet losses and when some unauthorized node tries to enter the network. Since AODV is the routing protocol used, by monitoring the routing information stored in routing table at each sensor node, attacks such as false destination sequence numbers can be detected. We use reverse labeling mechanism to identify and isolate the malicious nodes in sensor networks. TOSSIM traces back the propagation paths of false routing information through reverse labeling. Model of trust management can also be simulated in TOSSIM. The mobile nodes reach consistent conclusions on malicious nodes by

Figure 6. Moving direction of mobile sensor nodes

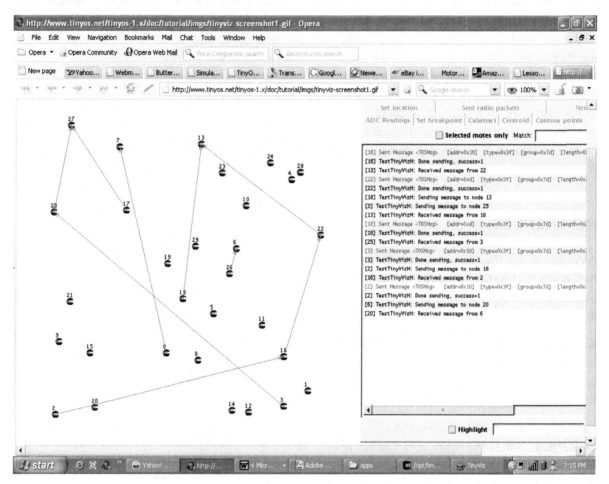

combining local decisions with knowledge from other nodes. Four performance metrics, namely, percentage of packets dropped, percentage of packets authenticated, node mobility and the number of independent malicious nodes, can be used to study the effectiveness, accuracy, and overhead of simulations.

5. CONCLUSION AND FUTURE WORK

In this paper, we propose a formal model for secure sensor network systems. The model is based on an augmented Petri net formalism called Extended Elementary Object System. This proposed secure sensor network model has a multi-layered structure consisting of sink node layer, sensor node layer and security mechanism layer. The model focuses on the security requirements of authentication, confidentiality, non-repudiation and data integrity. Using EEOS to model the sensor network systems has several advantages. (1) It is a hierarchical model and hence supports encapsulation. (2) It accommodates the design and implementation of different security mechanisms. Therefore various security objectives of a sensor network can be easily incorporated according to application requirements. (3) It supports the modeling of mobility, which is unique among all the existing formal methods of modeling. (4)

Finally, the formal modeling of Petri nets allows for formal analysis.

Future work can be pursued in the following directions. (1) Establish a methodology to combine results from Design/CPN and TOSSIM for formal analysis of the EEOS model of secure sensor network systems. (2) Generate some guideline on how to specify the upper bounds on the state space of the model for a given sensor network.

REFERENCES

Akyldiz, I., Su, W., Sankarasubramaniam, Y., & Cayirci, E. (2002). A Survey on Sensor Networks. *IEEE Communications, 40*(8), 102–114. doi:10.1109/MCOM.2002.1024422

Karlof, C., & Wagner, D. (2003). Secure Routing in Wireless Sensor Networks: Attacks and Countermeasures. *Ad Hoc Networks, 1*(2-3), 293–315. doi:10.1016/S1570-8705(03)00008-8

Lakos, C. (2001). Object Oriented Modeling with Object Petri Nets. In G. Agha, F. D. Cindio, & G. Rozenberg (Eds.), *Concurrent Object-Oriented Programming and Petri Nets* (LNCS 2001, pp. 1-37). Berlin: Springer Verlag.

Levis, P., Gay, D., & Culler, D. (2005, May). Active Sensor Networks. In *Proceedings of the 2nd Symposium on Networked Systems Design & Implementation* (USENIX) (pp. 343-356).

Levis, P., & Lee, N. (n.d.). *TOSSIM: A Simulator for TinyOS Networks*. Retrieved from http://www.eecs.berkeley.edu/~pal/pubs/nido.pdf

Lewis, F. L. (2004). Wireless Sensor Networks. In Cook, D. J., & Das, S. K. (Eds.), *Smart Environments: Technologies, Protocols, and Applications*. New York: John Wiley.

Ma, L., & Tsai, J. J. P. (2008). Formal Modeling and Analysis of Secure Mobile Agent Systems. *IEEE Transactions on System, Man, and Cybernetics . Part A, 38*(1), 180–196.

Murata, T. (1989). Petri Nets: Properties, Analysis, and Applications. In *Proceedings of the IEEE* (pp. 541-580).

Perrig, A., Szewczyk, R., Wen, V., Culler, D., & Tygar, J. D. (2002). SPINS: security protocols for sensor networks. *Wireless Networks, 8*, 521–534. doi:10.1023/A:1016598314198

Romer, K., & Mattern, F. (2004). The Design Space of Wireless Sensor Networks. *IEEE Wireless Communications, 11*(6), 54–61. doi:10.1109/MWC.2004.1368897

Valk, R. (1998). Petri Nets as Token Objects - An Introduction to Elementary Object Nets. In *Proceedings of the 19th International Conference on Application and Theory of Petri Nets (ICATPN'98)* (LNCS 1420, pp. 1-25).

Walters, J. P., Liang, Z., Shi, W., & Chaudhary, V. (2007). Wireless Sensor Network Security: A Survey . In Xiao, Y. (Ed.), *Security in Distributed, Grid, Mobile and Pervasive Computing*. New York: Auerbach Publications.

Wang, Y. (2007). Toward Theoretical Foundations of Autonomic Computing. *International Journal of Cognitive Informatics and Natural Intelligence, 1*(3), 1–16.

This work was previously published in volume 4, issue 4 of the International Journal of Cognitive Informatics and Natural Intelligence, edited by Yingxu Wang, pp. 1-17, copyright 2010 by IGI Publishing (an imprint of IGI Global).

Chapter 19
Amplification of Signal Features Using Variance Fractal Dimension Trajectory

Witold Kinsner
University of Manitoba, Canada

Warren Grieder
University of Manitoba, Canada

ABSTRACT

This paper describes how the selection of parameters for the variance fractal dimension (VFD) multiscale time-domain algorithm can create an amplification of the fractal dimension trajectory that is obtained for a natural-speech waveform in the presence of ambient noise. The technique is based on the variance fractal dimension trajectory (VFDT) algorithm that is used not only to detect the external boundaries of an utterance, but also its internal pauses representing the unvoiced speech. The VFDT algorithm can also amplify internal features of phonemes. This fractal feature amplification is accomplished when the time increments are selected in a dyadic manner rather than selecting the increments in a unit distance sequence. These amplified trajectories for different phonemes are more distinct, thus providing a better characterization of the individual segments in the speech signal. This approach is superior to other energy-based boundary-detection techniques. Observations are based on extensive experimental results on speech utterances digitized at 44.1 kilosamples per second, with 16 bits in each sample.

INTRODUCTION

This work is motivated by the need for better human-machine interaction. We have reached a point at which our ability to create large computing systems and information has exceeded our ability to maintain and manage them manually. The developments towards cognitive machines and systems are intended to increase utilization of resources, as well as to ease their maintenance and their human-centric interactions (Kinsner, 2007, January). The semantic Web is intended to provide applications to alleviate the problem of manual keyword searches and blog surfing

DOI: 10.4018/978-1-4666-1743-8.ch019

through natural-language and semantic tools to determine the required content from any textual material through cognitive informatics (Wang, 2002) and other new developments in intelligent signal processing (Haykin, Principe, Sejnowski, & McWhirter, 2007), (Kinsner, 2007, April). However, non-textual materials such as non-annotated music, sounds, images, video, mathematical expressions, and chemical formulae are still largely inaccessible. More importantly, the vast amount of recorded acoustic speech and voices in their analog form (e.g., magnetic recordings) and digital form (uncompressed or compressed recordings) is largely inaccessible for browsing or real-time automatic translation at this stage.

This paper provides a small, but significant step towards not only an automatic speech recognition and translation into text, but also speech browsability (searching for specific phrases) and speech understanding. The technique described here is based on a multiscale information-theoretic approach to dealing with band-limited and broadband signals contaminated by noise. This approach differs fundamentally from the traditional energy-based approaches.

One major difficulty in the automatic recognition of speech by a machine is the unlimited number of possible utterances in a given language. This is further compounded by the non-stationary and variable nature of speech, where even two utterances of the same phrase, while perceptually identical to a human listener, contain several differences that make template matching of complete phrases impractical due to the extensive memory and search time requirements for a system with a large vocabulary. Thus, it is necessary to segment utterances into smaller units such as words, syllables, or phonemes. When the size of the segmentation units is reduced, there are fewer possible matching patterns, thus reducing both the size of the search for matching elements and the amount of storage required for pattern templates. Although still large on the word and syllable level,

pattern matching becomes more manageable on the phonemic level.

Many speech pre-processing techniques, which utilize various parameterization of speech, have been developed that can perform speech recognition (Bristow, 1986) with varying degrees of success. Among the parameterizations used are linear predictive coding (LPC) with dynamic time warping (Parsons, 1987; Rabiner & Schafer, 1978), used in formant tracking techniques, and fast Fourier transforms, used in the neural phonetic typewriter (Kohonen, 1988). Many segmentation and recognition techniques use wavelets (Mallat, 1998; Wornell, 1996), fractals (Al-Akaidi, 2004; Kinsner, 2007, October), higher-order statistics (Haykin, Principe, Sejnowski, & McWhirter, 2007), neuro-fuzzy classifications techniques (Haykin & Kosko, 2001, Ch. 5; Bishop, 2006). With a more accurate identification scheme of the segmentation boundaries, further analysis using these and other techniques on the speech segments may result in increased performance.

In a previous paper (Kinsner & Grieder, 2008), we have shown how the variance fractal dimension (VFD) algorithm can be used to calculate a dimension value of the speech samples contained in a window within the speech utterance. By shifting this window to different positions spaced at regular intervals along the utterance and calculating the dimension for each window, a trajectory for the speech in the variance fractal dimension domain can be obtained, which can then be analyzed to provide a segmentation of the utterance. This variance fractal dimension trajectory (VFDT) follows a path that is determined by the characteristics of the utterance, with each phoneme exhibiting a characteristic trajectory pattern and transitions between adjacent phonemes generally indicated by a change in the trajectory. The beginning and end of an utterance can be determined by transitions between silence, which contains low level noise with a high dimension, and the more correlated speech waveform, which has a lower dimension. Most importantly, transitions between consonants and vowels can also be noted within utterances, the consonants have noise-like properties and thus have higher dimensions than the vowels which have very regular waveforms. As well, segmentation within consonant clusters is possible due to the distinctive trajectories of each phoneme.

Speech is very difficult to recognize by machines because of the inherent variability of its features. For the same speaker, the features change from morning to noon to evening, from calm speech to agitated speech, from natural speech to speech with some impediments such as the common cold. Even if all this variability were to be minimized, there is an inherent variability that cannot be eliminated: the natural variability of phonemes within an utterance. For example, the stop consonant "t" in "start" is very different in the first and second appearance. This paper is dedicated to this problem, and provides a solution by amplification of the multiscale measures of each phoneme in the utterance.

The manner of selection of time increments for the VFD algorithm can create an amplification of the fractal dimension trajectory for a given waveform. When a unit distance selection of the time increments used in the calculation of the variance fractal dimension is chosen, the trajectory exhibits a significant transition from a high dimension for the background noise during periods of silence to a lower dimension for the speech utterances. However, the transitions within the speech utterance itself are less pronounced. The degree of distinction between internal segments is amplified by choosing a dyadic selection of the time increments. Another parameter in the VFD algorithm is the window displacement.

The amplification for the dyadic selection results from a combination of the exclusion of the unit distance increment and a broader range of time increments. With the unit distance selection, the inclusion of the unit increment and the narrower range of time increments selected cause the measured dimension to be dependent on the degree of correlation between adjacent samples (Kinsner & Grieder, 2008). With the dyadic selection these correlations have a lesser effect which results in increased distinction between the trajectories of individual segments within the utterances.

The VFDT technique described in this paper has also been used by the first author to segment and classify temporal signals found in dishabituation studies (Kinsner, Cheung, Cannons, Pear, & Martin, 2006), and radio transmitter fingerprinting.

VARIANCE FRACTAL DIMENSION TRAJECTORY ALGORITHM

Formulation of the VFD for Analog Signals

The multiscale variance-based technique of calculating a fractal dimension is derived from the properties of an analog (continuous) locally stationary fractional Brownian motion, $s(t)$, and other related stationary fractional broadband correlated stochastic processes, sampled at a sufficiently high sampling frequency, f_s, or the atomic sampling interval $\delta t = 1/f_s$. The sampling frequency is usually much higher than the Nyquist sampling frequency (as referenced by the 3dB cutoff frequency in the signal), and is referenced by the point where the signal drops below the floor noise. The variance fractal dimension, D_σ, of a fractional Brownian motion is determined by the so-called Hurst exponent, H, (Kinsner, 1994, May; Kinsner, 2007, October; Kinsner & Grieder, 2008; Gache, Flandrin, & Garreau, 1991; Zhang, Barad, & Martinez, 1990; Peitgen, Jürgens, & Saupe, 2004), according to

$$D_\sigma = D_E - H \qquad (1)$$

265

where D_E is the embedding dimension. For a one-dimensional analog signal, the embedding dimension is $D_E = 2$, which is the dimension of a white noise for which $H = 0$. So, what is H, and how do we obtain the desired value of H? The Hurst exponent H relates the increments in the amplitude to the time increments in self-affine signals, and it can be computed by measuring the variance of such signals at different scales (coverings), according to the fundamental Hausdorff principle of multiscale measurements.

The increments for a fractional Brownian motion are denoted by

$$d(t_n, \Delta t) = s(t_n + \Delta t) - s(t_n) \tag{2}$$

where $s(t_n)$ is the amplitude of the analog signal at time t_n, and Δt is the time displacement over which the increment is measured. For a self-affine signal such as the Brownian motion, these increments satisfy the following power-law property

$$d(t_n, \Delta t) = \lim_{\Delta t \to 0} c_1 \xi |\Delta t|^H \tag{3}$$

where c_1 is a proportionality constant, and ξ is a normalized Gaussian random variable. Notice that since Δt represents the scale of measurement during the successive coverings, it is also called a *volume element*, or *vel* for short (Kinsner, 1994, May; Kinsner, 2007, October). In general, this name applies to both time and space coverings.

The increments $d(t_n, \Delta t)$ have a zero mean, and a variance, Var[$d(t_n, \Delta t)$], denoted by

$$\text{Var}[d(t_n, \Delta t)] \equiv \left\langle d^2(t_n, \Delta t) \right\rangle = \lim_{\Delta t \to 0} c_2 |\Delta t|^{2H} \tag{4}$$

where the bra-cket notation signifies the expected value, and c_2 is a proportionality constant. Taking the logarithm of both sides gives

$$\log \left\langle d^2(t_n, \Delta t) \right\rangle = 2H \log \Delta t + c_3 \tag{5}$$

where Δt is always made to be positive, and c_3 is a constant. It is evident that this is a line in the log-log space with a slope of $2H$ and an offset c_3. Thus, for a given time series and a selected jth scale of Δt, this calculation produces a single ordered pair

$$(x_j, y_j) \equiv \left(\log \Delta t, \log \left\langle d^2(t_n, \Delta t) \right\rangle \right) \tag{6}$$

The calculations must be repeated for a sufficiently large number M of scales of Δt within which the power law applies. Since the self-affine signal satisfies the power law (4), the M ordered pairs constitute points on a straight line in the log-log plot, the value of H can be calculated by using a robust least-squares regression, based on (Kinsner, 1994, June)

$$H = \frac{1}{2} \frac{M \sum_{j=1}^{M} x_j y_j - \left(\sum_{j=1}^{M} x_j \right) \left(\sum_{j=1}^{M} y_j \right)}{M \sum_{j=1}^{M} x_j^2 - \left(\sum_{j=1}^{M} x_j \right)^2} \tag{7}$$

Notice that this linear regression applies if and only if the pairs form a line. If the points do not form a line, the power law does not apply, and the signal is not self affine. Thus, the variance fractal dimension D_σ should not be calculated as it would be meaningless. If the majority of the pairs form a line, but saturations occur at the extreme pairs, the saturations must be removed before computing H. Extreme attention must be paid to the robustness of the linear regression algorithm.

The actual VFD algorithm to calculate D_σ of a stationary sequence of a digital (discrete and quantized) signal (time series) is described in detail in (Kinsner & Grieder, 2008). That paper also describes the VFDT algorithm.

THE TIME INCREMENT SELECTION IN VFD ALGORITHM

Let us assume that the sequence contains N samples, each acquired at times t_n given by

$$t_n = n\delta t, \quad n = 0, 1, 2, , ..., N-1 \quad (8)$$

where n is the time index, and δt is the atomic time displacement between individual samples.

The vel size (i.e., the cumulative time displacement Δt for the measurement of the amplitude increments) can be chosen as a multiple m of the atomic time displacement δt, as given by

$$\Delta t_m = m_i \delta t \quad (9)$$

where m_i can be selected so that the sequence of the coverings is either monadic, or dyadic, or triadic, as given by

$$m_k = b^k, \quad k = 0, 1, 2, ..., K-1 \quad (10)$$

where b is the base for a covering, and K is the number of required coverings, from the smallest to the largest vel size, and selected according to statistical considerations (Kinsner, 1994, June). The monadic covering ($m_m = 1,2,3,4,5,...M_m$) is produced for $b = 1$ and $M_m = 5$, and is best suited for utterance boundary detection. The dyadic sequence ($m_d = 1,2,4,8,16,...M_d$) is obtained for $b = 2$ and $M_m = 16$, and is the most common choice, as it can reveal long-range relations between the samples in the time series. This sequence is best suited for differentiation between internal feature of utterances, including phonemes because it has the feature amplification capability. The triadic sequence ($m_t = 1,3,9,27,81,...M_t$) is obtained for $b = 3$ may also be used to reveal even longer-range relations between the samples. Since each covering for $k = 0$ considers samples separated by just one atomic distance, this value of k may be omitted to reduce the effect of correlation between adjacent signal samples.

For a specific starting time, $n\delta t$, and a selected vel size (time displacement), $m\delta t$, the signal increment, $d(n\delta t, m\delta t)$, between speech samples is determined from

$$d(n\delta t, m\delta t) = s(n\delta t + m\delta t) - s(n\delta t) \quad (11)$$

where $s(\bullet)$ is a digital signal sample.

The variance of the digital signal increments, $\langle d^2(n\delta t, m_k\delta t)\rangle$, is calculated for each kth covering, with a specific vel size $m_k\delta t$. The covering may be *nonoverlapping* (i.e., each vel $m_k\delta t$ is adjacent to the next), as given by

$$\left\langle d^2(n\delta t, m_k\delta t)\right\rangle_n = \frac{\displaystyle\sum_{j=0}^{N_k^*-1}\left[d(jm_k\delta t, m_k\delta t)\right]}{N_k^*} \quad (12)$$

where the subscript outside the bra-cket on the left-hand side signifies the type of covering (n for nonoverlapping), and

$$N_k^* = \left\lfloor \frac{N}{m_k} \right\rfloor \quad (13)$$

is number of vels in the kth covering, with $\lfloor \bullet \rfloor$ denoting the floor function. Alternatively, the covering may also be *overlapping*. In the extreme, when the starting point of the next vel is located at each successive signal sample, then the variance at the kth covering is

$$\left\langle d^2(n\delta t, m_k\delta t)\right\rangle_1 = \frac{\displaystyle\sum_{n=0}^{N-m-1}\left[d(n\delta t, m_k\delta t)\right]}{N-m_k} \quad (13)$$

The logarithmic form of the power law (5) can now be rewritten for each kth covering as

$$\log \left\langle d^2(n\delta t, m_k\delta t) \right\rangle = 2H \, \log(m_k\delta t) + c_3$$
$$= 2H \, \log(m_k) + 2H \, \log(\delta t) + c_3$$
$$= 2H \, \log(m_k) + c_4$$

(14)

where c_4 is a constant. Thus, it is sufficient to calculate the logarithms of the vel size index, rather than the logarithms of the time displacements themselves.

Other improvements on the scheme are discussed in (Kinsner, 1994, June).

REDUCING ERROR IN D_σ DUE TO SIGNAL CORRELATION

To advance the argument quickly, let us simplify the problem from the VDFT to VFD algorithm which produces a single value of D_σ within a single window of the time series of size N. With the notation from the previous sections, we can write an explicit expression for the variance at atomic displacements δt as

$$\left\langle d^2(t_n, \delta t) \right\rangle = \frac{1}{N} \sum_{j=0}^{N-1} \{ s[(j+1)\delta t] - s(j\delta t) \}^2$$

(15)

In order to see the impact of correlation between samples, let us expand the variance as

$$\left\langle d^2(t_n, \delta t) \right\rangle = \frac{1}{N} \Big\{ \sum_{j=0}^{N-1} s^2[(j+1)\delta t] + \sum_{j=0}^{N-1} s^2(j\delta t)$$
$$+ \sum_{j=0}^{N-1} 2s[(j+1)\delta t]s(j\delta t) \Big\}$$

(16)

The third term in Eq. (16) is affected by the degree of correlation between the adjacent samples. An increased correlation for the smallest $\Delta t = \delta t$ may reduce the value of the variance considerably, as shown in Figure 1.

It is seen that the decreased variance pulls the fitted line down, thus resulting in an increased value of the Hurst exponent due to its steeper slope. This increased value of the Hurst exponent results in a decreased dimension D_σ. By eliminating the atomic increment $\Delta t = \delta t$, as well as the selection of the dyadic (rather than monadic) time increments over a larger range, a reliable amplification of the fractal dimension can be obtained.

EXPERIMENTS AND RESULTS

Experimental Setup

All our experiments are based on the natural speech of a single speaker, sampled at 44.1 ksps and 16 bits per sample, and recorded in a contiguous session. In order to test for all the phonemes and to provide a repeatable set of utterances, we have selected the Edinburgh *machine-readable phonetic alphabet* (MRPA) representation of phonemes and keywords (e.g., Bristow, 1986), as described in (Kinsner & Grieder, 2008). Notice that the *international phonetic alphabet* (IPA) is not machine readable.

The minimum set of recordings included all the keywords from Table 1. By examining the variance fractal dimension trajectories of the recordings calculated for a certain control setting for the VFDT algorithm, one can determine if the utterance boundary segmentation is possible or not. Furthermore, by changing the control settings, investigation of phonemic segmentation is also feasible.

A window size of N = 512 samples was used to provide an adequate width to prevent erratic behaviour of the dimension trajectory without being so large as to suffer the loss of features. This width corresponds to 11.6 ms, a value that is in agreement with the 10 - 30 ms window sizes for energy measurements established in (Schafer & Rabiner, 1975). This window size is also consistent with the accepted stationarity

Figure 1. Impact of signal correlation on D_σ

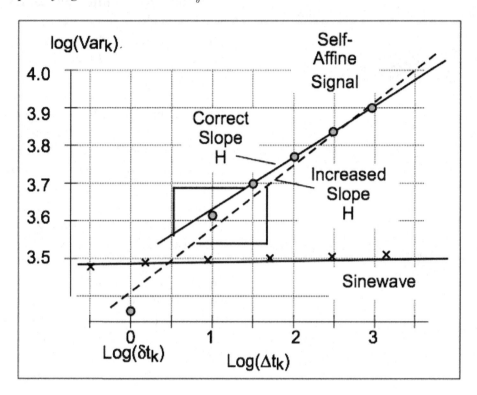

Table 1. Machine Readable Phonetic Alphabet (MRPA) representation of english phonemes and keywords. (After Bristow, 1986)

MRPA	Key word	MRPA	Key word	MRPA	Key word
/p/	*pip*	/zh/	*measure*	/oo/	*for*
/b/	*barb*	/h/	*hand*	/u/	*book*
/t/	*tight*	/r/	*rear*	/uu/	*boot*
/d/	*deed*	/l/	*loyal*	/uh/	*bud*
/k/	*kick*	/m/	*mime*	/@@/	*bird*
/g/	*gag*	/n/	*none*	/@/	*banana*
/ch/	*church*	/ng/	*ringing*	/ei/	*bay*
/jh/	*judge*	/y/	*year*	/ou/	*boat*
/f/	*fife*	/w/	*weal*	/ai/	*buy*
/v/	*verve*	/ii/	*bead*	/au/	*bough*
/th/	*thirtieth*	/i/	*bid*	/oi/	*boy*
/dh/	*other*	/e/	*bed*	/i@/	*beer*
/s/	*cease*	/a/	*bad*	/e@/	*bear*
/z/	*zoos*	/aa/	*bard*	/u@/	*poor*
/sh/	*sheepish*	/o/	*body*		

window for speech. A window interval spacing of a quarter of the window size (I = 128 samples) was used so that the trend of the dimension is noticeable, with few redundant calculations required.

Utterance Boundary Separation from Noise

To achieve the separation of an utterance from noise, we examined the monadic sequence of coverings with the set of $\Delta t = m_k \delta t$ containing $\{1\delta t, 2\delta t, 3\delta t, 4\delta t, 5\delta t\}$.

The monadic coverings involve highly-correlated adjacent samples, thus having a low dimension in comparison to less correlated samples. The dyadic selection provides information over a larger range, thus distinguishing features that are not noticeable in the unit-distance selection although other features may no longer be noticed.

Figure 2. VFDT for (a) "bad," (b) "bed," (c) "bid," and (d) "bud," using the monadic coverings (segmentation)

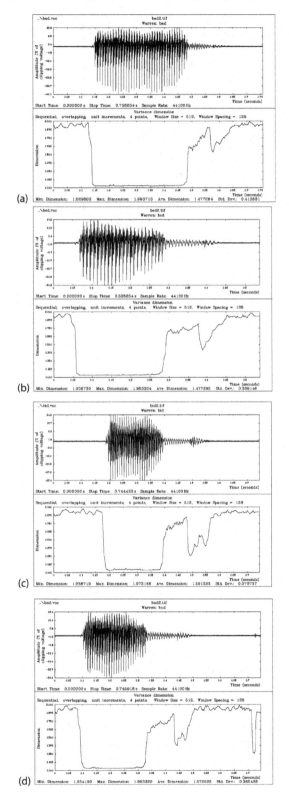

Figure 2. VFDT for (a) "bad," (b) "bed," (c) "bid," and (d) "bud," using the monadic coverings (segmentation)

Figure 2 shows **utterance separation** from noise through VFD trajectories obtained using monadic coverings for four utterances "bad" (Figure 2a), "bed" (Figure 2b), "bid" (Figure 2c), and "bud" (Figure 2d). Each Figure 2 a-d consists of two panels: the upper panel shows the time-domain signal of the corresponding utterance, while the lower panel depicts its variance fractal dimension trajectory (VFDT) computed from the time waveform. The horizontal axes in each panel represent time in seconds. The amplitude of the time waveform is displayed as percentage of the clipping voltage to assure that the signal is not clipped in any of the experiments. The maximum values for the above utterances are 18.9, 17.5, 24.2, and 18.4%, and the negative values are 41, 30, 35.4, and 31.9%. The duration of the utterances is approximately 0.74 s, except for he shorter "bed" (0.54 s). The window size for each VFD analysis is 512 samples, and the window displacement is 128 samples (overlapping by 75%).

Figure 2 shows clearly that the monadic coverings produce a VFDT in which all the utterances have a lower dimension (close to 1) than the internal noise contained with the periods of silence (close to 2). Each transition between the silence and the speech utterance is very abrupt. This gives us the ability to determine the beginning and end of isolated speech utterances, as well as identify intermediate periods of silence such as stop gaps. Notice that another example of separation of the utterance "tight," is discussed in (Kinsner & Grieder, 2008).

It is evident that this remarkable result is due to the multiscale technique which is based on the complexity measure of the signal, rather than on its energy.

Fractal Feature Amplification

To achieve the fractal amplification of features within an utterance, we examined the dyadic sequence of coverings with the set of Δt containing the following successive partitioning sizes $\{2\delta t, 4\delta t, 8\delta t, 16\delta t\}$.

Figure 3 shows **feature amplification** through VFD trajectories obtained using dyadic coverings for the same four utterances "bad," "bed," "bid" and "bud". It is seen that the variability of the VFDT is much greater within each utterance, as compared with the monadic coverings of Fig. 2. It is also seen that each utterance has a distinct VFDT. What is also remarkable is that the shape of the VFDT does not change with energy of the signal. Thus, the VFDT is a good candidate for utterance recognition. Furthermore, since the phonemes in each utterance have characteristic VFDT segments, one can also distinguish between various parts of each utterance easier. This methodology can be used for phoneme segmentation.

Examples of trajectories obtained for the words "tight" and "test" are discussed in (Kinsner & Grieder, 2008). We have also studied the characteristic properties of the trajectories for vowels, as well as for each class of consonant phonemes, including stop consonants, /p/, /b/, /t/, /d/, /k/, and /g/, the fricatives, /ch/ and /jh/, and another class of fricatives, /f/, /v/, /th/, /dh/, /s/, /z/, /sh/, /zh/. A discussion of those results is given in (Kinsner & Grieder, 2008).

Verification of Results

Since speech is a complicated nonstationary signal, the VFD and VFDT results must be verified by comparing them with monofractals such as the fractional Brownian motion and the Weierstrass function, using the same selections of the Δt for the desired segmentation and amplification.

Fractional Brownian Motion Tests

The fractional Brownian motion (fBm) is generated using the Gaussian random midpoint displacement algorithm (Kinsner, 1994, May;

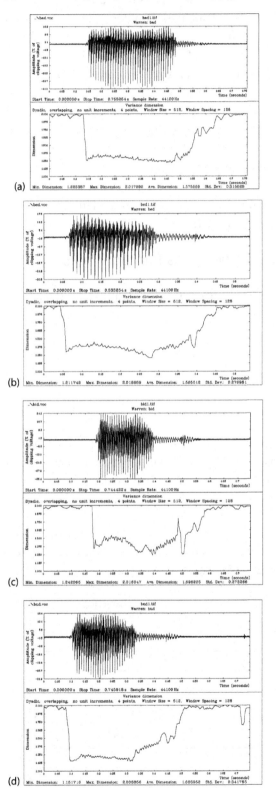

Figure 3. VFDT for (a) "bad," (b) "bed," (c) "bid," and (d) "bud," using the dyadic coverings (amplification)

Peitgen, Jürgens, & Saupe, 2004; Turcotte, 1997; Schroeder, 1991). The fractal dimension, D_σ, of such an fBm depends on the Hurst exponent, H, as given by (7). An example of the fBm with $H = 0.5$ is shown in Fig. 4. Notice that since there is very little correlation between the adjacent samples in fBm (due to its individual increments being related to a Gaussian random variable), there is little difference in the dimension values obtained using the noise separation set and fractal amplification set of time increments. The average dimension values obtained for nine values of the Hurst exponent are given in Table 2.

The Weierstrass Function Tests

The Weierstrass function is given by (Harrison, 1989)

$$w(x) = \sum_{j=1}^{\infty} \frac{\sin\left(\lambda^j x\right)}{\lambda^{j\varepsilon}} \qquad (17)$$

where $\lambda > 1$ and $0 < \varepsilon < 1$ are constants (Harrison, 1989). Although it has not been proven rigorously, it seems likely that the coefficient ε is equivalent numerically to the Hurst exponent,

H (West, Bologna, & Grigolini, 2003). Thus, for the 1D Weierstrass function, the fractal dimension is given by

$$D_\sigma = 2 - \varepsilon \qquad (18)$$

An example of the Weierstrass function waveform is shown in Figure 5. Notice that since the degree of correlation between the adjacent samples in the Weierstrass function is much larger than in the fBm, there is a significant difference in the dimension values D_σ obtained using the noise-separation and the fractal-amplification algorithms. The average D_σ dimension values obtained for $\lambda = 2.0$ and nine values of ε are given in Table 3. Notice that the noise separation algorithm underestimates the value of D_σ, while the amplification algorithm slightly overestimates the values of D_σ. Also notice that when $D_\sigma = 1.2$, the curve resembles terrestrial mountains, while the mountains on the Moon and Mars have higher dimensions due to lack of erosion from wind and water (Turcotte, 1997).

Computationally, the summation in (17) should be truncated when λ^j exceeds the number of pixels in either the display or the dots-per-inch in the graphical diagram required, and the calculations

Table 2. D_σ values for Fractional Brownian Motion with $H = 0.5$

Hurst Exponent, H	VFD Values		
	Exp-ected	Noise Separation	Fractal Amplification
0.9	1.1	1.15	1.13
0.8	1.2	1.23	1.22
0.7	1.3	1.33	1.32
0.6	1.4	1.42	1.41
0.5	1.5	1.50	1.51
0.4	1.6	1.57	1.59
0.3	1.7	1.63	1.67
0.2	1.8	1.69	1.73
0.1	1.9	1.73	1.78

Figure 4. VFDT for fBm with H = 0.5 for (a) separation, and (b) amplification

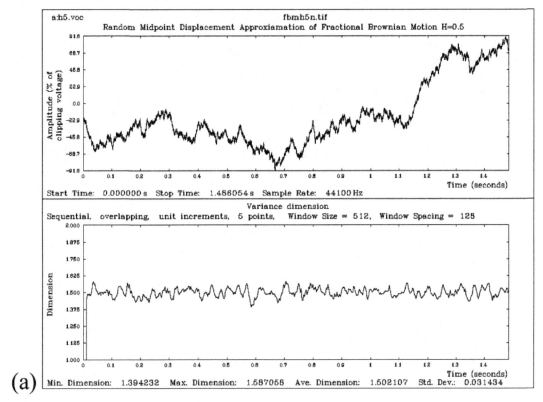

(a)

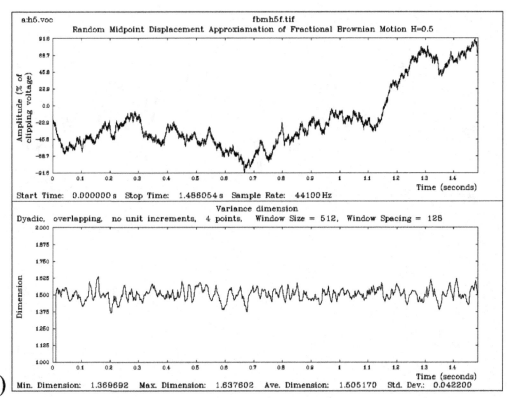

(b)

Figure 5. VFDT for a Weierstrass function with λ = 2.0 and ε = 0.5 for (a) separation, and (b) amplification

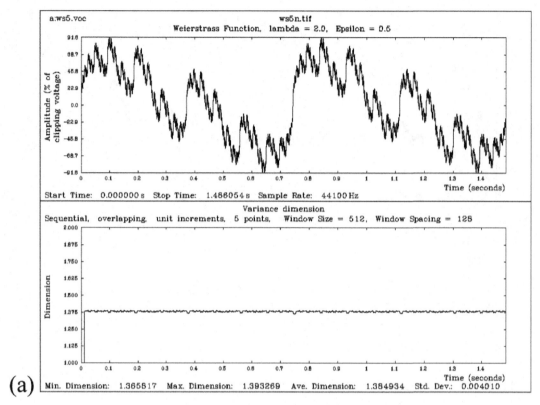

(a)

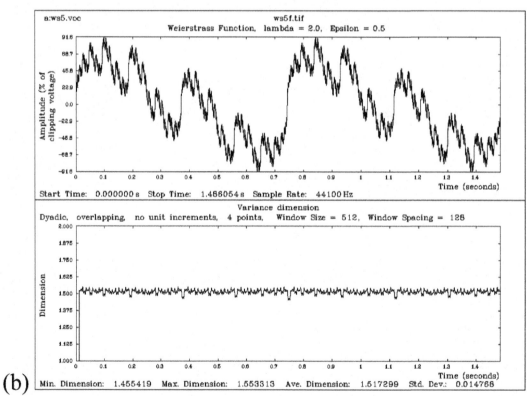

(b)

Table 3. Dimension values for Weierstrass function, $\lambda = 2.0$

ε	VFD Values		
	Exp-ected	Noise Separation	Fractal Amplification
0.9	1.1	1.11	1.15
0.8	1.2	1.18	1.22
0.7	1.3	1.25	1.32
0.6	1.4	1.32	1.42
0.5	1.5	1.38	1.52
0.4	1.6	1.45	1.62
0.3	1.7	1.51	1.72
0.2	1.8	1.57	1.82
0.1	1.9	1.64	1.92

should be done in at least double precision (Sprott, 2003). Often, it is computed for a quarter of the fundamental harmonic.

Notice that there are many other formulations of the Weierstrass function. It is quite clear that a trivial reformulation of the function is to express it in terms of cosines, rather than sines (Sprott, 2003; Schroeder, 1991). A more fundamental extension is to expand it from the positive harmonics to the whole spectrum. The most important extension is to make the function complex, thus leading to complex fractal dimensions. Such functions are called Weierstrass-Mandelbrot functions (Mandelbrot, 2002; West, Bologna, & Grigolini, 2003).

DISCUSSION

The variance fractal dimension (VFD), D_σ, is often used to estimate the complexity of a stationary self-affine (monofractal) time series. If the time series is multifractal in time, a single scalar value of D_σ cannot represent the complexity. Instead, repeated calculations of D_σ over a window containing a stationary segment of the time series can produce a VFD trajectory (VFDT). When applied to natural speech, the VFDT can be generated using different vel covers of the time series: The monadic cover suitable for segment-ing the speech signal from ambient noise, and the dyadic cover suitable for feature extraction from an isolated utterance. Both algorithms offer an important alternative for increasing performance of speech recognition and translation systems. Since the segmentation algorithm uses complexity measures to identify the utterance boundary, it is inherently stronger than other energy-based thresholding algorithms. Since the amplification algorithm produces well-defined differences between various classes of phonemes, it offers the possibility of separating speech utterances into specific phonemic regions. The segmentation of utterance boundaries can provide a starting point for various speech processing schemes such as linear-predictive coding (LPC), fast Fourier transform (FFT), as well as wavelet and fractal analyses for speech recognition and translation. Since the VFDT amplification algorithm produces multiscale measures of the complexity of individual phonemes of a given speech utterance, the trajectory can be used directly as an input to a neural network acting as a classifier. For the system to operate reliably, a number of computational issues must be taken into account.

In summary, this paper has described an implementation of the VFD algorithm, and how it can be used to produce the VFD trajectories as features of natural speech. The characteristics of these trajectories can be used to segment digital speech signals. The method has also been used by us to segment and classify many other signals. Major advantages of the VFDT is that it measures complexity of the signal (and not its energy), and it operates in the time domain, not only in a batch mode, but also in a real-time mode.

ACKNOWLEDGMENTS

This work was supported in part through a research grant from the Natural Sciences and Engineering Research Council (NSERC) of Canada, the Manitoba Telephone System (MTS), and the Telecommunication Research Laboratories (TRLabs).

REFERENCES

Al-Akaidi, M. (2004). *Fractal Speech Processing*. Cambridge, UK: Cambridge University Press. doi:10.1017/CBO9780511754548

Bishop, C. M. (2006). *Pattern Recognition and Machine Learning* (2nd ed.). New York: Springer.

Bristow, G. (1986). *Electronic Speech Recognition*. New York: McGraw-Hill.

Gache, N., Flandrin, P., & Garreau, D. (1991). Fractal dimension estimators for fractional Brownian motions. In *Proceedings of the IEEE International Conference Acoust, Speech, Signal Processing*, Toronto, ON. Washington, DC: IEEE.

Harrison, J. (1989). Introduction to Fractals . In Devaney, R. (Ed.), *Chaos and Fractals: The Mathematics Behind the Computer Graphics* (*Vol. 39*, pp. 107–126). Providence, RI: American Mathematical Society.

Haykin, S., & Kosko, B. (Eds.). (2001). *Intelligent Signal Processing*. Washington, DC: IEEE Press. doi:10.1109/9780470544976

Haykin, S., Principe, J. C., Sejnowski, T. J., & McWhirter, J. (Eds.). (2007). *New Directions in Statistical Signal Processing*. Cambridge, MA: MIT Press.

Kinsner, W. (1994, May). *Fractal dimensions: Morphological, entropy, spectra, and variance classes* (Tech. Rep. No. DEL94-4). Winnipeg, MB: University of Manitoba, Dept. Electrical & Computer Engineering.

Kinsner, W. (1994, June). *Batch and real-time computation of a fractal dimension based on variance of a time series* (Tech. Rep. No. DEL94-6). Winnipeg, MB: University of Manitoba, Dept. Electrical & Computer Engineering.

Kinsner, W. (2007, January). Towards Cognitive Machines: Multiscale Measures and Analysis. *International Journal of Cognitive Informatics and Natural Intelligence, 1*(1), 28–38.

Kinsner, W. (2007, April). Is entropy suitable to characterize data and signals for cognitive informatics? *International Journal of Cognitive Informatics and Natural Intelligence, 1*(2), 34–57.

Kinsner, W. (2007, October). A unified approach to fractal dimensions. *International Journal of Cognitive Informatics and Natural Intelligence, 1*(4), 26–46.

Kinsner, W., Cheung, V., Cannons, K., Pear, J., & Martin, T. (2006). Signal classification through multifractal analysis and complex domain neural networks. *IEEE Trans. Systems, Man, and Cybernetics . Part C, 36*(2), 196–203.

Kinsner, W., & Grieder, W. (2008). Speech segmentation using multifractal measures and amplification of signal features. In *Proceedings of the IEEE 7th Intern. Conf. Cognitive Informatics (ICCI08)*, Palo Alto, CA (pp. 351-357).

Kohonen, T. (1988, March 11-22). The neural phonetic typewriter. *Computer*.

Mallat, S. (1998). *A Wavelet Tour of Signal Processing*. San Diego, CA: Academic.

Mandelbrot, B. B. (2002). *Gaussian Self-Similarity and Fractals: Globality, The earth, 1/f noise, and R/S*. New York: Springer Verlag.

Parsons, T. (1987). *Voice and Speech Processing*. New York: McGraw-Hill.

Peitgen, H.-O., Jürgens, H., & Saupe, D. (2004). *Chaos and Fractals* (2nd ed.). New York: Springer Verlag.

Rabiner, L. R., & Schafer, R. W. (1978). *Digital Processing of Speech Signals*. Upper Saddle River, NJ: Prentice-Hall.

Schafer, R. W., & Rabiner, L. R. (1975). Parametric representations of speech. In *Proceedings of the Speech Recognition Invited Paper Presented at the 1974 IEEE Symposium*. New York: Academic Press.

Schroeder, M. (1991). *Fractals, Chaos, Power Laws: Minutes from an Infinite Paradise*. New York: W. H. Fremman.

Sprott, J. C. (2003). *Chaos and Time-Series Analysis*. Oxford, UK: Oxford University Press.

Turcotte, D. L. (1997). *Fractals and Chaos in Geology and Geophysics* (2nd ed.). New York: Springer Verlag.

Wang, Y. (2002). On cognitive informatics. In *Proceedings of the 1st IEEE Intern. Conf. Cognitive Informatics*, Calgary, AB (pp. 34-42).

West, B. J., Bologna, M., & Grigolini, P. (2003). *Physics of Fractal Operators*. New York: Springer.

Wornell, G. W. (1996). *Signal Processing with Fractals: A Wavelet-Based Approach*. Upper Saddle River, NJ: Prentice-Hall.

Zhang, P., Barad, H., & Martinez, A. (1990). Fractal dimension estimation of fractional Brownian motion. In *. Proceedings of the IEEE Southeastcon, 3*, 934–939. doi:10.1109/SECON.1990.117957

This work was previously published in volume 4, issue 4 of the International Journal of Cognitive Informatics and Natural Intelligence, edited by Yingxu Wang, pp. 1-17, copyright 2010 by IGI Publishing (an imprint of IGI Global).

Chapter 20
Some Remarks on the Concept of Approximations from the View of Knowledge Engineering

Tsau Young Lin
San Jose State University, USA

Rushin Barot
San Jose State University, USA

Shusaku Tsumoto
Shimane Medical University, Japan

ABSTRACT

The concepts of approximations in granular computing (GrC) vs. rough set theory (RS) are examined. Examples are constructed to contrast their differences in the Global GrC Model (2nd GrC Model), which, in pre-GrC term, is called partial coverings. Mathematically speaking, RS-approximations are "sub-base" based, while GrC-approximations are "base" based, where "sub-base" and "base" are two concepts in topological spaces. From the view of knowledge engineering, its meaning in RS-approximations is rather obscure, while in GrC, it is the concept of knowledge approximations.

INTRODUCTION

Approximation is a serious concept in rough set theory (*RS*); it defines the rough sets. While in granular computing (GrC), it can be considered from three semantic views: Knowledge Engineering (KE), Uncertainty mathematics, and how-to-compute/solve-it [5]. Each view will have its own theory. In this paper, we will focus on KE view.

DOI: 10.4018/978-1-4666-1743-8.ch020

This paper is a continuous effort that was initiated in Lin (2006b) and Barot and Lin (2008).

RS-APPROXIMATIONS IN (INFINITE) UNIVERSE

The approximation theory of RS is well known. For preciseness, we will recall the notion here. Let U be a classical set, called the universe. Let β be a partition, namely, a family of subsets, called equivalence classes, that are mutually disjoint and their union is the whole universe U. Then the pair (U, β) is called approximation space in RS. Pawlak introduced following two definitions. Observe that Pawlak focus on finite universe. However we allow U to be infinite.

Let X be an arbitrary subset of the universe U.

Definition (RS) 1 Let E be an arbitrary equivalence class of R.

Upper approximation:

$$U[X] = \cup \{E | E \cap X \neq \varnothing\}$$

Lower approximation:

$$L[X] = \cup \{E | E \subseteq X\}$$

This definition is the formal form of the intuitive upper and lower approximations

Definition (RS)2 Let p be an arbitrary element of U.

Closure

$$C[X] = \{p | \forall E, \text{ if } p \in E, \text{ then } E \cap X \neq \varnothing\};$$
note that C[X] is a closed set in the sense of topological spaces.

Interior

I[X] = { $p \parallel \exists E$ such that $p \in E$ & $E \subseteq X$ }.

In RS community, the previous definitions are directed generalized to Covering *Cov* by interpreting E as member of *Cov*.

COUNTER INTUITIVE PHENOMENA

In this section, we present some Counter Intuitive phenomena of approximations. The first example was generated to answer some questions raised in

a conversation with Tian Yang, Guangming Lang, Jing Hao from Hunan University.

Example 1. Let the universe U be the real line. Let us consider the collection *COV* of all open half lines, namely, the sets of the following form {u | u < a} and {u | a < u} for a $\in$ U. These half lines form a sub-base of the usual topology in real line; Here the "usual topology" is a technical term referring to the topology of commonly known closure of the whole set.

In RS community, the approximations are defined by Definitions RSD1 or RSD2 given below, based on such definitions, one can readily see that the upper approximation of any finite interval, in fact any bounded sub-set, is the whole real line and its lower approximations is empty set.

- The RS-approximation space of a covering is too coarse.

This is an example of infinite universe; we will transform it into a finite universe.

Example 2. By considering any finite interval of integers, we have a similar example for a finite universe. Let U be set of the integers, say [1, 1000]. Let COV ∩ U be the collection of all open half lines restricted to U. Then any open sub-interval, say (a, b), has the itself as upper approximation and empty set as lower approximation.

The approximation spaces of RS and some GrC models are actually NS-spaces, where NS is neighborhood systems (Barot & Lin, 2008; Lin, 1989a; Lin, 1989b; Lin, 2009a; Lin, 2009b). For convenience of readers, we recall the definition of NS-space here

Definition (NS)3: The pair (U, β) is called a NS-space, if β associates to each point of U a family of subsets of U, formally

$\beta : U \rightarrow P(P(U))$

where P(X) is the power set of X; X is U or P(U). β is called a neighborhood system(NS). Note that in the case that every family is a singleton, then β, by abuse of notation, will be regarded as an association from U to P(U).

$\beta : U \rightarrow P(U)$

Let us consider a special NS-space that is based on a family of "convergent" partitions (equivalence relations.) Note that Lin (1992) (on the section of Exact information via Approximations) and Polkowski (1992) had considered such cases in Slowinski's Book (1992).

KNOWLEDGE THEORY ON GrC

The concept of approximations in RS was based on Pawlak's view of knowledge; it is used to approximate any unknown concept (represented by arbitrary subsets of the universe) by given basic knowledge (represented by equivalence classes (granules). GrC has three semantics views: each has its own meaning of approximations

1) Uncertainty theory: A granule represents a basic unit of uncertainty (lacking precise knowledge).
    ◦ The meaning of approximations by granules (units of uncertainty) is not clear

In this view, the approximations are not the main issues. In (Lin, 2009b), there are some exploration on Uncertainty reasoning - The Meaning of "Near".

2) How-to-Solve/Compute-it: A granule represents a sub-problem or software unit.
    ◦ Is it related to approximate computing/proof ?

3) Knowledge Engineering: A granule represents a basic unit of knowledge.

The concept of approximations are similar to RS. Following Pawlak, approximations is regarded as

• Expressing an unknown concept by available knowledge

In this paper, we will focus on KE view.

Admissible Operators in KE View

An important question associated with KE view is: What are the admissible operations used in expressing a concept? Conceptually, they are knowledge operations (Barot & Lin, 2008; Lin, 2009a). For simplicity we will use Coverings to illustrate the idea. A covering is a collection of subsets (granules) whose union is the total space. It is a special example of global GrC Model (2nd GrC Model) and a generalization of RS.

In KE view, a granule represents a piece of known knowledge, so "or" and "and" of two pieces of knowledge, should be a new piece of knowledge. Hence

• Finite intersections and finite unions are the admissible operations of granules in KE view. The two operators generate respective semi group of granules, and jointly generate a Boolean algebra.

This Boolean algebra is a generalization of Pawlak's definable sets. These granules represent some "definable knowledge" that can be precisely defined/described by the given granules (basic knowledge).

In current practices of RS (finite universe), only one operation "finite union" has been used. We believe this is a miss-interpretation; in classical RS, "finite intersection" is always empty, so explicit formulation is unnecessary.

Admissible Approximate Operators in KE View

Next we shall consider infinite unions. The following consideration seems reasonable:

- A proposition is evaluated to be true based on a given collection (may be infinite) of granules iff this proposition is true on one of them.

This proposition can be reformulated into

- A proposition is evaluated to be true based on the union of those granules in the given collection of granules iff this proposition is true on one of the granule.

Observe that infinite union do not really involve with infinite operations on those granules. So we shall accept infinite unions as admissible operators. Nevertheless, we will regard it as a derived knowledge of *lesser quality*, so we will call the infinite unions as *admissible approximate knowledge* and the operator *admissible approximate operator*.

- Infinite unions, together with the admissible operators, are called approximate operators.

Now we shall observe that the new collection of new granules that are generated by finite intersections and infinite unions of given granules actually form a topology in the theory of topological space. Let us collect the know term as well as new term in the following definition

Definitions (GrC)4

1. The collection of granules that are given aprior is called Granular Structure (GrS).
2. The collection of all possible finite intersection of GrS is called Base of GrS (BGrS)

2. The collection of granules that are generated from GrS by applying approximate operators (finite intersections and infinite unions) is called the topology of GrS (TGrS)..

APPROXIMATIONS IN KE VIEW OF PARTIAL COVERINGS

GrC has nine models; each has its own approximation theory. We will illustrate the idea in Partial Covering, which is the Global GrC model and also be referred to as 2nd GrC model.

Let (U, β) be a global GrC Model, where U is a classical set and β be a collection of subsets in U, In pre-GrC period, β is called a partial covering. Let G_1 be the collection of all possible finite intersections in β . Let G be a variable that varies through the member of the collection G_1, then we define the following topology based concepts. In (Lin, 1992), we have introduced the closure based on *Cov*. Note that the definition of closure used in (Lin, 1992) is the same as this article, which is adopted directly from the theory of topological spaces. However, the "closure" or "closed set" in that article is not the same as those in topological sense. The closure in the sense of topological spaces is called closed set based closure in present paper.

Definition (GrC)5

Upper approximation (Closure)

$$C[X] = \overline{\beta}\,[X] = \{p \mid \forall\, G, \text{ such that,}$$
$p \in G \ \& \ G \cap X \neq \varnothing \}$; C[X] is not necessarily closed in the sense of topological spaces

Lower approximation (Interior)

$$I[X] = \underline{\beta}\,[X] = \{\, p \mid \exists G, \text{ such that,}$$
$p \in G \ \& \ G \subseteq X \}$; I[X] is not necessarily open in the sense of topological spaces

Closed set based Closure: Lin (2006a) introduced closed closure operator. It applies closure operator repeatedly (for transfinite times) until the resultants stop growing.

CC[X] = X ∪ C[X] ∪ C[C[X]] ∪ C[C[C[X]]]
    . . . (transfinite).

For such a closure, it is a closed set in the sense of topological spaces.

The concept of approximations just defined is derived from topological spaces. Let us recall a theorem from (Barot & Lin, 2008)

Theorem 1 *The approximation space of Full Covering Model is a topological space. However, generalized rough set approximation space may not be a topological space.*

Following RS, we may define:
Definition (GrC)6
Upper approximation H:

$U[X] = \overline{\beta}[X] = \cup\{G|\forall G$, such that, $G \cap X \neq \varnothing\}$.

Lower approximation L:

$L[X] = \underline{\beta}[X] = \cup\{G|\exists G$, such that, $G \subseteq X\}$.

For Covering these definitions do not work well, For example, if we take β to be the topology. Then U[X]=U for every X.

CONCLUSIONS

We have examined the concept of approximations on the coverings from the perspective of knowledge engineering. First we use examples to indicate that

• RS-approximations are very coarse

Next, the concept of approximations in global GrC model (partial covering) is examined from the KE view. Based on intuitive view of knowledge, the concept of admissible and approximate knowledge operations are introduced. They are finite intersections and infinite unions. In partial covering we observe (Theorem 1)

• Approximations in KE view is the topological approximations

In the special session in RSCTC2008, Lin showed that even in such considerations, the classical approximations has some "pathological phenomena" that is the approximation is very different from usual topology. The example is included in appendix.

In future work, we may, more generally, mimic the descriptive set theory allow more advanced operations.

Observe that RS-approximations are actually a sub-base approximation, while current GrC-approach (this paper) is a base approximation. In the theory of topological spaces, a base is a collection of open sets that can express every open sets as their union, while a sub-base is a collection of open sets whose finite intersection forms a base. Clearly, GrC-approximation is a topological concept, while generalized RS-approximation is not; Note that classical RS-approximation is a topological concept as intersections are all empty.

REFERENCES

Barot, R. B., & Lin, T. Y. (2008). Granular Computing on Covering from the aspects of Knowledge Theory. In *Proceedings of the IEEE NAFIPS 2008*.

Lin, T. T. (1990). Relational Data Models and Category Theory (Abstract). In *Proceedings of the ACM Conference on Computer Science 1990* (p. 424).

Lin, T. Y. (1989a, October 12-15). Neighborhood Systems and Approximation in Database and Knowledge Base Systems. In *Proceedings of the Fourth International Symposium on Methodologies of Intelligent Systems* (pp. 75-86).

Lin, T. Y. (1989b, December 4-8). Chinese Wall Security Policy-An Aggressive Model. In *Proceedings of the Fifth Aerospace Computer Security Application Conference* (pp. 286-293).

Lin, T. Y. (1992). Topological and Fuzzy Rough Sets . In Slowinski, R. (Ed.), *Decision Support by Experience - Application of the Rough Sets Theory* (pp. 287–304). London: Kluwer Academic Publishers.

Lin, T. Y. (2006a). A Roadmap from Rough Set Theory to Granular Computing. In . *Proceedings of the RSKT, 2006, 33*–41.

Lin, T. Y. (2006b). Granular Computing on Partitions, Covering and Neighborhood system. *Journal of Nanchan Institute of Technology, 25*(2), 1–7.

Lin, T. Y. (2009a). Granular Computing: Practices, Theories, and Future Directions. *Encyclopedia of Complexity and Systems Science 2009* (pp. 4339-4355).

Lin, T. Y. (2009b). Granular computing I: the concept of granulation and its formal model. *Int. J. Granular Computing . Rough Sets and Intelligent Systems, 1*(1), 21–42. doi:10.1504/IJGCRSIS.2009.026723

Polkowski, L. (1992). On convergence on rough sets . In Slowinski, R. (Ed.), *Decision Support by Experience - Application of the Rough Sets Theory* (pp. 305–309). London: Kluwer Academic Publishers.

Zadeh, L. A. (1979). Fuzzy sets and information granularity . In Gupta, M., Ragade, R., & Yager, R. (Eds.), *Advances in Fuzzy Set Theory and Applications* (pp. 3–18). Amsterdam: North-Holland.

Zadeh, L. A. (1996, September 8-11). The key roles of information granulation and fuzzy logic in human reasoning. In *Proceedings of the 1996 IEEE International Conference on Fuzzy Systems*, New Orleans, Louisiana.

Zadeh, L. A. (1997). Toward a theory of fuzzy information granulation and its centrality in human reasoning and fuzzy logic. *Fuzzy Sets and Systems, 90*, 111–127. doi:10.1016/S0165-0114(97)00077-8

Zadeh, L. A. (1998). Some reflections on soft computing, granular computing and their roles in the conception, design and utilization of information/ intelligent systems. *Soft Computing, 2*, 23–25. doi:10.1007/s005000050030

APPENDIX- COUNTER INTUITIVE APPROXIMATIONS IN CLASSICAL RS

Example 3. We shall consider a sequence of partitions of the real line by semi-closed intervals:

$S_1 = ...$ [−2, −1), [−1, 0), [0, 1), [1, 2) ...

$S_2 = ...$ [−1, −1/2), [−1/2, 0), [0, 1/2), [1/2, 1), [1, 3/2)...

,,,

$S_n = ...$ [−1/2$^{(n+1)}$, −1/2^n), [−1/2^n, 0), [0, 1/2^n), [1/2^n, 1/2^{n-1})...

For each n, the sequence S_n defines an RS-approximation space on real numbers S. Next, we consider the union S_∞ of all such S_n, n = ...−1, 0, 1, ...

This family of granulations is very interesting: for finite n, S_n is a partition, however for n=∞, S_∞ (= $\cup_n S_n$) is a covering, not a partition. The approximations in (S, β), where β = S_n or S_∞ is quite counter intuitive:

1. The sequence, 1 / m, m = 1, 2, ...converges to 0. In other words, 0 is a limiting point
2. The sequence, −1 / m, m = 1, 2, ... does NOT converges to 0. In other words, 0 is not a limiting point.
3. The RS-approximations are very different from usual topology.

Again, we will transform this example into a finite universe.

Example 4. Let U ={z/2^x | z, x are integers, 0 $\leq$ x $\leq$ L and 0 $\leq$ z $\leq$ 2^L }, where L is a large number. To be definitive, we choose L=2000 in this discussion. Now we consider the partition $S_n \cap$ U. Here are the conclusions:
1. 0 is a limiting point the sequence, 1 / m, m = 1, 2, ...; 2^L
2. 0 is not a limiting point of the sequence, −1 / m, m = 1, 2, ... does NOT converges to 0.

Again, we observe that RS-approximation is quite different from that of the usual topology. In many RS applications, these differences are not properly observed.

Appendix- Granular Computing

Briefly speaking the term was coined by T. Y. Lin in the fall of 1996 to label a subset of Zadeh's granular mathematics (Zadeh, 1998). The idea was implicitly explained in (Zadeh, 1979). In (Zadeh, 1997), he outlined his main idea in the seminal paper, where he said,
    'Basically, TFIG...

...... its foundation and methodology are **mathematical** in nature'.

Here TFIG is theory of fuzzy information granulation, which is precisely the GrC. Lin has adopted an incremental approach; Nine GrC models have been accumulated. In GrC 2008, Lin finally proposed his 8th GrC model as the "Final" Formal GrC Model. It is important to note that the categorically GrC model is the "same" as the category model of relational databases that we have proposed in (Lin, 1990). At first this seems a surprise, however, after analysis, this should be natural, as we have regarded knowledge is a granule of data. So Category Theory Based GrC Models is a "higher level" view.

We shall recall from (Zadeh, 1996; Lin, 2009a; Lin, 2009b) the following definitions

Definition (GrC)7: Informal definition

Information granulation involves partitioning a class of objects (points) into granules, with a granule being a clump of objects (points) which are drawn together by some constraints or forces, such as 'indistinguishability, similarity or functionality'. Intuitively, a class of objects that are drawn by some constraints forms a tuple with these constraints as the schema of the tuple.

Let CAT be a given category.

Definition (GrC)8: Category Theory Based GrC Model

1. Let $C=\{C_j^h \mid h \in H \text{ and } j \in J_h\}$ be a family of objects in the Category CAT; it is called the universe (of discourse).
2. Consider a family Π of product objects (same objects may appear several times in the products) in C
3. Consider a family β of relation objects, which are sub-objects of Π.

Then the pair (C, β) is the "final" Formal GrC Model that has been called the Category Theory Based GrC Model (also 8th GrC Model).

Remark: Note that if CAT is the category of sets, then we can regard C as the union of these sets C_j^h.

If CAT is specified into the categories of sets (or type I fuzzy sets), functions, Turing machines, or qualitative fuzzy sets, they are called 5th, 6th 7th or 9th GrC Models. By restricting the relations in 5th GrC model to be symmetric, we have Second GrC Model (Global GrC Model), informally speaking, it is a Partial Covering. By restricting the relations in 5th GrC model to be binary relations, we have 4th GrC Models. By restricting the number of relations to one, we have 3rd GrC Model (Binary GrC Model)}.

Note that a binary relation B defines a binary (right) neighborhood system as follows: Let $p \in U$ be an arbitrary point in the universe U

$$B(p)=\{y \mid (p, y) \in B\}$$

By considering the collection of B(p) for every binary relation in the Fourth GrC Model, we have 1st GrC Model (Local GrC Model); see Definition (NS)3

In this paper, we focus on Global GrC Model (2nd GrC model).

Definition (GrC)9: GrC Model in the category of sets

1. Let C be a set, called the universe (of discourse).
2. Let $\prod_i$, $i \in I$, be some product of C, where I is an index set
   2. Consider a family β of relation objects, each is a subset of some $\prod_i$.

Then, we have two views:

3a. The pair (C, β) is relational GrC Model (5th GrC Model.)

Or by abuse of notation, we will use β again to denote the collection of all tuples in the relations β

.

3b. The new pair (C, β), with β as the collection of tuples, is another view of relational GrC Model (5th GrC Model.)

Next, we will consider a special case
Definition (GrC)10: Partial Covering (Global GrC Model or 2nd GrC model)

1. Let C be a set, called the universe (of discourse).
2. Consider a family β of subsets
    3b. Observe that subsets are tuples of symmetric relations, so this is a special case of 5th GrC Model. The pair (C, β), with β as the collection of tuples, is a global GrC Model (2nd GrC model). Its pre-GrC term is a partial covering.

This work was previously published in volume 4, issue 2 of the International Journal of Cognitive Informatics and Natural Intelligence, edited by Yingxu Wang, pp. 1-11, copyright 2010 by IGI Publishing (an imprint of IGI Global).

Chapter 21
Giving Personal Assistant Agents a Case-Based Memory

Ke-Jia Chen
Nanjing University of posts and telecommunications, China, and Université de Technologie de Compiègne, France

Jean-Paul A. Barthès
Université de Technologie de Compiègne, France

ABSTRACT

We consider Personal Assistant (PA) agents as cognitive agents capable of helping users handle tasks at their workplace. A PA must communicate with the user using casual language, sub-contract the requested tasks, and present the results in a timely fashion. This leads to fairly complex cognitive agents. However, in addition, such an agent should learn from previous tasks or exchanges, which will increase its complexity. Learning requires a memory, which leads to the two following questions: Is it possible to design and build a generic model of memory? If it is, is it worth the trouble? The article tries to answer the questions by presenting the design and implementation of a memory for PA agents, using a case approach, which results in an improved agent model called MemoPA.

INTRODUCTION

Computer applications require efficient interfaces. Complex applications have shown the limits of "point & click" interfaces. Such direct manipulations are no longer ideal especially for untrained users. Consequently, a new style of interface has been proposed, using the concept of intelligent agent. It was introduced into the Human-Machine Interaction (Lieberman, 1997; Maes, 1994), giving birth to the concept of *personal assistant* (PA) agent, also called *interface agent* in the literature (Middleton, 2002). Unlike the direct manipulation approach, the PA agent is regarded as a virtual secretary that can execute tasks autonomously by interacting with a set of service agents (Figure 1). As indicated by Lieberman, the approach has potential productivity advantages.

PA agents are one of the most compelling sub-domains of agent research (Modi, Veloso, Smith,

DOI: 10.4018/978-1-4666-1743-8.ch021

Figure 1. A prototype of PA agent by Maes (1994)

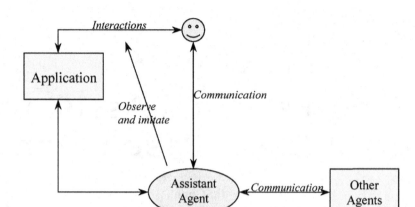

& Oh, 2004). In the early works (Maes & Kozierok, 1993; Mitchell, Caruana, Freitag, McDermott, & Zabowski, 1994), PA agents were developed for reducing the workload of the user by handling tasks on his behalf, hiding the task complexity, learning and adapting to the users' preferences, as well as collaborating with other agents (Lashkari, Metral, & Maes, 1994). The tasks could be either routine tasks like scheduling meeting or handling email (Modi et al., 2004), or more specific tasks like browsing and suggesting web links (Lieberman, 1995). After that, many systems and prototypes of PA agents have been built for a variety of areas, but recently personal assistants have raised a great interest as can be seen from specialized meetings like the AAAI 2007 Spring Symposium, Interaction for Intelligent Assistants[1] or important programs like DARPA PAL[2] (Personal Assistants that Learns).

Designing and building PAs is a difficult task since it requires integrating different research domains like reasoning, planning, scheduling, natural language processing, or multi-modal interfaces (Guzzoni, Baur, & Cheyer, 2007). Most of the previous work has focused on learning and adapting to the user's preferences and goals, assuming that once the agent knows what a user wants, it can provide effective assistance. In practice, a successful PA agent is supposed to possess many

kinds of knowledge to perform tasks autonomously by inferential reasoning. It can learn from failures and adapt to new tasks (Wobcke, Ho, Nguyen, & Krzywicki, 2005). However, if the agent has no memory it will ignore past experiences. Thus, when dealing with a new task similar to a task it has already performed, the agent will reprocess the task from scratch. Therefore, it is important to give PAs a memory mechanism. However, doing so increases the complexity of the agent, which leads to two questions: Is it feasible? Is it worth it?

In the article we address the issue of developing a generic mechanism that can be integrated seamlessly into the previous dialog mechanism of the agent, and that should be transparent for the user and easy to implement for the application designer. The work concerns a new research field, Cognitive Informatics (CI) (Wang, 2003), a study of cognitive and information sciences that investigates the internal information processing mechanisms and processes of the natural intelligence generated by the human brain. A major problem of our work is to acquire and formalize situations automatically from the natural language dialogs and from the results of the tasks that were completed. In order to explain our design choices we need first to describe the structure and behavior of our assistant agent, which is done briefly in the next section.

Figure 2. The SCA PA agent model

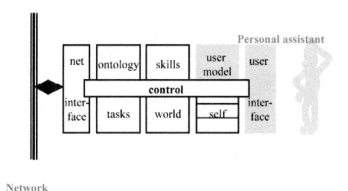

CONTEXT

Our laboratory contributed to the development of assistant agents, proposing a specific PA architecture (Barthès & Ramos, 2002), then implementing several models of agents capable of interacting with the user in natural language (Enembreck & Barthès, 2003; Paraiso & Barthès, 2004). We build our cognitive agents using a specific platform supporting a high level model of agent (SCA for Structured Cognitive Agent). The middleware takes care of all ancillary problems like handling threads or distributing messages to the right process. Our agents are totally independent and do not have to register anywhere. They can join or leave the platform at any time. Building an application is done by plugging the agent skills, ontologies, task models and dialogs into the agent structure[3].

The PA Model

A PA is built upon the SCA model and its structure is represented in Figure 2.

The different parts of a PA are the following.

the **net interface** connects an agent to other agents (service agents or PAs) on the network.
the **skills** define and implement what the agent can do, but not its goals.

the **ontology** module contains the various ontologies that an agent can have (agent ontology, domain ontology, task ontology). All ontologies use a frame language, MOSS[4], which can represent multi-lingual ontologies and knowledge bases.
the **world** model contains a representation of other agents and is upgraded dynamically (our agents are purely intellectual and not situated, thus it is not a representation of the physical world).
the **self** representation is the most important part since it contains the model of the agent, of its skills, its memory and its goals.
the **user interface** is the interface allowing communicating with the human user. It can be rather complex for multimodal communication involving speech.
the **user model** contains a library of tasks that the agent knows how to do or sub-contract, and sub-dialogs associated with each task. Preferences are not handled at this level.
the **control** module contains the functions to coordinate the agent behavior.

The behavior of an agent is handled by the control module through a number of threads (Figure 3), including a thread for receiving messages, a thread for managing the agenda, two threads per task being executed, and several other threads for

Figure 3. Some of the threads associated with a SCE agent (ovals)

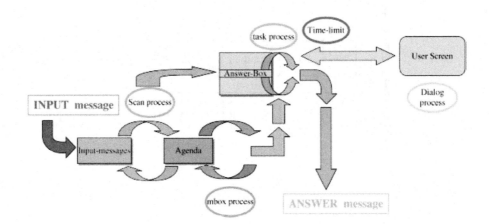

communicating with the user (only one is shown on the figure).

In addition, in order to limit the complexity of our PAs, we implemented the PA as a *digital butler* as proposed by Negroponte (1997). The PA is restricted to handling communications with the user, and has a staff of specialized agents in charge of technical matters. Such a group of agents constitutes a small society that lives normally in the user's computer. The memory mechanism is built to be inserted into the butler (The butler is our actual PA). Such an organization is different from the usual approach that regards the PA agent as a single entity in charge of solving all problems and eventually explaining how it has done it (Lopez de Mantara et al., 2006). In our case the PA does not solve the problems but simply transfers the problems to a more technical staff agent. It can be regarded as a broker.

Agent Behavior and Dialogs

To further limit the complexity of our PA, we assume that it evolves in a professional environment where possible actions are predefined and have been modelled as a library of tasks. The dialog system is implemented using conversation graphs (finite state machines). A dialog has two steps:

1. The first step involves a very general dialog (Figure 4). Linguistic elements are extracted from the user input and analyzed to determine what kind of task the user wants to do, and if the input is a request, a command, or a statement. To do so, each task in the task library is examined and is assigned a score according to the presence of linguistic markers. Tasks are then ranked and only those above a predefined threshold are kept. Then the task with the highest score is launched. If it fails the next task will be considered.

2. Launching a task triggers an associated sub-dialog. Its role is to gather eventual additional information necessary to sub-contract the task to a service agent. An example of the graph of such a sub-dialog is given Figure 5. It corresponds to the task of getting somebody's address (*get-email-address-conversation*).

Once a task is completed, the PA processes the next input. Apart from possible interrupts, there is no memorization of the results of the task (except for the availability of a simple cache memory). There is no taking into account of the context except through the knowledge bases of the staff agents.

Figure 4. A graph of the top level conversation of a PA agent

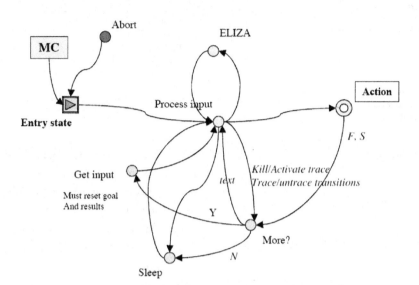

Ontologies

The previous process uses various ontologies: a general ontology, letting the PA describe its structure and the tasks it can undertake; more detailed ontologies, used by the staff agents to process the technical problem. Ontologies are represented using the MOSS formalism (Shen & Barthés, 1995).

Representation of Ontologies and Knowledge Base

Table 1 gives an example of simple concepts of **person**, **student** and **organization**. In the definition of concepts, **:is-a** indicates a relation of subsumption; **:att** defines an attribute for the concept; **:rel** defines a relation onto another concept.

Figure 5. A graph of the _get-email-address-conversation sub-dialog

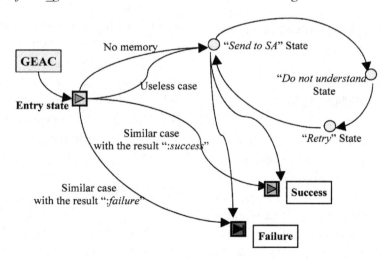

Table 1. Definition of some concepts of the MemoPA ontology

```
...
(defconcept "person"
(:att "name" (:entry))
(:att "first-name")
(:rel "phone" (:to "phone"))
(:rel "address" (:to "address"))
(:rel "email" (:to "email")))
(defconcept "student"
(:is-a "person")
(:rel "school" "university"))
...
(defconcept "organization"
(:att "name" (:entry))
(:att "acronym" (:entry))
(:rel "address" (:to "address"))
(:rel "phone" (:to "phone")))
```

Table 2. Knowledge about a specific student

```
defindividual "student"
("name" "Wang")
("first name" "Kelly")
("email" (:new "email"
("code" "kellyw@utc.fr")))
(:var _kw)
(:doc "Kelly Wang is a PhD student at UTC"))
```

The knowledge base of a MemoPA is actually made of *individuals* of some concepts of its ontology. Table 2 gives an example of a student named "Kelly" who is a PhD student at UTC and has an email address "kellyw@utc.fr".

New concepts or new individuals appearing during execution of a task may be added to the knowledge base dynamically.

The Memory Problem

In our approach the interests of having a structured memory are obvious. A memory would allow on one hand reusing results, positive or negative, of past experiences, on the other hand defining a context for interpreting dialogs. The main question is: what formalism should we select?

THE MEMORY FORMALISM

Several principles should be considered while selecting a memory representation: the representation language must be quite expressive, the expense of storage and calculation should be minimal, and memory retrieval should be easy. Artificial intelligence has provided a wide range of representation formalisms, such as frames, scripts, semantic networks, predicates, objects, rules and so on (Davis, Shrobe, & Szolovits, 1993). In previous assistant systems memory was often implemented as a stack of *salient features*, which consisted in saving important elements, thus providing a local context for the conversation. Such a mechanism allows building a short term memory ensuring some continuity in the conversation. However it is too limited for implementing a long term memory.

In our case, considering the global environment and the way tasks are selected at the end of specialized sub-dialogs, it was rather natural to select a case approach derived from case-based reasoning (CBR). The current research in CBR has been described in a review paper by Lopez de Mantara et al. (2006). However, we are not so much interested in the problem solving aspects, which for us are implemented through the dialogs and processed by the staff agents, but in the possibility of structuring the memory. This led us to select a dynamic memory model and to reuse the code proposed by Kolodner (1993) a long time ago, correcting some mistakes and adapting it to our representation formalism.

Structuring the memory is based on the use of Memory Organization Packets (Riesbeck & Schank, 1989) (MOPs) that define a semantic lattice to which we added indexes for improving retrieval. The following paragraph recalls and summarizes the approach.

MOP Structures

In the dynamic memory model, both domain knowledge and episodes are translated and or-

Figure 6. A segment of the MOP-based memory for a MemoPA

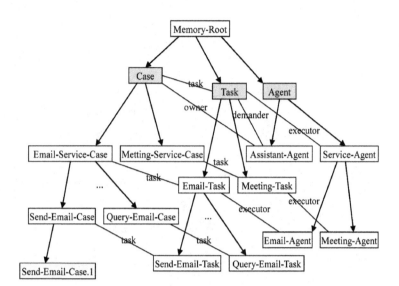

ganized into MOPs. A MOP may contain a set of norms representing the basic elements of this MOP: occurring events, objectives to achieve, involved actors, and so on.

There are basically two kinds of MOPs: *instance MOPs* and *abstraction MOPs*. The former concern a particular occurrence of an event, and the latter concern the specializations of instance MOPs. In this article, the term "case" normally refers to instance MOPs, an event or a situation in which a problem has been solved. MOPs are interconnected with two kinds of relations: *abstraction relations* and *packaging relations* (pairs of role and filler, where a filler can also be a MOP).

Figure 6 shows a segment of the MOP-based memory designed for an office PA. The agent is capable of performing the office tasks in daily life like email or calendar management. In Figure 6, all rectangles represent abstraction MOPs with the exception of the bottom left one that represents an instance MOP, that is, an episodic case. Arrows represent abstraction relations and finer lines represent packaging relations. Instance MOPs can be connected to their abstract MOP with abstraction relations (e.g. the MOP "Send-Email-Case" is the

abstraction of the MOP "Send-Email-Case.1"). It is interesting to note that along with the memory activities like memorization, instance MOPs, once generated, must be refined and inserted at the lowest possible level of the MOP hierarchy.

Inserting a New Case

A new episodic case can be automatically installed in memory during the activity of a PA agent, which leads to a structural adjustment of the memory.

For example (Figure 7), the agent now deals with the task "send an email to Mike", represented by the MOP "Send-Email.16". In memory, a new "Case.42" for this task is created under the MOP "Case". The MOP "Case.42" can be refined as MOP "Email-Service-Case.38" under the MOP "Email-Service-Case", moreover the MOP "Email-Service-Case.38" is refined as the MOP "Send-Email-Case.16" under the MOP "Send-Email-Case". The new case is finally integrated in the memory as the MOP "Send-Email-Case.16".

At the same time, a case retrieval (or a remembering process) is normally done along with a dynamic memory update. The objective is to

Figure 7. A dynamic installation of an episodic case in memory

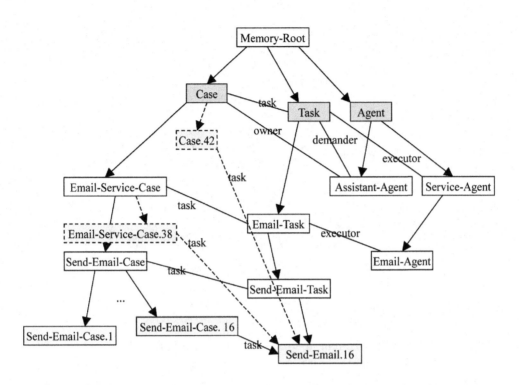

search an episodic case similar to the new case by following the abstraction links in the current MOP-based memory. The case is the most specific MOP that has slots compatible with the slots in the new case.

Advantages

As a memory modeling method, MOPs enable effective categorization of knowledge and experiences in a lattice memory structure.

Memory Organizer and Processor

A MOP serves both as an organizer and a processor of knowledge in memory. Sets of MOPs are organized around specific topics, using different links. The organization of MOPs determines the information that is accessible in the process of memorization.

Dynamic Structure

The memory changes when used. The MOP representation is not a static structure, but can be adapted dynamically. Adaptation occurs in the central process of MOP-based memory when processing a new input. Processing an input begins with a root MOP and a set of input "slots" (properties and their values) describing an instance of this MOP. Each slot has a packaging link (role and filling, role: a symbol representing the link name, filling: a MOP or nil). Then, the most specific specializations of this MOP having the slots compatible with the input slots are localized. If the input slots do not exist in some instance MOP, a new instance MOP (case) is built. During this process, the memory structure can be modified by adding a new case. The memory can also change when some abstraction MOPs are created automatically, e.g. when new cases are added to the memory, or when some

Table 3. Representation of "Case" in MOSS

```
(defconcept "Case"
 (:doc "A CASE represents an episode of memory.")
 (:att "time")
 (:rel "owner" (:to "Assistant Agent"))
 (:att "term" (:one-of:short:long))
 (:att "rtag")
 (:att "rcount")
 (:rel "task" (:to "Service Task")))
```

outdated cases are removed from the memory. The main idea is that if several cases under a given MOP share slots, an abstraction including these slots can be created. While most of the instances of an abstraction MOP move under one of its specializations, some MOPs will be merged by removing unnecessary abstraction MOPs.

IMPLEMENTATION

This section details the design of a MemoPA agent. First of all, we show how a case is represented. Then a memory mechanism is proposed that should be general enough to be easily integrated into any PA agent. Finally, the integration of the memory mechanism into a PA agent is discussed.

Representation of MOPs

The MOP memory uses the same formalism than the ontology and knowledge base. Table 3 shows the definition of the "Case" MOP (represented as a concept) that plays a key role in the memory.

Under the "Case" MOP, several new MOPs can be defined using **:is-a** field. Those MOPs form a hierarchy of cases concerning email task and a hierarchy of cases concerning the meeting task. For example, in Table 4, the "Email Service Case" MOP is a "Case" MOP, and the "Send Email Case" MOP is an "Email Service Case" MOP. The more precise the MOPs, the more precise the tasks involved.

In the memory of a MemoPA agent, there is also a conceptualization of service tasks (Table 5) to fill the content of cases. Therefore, the hierarchy of the "Service Task" MOP is defined in the same fashion as the hierarchy of the "Case" MOP. The "Task Arg" MOP defines task arguments. Each argument is described by its name, its value and its weight. The attribute "weight" is used to calculate the similarity between cases in the Remember process.

Information about agents is also important to represent a task or a case: the task in each case is normally executed by a service agent; a PA agent that works for a user can be linked to several service agents; the agents involved in a case can be local or remote.

Management of the Memory Process

The memory mechanism of a MemoPA consists of two basic components (Figure 8): (i) case memory; and (ii) memory processor.

Case Memory

For a MemoPA agent, *short-term memory* and *long-term memory* play a central role in the memory process. The short-term memory exists in the working memory and provides a context for the current task that the agent is performing. Thus, the short-term memory must be activated during the interaction with a user to receive the information required for a task. The long-term memory plays an essential role in the cognitive activities of a MemoPA agent. Past experiences are stored in the long-term memory.

As mentioned before, the case memory contains a number of MOP-based episodic cases. Inspired by the human memory model, we divide the episodic cases into two types: (i) Short-term cases (STC); and (ii) Long-term cases (LTC). Short-term cases provide a context for the whole task that the agent currently processes, and long-term cases contain the situations of the tasks handled

Table 4. Representation of several MOPs under "Case"

```
...
(defconcept "Email Case"
(:is-a "Case")
(:rel "task" (:to "Email Task")))
(defconcept "Send Email Case"
(:is-a "Email Case")
(:rel "task" (:to "Send Email")))
...
(defconcept "Meeting Case"
(:is-a "Case")
(:rel "task" (:to "Meeting Task")))
(defconcept "Arrange Meeting Case"
(:is-a "Meeting Case")
(:rel "task" (:to "Arrange Meeting")))
(defconcept "Cancel Meeting Case"
(:is-a "Meeting Case")
(:rel "task" (:to "Cancel Meeting")))
...
```

Table 5. Representation of "Service Task" and "Task Arg"

```
(defconcept "Service Task"
(:rel "executor" (:to "Service Agent"))
(:rel "applicant" (:to "Assistant Agent"))
(:att "result" (:one-of:success:failure))
(:att "return value")
(:att "fail reason")
(:rel "target" (:to "Universal Class"))
(:rel "arg" (:to "Task Arg")))
(defconcept "Task Arg"
(:doc "A TASK-ARG is an argument required or optional to
the task.")
(:att "name")
(:att "val")
(:att "weight"))
```

Table 6. Representation of "Agent"

```
(defconcept "Agent"
(:att "name")
(:att "position" (:one-of:local:remote)))
(defconcept "Assistant Agent"
(:doc "An ASSISTANT-AGENT is a personal assistant agent to help user.")
(:is-a "Agent")
(:rel "master" (:to "Person"))
(:rel "staff" (:to "Service Agent")))
(defconcept "Service Agent"
(:doc "A SERVICE-AGENT owns a domain-related knowledge and processes domain-related tasks.")
(:is-a "Agent")
(:rel "skill" (:to "Skill")))
```

Figure 8. A diagram of the memory mechanism in MemoPA

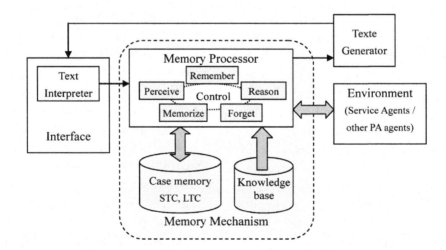

previously. The type of memory can be indicated in the representation of the case. A new case is generated first as a short-term case. When the case is finally saved into the memory, it is transformed into a long-term case. In fact, both kinds of cases contribute to the cognition of MemoPA.

Memory Processor

The second component of the memory mechanism is the *memory processor* (Figure 9) aiming at retrieving cases, processing the cases and updating the memory. The memory processor is composed of five cognitive processes and an Engine to trigger some of the cognitive processes depending on the current state of the agent. The processes are: (i) perceive; (ii) remember; (iii) reason; (iv) memorize; and (v) forget. They are built in reference to the process of human memory, which is similar to the classical cycle of CBR (retrieval, reuse, revision and retention, see Watson & Marir, 1994).

- The **Perceive process** is activated when a message arrives from the user or from other agents. If the message concerns a new task, a new short-term memory case is generated. Otherwise, an old short-term memory case is retrieved and then enriched by

the new information involving the current environment. When the agent has collected all necessary information for the task, it triggers the Remember process and the Reason process.

- The **Remember process** plays an essential role in the memory processor. It has to find cases similar to the current one in the agent memory. We propose a two-step searching method: (i) an abstract MOP is found using a dynamic memory process. The abstract MOP contains several features (e.g. the task type) that best match the current situation; and (ii) the most similar episodic cases under that MOP are selected. A weighted NN (Nearest Neighbor) method is adopted to calculate the feature distance between cases. If no similar case can be found, the task then is processed from scratch.

- The **Reason process** is activated when a similar past case is found. How to use the remembered case is different for different tasks. For example, if the remembered case concerns a query task like "get email address," the result of the task in the remembered case is checked to find out if it is the expected answer to the current case. If the remembered case concerns an "arrange

Figure 9. A diagram of cognitive activities in memory processor

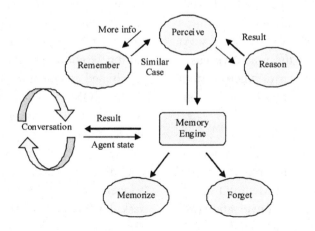

Figure 10. A diagram of Perceive process

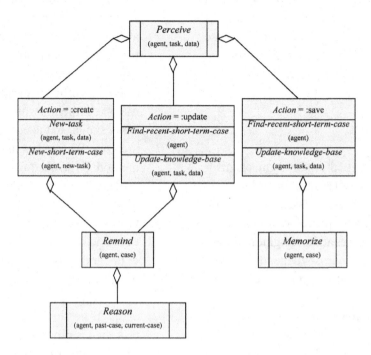

meeting" task, the "meeting time" information will be checked in both the remembered case and the current one to avoid a time conflict.

- The **Memorize process** is triggered once a task is finished. The short-term memory case of that task is transformed into a long-term memory case and then saved into the long-term memory.
- The **Forget process** removes regularly some useless (repetitive) or outdated experiences in order to maintain the correctness and the efficiency of the case memory. At present, we consider the repetitive cases as useless cases. The cases where certain information is not true any more are considered outdated.

The Memory Engine is a control component. Once the engine memory is triggered, it analyzes the data in the current state of MemoPA agent, including the current state of a conversation (beginning, middle or end of a task), and the data describing this task (Figure 10). The result of the analysis determines where the data should be sent: either to the Perceive process when a task is just started or processed by the agent or to the Memorize process or the Forget process when the task is completed.

Integration into the Dialog Mechanism

Once the memory mechanism built, it is integrated into the dialog system of the MemoPA. In our implementation, the memory mechanism is activated during the entire conversation. When a new dialog is initiated, the memory mechanism is triggered.

In the OMAS-MOSS system, the PA agent has a text parser that can recognize the task by analyzing the statements of a user. Once a task is recognized, the agent initiates the (sub-)conversation corresponding to the task (an entry of dialog) and then triggers one or more sub-dialogs to process the task. Each dialog is defined as a series of states. Once a state is activated, an **=execute**[5] method is applied to this state. If in this state a question is asked to the user or to other agents, the response will be handled by a **=resume** method. If no question is asked, there will be a state transition in the **=execut**e method. The MemoPA memory engine is integrated in both the **=execute** methods and **=resume** methods and should be manually programmed for each particular dialog.

At the beginning of each dialog, the MemoPA extracts task data from the user's statement. Pronominal references are removed and replaced by the corresponding entities taken from the latest case. For a personal pronoun, the entity must be the value of a task argument related to the concept of "person." For an object pronoun, the entity must be the value of an argument "target" of the task stored in this case.

Relations Between the Memory Mechanism and the Other Modules

The new memory mechanism installed in the Self module is not independent from the other modules, especially the Ontology module, the World module and the Interface module.

Relation with the Ontology Module

In our approach, the ontology plays three principal roles for PA agents: (i) it can be used to extract information from the messages from a user or from other agents; (ii) it can help select a service agent able to process the user tasks; and (iii) it plays a fundamental role in structuring the memory.

The memory is essentially structured on the basis of the ontology because the events (cases) stored in memory are defined using the concepts from the ontology (Figure 11), and those events (cases) may involve certain facts or certain individuals from the knowledge base.

Moreover, all the information stored in the memory must be known and understood by the agent. Thus, before memorizing a new case, the agent should update its knowledge base by adding new knowledge perceived from the environment. For example, assume that the user requests personal information concerning a person named "Kelly". At first the MemoPA agent does not know the person, and will ask a service agent to perform the task. After that, the MemoPA stores the case into memory, and updates its knowledge base by

Figure 11. An example of ontology for a PA agent

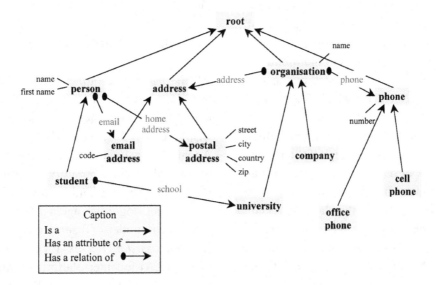

Figure 12. A segment of the structure of the knowledge "who can do what"

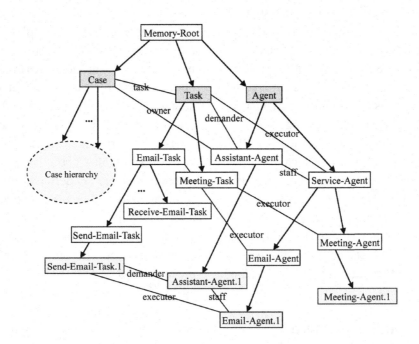

recording new knowledge, i.e., it builds a person concept representing "Kelly".

Relation with the World Module

The MemoPA agent needs to create an internal representation of other agents in the environment. The knowledge "who can do what" in the World module is represented in the knowledge base of MemoPA. In Figure 12 for example, the task "Send-Email-Task.1" delegated to the MemoPA "Assistant-Agent.1" can be executed by the service agent "Email-Agent.1", which is a staff of "Assistant-Agent.1".

Once a task is recognized, MemoPA first consults its World module to check if there is an agent (a PA agent or a local service agent) that can handle this task. Otherwise, MemoPA will consult its memory to see whether there is a recent case in which this task has been successfully completed. Such a case can provide an answer to the question: "whom the agent should ask to do this task?"

Relation with the Interface Module

The memory mechanism is activated only after the MemoPA agent has received information from the environment. Consequently, the integration of the memory mechanism requires a thorough study of the Interface module, especially of the dialog mechanism.

The Agents Platform

All the agents are implemented on the OMAS multi-agent platform (Barthès & Ramos, 2002) using the environment of Allegro Common Lisp®Version 8.1. The OMAS (Open Multi-Agent System) platform is a research platform developed in our laboratory several years ago. It aims at designing and implementing applications using cognitive agents. OMAS contains three agent models: (i) *service agents* (SA); (ii) *personal assistant agents* (PA); and (iii) *transfer agents* (XA) for inter-platform communication. Service agents dedicated to a PA agent form the *staff* of the PA agent (Tacla, 2003). They generally run on the user's computer. Other SAs and XAs usually run on different machines.

The MOP-based memory of the MemoPA agent is represented using a knowledge representation language named MOSS, which is based on a model, PDM (Property Driven Model, see Shen & Barthès, 1995).

TESTS

Traditionally, tests for personal assistant involve two types of situations: (i) handling emails; and (ii) organizing meetings. In our experiments, we used three agents: a MemoPA, and two service agents (SAs). The MemoPA agent embodies an *office* assistant, which is a traditional test example. The office assistant can help the user to deal with her daily work: sending emails, arranging meetings, asking information about meetings, and so on. The service SAs include an email service agent and a meeting service agent that are able to handle those specific tasks. The MemoPA agent has a basic ontology modelling the domain knowledge. The email agent has skills for answering requests about email addresses, for sending emails and receiving emails, and the meeting agent has skills for organizing meetings, canceling meetings and answering requests about meetings. Both service agents have their own domain ontology.

Table 7. A conversation for querying Kejia's email address

```
...
User: Please arrange a meeting for tomorrow 10am.
Agent: Who will attend the meeting?
User: Kejia and kelly.
...
User: What is Kejia's email address?
Agent: As far as I recall, the email address you want should
be:("kejia.chen@utc.fr").
Agent: Would you like to do something else?
User: Send a mail to her.
Agent: What is the object?
...
```

We conducted several experiments in the OMAS-MOSS V7.0 environment. Compared to a PA agent without memory, MemoPA is obviously more efficient in processing tasks and in interacting with users as shown by the following scenarios. The improvements concern primarily the help in solving new problems, in warning of a possible failure, and in processing pronominal references.

Results are similar to those reported by others (Nguyen, 2007; Guzzoni et al., 2007) as shown by the following conversation abstracts.

Table 7 contains a request for an address and shows the handling of a pronominal reference.

Table 8 shows how an object pronoun is taken into account.

Table 9 shows that the agent can issue warnings in case of conflicts.

DISCUSSION

A number of researchers have addressed the problem of personal assistant agent.

- Vere and Bickmore (1990) created the HOMER agent. HOMER has a limited episodic memory (a set of previous joint statements), which was simply used to answer questions on past experiences of HOMER.
- Lashkari et al. (1994) selected a Memory-Based Reasoning method to capture user patterns. Each pair of a user action and the corresponding situation is recorded in the agent memory. After gathering the closest

Table 8. Using object pronouns

```
...
User: Do I have a meeting tomorrow?
Agent: Yes. You have meetings:
("time: 10; Attendees: Kejia; Room: C230; Topic: About thesis
modification.")
User: I want to cancel it.
Agent: Well, this meeting has been cancelled.
...
```

Table 9. A warning message in the "arrange meeting" task

```
...
User: Please arrange a meeting for tomorrow 10 am.
Agent: Who will attend the meeting?
User: Kejia and Kelly.
Agent: Where will be hold the meeting?
User: Room C230.
Agent: What is the meeting topic?
User: About thesis modification.
Agent: This meeting has been arranged. (A new case has been
added in the memory)
Agent: What else can I do for you?
...
User: Please arrange a meeting for tomorrow 10am.
Agent: Sorry, you have arranged a meeting at that time. What
about anthor time?
User: At 3 pm.
Agent: Who will attend the meeting?
...
```

matching situations in memory, the agent calculates a prediction for an action in the new situation.

- Ferret and Grau (1997) proposed a system called MLK (Memorization for Learning Knowledge) that organizes specific situations in episodic memory in the form of conceptual graphs. MLK tries to solve the problem of understanding and learning even when it lacks domain knowledge.

- Koide and Yamauchi (1999) implemented a case-based memory for an interface agent operating in a process plant. The interface agent could discriminate among experienced plant states and unexperienced plant states. This dialog agent works in a quite specific domain without interacting with a multi-agent environment.

- Lerman and Galstyan (2003) incorporated the history of agent actions into the mathematical model of a multi-agent system. The agents use their memory to estimate the global state of the system from the states of agents or of the environment from the situations they have encountered in the past.

Two projects are closer to what we propose:

- The personal assistant agent developed by Nguyen (2007) that provides essentially the same services than our MemoPA. This agent has been built around a BDI mode, which makes controlling the conversation a delicate business because it is indirect.

- The approach proposed by Guzzoni et al. (2007) in the CALO project of the DARPA PAL program is also developed around a BDI model. However, the project is intended for developing cognitive systems by using wizzards and graphics programming. We share with this project the fact that the resulting system is fully integrated.

CONCLUSION AND FUTURE WORK

Let us come back to the original questions: is developing a generic memory mechanism for a personal assistant agent feasible? Is it worth it?

The work that we have reported in this article demonstrates that in our case it is indeed feasible. Our work focused especially on structuring a generic memory mechanism for PA agents based on a cognitive model. The work covers representation of cases, organization of cases, generation of cases, and use of cases. Thus, it is possible to build a short-term and a long-term memory. In the digital butler approach the memory is not used for problem solving but for information extraction to prepare job requests. Thus, it serves to improve the conversation and to avoid asking for already known things.

Concerning the second question: is the increased complexity worth it? I.e. is the result efficient? It is too early to conclude. It seems that the price to pay for the increased complexity is bearable. However, one needs to experiment in more complex situations, other than those used to test the approach in the literature. In this perspective an interesting question relates to the work needed to build a new application. In the framework of our approach and agent model (SCA), the additional required work involves extending the PA ontology and writing additional sub-dialogs. The specific domain is not taken into account at the memory level.

Future work should include the question of learning. There is room for two kinds of learning: (i) increasing and updating the knowledge of MemoPA through interaction with the user; (ii) trying to generalize rules for example after discovering that some task is always followed by some other task). Such rules would let the agent predict future tasks and even their solutions. To learn these rules, machine learning methods can be used.

REFERENCES

Atkinson, R. C., & Schiffrin, R. M. (1968). Human Memory: A Proposed System and its Control Processes. *Psychology of Learning and Motivation, 2,* 742–775.

Barthès, J.-P. A., & Ramos, M. (2002). Agents Assistants Personnels dans les Systèmes Multi-Agents Mixtes - Réalisation sur la Plate-forme OMAS. *Technique et Science Informatiques, 21*(4), 473–498.

Davis, R., Shrobe, H., & Szolovits, P. (1993). What is a Knowledge Representation? *AI Magazine, 14*(1), 17–33.

Enembreck, F., & Barthès, J.-P. A. (2003). Architecture d'un système de dialogue avec un agent assistant. In *Proceedings of the 15th Conference Francophone sur l'interaction Homme-Machine* (pp. 95-105). New York: ACM Publishing.

Ferret, O., & Grau, B. (1997). An Aggregation Procedure for Building Episodic Memory. In *Proceedings of the 15th International Joint Conference on Artificial Intelligence,* Nagoya, Japan (pp. 280-285).

Guzzoni, D., Baur, C., & Cheyer, A. (2007). Modeling Human-Agent Interaction with Active Ontologies (Tech. Rep. SS-07-04). In *Proceedings of the AAAI Spring Symposium: Interaction Challenges for Intelligent Assistants,* Palo Alto, CA (Vol. 1, pp. 52-59). AAAI Press.

Koide, S., & Yamauchi, S. (1999, September). Interface Agent for Process Plant Operation towards the Next Generation Interface. In *Proceedings of the IEEE/ASME International Conference on Advanced Intelligent Mechatronics,* Atlanta, GA (pp.197-202).

Kolodner, J. L. (1993). *Case-Based Reasoning.* San Mateo, CA: Morgan Kaufmann.

Lashkari, Y., Metral, M., & Maes, P. (1994, August). Collaborative Interface Agents. In *Proceedings of the 12th National Conference on Artificial Intelligence,* Seattle, WA (pp. 1-6).

Lerman, K., & Galstyan, A. (2003, July). Agent Memory and Adaptation in Multi-Agent Systems. In *Proceedings of the 2nd International Joint Conference on Autonomous Agents and Multi-Agent Systems,* Melbourne, Australia (pp.797-803).

Lieberman, H. (1995, August). Letizia: An Agent That Assists Web Browsing. In *Proceedings of the 14th International Joint Conference on Artificial Intelligence,* Montreal, QB, Canada (pp. 924-929).

Lieberman, H. (1997, March). Autonomous Interface Agents. In *Proceedings of the ACM Conference on Computers and Human Interface,* Atlanta, GA (pp. 67-73).

Lopez de Mantara, R., McSherry, D., Bridge, D., Leake, D., Smyth, B., & Craw, S. (2006). Retrieval, reuse, revision and retention in case-based reasoning. *The Knowledge Engineering Review, 20*(3), 215–240. doi:10.1017/S0269888906000646

Maes, P. (1994). Agents that Reduce Work and Information Overload. *Communications of the ACM, 37*(7), 30–40. doi:10.1145/176789.176792

Maes, P., & Kozierok, R. (1993, July). Learning Interface Agents. In *Proceedings of the 11th National Conference on Artificial Intelligence*, Washington, DC (pp. 459-465).

Middleton, S. E. (2002). *Interface Agent: A review of the field* (Tech. Rep. ECSTR-IAM01-001). Southampton, UK: School of Electronics and Computer Science, University of Southampton.

Mitchell, T., Caruana, R., Freitag, D., McDermott, J., & Zabowski, D. (1994). Experience with a Learning Personal Assistant. *Communications of the ACM, 37*(7), 81–91. doi:10.1145/176789.176798

Modi, P. J., Veloso, M., Smith, S. F., & Oh, J. (2004). *CMRadar: A Personal Assistant Agent for Calendar Management*. In Proc. of the 6th International Workshop on Agent-Oriented Information Systems, pp. 134-148, Riga, Latvia, June, 2004.

Negroponte, N. (1997). Agents: From Direct Manipulation to Delegation. In J. M. Bradshaw (Ed.), *Software Agents* (pp. 57-66). Cambridge, MA: MIT Press.

Nguyen, A. (2007). *An Agent-Based Approach to Dialogue Management in Personal Assistants*. Unpublished PhD thesis, School of Computer Science and Engineering, University of New South Wales, Sydney, Australia.

Paraiso, E. C., & Barthμes, J-P. A. (2004). Une interface conversationnelle pour les agents assistants appliqués à des activités professionnelles. In *Proceedings of Actes IHM 04*, Namur, Belgium (pp. 243-246). New York: ACM Publishing.

Riesbeck, C. K., & Schank, R. C. (1989). *Inside Case-Based Reasoning*. Hillsdale, NJ: Lawrence Erlbaum.

Shen, W., & Barthés, J.-P. A. (1995). Description and Applications of an Object-Oriented Model PDM. In *Modeling Complex Data for Creating Information: Real and Virtual Objects* (pp. 15-24).

Tacla, C. A. (2003). *De l'utilité des systèmes multi-agents pour l'acquisition des connaissances au fil de l'eau*. Unpublished doctoral dissertation, Université de Technologie de Compiègne, France.

Vere, S. A., & Bickmore, T. W. (1990). A Basic Agent. *Computational Intelligence, 6*, 41–60. doi:10.1111/j.1467-8640.1990.tb00128.x

Wang, Y. (2003). Cognitive Informatics: A New Transdisciplinary Research Field. *Brain and Mind, 4*(2), 115–127. doi:10.1023/A:1025419826662

Watson, I., & Marir, F. (1994). Case-Based Reasoning: A Review. *The Knowledge Engineering Review, 9*(4), 355–381. doi:10.1017/S0269888900007098

Wobcke, W. R., Ho, V., Nguyen, A., & Krzywicki, A. (2005, September). A BDI Agent Architecture for Dialogue Modeling and Coordination in a Smart Personal Assistant. In *Proceedings of the IEEE/WIC/ACM International Conference on Web Intelligence and Intelligent Agent Technology*, Compiègne, France (pp. 323-329).

ENDNOTES

[1] http//www.aai.sri.com/nysmith/organizing/sss07/

[2] http://www.darpa.mil/IPTO/programs/pal/pal.asp

[3] A detailed documentation is available at the following address: http://www.utc.fr/barthes/OMAS/

[4] A detailed documentation is available at the following address: http://www.utc.fr/barthes/MOSS/

[5] The = sign is a MOSS convention.

This work was previously published in volume 4, issue 1 of the International Journal of Cognitive Informatics and Natural Intelligence, edited by Yingxu Wang, pp. 45-64, copyright 2010 by IGI Publishing (an imprint of IGI Global).

Chapter 22
An Evaluation Method of Relative Reducts Based on Roughness of Partitions

Yasuo Kudo
Muroran Institute of Technology, Japan

Tetsuya Murai
Hokkaido University, Japan

ABSTRACT

This paper focuses on rough set theory which provides mathematical foundations of set-theoretical approximation for concepts, as well as reasoning about data. Also presented in this paper is the concept of relative reducts which is one of the most important notions for rule generation based on rough set theory. In this paper, from the viewpoint of approximation, the authors introduce an evaluation criterion for relative reducts using roughness of partitions that are constructed from relative reducts. The proposed criterion evaluates each relative reduct by the average of coverage of decision rules based on the relative reduct, which also corresponds to evaluate the roughness of partition constructed from the relative reduct,

INTRODUCTION

In rough set theory (Pawlak, 1982; Pawlak, 1991), set-theoretical approximation of concepts and reasoning about data are the two main topics. In the former, lower and upper approximations of concepts and their evaluations are the main

DOI: 10.4018/978-1-4666-1743-8.ch022

topics. Accuracy, quality of approximation, and quality of partition are well-known criteria in evaluation of approximations; these criteria are based on the correctness of the approximation. However, the roughness of the approximation is not explicitly treated in these criteria. In reasoning about data, the relative reduct is one of the most important concepts for rule generation based on rough set theory, and many methods for exhaustive or heuristic calculation of relative reducts have been proposed (Bao, 2004; Guan, 1998; Heder, 2008; Hu, 2008; Hu, 2003; Ślęzak, 2002;, Pawlak, 1991; Skowron & Rauszer, 1992; Xu, 2008; Xu, 2007; Zhang, 2003). As an evaluation criterion for relative reducts, the cardinality of a relative reduct, i.e., the number of attributes in the relative reduct, is typical and is widely used (for example, in (Heder, 2008; Hu, 2008; Hu, 2003; Xu, 2008; Zhang, 2003)). In addition, other kinds of criteria related to evaluation of partitions are also considered with respect to the following evaluation functions: a normalized decision function generated from a relative reduct B (Ślęzak, 2000), the information entropy H(B) of B (Ślęzak, 2002), and the number of decision rules induced from B (Wróblewski, 2001).

In this paper, we consider evaluating relative reducts based on the roughness of partitions constructed from them. The outline of relative reduct evaluation we propose is:

"Good" relative reducts = relative reducts that provide partitions with approximations as rough and correct as possible.

In this sense, we think that evaluation of relative reducts is strictly concerned with evaluation of roughness of approximation.

The paper is structured as follows. First, we review the foundations of rough set theory as background for this paper. Then, we derive some properties related to roughness of partition and the average coverage of decision rules, and propose an evaluation criterion of relative reducts based on roughness of partition. We also demonstrate the proposed method for evaluating relative reducts. Finally, we discuss the results of this paper and present our conclusions.

ROUGH SET

We review the foundations of rough set theory as background for this paper. The contents of this section are based on (Polkowski, 2002).

In rough set data analysis, objects as targets of analysis are illustrated by a combination of multiple attributes and their values and is represented by the following decision table:

$$(U, C, d),$$

where U is the set of objects, C is the set of condition attributes such that each attribute $a \in C$ is a function $a : U \to V_a$ from U to the value set V_a of a, and d is a function $d : U \to V_d$ called the decision attribute.

The indiscernibility relation R_B on U with respect to a subset $B \subseteq C$ is defined by

$$(x, y) \in R_B \Leftrightarrow a(x) = a(y), \forall a \in B. \qquad (1)$$

It is easy to confirm that the indiscernibility relation R_B is an equivalence relation on U. The equivalence class $[x]_B$ of $x \in U$ by R_B is the set of objects which are not discernible with x even though they use all attributes in B.

Any indiscernibility relation provides a partition of U. We denote the quotient set of U, i.e., a partition of U, with respect to an equivalence relation R by U / R. In particular, the partition $\mathbf{D} = \{D_1, ..., D_m\}$ provided by the indiscernibility relation R_d with respect to the decision attribute d is called the set of decision classes.

For any decision class $D_i (1 \leq i \leq m)$, the lower approximation $\underline{B}(D_i)$ and the upper approximation $\overline{B}(D_i)$ of D_i with respect to the indiscernibility relation R_B are defined as follows, respectively:

$$\underline{B}(D_i) = \{x \in U \mid [x]_B \subseteq D_i\}, \qquad (2)$$

$$\overline{B}(D_i) = \{x \in U \mid [x]_B \cap D_i \neq \varnothing\}. \qquad (3)$$

A pair $(\underline{B}(D_i), \overline{B}(D_i))$ is called a rough set of D_i with respect to R_B.

As evaluation criteria of approximation, the accuracy measure and the quality of approximation are well known. Moreover, the quality of partition by R_B with respect to the set of decision classes $\mathbf{D}=\{D_1, ..., D_m\}$ is also defined as

$$\gamma_B(D) = \frac{\sum_{i=i}^{m}\left|\underline{B}(D_i)\right|}{|U|} \qquad (4)$$

where $|X|$ is the cardinality of the set X.

Table 1 represents a decision table consisting of the set of objects $U = \{x1, \cdots, x6\}$, the set of condition attributes $C = \{c1, \cdots, c6\}$, and the decision attribute d. For example, the attribute c2 is the function $c2 : U \to \{1, 2, 3\}$, and the value of an object $x3 \in U$ at c2 is 3, i.e., c2(x3)=3. Moreover, the decision attributed d provides the following three decision classes: $D_1 = \{x1, x2, x5\}$, $D_2 = \{x3, x4\}$, and $D_3 = \{x6\}$.

In this paper, we denote a decision rule constructed from a subset $B \subseteq C$ of condition attributes, the decision attribute d, and an object $x \in U$ by

$$(B, x) \to (d, x).$$

The concepts of certainty and coverage are well-known criteria in evaluation of decision rules. For any decision rule $(B, x) \to (d, x)$, the score

of certainty $Cer(\cdot)$ and the score of coverage $Cov(\cdot)$ are defined as follows:

$$Cer\left((B, x) \to (d, x)\right) = \frac{\left|[x]_B \cap D_i\right|}{\left|[x]_B\right|}, \qquad (5)$$

$$Cov\left((B, x) \to (d, x)\right) = \frac{\left|[x]_B \cap D_i\right|}{|D_i|}, \qquad (6)$$

where the set D_i is the decision class such that $x \in D_i$.

For example, a decision rule $(B, x1) \to (d, x1)$ constructed from a set $B = \{c2, c3\}$, the decision attribute d, and an object $x1 \in U$ has the form

$$(c2 = 1) \wedge (c3 = 1) \to (d = 1).$$

Its certainty is 1.0 and the coverage is 1/3.

Relative reducts are minimal subsets of condition attributes that provide the same result of classification of objects to decision classes by the indiscernibility relation R_C with respect to the set C of all condition attributes. Formally, a relative reduct for the partition $\mathbf{D}$ is a set of condition attributes $A \subseteq C$ that satisfies the following two conditions:

1. $Pos_A(\mathbf{D}) = Pos_C(\mathbf{D})$
2. For any proper subset $B \subset A$, $Pos_B(\mathbf{D}) \neq Pos_C(\mathbf{D})$,

where $Pos_X(\mathbf{D}) = \bigcup_{D_i \in \mathbf{D}} \underline{X}(D_i)$ is the positive region of $\mathbf{D}$ by $X \subseteq C$.

For example, there are the following seven relative reducts of Table 1: {c1, c3}, {c3, c5}, {c5, c6}, {c1, c2, c3}, {c1, c2, c4}, {c1, c2, c6}, and {c2, c4, c5}.

Table 1. Decision table

	c1	c2	c3	c4	c5	c6	d
x1	1	1	1	1	1	2	1
x2	2	2	1	1	1	2	1
x3	2	3	2	1	2	1	2
x4	2	2	2	2	2	1	2
x5	2	2	3	1	1	2	1
x6	1	2	1	1	2	2	3

EVALUATION OF RELATIVE REDUCTS USING PARTITIONS

In this section, we propose an evaluation method for relative reducts using partitions constructed from them. To summarize relative reduct evaluation, we consider that rougher partitions constructed by a relative reduct lead to better evaluation of the relative reduct.

However, the quality of partition defined by (4) does not consider roughness of partition, although it considers correctness of approximation. In fact, all relative reducts of a consistent decision table, i.e., a decision table that satisfies $Pos_C(\mathbf{D}) = U$, provide crisp approximations of all decision classes, i.e., $\underline{A}(D_i) = D_i = \overline{A}(D_i)$ for any relative reduct A and any decision class D_i, even though the difference of roughness of partitions based on relative reducts.

For example, because the decision table illustrated by Table 1 is consistent, all the relative reducts of Table 1 provide crisp approximation, and it is easy to confirm that the score of quality of partition by any relative reduct in Table 1 is equal to 1. However, the roughness of partitions based on the relative reducts differs, as follows:

- Partitions by the relative reduct {c1, c5}: {{x1}, {x2, x5}, {x3, x4}, {x6}}.
- Partitions by the relative reduct {c3, c5}: {{x1, x2}, {x3, x4}, {x5}, {x6}}.
- Partitions by the relative reduct {c5, c6}: {{x1, x2, x5}, {x3, x4}, {x6}}.
- Partitions by the relative reduct {c1, c2, c3}: {{x1}, {x2}, {x3}, {x4}, {x5}, {x6}}.
- Partitions by the relative reduct {c1, c2, c4}: {{x1}, {x2, x5}, {x3}, {x4}, {x6}}.
- Partitions by the relative reduct {c1, c2, c6}: {{x1}, {x2, x5}, {x3}, {x4}, {x6}}.
- Partitions by the relative reduct {c2, c4, c5}: {{x1}, {x2, x5}, {x3}, {x4}, {x6}}.

In particular, all equivalence classes in the partition by {c1, c2, c3} are singletons. Thus, the quality of approximation is not suitable for evaluating roughness of partition.

In addition, from the viewpoint of rule generation, such rough partitions constructed from relative reducts provide decision rules with higher scores of coverage than those of coverage of decision rules based on fine partitions. Moreover, the correctness of partitions based on relative reducts is guaranteed, because each relative reduct provides the same approximation as the one based on the set of all condition attributes. Thus, we consider evaluating relative reducts using the coverage of decision rules constructed from them.

Here, we consider deriving some relationship between the roughness of partitions based on relative reducts and the coverage of decision rules based on them. Suppose we fix a non-empty subset of condition attributes $B \subseteq C$. For any equivalence class $[x]_B \in U / R_B$, we define the set

$$Dec_B([x]_B) \stackrel{def}{=} \left\{ D_i \in \mathbf{D} \,\middle|\, [x]_B \cap D_i \neq \varnothing \right\}. \quad (7)$$

The set $Dec_B([x]_B)$ corresponds to the set of conclusions of decision rules, with the formula (B, x) as the antecedent. Thus, the value defined as

$$N_B \stackrel{def}{=} \sum_{[x]_B \in U / R_B} \left| Dec_B([x]_B) \right| \quad (8)$$

is the sum of the number of all decision rules constructed from B. Similarly, for any decision class $D_i \in \mathbf{D}$, we define the set

$$Cond_B(D_i) \stackrel{def}{=} \left\{ [x]_B \in U / R_B \,\middle|\, [x]_B \cap D_i \neq \varnothing \right\}. \quad (9)$$

The set $Cond_B(D_i)$ corresponds to the set of antecedents of decision rules with the formula (d, y) for some $y \in D_i$ as the conclusion. From the definitions of sets $Dec_B\left([x]_B\right)$ and $Cond_B\left(D_i\right)$, the following relationship is obvious:

$$D_i \in Dec_B\left([x]_B\right) \Leftrightarrow [x]_B \in Cond_B\left(D_i\right). \tag{10}$$

For evaluation of relative reducts using criteria involving decision rules, we use the following properties of the certainty and coverage of decision rules.

Lemma 1. Let $B \subseteq C$ be a non-empty subset of condition attributes. For any equivalence class $[x]_B \in U / R_B$, the sum of the certainty of all decision rules constructed from the equivalence class $[x]_B$ and decision classes $D_i \in Dec_B\left([x]_B\right)$ is equal to 1; i.e., the following equation is satisfied:

$$\sum_{D_i \in Dec_B([x]_B)} \frac{\left| [x]_B \cap D_i \right|}{\left| [x]_B \right|} = 1. \tag{11}$$

Similarly, for any decision class $D_i \in \mathbf{D}$, the sum of the coverage of all decision rules constructed from equivalence classes $[x]_B \in Cond_B\left(D_i\right)$ and the decision class D_i is equal to 1; i.e., the following equation is satisfied:

$$\sum_{[x]_B \in Cond_B(D_i)} \frac{\left|[x]_B \cap D_i\right|}{\left|D_i\right|}, \tag{12}$$

Proof. Here, we derive equation (11). Because the set $\mathbf{D} = \left\{D_1, \cdots, D_m\right\}$ of decision classes is a partition on U, it is clear that the set of non-empty intersections $[x]_B \cap D_i$ of decision classes D_i and a given equivalence class $[x]_B \in U / R_B$ is a partition on the equivalence class $[x]_B$. Thus, we have the following equation from (7):

$$[x]_B = \bigcup_{D_i \in Dec_B([x]_B)} \left([x]_B \cap D_i\right) \tag{13}$$

Moreover, any two intersections $[x]_B \cap D_i$ and $[x]_B \cap D_j$ are disjoint from each other if the decision classes are different; therefore, we can simplify the left side of equation (11) as follows:

$$\sum_{D_i \in Dec_B([x]_B)} \frac{\left| [x]_B \cap D_i \right|}{\left| [x]_B \right|} = \frac{\left| [x]_B \cap D_{j1} \right| + \cdots + \left| [x]_B \cap D_{jn} \right|}{\left| [x]_B \right|} \quad \left(\forall D_{jk} \in Dec_B\left([x]_B\right)\right)$$
$$= \frac{\left| \left([x]_B \cap D_{j1}\right) \cup \cdots \cup \left([x]_B \cap D_{jn}\right) \right|}{\left| [x]_B \right|}$$
$$= \frac{\left| [x]_B \right|}{\left| [x]_B \right|} \quad \left(\text{by (13)}\right)$$
$$= 1.$$

This concludes the derivation of (11).

Equation (12) being derived in a similar way, we omit the proof. (Q.E.D.)

Lemma 1 exhibits useful properties for considering the average certainty and the average coverage of decision rules constructed from non-empty subsets of condition attributes. This is because Lemma 1 indicates that the sum of the certainty (coverage) of all decision rules constructed from a given equivalence class (a fixed decision class) and decision classes (equivalence classes) relevant to the equivalence class (the decision class) is equal to 1, even though the detailed scores of certainty and coverage may differ because different equivalence classes and decision classes are used. Therefore, we do not need to consider detailed scores of certainty and coverage of each decision rule to calculate the average certainty and the average coverage.

We show the following theorem about the average certainty and the average coverage of all decision rules constructed from any non-empty subset of condition attributes. This theorem provides a basis for evaluating relative reducts we consider.

Theorem 1. For any non-empty subset $B \subseteq C$ of condition attributes, the average of the certainty $ACer(B)$ of all decision rules $(B, x) \rightarrow (d, x)$ $(\forall x \in U)$ constructed from equivalence classes $[x]_B \in U / R_B$ and decision classes $[x]_d \in \mathbf{D}$ is calculated using

$$ACer(B) = \frac{|U/R_B|}{N_B}, \qquad (14)$$

where N_B is the number of all decision rules constructed from B defined by (8).

Similarly, the average of the coverage $ACov(B)$ is calculated as

$$ACov(B) = \frac{|D|}{N_B} \qquad (15)$$

Proof. Here, we derive equation(15). Because $\mathbf{D} = \{D_1, \cdots, D_m\}$ is a partition on U, we can consider the sum of the coverage of all decision rules constructed from B by treating all decision classes $D_i \in \mathbf{D}$ in (12). Thus, using the number N_B of all decision rules defined by (8), we simplify the average coverage of all decision rules constructed from B as

$$ACov(B) = \frac{1}{N_B} \sum_{D \in D_i} \sum_{[x]_B \in Cond_B(D_i)} \frac{|[x]_B \cap D_i|}{|D_i|}$$

$$= \frac{1}{N_B} \sum_{D_i \in D} 1 (by(12))$$

$$= \frac{|D|}{N_B}$$

This concludes the derivation of (15).

Equation (14) being derived in a similar way, we omit the proof. (Q.E.D.)

Theorem 1 demonstrates that we can calculate the average certainty and the average coverage of decision rules based on any non-empty set $B \subseteq C$ by the following three parameters: the number of equivalence classes based on B, the number of decision classes, and the number of decision rules constructed from B. In particular, because the number of decision classes is uniquely determined for any decision table, the average coverage depends only on the number of decision rules.

By Theorem 1, if we use relative reducts as subsets of condition attributes in any consistent decision table, the average certainty values of decision rules constructed from the relative reduct are equal to 1 for any relative reduct. In addition, the smaller the number of decision rules constructed from the relative reduct, the higher the average coverage of decision rules constructed from the relative reduct.

Moreover, from Theorem 1, we can derive the relationship between the roughness of partitions based on relative reducts and the coverage of decision rules based on relative reducts. We use the following lemma to derive the relationship.

Lemma 2. Let $B \subseteq C$ be a non-empty set of condition attributes, and D_i be a decision class. For any object $x \in U$, we have $x \in \underline{B}(D_i)$ if and only if $Dec_B([x]_B) = \{D_i\}$.

Proof. Suppose $x \in \underline{B}(D_i)$. By the definition of lower approximation, we have $[x]_B \subseteq D_i$, which implies $[x]_B \cap D_i \neq \varnothing$ and $[x]_B \cap D_j = \varnothing$ for any $D_j \neq D_i$. This concludes $Dec_B([x]_B) = \{D_i\}$. Conversely, suppose $Dec_B([x]_B) = \{D_i\}$. This indicates that there is just one decision class D_i such that $[x]_B \cap D_i \neq \varnothing$, and $[x]_B \cap D_j = \varnothing$ for any other decision class $D_j \neq D_i$. This implies $[x]_B \subseteq D_i$, and thus we have $x \in \underline{B}(D_i)$. (Q.E.D.)

Theorem 2. Let E and F be relative reducts of a given decision table. The following properties are satisfied:

1. If $R_E \subset R_F$ holds, i.e., the partition U/R_F is rougher than the partition U/R_E, then $ACov(E) \leq ACov(F)$ holds.

2. If the given decision table is consistent and $R_E \subset R_F$ holds, then $ACov(E) < ACov(F)$ holds.

Proof. 1. By Theorem 1, it is sufficient to show that $R_E \subset R_F$ implies $N_E \geq N_F$, as defined by (8). It is easy to confirm that the condition $R_E \subset R_F$ implies $[x]_E \subseteq [x]_F$ for any $x \in U$, and there is at least one object $y \in U$ with $[y]_F = \bigcup_{j=1}^{p} [y_j]_E \ (p \geq 2)$. Because the set $Dec_F([y]_F)$ contains at least one decision class, for each decision class $D_i \in Dec_F([y]_F)$, we have $D_i \cap [y]_F = \bigcup_{j=1}^{p}(D_i \cap [y_j]_E)$. Then, the intersection $D_i \cap [y]_F$ is either identical to an intersection $D_i \cap [y_j]_E$ by just one equivalence class $[y_j]_E$ or the union of plural non-empty intersections $D_i \cap [y_j]_E$. This implies the inequality $\left| Dec_F([y]_F) \right| \leq \sum_{j=1}^{p} \left| Dec_E([y_j]_E) \right|$, which concludes $N_E \geq N_F$.

2. Suppose the given decision table is consistent and we have $R_E \subset R_F$. By this condition, for any $y \in U$ with $[y]_F = \bigcup_{j=1}^{p}[y_j]_E$ $(p \geq 2)$, $y \in D_i$ implies $y \in \underline{F}(D_i)$. By Lemma 2, we have $Dec_F([y]_F) = \{D_i\}$. Thus, similar to the case of 1, the following inequality

$$1 = \left| Dec_F([y]_F) \right| < \sum_{j=1}^{p} \left| Dec_E([y_j]_E) \right| \text{ is }$$

satisfied. This concludes $N_E > N_F$, and therefore we have $ACov(E) < ACov(F)$. (Q.E.D.)

Theorem 2 guarantees that relative reducts that provide rougher partitions receive better evaluations than those that provide finer partitions.

Combining Theorems 1 and 2, we can evaluate relative reducts of a given decision table by calculating the average coverage of decision rules constructed from the relative reducts. Therefore, we propose to use the average coverage of decision rules constructed from relative reducts as an evaluation criterion of the relative reducts based on roughness of partitions.

For example, we evaluate the relative reducts of Table 1 by calculating the average coverage of all decision rules constructed from these relative reducts. To calculate the average coverage, we need to get the number of decision rules constructed from each relative reduct. In the case of the relative reduct $A = \{c1, c5\}$, as we have illustrated in this section, the partition U / R_A consists of the following four equivalence classes: $\{x1\}$, $\{x2, x5\}$, $\{x3, x4\}$, and $\{x6\}$. For each equivalence class, the set of decision classes $Dec_A(\cdot)$ defined by (7) is calculated as

$$Dec_A([x1]_B) = \{D_1\}, \ Dec_A([x2]_B) = \{D_1\},$$
$$Dec_A([x3]_B) = \{D_2\}, \ Dec_A([x6]_B) = \{D_3\}.$$

Thus, the number N_A of all decision classes is 4, and therefore, according to Theorem 1, the evaluation score of A is 3/4 because the number of decision classes in Table 1 is 3.

We can construct the following four decision rules from $A = \{c1, c5\}$:

. $(c1 = 1) \wedge (c5 = 1) \rightarrow (d = 1)$, Certainty = 1, Coverage = 1/3.
. $(c1 = 2) \wedge (c5 = 1) \rightarrow (d = 1)$, Certainty = 1, Coverage = 2/3.
. $(c1 = 2) \wedge (c5 = 2) \rightarrow (d = 2)$, Certainty = 1, Coverage = 1.
. $(c1 = 1) \wedge (c5 = 2) \rightarrow (d = 3)$, Certainty = 1, Coverage = 1.

The average certainty of these rules is $(1 + 1 + 1 + 1) / 4 = 1$, and this score is equal to the value "the number of equivalence classes / the number of decision rules" from Theorem 1. Moreover, the average coverage is $(1/3 + 2/3 + 1 + 1) / 4 = 3/4$, and it is also equal to the value "the number of decision classes / the number of decision rules" from Theorem 1.

Table 2 shows the average scores of certainty and the average scores of coverage for each rela-

Table 2. Average certainty and average coverage calculated from relative reducts of Table 1

Relative reducts	Avg. of Certainty	Avg. of coverage
$\{c1, c5\}$	1	0.75
$\{c3, c5\}$	1	0.75
$\{c5, c6\}$	1	1
$\{c1, c2, c3\}$	1	0.5
$\{c1, c2, c4\}$	1	0.6
$\{c1, c2, c6\}$	1	0.6
$\{c2, c4, c5\}$	1	0.6

tive reduct. On the basis of this result, we regard the relative reduct $\{c5, c6\}$ to be the best one that provides the roughest and most correct approximations of decision classes. Actually, the partition constructed from the relative reduct $\{c5, c6\}$ is identical to the partition U / R_d, i.e., the set **D** of all decision classes.

EXAMPLE

To demonstrate our method of evaluation of relative reducts, we apply the proposed method to a dataset, Zoo (Forsyth, 1990), in the UCI Machine Learning Repository (http://archive.ics.uci.edu/ml/). The Zoo data consists of 101 samples and 17 attributes with discrete values. We use the attribute *type* as the decision attribute, and the remaining 16 attributes (*hair, feathers, eggs, milk, airborne, aquatic, predator, toothed, backbone, breathes, venomous, fins, legs, tail, domestic,* and *catsize*) as condition attributes.

The decision attribute *type* provides seven decision classes corresponding to kinds of animals: mammal, bird, reptile, fish, amphibian, insect, and other invertebrates. Note that the decision table based on the Zoo data is consistent.

Consequently, there are 33 relative reducts in the Zoo data. These include 7 relative reducts that consist of five attributes, 18 that consist of six, and 8 that consist of seven.

Table 3 presents the experimental results of evaluation of relative reducts consisting of five, six, and seven attributes. The maximum, minimum, and average scores of evaluation of the 33 relative reducts are 0.35, 0.167, and 0.260, respectively.

These results indicate that the smaller the number of attributes in a relative reduct, the higher the score of evaluation in general. However, even when the number of attributes is identical, big differences occur between the scores of evaluation of relative reducts. For example, the relative reduct with the highest evaluation, 0.35, is {milk, aquatic, backbone, fins, legs}, and this relative reduct generates 20 decision rules; thus, we have the score 7/20 = 0.35. In other words, because the decision table is consistent, this relative reduct divides 101 samples into 20 equivalence classes. In addition, even though the number of attributes is the same, the relative reduct with the lowest score of evaluation, 0.259, is {*eggs, aquatic, toothed, legs, catsize*}, which constructs 27 equivalence classes. Moreover, the worst relative reduct, with the evaluation score 0.167, is {*egg, aquatic, predator, breathes, venomous, legs, catsize*}, which constructs 42 equivalence classes.

Table 3. Experimental results of evaluation of relative reducts of Zoo data

Number of attributes	Number of relative reducts	Maximum score of evaluation	Minimum score of evaluation	Average of evaluation
5	7	0.35	0.259	0.306
6	18	0.318	0.189	0.260
7	8	0.233	0.167	0.201
Total	33	0.35	0.167	0.260

Decision rules constructed from the best relative reduct {*milk, aquatic, backbone, fins, legs*} represent characteristics of each decision class very well. For example, unlike the decision class "mammal," which is directly identified by the attribute *milk*, there is no attribute that identifies the decision class "fish" directly. However, the decision class fish, which consists of 13 kinds of fishes, is described just one decision rule:

- If (*milk* = no) and (*aquatic* = yes) and (*backbone* = yes) and (*fins* = yes) and (*legs* = 0), then (*type* = fish); Certainty = 1, Coverage = 1

Note that the attribute *fins* alone does not identify the decision class fish, because aquatic mammals in the Zoo data such as the dolphin, porpoise, and seal also have fins. Similarly, the decision class "bird," which consists of 20 kinds of birds, is described by two decision rules:

- If (*milk* = no) and (*aquatic* = no) and (*backbone* = yes) and (*fins* = no) and (*legs* = 2), then (*type* = bird); Certainty = 1, Coverage = 0.7
- If (*milk* = no) and (*aquatic* = yes) and (*backbone* = yes) and (*fins* = no) and (*legs* = 2), then (*type* = bird); Certainty = 1, Coverage = 0.3

These two decision rules describe the fact that all birds in the Zoo data are characterized as non-mammal vertebrates with two legs and no fins.

CONCLUSION

In this paper, we proposed a method of evaluating relative reducts of a given decision table by averages of the coverage of decision rules constructed from them. The proposed method is based on the roughness and correctness of partitions based on the relative reducts and evaluates the relative re-

ducts that provide the roughest and most correct approximations to be better. Moreover, when we evaluate a relative reduct by the proposed method, we do not need to calculate actual scores of coverage of decision rules constructed from the relative reduct; we just need to know how many decision rules are generated from the relative reduct. Experimental results of the proposed method indicate that even when the number of attributes making up relative reducts is identical, the evaluation results based on the proposed method may be quite different, and decision rules generated from a good relative reduct in the sense of the proposed evaluation represent the characteristics of decision classes very well. Thus, we believe that the proposed method is very important and useful as an evaluation criterion for relative reducts.

Several issues remain to be investigated. First, we need to compare the proposed method with other evaluation criteria for relative reducts related to evaluation of partitions (Ślęzak, 2000; Ślęzak, 2002; Wróblewski, 2001), in particular, the method proposed in (Wróblewski, 2001), which evaluates relative reducts by the number of decision rules induced from a relative reduct. This is because the basic idea in (Wróblewski, 2001) is similar to the proposed method, as described in Section 3. We also think that the idea of evaluation of subsets of condition attributes by the average coverage of decision rules is applicable to many extensions of rough set theory, such as variable precision rough sets (Ziarko, 1993) and dominance-based rough sets (Greco, 2001). Thus, application of this idea to these variations of rough sets is also an interesting issue.

ACKNOWLEDGEMENT

We appreciate the reviewer's helpful comments and suggestions that led us to improve the previous version of this paper. This work was partially supported by MEXT KAKENHI (20700192).

REFERENCES

Bao, Y., Du, X., Deng, M., & Ishii, N. (2004). An Efficient Method for Computing All Reducts. *Transactions of the Japanese Society for Artificial Intelligence, 19*(3), 166–173. doi:10.1527/tjsai.19.166

Forsyth, R. (1990). *Zoo Data Set*. Retrieved May 15, 1990, from http://archive.ics.uci.edu/ml/datasets/Zoo

Greco, S., Matarazzo, B., & Słowiński, R. (2001). Rough Set Theory for Multicriteria Decision Analysis. *European Journal of Operational Research, 129*, 1–47. doi:10.1016/S0377-2217(00)00167-3

Guan, J. W., & Bell, D. A. (1998). Rough Computational Methods for Information Systems. *Artificial Intelligence, 105*, 77–103. doi:10.1016/S0004-3702(98)00090-3

Hedar, A. H., Wang, J., & Fukushima, M. (2008). Tabu Search for Attribute Reduction in Rough Set Theory. *Soft Computing, 12*(9), 909–918. doi:10.1007/s00500-007-0260-1

Hu, F., Wang, G., & Feng, L. (2008). Fast Knowledge Reduction Algorithms Based on Quick Sort. In G. Wang et al. (Eds.), *Rough Sets and Knowledge Technology* (LNAI 5009, pp. 72-79). New York: Springer.

Hu, K., Diao, L., Lu, Y., & Shi, C. (2003). A Heuristic Optimal Reduct Algorithm. In K. S. Leung et al. (Eds.), *Intelligent Data Engineering and Automated Learning* (LNCS 1983, pp. 89-99). New York: Springer.

Pawlak, Z. (1982). Rough Sets. *International Journal of Computer and Information Science, 11*, 341–356. doi:10.1007/BF01001956

Pawlak, Z. (19921991). *Rough Sets: Theoretical Aspects of Reasoning about Data* (Theory and Decision Library). Dordrecht, The Netherlands: Kluwer Academic Publisher.

Polkowski, L. (2002). *Rough sets: Mathematical Foundations*. Advances in Soft Computing.

Skowron, A., & Rauszer, C. M. (1992). The Discernibility Matrix and Functions in Information Systems . In Słowiński, R. (Ed.), *Intelligent Decision Support: Handbook of Application and Advances of the Rough Set Theory* (pp. 331–362). Dordrecht, The Netherlands: Kluwer Academic Publisher.

Ślęzak, D. (2000). Normalized Decision Functions and Measures for Inconsistent Decision Table Analysis. *Fundamenta Informaticae, 44*(3), 291–319.

Ślęzak, D. (2002). Approximate Entropy Reducts. *Fundamenta Informaticae, 53*(3-4), 365–390.

Wróblewski, J. (2001), Adaptive Methods of Object Classification. Doctoral thesis, Institute of Mathematics, Warsaw University, Poland.

Xu, J., & Sun, L. (2008). New Reduction Algorithm Based on Decision Power of Decision Table. In G. Wang et al. (Eds.), *Rough Sets and Knowledge Technology* (LNAI 5009, pp. 180-188). New York: Springer.

Xu, Z., Zhang, C., Zhang, S., Song, W., & Yang, B. (2007). Efficient Attribute Reduction Based on Discernibility Matrix. In J. T. Yao et al. (Eds.), *Rough Sets and Knowledge Technology* (LNAI 4481, pp.13-21). New York: Springer.

Zhang, J., Wang, J., Li, D., He, H., & Sun, J. (2003). A New Heuristic Reduct Algorithm Based on Rough Sets Theory. In G. Dong et al. (Eds.), *Advances in Web-Age Information Management* (LNSC 2762, pp. 247-253). New York: Springer.

Ziarko, W. (1993). Variable Precision Rough Set Model. *Journal of Computer and System Sciences, 46*, 39–59. doi:10.1016/0022-0000(93)90048-2

This work was previously published in volume 4, issue 2 of the International Journal of Cognitive Informatics and Natural Intelligence, edited by Yingxu Wang, pp. 48-60, copyright 2010 by IGI Publishing (an imprint of IGI Global).

Compilation of References

Abrantes, G., & Pereira, F. (1997). Mpeg-4 facial animation technology: survey, implementation, and results. *IEEE Transactions on Circuits and Systems for Video Technology, 9*(2), 290–305. doi:10.1109/76.752096

Accardo, P., & Pensiro, S. (2003). Neural network based system for early keratoconous detection from corneal topography. *Journal of Biomedical Informatics, 35*, 151–159. doi:10.1016/S1532-0464(02)00513-0

Acero, A., Deng, L., Kristjansson, T., & Zhang, J. (2000). HMM adaptation using vector Taylor series for noisy speech recognition. In. *Proceedings of ICSLP, 3*, 869–872.

Acharya, R. (2007). Automatic identification of anterior segment eye abnormality. In . *Proceedings of the ITBM-RBM, 28*, 35–41.

Ahn, H., & Picard, R. W. (2006). Affective cognitive learning and decision making: The role of emotions. In *Proceedings of the 18th European Meeting on Cybernetics and Systems Research*, Vienna, Austria (201-207).

Akers, S. B. (1978). Binary decision diagrams. *IEEE Transactions on Computers, 27*(6), 509–516. doi:10.1109/TC.1978.1675141

Akyldiz, I., Su, W., Sankarasubramaniam, Y., & Cayirci, E. (2002). A Survey on Sensor Networks. *IEEE Communications, 40*(8), 102–114. doi:10.1109/MCOM.2002.1024422

Al-Akaidi, M. (2004). *Fractal Speech Processing*. Cambridge, UK: Cambridge University Press. doi:10.1017/CBO9780511754548

Alani, H., Kim, S., Millard, D. E., Weal, M., Hall, W., & Lewis, P. H. (2003). Automatic Ontology-based Knowledge Extraction from Web Documents. *IEEE Intelligent Systems, 18*(1), 14–21. doi:10.1109/MIS.2003.1179189

Alpigini, J. J., Peters, J. F., Skowron, A., & Zhong, N. (2002). *Rough Sets and Current Trends in Computing* (LNAI 2475). Berlin: Springer Verlag.

Anahory, S., & Murray, D. (1997). *Data Warehousing in the Real World-A Practical Guide for Building Decision Support Systems*. Boston: Addison-Wesley.

Anderasen, T., Jensen, P. A., Nilsson, J. F., Paggio, P., Pederson, B. S., & Thomsen, H. E. (2004). Content-based text querying with ontological descriptors. *Data & Knowledge Engineering, 48*, 199–219. doi:10.1016/S0169-023X(03)00105-8

Ando, M., Sekine, S., & Ishizaki, S. (2003). *Automatic Extraction of Hyponyms from Newspaper Using Lexicon-syntactic Patterns* (IPSJ SIG Technical Report 2003-NL-157). Tokyo: Information Processing Society in Japan.

Antani, S., Kasturi, R., & Jain, R. (2002). A survey on the use of pattern recognition methods for abstraction, indexing and retrieval of images and video. *Pattern Recognition, 35*(4), 945–965. doi:10.1016/S0031-3203(01)00086-3

Atkinson, R. C., & Schiffrin, R. M. (1968). Human Memory: A Proposed System and its Control Processes. *Psychology of Learning and Motivation, 2*, 742–775.

Baader, F., & Hollunder, B. (1992). Embedding defaults into terminological knowledge representation formalisms. In *Proceedings of the 3rd International Conference on Principles of Knowledge Representation and Reasoning (KR-92)* (pp. 306-317). San Francisco, CA: Morgan Kaufmann.

Baader, F., Calvanese, D., McGuinness, D. L., Nardi, D., & Patel-Schneider, P. F. (Eds.). (2002). *The Description Logic Handbook*. Cambridge, UK: Cambridge University Press.

Baciu, G., Wang, Y., Yao, Y., Chan, K., Kinsner, W., & Zadeh, L. A. (Eds.). (2009). *Proceedings of the 8th IEEE International Conference on Cognitive Informatics (ICCI'09)*. Los Alamitos, CA: IEEE Computer Society Press.

Banerjee, M. (1997). Rough sets and 3-valued Lukasiewicz logic. *Fundamenta Informaticae, 31*, 213–220.

Banerjee, M., & Chakraborty, M. K. (1996). Rough sets through algebraic logic. *Fundamenta Informaticae, 28*(3-4), 211–221.

Bao, Y., Du, X., Deng, M., & Ishii, N. (2004). An Efficient Method for Computing All Reducts. *Transactions of the Japanese Society for Artificial Intelligence, 19*(3), 166–173. doi:10.1527/tjsai.19.166

Bargiela, A., & Pedrycz, W. (Eds.). (2009). *Human-Centric Information Processing Through Granular Modelling*. Berlin, Germany: Springer.

Barker, K., & Szpakowicz, S. (1998). Semi-automatic recognition of noun modifier relationships. In *Proceedings of the 36th Annual Meeting of the Association for Computational Linguistics, 17th International Conference on Computational Linguistics* (Vol. 1, pp. 96-102). ACL/Morgan Kaufmann Publishers.

Barnhill, D., et al. (2005). Measurement of the lateral distribution function of UHECR air showers with the Pierre Auger observatory. In *Proceedings of the 29th International Cosmic Ray Conference*, Pune, India (pp. 101-104).

Barot, R. B., & Lin, T. Y. (2008). Granular Computing on Covering from the aspects of Knowledge Theory. In *Proceedings of the IEEE NAFIPS 2008*.

Barthès, J.-P. A., & Ramos, M. (2002). Agents Assistants Personnels dans les Systèmes Multi-Agents Mixtes - Réalisation sur la Plate-forme OMAS. *Technique et Science Informatiques, 21*(4), 473–498.

Beeferman, D. (1998). Lexical discovery with an enriched semantic network. In *Proceedings of the ACL/COLING Workshop on Applications of WordNet in Natural Language Processing Systems* (pp. 135-141). Association of Computational Linguistics.

Beh, J., & Ko, H. (2003). A novel spectral subtraction scheme for robust speech recognition: spectral subtraction using spectral harmonics of speech. In *Proceedings of ICASSP* (pp. 648-651).

Bell, D. A., & Wang, H. (2000). A formalism for relevance and its application in feature subset selection. *Machine Learning, 41*(2), 175–195. doi:10.1023/A:1007612503587

Benson, S., & Yan, H. (2008). A Novel vessel segmentation algorithm for pathological retinal images based on the divergence of vector fields. *IEEE Transactions on Medical Imaging, 27*(2), 237–246. doi:10.1109/TMI.2007.909827

Bishop, C. M. (2006). *Pattern Recognition and Machine Learning* (2nd ed.). New York: Springer.

Blum, A., & Langley, P. (1997). Selection of relevant features and examples in machine learning. *Artificial Intelligence, 97*(1-2), 245–271. doi:10.1016/S0004-3702(97)00063-5

Bollig, B., Löbbing, M., & Wegener, I. (1995). Simulated Annealing to Improve Variable Orderings for OBDDs. In *Proceedings of the International Workshop on Logic Synthesis*.

Bollig, B., & Wegener, I. (2002). Improving the variable ordering of OBDDs is NPcomplete. *IEEE Transactions on Computers, 45*(9), 993–1002. doi:10.1109/12.537122

Bonikowski, Z., Bryniarski, E., & Wybraniec, U. (1998). Extensions and intentions in the rough set theory. *Information Sciences, 107*, 149–167. doi:10.1016/S0020-0255(97)10046-9

Bonnet, P., Gehrke, J., & Seshadri, P. (2000). Querying the physical world. *IEEE Pervasive Communication, 7*, 10–15. doi:10.1109/98.878531

Borgida, A., & Brachman, R. J. (2002). Conceptual Modeling with description logics . In Baader, F., Calvanese, D., McGuiness, D. L., Nardi, D., & Patel-Schneider, P. F. (Eds.), *The Description Logic Handbook* (pp. 359–381). Cambridge, UK: Cambridge University Press.

Brachman, R. J., & Levesque, H. J. (2004). *Knowledge representation and reasoning*. San Francisco: Morgan Kaufmann Publishers.

Brachman, R. J. (1979). On the epistemological status of semantic networks . In Findler, N. V. (Ed.), *Associative Networks: Representation and Use of Knowledge by Computers*. New York: Academic Press.

Briscoe, T., & Carroll, J. (1997). Automatic extraction of subcategorization from corpora. In *Proceedings of the 5th Conference on Applied Natural Language Processing* (pp. 356-363).

Bristow, G. (1986). *Electronic Speech Recognition*. New York: McGraw-Hill.

Bryant, R. (1986). Graph-Based Algorithms for Boolean Function Manipulation. *IEEE Transactions on Computers, 35*(8), 677–691. doi:10.1109/TC.1986.1676819

Cao, C., & Shi, Q. (2001). Acquiring Chinese Historical Knowledge from Encyclopedic Texts. In *Proceedings of the International Conference for Young Computer Scientists* (pp. 1194-1198). IEEE Computer Society Press.

Caraballo, A. S. (1999). Automatic construction of a hypernym-labeled noun hierarchy from text. In *Proceedings of 37ʰ Annual Meeting of the Association for Computational Linguistics* (pp. 120-126). Association for Computational Linguistics.

Cardie, C. (1993). Using Decision Trees to Improve Case-based Learning. In *Proceedings of Tenth International Conference on Machine Learning* (pp. 25-32).

Carpineto, C., & Romano, G. (2004). *Concept Data Analysis: Theory and Applications*. New York: John Wiley & Sons.

CC. (2007). *Cognitive Computing, A Multidisciplinary Synthesis of Neuroscience, Computer Science, Mathematics, Cognitive Neuroscience, and Information Theory*. Retrieved from http://wwwbisc.eecs.berkeley.edu/CognitiveComputing07/

Chaitin, G. (1987). *Algorithmic Information Theory*. Reading, MA: Addison-Wesley.

Chang, C.-H., Kayed, M., Girgis, M. R., & Shaalan, K. (2006). A Survey of Web Information Extraction System. *IEEE Transactions on Knowledge and Data Engineering, 18*(10), 1411–1428. doi:10.1109/TKDE.2006.152

Chen, P. J., Wang, G. Y., Yang, Y., & Zhou, J. (2006). Facial expression recognition based on rough set theory and SVM. In G. Y. Wang (Ed.), *First International Conference on Rough Sets and Knowledge Technology*, Chongqing (pp. 772-777). New York: Springer.

Chen, D., Zhang, W., Yeung, D., & Tsang, E. (2006). Rough approximations on a complete completely distributive lattice with applications to generalized rough sets. *Information Sciences, 176*, 1829–1848. doi:10.1016/j.ins.2005.05.009

Chen, J., Paliwal, K. K., & Nakamura, S. (2003). Cepstrum derived from differentiated power spectrum for robust speech recognition. *Speech Communication, 41*, 469–484. doi:10.1016/S0167-6393(03)00016-5

Chung, A. J., Deliganni, F., & Yang, Z. (2005). Extraction of visual features with eye tracking for saliency driven 2D/3D registration. *Image and Vision Computing, 23*, 999–1008. doi:10.1016/j.imavis.2005.07.003

Cilibrasi, R. L., & Vitanyi, P. (2007). The Google Similarity Distance. *IEEE Transactions on Knowledge and Data Engineering, 19*(3), 370–383. doi:10.1109/TKDE.2007.48

Clarke, E. M., Grumberg, O., & Long, D. E. (1994). Model checking and abstraction. *ACM Transactions on Programming Languages and Systems, 16*(5), 1512–1542. doi:10.1145/186025.186051

Clark, M. C., Hall, L. O., Goldgof, D. B., & Murtagh, F. R. (2004). Brain tumor segmentation using knowledge-based and fuzzy techniques. *Journal of Fuzzy and Fuzzy-Neuro Systems in Medicine, 8*, 57–68.

Codin, R., Missaoui, R., & Alaoui, H. (1995). Incremental Concept Formation Algorithms Based on Galois (Concept) Lattices. *Computational Intelligence, 11*(2), 246–267. doi:10.1111/j.1467-8640.1995.tb00031.x

Cody, W. F., Haas, L. M., Niblack, W., Arya, M., Carey, M. J., Fagin, R., et al. (1995). Querying multimedia data from multiple repositories by content: the Garlic project. In *Proceedings of the third IFIP WG2.6 working conference on Visual database systems 3* (VDB-3) (pp. 17 - 35). New York: Lausanne, Chapman & Hall.

Cohen, F. S., Huang, Z., & Yang, Z. (1995). Invariant matching and identification of curves using B-splines curve representation. *IEEE Transactions on Image Processing, 4*(1), 1–10. doi:10.1109/83.350818

Comer, S. (1993). On connections between information systems, rough sets and algebraic logic . In *Algebraic methods in logic and computer science* (pp. 117–124). Warszawa, Poland: Banach Center Publications.

Cootes, T. F., Edwards, G. J., & Taylor, C. J. (2001). Active appearance models. *IEEE Transactions on Pattern Analysis and Machine Intelligence, 23*(6), 681–685. doi:10.1109/34.927467

Cootes, T. F., Taylor, C. J., Cooper, D. H., & Graham, J. (1995). Active shape models-Their training and application. *Computer Vision and Image Understanding, 61*(1), 38–59. doi:10.1006/cviu.1995.1004

Costa, U. S., Déharbe, D., & Moreira, A. M. (2000). Variable ordering of BDDs with parallel genetic algorithms. In *Proceedings of the International Conference on Parallel and Distributed Processing Techniques and Applications.*

Dai, J. H. (2004). Structure of rough approximations based on molecular lattices. In *Proceedings of 4th International Conference on Rough Sets and Current Trends in Computing (RSCTC2004)* (LNAI 3066, pp. 69-77). Berlin: Springer Verlag.

Dai, J. H. (2005). Logic for rough sets with rough double Stone algebraic semantics. In *Proceedings of the 10th International Conference on Rough Sets, Fuzzy Sets, Data Mining, and Granular Computing (RSFDGrC 2005)* (LNAI 3641, pp. 141-148). Berlin: Springer Verlag.

Dai, J. H., Chen, W. D., & Pan, Y. H. (2005). Sequent calculus system for rough sets based on rough Stone algebras. In *Proceedings of the IEEE International Conference on Granular Computing (IEEE GrC2005)* (pp. 423-426). Washington, DC: IEEE Press.

Dai, J. H., Chen, W. D., & Pan, Y. H. (2006a). Rough sets and Brouwer-Zadeh lattices. In *Proceedings of First International Conference on Rough Sets and Knowledge Technology* (pp. 200-207). Berlin: Springer Verlag.

Dai, J. H., Lv, H. F., Chen, W. D., & Pan, Y. H. (2006b). Two kinds of rough algebras and Brouwer-Zadeh lattices. In *Proceedings of 5th International Conference on Rough Sets and Current Trends in Computing (RSCTC2006)* (pp. 99-106). Berlin: Springer Verlag.

Dai, J. H. (2007). Rough algebras and 3-valued Lukasiewicz algebras. *Chinese Journal of Computers, 30*(2), 161–167.

Dai, J. H. (2008). Rough 3-valued algebras. *Information Sciences, 179*(8), 1986–1996. doi:10.1016/j.ins.2007.11.011

DARPA. (2008). *Systems of Neuromorphic Adaptive Plastic Scalable Electronics* (Defense Sciences Office, DARPA-BAA 08-28). Alrington, VA: Author.

DARPA. (2009). *SyNAPSE Project*. Retrieved from http://www.fbo.gov/index?s=opportunity&mode=form &id= b7b66ad9c0d5a7df21d9488b107256ae&tab=co re&_cview=1&cck=1&au=&ck=

Dash, M., & Liu, H. (2003). Consistency-based Search in Feature Selection. *Artificial Intelligence, 151*, 155–176. doi:10.1016/S0004-3702(03)00079-1

Davis, R., Shrobe, H., & Szolovits, P. (1993). What is a Knowledge Representation? *AI Magazine, 14*(1), 17–33.

De Meo, P., Terracina, G., Quattrone, G., & Ursino, D. (2004). Extraction of synonymies, hyponymies, overlappings and homonymies from XML schemas at various "severity" levels. In *Proceedings of the International Conference on Database Engineering and Application Symposium* (pp. 389-394). IEEE Computer Society Press.

Dolan, W., Vanderwende, L., & Richardson, S. D. (1993). Automatically Deriving Structured Knowledge Bases from Online Dictionaries. In *Proceedings of the 1993 Pacific Association for Computational Linguistics* (pp. 5-14). Pacific Association for Computational Linguistics.

Draa, A., Meshoul, S., Talbi, H., & Batouche, M. (2010). A Quantum-Inspired Differential Evolution Algorithm for Solving the N-Queens Problem. *Int. Arab J. Inf. Technol., 7*(1), 21–27.

Drechsler, R., Becker, B., & Göckel, N. (1996). A Genetic Algorithm for Variable Ordering of OBDDs. In *Proceedings of the IEEE on Computers and Digital Techniques* (pp. 363-368).

Drechsler, R., Drechsler, N., & Slobodova, A. (1998). Fast exact minimization of BDDs. In *Proceedings of the 35th Design Automation Conference* (pp. 200-205).

Drechsler, R., & Becker, B. (1998). *Binary Decision Diagrams: Theory and Implementation*. Boston: Kluwer Academic Publisher.

Duan, H., Cheng, Y. M., Wang, Y. X., & Cai, S. H. (2004). Tracking facial feature points using Kanade-LucasTomasi Approach. *Journal of Computer-aided Design & . Computer Graphics, 16*(3), 279–283.

Dubois, D., & Prade, H. (1990). Rough Fuzzy Sets and Fuzzy Rough Sets. *International Journal of General Systems*, 191–209. doi:10.1080/03081079008935107

Dubois, D., & Prade, H. (1992). Putting Rough Sets and Fuzzy Sets Together . In Słowiński, R. (Ed.), *Intelligent Decision Support* (pp. 203–232). Dordrecht, The Netherlands: Kluwer.

Duentsch, I. (1997). A logic for rough sets. *Theoretical Computer Science*, *179*(1-2), 427–436. doi:10.1016/S0304-3975(96)00334-9

Du, X., & Li, M. (2006). A Survey of Ontology Learning Research. *Journal of Software*, *17*(9), 1837–1847. doi:10.1360/jos171837

Dvorak, V. F. (1975). Tropical cyclone intensity analysis and forecasting from satellite imagery. *Monthly Weather Review*, *103*, 420–430. doi:10.1175/1520-0493(1975)103<0420:TCIAAF>2.0.CO;2

Ekman, P., & Friesen, W. V. (1978). *Facial Action Coding System (FACS): manual*. Palo Alto, CA: Consulting Psychologist Press.

Enembreck, F., & Barthès, J.-P. A. (2003). Architecture d'un système de dialogue avec un agent assistant. In *Proceedings of the 15th Conference Francophone sur l'interaction Homme-Machine* (pp. 95-105). New York: ACM Publishing.

Fan, T. F., Liau, C. J., & Yao, Y. Y. (2002). On modal and fuzzy decision logics based on rough set theory. *Fundamenta Informaticae*, *52*(4), 325–344.

Fan, T. F., Liau, C. J., & Yao, Y. Y. (2002). On modal decision logics. *Communications of Institute of Information and Computing Machinery*, *5*(2), 21–26.

Feder, J. (2006). The Roland Maze project: School-based extensive air shower network. *Nucl. Phys. Proc.*, *151*(Suppl.), 430–433. doi:10.1016/j.nuclphysbps.2005.07.078

Fellbaum, C. (Ed.). (1998). *WordNet: An Electronic Lexical Database*. Cambridge, MA: Bradford Books.

Fensel, D., van Harmelen, F., Horrocks, I., McGuinness, D., & Patel-Schneider, P. F. (2001). OIL: An ontology infrastructure for the semantic web. *IEEE Intelligent Systems*, *16*, 38–45. doi:10.1109/5254.920598

Ferret, O., & Grau, B. (1997). An Aggregation Procedure for Building Episodic Memory. In *Proceedings of the 15th International Joint Conference on Artificial Intelligence*, Nagoya, Japan (pp. 280-285).

Fitting, M. C., & Mendelsohn, R. (1998). *First-order modal logic*. Dordrecht, The Netherlands: Kluwer.

Fleming, A. D. (2006). Automated microaneursym detection using local contrast normalization and local vessel detection. *IEEE Transactions on Medical Imaging*, *25*(9), 1223–1232. doi:10.1109/TMI.2006.879953

Flickner, M., Sawhney, H., Niblack, W., & Ashley, J. (1995). Query by image and video content: The QBIC system. *IEEE Computer Society Press*, *28*(9), 23–32.

Forsyth, R. (1990). *Zoo Data Set*. Retrieved May 15, 1990, from http://archive.ics.uci.edu/ml/datasets/Zoo

Freund, Y. (1995). Boosting a weak algorithm by majority. *Information and Computation*, *121*(2), 256–285. doi:10.1006/inco.1995.1136

Friedman, S. J., & Supowit, K. J. (1987). Finding the Optimal Variable Ordering for Binary Decision Diagrams Design. In *Proceedings of the Automation Conference* (pp. 348-356).

Fujii, H., Ootomo, G., & Hori, C. (1993). Interleaving based variable ordering methods for ordered binary decision diagrams. In *Proceedings of the International Conference on Computer-Aided Design* (pp. 38-41).

Fujita, M., Fujisawa, H., & Kawato, N. (1988). Evaluation and improvements of Boolean comparison method based on binary decision diagrams. In *Proceedings of the International Conference on Computer-Aided Design* (pp. 2-5).

Fujita, M., Matsunaga, Y., & Kakuda, T. (1991). On Variable Orderings of Binary Decision Diagrams for the Application of Multi-Level Logic Synthesis. In *Proceedings of the European Conference on Design Automation* (pp. 50-54).

Gache, N., Flandrin, P., & Garreau, D. (1991). Fractal dimension estimators for fractional Brownian motions. In *Proceedings of the IEEE International Conference Acoust, Speech, Signal Processing,* Toronto, ON. Washington, DC: IEEE.

Gales, M. J. F., & Young, S. J. (1995). Robust speech recognition in additive and convolutional noise using parallel model combination. *Computer Speech & Language*, *9*, 289–307. doi:10.1006/csla.1995.0014

Gales, M. J. F., & Young, S. J. (1996). Robust continuous speech recognition using parallel model combination. *IEEE Transactions on Speech and Audio Processing,* *4*(5), 352–359. doi:10.1109/89.536929

Ganter, B., & Wille, R. (1999). *Formal Concept Analysis.* Berlin: Springer.

Gdalyahu, Y., & Weinshall, D. (1999). Flexible syntactic matching of curves and its applications to automatic hierarchical classification of silhouettes. *IEEE Transactions on Pattern Analysis and Machine Intelligence,* *12*(2), 1312–1328. doi:10.1109/34.817410

Gehrke, M., & Walker, E. (1992). On the structure of rough sets. *Bulletin of the Polish Academy of Sciences: Mathematics,* *40*(3), 235–255.

Gerrans, P., & Kennett, J. (2006). Is cognitive penetrability the mark of the moral? *Philosophical Explorations,* *9*(1), 3–12. doi:10.1080/13869790500492284

Ginsber, M. (Ed.). (1987). *Readings in Nonmonotonic Reasoning.* San Francisco, CA: Morgan Kaufmann.

Gleason, J. B. (1997). *The Development of Language, Introduction to Descriptive Linguistics* (4th ed.). Boston: Allyn and Bacon.

Goertzel, B. (2006a). *Patterns, Hypergraphs and General Intelligence.* Paper presented at WCCI-06, Vancouver, BC, Canada.

Goertzel, B. (2006b). *The Hidden Pattern.* Boca Raton, FL: Brown Walker.

Goertzel, B. (2009a). *Cognitive Synergy: A Universal Principle of Feasible General Intelligence?* Paper presented at ICCI'09, Hong Kong.

Goertzel, B. (2009b). *OpenCogPrime: A Cognitive Synergy Based Architecture for Embodied General Intelligence.* Paper presented at ICCI-09, Hong Kong.

Goldberg, D. E. (1989). *Genetic algorithm in search, optimization and machine learning.* Reading, MA: Addison Wesley.

Gómez-Pérez, A., & Corcho, O. (2002). Ontology languages for the semantic web. *IEEE Intelligent Systems,* 54–60. doi:10.1109/5254.988453

Gong, X., & Wang, G. Y. (2008). A novel deformation framework for face modeling from a few control points. In G. Wang, et al. (Eds.), *RSKT 2008* (LNAI 5009, 434-441).

Gong, X., & Wang, G. Y. (2009). Based on the feature points of three-dimensional face variable model. *Journal of Software,* *20*(3), 724–733.

Greco, S., Inuiguchi, M., & Słowiński, R. (2003). Rough Sets and Gradual Decision Rules . In Wang, G., (Eds.), *Rough Sets, Fuzzy Sets, Data Mining, and Granular Computing* (pp. 156–164). Berlin: Springer Verlag. doi:10.1007/3-540-39205-X_20

Greco, S., Matarazzo, B., & Słowiński, R. (1999). The Use of Rough Sets and Fuzzy Sets in MCDM . In Gal, T., Stewart, T. J., & Hanne, T. (Eds.), *Multicriteria Decision Making: Advances in MCDM Models, Algorithms, Theory, and Applications.* Boston: Kluwer Academic Publishers.

Greco, S., Matarazzo, B., & Słowiński, R. (2001). Rough Set Theory for Multicriteria Decision Analysis. *European Journal of Operational Research,* *129*, 1–47. doi:10.1016/S0377-2217(00)00167-3

Griffith, D. G., & Greitzer, F. (2007). Neo-symbiosis: the next stage in the evolution of human information interaction. *International Journal of Cognitive Informatics and Natural Intelligence,* *1*(1), 39–52.

Grisé, M. L., & Gallupe, R. B. (1999). Information overload: Addressing the productivity paradox in face-to-face electronic meetings. *Journal of Management Information Systems,* *16*(3), 157–185.

Gruber, T. R. (1995). Toward principles for the design of ontologies used for knowledge sharing. *International Journal of Human-Computer Studies,* *43*, 907–928. doi:10.1006/ijhc.1995.1081

Guan, J. W., & Bell, D. A. (1998). Rough Computational Methods for Information Systems. *Artificial Intelligence,* *105*, 77–103. doi:10.1016/S0004-3702(98)00090-3

Guarino, N. (1994). The ontological level . In Casati, R., Smith, B., & White, G. (Eds.), *Philosophy and the Cognitive Science* (pp. 443–456). Vienna, Austria: Höder-Pichler-Tempsky.

Guarino, N. (1995). Formal ontology, conceptual analysis and knowledge representation. *International Journal of Human-Computer Studies,* *43*, 625–640. doi:10.1006/ijhc.1995.1066

Gusfield, D. (1997). *Algorithms on Strings, Trees and Sequences: Computer Science and Computational Biology.* Cambridge, UK: Cambridge University Press.

Guzzoni, D., Baur, C., & Cheyer, A. (2007). Modeling Human-Agent Interaction with Active Ontologies (Tech. Rep. SS-07-04). In *Proceedings of the AAAI Spring Symposium: Interaction Challenges for Intelligent Assistants*, Palo Alto, CA (Vol. 1, pp. 52-59). AAAI Press.

Haarlick, R. M. (1979). Statistical and structural approaches to texture. *Man and Cybernatics, 67*, 786–804.

Hachtel, G. D., & Somenzi, F. (2006). *Logic Synthesis and Verification Algorithms*. New York: Springer Verlag.

Hampton, J. A. (1997). *Psychological Representation of Concepts of Memory* (pp. 81–110). Hove, UK: Psychology Press.

Han, J. K., Hu, X. H., & Lin, T. Y. (2004). *Feature Subset Selection Based on Relative Dependency between Attributes* (pp. 176–185). Rough Sets and Current Trends in Computing.

Han, K. H., & Kim, J. H. (2004). Quantum-inspired Evolutionary Algorithms with a New Termination Criterion, Hε Gate, and Two Phase Scheme. *IEEE Transactions on Evolutionary Computation, 8*(2), 156–169. doi:10.1109/TEVC.2004.823467

Haralick, R. M. (1979). Statistical and structural approaches to texture. *Proceedings of the IEEE, 67*(5), 786–804. doi:10.1109/PROC.1979.11328

Harrison, J. (1989). Introduction to Fractals . In Devaney, R. (Ed.), *Chaos and Fractals: The Mathematics Behind the Computer Graphics* (Vol. 39, pp. 107–126). Providence, RI: American Mathematical Society.

Hawkins, J., & Blakeslee, S. (2004). *On Intelligence*. New York: Henry Holt and Company.

Haykin, S., & Kosko, B. (Eds.). (2001). *Intelligent Signal Processing*. Washington, DC: IEEE Press. doi:10.1109/9780470544976

Haykin, S., Principe, J. C., Sejnowski, T. J., & McWhirter, J. (Eds.). (2007). *New Directions in Statistical Signal Processing*. Cambridge, MA: MIT Press.

Hearst, A. M. (1992). Automatic acquisition of hyponyms from large text corpora. In *Proceedings of the 14th International Conference on Computational Linguistics* (pp. 539-545). Association of Computational Linguistics.

Hedar, A. H., Wang, J., & Fukushima, M. (2008). Tabu Search for Attribute Reduction in Rough Set Theory. *Soft Computing, 12*(9), 909–918. doi:10.1007/s00500-007-0260-1

Heisterkamp, D. R., & Bhattacharya, P. (1998). Matching 2D polygonal arcs by using a subgroup of the unit quaternions. *Computer Vision and Image Understanding, 69*(2), 246–249. doi:10.1006/cviu.1997.0566

Hemanth, J., Selvathi, D., & Anitha, J. (2010). *Artificial Intelligence Techniques for Medical Image Analysis: Basics, Methods, Applications*. Berlin: VDM-Verlag.

Hernando, J., & Nadeu, C. (1997). Linear prediction of the one-sided autocorrelation sequence for noisy speech recognition. *IEEE Transactions on Speech and Audio Processing, 5*(1), 80–84. doi:10.1109/89.554273

Hou, Z. Q., & Han, C. Z. (2006). A survey of visual tracking. *Acta Automatica Sinica, 32*(4), 603–617.

Hu, A. J., Dill, D. L., Drexler, A. G., & Yang, C. H. (1992). Higher-Level Specification and Verification With BDDs. In *Proceedings of the Workshop on Computer-Aided Verification* (pp.82-95).

Hu, F., Wang, G., & Feng, L. (2008). Fast Knowledge Reduction Algorithms Based on Quick Sort. In G. Wang et al. (Eds.), *Rough Sets and Knowledge Technology* (LNAI 5009, pp. 72-79). New York: Springer.

Hu, K., & Wang, Y. (2007). Autolearner: An Autonomic Machine Learning System Based on Concept Algebra. In *Proceedings of the 6th International Conference on Cognitive Informatics (ICCI'07)*, Lake Tahoe, CA (pp. 502-512).

Hu, K., Diao, L., Lu, Y., & Shi, C. (2003). A Heuristic Optimal Reduct Algorithm. In K. S. Leung et al. (Eds.), *Intelligent Data Engineering and Automated Learning* (LNCS 1983, pp. 89-99). New York: Springer.

Hu, X. H. (1995). Knowledge discovery in database: an attribute-oriented rough set approach. Unpublished doctoral dissertation, Regina.

Huang, T. S., & Naphade, M. R. (2000). MARS (Multimedia Analysis and Retrieval System): A test bed for video indexing, browsing, searching, filtering, and summarization. In *Proceedings of the IEEE International Workshop on Multimedia Data Storage, Retrieval, Integration and Applications*, Hong Kong, China (pp. 1-7).

Hu, M. K. (1962). Visual pattern recognition by moment invariants. *IEEE Transactions on Information Theory*, 8(2), 179–187. doi:10.1109/TIT.1962.1057692

Hung, W. N., & Song, X. (2001). BDD Variable Ordering By Scatter Search. In *Proceedings of the International Conference on Computer Design: VLSI in Computers & Processors* (pp. 368-373).

Hu, Q. H., Zhao, H., Xie, Z. X., & Yu, D. R. (2007). Consistency Based Attribute Reduction. In . *Proceedings of PAKDD, 2007*, 96–107.

Hurley, P. J. (1997). *A Concise Introduction to Logic* (6th ed.). Belmony, CA: Wadsworth.

Hussein, A., & Thomas, G. D. (1994). Learning Boolean Concepts in the Presence of Many Irrelevant Features. *Artificial Intelligence*, 69(1-2), 279–305. doi:10.1016/0004-3702(94)90084-1

Huttenlocher, D. P., Klanderman, G. A., & Rucklidge, W. J. (1993). Comparing images using the Hausdorff distance. *IEEE Transactions on Pattern Analysis and Machine Intelligence*, 15(9), 850–863. doi:10.1109/34.232073

IBM. (2001). *Autonomic Computing Manifesto*. Retrieved from http://www.research.ibm.com/autonomic/

Inuiguchi, M. (2004). Generalizations of Rough Sets and Rule Extraction . In Peters, J. F., Skowron, A., Grzymała-Busse, J. W., Kostek, B., Świniarski, R., & Szczuka, M. (Eds.), *Transactions on Rough Sets I* (pp. 96–119). Berlin: Springer Verlag.

Inuiguchi, M., Hirano, S., & Tsumoto, S. (2003a). *Rough Set Theory and Granular Computing*. Berlin: Springer Verlag.

Inuiguchi, M., & Tanino, T. (2003b). Two Directions toward Generalization of Rough Sets . In Inuiguchi, M., Hirano, S., & Tsumoto, S. (Eds.), *Rough Set Theory and Granular Computing* (pp. 47–57). Berlin: Springer Verlag.

Inuiguchi, M., & Tanino, T. (2003c). New Fuzzy Rough Sets Based on Certainty Qualification . In Pal, K., Polkowski, L., & Skowron, A. (Eds.), *Rough-Neural Computing* (pp. 278–296). Berlin: Springer Verlag.

Ishiura, N., Sawada, H., & Yajima, S. (1991). Minimization of binary decision diagrams based on exchange of variables. In *Proceedings of the International Conference on Computer-Aided Design* (pp. 472-475).

Iwinski, T. B. (1987). Algebraic approach to rough sets. *Bulletin of the Polish Academy of Sciences: Mathematics*, 35(9-10), 673–683.

Jaeger, G. (2006). *Quantum Information: An Overview*. Berlin: Springer.

Jahn, R., Dunne, B. J., Bradish, G., Dobyns, Y., Lettieri, A., & Nelson, R. (2000). Mind/Machine Interaction Consortium: PortREG Replication Experiments. *Journal of Scientific Exploration*, 14(4), 499–555.

James, F., & Roos, M. (1975). MINUIT: A System for Function Minimization and Analysis of the Parameter Errors and Correlations. *Computer Physics Communications*, 10, 343–367. doi:10.1016/0010-4655(75)90039-9

Jarvinen, J. (2002). On the structure of rough approximations. In *Proceedings of 3rd International Conference on Rough Sets and Current Trends in Computing (RSCTC2002)* (LNAI 2475, pp. 123-130). Berlin: Springer Verlag.

Jelink, H. F., et al. (2005). Classification of pathology in diabetic eye diseases. In *Proceedings of the ARPS workshop on digital image computing* (pp. 9-13).

Jelonek, J., Krawiec, K., & Slowinski, R. (1995). Rough set reduction of attributes and their domains for neural networks. *Computational Intelligence*, 11, 339–347. doi:10.1111/j.1467-8640.1995.tb00036.x

Jensen, R., & Shen, Q. (2004). Semantics-preserving dimensionality reduction: rough and fuzzy-rough-based approaches. *IEEE Transactions on Knowledge and Data Engineering*, 16(12), 1457–1471. doi:10.1109/TKDE.2004.96

Jiao, B., Son, S. H., & Stankovic, J. A. (2005). *Gem: Generic event service middleware for wireless sensor networks*. Paper presented at the Second International Workshop on Networked Sensing Systems (INSS05).

JUNG. (2007). *Java Universal Network/Graph Framework*. Retrieved from http://jung.sourceforge.net/

Karlof, C., & Wagner, D. (2003). Secure Routing in Wireless Sensor Networks: Attacks and Countermeasures. *Ad Hoc Networks*, 1(2-3), 293–315. doi:10.1016/S1570-8705(03)00008-8

Kass, M., Witkin, A., & Terzopoulos, D. (1987). Snakes: Active contour models. In *Proceedings of the First International Conference on Computer Vision*, London (pp. 259-268).

Kawahara, D., & Kurohashi, S. (2006). Case frame compilation from the web using high-performance computing. In *Proceedings of the 5th International Conference on Language Resources and Evaluation (LREC2006)* (pp. 1344-1347).

Kay, S. (1988). *Modern Spectral Analysis*. Upper Saddle River, NJ: Prentice Hall.

Kay, S. M. (1979). The effects of noise on the autoregressive spectral estimator. *IEEE Transactions on Acoustics, Speech, and Signal Processing, 27*(5), 478–485. doi:10.1109/TASSP.1979.1163275

Kelley, P. M., Cannon, T. M., & Hush, D. R. (1995). Query by example: The CANDID approach. *SPIE Storage and Retrieval for Image and Video Databases II, 2420*, 238–248.

Kim, D. Y., Un, C. K., & Kim, N. S. (1998). Speech recognition in noisy environments using first-order vector Taylor series. *Speech Communication, 24*(1), 39–49. doi:10.1016/S0167-6393(97)00061-7

Kinsner, W. (1994, June). *Batch and real-time computation of a fractal dimension based on variance of a time series* (Tech. Rep. No. DEL94-6). Winnipeg, MB: University of Manitoba, Dept. Electrical & Computer Engineering.

Kinsner, W. (1994, May). *Fractal dimensions: Morphological, entropy, spectra, and variance classes* (Tech. Rep. No. DEL94-4). Winnipeg, MB: University of Manitoba, Dept. Electrical & Computer Engineering.

Kinsner, W., & Grieder, W. (2008). Speech segmentation using multifractal measures and amplification of signal features. In *Proceedings of the IEEE 7th Intern. Conf. Cognitive Informatics (ICCI08)*, Palo Alto, CA (pp. 351-357).

Kinsner, W. (2007). Towards cognitive machines: Multiscale measures and analysis. *International Journal of Cognitive Informatics and Natural Intelligence, 1*, 28–38.

Kinsner, W. (2007, April). Is entropy suitable to characterize data and signals for cognitive informatics? *International Journal of Cognitive Informatics and Natural Intelligence, 1*(2), 34–57.

Kinsner, W. (2007, January). Towards Cognitive Machines: Multiscale Measures and Analysis. *International Journal of Cognitive Informatics and Natural Intelligence, 1*(1), 28–38.

Kinsner, W. (2007, October). A unified approach to fractal dimensions. *International Journal of Cognitive Informatics and Natural Intelligence, 1*(4), 26–46.

Kinsner, W., Cheung, V., Cannons, K., Pear, J., & Martin, T. (2006). Signal classification through multifractal analysis and complex domain neural networks. *IEEE Trans. Systems, Man, and Cybernetics . Part C, 36*(2), 196–203.

Kipp, M. (2001). Anvil – a generic annotation tool for multimodal dialogue. In *Proceedings of the 7th European Conference on Speech Communication and Technology (Eurospeech)* (pp. 1367-1370).

Kitagawa, G., & Gersh, W. (1984). A smoothness priors-state space modeling of time series with trend and seasonality. *Journal of the American Statistical Association, 79*, 378–389. doi:10.2307/2288279

Klages, H. O. (1997). The KASCADE Experiment. *Nucl. Phys. Proc., 52B*(Suppl.), 92–102. doi:10.1016/S0920-5632(96)00852-3

Kohonen, T. (1988, March 11-22). The neural phonetic typewriter. *Computer*.

Koide, S., & Yamauchi, S. (1999, September). Interface Agent for Process Plant Operation towards the Next Generation Interface. In *Proceedings of the IEEE/ASME International Conference on Advanced Intelligent Mechatronics*, Atlanta, GA (pp.197-202).

Koller, D., & Sahami, M. (1996). Towards Optimal Feature Selection. In *Proceedings of the Thirteenth International Conference on Machine Learning*. San Francisco, CA: Morgan Kaufumann.

Kolodner, J. L. (1993). *Case-Based Reasoning*. San Mateo, CA: Morgan Kaufmann.

Kondo, M. (2005). *Algebraic approach to generalized rough sets (. LNAI, 3641*, 132–140.

Kondo, M. (2006). On the structure of generalized rough sets. *Information Sciences, 176*, 589–600. doi:10.1016/j.ins.2005.01.001

Kononenko, I. (1994). Estimating Attributes: Analysis and Extension of RELIEF. In *Proceedings of the Sixth European Conf. Machine Learning* (pp. 171-182).

Lakos, C. (2001). Object Oriented Modeling with Object Petri Nets. In G. Agha, F. D. Cindio, & G. Rozenberg (Eds.), *Concurrent Object-Oriented Programming and Petri Nets* (LNCS 2001, pp. 1-37). Berlin: Springer Verlag.

Larish, J. (1995). Kodak's still picture exchange for print and film use. *Advanced Imaging (Woodbury, N.Y.), 10*, 38–39.

Lashin, E. F., Kozae, A. M., Khadra, A. A., & Medhat, T. (2005). Rough set theory for topological spaces. *International Journal of Approximate Reasoning, 40*, 35–43. doi:10.1016/j.ijar.2004.11.007

Lashkari, Y., Metral, M., & Maes, P. (1994, August). Collaborative Interface Agents. In *Proceedings of the 12th National Conference on Artificial Intelligence,* Seattle, WA (pp. 1-6).

Layeb, A., & Saidouni, D. E. (2008). A New Quantum Evolutionary Local Search Algorithm for Max 3-SAT Problem. In *Proceedings of the 3rd International Workshop on Hybrid Artificial Intelligence Systems* (Vol. 5271, pp. 172-179).

Layeb, A., Meshoul, S., & Batouche, M. (2006). Multiple Sequence Alignment by Quantum Genetic Algorithm. In *Proceedings of the 7th International Workshop on Parallel and Distributed Scientific and Engineering Computing of the 20th IPDPS* (pp. 1-8).

Layeb, A., & Saidouni, D. E. (2007). Quantum Genetic Algorithm for Binary Decision Diagram Ordering Problem. In . *Proceedings of the International Journal of Computer Science and Network Security, 7*(9), 130–135.

Lee, C. H., Soong, F. K., & Paliwal, K. K. (1996). *Automatic speech and speaker recognition.* Dordrecht, The Netherlands: Kluwer Academic Publishers.

Lerman, K., & Galstyan, A. (2003, July). Agent Memory and Adaptation in Multi-Agent Systems. In *Proceedings of the 2nd International Joint Conference on Autonomous Agents and Multi-Agent Systems,* Melbourne, Australia (pp.797-803).

Levis, P., & Lee, N. (n.d.). *TOSSIM: A Simulator for TinyOS Networks.* Retrieved from http://www.eecs.berkeley.edu/~pal/pubs/nido.pdf

Levis, P., Gay, D., & Culler, D. (2005, May). Active Sensor Networks. In *Proceedings of the 2nd Symposium on Networked Systems Design & Implementation* (USENIX) (pp. 343-356).

Lewis, F. L. (2004). Wireless Sensor Networks . In Cook, D. J., & Das, S. K. (Eds.), *Smart Environments: Technologies, Protocols, and Applications.* New York: John Wiley.

Li, X., Kim, Y. J., Govindan, R., & Hong, W. (2002). Multi-dimensional range queries in sensor networks. In *Proceedings of the ACM Conference on Embedded Networked Sensor Systems (SenSys '03)* (pp. 63-73).

Liau, C. J. (2000). An overview of rough set semantics for modal and quantifier logics. *International Journal of Uncertainty, Fuzziness and Knowledge-based Systems, 8*(1), 93–118. doi:10.1016/S0218-4885(00)00007-1

Lieberman, H. (1995, August). Letizia: An Agent That Assists Web Browsing. In *Proceedings of the 14th International Joint Conference on Artificial Intelligence,* Montreal, QB, Canada (pp. 924-929).

Lieberman, H. (1997, March). Autonomous Interface Agents. In *Proceedings of the ACM Conference on Computers and Human Interface,* Atlanta, GA (pp. 67-73).

Lin, T. T. (1990). Relational Data Models and Category Theory (Abstract). In *Proceedings of the ACM Conference on Computer Science 1990* (p. 424).

Lin, T. Y. (1989). Neighborhood Systems and Approximation in Database and Knowledge Base Systems. In *Proceedings of the Fourth International Symposium on Methodologies of Intelligent Systems* (pp. 75-86).

Lin, T. Y. (1989a, December 4-8). Chinese Wall Security Policy: An Aggressive Model. In *Proceedings of the Fifth Aerospace Computer Security Application Conference* (pp. 286-293).

Lin, T. Y. (1989a, October 12-15). Neighborhood Systems and Approximation in Database and Knowledge Base Systems. In *Proceedings of the Fourth International Symposium on Methodologies of Intelligent Systems* (pp. 75-86).

Lin, T. Y. (1989b, December 4-8). Chinese Wall Security Policy-An Aggressive Model. In *Proceedings of the Fifth Aerospace Computer Security Application Conference* (pp. 286-293).

Lin, T. Y. (1989b, October 12-15). Neighborhood Systems and Approximation in Database and Knowledge Base Systems. In *Proceedings of the Fourth International Symposium on Methodologies of Intelligent Systems* (pp. 75-86).

Lin, T. Y. (1992). Topological and Fuzzy Rough Sets. In R. Słowiński (Ed.), *Intelligent Decision Support: Handbook of Applications and Advances of the Rough Sets theory* (287-304). Dordrecht, The Netherlands: Kluwer Academic Publishers.

Lin, T. Y. (2009a). Granular Computing: Practices, Theories, and Future Directions. *Encyclopedia of Complexity and Systems Science 2009* (pp. 4339-4355).

Lin, T. Y., & Yin, P. (2004). Heuristically Fast Finding of the Shortest Reducts. *Rough Sets and Current Trends in Computing*, 465-470.

Lin, T. Y., Huang, K. J., Liu, Q., & Chen, W. (1990). Rough sets, neighborhood systems and approximation. In *Proceedings of the Fifth International Symposium on Methodologies of Intelligent Systems*, Knoxville, Tennessee (pp. 130-141).

Lin, T. Y., Yao, Y. Y., & Zadeh, L. A. (Eds.). (2002). *Data Mining, Rough Sets and Granular Computing*. Heidelberg, Germany: Physica-Verlag.

Lind-Nielsen, J. (1999). *BuDDy - A Binary Decision Diagram Package* (Tech. Rep. No. 1999-028). Denmark: Institute of Information Technology, Technical University.

Lin, T. Y. (1992). Topological and fuzzy rough sets . In Slowinski, R. (Ed.), *Intelligent Decision support: Hand book of Applications and Advances of rough set theory* (pp. 287–304). London: Kluwer Academic Publishers.

Lin, T. Y. (1997). Neighborhood Systems-A Qualitative Theory for Fuzzy and Rough Sets . In Wang, P. (Ed.), *Advances in Machine Intelligence and Soft Computing* (Vol. 4, pp. 132–155). Durham, NC: Duke University.

Lin, T. Y. (1998a). Granular Computing on Binary Relations I: Data Mining and Neighborhood Systems . In Skowron, A., & Polkowski, L. (Eds.), *Rough Sets In Knowledge Discovery* (pp. 107–121). Berlin: Physica Verlag.

Lin, T. Y. (1998b). Granular Computing on Binary Relations II: Rough Set Representations and Belief Functions. In Skowron, A., & Polkowski, L. (Eds.), *Rough Sets In Knowledge Discovery* (pp. 121–140). Berlin: Physica Verlag.

Lin, T. Y. (2006a). A Roadmap from Rough Set Theory to Granular Computing. In . *Proceedings of the RSKT, 2006*, 33–41.

Lin, T. Y. (2006b). Granular Computing on Partitions, Covering and Neighborhood system. *Journal of Nanchan Institute of Technology*, 25(2), 1–7.

Lin, T. Y. (2009b). Granular computing I: the concept of granulation and its formal model. *Int. J. Granular Computing . Rough Sets and Intelligent Systems*, 1(1), 21–42. doi:10.1504/IJGCRSIS.2009.026723

Lin, T. Y., & Liu, Q. (1994). Rough approximate operators-Axiomatic Rough Set Theory . In Ziarko, W. P. (Ed.), *Rough sets, fuzzy sets and knowledge Discovery* (pp. 256–260). London: Springer Verlag.

Lin, T. Y., & Liu, Q. (1996). First-order rough logic I: approximate reasoning via rough sets. *Fundamenta Informaticae*, 27(2-3), 137–144.

Liu, L., Cao, C., Wang, H., & Chen, W. (2006). A Method of Hyponym Acquisition Based on "isa" Pattern. *Journal of Computer Science*, 146-151.

Liu, G. L. (2006). The axiomatization of the rough set upper approximation operations. *Fundamenta Informaticae*, 69, 331–342.

Liu, G. L. (2008). Generalized rough sets over fuzzy lattices. *Information Sciences*, 178, 1651–1662. doi:10.1016/j.ins.2007.11.010

Liu, G. L., & Zhu, W. (2008). The algebraic structures of generalized rough set theory. *Information Sciences*, 178(21), 4105–4113. doi:10.1016/j.ins.2008.06.021

Liu, H., & Singh, P. (2004). ConceptNet - A Practical Commonsense Reasoning Toolkit. *BT Technology Journal*, 22(4), 211–225. doi:10.1023/B:BTTJ.0000047600.45421.6d

Liu, L., Cao, C., & Wang, H. (2005). Acquiring Hyponymy Relations from Large Chinese Corpus. *WSEAS Transactions on Business and Economics*, 2(4), 211–218.

Liu, Y., Xiong, R., & Chu, J. (2009). Quick Hash based Attribute Reduction. *Chinese Journal of Computers, 32*(8), 1493–1499.

Lopez de Mantara, R., McSherry, D., Bridge, D., Leake, D., Smyth, B., & Craw, S. (2006). Retrieval, reuse, revision and retention in case-based reasoning. *The Knowledge Engineering Review, 20*(3), 215–240. doi:10.1017/S0269888906000646

Lucas, B., & Kanade, T. (1981). An iterative image registration technique with an application to stereo vision. In P. J. Hayes (Ed.), *Proceedings of the 7th Int'l Joint Conf. on Artificial Intelligence*, Vancouver, Canada (pp. 674-679). San Francisco: Morgan Kaufmann Publishers.

MacQueen, J. (1967). Some Methods for classification and Analysis of Multivariate Observations. In *Proceedings of the 5th Berkeley Symposium on Mathematical Statistics and Probability* (pp. 281-297). Berkeley, CA: University of California Press.

Madden, S., Franklin, M. J., Hellerstein, J. M., & Hong, W. (2003). The design of an acquisitional query processor for sensor networks. In *Proceedings of the ACM SIGMOD Conference (SIGMOD2003)* (pp. 491-502).

Madhyastha, H. V., Balakrishnan, N., & Ramakrishnan, K. R. (2003). *Event Information Extraction Using Link Grammar*. Paper presented at the 13th International Workshop on Research Issues in Data Engineering: Multi-lingual Information Management (RIDE'03).

Maekawa, T., Yanagisawa, Y., & Okadome, T. (2007). Towards environment generated media: object-participation-type weblog in home sensor network. In *Proceedings of the 16th International Conference on World Wide Web (WWW2008)* (pp. 1267-1268).

Maes, P., & Kozierok, R. (1993, July). Learning Interface Agents. In *Proceedings of the 11th National Conference on Artificial Intelligence*, Washington, DC (pp. 459-465).

Maes, P. (1994). Agents that Reduce Work and Information Overload. *Communications of the ACM, 37*(7), 30–40. doi:10.1145/176789.176792

Ma, L., & Tsai, J. J. P. (2008). Formal Modeling and Analysis of Secure Mobile Agent Systems. *IEEE Transactions on System, Man, and Cybernetics . Part A, 38*(1), 180–196.

Malik, S., Wang, A. R., Brayton, R. K., & Sangiovanni-Vincentelli, A. (1988). Logic Verification using Binary Decision Diagrams in a Logic Synthesis Environment. In *Proceedings of the International Conference on Computer-Aided Design* (pp. 6-9).

Mallat, S. (1998). *A Wavelet Tour of Signal Processing*. San Diego, CA: Academic.

Mandelbrot, B. B. (2002). *Gaussian Self-Similarity and Fractals: Globality, The earth, 1/f noise, and R/S*. New York: Springer Verlag.

Mansour, D., & Jaung, B. H. (1989b). The short-time modified coherence and noisy speech recognition. *IEEE Trans. Acoustics and signal processing, 37*(6), 795-804.

Mansour, D., & Jaung, B. H. (1989a). A family of distortion measures based upon projection operation for robust speech recognition. *IEEE Transactions on Speech and Audio Processing, 37*(11), 1659–1671.

Martucci, M. (1995). Digital still marketing at PressLink. *Advanced Imaging (Woodbury, N.Y.), 10*, 34–36.

Masulli, F., & Petrosino, A. (2006). Advances in fuzzy sets and rough sets. *International Journal of Approximate Reasoning, 41*, 75–76. doi:10.1016/j.ijar.2005.06.010

Matlin, M. W. (1998). *Cognition* (4th ed.). New York: Harcourt Brace College Pub.

McGuinness, D. (2002). Ontologies come of age . In Fensel, D., (Eds.), *The Semantic Web: Why, What, and How*. Cambridge, MA: MIT Press.

McMillan, K. L. (1992). *Symbolic Model Checking: An Approach to the State Explosion Problem*. Unpublished doctoral dissertation, Carnegie-Mellon university, School of Computer Science, Pittsburgh, PA.

Medin, D. L., & Shoben, E. J. (1988). Context and Structure in Conceptual Combination. *Cognitive Psychology, 20*, 158–190. doi:10.1016/0010-0285(88)90018-7

Meinel, C., & Slobodova, A. (1997). Speeding up variable ordering of OBDDs. In *Proceedings of the International Conference on Computer-Aided Design* (pp. 338-343).

Middleton, S. E. (2002). *Interface Agent: A review of the field* (Tech. Rep. ECSTR-IAM01-001). Southampton, UK: School of Electronics and Computer Science, University of Southampton.

Miller, G. A., Beckwith, R., Felbaum, C., Gross, D., & Miller, K. J. (1990). Introduction to WordNet: An On-line Lexical Database. *International Journal of Lexicography, 3*(4), 235–244. doi:10.1093/ijl/3.4.235

Minsky, M. (2006). *The Emotion Machine: Commonsense Thinking, Artificial Intelligence, and the Future of the Human Mind*. New York: Simon & Schuster.

Mitchell, T., Caruana, R., Freitag, D., McDermott, J., & Zabowski, D. (1994). Experience with a Learning Personal Assistant. *Communications of the ACM, 37*(7), 81–91. doi:10.1145/176789.176798

Modi, P. J., Veloso, M., Smith, S. F., & Oh, J. (2004). *CMRadar: A Personal Assistant Agent for Calendar Management*. In Proc. of the 6th International Workshop on Agent-Oriented Information Systems, pp. 134-148, Riga, Latvia, June, 2004.

Moeslund, T. B., & Granum, E. (2001). A survey of computer vision-based human motion capture. *Computer Vision and Image Understanding, 81*(3), 231–268. doi:10.1006/cviu.2000.0897

Montoro, G., Alaman, X., & Haya, P. A. (2004). A plug and play spoken dialogue interface for smart environments. In *CICLing (*LNCS 2945, pp. 360-370).

Moreno, P. J. (1996). *Speech recognition in noisy environment*. Unpublished doctoral dissertation, Carnegie-Mellon University, Pittsburgh, PA.

Moreno, P. J., Raj, B., & Stern, R. M. (1996). A vector Taylor series approach for environment independent speech recognition. In *Proceedings of ICASSP* (pp. 733-736).

Morris, R., Tarassenko, L., & Kenward, M. (Eds.). (2006). *Cognitive Systems: Information Processing Meets Brain Science*. New York: Elsevier.

Murata, T. (1989). Petri Nets: Properties, Analysis, and Applications. In *Proceedings of the IEEE* (pp. 541-580).

Murphy, G. L. (1993). Theories and Concept Formation . In Mechelen, I. V., (Eds.), *Categories and Concepts, Theoretical Views and Inductive Data Analysis* (pp. 173–200). New York: Academic Press.

Na, S. H., Kang, I. S., Roh, J. E., & Lee, J. H. (2005). An Empirical Study of Query Expansion and Cluster-Based Retrieval in Language Modeling Approach. In *Information Retrieval Technology* (LNCS 3689, pp. 274-287).

Negroponte, N. (1997). Agents: From Direct Manipulation to Delegation. In J. M. Bradshaw (Ed.), *Software Agents* (pp. 57-66). Cambridge, MA: MIT Press.

Nelson, R. (2000, July 2-7). *Subtle Energies and Uncharted Realms of the Mind*. Paper presented at the Esalen Conference.

Nguyen, A. (2007). *An Agent-Based Approach to Dialogue Management in Personal Assistants*. Unpublished PhD thesis, School of Computer Science and Engineering, University of New South Wales, Sydney, Australia.

Nielsen, M. A., & Chuang, I. (2000). *Quantum Computation and Quantum Information*. Cambridge, UK: Cambridge University Press.

Niemeijer, M. (2006). Image structure clustering for image quality verification of color retinal images in diabetic retinopathy screening. *Medical Image Analysis, 10*, 888–898. doi:10.1016/j.media.2006.09.006

Niemeijer, M. (2007). Automated detection and differentiation of exudates in digital color fundus photographs for DR diagnosis. *Investigative Ophthalmology & Visual Science, 48*(5), 2260–2267. doi:10.1167/iovs.06-0996

Noble, J. A. (1988). Finding corners. *Image and Vision Computing, 6*(2), 121–128. doi:10.1016/0262-8856(88)90007-8

Noma, H., Ohmura, A., Kuwahara, N., & Kogure, K. (2004). Wearable sensors for auto-event-recording on medical nursing – user study of ergonomic design. In *Proceedings of the 8th IEEE Intl. Symposium on Wearable Computers (ISWC'04)* (pp. 8-15).

Okadome, T. (2006). Event representation for sensor data grounding. *International Journal of Computer Science and Network Security, 6*, 187–193.

Oppenheiem, C., Moris, A., Mcknight, C., & Lowley, S. (2000). The evaluation of www search engines. *The Journal of Documentation, 56*, 190–211. doi:10.1108/00220410010803810

Osareh, A. (2002). Comparative exudate classification using support vector machine and neural networks. In . *Proceedings of MICCAI, 2489*, 413–420.

Osareh, A. (2003). Automated identification of diabetic retinal exudates in digital colour images. *The British Journal of Ophthalmology, 87*, 1220–1223. doi:10.1136/bjo.87.10.1220

Padmanabhan, M. (2000). Spectral peak tracking and its use in speech recognition. In *Proceedings of the ICSLP.*

Pagliani, P. (1996). Rough sets and Nelson algebras. *Fundamenta Informaticae, 27*(2-3), 205–219.

Palaniappan, R., & Eswaran, C. (2009). Using genetic algorithm to select the presentation order of training patterns that improves ARTMAP classification performance. *Applied Soft Computing, 9*, 100–106. doi:10.1016/j.asoc.2008.03.003

Panda, S., & Somenzi, F. (1995). Who are the variables in your neighborhood. *In Proceedings of the International Conference on Computer-Aided Design* (pp. 74-77).

Paraiso, E. C., & Barthµes, J-P. A. (2004). Une interface conversationnelle pour les agents assistants appliqués à des activités professionnelles. In *Proceedings of Actes IHM 04,* Namur, Belgium (pp. 243-246). New York: ACM Publishing.

Parsi, B., Margalit, A., & Rosenfeld, A. (1991). Matching general polygonal arcs. *Computer Vision . Graphics and Image Processing: Image Understanding, 53*(2), 227–234.

Parsons, T. (1987). *Voice and Speech Processing.* New York: McGraw-Hill.

Parsons, T. (2006). *The traditional square of opposition.* Stanford Encyclopedia of Philosophy.

Paul, V., & Michael, J. (2001). Rapid Object Detection using a Boosted Cascade of Simple Features. In *Computer Vision and Pattern Recognition* (pp. 511-518).

Pawlak, Z. (1982). Rough sets. *International Journal of Computer and Information Sciences, 11*, 341–356. doi:10.1007/BF01001956

Pawlak, Z. (1987). Rough Logic. *Bulletin of the Polish Academy of Science . Technical Science, 5-6*, 253–258.

Pawlak, Z. (1991). *Rough sets: theoretical aspects and reasoning about data.* Boston: Kluwer Academic Publishers.

Pedrycz, W., Skowron, A., & Kreinovich, V. (Eds.). (2008). *Handbook of Granular Computing.* Chichester, UK: Wiley.

Pei, D. (2005). A generalized model of fuzzy rough sets. *International Journal of General Systems, 34*(5), 603–613. doi:10.1080/03081070500096010

Peitgen, H.-O., Jürgens, H., & Saupe, D. (2004). *Chaos and Fractals* (2nd ed.). New York: Springer Verlag.

Pentland, A., Picard, R. W., & Sclaroff, S. (1996). Photobook: tools for content-based manipulation of image databases. *International Journal of Computer Vision, 18*(3), 233–254. doi:10.1007/BF00123143

Perkowitz, M., Philipose, M., Fishkin, K. P., & Patterson, D. (2004). Mining models of human activities from the web. In *Proceedings of the 13th International Conference on World Wide Web (WWW2004)* (pp. 573-582).

Perrig, A., Szewczyk, R., Wen, V., Culler, D., & Tygar, J. D. (2002). SPINS: security protocols for sensor networks. *Wireless Networks, 8*, 521–534. doi:10.1023/A:1016598314198

Peterson, R., Doom, T., & Raymer, M. (2005). GA facilitated KNN classifier optimization with varying similarity measures. In *Proceedings of Conference on Genetic and evolutionary computation* (pp. 1549-1550).

Philipose, M., Fishkin, K. P., Perkowitz, M., Patterson, D. J., Fox, D., & Kautz, H. (2004). Inferring activities from interactions with objects. *IEEE Pervasive Computing / IEEE Computer Society [and] IEEE Communications Society, 3*, 50–57. doi:10.1109/MPRV.2004.7

Picard, R. W. (2003). Affective Computing: Challenges. *International Journal of Human-Computer Studies, 59*(1), 55–64. doi:10.1016/S1071-5819(03)00052-1

Pirolli, P. (2009). Powers of 10: Modeling Complex Information-Seeking Systems at Multiple Scales. *IEEE Computer, 42*(3), 33–40.

Polkowski, L. (1992). On convergence on rough sets . In Slowinski, R. (Ed.), *Decision Support by Experience - Application of the Rough Sets Theory* (pp. 305–309). London: Kluwer Academic Publishers.

Polkowski, L. (2002). *Rough sets: Mathematical Foundations.* Advances in Soft Computing.

Polkowski, L., & Skowron, A. (Eds.). (1998). *Rough sets in knowledge discovery (Vol. 1).* Heidelberg, Germany: Physica Verlag.

Polkowski, L., & Skowron, A. (Eds.). (1998). *Rough sets in knowledge discovery (Vol. 2).* Heidelberg, Germany: Physica Verlag.

Pols, L. (1999). Flexible, robust, and efficient human speech processing versus present-day speech technology. In *Proceedings of 14th Int. Congress of Phonetic Sciences (ICPhS-99)*, San Francisco, CA (pp. 9-16).

Polya, G. (1957). *How to Solve It*. Garden City, NY: Doubleday Anchor.

Pomykala, J., & Pomykala, J. A. (1988). The Stone algebra of rough sets. *Bulletin of the Polish Academy of Sciences: Mathematics, 36*(7-8), 495–508.

Pylyshyn, Z. (1989). Computing in cognitive science. In M. I. Posner (Ed.), *Foundations of cognitive science* (pp. 49-92). Cambridge, MA: MIT Press.

Pylyshyn, Z. (1999). Is vision continuous with cognition? The case for cognitive impenetrability of visual perception. *The Behavioral and Brain Sciences, 22*, 341–423.

Qi, G., & Liu, W. (2004). Rough operations on Boolean algebras. *Information Sciences, 173*, 49–63. doi:10.1016/j.ins.2004.06.006

Quantz, J., & Royer, V. (1992). A preference semantics for defaults in terminological logics. In *KR-92* (pp. 294-305).

Quellec, G. (2008). Optimal wavelet transform for the detection of microaneurysms in retinal photographs. *IEEE Transactions on Medical Imaging, 27*(9), 1230–1241. doi:10.1109/TMI.2008.920619

Quillian, M. R. (1968). Semantic Memory . In Minsky, M. (Ed.), *Semantic Information Processing*. Cambridge, MA: MIT Press.

Rabiner, L. R., & Sambur, M. R. (1975). An algorithm for determining the endpoints of isolated utterances. *The Bell System Technical Journal, 54*, 297–315.

Rabiner, L. R., & Schafer, R. W. (1978). *Digital Processing of Speech Signals*. Upper Saddle River, NJ: Prentice-Hall.

Radzikowska, A. M., & Kerre, E. E. (2004). Fuzzy rough sets based on residuated lattices. In *Transactions on Rough Sets* (LNCS 3135, pp. 278-296).

Rasiowz, H. (1974). *An algebraic approach to non-classical logics*. Amsterdam: North Holland.

Reeve, L., & Han, H. (2005). Survey of semantic Annotation Platforms. In *Proceedings of the ACM Symposium on Applied Computing* (pp. 1634-1638).

Riesbeck, C. K., & Schank, R. C. (1989). *Inside Case-Based Reasoning*. Hillsdale, NJ: Lawrence Erlbaum.

Robert, J. S., & Jeffery, S. M. (2005). *Cognition psychology*. Belmont, CA: Wadsworth.

Romer, K., & Mattern, F. (2004). The Design Space of Wireless Sensor Networks. *IEEE Wireless Communications, 11*(6), 54–61. doi:10.1109/MWC.2004.1368897

Rudell, R. (1993). Dynamic variable ordering for ordered binary decision diagrams. In *Proceedings of the International Conference on Computer-Aided Design* (pp. 42-47).

Rui, R., Huang, T. S., & Chang, S. F. (1999). Image retrieval: current techniques, promising directions, and open issues. *Journal of Visual Communication and Image Representation, 10*(1), 39–62. doi:10.1006/jvci.1999.0413

Rydin, S. (2002). Building a hyponymy lexicon with hierarchical structures. In *Proceedings of the ACL-02 Workshop on Unsupervised Lexical Acquisition* (Vol. 9, pp. 26-33). Association of Computational Linguistics.

Schafer, R. W., & Rabiner, L. R. (1975). Parametric representations of speech. In *Proceedings of the Speech Recognition Invited Paper Presented at the 1974 IEEE Symposium*. New York: Academic Press.

Schroeder, M. (1991). *Fractals, Chaos, Power Laws: Minutes from an Infinite Paradise*. New York: W. H. Fremman.

Segen, J. (1984). Feature Selection and Constructive Inference. In *Proceedings of the Seventh Int'l Conf. Pattern Recognition* (pp. 1344-1346).

Sen, J., & Chakraborty, M. K. (2002). A study of interconnections between rough and 3-valued Lukasiewicz logics. *Fundamenta Informaticae, 51*, 311–324. doi:10.1046/j.1472-8206.2002.00092.x

Shannon, B. J., & Paliwal, K. (2006). Feature extraction from higher-lag autocorrelation coefficients for robust speech recognition. *Speech Communication, 48*(11), 1458–1485. doi:10.1016/j.specom.2006.08.003

Shapira, B., & Meirav, T. M. (2005). Subjective and Objective Evaluation of Interactive and Automatic Query Expansion. *Online Information Review, 29*(4), 374–390. doi:10.1108/14684520510617820

Sheinvald, J., Dom, B., & Niblack, W. (1990). A Modelling Approach to Feature Selection. In *Proceedings of Tenth International Conference on Pattern Recognition* (Vol. 1, pp. 535-539).

Shen, J. L., Hung, J. W., & Lee, L. S. (1998). Improved robust speech recognition considering signal correlation approximated by Taylor series. In *Proceedings of ICSLP.*

Shen, W., & Barthés, J.-P. A. (1995). Description and Applications of an Object-Oriented Model PDM. In *Modeling Complex Data for Creating Information: Real and Virtual Objects* (pp. 15-24).

Shi, J. B., & Tomasi, C. (1994). Good features to track . In *Proceedings of Computer Vision and Pattern Recognition 1994, Seattle, WA* (pp. 593–600). Washington, DC: IEEE Press.

Shi, Z. W., Hu, H., & Shi, Z. Z. (2008). A computational cognitive model for the brain. *International Journal of Cognitive Informatics and Natural Intelligence, 2*(4), 85–99.

Skowron, A., & Rauszer, C. M. (1992). The Discernibility Matrix and Functions in Information Systems . In Słowiński, R. (Ed.), *Intelligent Decision Support: Handbook of Application and Advances of the Rough Set Theory* (pp. 331–362). Dordrecht, The Netherlands: Kluwer Academic Publisher.

Ślęzak, D. (2000). Normalized Decision Functions and Measures for Inconsistent Decision Table Analysis. *Fundamenta Informaticae, 44*(3), 291–319.

Ślęzak, D. (2002). Approximate Entropy Reducts. *Fundamenta Informaticae, 53*(3-4), 365–390.

Słowiński, R., & Vanderpooten, D. (2000). A Generalized Definition of Rough Approximations Based on Similarity. *IEEE Transactions on Data and Knowledge Engineering, 2*, 331–336. doi:10.1109/69.842271

Smith, E. E., & Medin, D. L. (1981). *Categories and Concepts*. Cambridge, MA: Harvard University Press.

Smith, J. R., & Chang, S. F. (1997). Visually searching the web for content. *IEEE MultiMedia, 4*(3), 12–20. doi:10.1109/93.621578

Solis, M., et al. (2001). Pattern recognition of wavelets decomposition using ART2 networks for echoes analysis. In *Proceedings of the IEEE ultrasonic symposium, 1*, 679-682.

Song, G., Ai, H. Z., & Xu, G. Y. (2004). Texture Constrained Facial Feature Point Tracking. *Journal of Software, 15*(11), 1607–1615.

Sopharak, A., & Uyyanonvara, B. (2007). Automatic exudates detection from DR images using FCM and morphological methods. In *Proceedings of the IASTED International conference on advances in computer science and technology* (pp. 359-364).

Spink, A., Wolfram, D., Jansen, M. B. J., & Saracevic, T. (2002). From E-sex to E-commerce: Web search changes. *IEEE Computer, 35*(3), 107–109.

Sprott, J. C. (2003). *Chaos and Time-Series Analysis*. Oxford, UK: Oxford University Press.

Sroka, J. J., & Braida, L. D. (2005). Human and machine consonant recognition. *Speech Communication, 45*(4), 401–424. doi:10.1016/j.specom.2004.11.009

Stall, J. (2004). Ridge based vessel segmentation in color images of the retina. *IEEE Transactions on Medical Imaging, 23*(4), 501–509. doi:10.1109/TMI.2004.825627

Strope, B., & Alwan, A. (1998). Robust word recognition using threaded spectral peaks. In *Proceedings of the ICASSP* (pp. 625- 628).

Strope, B., & Alwan, A. (1997). A model of dynamic auditory perception and its application to robust word recognition. *IEEE Transactions on Speech and Audio Processing, 5*(5), 451–464. doi:10.1109/89.622569

Sugawara, K., Fujita, S., Kinoshita, T., & Shiratori, N. (2008). A design of cognitive agents for recognizing real space—towards symbiotic computing. In *Proceedings of the 7th International Conference on Cognitive Informatics (ICCI '08)* (pp. 277-285).

Sujatha, J., Prasanna, K. R., Ramakrishnan, K. R., & Balakrishnan, N. (2003). Spectral maxima representation for robust automatic speech recognition. *In Proceedings of the Eurospeech* (pp. 3077-3080).

Swiniarski, R. W., & Skowron, A. (2003). Rough set methods in feature selection and recognition. *Pattern Recognition Letters, 24*(6), 833–849. doi:10.1016/S0167-8655(02)00196-4

Tacla, C. A. (2003). *De l'utilité des systèmes multi-agents pour l'acquisition des connaissances au fil de l'eau*. Unpublished doctoral dissertation, Université de Technologie de Compiègne, France.

Tan, J. G., Zhang, D., Wang, X., & Cheng, H. S. (2005). Enhancing semantics spaces with event-driven cotnext interpretation. In *PERVASIVE2005* (LNCS 3468, pp. 80-97).

Taylor, J. G. (2009). Cognitive computation. *Cognitive Computation, 1*, 4–16. doi:10.1007/s12559-008-9001-8

Tian, Y., Wang, Y., & Hu, K. (2009). A Knowledge Representation Tool for Autonomous Machine Learning Based on Concept Algebra. *Transactions of Computational Science, 5*, 143–160. doi:10.1007/978-3-642-02097-1_8

Timothy, J. R. (2004). *Fuzzy logic with engineering applications* (2nd ed.). New York: Wiley and sons.

Tomasi, C., & Kanade, T. (1991). *Detection and tracking of point features* (Tech. Rep. No. CMU-CS-91-132). Pittsburgh, PA: Carnegie Mellon University.

Touretzky, D. S. (1986). *The Mathematics of Inheritance Systems*. San Francisco, CA: Morgan Kaufmann.

Treigys, P., & Saltenis, V. (2007). Neural network as an ophthalmologic disease classifier. *Information Technology and Control, 36*(4), 365–371.

Tsang, E., Cheng, D., Lee, J., & Yeung, D. (2004). On the upper approximations of covering generalized rough sets. In *Proceedings of the Third International Conference on Machine Learning and Cybernetics* (pp. 4200-4203).

Tsang, P. S. (2001). Mental workload. In *International encyclopedia of ergonomics and human factors* (pp. 809-813).

Turcotte, D. L. (1997). *Fractals and Chaos in Geology and Geophysics* (2nd ed.). New York: Springer Verlag.

Valk, R. (1998). Petri Nets as Token Objects - An Introduction to Elementary Object Nets. In *Proceedings of the 19th International Conference on Application and Theory of Petri Nets (ICATPN'98)* (LNCS 1420, pp. 1-25).

Varga, A., & Steeneken, H. J. M. (1993). Assessment for automatic speech recognition: II. NOISEX-92: A database and an experiment to study the effect of additive noise on speech recognition systems. *Speech Communication, 12*, 247–251. doi:10.1016/0167-6393(93)90095-3

Vere, S. A., & Bickmore, T. W. (1990). A Basic Agent. *Computational Intelligence, 6*, 41–60. doi:10.1111/j.1467-8640.1990.tb00128.x

Wallas, G. (1926). *The Art of Thought*. New York: Harcourt-Brace.

Walters, J. P., Liang, Z., Shi, W., & Chaudhary, V. (2007). Wireless Sensor Network Security: A Survey . In Xiao, Y. (Ed.), *Security in Distributed, Grid, Mobile and Pervasive Computing*. New York: Auerbach Publications.

Wang, F., Liu, S., Liu, P., & Bai, Y. (2006). Bridging physical and virtual worlds: complex event processing for RFID data stream. In *Proceedings of the 10th International Conference on Extending Database Technology (EDBT 2006)* (pp. 588-607).

Wang, G., Liu, Q., Yao, Y., & Skowron, A. (2003). *Rough Sets, Fuzzy Sets, Data Mining, and Granular Computing* (LNAI 2639). Berlin: Springer Verlag.

Wang, S., Cao, Y., Cao, X., & Cao, C. (2007). Learning concepts from text based on the inner-constructive model. In Z. Zhang & J. Siekmann (Eds.), *2nd International Conference on Knowledge Science, Engineering, and Management* (pp. 255-266). Springer.

Wang, Y. (2002). On cognitive informatics. In *Proceedings of the 1st IEEE Intern. Conf. Cognitive Informatics*, Calgary, AB (pp. 34-42).

Wang, Y. (2002a, August). Keynote: On Cognitive Informatics. In *Proceedings of the 1st IEEE International Conference on Cognitive Informatics (ICCI'02)*, Calgary, Alberta, Canada (pp. 34-42). IEEE CS Press.

Wang, Y. (2003). On Cognitive Informatics. *Brain and Mind: A Transdisciplinary Journal of Neuroscience and Neurophilosophy, 4*(2), 151-167.

Wang, Y. (2003b). Cognitive Informatics: A New Transdisciplinary Research Field. *Brain and Mind: A Transdisciplinary Journal of Neuroscience and Neurophilosophy, 4*(2), 115-127.

Wang, Y. (2004, August). On Autonomic Computing and Cognitive Processes (Keynote Speech). In *Proceedings of the 3rd IEEE International Conference on Cognitive Informatics (ICCI'04)*, Victoria, BC, Canada (pp. 3-4). IEEE CS Press.

Wang, Y. (2006, July). Keynote: Cognitive Informatics - Towards the Future Generation Computers that Think and Feel. In *Proceedings of the 5th IEEE International Conference on Cognitive Informatics (ICCI'06)*, Beijing, China (pp. 3-7). IEEE CS Press.

Wang, Y. (2006b, July). Cognitive Informatics and Contemporary Mathematics for Knowledge Representation and Manipulation, Invited Plenary Talk. In *Proceedings of the 1st International Conference on Rough Set and Knowledge Technology (RSKT'06),* Chongqing, China (LNAI 4062, pp. 69-78).

Wang, Y. (2007a). *Software Engineering Foundations: A Software Science Perspective, CRC Series in Software Engineering, Vol. II.* Boca Raton, FL: Auerbach Publications.

Wang, Y. (2007a, July). *Software Engineering Foundations: A Software Science Perspective* (CRC Series in Software Engineering, Vol. 2). New York: Auerbach Publications.

Wang, Y. (2007d). The Theoretical Framework and Cognitive Process of Learning. *Proc. 6th International Conference on Cognitive Informatics* (ICCI'07), IEEE CS Press, Lake Tahoe, CA., Aug., 470-479.

Wang, Y. (2008a). On Contemporary Denotational Mathematics for Computational Intelligence. In *Transactions of Computational Science* (Vol. 2, pp. 6-29). New York: Springer.

Wang, Y. (2008b). Novel Approaches in Cognitive Informatics and Natural Intelligence. In *ISR Series in Advances of Cognitive Informatics and Natural Intelligence* (Vol. 1). Hershey, PA: Information Science References.

Wang, Y. *(2009h, June). Granular Algebra for Modeling Granular Systems and Granular Computing. In* Proceedings of the 8th IEEE International Conference on Cognitive Informatics (ICCI'09), *Hong Kong, China (pp. 145-154). IEEE CS Press.*

Wang, Y. (2010b). Keynote: Cognitive Informatics and Denotational Mathematics Means for Brain Informatics. In *Proceedings of the 1st Int'l Conference on Brain Informatics* (ICBI'10), Toronto, Canada.

Wang, Y., Johnston, R. H., & Smith, M. R. (Eds.). (2002). *Proceedings of the 1st IEEE.* Los Alamitos, CA: IEEE Computer Society Press.

Wang, Y., Zhang, D., Latombe, J.-C., & Kinsner, W. (Eds.). (2008). *Proceedings of the 7th IEEE International Conference on Cognitive Informatics (ICCI'08).* Los Alamitos, CA: IEEE Computer Society Press.

Wang, L., Hu, W. M., & Tan, T. N. (2002). A survey of visual analysis of human motion. *Chinese Journal of Computers, 25*(3), 225–237.

Wang, Y. (2002b). The Real-Time Process Algebra (RTPA). *Annals of Software Engineering, 14,* 235–274. doi:10.1023/A:1020561826073

Wang, Y. (2003). Cognitive Informatics: A New Transdisciplinary Research Field. *Brain and Mind, 4*(2), 115–127. doi:10.1023/A:1025419826662

Wang, Y. (2003). On cognitive informatics. *Brain and Mind, 4,* 151–167. doi:10.1023/A:1025401527570

Wang, Y. (2006a). On the Informatics Laws and Deductive Semantics of Software. *IEEE Transactions on Systems, Man, and Cybernetics . Part C, 36*(2), 161–171.

Wang, Y. (2007). The theoretical framework of cognitive informatics. *International Journal of Cognitive Informatics and Natural Intelligence, 1*(1), 1–27.

Wang, Y. (2007). Toward theoretical foundation of autonomic computing. *International Journal of Cognitive Informatics and Natural Intelligence, 1*(3), 1–16.

Wang, Y. (2007a). The Cognitive Processes of Formal Inferences. *International Journal of Cognitive Informatics and Natural Intelligence, 1*(4), 75–86.

Wang, Y. (2007b). On The Cognitive Processes of Perception with Emotions, Motivations, and Attitudes. *International Journal of Cognitive Informatics and Natural Intelligence, 1*(4), 1–13.

Wang, Y. (2007c). The OAR Model of Neural Informatics for Internal Knowledge Representation in the Brain. *International Journal of Cognitive Informatics and Natural Intelligence, 1*(3), 64–75.

Wang, Y. (2008a). On Concept Algebra: A denotational mathematical structure for knowledge and software modeling. *International Journal of Cognitive Informatics and Natural Intelligence, 2*(2), 1–19.

Wang, Y. (2008b). Mathematical Laws of Software. *Transactions of Computational Science, 2,* 46–83. doi:10.1007/978-3-540-87563-5_4

Wang, Y. (2008b). On system algebra: A denotational mathematical structure for abstract systems, modeling. *International Journal of Cognitive Informatics and Natural Intelligence, 2*(2), 20–43.

Wang, Y. (2008d). Deductive Semantics of RTPA. *International Journal of Cognitive Informatics and Natural Intelligence, 2*(2), 95–121.

Wang, Y. (2008e). RTPA: A Denotational Mathematics for Manipulating Intelligent and Computational Behaviors. *International Journal of Cognitive Informatics and Natural Intelligence, 2*(2), 44–62.

Wang, Y. (2009). On Cognitive Computing. *International Journal of Software Science and Computational Intelligence, 1*(3), 1–15.

Wang, Y. (2009a). On Abstract Intelligence: Toward a Unified Theory of Natural, Artificial, Machinable, and Computational Intelligence. *International Journal of Software Science and Computational Intelligence, 1*(1), 1–17.

Wang, Y. (2009c). A Cognitive Informatics Reference Model of Autonomous Agent Systems (AAS). *International Journal of Cognitive Informatics and Natural Intelligence, 3*(1), 1–16.

Wang, Y. (2009c). Paradigms of Denotational Mathematics for Cognitive Informatics and Cognitive Computing. *Fundamenta Informaticae, 90*(3), 282–303.

Wang, Y. (2009d). Toward a Formal Knowledge System Theory and Its Cognitive Informatics Foundations. *Transactions of Computational Science, 5*, 1–19. doi:10.1007/978-3-642-02097-1_1

Wang, Y. (2009e). A Formal Syntax of Natural Languages and the Deductive Grammar. *Fundamenta Informaticae, 90*(4), 353–368.

Wang, Y. (2009f). On Visual Semantic Algebra (VSA): A Denotational Mathematical Structure for Modeling and Manipulating Visual Objects and Patterns. *International Journal of Software Science and Computational Intelligence, 1*(4), 1–15.

Wang, Y. (Ed.). (2009g). Special Issue on Cognitive Computing, On Abstract Intelligence. *International Journal of Software Science and Computational Intelligence, 1*(3), 1–116.

Wang, Y., & Kinsner, W. (2006). Recent Advances in Cognitive Informatics. *IEEE Transactions on Systems, Man and Cybernetics. Part C, Applications and Reviews, 36*(2), 121–123. doi:10.1109/TSMCC.2006.871120

Wang, Y., Kinsner, W., Anderson, J. A., Zhang, D., Yao, Y., & Sheu, P. (2009c). A Doctrine of Cognitive Informatics. *Fundam. Informatic., 90*(3), 203–228.

Wang, Y., Kinsner, W., & Zhang, D. (2009). Contemporary Cybernetics and its Faces of Cognitive Informatics and Computational Intelligence. *IEEE Trans. on System, Man, and Cybernetics (B), 39*(4), 823–833. doi:10.1109/TSMCB.2009.2013721

Wang, Y., & Wang, Y. (2006). Cognitive Informatics Models of the Brain. *IEEE Transactions on Systems, Man and Cybernetics. Part C, Applications and Reviews, 36*(2), 203–207. doi:10.1109/TSMCC.2006.871151

Wang, Y., Wang, Y., Patel, S., & Patel, D. (2006). A Layered Reference Model of the Brain (LRMB). *IEEE Trans. on Systems, Man, and Cybernetics . Part C, 36*(2), 124–133.

Wang, Y., Zadeh, L. A., & Yao, Y. (2009). On the System Algebra Foundations for Granular Computing. *International Journal of Software Science and Computational Intelligence, 1*(1), 64–86.

Watson, I., & Marir, F. (1994). Case-Based Reasoning: A Review. *The Knowledge Engineering Review, 9*(4), 355–381. doi:10.1017/S0269888900007098

Wehmeier, S. (Ed.). (2005). *Oxford Advanced Learner's Dictionary of Current English* (7th ed.). Oxford, UK: Oxford University Press.

West, B. J., Bologna, M., & Grigolini, P. (2003). *Physics of Fractal Operators*. New York: Springer.

Whaley, J. (2007). *JAVABDD: a Java Binary Decision Diagram Library, Stanford University*. Retrieved October 29, 2007, from http://javabdd.sourceforge.net/

Wibig, T. (1998). The Artificial Neural Networks in Cosmic Ray Physics Experiment; I. Total Muon Number Estimation. In A. P. del Pobil & J. Mira (Eds.), *Tasks and Methods in Applied Artificial Intelligence* (LNAI 2, p. 867). Berlin: Springer Verlag.

Wille, R. (1982). Restructuring Lattice Theory: An Approach Based on Hierarchies of Concepts. In I. Rival (Ed.), *Ordered Sets* (pp. 445-470). Dordrecht, The Netherlands: Reidel.

William, S., & Austin, T. (1999). Ontologies. *IEEE Intelligent Systems*, 18-19.

Williams, C. P., & Clearwater, S. H. (1998). *Explorations in quantum computing*. Berlin: Springer.

Wilson, R. A., & Keil, F. C. (2001). *The MIT Encyclopedia of the Cognitive Sciences*. Cambridge, MA: MIT Press.

Wobcke, W. R., Ho, V., Nguyen, A., & Krzywicki, A. (2005, September). A BDI Agent Architecture for Dialogue Modeling and Coordination in a Smart Personal Assistant. In *Proceedings of the IEEE/WIC/ACM International Conference on Web Intelligence and Intelligent Agent Technology,* Compiègne, France (pp. 323-329).

WordNet. (1993). *About WordNet*. http://wordnet.princeton.edu/

Wornell, G. W. (1996). *Signal Processing with Fractals: A Wavelet-Based Approach*. Upper Saddle River, NJ: Prentice-Hall.

Wróblewski, J. (2001), Adaptive Methods of Object Classification. Doctoral thesis, Institute of Mathematics, Warsaw University, Poland.

Wyatt, D., Philipose, M., & Choudhury, T. (2005). Unsupervised activity recognition using automatically mined common sense. In . *Proceedings of AAAI, 2005*, 21–27.

Xu, J., & Sun, L. (2008). New Reduction Algorithm Based on Decision Power of Decision Table. In G. Wang et al. (Eds.), *Rough Sets and Knowledge Technology* (LNAI 5009, pp. 180-188). New York: Springer.

Xu, Z., Zhang, C., Zhang, S., Song, W., & Yang, B. (2007). Efficient Attribute Reduction Based on Discernibility Matrix. In J. T. Yao et al. (Eds.), *Rough Sets and Knowledge Technology* (LNAI 4481, pp.13-21). New York: Springer.

Xue, W., & Luo, Q. (2005). Action-oriented query processing for pervasive computing. In *Proceedings of the Second Biennaial Conference on Innovative Data Systems Research (CIDR2005)* (pp. 305-316).

Yan, C., & Su, G. D. (1998). Location and acquisition of characters of human face. *Journal of Image and Graphics, 3*(5), 375–379.

Yang, Y., Wang, G. Y., Chen, P. J., & Zhou, J. (2006). An Emotion Recognition System Based on Rough Set Theory . In Li, Y. F. (Ed.), *Active Media Technology 2006, Sydney, Australia* (pp. 293–297). Paris: IOS Press.

Yang, Y., Wang, G. Y., Chen, P. J., Zhou, J., & He, K. (2007). Feature Selection in Audiovisual Emotional Recognition Based on Rough Set Theory. *Transactions on Rough Sets, 7*, 283–294.

Yang, Y., Wang, G. Y., & Kong, H. (2009). Self-Learning Facial Emotional Feature Selection Based on Rough Set Theory. *Mathematical Problems in Engineering*. .doi:10.1155/2009/802932

Yao, Y. Y. (2005). Perspectives of Granular Computing. In *Proceedings of the 2005 IEEE International Conference on Granular Computing* (Vol. 1, pp. 85-90).

Yao, Y. Y. (2008). A unified framework of granular computing. In W. Pedrycz, A. Skowron, & V. Kreinovich (Eds.), *Handbook of Granular Computing* (pp. 401-410). New York: Wiley.

Yao, Y. Y. (in press). Human-Inspired Granular Computing. In J.T. Yao (Ed.), *Novel Developments in Granular Computing: Applications for Advanced Human Reasoning and Soft Computation*.

Yao, Y. Y. (2006). Three perspectives of granular computing. *Journal of Nanchang Institute of Technology, 25*, 16–21.

Yao, Y. Y., & Lin, T. Y. (1996). Generalization of Rough Sets Using Modal Logics. *Intelligent Automation and Soft Computing, 2*, 103–120.

Yap, K. K., Srinivasan, V., & Motani, M. (2005). Max: Human-centric search of the physical world. In *Proceedings of the 3rd ACM Conference on Embedded Networked Sensor Systems (Sen-Sys '05)* (pp.166-179).

Yeung, D., Chen, D., Tsang, E., Lee, J., & Xizhao, W. (2005). On the generalization of fuzzy rough sets. *IEEE Transactions on Fuzzy Systems, 13*(3), 343–361. doi:10.1109/TFUZZ.2004.841734

You, K.-H., & Wang, H.-C. (1999). Robust features for noisy speech recognition based on temporal trajectory filtering of short-time autocorrelation sequences. *Speech Communication, 28*, 13–24. doi:10.1016/S0167-6393(99)00004-7

Young, M. S., & Stanton, N. A. (2001). Mental workload: Theory, measurement, and application. In *International encyclopedia of ergonomics and human factors* (pp. 818-821).

Yousoof, M., Sapiyan, M., & Kamaluddin, K. (2006). Reducing Cognitive Load in Learning Computer Programming. In *Proceedings of the World Academy of Science, Engineering and Technology* (Vol. 12, pp. 259-262).

Yu, M. S., & Li, S. F. (2005). Dynamic facial expression recognition based on optical flow. *Microelectronics & Computer*, *22*(7), 113–119.

Yun, W. (2008). Identification of different stages of Diabetic Retinopathy using retinal optical images. *Information Sciences*, *178*, 106–121. doi:10.1016/j.ins.2007.07.020

Zadeh, L. A. (1996, September 8-11). The key roles of information granulation and fuzzy logic in human reasoning. In *Proceedings of the 1996 IEEE International Conference on Fuzzy Systems*, New Orleans, Louisiana.

Zadeh, L. (1972). A fuzzy-set-theoretical interpretation of linguistic hedges. *Journal of Cybernetics*, *2*, 4–34. doi:10.1080/01969727208542910

Zadeh, L. A. (1979). Fuzzy sets and information granularity . In Gupta, M., Ragade, R., & Yager, R. (Eds.), *Advances in Fuzzy Set Theory and Applications* (pp. 3–18). Amsterdam: North-Holland.

Zadeh, L. A. (1997). Toward a theory of fuzzy information granulation and its centrality in human reasoning and fuzzy logic. *Fuzzy Sets and Systems*, *90*, 111–127. doi:10.1016/S0165-0114(97)00077-8

Zadeh, L. A. (1998). Some reflections on soft computing, granular computing and their roles in the conception, design and utilization of information/ intelligent systems. *Soft Computing*, *2*, 23–25. doi:10.1007/s005000050030

Zelenko, D., Aone, C., & Richardella, A. (2003). Kernel Methods for Relation Extraction. *Journal of Machine Learning Research*, *3*, 1083–1106. doi:10.1162/153244303322533205

Zhang, B., & Zhang, L. (2002). Granular computing and human cognition. In *Proceedings of the KAIST-Tsinghua Joint Workshop on Brain Science and Human-like Technology* (pp. 37-49).

Zhang, C., Cao, C., Liu, L., Niu, Z., & Lin, J. (2007). Extracting hyponymy relations from domain-specific free texts. In *Proceedings of the 9th International Conference on Machine Learning and Cybernetics* (pp. 3360-3365). IEEE Computer Society Press.

Zhang, J., Wang, J., Li, D., He, H., & Sun, J. (2003). A New Heuristic Reduct Algorithm Based on Rough Sets Theory. In G. Dong et al. (Eds.), *Advances in Web-Age Information Management* (LNSC 2762, pp. 247-253). New York: Springer.

Zhang, C. (2005). The State of the Art and Difficulties in Automatic Chinese Word Segmentation. *Journal of System and Simulation*, *17*(1), 138–143.

Zhang, D. (2007). Fixpoint Semantics for Rule Base Anomalies. *International Journal of Cognitive Informatics and Natural Intelligence*, *1*(4), 14–25.

Zhang, D. (2008). On temporal properties of knowledge base inconsistency. *Springer Transactions on Computational Science*, *2*, 20–37.

Zhang, D. (2009). Quantifying knowledge base inconsistency via fixpoint semantics. *Springer Transactions on Computational Science*, *2*, 145–160.

Zhang, P., Barad, H., & Martinez, A. (1990). Fractal dimension estimation of fractional Brownian motion. In . *Proceedings of the IEEE Southeastcon*, *3*, 934–939. doi:10.1109/SECON.1990.117957

Zhang, W. X., & Xu, W. H. (2007). Granular computing based on the cognition model. *Journal of Engineering Mathematics*, *6*(24), 957–971.

Zhong, N., Liu, J., Yao, Y. Y., Wu, J., Lu, S., & Li, K. (Eds.). (2007). *Web Intelligence Meets Brain Informatics (LNAI 4845)*. Berlin, Germany: Springer.

Zhong, N., Dong, J., & Ohsuga, S. (2001). Using rough sets with heuristics for feature selection. *Journal of Intelligent Information Systems*, *16*(3), 199–214. doi:10.1023/A:1011219601502

Zhou, J., Wang, S., & Cao, C. (2007). A Google-based statistical acquisition model of Chinese lexical concepts. In Z. Zhang & J. Siekmann (Eds.), *2nd International Conference on Knowledge Science, Engineering, and Management* (pp. 243-254). Springer.

Zhou, X., & Dillon, T. S. (1991). A statistical-heuristic feature selection criterion for decision tree induction. *IEEE Transactions on Pattern Analysis and Machine Intelligence*, *13*(8), 834–841. doi:10.1109/34.85676

Zhu, Q., Iseli, M., Cui, X., & Alwan, A. (2001). Noise robust feature extraction for ASR using the AURORA2 database. *In Proceedings of Eurospeech.*

Zhu, W., & Wang, F. Y. (2006). A new type of covering rough sets. In *Proceedings of the Third IEEE International Conference on Intelligent System* (pp. 444-449).

Zhu, H., & Zhou, M. C. (2006). Role-based Collaboration and its Kernel Mechanisms. *IEEE Transactions on Systems, Man, and Cybernetics . Part C, 36*(4), 578–589.

Zhu, H., & Zhou, M. C. (2008). Roles in Information Systems: A Survey. *IEEE Transactions on Systems, Man, and Cybernetics . Part C, 38*(3), 57–589.

Zhu, W. (2007). Generalized rough sets based on relations. *Information Sciences, 177*(22), 4997–5011. doi:10.1016/j.ins.2007.05.037

Zhu, W. (2007). Topological approaches to covering rough sets. *Information Sciences, 177*(6), 1499–1508. doi:10.1016/j.ins.2006.06.009

Zhu, W., & Wang, F. Y. (2007). On three types of covering rough sets. *IEEE Transactions on Knowledge and Data Engineering, 19*(8), 1131–1144. doi:10.1109/TKDE.2007.1044

Ziarko, W. (1993). Variable Precision Rough Set Model. *Journal of Computer and System Sciences, 46*, 39–59. doi:10.1016/0022-0000(93)90048-2

About the Contributors

Yingxu Wang is professor of cognitive informatics, cognitive computing, and software engineering, President of International Institute of Cognitive Informatics and Cognitive Computing (ICIC), Director of Laboratory for Cognitive Informatics and Cognitive Computing, and Director of Laboratory for Denotational Mathematics and Software Science at the University of Calgary. He is a Fellow of WIF (UK), Fellow of ICIC, P.Eng of Canada, a Senior Member of IEEE and ACM, and a member of ISO/IEC JTC1 and the Canadian Advisory Committee (CAC) for ISO. He received a PhD in Software Engineering from the Nottingham Trent University, UK, and a BSc in Electrical Engineering from Shanghai Tiedao University. He has industrial experience since 1972 and has been a full professor since 1994. He was a visiting professor on sabbatical leaves in the Computing Laboratory at Oxford University in 1995, Dept. of Computer Science at Stanford University in 2008, the Berkeley Initiative in Soft Computing (BISC) Lab at University of California, Berkeley in 2008, and MIT (2012), respectively. He is the founder and steering committee chair of the annual IEEE International Conference on Cognitive Informatics and Cognitive Computing (ICCI*CC). He is founding Editor-in-Chief of *International Journal of Cognitive Informatics and Natural Intelligence* (IJCINI), founding Editor-in-Chief of *International Journal of Software Science and Computational Intelligence* (IJSSCI), Associate Editor of *IEEE Trans on System, Man, and Cybernetics* (Part A), and associate Editor-in-Chief of *Journal of Advanced Mathematics and Applications*. Dr. Wang is the initiator of several cutting-edge research fields or subject areas such as cognitive informatics (CI, such as the theoretical framework of CI, Neuroinformatics, the layered reference model of the brain (LRMB), the cognitive model of brain informatics (CMBI), the mathematical model of consciousness, and the cognitive learning engine), abstract intelligence, cognitive computing (such as cognitive computers, cognitive robots, cognitive agents, and cognitive Internet), denotational mathematics (i.e., concept algebra, inference algebra, real-time process algebra, system algebra, granular algebra, and visual semantic algebra), software science (on unified mathematical models and laws of software, cognitive complexity of software, and automatic code generators, coordinative work organization theory, and built-in tests (BITs)), basic studied in cognitive linguistics (such as the cognitive linguistic framework, the deductive semantics of languages, deductive grammar of English, and the cognitive complexity of text comprehension). He has published over 130 peer reviewed journal papers, 220+ peer reviewed full conference papers, and 18 books in cognitive informatics, cognitive computing, denotational mathematics, software science, cognitive linguistics, and computational intelligence. He is the recipient of dozens international awards on academic leadership, outstanding contributions, research achievement, best papers, and teaching in the last three decades. He can be reached at: yingxu@ ucalgary.ca.

* * *

J. Anitha received her Bachelor degree in Electronics and Communication Engineering from Bharathiar University, India in 2002 and her Master degree in Applied Electronics from Anna University, India in 2004. Currently, she is working as Assistant Professor in the Department of ECE of Karunya University, India. Her research interests include neural networks, retinal image processing and optimization algorithms.

George Baciu is Professor and Associate Head of the Department of Computing at the Hong Kong Polytechnic University. He holds degrees in Computer Science, Applied Mathematics and Systems Design Engineering from University of Waterloo. He is a member of the Computer Graphics Lab and the Pattern Analysis and Machine Intelligence group. Professor George Baciu is the founding director of the Graphics and Multimedia Applications (GAMA) Laboratory at the Hong Kong Polytechnic University. His group conducts research in 3D motion tracking, Animation, Collision Detection, Deformable Objects, Geometric Modeling. He has published extensively in IEEE Transactions and ACM conferences and has served as chair in international conference committees such as Game Technology Conference (GTEC), Pacific Graphics, ACM Virtual Reality Software and Technology (VRST), Eurographics, Computer Graphics International, CAD/Graphics, and Computer Animation and Social Agents (CASA), ACM VRCIA and IEEE International Conference on Cognitive Informatics (ICCI). His research interests include real-time motion tracking, collision detection, dynamics of large scale deformable surfaces, virtual clothing, geometric modeling, and scalable micro-surface reconstruction. He is a member of IEEE and ACM.

Poonam Bansal obtained her M.Tech. degree in Computer Science & Engineering from Delhi College of Engineering, Delhi University, in 2001. Presently she is associate professor in the Computer Science & Engineering department of Amity school of Engineering and Technology (A premier Institute affiliated to GGSIP university) New Delhi. She is pursuing her Ph.D. in the area of **Speech Recognition** from Guru Gobind Singh Inderprastha University, New Delhi, India. She has published various papers in renowned national and international journals & in the proceedings of leading conferences. Her research interests include Speech Recognition and Speaker Identification. She is a member of IEEE, IETE, IEICE and Acoustic society of India (ASI).

Rushin Barot obtained his MS in Computer Science from San Jose State University in May 2009. His primary interests are algorithms for large data sets and theory of computation.

Jean-Paul Barthès was born in France, on July 9, 1945. He graduated from the École Centrale des Arts et Manufactures, Paris, and obtained a PhD degree from the University of Stanford, USA. His employment experience included the Société Générale pour les Techniques Nouvelles, a branch of the nuclear industry, in Paris, and the Université de Technologie de Compiègne. His special fields of interest include artificial intelligence, knowledge representation, and multi-agent systems. Barthès developed a number of software systems including MOSS, a knowledge representation system, an object database that led to the MATISSE™ product and several multi-agent platforms, in particular, a multi-agent platform, OMAS, for developing systems of cognitive agents.

Ke-jia Chen received her BSc and MSc degrees in computer science from Nanjing University, China, in 2002 and 2005, respectively, and her PhD degree in computer science from Université de Technologie de Compiègne, France, in 2008. She joined the College of Computer Science of Nanjing University of Posts and Telecommuncations as an assistant professor in 2009. Her research interests include artificial intelligence, intelligent agent, machine learning, information retrieval. In these areas she has published more than 10 papers in international journals or conference proceedings.

Keith Chan is Professor and former Head of the Department of Computing at the Hong Kong Polytechnic University, Hong Kong. He holds a PhD in Computer Science, Applied Mathematics and Systems Design Engineering from University of Waterloo. He is a member of IEEE and ACM. He has published numerous papers in research journals and international conferences, as well as two books. His research interest is in software engineering, computer engineering, cognitive computing, and heir applications.

Cao Cungen, born in 1964, is a Professor and doctoral supervisor in Key Laboratory of Intelligent Information Processing, Institute of Computing Technology, Chinese Academy of Sciences. His main research interests include large-scale knowledge processing, knowledge engineering and intelligent software.

Amita Dev has obtained her B.Tech degree from Punjab University and completed her post graduation from BITS, Pilani. She has completed her PhD. from Delhi University in the area of Speech Recognition. She has more than Twenty Two years of working experience and presently she is working as Principal of Ambedkar Polytechnic, New Delhi and Bhai Parmanand Institute of Business Studies, New Delhi. She has been awarded "National Level Best Engineering Teacher Award" in year 2001 by **ISTE** for significant contribution in the field of Engineering and Technology. She has also been awarded "State Level Best Teacher Award" awarded by Department of Training & Technical Education. Govt. of Delhi. She is recipient of "National Level AICTE Young Teacher Career Award" for pursuing Advance research in the field of Speech Recognition. She has written several text and reference books in the area of Computer Science & Engineering. She has published more than 20 papers in the renowned national and international journals & in the proceedings of leading conferences.

V. Devarashetty received a M.S. degree from the Department of Computer Science at the University of Illinois at Chicago. Her research interests include Software engineering, distributed systems, and sensor networks.

D. Gafurov received his Diploma in Computer Engineering from Technological University of Tajikistan (Tajikistan) in 2000 and his PhD in Computer Science from University of Oslo (Norway) in 2008. Previously he worked as an engineer-programmer at the Computer Center of Technological University of Tajikistan, and at the same time he was a part-time lecturer at the department of Programming and Information Technology at TUT (2000-2004). D. Gafurov also had visits at International Institute for Software Technology, United Nations University (Macau, China) in 2001 and at the department of Electrical and Computer Engineering of University of Calgary (Canada) in 2002. He is currently a researcher at Norwegian Information Security Laboratory, Gjøvik University College (Norway) and involved in EU funded project TURBINE (ICT-2007-216339, www.turbine-project.eu). His current research interest includes biometrics, in particular performance evaluation of biometrics systems and human movement analysis for security applications.

Ben Goertzel is CEO and Chief Scientist of AI firm Novamente LLC, a company focused on creating powerfully intelligent NPC's for online games and virtual worlds. He is also CEO of bioinformatics firm

Biomind LLC, and Director of Research of the nonprofit Singularity Institute for AI. Dr. Goertzel is the originator of the OpenCog open-source AGI framework, as well as the proprietary Novamente Cognition Engine AGI system. A research faculty for 8 years in several universities in the US and Australasia, he remains active in the academic AI community. He is the Chair of the Steering Committee for the Artificial General Intelligence conference series, and was the Conference Chair for AGI-09 which was held in March 2009 in Washington DC. He currently serves on the Board of the World Transhumanist Association. Dr. Goertzel has authored eight technical monographs in the computing and cognitive sciences, published by leading scientific publishers, most recently Probabilistic Term Logic, to be published by Springer in mid-2008; and also edited four technical volumes. He has also published over 80 research papers in journals, conferences and edited volumes, in disciplines spanning AI, mathematics, computer science, cognitive science, philosophy of mind and bioinformatics; and has developed two AI-based trading systems for hedge funds in Connecticut and San Francisco. AI software created by his teams at Novamente LLC and Biomind LLC has been used in numerous government agencies and corporations.

Warren Grieder is Consultant on Internet Technology for Merlin, a special operating agency with the Department of Innovation, Energy and Mines, Government of Manitoba, Manitoba, Canada. He obtained his BSc and MSc in computer engineering from the University of Manitoba, Winnipeg in 1991 and 1996 respectively.

Stuart Hameroff MD is Professor of Anesthesiology and Psychology, and Director of the Center for Consciousness Studies at the University of Arizona in Tucson. Hameroff is known for the Orch OR theory of consciousness with Sir Roger Penrose based on quantum computation in intra-neuronal microtubules, and organizing the Toward a Science of Consciousness conference series. He has recently developed a cognitive model for the neural correlate of consciousness called the 'Conscious pilot', a self-organizing mobile agent moving through the brain's neuronal networks.

Kun He received a master degree in computer science from Chongqing University of Posts and Telecommunications, China (2008). He is working in Tecent Cororperation.

Kai Hu is an MSc candidate at International Center for Cognitive Informatics (ICfCI) as well as Theoretical and Empirical Software Engineering Center (TESERC) in Dept. of Electrical and Computer Engineering at the University of Calgary. He received a MEng from Zhejiang University, China, in Electrical Engineering in 1986. He is also a software engineer working at ITSportsnet Inc., Calgary. His research interest is in cognitive informatics, cognitive computing, software engineering, cognitive search engines, and machine learning.

Chu-Ren Huang is Dean of Faculty of Humanities and Chair Professor of Applied Chinese Language Studies at the Hong Kong Polytechnic University and a research fellow at the Institute of Linguistics, Academia Sinica. He received his PhD in linguistics from Cornell University in 1987 and has since played a central role in developing Chinese language resources. He directed or co-directed the construction of the CKIP lexicon and ICG Grammar, Sinica Corpus, Sinica Treebank, Academia Sinica Bilingual Ontological WordNet, Chinese WordSketch, Tagged Chinese Gigaword Corpus, Hantology and Chinese WordNet. He has ensured that most of the above resources are available online and has spearheaded the efforts to create language learning sites, such as Adventures in Wen-Land and SouWenJieZi. He also pioneered the use of corpus, especially automatically extracted collocations, in creating Chinese dictionaries with the Mandarin Daily Classifier Dictionary in 1996. He has published over 70 journal and book articles and over 280 conference papers on different aspects of Chinese linguistics. He has also edited over 14 books or journal special issues, including the just completed volume entitled Ontology and the Lexicon, to be published by Cambridge University Press in the Cambridge Studies in Natural Language Processing Series.

D. Jude Hemanth received his Bachelor degree in Electronics and Communication Engineering from Bharathiar University, India in 2002 and his Master degree in Communication Systems from Anna University, India in 2006. Currently, he is working as Assistant Professor in the Department of ECE of Karunya University, India. His research interests include brain image analysis, computer vision and artificial intelligence techniques. He has published several research papers in reputed International Journals. He is a life member of ISTE, IACSIT and IAENG.

Shail Bala Jain received her Ph.D degree in Electronics & Communication Engineering from Delhi University, New Delhi India. She has thirty one years of teaching and research experience at Delhi College of Engineering, New Delhi, India. Presently she is heading Electronics & Communication Engineering department of "Indira Gandhi Institute of Technology", premier Institute under Guru Gobind Singh Inderprastha University. She has also Co-authored a book "Linear Integrated circuits" published by Wiley Eastern India Ltd. She is senior member in IEEE and fellow member in IETE.

Yunliang Jiang is a Professor of the School of Information Engineering of Huzhou Teachers College, China. He obtained the B.S. degree in Mathematics from Zhejiang Normal University in 1989, the M.E. degree in Computer Science and Technology from Zhejiang University in 1997, and the Ph.D. degree in Computer Science and Technology from Zhejiang University in 2006, respectively. His research interests include information fusion, artificial intelligence, and geographic information system. He has published over 20 papers in journals such as Lecture Notes in Artificial Intelligence, Lecture Notes in Computer Science, Pattern Recognition and Artificial Intelligence (in Chinese), and others.

Koji Kamei is a researcher at NTT Communication Science Laboratories in Kyoto, Japan. His research interests focus on sharing of real-world events, including event extraction from sensors and ontology construction for realworld events. Kamei received his ME in electronics and communication engineering from Kyoto University.

Witold Kinsner is Professor and Associate Head at the Department of Electrical and Computer Engineering, University of Manitoba, Winnipeg, Canada. He is also Affiliate Professor at the Institute of Industrial Mathematical Sciences, and Adjunct Scientist at the Telecommunications Research Laboratories, Winnipeg. He obtained the Ph.D. degree in Electrical Engineering from McMaster University in 1974. He was Assistant Professor in Electrical Engineering at McMaster University and McGill University. He is a co-founder of the first Microelectronics Centre in Canada, and was its Director of Research from 1979 to 1987. He also was designing configurable self-synchronizing CMOS memories at the ASIC Division, National Semiconductor, Santa Clara, California. Dr. Kinsner has been involved in research on algorithms and software/hardware computing engines for real-time multimedia, using wavelets, fractals, chaos, emergent computation, genetic algorithms, rough sets, fuzzy logic, neural networks. Applications included signal and data compression, signal enhancement, classification, segmentation, and feature extraction in various areas such as real-time speech compression for multimedia, wideband audio compression, aerial and space ortho image compression, biomedical signal classification, severe weather classification from volumetric radar data, radio and power-line transient classification, image/video enhancement, and modeling of complex processes such as dielectric discharges. He also spent many years in VLSI design (configurable high-speed CMOS memories, as well as magnetic bubble memories), and computer-aided engineering of electronic circuits (routing and placement for VLSI, and field-programmable gate arrays). He has authored and co-authored over 500 publications in the above areas. Dr. Kinsner is a senior member of the Institute of Electrical & Electronics Engineers (IEEE), a member of the Association of Computing Machinery (ACM), a member of the Mathematical and Computer Modeling Society, a member of Sigma Xi, and a life member of the Radio Amateurs of Canada.

Yasue Kishino is a researcher at NTT Communication Science Laboratories in Kyoto, Japan. Her research interests include ubiquitous computing and human interfaces. Kishino received her PhD in information science and technology from Osaka University.

Yasuo Kudo received the M. Eng. degree and the Ph.D. degree in Engineering from Hokkaido University, Hokkaido, Japan, in 1997 and 2000, respectively. From 2003 to 2005 and 2005 to 2009, he was a Research Associate and an Assistant Professor with the Department of Computer Science and Systems Engineering, Muroran Institute of Technology, Japan, respectively. He is currently an Assistant Professor with College of Information and Systems, Muroran Institute of Technology. He has authored and coauthored more than 50 papers in international journals, book chapters and conferences. His current research interests include theory and application of rough set, non-classical logic, data base, and data mining.

Abdesslem Layeb was born in Algeria in 1977. He received his PhD degree in computer science from the University Mentouri of Constantine, Algeria. Member of MISC laboratory. Dr. Layeb is interested to the combinatorial optimization methods and its application to solve several problems from different domains like Bioinformatics, imagery, formal methods. Dr. Layeb has many publications in theoretical computer science, bioinformatics, and formal methods. Dr. Layeb is currently an assistant professor in the department of computer science at the University of Constantine.

Qin Li received his B.Eng. degree in computer science from China University of Geoscience, the M.Sc. degree (with distinction) in computing from the University of North-Umbria at Newcastle, and the Ph.D. degree from the Hong Kong Polytechnic University. His current research interests include medical image analysis, biometrics, image processing, and pattern recognition.

Tsau Young (T.Y.) Lin received his PhD in Mathematics from Yale University. He is a Professor of Computer Science at San Jose State University and a fellow in Berkeley Initiative in Soft Computing, University of California. He is the President of International Granular Computing Society and the Founding President of International Rough Set Society. He shares the Editor-in-Chief with Tony Xiaohua Hu for the International Journal of Granular Computing, Rough Sets and Intelligent Systems. He has served on various roles in reputable international journals and conferences. His interests include data/

text/web mining, data security and granular/rough/soft computing. He received the best contribution awards from ICDM01 and International Rough Set Society (2005), best service award from IEEE/WIC/ACM WI-IAT2007 and a pioneer award from GrC 2008.

Yong Liu (yongliu@iipc.zju.edu.cn) received his PhD in Computer Science from Zhejiang University in 2007, and he is a lecture in the institute of Cyber-Systems and Control. His research interests include machine learning, computer vision, information processing.

Lu Ma received a Ph.D. degree from the Department of Computer Science at the University of Illinois at Chicago. She is now a computer Scientist at NCR. Her research interests include Petri nets, formal modeling and Verification, software engineering, distributed systems, and computer security.

Takuya Maekawa is a researcher at NTT Communication Science Laboratories in Japan. His research interests include Web content engineering in mobile and ubiquitous environment. He received his Ph.D. in information science and technology from Osaka University in 2006.

Duoqian Miao received his Bachelor of Science degree in Mathematics in 1985, Master of Science degree in Probability and Statistics in 1991 both from Shanxi University, and Doctor of Philosophy in Pattern Recognition and Intelligent System at Institute of Automation, Chinese Academy of Sciences in 1997. Prof. Miao is a Professor and Vice dean of the school of Electronics and Information Engineering of Tongji University, China. Prof. Miao's present research interests include: Rough Sets, Granular Computing, Principal Curve, Web Intelligence, and Data Mining etc. Prof. Miao has published over 80 scientific articles in refereed international journals, books, and conferences. In addition, he has published 2 academics books. Prof. Miao is a committee member of International Rough Sets Society, a senior member of the China Computer Federation (CCF), a committee member of the CCF Artificial Intelligence and Pattern Recognition, a committee member of the CCF Machine Learning, a committee member of the Chinese Association for Artificial Intelligence(CAAI), a vice chair of the CAAI Rough Set and Soft Computing Society, a committee member of the Chinese Association of Automation(CAA) Intelligent Automation and CAA Youth Activities, a committee member and a vice chair of Shanghai Computer Society(SCA)Computing Theory and Artificial Intelligence.

Tetsuya Murai graduated from Department of Mathematics, Faculty of Science, Hokkaido University in 1987 (B.Sc). He graduated from Division of Information Engineering, Graduate School of Engineering, Hokkaido University in 1987 (M.Eng). He received his Dr. Eng degree in mathematical information engineering from Hokkaido University, Sapporo, Japan, in 1994. From 1987 to 1992, he was a Lecturer at School of Allied Health Professions in Sapporo Medical College, Japan. From 1992 to 1995, he was an Associate Professor at Hokkaido University of Education at Hakodate, Japan. Since 1995, he has been an Associate Professor at Hokkaido University. In 1998, he was a Visiting Professor in Catholic University at Brescia, Italy supported by il Consiglio Nazionale delle Richerche (CNR) in Italy and the Japan Society for the Promotion of Sciences (JSPS) for collaboration with Professor G. Resconi.

Takeshi Okadome (Ph.D.) is a professor of Kwansei Gakuin University. His current interest is the media design and contents creation using sensors. He received the Doctor of Science degree in Computer

Science from the University of Tokyo in 1988. During Apr. 1988-March 2009, as a computer scientist, he stayed in NTT Laboratories and he now with Kwansei Gakuin University. He is a member of the ACM.

Djamel Eddine Saidouni was born in Algeria in 1968. He obtained his PhD degree from Paul Sabatier university, France, in 1996. Djamel Eddine is interested to the following topics: maximality semantics, formal methods, real time system, state explosion problem, models for concurrency, refinement. Dr Djamel Eddine is currently member of the RT-LOTOS project and the author of the true concurrency model for process algebra called Maximality Labeled Transition system. Dr Djamel Eddine has many publications in theoretical computer science and formal methods. Dr Djamel Eddine is currently an assistant professor in the department of computer science at the University of Constantine. He is also the head of the research group on formal methods.

Yasushi Sakurai is a senior research scientist at NTT communication Science Laboratories in Kyoto, Japan. His research interests include indexing and search algorithms, data mining, and sensor data processing. Sakurai received his PhD in engineering from the Nara Institute of Science and technology. He is a member of the ACM.

Wang Shi, born in 1981, is an assistant researcher in Key Laboratory of Intelligent Information Processing, Institute of Computing Technology, Chinese Academy of Sciences. His current research interests include entity recognition and deep semantic analysis, knowledge discovery from text and phrases, large-scale knowledge processing.

Kenji Sugawara is a professor of the Department of Information and Network Science, and a dean of Faculty of Information and Computer Science, Chiba Institute of Technology, Chiba, Japan. He received BS (1972), his doctorate degree in Engineering (1983) from Tohoku University, Japan. His research interests include Multi-agent System, Artificial Intelligence, Ubiquitous Computing and Symbiotic Computing. Prof. Sugawara is a Fellow of IEICE Japan and a member of IEEE, ACM, and IPSJ.

Yuefei Sui (yfsui@ict.ac.cn) is professor of artificial intelligence and applied logic. He received the PhD in Mathematics from the Institute of Software, Chinese Academy of Sciences in 1988.

Yu Sun (ysun@ict.ac.cn) is professor of Artificial intelligence and ontology engineering. She is working at the Department of Computer Science, Yunnan Normal University, Kunming, Yunnan, China. She received the PhD in computer science from the Institute of Computing Technology, Chinese Academy of Sciences in 2005.

Tadeusz Wibig is the professor of Physics at the University of Lodz, Poland. He works in the fields of cosmic ray and high energy physics. He is the Head of the Department of Modeling of the Learning Processes in the Physics Institute at the University. He also works in the Department of the Cosmic Ray Physics of the Andrzej Soltan Institute of Nuclear Studies. He is President of Lodz Division of Polish Physical Society.

Yousheng Tian is a research fellow at the International Center for Cognitive Informatics (ICfCI) as well as Theoretical and Empirical Software Engineering Center (TESERC) in Dept. of Electrical and

Computer Engineering at the University of Calgary. He received a PhD from Xian Jiantong University, China, in Computer Science in 2002 and was a Post Doctoral Fellow at ICfCI during 2006 to 2007. His research interest is in cognitive informatics, cognitive computing, software engineering, machine learning, and denotational mathematics.

Jeffrey J.P. Tsai received a Ph.D. degree in Computer Science from the Northwestern University, Evanston, Illinois. He is a Professor of Computer Science at the University of Illinois at Chicago. He is also a Senior Research Fellow of IC2 at the University of Texas at Austin. His current research interests include sensor networks, ubiquitous computing, services computing, intrusion detection, bioinformatics, knowledge-based software engineering, formal modeling and verification, distributed real-time systems, multimedia systems, and intelligent agents. From 2000 to 2003, he chaired the IEEE/CS Technical Committee on Multimedia Computing and served on the steering committee of the IEEE Transactions on Multimedia. From 1994 to 1999, he was an Associate Editor of the IEEE Transactions on Knowledge and Data Engineering and he is currently an Associate Editor of the IEEE Transactions on Services Computing. He is a Fellow of the AAAA, the IEEE, and the SDPS.

Shusaku Tsumoto graduated from Osaka University, School of Medicine in 1989. After a resident of neurology in Chiba University Hospital, he was involved in developing hospital information system in Chiba University Hospital from 1991. He moved to Tokyo Medical University in 1993 and started his research on rough sets and data mining in biomedicine. He received his Ph.D (Computer Science) on application of rough sets to medical data mining from Tokyo Institute of Technology in 1997 and has become a Professor at Department of Medical Informatics, Shimane University in 2000. His interests include approximate reasoning, data mining, fuzzy sets, granular computing, knowledge acquisition, mathematical theory of data mining, medical informatics and rough sets (alphabetical order). He served as President of International Rough Set Society from 2000 to 2005 and served as a PC chair of RSCTC2000, IEEE ICDM2002, RSCTC2004, ISMIS2005 and IEEE GrC2007, as a Conference chair of PAKDD 2008. Shusaku Tsumoto graduated from Osaka University, School of Medicine in 1989. After a resident of neurology in Chiba University Hospital, he was involved in developing hospital information system in Chiba University Hospital from 1991. He moved to Tokyo Medical University in 1993 and started his research on rough sets and data mining in biomedicine. He received his Ph.D (Computer Science) on application of rough sets to medical data mining from Tokyo Institute of Technology in 1997 and has become a Professor at Department of Medical Informatics, Shimane University in 2000. His interests include approximate reasoning, data mining, fuzzy sets, granular computing, knowledge acquisition, mathematical theory of data mining, medical informatics and rough sets (alphabetical order). He served as President of International Rough Set Society from 2000 to 2005 and served as a PC chair of RSCTC2000, IEEE ICDM2002, RSCTC2004, ISMIS2005 and IEEE GrC2007, as a Conference chair of PAKDD 2008.

C.Kezi Selva Vijila is currently working as Professor & Head in the Department of ECE, Karunya University. Her areas of interests include Signal Processing, Biomedical applications, soft computing, etc.

Guoyin Wang was born in Chongqing, China, in 1970. He received a BSc in computer software, an MSc in computer software, and a PhD in computer organization and architecture from Xi'an Jiaotong University, China, in 1992, 1994, and 1996, respectively. He worked at the University of North Texas,

USA, and the University of Regina, Canada, as a visiting scholar during 1998-1999. Since 1996, he has been working at the Chongqing University of Posts and Telecommunications, where he is currently a professor and PhD supervisor, the Dean of the College of Computer Science and Technology. Professor Wang is the Chairman of the Advisory Board of International Rough Set Society (IRSS), Chairman of the Rough Set Theory and Soft Computation Society, Chinese Association for Artificial Intelligence. He served or is currently serving on the program committees of many international conferences and workshops, as program committee member, program chair or co-chair. He is an editorial board member of several international journals. Professor Wang has won many governmental awards and medals for his achievements. He was named as a national excellent teacher and a national excellent university key teacher by the Ministry of Education, China, in 2001 and 2002 respectively. Professor Wang was elected into the Program for New Century Excellent Talents in University by the Ministry of Education of P R China in 2004, and won the Chongqing Science Fund for Distinguished Young Scholars in 2008. He has delivered many invited talks at international and national conferences, and has given many seminars in USA, Canada, Poland, and China. Professor Wang is the author of 2 books, the editor of many proceedings of international and national conferences, and has over 200 research publications. His books and papers have been cited over 3000 times. His research interests include rough set, granular computing, knowledge technology, data mining, machine learning, neural network, soft computing, cognitive computing.

Jinghua Wang received his B.S. degree in Computer Science from Shandong University and his M.S. degree from Harbin Institute of Technology. He is currently a Ph.D. candidate in the Department of Computing, The Hong Kong Polytechnic University. His current research interests are in the areas of pattern recognition and image processing.

Yutaka Yanagisawa is a researcher at NTT Communication Science Laboratories, in Kyoto, Japan. His research interests include locating systems for mobile computing environments, programming languages to develop middleware and operating systems for small mobile devices, and augmented-reality systems to support mobile device users. Yanagisawa received his PhD in engineering from Osaka University.

Jianhua Yang received the Ph.D. degree from Zhejiang University, Hangzhou, China, in 2007. He is an associate professor at Zhejiang University of China. His research interests include artificial intelligence and robot, sensor network and large-scale information processing, and related algorithms and applications, he is the corresponding author of this paper.

Yiyu Yao is a professor of computer science in the Department of Computer Science, University of Regina, Regina, Saskatchewan, Canada. His research interests include information retrieval, rough sets, interval sets, granular computing, Web intelligence, cognitive informatics, data mining and fuzzy sets. He is an area editor of International Journal of Approximate Reasoning, a member of the editorial boards of the Web Intelligence and Agent Systems journal, Transactions on Rough Sets, Journal of Intelligent Information Systems, Journal of Chongqing University of Posts and Telecommunication, The International Journal of Cognitive Informatics & Natural Intelligence (IJCINI), International Journal of Software Science and Computational Intelligence (IJSSCI). He has served and is serving as a program co-chair of several international conferences. He is a member of ACM and IEEE.

Jane You received her B.Eng. degree in electronic engineering from Xi'an Jiaotong University, P.R. China, in 1986, and obtained her Ph.D degree in Computer Science from La Trobe University, Australia, in 1992. She was awarded a French Foreign Ministry International Fellowship in 1993. From 1993 to 1995, Dr. You was a lecturer in School of Computing and Information Science, the University of South Australia. From 1996 to 2001, she was with School of Computing and Information Technology, Griffith University, Australia, where she was a lecturer (1996-1998) and later a senior lecturer (1999-2001). Currently Dr. You is an associate professor in Department of Computing, the Hong Kong Polytechnic University. Her research interests include medical imaging, visual information retrieval, image processing, pattern recognition, multimedia systems, biometrics computing and data mining. So far, she has over 170 research papers published as journal articles, book chapters and conference publications in these areas.

Bo Zhang is a professor of Computer Science and Technology Department, Tsinghua University, Beijing, China, and the fellow of Chinese Academy of Sciences. He graduated from Dept. of Automatic Control, Tsinghua University in 1958. His main research interests include artificial intelligence, robotics, intelligent control and pattern recognition. He has published over 150 papers and 3 monographs in these fields. He is the General Co-Chair of IEEE ICCI 2010 at Tsinghua University.

Du Zhang received his Ph.D. degree in Computer Science from the University of Illinois. He is a Professor and Chair of the Computer Science Department at California State University, Sacramento. His current research interests include: knowledge base inconsistency, machine learning in software engineering, and knowledge-based systems and multi-agent systems. He has authored or coauthored over 130 publications in journals, conference proceedings, and book chapters in these and other areas. He has served as the conference general chair, the program committee chair, a program committee co-chair, or a program area chair for numerous IEEE international conferences. Currently, he is an Associate Editor for International Journal on Artificial Intelligence Tools, a member of editorial board for International Journal of Cognitive Informatics and Natural Intelligence, and a member of editorial board for International Journal of Software Science and Computational Intelligence. In addition, he has served as a guest editor for special issues of International Journal of Software Engineering and Knowledge Engineering, Software Quality Journal, IEEE Transactions on SMC-Part B, EATCS *Fundamenta Informaticae*, and International Journal of Computer Applications in Technology. Du Zhang is a senior member of IEEE and a member of ACM.

Ning Zhong received the Ph.D. degree in the Interdisciplinary Course on Advanced Science and Technology from the University of Tokyo. He is currently head of Knowledge Information Systems Laboratory, and a professor in Department of Life Science and Informatics at Maebashi Institute of Technology, Japan. He is also director and an adjunct professor in the International WIC Institute (WICI), Beijing University of Technology. He has conducted research in the areas of knowledge discovery and data mining, rough sets and granular-soft computing, Web intelligence, intelligent agents, brain informatics, and knowledge information systems, with over 200 journal and conference publications and 20 books. He is the editor-in-chief of the Web Intelligence and Agent Systems journal (IOS Press), associate editor of IEEE Transactions on Knowledge and Data Engineering (2005-2008), and the Knowledge and Information Systems journal (Springer), a member of the editorial board of Transactions on Rough Sets (Springer), International Journal of Cognitive Informatics and Natural Intelligence (IJCINI), and the editorial board of Advanced Information and Knowledge Processing (AI&KP) book series (Springer), Frontiers in AI and Applications book series (IOS Press), Chapman&Hall/CRC Data Mining and

Knowledge Discovery book series, and editor (the area of intelligent systems) of the Encyclopedia of Computer Science and Engineering (Wiley). He is the co-chair of Web Intelligence Consortium (WIC), chair of the IEEE Computer Society Technical Committee on Intelligent Informatics (TCII), member of the steering committee of IEEE International Conferences on Data Mining (ICDM), vice chair of IEEE Computational Intelligence Society Technical Committee on Granular Computing, the steering committee of International Rough Set Society. He has served or is currently serving on the program committees of over 100 international conferences and workshops, including IEEE ICDM'02 (conference chair), IEEE ICDM'06 (program chair), IEEE/WIC WI-IAT'03 (conference chair), IEEE/WIC/ACM WI-IAT'04 (program chair), and IJCAI'03 (advisory committee member). He was awarded the best paper awards of AMT'06, JSAI'03, IEEE TCII/ICDM Outstanding Service Award in 2004, and Pacific-Asia Conference on Knowledge Discovery and Data Mining (PAKDD) Most Influential Paper Award (1999-2008).

Jiayu Zhou, born in 1985, is a computer science PhD student in Ira A Fulton School of Engineering, Arizona State University. His main research interests include natural language processing, text mining, information retrieval, knowledge engineering, cognitive science and informatics.

Haibin Zhu is an Associate Professor of the *Department of Computer Science and Mathematics, Nipissing University, Canada* and has published more than ninety research papers, four books and two book chapters on object-oriented programming, distributed systems, collaborative systems, agent systems and computer architecture. He is *a senior member of IEEE, a member of ACM*, and *a life member of the Chinese Association for Science and Technology, USA*. He is a senior member of *IEEE* and a member of *ACM*. He is serving and served as co-chair of the technical committee of *Distributed Intelligent Systems of IEEE SMC Society*, guest (co-)editor for 3 special issues of prestigious journals, PC vice chair, poster co-chair, and publicity co-chair for many IEEE conferences. He is the recipient of the 2006-2007 research award from Nipissing University, the 2004 and 2005 IBM Eclipse Innovation Grant Awards, the Best Paper Award from the 11th ISPE Int'l Conf. on Concurrent Engineering (ISPE/CE2004), the Educator's Fellowship of OOPSLA'03, and several awards of research and textbook in China.

Index